THE ANCIENT D...
THE MODEI

Clod Ensemble: *Red Ladies* (2008).

The Ancient Dancer in the Modern World

Responses to Greek and Roman Dance

Edited by
FIONA MACINTOSH

OXFORD
UNIVERSITY PRESS

OXFORD
UNIVERSITY PRESS

Great Clarendon Street, Oxford OX2 6DP,
United Kingdom

Oxford University Press is a department of the University of Oxford.
It furthers the University's objective of excellence in research, scholarship,
and education by publishing worldwide. Oxford is a registered trade mark of
Oxford University Press in the UK and in certain other countries

© Oxford University Press 2010

The moral rights of the author have been asserted

First published 2010
First published in paperback 2012

British Library Cataloguing in Publication Data
Data available

Library of Congress Cataloguing in Publication Data
Library of Congress Control Number: 2010933147

ISBN 978–0–19–954810–1
ISBN 978–0–19–965693–6 (Pbk)

Printed and bound by
CPI Group (UK) Ltd, Croydon, CR0 4YY

Contents

V THE ANCIENT CHORUS IN CONTEMPORARY PERFORMANCE

Acknowledgements

The research for this book has been made possible by generous support of the Arts and Humanities Research Council, which has funded the Archive of Performances of Greek and Roman Drama (APGRD) at the University of Oxford for ten years following an initial three-year grant from the Leverhulme Trust. The conference, 'Greek Drama and Modern Dance', from which the preliminary ideas for this book sprung, was held in July 2006 at Magdalen College, Oxford. The conference benefited from funds kindly granted by the British Academy, the Classics Faculty of the University of Oxford, the Passmore Edwards Fund and the Society for the Promotion of Hellenic Studies. It also hosted a marvellous exhibition of photos from the Waldman Archive, New York of Martha Graham's dances, which was organized by Amanda Wrigley. Financial assistance for the pictures for this volume has been given by the Jowett Fund of the University of Oxford. To all these bodies I am most grateful.

There are numerous people without whom this volume would not have been possible. Preliminary discussions with Richard Cave, Helen Eastman, Martha Oakes, Yopie Prins, Michael Walton, Ruth Webb, David Wiles, Libby Worth, and Yana Zarifi enabled me to make invaluable contacts within the world of academic and professional dance. I am extremely grateful to all of them for having helped in those first stages. Since then I have gathered debts in numerous circles, especially from Emily Churchill and Laura Griffiths at the National Resource Centre for Dance (NRCD) at the University of Surrey, and to Alexandra Carter and Rachel Fenshaw, whose AHRC-funded project 'Pioneer Women: Early British Modern Dancers' has organized two one-day workshops, one on Classical Greek Dance (by Carol Vasko) and one on 'Natural Movement' (by Jean Kelly and Jacqueline Ferguson), which have not only been enormous fun but given me practical insights into what was otherwise a purely academic curiosity. I am also grateful to Miranda Laurence for organizing various academic events around the Oxford Festival of Greek Dance, to which we at the Archive have been able to contribute. To Rosemary Pountney, I am also indebted for sharing with me her memories of Irene Mawer.

The greatest debts, as ever, are to my colleagues at the Archive, past and present: to Peter Brown, Felix Budelmann, Edith Hall, Stephen Harrison, Stephe Harrop, Pantelis Michelakis, Scott Scullion, Naomi Setchell, Oliver Taplin, and Amanda Wrigley. I am also extremely grateful to Arabella Stanger and Lucy Jackson for help with the References. It has been a pleasure to work once more with Hilary O'Shea and Dorothy McCarthy at OUP and I am indebted to Tom Chandler, Tessa Eaton, and Carolyn McAndrew for their professional support during the book's production process. Brenda Hall, yet again, has done an excellent job on the index. Special mention must go to Helen Damon who worked extremely hard on the pictures, during her time with us; and to Michelle Paull for her help with pictures in the APGRD's Leyhausen-Spiess Collection. Finally, for help with the paperback edition, I must give special thanks to Taryn Das Neves at OUP and, for their unstinting efforts, I remain indebted to both Paul Cartledge and Martha Oakes.

F.M.

Note on the Text

In order to avoid confusion, this volume uses the lower case to refer to the 'modern' world—in contrast to the 'ancient' world—and adopts, contrary to what has become standard usage, an upper case 'M' to refer to the literary, historical, cultural movement of Modernism.

Any abbreviations to ancient texts follow the practice employed in the *Oxford Classical Dictionary* (3rd edition Oxford 1996). Translations are by the authors, unless otherwise indicated.

List of Illustrations

List of Contributors

DANIEL ALBRIGHT is the Ernest Bernbaum Professor of Literature at Harvard University. He has a longstanding interest in theatre, music and Modernism and has published widely on Yeats and Beckett. His recent publications include *Modernism and Music: An Anthology of Sources* (2004) and *Beckett and Aesthetics* (2003).

HENRIETTA BANNERMAN is Head of Research at London Contemporary Dance School. She trained with the Martha Graham Company in New York in the 1960s and has published numerous articles on Graham and contemporary American and British dancers in *Dance Research, Dance Theatre Journal* and *Dancing Times.*

RICHARD CAVE is Professor of Drama and Theatre Arts at Royal Holloway, University of London. He has published widely on many aspects of theatre history from the Renaissance to the present and is a leading authority on Irish literature. He edited the plays of Yeats (1997) and Wilde (2000) for Penguin Classics. His interest in dance and movement is both theoretical and practical and as a qualified practitioner of the Feldenkrais Method, he has worked regularly with actors in The Royal Shakespeare Company.

ANN COOPER ALBRIGHT is a performer, choreographer, and feminist scholar. She is Professor of Dance and Theater and Chair of the Gender and Women's Studies program at Oberlin College. She is the author of *Choreographing Difference: The Body and Identity in Contemporary Dance* (1997), and co-editor of *Moving History/Dancing Cultures* (2001), and *Taken By Surprise: Improvisation in Dance and Mind* (2003). Her most recent publication is *Traces of Light: Presence and Absence in the Work of Loïe Fuller* (2007).

HELEN EASTMAN is the producer for The Onassis Programme at the University of Oxford. She trained as a director at LAMDA after graduating from Oxford where she was the Passmore Edwards Scholar in Classics and English. Helen is Visiting Lecturer in Contemporary Performance Practice at the University of Westminster and a freelance director.

EDITH HALL is Professor of Classics and Drama at Royal Holloway, University of London, co-Founder with Oliver Taplin and Consultant Director of the APGRD at the University of Oxford. Her recent publications include *Greek Tragedy and the British Theatre 1660–1914* (co-authored with Fiona Macintosh, 2005), *The Theatrical Cast of Athens: Interactions between Ancient Greek Drama and Society* (2006), and *Suffering under the Sun* (2010). She is co-editor with Rosie Wyles of the APGRD volume, *New Directions in Ancient Pantomime* (2008).

SUSAN JONES spent fifteen years as a soloist with The Scottish Ballet, Glasgow before beginning a career in academia and she is currently Tutorial Fellow in English at St Hilda's College, University of Oxford. She is the author of *Conrad and Women* (1999) and is completing a book for Oxford University Press on Dance and Modernism.

ISMENE LADA-RICHARDS is Reader in Greek Literature and Culture and author of *Initiating Dionysus: Ritual and Theatre in Aristophanes' Frogs* (1999), *Silent Eloquence: Lucian and Pantomime Dancing* (2007) and numerous articles on aspects of ancient drama, most recently, pantomime dancing.

STRUAN LESLIE is a freelance choreographer, movement director and director, and Director of Movement at The Royal Shakespeare Company.

FIONA MACINTOSH is Reader in Greek and Roman Drama, University Lecturer in Classical Reception and Fellow of St Hilda's College, University of Oxford. Since 2010 she has been Director of the APGRD. Her publications include *Dying Acts: Death in Ancient Greek and Modern Irish Tragic Drama* (1994), *Greek Tragedy and the British Theatre 1660–1914* (2005—with Edith Hall), *Sophocles' Oedipus Tyrannus* (2009). She has co-edited numerous previous APGRD volumes: *Medea in Performance 1500–2000* (2000); *Dionysus Since 69* (2004); *Agamemnon in Performance 458 BC to AD 2004* (2005).

NADINE MEISNER was Dance Critic for *The Independent* for many years and continues to work as a freelance Dance Journalist whilst completing an academic study of the 'Russification' of Russian Ballet at Churchill College, Cambridge.

PANTELIS MICHELAKIS is Consultant Director of the APGRD and Senior Lecturer in the Department of Classics and Ancient History at the University of Bristol. He is the author of *Achilles in Greek Tragedy* (2002) and *A Companion to Euripides' Iphigenia at Aulis* (2006), and co-editor of *Homer, Tragedy and Beyond: Essays in honour of P. E. Easterling* (2001) and *Agamemnon in Performance, 458 BC to AD 2004* (2005). He is currently working on the reception of Greek tragedy on the modern stage and on screen.

FREDERICK NAEREBOUT is Senior Lecturer in the Department of History, University of Leiden. He is author of *Attractive Performances: Ancient Greek Dance: Three Preliminary Studies* (1997).

BARBARA RAVELHOFER is Reader in English Literature at the University of Durham and a Research Associate of the Centre for History and Economics at the University of Cambridge. Her publications include *The Early Stuart Masque: Dance, Costume, and Music* (2006) and *English Historical Drama, 1500–1660: Forms Outside the Canon* (co-edited with T. Grant, 2007).

KATHLEEN RILEY was until recently a British Academy Postdoctoral Fellow in Classics at the University of Oxford and a Junior Research Fellow of Corpus Christi College. She is also a Post-Doctoral Research Associate of the APGRD. Her current research involves an international and interdisciplinary study of the reception of Greek tragedy in the Modernist period. Kathleen's first book, published in 2004, was the authorized biography *Nigel Hawthorne on Stage*. Her second book, *The Reception and Performance of Euripides' Herakles: Reasoning Madness* was published by Oxford University Press in 2008. A lifelong Astaire enthusiast, Kathleen is presently at work on a history of the stage career of Fred and Adele Astaire (Oxford University Press 2011).

TYLER JO SMITH is Assistant Professor of Greek Art and Archaeology at the University of Virginia. She is a specialist in iconography and performance and author of *Komast Dancers in Archaic Greek Art* (2010).

ARABELLA STANGER trained with the English National Ballet before studying for a degree in Classics at King's College, London. She went on to take a Masters in Drama at Goldsmiths where she is now studying under Professor Maria Shevtova for a doctorate in contemporary performance theory.

JENNIFER THORP is Archivist of New College, University of Oxford, co-organizer with Michael Burden of the Annual New College Dance Symposium and specialist (as practitioner and author) in baroque dance.

RUTH WEBB is Professor of Greek at the Université de Lille3 and a member of the UMR 8163, Savoirs, Textes, Langage. She is also a member of the APGRD Advisory Board. She is the author of *Demons and Dancers: Performance in Late Antiquity* (2008) and *Ekphrasis, Imagination and Persuasion in Ancient Rhetorical Theory and Practice* (2009), and a teacher of Egyptian dance.

SUZY WILLSON is Co-Artistic Director of Clod Ensemble, which is based in London, and has directed all the company's performance pieces to date. Suzy has been teaching in the UK and internationally for over ten years and is currently an Honorary Senior Lecturer at Barts and the London Hospital, Queen Mary's School of Medicine and Dentistry, University of London. She specializes in teaching movement work and has led innovative education programmes for doctors in hospital settings and for young people in conflict with the law. She also works with People's Palace Projects on their Human Rights Project in Rio, Brazil.

ALESSANDRA ZANOBI recently completed her doctorate on Seneca in the Classics Department at the University of Durham, and is Post-Doctoral Associate of the APGRD. Her chapter on Seneca and ancient pantomime appears in Edith Hall and Rosie Wyles (eds.), *New Directions in Ancient Pantomime* (2008). She is also a dancer and trained in Italy.

YANA ZARIFI is Artistic Director of Thiasos Theatre Company. Her academic background is in Classics and the Social Sciences. She is an Honorary Research Fellow of Royal Holloway, University of London. She has directed classical Greek plays— including most of Aristophanes'—in London, Paris, and in the US. The Thiasos Theatre Company arose from her dedication to the re-performance of Greek drama through the use of Eastern theatrical traditions and her desire to reinstate the dancing and singing chorus to the central place it once occupied in Greek theatre. Her next project will be to produce Euripides' *Helen*, which she hopes to perform in Egypt, where she grew up.

VANDA ZAJKO is Senior Lecturer in the Department of Classics and Ancient History at the University of Bristol. She has published widely on the reception of classical literature, particularly in the twentieth century, and in mythology, psychoanalytic theory, and feminist thought. She is co-editor (with Miriam Leonard) of *Laughing with Medusa: Classical Myth and Feminist Thought* (2006) and (with Alexandra Lianeri) *Translation and the Classic: Identity as Change in the History of Culture* (2008).

List of Dances Discussed in this Volume with Première Dates

Introduction

Fiona Macintosh

In June 2007, the British choreographer Mark Bruce announced that his next project was to be based on Agamemnon and Clytemnestra.[1] Both the Aeschylean and Senecan versions of the *Agamemnon* have provided the subject matter for many ballets: in the twentieth century alone, and knowingly or not, Bruce is following in the footsteps of no lesser luminaries of the dance world than Rudolf von Laban, Ninette de Valois, and Martha Graham.[2]

Laban's *Agamemnons Tod*, which premiered in Hamburg in 1924, was in fact inspired by the *Agamemnon* ballet of the founding father of modern ballet, Jean-Georges Noverre. Noverre's *Der Tod Agamemnon*, with music by Joseph Starzer, was first performed in Vienna in 1771 and was one of the early *ballets d'action*, which Noverre, in particular, developed in direct imitation of ancient pantomime. Noverre worked on ideas explored by earlier choreographers—notably John Weaver, Franz Hilverding, and Gasparo Angiolini (see Lada-Richards, this volume)—and with the aid of ancient authorities such as Lucian and Libanius, he developed what he called his 'danced drama' (*ballet d'action*).[3]

At a time when ballet was no longer allied to opera or spoken theatrical entertainment, it had to find its own genealogy. Aristotle's idea of dance as mimetic action, combined with treatises on Roman pantomime (itself a direct descendant of Greek tragedy), provided the theoretical underpinning for the eighteenth-century *ballets d'action*. Dance was to follow the ancients in having something important to say; and Greek tragic drama was realized in eighteenth-century danced drama without the aid of either speech or (unlike ancient pantomime) song. Noverre's ballets very often turned to Greek tragedies for

---

[1] 'Donnachadh McCarthy in conversation with Mark Bruce', *Dance Europe* 108 (June 2007), 19. The project toured Britain in the summer of 2010 as *Love and War*.

[2] Laban's *Agamemnons Tod* (1924); Ninette de Valois' *Oresteiad* (1926); Martha Graham's *Clytemnestra* (1956). De Valois also did the choreography for *Oedipus the King, Antigone, Prometheus*, and a musical comedy version of Aristophanes, *The Birds*, all of which were staged at the Cambridge Arts Theatre. For Graham's other Greek-inspired works, see Bannerman and Zajko, this volume.

[3] See further Lada-Richards (2007), 166–71; and Hall (2008*b*). For the ancient sources (in the originals and translations), see the excellent Appendix in Hall and Wyles (2008).

their subject matter: in addition to *Der Tod Agamemnon* (1771) (also known as *Agamemnon Vengé*), he choreographed *Alceste et Admète* (1761), *La Mort d'Hercule* (1762), *Medée et Jason* (1763), *Alceste* (1767), *Iphigénie en Tauride* (1772/1779), and *Iphigénie en Aulide* (1777/1793). By the last quarter of the eighteenth century, ballet had acquired sufficient status to become a high cultural art form *sui generis*: and it had done so with the ancient example as both guide and legitimizing authority.

Ballet, like other performance arts, depends very much on its genealogy: not least because its major stars very often belong (like Mark Bruce himself, son of Christopher Bruce, Artistic Director of the Rambert Dance Company until 2002) to dancing dynasties. But this dependence on ancestry also occurs because 'looking back' is a sure way of acknowledging both debt and position within a tradition. In the case of ballet, that tradition regularly involves looking back to antiquity; and it is the aim of this volume to attempt to trace this perceived, occasionally actual, and very often tactical, debt to the ancient dancer.

The fascination with ancient dance in the twentieth century—especially as a means of liberating the body and soul from the repressive forces of nature and society and in turn from the strictures of balletic tradition itself—led to the conference on 'Greek Drama and Modern Dance', held in July 2006 at Magdalen College, Oxford. Some of the chapters in this volume grew out of papers presented at the conference (Cooper Albright, Webb, Bannerman, Meisner, Cave, and Leslie), whereas others were presented in the Archive's lecture series in 2006–7 (Lada-Richards, Naerebout, Ravelhofer, and Jones) or were especially commissioned (Smith, Thorp, Albright, Zajko, and Zarifi). The remaining chapters are written by Archive personnel (Riley, Hall, Macintosh, Michelakis) and young classical scholars, who are also trained in dance (Zanobi and Stanger). The final chapter in the book—a transcript of a discussion between the APGRD Onassis Producer, Helen Eastman and Suzy Willson, Co-artistic Director of Clod Ensemble, on the ancient chorus in modern devised dance—dates from May 2008, when Clod Ensemble brought *Red Ladies* to Oxford under the auspices of the Onassis Programme.

WHY IS ANCIENT DANCE RECEPTION NECESSARY?

Working on the performance history of ancient plays at the Archive of Performances of Greek and Roman Drama at the University of Oxford,[4] it became

---

[4] The APGRD was founded with a Leverhulme Trust three-year grant in 1996 by Edith Hall and Oliver Taplin in response to the need for a co-ordinated research effort devoted to the international production and reception of ancient plays since the Renaissance. From October 1999 it enjoyed ten years' funding from the AHRC and from January 2010 has benefited from a five-year Mellon Foundation award in conjunction with funding from the University of Oxford.

increasingly evident that to consider the Renaissance as the start date for the project was not just arbitrary; it was also highly restrictive. It was not simply that the term 'Renaissance' had recently come under scrutiny from wide quarters—ignoring as it does the uninterrupted tradition of 'classical learning' that was sustained in Byzantium and the Arabic and Syriac scholarly traditions, especially Baghdad. It was also because there was a growing awareness of the rich performance tradition in antiquity from almost immediately following the première of the tragedies in the fifth century BCE until beyond St Augustine, not only in the tragic theatre but in comedy, mime, dance, and sung recital, which cried out to be told within any such diachronic overview. The pioneering volume, edited by Pat Easterling and Edith Hall, *Greek and Roman Actors: Aspects of an Ancient Profession* (Cambridge 2002), shows how vibrant a performance tradition there was in late antiquity.

The Archive's research from 2005 therefore moved back into antiquity, in order to piece together that complex early history from disparate Christian and pagan sources, including visual records, literary testimonia, papyri, graffiti, and other inscriptions. The APGRD volume of essays edited by Edith Hall and Rosie Wyles, *New Directions in Ancient Pantomime* (Oxford 2008) focuses on one major aspect of that tradition, whose legacy was fundamental to the development of dance in the modern world. The collection explores the art of ancient pantomime from a wide range of perspectives—with reference to its relation to and influence on other literary and artistic media, in formal terms, as well as drawing attention to its legacy in the modern world.[5]

The Archive's research on ancient pantomime is part of a wider scholarly engagement with the performance tradition of late antiquity over the last few years, and especially those performance arts (such as mime and pantomime) that have hitherto been designated both the cause and symptom of so-called cultural decadence. Frederick Naerebout's pathbreaking and compendious study, *Attractive Performances: Ancient Greek Dance: Three Preliminary Studies* (1997) led the way towards an understanding of the need for a systematic investigation of non-verbal reception in music and movement. Naerebout reminded readers that ancient information about the theatre (not just the dramatic texts themselves)—for example, in anecdotes preserved in Plutarch or Philostratus, and treatises on dance by Lucian and Choricius—had exerted a continual influence on the western founding fathers and practitioners of new genres of musical theatre. Yana Zarifi's chapter in *The Cambridge Companion to Greek and Roman Theatre* (2007) provided a much-needed and scholarly overview of the role of chorus and dance in the ancient world, which showed how comparative material and ancient dance reception can cast light on the ancient sources.

---

[5] See esp. Hall (2008*b*).

The more recent wave of scholarship on ancient pantomime, in particular, owes more than a passing debt to the chapter by Pat Easterling, 'From Repertoire to Canon' in *The Cambridge Companion to Greek Tragedy* (1997), in which she pointed out that the survival of Greek tragedy was due in no small degree to ancient pantomime—sometimes referred to in inscriptions as 'rhythmic tragic dancing'—with its solo (usually masked) dancer, a musician, and a singing chorus who performed scenes from the fifth-century tragedians' works throughout the Roman empire. A number of recent studies have guaranteed that ancient pantomime has been rightly restored to cultural, and more specifically, theatre history.[6] Lada-Richards (2007) provides an illuminating reading of Lucian's *On Dancing* as the first serious account of the corporeal and mental skills demanded of a dancer. The wide-ranging and rich study by Webb (2008) not only provides careful scrutiny of tragedy's successor in the form of pantomime, it also examines ancient (Old and New) comedy's descendant in the mime. By reading the ancient (frequently prejudicial) sources 'against the grain', Webb is able to focus on the performers' practical skills, which the literary sources (in marked contrast to the epitaphs and inscriptions) choose to omit.

This present collection of essays is intended to complement these studies of antiquity and to serve as a companion piece to Hall and Wyles' APGRD ancient pantomime volume, in particular. Working on *Greek Tragedy and the British Theatre 1660–1914* (2005) with Edith Hall, it became more than apparent that modern appropriations of the chorus in the theatre could not be considered independently of a serious understanding of contemporary developments in both opera and dance. Non-verbal reception in music and movement had not received any refined and thoroughgoing treatment; and yet the ancient theatrical and theoretical sources have often been plundered and distorted whilst regularly acting as a starting point and/or foil for creative endeavour (see the chapters in Part I, this volume). As Naerebout writes in this volume: 'The inspiration derived from ancient Greek and Greco-Roman examples has been at work throughout the history of western theatrical dancing, as a major driving force in its development—a fact that is not given nearly enough attention in our teleological and self-centred "histories of the dance"' (p. 41). For this reason, the APGRD embarked on a rigorous and systematic study of both operatic and danced treatments of the ancient plays so that the sheer breadth of influence exerted by ancient Greek and Roman drama throughout the entire modern period could be appreciated. The present volume forms the second in this APGRD series, the third of which is Peter Brown and Suzana Ogranjenšek (eds.), *Ancient Drama in Music for the Modern Stage* (Oxford University Press 2010).

---

[6] Garelli (2007); Lada-Richards (2007); Webb (2008); and Hall & Wyles (2008).

DANCE HISTORY AND CLASSICAL
RECEPTION STUDIES

In September 2007, there was a rare treat: the first staging of Gluck's *Iphigénie en Tauride* at Covent Garden since 1973, in Robert Carsen's production that had previously been mounted in Chicago and San Francisco. The singing (from the mezzo Susan Graham and especially from the versatile baritone, Simon Keenly-side) was generally applauded; the music (from the Orchestra of the Age of Enlightenment under Ivor Bolton) similarly met with critical approval. What caused consternation in some circles, though, was the streamlined, black-box set designed by Tobias Hoheisel, which served as a blackboard upon which the names of the victims of the tragedies of the House of Atreus were literally chalked up—first Iphigenia, then (during Iphigenia's recitation of her dream of her parents) Agamemnon and Clytemnestra.

What offended most, however, was not the set, but the busy-ness of the production—and especially the fact that the chorus *on* stage were in fact dancers, not static singers because Carsen had chosen, apparently heretically, to confine the Covent Garden chorus to the wings. Representative of this general criticism was Tim Ashley's comment in *The Guardian*:

Carsen gives us too much distraction. He banishes the all-important chorus to the wings, replacing them with dancers who indulge in a considerable amount of throat-slitting during the Prelude, chalking the names of the previous Atreidae on the walls, then washing them off as the death toll mounts. Eventually they partly obstruct one's view of the crucial recognition scene between estranged brother and sister.[7]

What is, perhaps, most surprising about the tenor of Ashley's and others' criticisms of Carsen's directorial decisions—and especially regarding his decision to give the choreography by Philippe Giraudeau such a prominent role within his production—is that it presupposes that Carsen's staging—like his postmodern set (which Ashley compares to Martin Creed's 2001 Turner Prize winning entry 'The Lights Going On and Off')—was bold, innovative and frankly unorthodox. But it had been done before—no doubt unbeknown to either Carsen or Giraudeau.[8] The singers in Gluck's operas had previously been confined to the wings whilst the dancers had been placed centre stage; and this wasn't by some avant-garde director. No, it was by Gluck himself, together with the leading choreographer of the late eighteenth century, Noverre.

According to Noverre in his *Letters on Dancing and Ballet* (first published 1760 and then in an expanded edition of 1803–4 in St Petersburg), when Gluck's

---

[7] *The Guardian*, 12 Sept. 2007.
[8] Giraudeau worked for some years with Second Stride and danced the role of Dionysus in the Churchill/Spink, *A Mouthful of Birds* (1986)—see Cave, this volume.

Alceste was in rehearsal in Vienna in 1767, the composer despaired at his wooden and immobile chorus and turned to Noverre in desperation for help. Noverre's suggestion was that Gluck

> should break up the choruses and conceal them in the wings so the public would not see them and I promised to replace them by the elite of my *corps de ballet* who would perform the gestures appropriate to the song and so dovetail the action that the public would believe that the moving figures were in fact the singers. Gluck nearly smothered me in this excess of joy; he found my project excellent and its realisation created the most perfect illusion.[9]

Here, in Noverre's account, albeit in illusory form, we have the singing, dancing ancient chorus incarnate on the eighteenth-century stage. Whilst eighteenth-century attitudes to the ancient chorus are generally regarded by classical reception scholars as simply a 'theoretical' preoccupation of a few German intellectuals, Noverre's important collaboration with Gluck was a seminal practical experiment that had wide repercussions.[10]

Indeed, modern dance reception needs to be a major component in the armoury of anyone engaged in classical performance reception—not least because it is often the dancers who get there first. The dancer, Marie Sallé, who had learned much from John Weaver's pantomimes 'in imitation of the . . . Ancient Greeks and Romans' (see Lada-Richards and Thorp, this volume), provided the first classical *tableau vivant* at Covent Garden in 1734 as she performed as a statue in loose hair and scant garment in *Pygmalion*. This was some five decades before the much better known 'Attitudes' of Emma Hamilton, which attracted vase collectors and aristocratic voyeurs alike to Lord Hamilton's home in Naples at the end of the century. Hamilton's 'Attitudes' bore many striking similarities with art of pantomime, not least the way in which one 'Attitude' was said to have 'melted' into another.[11]

The philosophical and archaeological privileging of ancient sculpture casts a long shadow in theatre and dance history because Greek statues, as one early nineteenth-century commentator on Greek tragedy observed, did 'not appear so much to be imitations of nature, as nature herself, starting into life'.[12] Once the statue comes alive on stage, it exerts powers way beyond those originally intended by its Prometheus/Pygmalion. Not only can Modernist theatrical aesthetics be ultimately traceable to this longstanding fascination with the ancient moving statue (see Albright, this volume), it could also be argued that Modern Dance itself stems from this same source. When Genevieve Stebbins took François Delsarte's system of expressive action to America towards the end of the

---

[9] Novere (1807), I, 359.
[10] For wider discussion of the chorus in the 18th cent., see Macintosh (2009*b*); for Gluck as 'radical', see Goldhill (2010).
[11] Lada-Richards (2003*a*).
[12] Lockhart (1817).

nineteenth century, she popularized a method founded upon twelve poses based upon classical sculpture. She held an annual 'Delsarte Matinée', in which she assumed various poses, not as 'a series of tableaux, or a collection of poses each one starting from a base position . . . Instead, they melt[ed] into one another'.[13]

The first female actor-manager of a London theatre, Eliza Vestris took over the Olympic in 1830 and developed, together with the writer J. R. Planché, the hugely popular nineteenth-century theatrical form, the classical tragic burlesque. Vestris was first and foremost a dancer and singer, whose name came from her brief marriage into the most famous dance dynasty of the eighteenth century; and it was her singing and dancing skills that made the tragic burlesques so much closer to the ancient prototype than other modern adaptations of ancient tragedy.[14] And just as Sallé and Vestris were pioneers and major innovators in classically-inspired performances, so too Isadora Duncan and Diaghilev's Ballets Russes were to provide the cues for productions of ancient plays in the early twentieth century: Duncan with her bare-foot, tunic-clad performances; the Ballets Russes with Nijinsky's red-figure-vase-style, profile performance against a backdrop of Greek-style friezes by Léon Bakst in *L'Après-midi d'un faune* (1912) (see further Cooper Albright, Macintosh, Zanobi, and Jones, this volume).

However, it is not simply that dancers have led the way with bold formal innovations in the stagings of ancient material. It is also true that their danced versions of the ancient plays have often reflected and even on occasions anticipated, other theatrical, and wider intellectual, trends. This was the case, as we have seen, in the eighteenth century with the collaborative work of Gluck and Noverre. It was also true towards the end of the nineteenth century when Nietzsche's *The Birth of Tragedy* (1872) put the singing/dancing chorus (the Dionysiac) at the centre of ancient tragedy and in turn the dancer at the heart of Modernist aesthetics. When George Balanchine reworked his *Apollon Musagète* (1928) as *Apollo* (1937), the retitling was significant because he put the formal, angular, 'Apolline' qualities of high Modernism firmly centre stage (see Figure 1 and Jones, this volume).

The Symbolists saw in dance the ideal means of expressing the multiple layers of reality that eluded the spoken word; and once dance met with emergent psychoanalytical theory, the layers were perfectly explored through danced realizations of ancient myth (see Zajko, this volume). The danced versions often articulate shifts in the reception of particular myths long before they are formally acknowledged. This has notably been the case with the late twentieth-century reception of Oedipus, when psychoanalytical theory has tended to shun

---

[13] Ruyter (1996*b*), 70–89 for the influence of Stebbins on Modern Dance; for Stebbins' performances, see Elsie M. Wilbor in Stebbins (1902), 485–6. Raymond Duncan's method was based on six (rather than twelve) 'Greek Positions' but is also indebted, via Stebbins, to Delsarte.

[14] Hall and Macintosh (2005), esp. 395–9. It is perhaps equally significant that the dancer, Margaret Morris is billed in the 1920s as the first female actor-manager (on Morris, see Macintosh, this volume).

Figure 1 Souvenir programme cover, *Apollon Musagète* (1928).

the son of the Freudian bourgeois familial romance in favour of the pre-Oedipal
mother–child relationship of Kleinian theory.[15] Theatrical versions of the myth
in this period tend to mirror the theoretical trend and to marginalize the
protagonist while they bring Jocasta to the fore. This development may well

[15] See generally Macintosh (2009).

seem like a post-Lacanian or a post-feminist (particulary Kristeva-inspired) move, but it is in fact fully explored some thirty years earlier in dance. In Martha Graham's *Night Journey* of 1947, Jocasta comes centre stage—an inconceivable move in late 1940s Paris (see Bannerman, Zajko, this volume). In putting Jocasta at the heart of the Oedipus legend, Martha Graham anticipated just about every shift that has become emblematic in the reception of Sophocles' play in the last four decades. Whilst these pathbreaking moves may come as no surprise to the historian of dance, to those who come at the performance reception of ancient plays from a more text-based position, they bring with them a significant *caveat*—we ignore dance history at our peril.

THE ANCIENT DANCER

The ancient dancer, or rather the 'idea' of the ancient Greek and Roman dancer, has exerted an extraordinarily powerful fascination in the modern world. The ancient dancers who have exerted the most notable influence are the Roman pantomime dancers, Pylades and Bathyllus. Guillaume-Louis Pécour, the illustrious dancer of the court of Louis XIV was referred to as Bathyllus (see Thorp, this volume); and Noverre himself was dubbed 'the worthy rival of Pylades and Bathyllus in the art of speaking to the eyes and soul through gesture and movement'.[16] From Kathleen Riley's chapter in this volume, we see that Pylades' heir in the twentieth century was, in many ways, the consummate, seemingly effortless and truly popular gestural dancer, Fred Astaire. Even though Astaire's art did not involve any conscious appropriation of the ancient sources, his success and achievement demonstrates how classical material often penetrates western cultural history by subterranean and unconscious means. Astaire's career parallels that of the pantomime artist in effecting a bridge between high and low culture; and his use of dance to tell a story on stage and on screen earned him adulation from diverse quarters—from the cinema enthusiast, who would never dream of purchasing a ticket for the ballet, to the great high Modernist of twentieth-century dance, George Balanchine.

However, despite Pylades and Bathyllus' paradigmatic status, the ancient male dancers were in reality problematic figures for the advocates of dance in the modern world. It is often held that the male dancer was eclipsed after the demise of Louis XIV, once the associations between dance and effeminacy became deeply entrenched. But the negative associations between dance and gender transgression date from at least the founding texts of antiquity, Homer's *Iliad* and *Odyssey* (see Hall, this volume). For the male dancer was not only considered

---

[16] Cited by Guest (1996), 101. For other 'modern' Bathyllus figures, see Hall (2008*b*), 375–6.

to transgress in terms of gender, but was also susceptible to charges of moral and social degeneracy from the outset. These terms of opprobrium gathered greater force and resonance during the early years of Christianity, when the female dancer in particular was subjected to even closer scrutiny (see Webb, this volume). The ambiguous status of the professional dancer in antiquity, especially as it was codified by the Church, extends well into the baroque period, when the prejudices towards the dancer began to be robustly countered by the founders of *ballet d'action* with the aid of the 'legitimizing' rhetoric of Libanius (see Thorp, this volume). In the late nineteenth and early twentieth century, attitudes towards the ancient Greek and Roman dancer encompassed wider anxieties about both gender and race. The ancient dancer was, on the one hand, co-opted into the vanguard of women's liberation, whilst being charged with the seemingly contrary task of providing a healthy and 'pure' alternative to what was deemed moral and racial degeneration (see Webb and Macintosh, this volume).

Modernism—very much under the influence of Nietzsche's privileging of dance in *The Birth of Tragedy*—gave especial prominence to the ancient female dancer. When W. B. Yeats asks the teasingly elegant question in 'Among School Children' (1926):

> O body swayed to music, O brightening glance
> How can we know the dancer from the dance?[17]

he is implying that dance is the supreme art form in Nietzschean terms because it embodies the Modernist idea of unity between the artist and his/her art work. Yeats's ideal dancer—first Loïe Fuller and later Duncan (see Cooper Albright, Zanobi, and Smith, this volume)—is a direct descendant of the ancient dancer. In many respects, the dancer for Yeats was always intrinsically 'ancient'. When he embarked on his *Plays for Dancers* from 1914 onwards, he did so with the aid of Greek tragedy no less than Noh drama since he worked with the (Dalcroze-trained) Japanese dancer and choreographer, Michio Ito, who subsequently went to the States to work with Martha Graham.[18] Yeats's subsequent dancer and choreographer for these Greek/Japanese plays at the Abbey, and the one to whom he deferred for numerous changes in the text, was the emergent Ninette de Valois, the future founder of the Vic–Wells Ballet, eventually to become the Royal Ballet, whose early choreographies were of ancient Greek tragedies.[19]

The content of dance in the modern world, like so much of western culture and especially western performance culture, has been shaped by antiquity. This is true even in the twentieth century (see Bannerman, this volume), when the formalists (notably Balanchine) mounted a successful challenge to the Aristotelian notion of dance as a form of imitation and to the idea that dance must 'say'

---

[17] Yeats (1977), 446.
[18] On Ito, see Foster (2003), 38–9.
[19] See Cave (1980); Genné (1996). For de Valois's work on Greek tragedies, see n. 2 above.

something rather than simply 'be' (see Jones, this volume). Myth has often provided a means to express what is either difficult or impossible to say or has simply furnished a space in which to negotiate competing ideas or pressures. Myth in dance is no different from other media; and Barbara Ravelhofer shows how ancient myth in the Stuart Masque (where dance, music, and poetry often competed in performance as they had done in ancient pantomime) is often employed in order to express controversial ideas and promote a particular political agenda. Pina Bausch's choreography for Gluck's *Orpheus und Eurydike* and *Iphigenie auf Tauris* (both 1975) is atypical of her *oeuvre*, yet both seminal and pivotal in her career. For Bausch, ancient myth acted as a kind of *lingua franca* allowing her work to become international; but it also provided a kind of *rite de passage* in freeing her subsequent *Tanztheater* from the bounds of narrative (see Meisner, this volume).

Certain myths have had an undoubted allure to modern choreographers. When dance was deemed by Modernist anthropologists, and the Cambridge Ritualists in particular, as the most 'authentic' and 'primitive' means of communicating with the divine, the ritual sacrifice at the heart of the two Iphigenia tragedies by Euripides made them equally powerful foundational texts for Modern Dance (see Zanobi, this volume). Prometheus has appealed as fire-bringer and therefore liberator of humankind from at least the Romantic period onwards, when Viganò's first treatment of the myth (*The Creatures of Prometheus* 1801 to Beethoven's score—see Albright, this volume) caught the revolutionary spirit of the age. In Viganò's 1813 expanded version to Beethoven and other scores, the action of the *Prometheus Bound* and *Unbound* are incorporated; and it is the second part of the myth—in which the pinioned Prometheus rails against the forces of oppression—that has paradoxically appealed to modern choreographers by the very challenges it poses to orthodox movement (see Michelakis, this volume).

Even if Nietzsche's loathing of Euripides meant that he bizarrely omitted *Bacchae* from his discussion in *The Birth of Tragedy* (1872), his readers immediately found in the dancing Maenad an embodiment of the Dionysiac force. Indeed, Euripides' *Bacchae* has informed much of the content and the debate about Modern Dance, and especially its early 'Dionysiac' phase (see Macintosh, this volume). Even if Balanchine's increasing move towards the 'Apolline' in his work (see Jones, this volume) can be seen as the hallmark of much late twentieth-century dance, both the idea of the Dionysiac as ecstatic dance and the Dionysiac ritual of *sparagmos* (the tearing apart of the animal flesh) are deeply embedded in post-modern choreographies as well. In Greece the work of the theatre director, Theodoros Terzopoulos's company Attis depends on traditional ancient and modern examples of ecstastic dance; and the chapters by Stanger and Cave explore the Dionysiac in the choreographies of Forsythe, Clark, and Spink respectively.

THE ANCIENT CHORUS

If the ancient dancer has often acquired iconic status in the modern world, it is the dancing collectivities of the ancient world that have exerted a particularly powerful influence in performances of ancient plays in recent years. Ancient drama, as Wagner pointed out, was a veritable *Gesamtkunstwerk*—a combination of all the performing arts, song, speech and dance. Whilst synthesis of the parts was the ideal in the classical theatre, the ancient chorus very rapidly lost its central position within the drama. As the actors became stars within antiquity, the chorus members too became professionals, offering a kind of 'support act' with songs and dances for interludes between the acts—entertainment that could act as fillers for any kind of entertainment, rather than choral performances that were integral to a particular play. This happened very early in comedy in ancient Greece and it was the case in Roman tragedy of the Republican period.[20]

This compartmentalization of the arts was to become the norm in the modern world: early experiments in Italy in the late sixteenth century to revive ancient drama, where a singing chorus remained on stage throughout the spoken drama and ballet provided more than simply interludes, were shortlived. The ancient chorus, or its direct descendants, were transmogrified into the operatic chorus, once the separation between music and serious drama became entrenched with the development of Continental opera.

Indeed, in the modern world the ancient singing and dancing Greek chorus has generally been considered a problem—at best an intellectual curiosity, at worst an embarrassment consisting of diaphonously clad 'gals', with crystal-cut accents, langorously swaying and chanting in unison. French neoclassical theorists of the seventeeth and eighteenth centuries viewed the inclusion of an onstage chorus as working contrary to the dictates of verisimilitude. How could one hatch a plot, they reasonably asked, with a fifteen-strong chorus hanging around in the background? And how, we might infer, could the French monarch comfortably witness a chorus questioning the wisdom of a ruler? When dance no longer had the spoken/sung word to aid its narrative function, it turned, as we have heard, to ancient pantomime rather than the ancient chorus for inspiration. It was in collaboration with Gluck that Noverre, above all, was able to appreciate the full possibilities afforded by the ancient choric model.

Given the generic and institutionalized divisions between the performing arts, it is perhaps not surprising that Wagner should have developed his ideal of the *Gesamtkunstwerk*. Wagner had no desire to include either the ancient chorus (and definitely not its modern descendants in the nineteenth-century operatic chorus) or the *corps de ballet* in his highly hierarchical version of the *Gesamtkunstwerk*.

---

[20] On the ancient chorus, see Easterling (1997*b*); Wilson (2000); Gould (2001); Ley (2007).

He dispenses with the chorus altogether and substitutes the modern orchestra, thereby making music the dominant element. The Symbolists, by contrast, advocated and demonstrated in practice a new synthesis between the arts; and they found with the advent of the Ballets Russes, under the tutelage of Diaghilev, that both the Wagnerian ideal of the *Gesamtkunstwerk* and their ideals were now incorporated within ballet.

Max Reinhardt's landmark production of *Oedipus Rex* that premiered in Berlin and went on to be performed throughout the stages of Europe from 1910 onwards was one of the first stagings of an ancient drama in the modern world to incorporate a singing and dancing chorus successfully.[21] It was by no means fortuitous that Reinhardt's singing/dancing chorus should appear at this time on the stages of Europe: for the performing body was ubiquitous in the first decade of the twentieth century, in the innovative work of the Ballets Russes, Duncan, and Dalcroze, all of whom (like Reinhardt) challenged nineteenth-century stage pictorialism and its confined, distanced set of spatial relationships between performer and audience.

Yet despite all the advances in dance in the pre-World War I period and the inter-war choric experiments of Laban, Denishawn, Palmer, and Martha Graham (see Cooper Albright, Jones, Michelakis, and Bannerman, this volume), it wasn't until new inter-cultural perspectives were afforded from the east from the 1950s onwards that the ancient chorus found a role in performances of ancient plays.[22] The examples of choral traditions still alive in other non-western theatrical traditions provided a clue to how the ancient chorus may have worked in performance. The work of Tadashi Suzuki in Japan, though rarely seen in the West, began to fuel new scholarly and aesthetic interest in choruses.[23]

When Ninagawa's Japanese production of *Medea* first came to Europe in the mid-1980s, it provided western choreographers with new possibilities for ancient choruses.[24] Ninagawa's Kabuki-style chorus of sixteen, in brilliant blue-black cloaks and wide-brimmed hats with veils, entered in groups of four from both sides of the set vigorously plucking the strings of their shamisens and intersecting across the diagonals of the circular performance space. At moments of high tension, they tossed back their cloaks to reveal a vibrant red lining, sometimes wheeling around Medea, sometimes surging towards the central door to the house with astonishing rapidity. This chorus wasn't simply decorative; it provided emotional amplitude and counterpoint to every twist and turn in the life of the play's protagonist.

From the late 1980s on, it became impossible to ignore the ancient chorus in relation to Greek tragedy—both as practitioner and scholar. And although financial

---

[21] Macintosh (2009).
[22] Hall, Macintosh, and Wrigley (2004).
[23] McDonald (1992), 21–74.
[24] Smethurst (2000).

constraints have often reduced the role of the chorus in recent productions of ancient plays to that of one to three confidants, there has also been much interesting work done with larger-scale choruses in the subsidized theatres. This work in many ways chimes with recent interest in the chorus in scholarship: the multiplicity of responses engendered and embodied by a singing/dancing chorus extends the emotional range and tempo of the production; and the chorus' political significance is evident in its collective response to urgent contemporary concerns.

Théâtre du Soleil's production of *Les Atrides* (a tetralogy, directed by Ariane Mnouchkine, made up of Euripides' *Iphigenia at Aulis*, and Aeschylus' trilogy, *The Oresteia* (1990–2)) also put a singing and dancing chorus centre stage. The potent energy of the voluminously clad choruses was made palpable here through the percussive, largely Kathakali-inspired dancing (Figure 2). In many ways Ariane Mnouchkine's Théâtre du Soleil based at La Cartoucherie in Paris embodies a new egalitarian, anti-star-system ethos, in which ensemble performance is the aesthetic correlative to the social ideal of the classless society. In this sense the dominant role afforded to the chorus in Mnouchkine's production of *Les Atrides* is as much a product of political as aesthetic preferences.

Figure 2 Chorus from *Les Atrides* at La Cartoucherie de Vincennes, Paris, directed by Ariane Mnouchkine (1990).

The collaborative work of Gardzienice, the theatre company founded by the Polish director, Włodzimierz Staniewski, depends on collaboration and communal living. At the heart of its productions is choric work, which amplifies the emotional response of the protagonist (see Zarifi, this volume). The British theatre director, Katie Mitchell spent some time training with Gardzienice and Staniewski's imprint is registered in her multi-layered approach to direction, in which textual meaning is conveyed through movement and music as readily as it is through the modulation of the spoken word. This has meant that her ten-year collaboration with the Movement Director, Struan Leslie, whose original training was in dance, is central to the directorial process (see Leslie, this volume). Their work with the ancient chorus was especially powerful in the *Iphigenia at Aulis* production (2004), where physical movement carried the play's meaning. As Mitchell explained in an article in *The Guardian* (25 Sept, 2004), they were concerned to exemplify the ideas of the Portuguese-American neuro-scientist, Antonio Damasio, for whom the physicality of emotional response is prior to the cognitive one. The Mitchell/Leslie chorus brilliantly and evocatively conveyed their powerful emotional responses to the events being enacted before their eyes as if they were a flock of twittering birds. Clutching their handbags, and tottering on their 1950s stilettos, they quivered, bristled and then rippled in perfectly fluid formations. This was no decorous, marginal chorus: it provided the pulse of the entire performance (see Figure 21.2).

The music for the *Iphigenia at Aulis* choral odes was by Paul Clark, who also composed the score for Clod Ensemble's devised choral piece, *Red Ladies* (2005–8—see frontispiece and Figure 22.1). As with Ariane Mnouchkine, it was the director, Suzy Willson's training with Lecoq that led her to the tragic chorus: its potential for expressing collectivity both on account of its use of masks (the costuming functions as mask in *Red Ladies*) and in the way that it can be choreographed like materials from nature (it can be crumpled and then unfurl, as Lecoq famously explained, like a piece of paper). A chorus of women, indeed at one moment in fact a chorus of Trojan women (as they chant words from the ode from Euripides' play of that name) was the starting point for the dance piece. It would seem that Willson is saying, with the help of *Red Ladies*, that a perception of underlying pattern in otherwise apparently random movements (such as knitting, reading, running, eating) is what makes humankind connect both with the spaces around them and with each other.

Indeed, if the solipsistic modern western world has found the ancient Greek ritualized chorus generally hard to understand, it may well be that companies such as Clod Ensemble have found a way to understand our communality in a world of fractured, virtual communication. Here, as with the work of Suzuki, Ninagawa, Mnouchkine, Mitchell/Leslie, the chorus is far from being the otiose encumbrance and/or embarrassment it has generally been in the modern world. Instead, the example of the ancient dancing collectivity has now become a powerful means of exploring emotion and meaning in what is understood to be an alarmingly irrational and atomizing world.

I

DANCE AND THE ANCIENT SOURCES

1

Dead but not Extinct: On Reinventing Pantomime Dancing in Eighteenth-Century England and France

Ismene Lada-Richards

One of the greatest aesthetic attractions in the ancient world—emotionally absorbing, technically staggering, and hauntingly beautiful—was pantomime dancing, a ballet-style form of stage-entertainment which captivated and enthralled the highest and the lowest alike for approximately seven entire centuries, starting from 23 or 22 BCE, when star dancers Pylades from Cilicia and Bathyllus from Alexandria are credited with its introduction into Rome.[1] That most intriguing and flamboyant of spectacles was an expression-filled dance form predicated on the human body's mute delineation of action, character, and passion. Impersonating in close succession a series of mythical characters to the accompaniment of instrumental music and verbal narrative (partly recited and partly sung), a (predominantly male) masked, silent dancer celebrated the spectacle of form 'in flux', the human body's marvellous capacity to mould and re-mould itself in a fascinating array of sensational configurations.

As we can read in Lucian's *De Saltatione* (*On Dancing*), a witty little dialogue of the second century CE:

On the whole, pantomime dancing promises to demonstrate and enact characters and passions, introducing now someone in love now someone in the grip of anger, another afflicted with madness, another yet again plunged in sadness—and all these things in due measure. Indeed, its most incredible feature is that, within the selfsame day, now Athamas is shown overcome with madness now Ino in fear, and sometimes the same person is Atreus and after a while Thyestes, then Aegisthus or Aerope. Yet all these (characters) are but a single man.[2]

---

[1] In reality pantomime was an aesthetic form with a long period of evolution extending at least as far back as the third century BCE; nevertheless, the contribution of the two eastern performers must have been significant enough to signal a second beginning for the genre (see Jory (1981)). For a brief chronological sketch, see Lada-Richards (2007), 19–28 and (including mime) Webb (2008), 24–43.

[2] *Salt.* 67. All translations are my own, unless otherwise indicated.

With every nerve and muscle under perfect rhythmical control, the dancing-soloist reached out to his audience by means of an affective vocabulary of steps and gestures: speaking through 'the entrancing quiver of the palm',[3] he was master of a 'wonderful art' (*mirabilis ars*),[4] which downplayed verbal language as a mode of communication in favour of conversing 'through gesture, nod, leg, knee, hand and spin' (*gestu, nutu, crure, genu, manu, rotatu*).[5]

After successive knocks from the Church and Christian emperors, ancient pantomime finally breathed its last towards the end of the seventh century CE.[6] Yet the fascination that had always surrounded pantomime dancers lived on. Smouldering under the ashes, the secret that some time in the past there existed a wonderful stage-art, which knew how to speak without opening the mouth, was never extinguished:

Where could you find today a dancer or a mime who would know how to narrate whichever stories you want by means of bodily movement only; who, by mere nods and corporeal gesture, would expound things one by one no less clearly than some eloquent orator, so that he would seem to have as many tongues as limbs?[7]

cries the seventeenth-century philologist Isaac Vossius, appropriating a famous line from an anonymous Latin epigram.[8] Fully quoted by Andrea Perrucci, the seventeenth-century Neapolitan poet, amateur actor, and composer of a seminal treatise on the workings of the *commedia dell'arte*, this same ancient epigram was accompanied by the author's comment: 'most beautiful is the description written by an ancient poet of the movements of a dancer' (*bellissima è la descrizione fatta da un Poeta antico dell'azioni d'un Saltatore*).[9] Indeed, several Italian early seventeenth-century theatrical treatises discussing dance in the context of the new genre opera make a concerted effort to legitimize contemporary choreographic choices by means of establishing a crucial link with Greek and Roman practice, in particular the use of bodily communication in dramatic dancing.[10]

---

[3] *Greek Anthology* 9. 505, 17.
[4] Anonymous, *Latin Anthology*, I.1 (Shackleton Bailey) 100, 9.
[5] Sidonius Apollinaris, *Carmina* 23. 269–70.
[6] The decisive blow must have been given by canons 51 and 62 of the Council in Trullo (691/2) which banned all 'dancing on the stage'; see Lada-Richards (2007), 25 with primary sources; Webb (2008), 39 and 222–3.
[7] 'Ubinam hodie saltatorem aut mimum invenias, qui solo corporis motu, quasvis sciat narrare historias, qui solo nutu et corporis gestu non minus manifeste, quam disertus aliquis orator singula explicet, ita ut quot membra, totidem quoque linguas habere videatur?' Vossius (1673), 135. Indicative examples of early dance writings where the ancient pantomime's art is treated at length: de Pure (1972 [1688]); Ménestrier (1984 [1682]); Burette (1717); Calliachius (1718 [1713]); Ferrarius (1718 [1714]); Bonnet (1969 [1723]).
[8] *Latin Anthology*, I.1 (Shackleton Bailey) 100, 9.
[9] Perrucci (1699), 184, quoted by Alm (1996a), 87 and Alm (2003), 217. Perrucci's treatise is newly edited and translated by Heck (2007).
[10] This is the case especially on the Venetian operatic stage, where *balli* became an integral part of the entire spectacle. Most important in this respect are the erudite music theorist Giovanni Battista Doni's *Trattato della Musica Scenica* (*ca.* 1635–9; published in his posthumous *Lyra Barberina* II

Not surprisingly, ancient pantomime, as the art of those who, 'without speaking but simply with gestures' (*senza favellare ma solamente con i gesti*),[11] 'expressed anything and imitated that which was sung' (*esprimevano qualunque cosa, e imitavano quello, che si cantava*),[12] was given pride of place in aesthetic writings emanating from a theatrical tradition heavily reliant on the use of expressive gesture and mime in its danced parts.[13]

Despite pockets of expressive dance mimeticism dotted on the European map from the Renaissance onwards,[14] and unmistakeable peaks of pantomime style dancing in seventeenth-century choreographies in both Italy and France, the eighteenth century remains the time *par excellence* when, on both sides of the English channel, the cries increased from those who wished contemporary stage-dancing to move wholesale in the direction indicated by ancient pantomime. The advocates of a new kind of dance wanted to narrate an entire story in mute, gestural language in the manner of the ancients, and 'paint' vivid, striking pictures on the stage. Restricting the focus to eighteenth-century England and France, this chapter (*a*) outlines with the broadest possible brushstrokes some of the most significant moments of the dance reform gathering pace in the two neighbouring countries from the early 1700s; (*b*) takes some tentative steps towards explaining why it was only in these particular contexts that the 'idea' of ancient pantomime spawned the autonomous art form we now consider as the direct ancestor of the 'classical' ballet; and (*c*) draws attention to some of the intricate ways in which the ancient genre enjoyed a new lease of life by becoming assimilated and blended with some of the dominant aesthetic and cultural preoccupations of the Enlightenment in England and France.

[Florence 1763]) and the anonymous theatrical work *Il Corago* (*c*. 1628–37, first published by Fabbri and Pompilio 1983), which devotes several chapters to dance. On the latter, see Savage and Sansone (1989); on 17th-cent. theatrical treatises, see Alm (1995), (1996*a*), (1996*b*), (2003).

[11] Anon. *Il Corago*, in Fabbri and Pompilio (1983), 126.

[12] Doni (1763), 93.

[13] For example, mimed dancing was an important element in the Italian *Commedia dell'Arte* tradition; for the importance of mime in 17th-cent. Venetian dance, see below p. 27.

[14] Eminent examples of pantomimic dancing positioned by experts in the direct line of ancestry leading to the theatrical ballet (see Sparti (1993*a*), 54) are the so-called *moresche*, 15th-cent. mimed and danced interludes also known as *intermezzi* or *tramezzi* because they broke up lengthy plays, banquets, marriage celebrations, etc. Their themes were often mythological or heroic—we hear, for example, of a balletic battle between Heracles and the Centaurs or a danced contest between Neptune and Minerva for the control of Attica (Sparti (1996*a*), 44–5). Whatever their theme, *moresche* exhibited mimed actions (e.g. agricultural tasks, such as harvesting, sowing, mowing, threshing and shovelling) executed in time with the music; see Pirrotta (1982), esp. 49–55; Nevile (2004), esp. 33–9. In the 16th cent. too, Italian mascarades, *intermedii* and pastorals were also distinguished by their pantomimic elements (Sparti (1996*b*), 263). Nevertheless, 'we shall probably never know if and in what ways' the creators of *moresche* thought they were reviving ancient dance spectacles (Sparti 1993b: 385).

SETTING THE SCENE

From the last decades of the seventeenth and throughout the eighteenth century, the 'pinnacle of choreographic achievement' was widely felt to be ancient pantomime.[15] As dance historian, Susan Leigh Foster puts it,

> For almost every author, the most significant moment in the development of dance, the dancing against which all subsequent dances would necessarily be compared, occurred in the ancient Greek and Roman amphitheaters.[16]

What is most remarkable, however, is that theoretical interest in Greco-Roman pantomime was never far away from real attempts to revive the lost ancient art.

The process begun as early as 1712, when John Weaver, a dancing master from Shrewsbury, published his landmark *An Essay Towards an History of Dancing*, becoming thus the undisputed catalyst for the popularization of the ideal of Greco-Roman pantomime in the eighteenth century.[17] With his *Essay* and several subsequent treatises, he aimed to restore theatrical dancing to the standing of ancient pantomime as 'a Science Imitative and Demonstrative', capable of explaining

> Things conceiv'd in the Mind, by the *Gestures* and *Motions* of the Body, and plainly and intelligibly representing *Actions, Manners*, and *Passions*; so that the Spectator might perfectly understand the *Performer* by these his *Motions*, tho' he say not a Word.[18]

A mere two years after the publication of Weaver's *Essay*, the first practical experiment for the revival of ancient pantomime took place in France in the magnificent Château de Sceaux, near Paris. The cultured and extravagant Anne Louise Bénédicte, Duchesse du Maine, daughter-in-law of Louis XIV, 'had a mind to see an essay of the art of the ancient pantomimes, in order to acquire a clearer idea of their representations than that which she had conceived by reading'.[19] She therefore asked the first dancers of the Paris Opéra, namely Jean Balon and Françoise Prévost, to dance in mute, gestural language and to the accompaniment of specially composed music (by Jean-Joseph Mouret) the fourth Act of Corneille's *Horace*. According to the Abbé Du Bos, whose elegant prose popularized the experiment, the dancers, 'our two new Pantomimes', stimulated each other so effectively, that they brought themselves to the point

---

[15] Foster (1996*a*), 13.
[16] Ibid., 13.
[17] Weaver's works are reprinted in fascimile in Ralph (1985).
[18] Weaver, cited in Ralph (1985), 688, 652. The most important treatises in this context are: *Anatomical and Mechanical Lectures upon Dancing* (1721) and *The History of the Mimes and Pantomimes* (1728).
[19] Du Bos (1748), 220.

of shedding real tears.[20] So, the first modern age conscious attempt to revive the lost ancient art 'focused attention on narrative mimicry through expressive manual and bodily gesture'[21] and took place on 20 April 1714, the Fourteenth Night of the so-called *Grandes Nuits de Sceaux*, nightlong entertainments staged by the Duchess from April 1714 to May 1715.

The second practical experiment followed relatively shortly afterwards. It was John Weaver's *The Loves of Mars and Venus*, first performed as an afterpiece at Drury Lane Theatre on 2 March 1717. It was described in the programme accompanying the production as 'A Dramatick Entertainment of Dancing, Attempted in Imitation of the Pantomimes of the Ancient Greeks and Romans'; and, as Moira Goff writes, it 'skillfully integrated conventional dances with expressive gestures in order to convey a complete narrative without the help of sung or spoken words'.[22] In addition, putting theory into practice in unprecedented ways, Weaver produced two further dance-dramas in the same vein: *The Fable of Orpheus and Eurydice* (Drury Lane, 6 March 1718), advertised as 'Attempted in Imitation of the Ancient *Greeks* and *Romans*', and *The Judgment of Paris* (Drury Lane, 6 February 1733), described as 'A Dramatic Entertainment in Dancing and Singing, After the Manner of the Ancient *Greeks* and *Romans*'.[23]

Weaver's theatrical creations were not the crowd-pullers that the Drury Lane management had hoped for, primarily because the public's appetite, whetted by the ingenious mélange of slapstick and seriousness provided by John Rich at the rival patent playhouse of Lincoln's Inn Fields, inclined towards the more traditional types of pantomime entertainment, which combined classically inspired plots with the all-time favourite *Commedia dell' Arte* characters, such as Harlequin and Colombine.[24] However, even if his attempts had no immediate impact on theatrical dancing, Weaver does deserve the credit for having been the first dancing-master to fully recognize 'the sufficiency of bodily movement to communicate plot, character and emotion', and the first to present his efforts at composing dances 'altogether of the *Pantomimic* Kind' as an attempt to resurrect and rescue from oblivion the ancient art, whose practitioners he understood as '*Imitators of all Persons and of all Things*, as the Name imports'.[25]

---

[20] This most popular narrative, however, reached audiences a couple of decades after the event, since the description was only included in the third volume of Du Bos's work, not published until 1733. Du Bos's treatise was extremely fashionable in high intellectual circles, and enjoyed multiple editions throughout the eighteenth century, not just in French but also in English and Dutch. Du Bos (1748), 220.

[21] Chazin-Bennahum (1988), 303.

[22] Weaver *ap.* Ralph (1985), 737; Goff (2005), 214.

[23] See Weaver in Preface to *The Loves of Mars and Venus* in Ralph (1985), 767 and 841 respectively.

[24] On pantomime in 18th-cent. London, see e.g. Avery (1934), (1938); Sawyer (1990); O'Brien (1998), (2004).

[25] Cohen (1960), 43; *Preface to The Loves of Mars and Venus* in Ralph (1985), 752; Weaver in Ralph (1985), 685. On Weaver's importance in 18th-cent. dance history, see e.g. Cohen (1960); Ralph (1983), (1985); Goff (1995), (1998), (2005), 210–17; Taylor (2001); Blanning (2007); Weickmann (2007), 54. On dancing masters in the cultural context of early 18th-cent. London, see Goff (1994); Thorp (1997).

After Weaver's productions, the most memorable name along the line that starts from antiquity and culminates in the eighteenth-century *ballet d'action* or 'pantomime ballet' is Marie Sallé, member of a dynasty of well-established French fairground performers and undisputed star in the danced divertissements of some of Jean-Philippe Rameau's most famous operas.[26] Admired by dance reformer Jean-Georges Noverre (see below) as well as by Voltaire for her expressive style, she made history with her *Pygmalion* (Drury Lane 1734), where pantomime was 'invoked as the principal medium for sustaining a coherent exchange of thoughts and feelings' on the stage and used 'to portray faithfully the sincere feelings of danced characters'.[27] Despite the many isolated steps down the path to a complete reform of theatrical dancing, however, the single choreographer who ultimately 'succeeded in breaking the mould of performing-style in ballet', and therefore, as Angelica Goodden put it, removed the genre 'from the non-dramatic realms which dance had previously inhabited', was the French/Swiss ballet-master Jean-Georges Noverre (1727–1809).[28]

After a period in England in the close company of David Garrick, Noverre expounded his thoughts in a series of fifteen interrelated letters (first published in Stuttgart and Lyon in 1760)—a manifesto with 'immediate repercussions on the art of ballet throughout Europe'.[29] Naturally, what is of particular consequence in the context of pantomime's afterlife is that Noverre himself thought of his *Letters* as

the first stone of the monument which I desired to erect to that form of expressive dancing which the Greeks called pantomime.[30]

And it certainly looks as though his efforts in this direction did not get lost on his contemporaries, who styled him as

the greatest composer of ballet pantomimes since the Renaissance of the Arts, and the worthy rival of Pylades and Bathyllus in the art of speaking to the eyes and the soul through gesture and movement.[31]

Noverre came upon the scene after at least half a century of turmoil and ferment in the domain of the dance. He was notoriously reluctant to acknowledge Hilverding and Angiolini, his immediate predecessors in the revival of

---

[26] Primarily *Les Fêtes d' Hébé* (prem. 1739) and *Les Indes galantes* (prem. 1735).

[27] Foster (1996*a*), 2. For Noverre and Voltaire's admiration, see Nye (2005*a*), 209 and (2005*b*), 123–32; for her *Pygmalion* as 'poised on the brink of dance's narrativization', see McCleave (1998); as, in effect, a 'ballet d'action', see Weickmann (2007), 60 for further discussions, see Vince (1957); Foster (1996*a*), 1–12 and (1996*b*).

[28] Goodden (1986), 137. Athough there is no doubt that Noverre exaggerated his own contribution, the precise amount of credit owed to him as an 'inventor' of the *ballet d'action* and innovator in the context of the operatic dance tradition is a disputed point; see e.g. Nye (2007). On Noverre's contribution to ballet, see Lynham (1950); Winter (1974), esp. 113–22; Goodden (1986); Hansell (1998) and (2002), 198–251; Nye (2005*a*); Chazin-Bennahum (2007).

[29] Guest (1996), 8.

[30] Noverre (1930), 2.

[31] Guest (1996), 101, translating from a contemporary document.

ancient pantomime,[32] but he *did* pay tribute to the one stage-performer of his time who exercised the most formative influence on him, and strengthened his desire to unlock the hidden powers of body language, marry them even with the technical steps and attitudes of his dancers: David Garrick. According to Noverre, who saw Garrick perform during a whole theatrical season in London:

Mr Garrick, the celebrated English actor, is the model I wish to put forward. Not only is he the most handsome, the most perfect and the most worthy of admiration of all actors, he may be regarded as the Proteus of our own time.

Garrick built himself a reputation as the most ingeniously versatile of all performers, wearing, as Noverre put it, 'a different face for each part'.[33]

Compared to the unvarying, monotonous declamatory style that was the norm among his predecessors and early rivals, Garrick's non-stylized approach to acting was nothing less than revolutionary.[34] We must not forget, however, that supreme versatility as well as adaptation to the particular needs of every stage-character were deeply ingrained in the profession of the ancient pantomimes, whose job was, in Lucian's words, to imitate Proteus himself, the archetypal shape-shifter of Greek legend (*Salt.* 19).[35] For Noverre, who dreamt of 'Proteus-like' dancers able to 'assume a thousand different attitudes according to the varied symptoms of their passions' and of gestures that could function as 'the faithful interpreters of every mood', the pantomime ideal of a wonderful ductility of body and of soul, newly illustrated in Garrick's art, was hugely inspirational.[36]

Above everything else, what must have struck Noverre with the force of a revelation was Garrick's intensely physical acting style, which consciously and systematically privileged nonverbal, corporeal crystallizations of emotional intensity over the established rules of sonorous declamation. Throughout his long stage-career, Garrick continued to conceptualize dramatic character in terms of corporeal movement. In the words of Richard Cumberland, who saw him

---

[32] Franz Anton Hilverding and his pupil Gasparo Angiolini accelerated the pace of dance reform in Vienna and Italy with choreographic experiments whose repercussions were felt throughout Europe. The learned treatises accompanying some of Angiolini's ballets (see Bellina 1994) styled them 'in the taste of the ancients' (*dans le goût des Anciens*) and discussed Lucian's *De Saltatione* and other evidence on ancient pantomime; see further Lada-Richards (2007), 169. On Hilverding and Angiolini, see Tozzi (1972–3); Winter (1974); Carones (1987); Bellina (1989); Brown (1991); Brainard (1996); Hansell (2002), 198–251.

[33] Noverre (1930), 82, 83.

[34] Among an immense bibliography, see Davies (1780), (1973 [1784]); Boaden (1831–2); Hedgcock (1912); Joseph (1959), 67–172; Taylor (1972); Woods (1981), (1984); Roach (1982), (1993); Rogers (1984); Powell (1988); Wilson (1990); West (1991); Holland (1996); Goring (2005), 114–41.

[35] On the ancient pantomime's somatic versatility, see e.g. Lucian, *Salt.* 19, 66; Anon., *Greek Anthology* 16.289; Plotinus, *Enn.* 6.1.27; Cassiodorus, *Variae* 4.51.9; Manilius, *Astron.* 5.482a and 480b.

[36] Noverre (1930), 52–3; 15. On the ancient pantomime's empathic versatility, i.e. his ability to signify a series of contradictory emotions, see e.g. Lucian, *Salt.* 67; Automedon, *Greek Anthology* 5.129.

perform at Covent Garden, he displayed character 'in every muscle and in every feature',[37] a comment which encapsulates perfectly well the feeling of ancient connoisseurs of pantomime art, like Plotinus, who knew that every single part of the dancer's body, down to the clenched fingers of the hand and the sinews and veins which are affected along with them, had something to contribute to the overall effect (Plotinus, *En.* 4.4.34).

Having made such a huge investment in his entire body as a privileged medium of communication in the stage-audience transaction, Garrick was credited by his contemporaries with precisely that marvellous ability to translate vision into hearing, for which the ancient pantomime was renowned. Noverre enthuses:

> He was so natural, his expression was so lifelike, his gestures, features and glances were so eloquent and so convincing, that he made the action clear even to those who did not understand a word of English.[38]

And in the memory of those privileged to witness Garrick's dumbshow in the various Parisian salons:

> One felt tempted to call out to him at every moment, as to those mimes whose gestures vied in eloquence with Cicero's speech: 'You speak to us with your hands'.[39]

In reality, the most appropriate point of reference here is not Cicero and mimes but Lucian's *De Saltatione* where, after having watched a leading pantomime dance with no musical or vocal accompaniment whatsoever, a philosopher is said to have exclaimed:

> I hear, man, the acts you are performing; I don't merely see, but you seem to me to be talking with your very hands. (*Salt.* 63)

To return to Noverre's balletic vision, it was precisely the principle of a powerfully expressive nonverbal communication—a principle *both* enshrined in the dramaturgy of ancient pantomime *and* impressively illustrated by Garrick's acting[40]—that Noverre was hoping to instil in the new ballet, so that dance and mimed action could be at last reunified. Fully in the spirit of ancient pantomime, Noverre determined the point of perfection in his pantomime ballet as the moment when

> Words will become useless, everything will speak, each movement will be expressive, each attitude will depict a particular situation, each gesture will reveal a thought, each glance will convey a new sentiment.[41]

---

[37] *Memoirs of Richard Cumberland* (London 1806), quoted in Goring (2005), 119.
[38] Noverre (1930), 82.
[39] Quoted in Hedgcock (1912), 219.
[40] The two are connected in Noverre's letter (not indisputably genuine) to Voltaire about Garrick, where he writes: 'Les talents extraordinaires de Garrick m'ont convaincu de l'existence des Protées, des Pylades, des Batyles et des Roscius. Il pouvait être regardé comme le légataire de ces hommes rares, qui firent jadis l'admiration d'Athènes et de Rome'; see Besterman (1962), 211.
[41] Noverre (1930), 53.

A FERTILE CONFLUENCE OF FACTORS

One of the commonest fallacies in eighteenth-century dance history is the assumption that the *ballet d'action* signalled a total *rupture* with previous operatic traditions.[42] Nothing, however, could be further from the truth. Recent ground-breaking studies of the danced *divertissements*, which formed an integral part of almost every act of Jean-Baptiste Lully's operas in seventeenth-century Paris, have dealt a blow to the impression that 'dance at the Paris Opéra was primarily decorative before 1776, when Jean-Georges Noverre first mounted his *ballet d'action Médée et Jason*' (see Figure 1.1).[43] As Rebecca Harris-Warrick argues, many such spectacles 'seemed to edge toward, if not to cross the line into, pantomime', not simply by being 'imitative of specific actions such as fighting', but, most importantly, because of their clear narrative function, that is to say their choreography's ability to portray an action that unfolds over time.[44] Similarly, *libretti*, choreographic sources, dance treatises, and eyewitness accounts indicate that a strong mimetic element was one of the most distinctive features of the *balli* (theatrical dances) which graced almost every performance on the operatic stage of seventeenth-century Venice.[45] Yet in neither context did the pantomimic aspect of the spectacles involved give rise to a new genre, as was the case in eighteenth-century England and France. Why was this so? The answer should be sought in the extraordinary confluence of factors which proved exceptionally fertile for the reception of the ancient pantomime seed.

Since the beginning of the century, a masterfully developed gestural 'language' was already in bloom on both sides of the Channel. In France the various fairgrounds of the capital, deprived of the right to stage drama with spoken dialogue, hosted an unlimited variety of corporeal entertainments (including rope-dancing and all kinds of acrobatic numbers), the speciality of the so-called *forains*, performers well-trained not just in breathtaking somersaults but, most importantly, in miming, singing, and dancing.[46] In London too, corporeal

---

[42] On the ballet-pantomime as a genre born well inside the French operatic tradition, see Nye (2005*a*).

[43] Harris-Warrick (2007), 209–10. Lully's own librettist, Philippe Quinault, was greatly admired by such ardent exponents of dance reform as Louis de Cahusac (see below) and Noverre, who saw in his work a 'project of integrating dance with the unfolding of the plot' (Harris-Warrick 1999: 190).

[44] Harris-Warrick (2007), 215 and (1999), 189 and further (1998), (1999); cf. Pierce and Thorp (2006), on the 'imitative' aspect of theatrical dance in Lully's work. Many thanks to Jennifer Thorp who kindly alerted me to this aspect of Lully's operas.

[45] See primarily Alm (1995), (1996*a*), (1996*b*), (2003); cf. Hansell (2002), 178–82. On Venetian pantomimic choreographies as providing 'significant evidence that the *ballet en action* also had historical roots in Italy as well as France', see Alm (2003), 238–9.

[46] See e.g. Brockett (1965); Lagrave (1979); Brown (1980); Crow (1985), 45–55; Isherwood (1981), (1986); Martin (2002). Best primary sources on the *spectacles de la foire*: Parfaict (1743); Compardon (1877).

Figure 1.1 *Médée et Jason*, Ballet tragique, London (1781).

dramaturgy was phenomenally successful not only at the various minor or illegitimate theatres which were not licensed for the production of spoken drama but also at the two rival patented playhouses, Drury Lane and Lincoln's Inn Fields, which kept afloat financially by staging (primarily as afterpieces) pantomime shows reliant on dance, music, and sensational spectacle.[47] Indeed, the undisputed king of this kind of nonverbal drama, the celebrated John Rich, manager of Lincoln's Inn Fields, was praised by his fans for his prowess as Harlequin in terms that would have made any ancient pantomime proud:

his gesticulation was so perfectly expressive of his meaning, that every motion of his hand or head, or any part of his body, was a kind of dumb eloquence that was readily understood by the audience.[48]

---

[47] See e.g. Rosenfeld (1960); O'Brien (2004).
[48] Davies (1780), 1. 368–9.

Simultaneously, however, the lost ancient art found powerful advocates at the higher end of the socio-cultural spectrum, with élite trend-setters, like the Abbé Du Bos (see above), writing about it in glowing prose, and important men of the theatre, like Charles Gildon, author of the most influential of acting manuals in the first half of the eighteenth century, musing aloud on the high desirability of its reintegration into mainstream theatrical business:

> ...but I am of Opinion, that the Hands in Acting ought very seldom to be wholly quiescent, and that if we had the Art of the *Pantomimes*, of expressing things so clearly with their Hands, as to make the Gestures supply Words, the joining these significant Actions to the Words and Passions justly drawn by the Poet, would be no contemptible Grace in the Player, and render the Diversion infinitely more entertaining, than it is at present. For indeed *Action* is the Business of the Stage.[49]

It cannot be stressed strongly enough that the corporeal aesthetics of English Harlequins and French *forains* was not exactly what aspiring reformers in the worlds of theatre and dance had in mind when encouraging a greater prominence of the bodily factor in performance. Consequently, the perceived asymmetry of cultural capital between the corporeal dramaturgy of contemporary non-verbal performers and that of the ancient pantomime dancers informs a variety of texts, from Gildon's *Life of Mr Thomas Betterton*, which opposes categorically 'our modern dancers' to 'the Mimes and Pantomimes of the Romans'[50] to Noverre himself, who stipulates that

> Students of dancing should not confuse the noble pantomime of which I speak with that low and trivial form of expression which Italian players have introduced into France, and which bad taste would appear to have accepted.[51]

Nevertheless, élite attempts at demarcating the boundaries of theatrical legitimacy notwithstanding, the crucial fact remains that since the early decades of the century, a powerful concatenation of forces created a congenial milieu for the kind of somatic techniques which formed the lifeblood of the ancient dancer's

---

[49] Gildon (1970 [1710]), 78. For Gildon, acting is not just a matter of proper declamation but also of appropriate bodily deportment, *actio* (Ibid. 51), precisely the realm wherein the ancient pantomime excelled (ibid. 23).

[50] See Gildon (1970), 144–5: 'Were our modern Dancers like the *Mimes* and *Pantomimes* of the *Romans*...our Dotage on them might have been thought more excusable; since one of them, as I have shewn from *Lucian*, by the Variety of his Motions and Gesticulations, would represent a whole History, with all the different Persons concerned in it so plainly and evidently, that every body, that saw him, perfectly understood what he meant.'

[51] Noverre (1930), 99. Crucially, however, this was not a judgement shared by all members of the socio-cultural élite. The most vocal exponent of an opposite opinion was the economist and critic Ange Goudar who, writing often in his wife Sarah's name, was keen to recognize merit 'in just those aspects of Itallian ballet that stood in sharpest contrast to the new style of heroic pantomimes': Hansell (2002), 225. Hitting at the cultural snobbism of Noverre and his followers, he famously declared that 'it is better to be a genuine Pierrot than a false Pyrrhus' (il vaut mieux être un vrai *Pierot* qu'un faux *Pyrrhus*): Goudar (1773), 133.

art. In both England and France, the erudite's word just as much as every other stage-Harlequin's performance demonstrated that the weight of theatrical communication could be carried perfectly well by body-language alone, and that non-verbal signs could be as effective vehicles of thoughts and feelings as complex verbal articulations.[52] The revival of interest in ancient pantomime in the eighteenth century, then, was facilitated immeasurably by the general popularity enjoyed by gestural eloquence,[53] its position, that is, as part and parcel of the wider public's theatrical experience or even more so as a force conditioning that public's 'horizon of expectations'[54] in the field of entertainment culture.

In addition, it is incalculably important that some features of the ancient genre found themselves in broad consonance with major artistic and aesthetic trends, concerns, preoccupations of the hosting cultural milieu. One example is, I hope, sufficient at this point, especially as it relates to what is perhaps the ancient genre's most neglected aspect, namely its character as a fully-fledged pictorial dramaturgy.

Plutarch, writing in the early second century CE, seems to understand pantomime as a spectacle that integrates the figurative arts, and refers to bodily configurations frozen in space and time, as if incorporated in a 'picture':

when the dancers, having arranged their overall appearance in the shape of Apollo or Pan or a bacchant, retain these attitudes, like figures in a painting.[55]

Similarly, Libanius, in the fourth century CE, draws our attention to the dancer's transition from dizzyingly swift movement to a statue-like stillness that culminates in a veritable *tableau vivant* on stage:

What would someone admire more? The continuity of their many pirouettes or, after this, their suddenly crystallised posture, or the figure held fixed in this position? For they whirl round, as if borne on wings, but conclude their movement in a static pose, as if glued to the spot; and with the stillness of the pose, the image presents itself.[56]

---

[52] My point here can easily mislead, if one fails to bear in mind the virulence of the opposing voice. For early 18th-cent. London was not only entertained by non-verbal acts but also constantly reprimanded by moralists and satirists warning against the ethical and intellectual dangers of succumbing to illegitimate visual attractions, such as 'monsters, tumblers, ladder-dancers, Italian shadows, dumb shews, buffoonery, and nonsense!': so William Popple in *The Prompter* of Thursday, 23 Dec. 1735, repr. in Appleton and Burnim (1966), 136; see further Avery (1938) and for parallels with the ancient world, Lada-Richards (2004*a*). On the other hand, enjoying the patent of antiquity in a century obsessed with Greece and Rome, ancient pantomime was easily immune from direct calumniation.

[53] Although restrictions of space prevent further discussion, it cannot be stressed strongly enough that the practical experiments of dance reformers in the eighteenth century are also to be seen in relation to one of the favourite Enlightenment topics, the power of wordless, gestural communication. Cf. below, p. 34 and n. 73.

[54] For the concept of the 'Erwartungshorizont', see primarily Jauss (1970).

[55] Plutarch, *Mor.* 747c.

[56] Libanius, *Oration* 64.118.

With the aid of Plutarch, Libanius, and several other texts we can easily imagine that one of the thrills of ancient pantomime would have consisted in watching the dancer's flowing movement stilled for a fraction of time, then artfully resumed. It is not at all improbable that, in competent choreographies, such pictorial configurations would have been exploited for their sheer expressive force, underscoring moments of extreme passion. Moreover, in a genre where the actor incarnated in turn all the characters in the dramatization of a myth, moments of suppressed action may well have served as pictorial 'transitions' between the roles of, say, Dionysus, Teiresias, Cadmus, the Messenger, and Agave, in a pantomime re-creation of the story told by Euripides' *Bacchae*.[57]

If my assumptions concerning the ancient genre's pictorial quality are essentially correct,[58] Greco-Roman pantomime must have been able to offer a ready-made answer to the prayers of Diderot, who was dreaming of plays able to transfix the viewer not by 'coups de théâtre' but by way of being punctuated by striking, emotionally laden, essentially silent 'tableaux', plays, that is, which would treat the spectator as if he were in front of a canvas on which a series of tableaux would follow one another as if by magic.[59] Similarly, the pantomime's statuesque poses, 'pregnant' with the possibility of imminent action, and attitudes only seemingly at rest but in reality spawning their sequel, would have satisfied Diderot's predilection for 'those paintings where the figures seem to me ready to move (*prêtes à se mouvoir*)', as he put it in a well-known letter to Mme Riccoboni, adding: 'I'm constantly in waiting' (*J'attends toujours*).[60]

Most importantly, Diderot, although the most prolific and ingenuous art-critic in France in the second half of the eighteenth century, was not alone in his views regarding the ideal of a close reciprocity between the theatrical and the pictorial arts. He did offer what is perhaps the most extreme articulation of such views in his *Entretiens sur le Fils Naturel* (1757) and the *Discours de la poésie dramatique* (1758), but he was nevertheless expressing sentiments that were very much in the air in wider circles among his contemporary men of letters. There is every reason to believe that the wonderful dovetailing between ancient and modern notions of stage-pictorialism at this particular juncture must have played a significant role in the supreme importance attached by all dance-reformers to the requirement that a ballet ought to 'paint', or even more so, 'look like', a picture.[61]

---

[57] *Greek Anthology* 16.289.

[58] See further Lada-Richards (2004*b*).

[59] See, most famously, in his *Discours de la poésie dramatique*, in Versini (1996), 4. 1342: 'Si le spectateur est au théâtre comme devant une toile où des tableaux divers se succéderaient par enchantement...'. On Diderot and painting, Fried (1988) is still unexcelled; cf. Barthes (1977); Caplan (1986); on Diderot's preference for 'tableaux' as opposed to coups de théâtre, see Szondi (1980).

[60] Diderot à Madame Riccoboni, Letter of 27 November 1758; text in Roth (1955–70), 2. 98.

[61] See e.g. Foster (1996*a*), esp. 13–15.

The dancing master, writes Weaver, 'ought to give his Performers, as the Painter does his Pictures, proper Attitudes', or, in Noverre's words,

A ballet is a picture, or rather a series of pictures connected one with the other by the plot which provides the theme of the ballet; the stage is, as it were, the canvas.[62]

A bad ballet, conversely, is one where movements and gestures do 'not afford a single picture worthy of a painter's attention'.[63] Most authors of dance manuals seem to be perfectly conscious that, by means of such requests, they are in the process of reviving an aspect of the ancient genre, whose dancers concentrated on 'selecting all the most proper situations for furnishing the most striking pictures', as ballet-master Giovanni Andrea Gallini wrote in his *Treatise on the Art of Dancing* of 1772.[64] Contemporary dance critics too were not slow to grasp that vital connection. As an art reviewer writes in the *Mercure de France* (October 1776):

pantomime dance is the art that most closely approximates painting. Both speak to the eyes, and they form in the same way tableaux where the passions and sentiments of the characters are rendered with the help of gesture, attitudes, positions, and groupings... it is by making dancing as close to painting as possible that M. Noverre has created a new art, or at least, brought back the dance pantomimes of the ancients (*la danse pantomime des Anciens*).[65]

NEW GESTATIONS

The story of ancient pantomime's revival is nevertheless infinitely more complex and therefore fascinating than my simple sketch suggests. In the first place, as the century advances, pantomime's influence becomes much more subtle, diffuse and as it were 'subterranean', so that, by the time we start considering the period's brightest stars, the threads become so many that the overall picture resembles an inextricable tangle. Diderot, with his calls for a gestural and pictorial dramaturgy; David Garrick, with his most intensely physical, supremely pantomimic acting; Jacques-Louis David, whose paintings celebrate the aesthetic of the body as the supreme bearer of character and passion; the inimitable Emma, Lady Hamilton, whose fascinating *Attitudes* took the aristocratic courts of Europe by storm, *as well as*, earlier in the century, that most innovative and pictorially expressive of French actors, LeKain, or the *castrato* opera singer of proverbial bodily expressiveness Nicolini Grimaldi, whose 'every Limb and every Finger contributes to the Part he acts, insomuch as a deaf Man might go along with him in the Sense of it': all these figures and many more besides have no place

---

[62] Weaver in Ralph (1985), 1019; Noverre (1930), 9.
[63] Noverre (1930), 17.
[64] Gallini (1772), 92.
[65] Translation in Foster (1996*a*), 120.

in the linear development of eighteenth-century dance.[66] Yet their work or their thought bears indelibly the imprint of the pantomime legacy, insofar as they advocate or exemplify in their respective media principles related to the aesthetic of bodily eloquence, the importance of the entire body for the effective communication of action, character, and passion. For this reason, if we really want to understand the afterlife of ancient pantomime and grasp its momentous import to eighteenth-century culture, we have to look into areas extending much further than the relatively narrow domain of ballet-dancing.[67]

Secondly, the story of ancient pantomime in the eighteenth century is not the story of a fossilized image, the relic of a glorious past adoringly preserved by overawed admirers. It should rather be seen as the story of pantomime's multiple, incessant, reciprocal interconnections with the age's *Zeitgeist*. If the eighteenth century appropriated pantomime's heritage, it also injected back into it its own cultural assumptions and aesthetic predilections, so that the ancient genre became progressively 'naturalized' in the century's literary, theatrical, aesthetic, moral, and philosophical landscapes.

Take, for example, the overarching eighteenth-century context of 'sensibility' or *sensibilité*, which colours areas as diverse as the novel, the fine arts, drama, political and moral philosophy, and much else besides. In its theatrical manifestation, it means not only the actor's 'sympathetic identification' with his characters, his ability to project himself imaginatively into their innermost being, feel with *their* feelings, become suffused with *their* passions; it also means the audience's predisposition for being deeply affected by the stage-action, in sympathy with the actor's own feelings and with the ultimate purpose of shedding copious tears.

Ancient pantomime, the genre *par excellence* which sought the sensational and the emotional among dramatic topics, *did* privilege emotional expressiveness. One might even claim that it challenged the boundaries of emotional expressiveness more than any other performative genre in the ancient world. It would certainly have ticked many of the boxes under the banner of *sensibilité*, especially in terms of acting style.[68] But it was only when appropriated by the aesthetic matrices of the eighteenth century that Pylades, the founder of the ancient genre,

---

[66] Among a vast bibliography for Diderot, indispensible are: Josephs (1969); Goodden (1986); (2001); Roach (1993), esp. 116–59; for David see e.g. Johnson (1989), (1993); for the close interrelation of theatre and David's art see Wind (1940), and Carroll (1990); on Emma Hamilton in relation to ancient pantomime, see Lada-Richards (2003*a*), with further bibliography; for Lekain and early 18th-cent. acting styles, see LeKain (1801), Talma (1883), Olivier (1907), Holmström (1967), 11–39. The comment on Grimaldi is by Richard Steele in *The Tattler*, no. 115, Tuesday 3 Jan. 1709—see further Roach (1976).

[67] Examples of important research aiming at a synthetic picture: Heartz (1967–8); Murphy (1976); Chazin-Bennahum (1983), (1988); Goodden (1986); Foster (1996*a*); Rosenfeld (2000).

[68] See e.g. *Greek Anthology* 5.129; Arnobius, *Gent.* 4.35; Claudian, *In Eutrop.* 2.405; Manilius, *Astron.* 5.483; *Greek Inscriptions* 14.2124 (a dead pantomime acclaimed for his ability to empathize, *sympaschein*, with his characters). See Lada-Richards (2007), 52 and now Webb (2008) 86.

became fashioned as something close to an emblem of *sensibilité* in his ability to move and touch the viewer's heart:

Pylade, dans toutes ses tragédies, arrachait des larmes aux spectateurs les moins sensibles.[69]

This view by Cahusac, one of the French pioneers of dance reform, is echoed later in the century by the dancer, choreographer, impresario, and writer Giovanni Andrea Gallini, who enthuses:

This dancer (Pylades) had such great powers in all his tragedies, that he could draw tears from even those of the spectators that were least used to the melting mood.[70]

Similarly, when Noverre states that the infusion of feeling into a ballet would make dancing in 'as flourishing a condition as pantomime was in the time of the ancients',[71] the real yardstick is not so much the pantomime of the ancients *per se*, but pantomime as refashioned *in accordance with prevalent aesthetic assumptions*. The catalyst inspiring Noverre's wish to reinvest the dance with 'the power of speaking to the heart'[72] is something considerably stronger than the art of the ancient masters: it is a genetically modified version of ancient pantomime, a fresh cultural amalgam consisting of the distant echoes of an ancient practice fortified with all the vigour of eighteenth-century *sensibilité*.

Comparable are the transformations undergone by the *sine qua non* principle of ancient pantomime, the 'speaking gesture'. In this case, the points of contact between ancient pantomime and eighteenth-century culture are immediately clear, especially with respect to the tremendous interest in gesture as the most immediate, primordial, universally comprehensible language of mankind, entertained in the circles of the Encyclopaedists.[73] Lucian's much loved story in *De Saltatione* 64, for example, regarding the foreign visitor at Nero's court, who asked the emperor to give him a VIP dancer as a farewell gift, so that his gestural clarity might help him communicate with his barbarian neighbours, resonates with ideas deeply entrenched in eighteenth-century mentality. Yet there

---

[69] De Cahusac (2004 [1754]), 108.
[70] Gallini (1772), 248; cf. Weaver in Ralph (1985), 590 on the ancient pantomimes as '*copying* all the *Force* of the *Passions* meerly by the *Motions* of the *Body*, to that degree, as to draw *Tears* from the *Audience* at their *Representations*'. The entire genre was imagined as exciting the most vivid emotions and making the tears fall ('elle faisoit couler des larmes') in a document coming from Hilverding's circle: see Brown (1991), 156. Cf. Angiolini in Bellina (1994), 161.
[71] See Noverre (1930), 87–8.
[72] Ibid. 11.
[73] Leading philosophers like Condillac and Rousseau became obsessed with a putative primordial and natural language of bodily gestures and inarticulate cries, better suited than verbal language to the expression of man's deepest feelings. See very briefly Rosenfeld (2000). Condillac in particular, taking his cue from Du Bos's special interest in ancient pantomime, devotes long sections of his essay to 'the art of gesture among the ancients' (e.g. *Essay* II. i. 30–42); he posits the 'dance of gestures' as an inextricable part of a powerfully affective 'language of action' and understands Roman pantomime as reflecting a kind of 'language which had been the first that mankind spoke' (*Essay* II. i. 34); see Condillac (2001 [1746]).

is a sense in which, by the time we reach Noverre's dance-manual, the power of the gestural eloquence attributed by ancient sources to the pantomime dancer and his art has grown.

Here is Noverre in the *Preface* to the 1803 enlarged edition of his *Letters*:

There are, undoubtedly, a great many things which pantomime can only indicate, but in regard to the passions there is a degree of expression to which words cannot attain or rather there are passions for which no words exist. Then dancing allied with action triumphs. A step, a gesture, a movement, and an attitude express what no words can say; the more violent the sentiments it is required to depict, the less able is one to find words to express them. Exclamations, which are the apex to which the language of passions can reach, become insufficient, and have to be replaced by gesture.[74]

There is a new, fresh coating here that takes ancient pantomime discourse one step further. Because, despite the fact that Lucian *does* appreciate very keenly the singular impact of pantomime's non-verbal language, he is primarily concerned with demonstrating a lower key proposition, namely that the dancer's silent eloquence does not lag behind the complexities of articulate speech: 'I hear, man, what you are doing—I don't merely see', shouts the philosopher Demetrius (*Salt.* 63; quoted above, p. 26). To the best of my knowledge, only *once* in ancient narratives do we find the realization that dance's unique value as a communicative channel resides in its ability to bring to life those ineffable, inaccessible regions of feeling and experience that verbal language can never reach. For if we forget Cassiodorus, the high-ranking Christian official of the sixth century CE, who states that the pantomime dancer 'renders intelligible what could hardly be expressed by means of oral narrative or written text' (*'facit intellegi, quod vix narrante lingua aut scripturae textu possit agnosci;' Variae* 1.20.5), no ancient author seems keen to impress on us that pantomime dancing expresses *more*, not less, than language is capable of verbalizing.

Once again, then, Noverre's statement bears the traces of an all-important cultural conflation between the pantomime of the ancient sources and the specific concerns of his own time. For Noverre seems to be fully in accord with the views pervading some of the mid-century writings of Diderot, who played the most pivotal role in pantomime's transformation from a lost genre to the lynchpin of a new-style stage-dramaturgy.[75] Diderot's famous distrust of the declamatory mode in theatrical representation combined with his demand that actors act not just with their face but with their whole body, liberates gestural expressiveness from the stigma of an alternative, inferior theatrical language, useful only on those stages where the language of legitimate drama is banned.[76]

---

[74] Noverre (1930), 4.

[75] See esp. Goodden (2001), 89–113.

[76] e.g. Diderot's *Second entretien sur le fils naturel*, in Versini (1996) 1143–4 (with reference to ancient pantomime); and his Letter to Madame Riccoboni (27 Nov. 1758), in Roth (1955–70), 2. 91.

Expressive movement, in its judicious alternation with words, is now positively exalted as the language *of choice*, the one best suited for epitomizing a play's central meanings or encapsulating its affective core. At moments of overwhelming passion silent gesture is primed to carry most effectively the burden of ineffable expression. As early as 1751, in his *Lettre sur les sourds et muets*, Diderot wrote: 'There are sublime gestures that all the eloquence of rhetoric will never express'; and he highlighted as such the obsessive washing of the hands of the sleepwalking Lady Macbeth: 'I know of nothing so full of *pathos* in discursive speech as this woman's silence and movement of the hands.'[77] And in a 1760 letter to Voltaire he comments on the superb pantomimic expression of *pathos* achieved by Mlle Clairon, acting in Voltaire's own *Tancrède*:

> if you could see Clairon crossing the stage, ... you would be more convinced than ever that sometimes silence and pantomime possess a degree of *pathos* that all the resources of the art of rhetoric do not attain.[78]

Here then we have the additional layer which bonds admirably well with the 'idea' of ancient pantomime: it is the new notion of artistic sublimity located in the regions that lie *beyond* the language of words, the regions that only become visible when linguistic discourse breaks down.

Nor was Diderot himself oblivious to the relevance of pantomimic action to the art of dancing. Writing the third of his *Entretiens sur le Fils naturel* in 1757, he was still awaiting the 'man of genius' (*un homme de génie*), who would restore dancing to its status as an imitative art by re-introducing to it the language of the entire body as the vehicle for the imitation of action, character and, especially, the finest shades of emotion.[79] The man of genius, of course, turned out to be Jean-Georges Noverre, but it is, I think, of the utmost importance for us to realize that the 'idea' of ancient pantomime reached the ingenuous ballet master by way of several, interlinked series of cross-fertilizations with eighteenth-century congenial matter, first and foremost the thought of Diderot himself. More generally speaking, the 'idea' of Greco-Roman pantomime functioned as a potent cultural adhesive, able to bind and keep together a multitude of disparate threads in the literary and philosophical, the theatrical and the artistic spheres of eighteenth-century life in both England and France.

---

[77] Diderot (1965 [1751]), 47–8.
[78] Diderot, in Roth (1955–70), 3. 272–3. On Voltaire's contribution to the 18th-cent.'s search for pictorial, pantomimic action, see Holmström (1967), 11–39; Carlson (1998).
[79] Diderot, in Versini (1996), 1182–3.

POSTLUDE

I will bring this chapter to an end by highlighting what is perhaps the greatest irony in the story of ancient pantomime's revival as expounded so far. Both Weaver and Noverre, the two choreographers whose writings were most influential in terms of popularizing the link of their experiments to ancient pantomime, the dance form they believed they were reviving, were also most clearly responsible for overlooking one of the fundamental dimensions of the ancient dancer's style, namely the fastness and sheer acrobatic brilliance of his leaps, pirouettes, and overall technique.[80] Consequently, they failed to appreciate that branch of theatrical dancing which appeared to preserve most faithfully the profile of the ancient genre, with its characteristic blending of gestural expressiveness with sequences of pure, aesthetically pleasing dancing. The despised tradition was that of the (primarily) Italian *grotteschi* dancers, renowned throughout Europe for their spectacular 'aerial style', 'technical virtuosity', 'rigorous athleticism', and 'enormous stylistic, technical and expressive range'.[81]

Noverre's *ballets d'action* on the other hand, restrained and static to the point of privileging measured walking above virtuosic dancing, crystallized in a style known as *terre à terre* dancing. They may well have revived the pictorial dimension of ancient pantomime but, if we trust Baron Grimm's often quoted impression that in Noverre's spectacles 'dancing for the sake of dancing cannot occur except when the danced drama is over', we can only conclude that the great master's ballets failed to do justice to the exhilarating, breathtaking aspect of the ancient dancer's flamboyant physical exploits.[82]

Be all this as it may, by the end of the century the silent art of Pylades and Bathyllus had acquired the aura of a legend, especially thanks to the celebrity status attained in the 1780s by Gaëtan Vestris, the so-called 'God of the Dance', and his marvellous son, Auguste Vestris. From learned connoisseurs to columnists of minor journals, the belief was ripe that contemporary dancing could only legitimize itself as a liberal art worthy of study and esteem by re-establishing the broken link with its remote ancestor, Greco-Roman pantomime dancing. As a result of these ferments in which the 'idea of the ancient pantomime' played a catalytic role, the 'romantic' or 'classical' ballet gradually emerged as an entirely distinct art-form, wherein a self-consistent plot was conveyed through danced

---

[80] Several ancient sources highlight the pantomime's rapid, gliding motion, his multiple sustained revolutions around the axis of his own body and his high, energetic leaps. See e.g. Lucian, *Salt.* 71; Galen, *On preserving one's health* 2.11.40; Libanius, *Or.* 64.104, 117, 118; John Chrysostom, *PG* 49.195; Claudian, *Against Eutropius* 2.359–61.

[81] On the 'grotesque' dancer's style and his ability to combine pantomimic and acrobatic skills, see the eminent contributions to Harris-Warrick and Brown (2005). For their virtuosity, see Harris-Warrick (2005), 10, 6, and 7 (and *passim*).

[82] Grimm (1879), 6. 300; quoted in Hansell (2005), 27 n. 22.

movement. In other words, with the aid of ancient pantomime, the eighteenth century rediscovered dance's ability to narrate a story. As for the idea of the marvellous ancient art itself, it proved to be an entirely dynamic, polymorphous, kaleidoscopic construct, as flexible and changeable as the ancient pantomimic body was in a perpetual process of self-transformation.[83]

[83] A first sketch for some of the material contained in this chapter can be found in Lada-Richards (2007), 163–73; for further angles in the exploration of the same ground, see now Hall (2008b), 363–77.

2

'In Search of a Dead Rat': The Reception of Ancient Greek Dance in Late Nineteenth-Century Europe and America

Frederick Naerebout

One hundred and thirty-five years ago the Dutch—or Frisian—painter Lourens Alma Tadema, who was based in Belgium, exhibited in London at the Royal Academy to huge popular success. For several reasons he decided to stay on in England, Anglicized his name as Lawrence Alma-Tadema, and became a member of the artistic establishment, a Royal Academician, and a recipient of a knighthood. After a period of neglect, he is now again counted as one of the most popular of nineteenth-century academic painters.[1] Alma-Tadema's speciality were scenes of ancient Greece and Rome, meticulously researched and rendered in painstaking detail.[2] His ability to make his audience feel the cool marble surfaces, gave rise to the quip 'a marbellous painter'.

One of the paintings that heralded his ultimate breakthrough in Britain, included in his 1869 London exhibition, was an image of the pyrrhic dance, a weapon dance, performed by soldiers in arms, in a Greek, supposedly classical Athenian setting (see Figure 2.1). In the foreground we see two hoplites in a crouching position, one leg stretched out in front to indicate the dynamism of their dance step, the big round shield, the *hoplon*, lifted with their left hands above their helmeted heads, while their right hands grasp a javelin. Others in the same position are seen coming up behind them.[3] The public loved the painting. Not every critic did: after seeing it at Alma-Tadema's 1882–3 one-man show at

---

[1] Swanson (1977); Becker et al. (1996); Barrow (2001).

[2] On Tadema carefully researching his paintings: Swanson (1977), 14, 36; Borger (1978), *passim*; Barrow (2001), 30, on Tadema's photographic collection and library, now housed at the University of Birmingham.

[3] The Pyrrhic dance, Opus LXIX [= Swanson (1990), 111 = Becker et al. (1996), 151 (no. 16)]. Painted April 1869, exhibited at the Royal Academy in the same year (no. 421), now in the Guildhall Art Gallery.

Figure 2.1 Alma-Tadema's *The Pyrrhic Dance* (1869).

the Grosvenor Gallery, Ruskin caustically described it as 'exactly like a micro-
scopic view of a small detachment of black-beetles, in search of a dead rat'.[4]
Ruskin was of the opinion that the painter had not quite succeeded in giving us a
true impression of what a pyrrhic dance performed by the flower of glorious
Athenian manhood looked like. Although others did find the painting aesthetically pleasing, most will have shared in Ruskin's scepticism: there was at the time
a general conviction that we did not know, and could not know, what ancient
Greek dancing was like. Certainly, Alma-Tadema's 'five o'clock tea Antiquity'
(in Whistler's equally caustic words[5]) was not going to bring us any closer to the
real thing, however well researched many aspects of it were. Still, Alma-Tadema's
paintings—in which quite a lot of dancing is going on[6]—can actually have
contributed to the steady erosion of that opinion, so that towards the end of
the century, we find that Greek dancing is no longer considered a lost art. How
did that come about?

[4] In an 1883 Oxford lecture on the 1882–3 Winter Exhibition at the Grosvenor Gallery: Ruskin
(1908), 319–21, where Alma-Tadema's treatment of marble (!) is called 'a fallacy in his classical
idealism', and in general the twilight atmosphere of his painted interiors, where people 'crouch and
loll' is bitterly attacked. 'The most dastardly of all these representations of classic life' is *The Pyrrhic
Dance*, with its 'fuliginous and cantharoid disfigurement and disgrace'. In 1875 Ruskin had already
written (Ruskin (1904), 263–4): 'The actual facts which Shakespeare knew about Rome were, in
number and accuracy, compared to those which M. Alma-Tadema knows, as the pictures of a child's
first story-book compared to Smith's *Dictionary of Antiquities*. But [Shakespeare] . . . knew Rome
herself, to the heart; and M. Tadema, after reading his Smith's *Dictionary* through from A to Z,
knows nothing of her but her shadow; and that, cast at sunset.'
[5] Quoted by Swanson (1977), 20.
[6] See Borger 1978; Swanson (1977) and (1990). Dance is an important subject in nine pictures
illustrated in Barrow (2001), ills. 14, 40, 44, 50, 68, 84, 86, 130, 136, ranging in date from 1863 to
1889. Add Becker et al. (1996), no. 46.

Here we step back for a moment, in order to sketch, in very broad outlines, some of the background.[7] In post-antique Europe ancient Greek dance was studied from the Renaissance onwards. There was a lot of antiquarian research, but since thoughts of imitating and emulating 'the ancients' and thoughts about the applicability of learning in general were always at least at the back of everybody's minds, we find a constant interplay between scholarship and theatre-making. The inspiration derived from ancient Greek and Greco-Roman examples has been at work throughout the history of western theatrical dancing, as a major driving force in its development—a fact that is not given nearly enough attention in our teleological and self-centred 'histories of the dance'. This interplay grew to a crescendo in the eighteenth century, especially towards the end of the century, with (what I have called elsewhere) the pantomimic craze. All ancient dance was looked at from the angle of Greco-Roman pantomime, and this too inspired performances (see further Lada-Richards, this volume). For the first time the iconographic sources played an important part: the rising tide of archaeological discovery—even though Greek vase-painting, Pompeian wall-painting, and sculpture from different ages were all indiscriminately thrown together—led to a movement in the direction of 'authentic' costuming, and a strong interest in gesture. Best known in England are the 'antique attitudes' by Lady Hamilton, but there were comparable experiments going on across Europe, Maria and Salvatore Viganò being the most famous examples. Soon a classicizing *pas de shawl* was danced on every stage.[8] Most of the time it appeared satisfactory to regard this as a *new* art inspired by classical ideals, and not as an exact reconstruction. Except for a few isolated experiments that did not meet with much enthusiasm, nobody ever actually spoke of reviving ancient dancing. As the great theorist of the pantomimic style of dancing, Jean-Georges Noverre, succinctly put it: 'We are no longer, Sir, in Athens. Everything has well and truly changed since then.'[9]

As the nineteenth century progresses, we can see a general shift towards new subject-matter, new performance styles, new costuming. In the theatre people slowly turned away from the Greeks and Romans and the dances of the ancient

---

[7] Discussed at length in the first part of Naerebout (1997). A revised Italian version of the same is Naerebout (2001), translated by Alessandro Arcangeli.

[8] For a general background, see the excellent study by Holmström 1967.

[9] 'Nous ne sommes plus à Athènes, Monsieur, tout est bien changé.' J.-G. Noverre's *Lettres* were first published in Lyon in 1760; many other editions followed, with new letters added (and letters repeatedly, and confusingly, renumbered); I used the magnificent four-volume edition: Noverre 1803–4. The quote is in vol. 2. 23; cf. 2. 75: 'des fanatiques et des bigots de l'Antiquité, acharnés de mépriser nos chefs-d'oeuvre', and 2. 105: 'Quant à notre danse . . . elle ne peut-être comparée qu'à elle-même.' Noverre argues that in a purely technical sense modern dancing reigns supreme, in the field of pantomime however the dance of the ancients: 'les anciennes avoient des bras, et nous avons des jambes' (1. 129); if the two are brought together, dancing will reach the pinnacles of perfection, see 2. 105, where it is said that the new dance will be far better than 'ces mimes, qui n'avoient que des gestes de convention, et qui ignoroient parfaitement la danse'.

world came to be considered irrelevant. Thus August Bournonville could state that 'we can actually form no clear idea of the manner in which the ancients danced', and that 'it is a mistake to assume that the pantomime which captivated the Romans . . . has something in common with the art form we call ballet'.[10] When the theatre started to look for its inspiration elsewhere, scholars henceforth studied the ancient dance in splendid isolation, as a self-sufficient exercise. This followed a common pattern: the ancient world became the preserve of specialist disciplines—classical philology, ancient history, classical archaeology—together with a diminishing belief in the immediate applicability of the sources. Modern industrial society had other concerns than imitating and emulating the ancients. That did not, or not necessarily, imply a loss of interest: indeed, interest flared up again and again and in many ways burned with an even brighter flame than before. But interest in the ancients was, and still is, enthusiasm for something that is intriguing because it is increasingly unfamiliar.

Then, quite unexpectedly the tables were turned, and towards the end of the nineteenth century ancient Greek dancing was no longer considered a lost art. Some scholars had come to the conclusion that individual movements and even bits of choreography could be reconstructed from the evidence. Wherever revival or reconstruction is accepted as a possibility, it will also be put into practice. So at the same time, there arose a proliferation of dancers who danced ancient dances. The central figure in this development is the French musicologist and composer, Maurice Emmanuel (1862–1938).[11] After some disappointments in his musical career, Emmanuel turned to a study of ancient Greek dance. Indeed, a substantial part of his scholarly activity is taken up with ancient Greece: ancient Greek music and rhythm. It was the study of rhythm that brought him to ancient Greek dance: he studied rhythm as such, in Greek poetry, in Greek music and in Greek dance—ancient Greek *mousikē*.

Emmanuel's thesis is an interesting and much undervalued analysis of the Greek vocabulary of the dance, along traditional lines. His *thèse supplémentaire*, however, is a very different kind of book: there Emmanuel rejects almost all written sources, except drama, as major evidence and focuses almost exclusively on iconography, mostly vase-paintings and some sculptural works. It is from the visual representations that he thought he could retrieve at least part of the art of ancient Greek dancing. What convinced Emmanuel that ancient dancing was not lost after all? Was what he did entirely new, or was he doing something that

---

[10] Clear examples of the shift away from antiquity can be seen in for example the following works: Voïart (1823); Baron (1824). For the quote, see Bournonville (1979), 7, 12.

[11] On Emmanuel, see *The New Grove Dictionary of Music and Musicians* s.v., with many references; more specifically on Emmanuel's work on the Greek dance: Prudhommeau (1982*b*). Emmanuel's studies of Greek dance: (1895*a*) thesis; (1895*b*) the accompanying *thèse supplémentaire*; (1896*a*) identical to the *thèse supplémentaire*, but aimed at a wider audience; translated into English by Harriet Jean Beauley as Emmanuel (1916) repr. New York and London 1927; (1896*b*) is an article summarizing his work.

was 'in the air', waiting to be done? I want to argue that Emmanuel's work was the logical outcome of a number of nineteenth-century interests, and not so unexpected at all when you read the signs of the times. I will discuss this under three headings: the ongoing tradition; the general concern with 'authenticity'; and technological advances.

1. *The Ongoing Tradition.* Not all 'antique dancing' disappeared around 1820: some survived as part of the 'night scene'. 'Greek dance' was an excellent pretext for women to undress; thus the 1841 *Swells' Night Guide through the Metropolis* directs young gentlemen in search of an enjoyable night about town in London to the 'Temples of Voluptuousness', the 'Hall of Rome' and so on, where one could see 'the slightly veiled daughters of Venus' and other women in varying states of undress perform *poses plastiques*, tableaux vivants, and 'spirit stirring dances' in 'imitation of the classic models'.[12] In this way the eighteenth-century *pas de shawl* and 'statue posing' survived in non-legitimate entertainment.[13]

Also important in this respect was the continued presence of the dance in novels, poems, sculpture, and paintings dealing with antiquity. Of course the classical subject-matter allowed otherwise impossible eroticism and nudity. Novels and poetry too contain 'antique' dance scenes, often of an erotic nature. An early instance can be found in the Lydian dancers figuring in the sybaritic banquet scene in Lytton's immensely popular *The Last Days of Pompeii* (first published in 1834); and later such items became fairly commonplace: Pierre Louÿs, *Les Chansons de Bilitis*, 1894 and *Aphrodite, moeurs antiques*, 1895, and Jean Bertheroy (Berthe le Barillier), *Le mime Bathylle*, 1894 and *La danseuse de Pompei*, 1899, all bestsellers.[14] All such things undoubtedly helped to keep alive interest in the dances of classical antiquity. Towards the end of the century 'things Greek' can be seen to return to the general stage: from the 1880s onwards there is a remarkable proliferation of Grecian balls, Greek tableaux vivants, and a new approach to classical drama. Emmanuel cannot have been completely immune to such trends.

2. *Authenticity.* Nowadays, we are completely obsessed with the concept of authenticity, in the sense of the 'real thing'.[15] The reason for our obsessive interest in 'the authentic' seems to be the quickening of change with a resulting sense of loss and alienation. It is not so much modernity replacing

[12] As quoted by Laver (1969), 103.
[13] For a lively description of burlesque and pageantry, such as Little Egypt and her hootchy-kootchy or Salomania, see Bentley (2002). On classical burlesques, see Hall and Macintosh (2009), 350–429.
[14] On the antiquarian-didactic trend in 19th-cent. literature, comparable to the one in painting, see Riikonen (1978).
[15] Naerebout (1994), (2002).

tradition, but relatively slow-moving communities, mainly agricultural, being eroded by relatively fast-moving communities, mainly urban. Several branches of eighteenth-century scholarship (not accidentally coinciding with the Industrial Revolution) sought to preserve the culture of disappearing communities, and gave the interest in 'the authentic' a big boost. We find this in emerging folklore studies, with its documenting of disappearing folk song and of dying handicrafts, but also in other fields, such as textual criticism, as in Malone's 1790 edition of Shakespeare. Nineteenth-century scholarship in general is preoccupied with 'the real'. Historical scholarship sets out to establish historical truth: 'wie es eigentlich gewesen'. There is everywhere an interest in preserving the real thing: museums, archives, the protection and restoration of monuments, and so on. If the real thing is already lost, one can try to retrieve it: we can always turn to folklore where age-old behaviour has been preserved, or to ethnographic parallels which show us in their present what existed in our past. There are several drives towards 'realism' or 'naturalism' in painting, in writing and dramatic performance. Painters of classical scenes were striving after a genuine archaeological exactness, as for instance Alma-Tadema, and his famous French counterparts, Gustave-Clarence-Rodolphe Boulanger, and Jean-Léon Gérôme, the centre of the group of the Néo-grecques or Pompéistes.[16] Such paintings may have influenced the direction into which theatrical tastes or even scholarly inquiry developed, not too a bold an assertion, when one takes into account their incredible popularity.[17] From about 1840 a strong interest in pre-nineteenth-century music developed, and by 1885 Arnold Dolmetsch was reviving old instruments and studying the way these should be played. His efforts became part of a wide-ranging ancient music movement. Dance followed suit.

Emmanuel cannot have been immune to these trends either: and here we can point to his work as a composer. He struggles against the traditional musical establishment, at the conservatory and in the church, turning instead to folk music and 'ancient music', such as plainchant. He is also a typical nineteenth-century educated gentleman in his quite fanatic pursuit of geology and botany.

3. *Technological Advances.* Emmanuel may have been interested in ancient Greece in general, and its dance in particular, and he may have thought that the real thing should be recovered, but how did he think that that could be done, when dance, an ephemeral art, is notoriously difficult to document, and choreographies are hard to preserve and to hand down? There are two possible answers. First, one could suppose that ancient Greek dance and some aspect of

---

[16] Whitely (1996); Harding (1979).

[17] See e.g. Treble (1978); Maas (1975); MacLeod (1996). Some painters literally worked for the theatre, as did Alma-Tadema in his stage and costume designs for Henry Irving and Beerbohm Tree: Swanson (1977), 27–8; Treuherz (1996), 15–16. On the influence of paintings on the cinema: Blom (2001).

present-day dance are genetically related—in other words, you decide that ancient Greek dance has not died, but that it still lives on somewhere, for all to see, if only you know where to look for it. You may have to tidy it up a bit, but there it is—'ancient Greek' dance. Second, you aver that the ancient world knew of ways in which to document dance movements so as to make them reproducible at any time—also many centuries later. It is this last idea, the idea that ancient Greek dance is documented in performative detail, and that it is possible to read such documentation, that we find in Emmanuel. The parallel hypothesis of an unbroken tradition stretching down from antiquity to the present was also put forward (it had been around for some time), but outside Greece it never gained a real foothold in scholarship. And even there, the thought that ancient dance was documented is primary: continuity is supposed, on the basis of certain identities, to be established by comparing ancient and modern documentation of the dance.

For Emmanuel, a new technology, photography in the particular shape of chronophotography and of cinematography, provided the key. Emmanuel was aware of several chronophotographical experiments that were going on, not just those by Étienne-Jules Marey, Demeney (Marey's assistant) and Jean-Louis Soret, a physicist in Le Havre, who published on photography in the 1890s, whom he explicitly mentions, but also those by Muybridge whom he simply cannot have missed (see Figure 2.2).[18] It is no coincidence that Emmanuel published his ideas on ancient Greek dance in the same year that the first cinematic exhibition with a projector in a room took place in Paris. Of course, the idea of 'authenticity' is now back: photography brought with it the notion of images as 'the analogue of the real', and chronophotography and film made it possible to capture movement, life itself. It is for this reason that painters also show an interest in this work: Alma-Tadema bought Muybridge's work and when Muybridge visited London it was Alma-Tadema who urged him to speak at the Royal Academy.

Emmanuel looked at ancient images of dancing in the same way that he looked at modern photographs (I wonder whether ancient Greek art in the guise of black-figure and red-figure vase-painting admitted of such an approach more than other imagery, because in its negative and positive aspects it already

---

[18] On chronophotography in France, see Braun (1992). Emmanuel mentions Marey in the introduction to (1895*b*); cf. the 'Repères biographiques' in *La Revue Musicale* 410–11 (1988), 6: 'Il soutient en Sorbonne sa thèse de Doctorat-ès-Lettres . . . séance illustrée par les mouvements chorégraphiques d'une danseuse et par de projections au moyen du Chronophotographe de J. Marey.' Prudhommeau (1982*b*), 22 gives the name of the dancer who assisted in Emmanuel's research as Mlle Montchanin. On Muybridge in Paris, see *Scientific American*, Suppl. vol. 13 n. 317 (28 Jan. 1882), 5058–9. Apparently Muybridge's work had been published in France as early as 1878 (*La Nature* Dec. 1878; non vidi: cf. Ott (2005), 422), and Marey befriended Muybridge and assisted in his zoöpraxiscope displays (Haas (1976), 127–32). Muybridge showed no particular interest in the dance, but *Animal Locomotion* pl. 187 is of 'Fancy dancing' (Miss Larrigan 28 July 1885). Prodger and Gunning (2003), 160 illustrates a zoöpraxiscope disc with a dancer from about 1893.

Figure 2.2 Photographs by Eadweard Muybridge (1890s) and (facing) taken from Emmanuel (1896).

had some 'photographic' quality). Speculating on *the decisive moment* captured by the artist, one could also speculate on the previous and subsequent moments in time.[19] Chronophotography and early cinema did the rest. Why shouldn't the

---

[19] Anonymus in *The Nation* 19 Jan. 1888 (quoted by Haas (1976), 156): 'the artist's true method of study is to master the whole movement, and then to select for representation the one or two phases that most nearly convey the sense of this movement as a whole.' Artists were much interested in Muybridge's work and were amongst those who bought *Animal locomotion*; there is a

artists have captured several moments from a single movement? One only had to put those images in sequence, in a zoötrope, or whatever name those optical instruments carried, for the movement to come back to life. The famous debate on what a horse did with its legs at full gallop, which chronophotography had to solve and did, is remarkable in this context, because there it turned out that artists had had it wrong—which, however, did not lead to the conclusion that artists might have got much more wrong. At least not with Emmanuel, as he came up with the idea that Greek vase-painters were chronophotographers *avant la lettre*.

As far as I can see, the idea of comparing ancient Greek art with chronophotography, and applying this to the art of dance, is Emmanuel's own. But his approach was rooted in general ideas, which had been gestating for a large part of the nineteenth century. That one could use the ancient evidence to gain immediate access to ancient Greek dancing, without being held back by any opaqueness or distortion inherent in that very evidence, is part and parcel of a nineteenth-century dream. They gathered all the evidence, used all available technology to interpret it, and concluded that they held 'reality' in their hands: the boundless optimism of a pessimistic age.

For some fifteen years, Emmanuel and 'revivalism' reigned supreme: Emmanuel's work became a bestseller, and others spread the word.[20] Other authors came up with their own recipes for the reconstruction of Greek movement.[21] Even scholars who rejected or ignored Emmanuel and were not interested in recreating or reviving ancient Greek movement, now published quite extensively on ancient Greek dance, and may have contributed to the overall popularity of that subject.[22] That so many embraced what Emmanuel had suggested, might seem remarkable considering that he was academically speaking an outsider, who did not really want to be a scholar.[23] He must have struck a chord. If I am right and his ideas are what the nineteenth century had, so to speak, been waiting for, it makes sense that they were readily embraced. His method looked so simple, and Emmanuel was quite

long list of subscribing artists in Haas (1976), 158, amongst whom we find Alma-Tadema, who was amongst the first to receive Muybridge in London in 1882 (Haas (1976), 132).

[20] Amongst early popularizers of Emmanuel we encounter De Soria (1897), 83, and Charbonnel (1899). Many others followed: De Ménil (1905), 12–13; Hincks (1906), 449 and (1907), 352–4; Khudekov (1913), 244–60. Louis Séchan was a convert amongst the more serious classical scholars, see Séchan (1909), esp. 1029, 1039 and Séchan (1930).

[21] For instance Watts (1914), or Gage (1929), an attempt to recreate floor patterns.

[22] Schnabel (1910) is the first monograph devoted to a single dance genre from the ancient world. Of much importance is Latte (1913). Jane Harrison in Harrison (1912) and (1913) was the first to integrate non-Greek material into an account of ancient Greek dancing on an appreciable scale.

[23] *Contra* Garelli (2006), who states that I 'mêle indistinctement les travaux d'une critique universitaire et érudite et la recherche créatrice d'artistes'. It is not I who do so, it is what *happened*: Emmanuel is no example of 'une critique universitaire': it was only from 1909 onwards that he was a professor of the history of music at the Paris Conservatoire, and even then he stressed 'nous sommes des musiciens' (quoted by Classens (1988), 118–19, who summarizes: 'en fait, c'est bien en artiste . . . qu'il s'exprimait'). In a letter of 1920 Emmanuel stressed: 'je ne suis pas un érudit . . . Mais—quoiqu'il n'y paraisse guère—je suis un artiste, peut-être un musicien' (*La Revue Musicale* (1988), 48).

confident about it (though careful in his ultimate claims—a carefulness that his followers tended to neglect). The general enthusiasm lasted until World War I; then, for another fifteen years, Emmanuel's reputation slowly declined, and around 1930 it was all but gone.

During the years of Emmanuel's success, there are countless dancers performing 'ancient dances' (Greek, but soon also Roman, Persian, Assyrian, Aztec and whatever one could think of) on stage, jumping on the bandwagon of 'authenticity', and only rarely carrying out any serious research. This huge amount of revivalism on stage was not all Emmanuel's doing. First, there is no direct link between him and any of those dancers. We have no indication that Emmanuel himself wanted to stage the movements he thought he had retrieved, other than in a small-scale experimental setting. Neither do I know of any opinion expressed by Emmanuel about 'revived dance'.[24] But several of the many revivalist dancers will have read or heard of Emmanuel's work. Whenever we find *theorizing* of any kind about the basis for reconstructionism, this certainly seems to be influenced by Emmanuel.

For instance, Isadora Duncan—to name but the most famous of the dancers who put 'ancient Greek dance' on stage—must have come into contact with Emmanuel or Emmanuel's ideas: anybody evincing the slightest interest in dance and in ancient Greece will have been aware of Emmanuel.[25] She herself mentions extensive reading in the library of the Opéra in Paris, where the archivist, Nuittier, had assisted Emmanuel in his researches.[26] It is obvious that full development of her ideas took place only after her arrival in Europe, especially after moving from London to Paris.[27] Indeed, Duncan went to museums everywhere to study Greek art. In London she was guided by Alma-Tadema and we have a report of his enthusiasm for Duncan: 'The Alma Tademas saw her dance and succumbed to her charm, that she became thenceforth their protégé and was made much of by London's exclusive aesthetic set.'[28]

---

[24] On music he said, in the preface to his *Salamine* (1928): 'il serait absurde et d'ailleurs impossible de tenter une imitation de la musique grecque antique' (quoted in Baud-Bovy (1988), 110).

[25] As was suggested twenty years ago by Deborah Jowitt, but to little avail: Jowitt (1987), 198. Jowitt diminished the persuasiveness of her argument by only mentioning the 1916 Beauley translation of Emmanuel.

[26] Duncan (1927), 80. Already back in California Duncan could have seen the book by Emmanuel, or reports of it in the press: her father, with whom she was in contact again from 1893 onwards, had some interest in classical antiquity, see Steegmuller (1974), 373–4. Daly (1994), 21, notes San Francisco's new collection of Greek vases in the California Midwinter Exposition Memorial Museum, which opened in March 1895.

[27] See MacDougall in Magriel (1947), 37. For the performances in New York, see Seroff (1972), and Blair (1986), 32. Jowitt (1987) also suggests a link to Hellenism by way of Gordon Craig, pointing out the Hellenism of Gordon Craig's father Godwin. Jenkyns (1980), 301, mentions the eclecticism of Godwin and his mistress Ellen Terry (Gordon Craig's mother): they saw, as did many others, an affinity between the arts of Greece and Japan. Compare Duncan's statement to the effect that she disliked all dance, except Japanese dance (Rosemont (1983), 52).

[28] *The World* 16 Dec 1900 (quoted by Daly (1994), 15). For Alma-Tadema guiding Duncan at the British Museum: see MacDougall (1960), 54 (quoting from a 1903 autobiographical note).

Duncan's reaction to the ancient works of art strongly suggests that she had read Emmanuel: 'there is not one [Greek vase or bas-relief] which in its movement does not presuppose another movement', she maintained in *The dance of the Future*.[29] In a 1903 open letter to the Berlin *Morgen Post* the statue of a Maenad is said to be the only real dancer in town, and Duncan speaks of 'reproducing in life' that sculpture's pose and movement.[30] But she never mentioned Emmanuel. This silence may have been because she obviously differed from Emmanuel when she put classical ballet and Greek dancing in opposition whereas he noted their parallels. But then she hardly ever referred to influences *within the field of dance*: she apparently did not intend to detract from her own originality. Rather than acknowledging precursors or influences, she decried others as imitators (see further, Macintosh, Zanobi, this volume).

In the last paragraph, I have presented Duncan as a straightforward revivalist. That is not generally acknowledged: she is presented as the godmother of 'modern dance', as an icon of 'American art' (see further Macintosh, Zanobi, this volume). Consequently, her embeddedness in Greek revivalism has not been fully explored.[31] The conviction that she was reviving ancient Greek dancing, or at least trying to do so, was, and is, however, widespread. The descriptions and praises of Duncan as a 'Greek' or 'antique' dancer, recreating a lost art, are numerous.[32] Sometimes she herself found it opportune to deny this, but several of her pronouncements and deeds clearly demonstrate her revivalist intentions.

First, there is the evidence of her studies in the vase rooms of the British Museum, the Louvre and the Munich Museum.[33] Next, there is the curious episode of the Duncan family's *séjour* in Athens.[34] The enthusiasm of the Duncans for ancient Greece, an enthusiasm later borne out most extremely by Raymond Duncan and his Greek wife, cannot be in doubt, and in Greece the idea to 'revivify the Greek chorus' is born.[35] Duncan says things like: 'I am trying to revive that beauty

---

[29] Quoted from Steinberg (1980), 38.

[30] The translated text is in Rosemont (1983), 34–5, and in Blair (1986), 65–6. Cf. Duncan's address to the Berlin Press Club in the same year (Rosemont (1983), 33): 'The Greek dances were spontaneous and natural. We must seek to revive them.' In 1903 there is more talk of reconstructing ancient dances and ancient dress (ibid. 51). Another bit on sculpture (tentatively dated to Berlin 1905–6) is in Duncan (1928), 71.

[31] As was rightly stated by S. A. Manning in Cohen (1982), 281, and still holds good, even though Jowitt (1987) has gone some way towards alleviating this deficiency.

[32] Several examples can be found in Blair (1986), and in McVay (1980). One could add the fulsome praise of 'la ricostitutrice delle antiche danze greco-romane' by an Italian epigone: Pichetti, s.a., 35. Séchan (1930), devotes a complete chapter to Duncan. See also Karl Federn's preface to Duncan (1903), 8: 'in wunderbaren antiken Bewegungen . . . Hellas vor uns auferstehen lässt . . . Wie viele Statuen sind in ihr lebendig geworden!'

[33] Duncan (1927), 51, 55, 67.

[34] Ibid. 129ff. Rosemont (1983), 36, prints a statement by Duncan on arrival in Greece in 1903: 'I came to Greece to study these forms of ancient art'.

[35] Duncan (1927), 136.

which—alas—is at present forgotten and buried', or 'to call back to life again
that ideal movement . . . and to awaken an art which has slept for two thousand
years'.[36] In 1903 she stresses that she does not seek to recreate Greek movement, but
a 1909 Paris programme again speaks of 'reconstitutions de danses antiques'. If
Duncan's position on this issue is unclear this is probably the result of both
confusion and opportunism, in differing combinations.[37] Whatever she said herself,
from the evidence a good case can be made for antiquity being the main inspirational force in her career, certainly in the early stages, but never quite relinquished.[38]
This inspiration seems to have gone beyond a mere recreation of 'spirit', and it
certainly was perceived as such by most contemporaries.

There are others who, either inspired by Duncan or of their own accord, show
themselves influenced by Emmanuel, directly or indirectly. Fokine is said to have
studied antique works of art in the Hermitage, and there certainly was an interest in
the dance of ancient Greece amongst the staff and audience of the St Petersburg
theatres.[39] Bakst, who designed remarkable Greek costumes and sets for Les Ballets
Russes, studied Greek art and even travelled to Greece.[40] Nijinsky's ballet *L'Après-
midi d'un faune* has been called 'a moving Greek frieze'.[41] Pavlova also went to
museums to study Greek art and performed several Greek dances, which were

---

[36] Thus Duncan in a 1904 St Petersburg interview, quoted by Steegmuller (1974), 39; cf. 42–5.
See also Duncan (1927,) 30–1. The 1906 prospectus of Duncan's Grünewald school has an
introduction by Duncan herself: 'Die schönen rhythmische Bewegungen des menschlichen
Körpers wieder zu finden, die ideale Bewegung, die in Harmonie mit der höchsten körperlichen
Form sein soll, wieder ins Leben zu rufen, eine Kunst wieder zu erwecken, die zweitausend Jahre
geschlafen hat, das ist das erste Zweck dieser Schule' (English in McVay (1980), 8, and Rosemont
(1983), 37, who erroneously dates this brochure to 1907–8).

[37] Outspoken on Duncan's opportunism is Daly (1994), 7–9: 'Duncan may not have intended
to copy ancient Greek dances per se', it was rather a rhetorical device, a 'gimmick', in Duncan's
strategies of difference and exclusion.

[38] Dillon (1990) sees a development from a time early in her career when Duncan saw and
presented herself and her work as closely allied to the ancient Greeks, to a later phase in which this
conviction was supplanted by other concerns. But in fact she is shifting back and forth all through
her career. Cf. Daly (1994), 8–10, on the Greekness of Duncan. Rosemont (1983), 39, quotes a
1915 speech at the Century Opera House, New York, from the season during which Duncan was
staging Greek tragedies in the United States: 'these beautiful children you have seen tonight are
doing things that have not been done for 2000 years.' This is not different from the 1904
pronouncements quoted above.

[39] On Fokine, see MacDonald (1983); Roslavleva (1966), 176; Romanovsky-Krassinsky (1960),
105. The interest in ancient dance in circles of the Imperial Theatres is reflected in Svetlov (1899–
1900), a comprehensive overview of the dance from 'Darwin' to the early Middle Ages, intended
for the general reader.

[40] On Fokine's ballets for Diaghilev, see Buckle (1979), 150, 229. On Bakst and ancient Greece:
ibid. 194 (with n.69); Lieven (1936), 173, 321. Illustrations of Bakst designs in Alexandre and
Cocteau (1972); Spencer (1973), *passim* (with text on 37, 86, 98 ff.); and Pruzhan (1988), *passim*.
Bakst's interest in Greece antedates Duncan's first arrival in Russia: Pruzhan (1988), 31.

[41] Buckle (1979), 185; cf. Buckle (1980), 187f., 279. There exists a splendid series of
photographs of Nijinsky's ballet by Baron de Meyer, published in 1914. Cf. Brandau (1976),
plates at no. 39. Nijinsky must have been working on an *Après-midi*-like version of *Les chansons de
Bilitis*, sometime in 1918 (Buckle (1980), 482); this was never finished.

mostly remakes of older ballets fitted out in a more authentic style.[42] Ruth St Denis sounded very Emmanuelish when she said: 'all I had to do was take the best poses [of ancient works of art], the most meaningful ones and set those poses dancing.'[43] Fokine, Nijinsky, Pavlova, or St Denis are well-known names. But Europe was knee-deep in revivalists, many of the Duncan type, the so-called 'barefoot dancers'. There are: Maud Allan; Michelle Azra Hincks; Ruby Ginner; Emma Sandrini; Olga Desmond; Margaret Morris; Mona Païva; Jeanne Rosay; Toula Paléologue; Nikolska; Mlle Isis; Auréa; Miss Wordsworth; Lina Imperia; The Moscow Athletic dancers; Lady Constance Stewart-Richardson; Jacoba and Helena van der Pas (see further, Webb, Macintosh this volume).[44]

Seen in retrospect Duncan has eclipsed all competitors, even if other dancers in 'Greek taste' must have been quite well known in their day. But already during her lifetime, everybody in Europe and America with some notion of the surrounding world must have heard about her.[45] Still, without Duncan everything would have happened much the same way, with one of the many comparable dancers taking her place. Duncan is a paradigm that monopolizes historical accounts, while the real Duncan was part of a broad movement both European and American. It was the widespread interest in and study of ancient Greek dancing, especially in nineteenth-century France, which gave birth to Isadora Duncan's art. It was Germany that nurtured it.

Germany enters the story when we seek to explain the remarkable success of the 'barefoot dancers'. Was everybody dying to see ancient Greek dance come back to life again? Some were, sometimes. But there were attractions other than historic sensation, such as the scanty costuming of the performers: several of the 'barefoot

---

[42] Lazzarini and Lazzarini (1980), 114 (cf. 212), 149, 152, 158, 170, 196; Money (1982), 206, 234, 268, 295f, 351. Cf. comments in Svetlov (1974), 102 f. Pavlova knew Ruby Ginner: see Hart (1991), 214.

[43] Quoted in Sherman (1979), 70.

[44] Many names in Ersky (1910); Khudekov (1913), 253–60; Genthe (1920); Philadelpheus (1926), 315–20, who mentions the many *danseuses* who came to Athens 'pour donner sous le ciel attique des reconstructions des danses antiques' (315). Some interesting pictures of foreign and Greek revivalists by the photographer Elly Sujulzoglu, known as Nelly, are brought together in Nelly (1989), and Efthimiou-Tsekoura, et al. (1997). On Maud Allan: Allan (1908); Cherniavsky (1991); and chapters by Webb and Macintosh (this volume). On Michelle Azra Hincks: Reinach (1908). On Ruby Ginner and Irene Mawer (who from 1915 taught Greek theatre arts and later founded the Greek Dance Association and associated organizations, such as Mawer's Institute of Mime): Ginner (1933); Mawer (1932); Hart (1991); and Macintosh (this volume). Further references in Naerebout (1997), 64–6, 84. On Ruth St Denis and Ted Shawn (together known as Denishawn, who did some Greek things, but specialized in Egyptian, Oriental, and pre-Columbian): Sherman (1979); Shelton (1990); and Michelakis (this volume). On Constance Stewart-Richardson: Goldhill (2002). On the Van der Pas sisters: Van Schaik (1981), 14–5; Fehling (2007).

[45] I limit references to some better known works of scholarship: praise for Duncan in Weege (1926), 3–4; Séchan (1930), 315 ff.; Van der Leeuw (1930), 62 (extravagant); strongest criticism by Warnecke (1932), 2247.

dancers' bared much more than their feet.[46] We should not play down the element of sexuality. There was a whiff, or more than a whiff, of scandal surrounding some of these performers. The argument that claiming Greek ancestry is a way to gain legitimacy, even to turn dance into a highbrow art, is not unconvincing.[47] But it is just not the whole story: Greece may be uplifting, but Greece is also associated with indecency. By referring to Greece, Duncan raises her dancing to the status of art for an upper-class audience; but at the same time risqué 'Greek dancing' is made legitimate by being danced by Duncan—who happens to be articulate enough to do so (see further Macintosh, this volume).

Even more important for the revivalists' success must have been the way their doings tied in with the wider phenomenon of the so-called *Körperkultur*. This is a German label for an international and many-faceted phenomenon consisting of back to nature movements, a preference for the primitive and archaic, improvement of health and hygiene by way of open air exercise, gymnastics of all sorts, eurhythmy, eurhythmics, bathing, nudism, vegetarianism, a whole complex of 'striving to be healthy and pure', and part of an even larger complex of folklorism, free sex, feminism, esotericism, spiritism, theosophy, anthroposophy, astrology, psychoanalysis, druidism, witchcraft, and what not.[48] Much of this *Körperkultur* looks back to the ancient Greeks for a theoretical background.[49] There do not seem to have been, however, many direct links between *Körperkultur* and the Greek revivalists—though it should be noted that François Delsarte's systems had a Greek flavour, certainly in the American versions as taught by, amongst others, Genevieve Stebbins, who influenced Duncan and St Denis.[50]

Duncan's relationship to Central European *Körperkultur* is quite unexplored, but I suggest there is much that links Duncan to these movements in their European and American guises. Such can be concluded from her eugenic ideas, and her concern with health and naturalness, which may even turn racist, for instance in its attack on modern social dances as the unwelcome influence by primitive races (as opposed to the wholesome Greek culture, the product of 'our race'; see further Webb and

[46] Genthe (1920) has a section titled 'classic dancers' consisting entirely of pictures of girls performing in the nude (with noble intentions expressed in the preface). On the many aspects of nudity at the time: Toepfer (1997).

[47] Daly (1994).

[48] Romein (1976), 646. Put in very broad perspective ibid. ch. 33; see also Kern (1975) (both authors mention Duncan). Excellent overview: Wedemeyer-Kolwe (2004); his chapter 'Rhythmus', 25–128, has much on *Körperkultur* and dance. In English: Hau (2003).

[49] For this sort of *mens sana in corpore sano* action programmes: Augustin (1924), 22–3; Winther (1920), 5 ff., and (1923), 8, 52. Alternatively, there is much *Körperkultur* in Weege (1926), 2, 14, 38, 152. Schröder (1927), 89–92, speaks of Greek dances and of *Wandervögel* emulating these dances.

[50] Blair (1986), 17–18, mentions Greek dress and 'statue posing'. In *The Director* of 1898 Duncan praises Delsarte (quoted by Shawn s.a., 79); Gordon Craig said in a 1952 radio-interview that Duncan owned a book by Delsarte (Steegmuller (1974), 363). In 1925 she seems to have referred to Delsarte in an interview: see Blair (1986), 165–9, Jowitt (1987), 196. In general: Ruyter (1996*a*) and (1999).

Macintosh, this volume).[51] But it is not influence that is the issue here, but the fact that the revivalists, with their 'back to basics' message (the past, nature, the body), certainly fitted into the concept of *Körperkultur*. *Körperkultur* welcomed them, and contributed to their popularity. But that same *Körperkultur* did not need them and it survived them; indeed, it is still alive in sports, the Olympic movement, bodybuilding, gymnastics, athletics, the Scouts, dieting, vegetarianism, homeopathy, biodynamics, sunbathing, seabathing, nudism, and so on—a rich inheritance of nineteenth-century common sense and idiocy (take your pick). Greek dance revivals, however, went out of fashion a long time ago.

Why was interest in Emmanuel and in revivalism waning by the time of World War I and dead by the time we reach 1930? As to Emmanuel himself, the few dissenting voices increased in number, and they insisted that everything was wrong with his ideas, whatever their success. Emmanuel was a good scholar and an honest man, but an easy target, because his point of departure was fatally flawed: reconstruction is an impossibility, on several different levels of enquiry. Emmanuel was flogging a dead rat—it had already been dead for many, many centuries when he stumbled on it. Some saw this from the moment he published his thesis, and were critical from the start—though when confronted with undoubtedly charismatic stage personalities such as Anna Pavlova, Vaslav Nijinsky, Isadora Duncan, Maud Allan, or Ruth St Denis and Ted Shawn they often forgot their reservations. Others became more critical as time went on. It is only in France that Emmanuel found a following after his own death, and there some researchers still embrace his ideas.

Revivalism on the stage waned because it was essentially nineteenth century in its spirit. So were *Körperkultur* and everything associated with it, so were sport, the Scouts—the whole lot. But they managed to associate themselves with 'modernity' in the sense of being contemporaneous with the twentieth century and able to compete—or integrate—with other twentieth-century trends. 'Greek dancing' did not manage to do so—if only because it was called 'Greek' or 'classical', and had so heavily invested in being the authentic *past*, instead of the authentic *present*. It goes out of the window—together with academic painting: Alma-Tadema died in 1912 and was already ridiculed in the press in 1913 on the occasion of a retrospective exhibition; he was last praised in 1924 and effectively damned and removed from public view in 1928.[52] 'Ancient Greek dance' was also subject to criticism and ridicule from the start, but the dissenting voices

---

[51]   Much on this in Francis (1994), 37–9, on Duncan's 'nationalist discourse of identity' (39), i.e. her rejection of the 'primitivism' of popular dance, stressing America, i.e. Anglo-Saxon America, and its classical inheritance. See Duncan (1928), 82, on Greece as 'our race'. See also Daly (1994), 17–19, and Ragona (1994), 59–60. Rosemont (1983), 38–9, gives a 1908 speech, as quoted in *Current literature* (New York 1908), wherein ragtime is equated with disease and death, and a 1915 speech at the Century Opera House, New York, with an attack on the tango.

[52]   Swanson (1977), 62–3.

became more incisive when such performances were seen as increasingly out of tune with the present.

Isadora Duncan and the many others like her are not harbingers of 'modern dance' or even the 'modern age', into which they have been turned retrospectively (what influence they have had on whom, is neither here nor there).[53] Their heyday was the final years of the long nineteenth century, until 1914. Duncan tried to reinvent herself, but it was the 'Greek' label—once a ticket to success—that stuck and that caused her to be out of fashion well before she died in 1927. Revealing in this respect are the condemnations of Duncan's dances by her contemporaries as being *too much* reconstructed. Some commentators stress that they would rather see something modern, instead of something Greek, if it can be called 'Greek' at all: Isadora stands accused of 'being Greek on Fourth Avenue', in a memorable phrase by George Copeland.[54] It reminds one of Ruskin or Whistler about Alma-Tadema. In 1932 the dancer Agna Enters in an eloquent and highly damaging, because cruelly satirical, essay describes 'Greek dance credoes' as 'nauseous cobwebby patter', while 'even the clearest vision of Greece is inescapably seen in terms of our own time'.[55]

So revivalism had run its course, except for a few who could not bring themselves to say goodbye to the idea: Ruby Ginner and those continuing her work in Britain, die-hard Duncanites in the United States, some theatre-makers and theorists in modern Greece for obvious, nationalistic reasons, and, as already mentioned, a number of French scholars, who down to this very day have been struggling to keep Emmanuel's work on the Greek dance alive—especially Louis Séchan, Germaine Prudhommeau (by whom Emmanuel's ideas have been perverted and turned into something very extreme—which should not be laid at Emmanuel's door, even if Prudhommeau claims him as her predecessor), and Marie-Hélène Delavaud-Roux. They have added their own nuances, but the basic idea that ancient Greek dance can be reconstructed from ancient Greek iconography, remains central to their undertakings.

---

[53] Cf. Garelli (2006), who wants to distinguish between the 'esprit classicisant' of the 'école reconstructioniste' versus the liberating movement exemplified by Duncan and Les Ballets Russes. The fact that Duncan and others—not so much Les Ballets Russes—rejected the artificialities of ballet does not make them much different from someone like Emmanuel. They use the same means, and not even to completely different ends, because Emmanuel may be a supporter of traditional forms of theatrical dancing, but not without criticism: (1895*b*), 322–9. Musically Emmanuel is not a traditionalist and describes his own work as 'extra-classique' (Landormy (1943), 206–7). Recently there have been several interesting attempts to rewrite aspects of Duncan's career: see Franko (1995), and Daly (1994), Francis (1994) and Ragona (1994). They lay bare some of the tensions and contradictions in the story of Duncan who tried to be modern on a traditional humanist basis. Ragona argues that Duncan reached to the primitive by way of Greece, but this is definitely not the case: she is an exclusivist who rejects 'the primitive' in racist terms (Daly (1994), 17–8, Francis (1994), 38–9).

[54] See Augustin (1924), 25–6; Thiess s.a., 121; Brandenburg (1921), 30, 35. Copeland is quoted by Blair (1986), 248.

[55] Enters (1931–2), 292–3.

Is this story of revivalism an interesting bit of cultural history? Certainly. Is it of any real consequence? Yes. The idea of reconstructionism has exerted a deep and baleful influence: not so much because a number of scholars have been keeping these ideas alive (they are barely alive within the scholarly community), but especially because the public at large has been much taken up with it and cannot let go of it. The iconic status of Isadora Duncan undoubtedly plays its part here. But the public, and not only the scholarly community, have to get rid of the very thought that the past can be recreated, because it is only when we realize that *nobody* has the ability to get it completely right, that we can critically review every interpretation put upon the past.

3

The Tanagra Effect: Wrapping the Modern Body in the Folds of Ancient Greece

Ann Cooper Albright

> As the dancer takes up the word, she problematizes her status as work of art and artist in one. Through a combination of performance, autobiography, and publicity, women artists reconceptualized the figure of the dancer while rewriting the aesthetics of femininity and women's sexuality.[1]

At the turn of a century which had consolidated the separation of private and public realms, to put one's body on display as a spectacle and still claim subjectivity onstage was a difficult and complex balancing act for a female performer. Equally difficult for women was claiming authority as writer, particularly if the writer had been known as a performer.[2] Resisting the societal strictures of 'appropriate' behaviour for women, Colette, Loïe Fuller, Isadora Duncan, and Eva Palmer found unique ways to negotiate their specific social and economic circumstances, not only to stage their bodies consciously, but also to produce written manifestos that articulated the artistic vision which inspired their work.

Whether they began in dance, pantomime, or theatre, these women all started with a corporeal practice, producing a physical language that focused on breath rhythms, the dynamic use of the torso, and the articulation of gestures that galvanized space in new and important ways. Then they articulated the cultural potency of that physical work while describing the meanings of their life missions. Their writings give us their ideas. The photographic images help us to infer their movement vocabulary and the stylistic aspects of the staging of their work. But these visual and written traces are necessarily fragmentary, and rarely do they directly address the implications of this physical engagement with the world—what we might call their corpo-realities. In this chapter, I propose to read

---

[1] Townsend (2001), 112.

[2] Throughout her life, Colette's past career as a music-hall entertainer caused various protests by an older generation whenever her name was suggested as the possible recipient of a literary prize. See Thurman (1999), xiii.

through the historical evidence with an attention to the physical practices (often inspired by conceptions of antiquity as a holistic trinity combining body, mind, and soul) that created a somatic foundation for these women's courageous and ambitious interventions in the performance culture of their time.

Working in between the stage and the text, my interpretative methodology aligns itself obliquely with one that feminist literary scholar, Nancy Miller proposes in her essay 'Writing Fictions: Women's Autobiography in France'. In the midst of a discussion that seeks to intervene in glib readings of women's fiction as always already autobiographical, Miller calls for a 'double reading', which she describes as 'an intratextual practice of interpretation which . . . would privilege neither the autobiography nor the fiction, but take the two writings together in their status as text'.[3] This strategy allows Miller to combine the pleasures of French literary theory with the critical attention to historical and material conditions that galvanized North American feminism in the 1980s, giving her access to both (as she terms it) 'tropes and sensible shoes'.[4] She concludes her essay with her usual panache by adding: 'The historical truth of a woman writer's life lies in the reader's grasp of her intratext: the body of her writing and not the writing of her body.'[5] Mirroring Miller's strategy of a 'double reading', I take as my intratext both the body of these women's writings and the writing (that is, the representations) of their bodies.

Performance and autobiography are genres of representation that foreground the problematic relationship of body to signature—of gender to power. Of course, at the beginning of the twentieth century, performing and writing were highly gendered occupations. With few exceptions, women performed onstage, and men wrote about them. This historical fact was reinforced by a cultural alignment of bodily display as feminized (whether the performer was a man or a woman—see further Hall, this volume), and the writer's signature as masculine (the pen as the phallus). In the nineteenth-century bourgeois culture which still reigned in Parisian society at the beginning of the twentieth century, these activities were imbued with class values as well. Refusing to be passive instruments of another's vision, Isadora Duncan, Loïe Fuller, Eva Palmer, and Colette all took responsibility for shaping both the larger theatrical frame and the expressive nuances of their (self-) representations.

While these women, three Americans and one French, all lived emancipated lives in Paris at the beginning of the twentieth century, and while they even sometimes shared a stage (or lawn, to be more precise) and a passion for performance as an ethical, life-affirming force, they developed radically different interests and aesthetics. Before she became a journalist and full-time writer, Colette worked on the stages of music-halls for seven years, travelling all over France with a small pantomime company. Loïe Fuller, who was at the height of

---

[3] Miller (1988), 60.   [4] Ibid. 17.   [5] Ibid. 61.

her career as the century turned, began to choreograph for her own group of dancers, as well as serving as an impresario for two Japanese theatre companies, and (very briefly) for Isadora Duncan, among others. Expounding a rhetoric of dance as Art, Duncan, in turn, shunned the music-hall stage and danced exclusively in the concert halls, opera houses, and salons of upper-class European society, launching a career of mythic proportions. Eva Palmer, who once shared a couple of afternoon performances with Colette at Natalie Barney's, and who would later marry the brother of Raymond Duncan's wife, recast an early infatuation with Sappho and Hellenism into an ambitious project to revive ancient Greek drama, producing at Delphi two of the biggest theatrical festivals in modern Greece.

There are, of course, overlapping spheres of influence between these women. Some of these have been routinely charted, including Fuller and Duncan's brief and mutually unsatisfactory professional relationship, or Colette and Eva Palmer's appearances at Nathalie Barney's home. Others which, to my knowledge, have never been explored, include Colette's invocation of Fuller's dancing and her short portrait of Duncan in *Paysages et Portraits*. In this chapter, I hope to map out the unique performance trajectories of these four women, and sketch in some of their commonalities. For, despite the quite different looks of their performances—these women were connected by the fact that, at some point in their careers, they all conjured a vision of ancient Greece to enhance the representation of their bodies as agents of self-expression. This, then, is what I refer to as the 'Tanagra Effect'.

Tanagra dresses, Tanagra scarves, Tanagra corsets that go from the armpits to the knees and don't allow one to sit, to eat, to bend over, or anything! This corset contains everything, holds everything back...Poor little 'Tanagras' of Paris, what can we make of this cruel fashion which places women, snake-like, sitting on their tails! Their dimpled backsides, restless and aggressive, their...expressive hips—all these are sacrificed to the Tanagra corset, a hard master who crushes their bodies...Their impatient bodies shake, fettered by this 'Tanagra' dress, which emphasizes their rumps and constrains their feet.[6]

These comments by Colette, the famed novelist, journalist, and woman–about–town in Paris, were occasioned by a review of a performance by Isadora Duncan at the beginning of the twentieth century. As always, Colette was watching the audience as much as the stage, and while she notes that Duncan danced with great expression and with her whole body engaged, Colette remarks on the contrast between Duncan's Greek tunics, which were loosely fitted and light-weight, and those 'Tanagra' dresses of the women applauding her. Colette also registers the irony that her audience was filled with women who were physically (not to mention psychically) bound by bourgeois conventions and idiotic fashions such as Fortuny's famous 'Tanagra' dresses. 'Let us not fool ourselves,' she

---

[6] Colette (1958), 153.

writes, '[these women] acclaim her but they don't envy her. They salute her at a distance, and they contemplate her, but as an escapee—not as a liberator.'[7]

When I originally titled this essay 'The Tanagra Effect', I was thinking, of course, of the Tanagra sculptures of ancient Greece, those carved figurines whose draping clothes and folded scarves brilliantly capture the underlying movement of their bodies. I wanted to compare the implications of the uses of this kind of Greek costume and humanist references to ancient civilization in performances by Isadora Duncan, Loïe Fuller, and Eva Palmer. But when I found the above quote, I realized that it was important first to foreground the extraordinary and often amusing range of popular interpretations of 'Tanagra' at the cusp of a new century. Although modelled on ancient costumes, the Tanagra style of dress most often symbolized a modern woman, one whose lifestyle literally incorporated choices (about career, leisure activities, dress, and family) with a mobility unheard of twenty years earlier. Yet this mobility was also partially suspect, and a looseness of clothing could also suggest a loose morality as well. This is certainly true of women dancers who wore Grecian-style tunics onstage (Isadora Duncan being the most famous example), which is why most of the women in their audiences were still bound by the paradoxical fashion of wearing a long corset underneath the mobile dress. In the publicity and press concerning performances by women dancers at this time, claims of 'aesthetic', 'intelligent', and 'chaste' dancing, or an appeal to the idealism of ancient Greek culture, all constitute various strategies to subvert this overdetermined social discourse.

In 1911, Colette appeared on the cover of *La Culture Physique*, a bimonthly journal which calls itself the 'organe de l'Énergie française' (the organ of French energy), thus invoking a provocative slippage between body and industry. In this issue, Colette is profiled as a fervent advocate of physical culture. Ironically, although Colette exercised in a sleeveless knit body-suit on assorted gymnastic equipment, the cover shot has her posing like a Grecian statue, standing in profile with one arm stretched up holding the white cloth which is artistically draped around her torso. This French voguing of Hellenism vacillates between an image of the middle-class aesthetic postures à la Delsarte and the more low-brow titillation implied by the fact that underneath the graceful folds of the fabric, she is naked.

By the time she posed as the cover girl for *La Culture Physique*, Colette had been seriously working out for about nine years, and her letters to her friends reveal how proud she was of her hard-earned muscles.[8] As a young girl, Colette was outdoorsy and a tomboy. Indeed, until arthritis crippled her in her old age, Colette prided herself on being robust and physically active. When in 1902, Colette moved to larger (and lighter) quarters on the rue de Courcelles with her husband, Willy, she claimed the artist's studio on the top floor. She outfitted this

---

[7] Colette (1958), 153–4.   [8] Thurman (1999), 210.

bachelorette pad with gymnastic equipment; she exercised and entertained her friends there to distract herself from her faltering marriage. In *My Apprenticeships*, Colette describes this austere, but inspiring, space of her own:

Mine had no ornaments beyond the fittings of a gymnasium, the horizontal bar, trapeze, rings, and knotted rope. I used to swing and turn over the bar, suppling my muscles half secretly, without any particular zeal or brilliance. Yet when I reflected on it later, it seemed to me that I was exercising my body in much the same way that prisoners, although they have no clear idea of flight, nevertheless tear up their sheets and plait the strands together, sew gold coins into their coat-linings, hide chocolate under the mattress.[9]

Whether she was conscious of it or not at the time, Colette was crafting a 'modern' woman's body, exploring through her exercise routine the psychosomatic experience of muscular stability and strength. Colette had begun to emerge from the bourgeois cocoon of domesticity, and the photographs of her in her gym reveal a self-possession that contrasts markedly with earlier images. Natalie Barney describes the change in Colette at this time: 'At the beginning of the century, when I saw Colette for the first time, she was no longer the thin, long-braided adolescent cradled in a hammock which a photograph shows us. She was a young woman firmly fixed on solid legs, with the small of her back arching down to a full behind; with manners as frank as her speech.'[10] In her biography of Colette, Judith Thurman affirms Barney's portrayal, connecting the literal to the metaphoric as she emphasizes the sociological implications of Colette's actions:

In the process of becoming fit, she discovered that exercise strengthens one's moral . . . She was also, consciously or not, training herself for the profession [as a dancer and a mime, that] she would take up when her marriage ended. Colette had understood, precociously, that the true beauty of a woman's muscles is identical with their purpose, and that's self-support.[11]

First came the focus on fitness, then the flight. By the time Colette was ready to leave the domestic hearth that had charred her provincial innocence, she had trained with the well-known mime Georges Wague. Eventually, she would join him and his partner on the professional stage. In *The Vagabond*, she describes the satisfactions of this new career: 'Solitude, freedom, my pleasant and painful work as mime and dancer, tired and happy muscles, and, by way of a change from all that, the new anxiety about earning my meals, my clothes, and my rent—such, all of a sudden, was my lot.'[12]

At the end of April 1907, Colette penned her response to socialites who considered that she was 'a woman of letters who has turned out badly' for *La Vie*

[9] Colette (1957), 104. [10] Phelps (1978), 62.
[11] Thurman (1999), 133. [12] Colette (1954), 32.

Parisienne. Entitled 'Toby-Chien Parle,' this ironic dialogue between her dog and cat contains the defiant language of a manifesto:

I want to do what I want. I want to play pantomime and also comedy. I want to dance nude if the leotard constrains me and humiliates my figure. I want to cherish who loves me and give him whatever is mine in the world: my body resists sharing my gentle heart and my independence![13]

In the midst of this fierce declamation, Colette describes in the future tense the kind of dancing that she envisions for herself:

I will dance nude or dressed for the sole pleasure of dancing, to time my movements to the rhythm of music . . . I will dance, I will invent slow beautiful dances where at times the veil will cover me, at times will surround me like a spiral of smoke, at times will stretch behind me like the sail of a boat.[14]

Colette's language here, her 'invented' dance with fabric that surrounds her like a spiral of smoke, or billows behind her like a sail, so closely resembles published descriptions of Loïe Fuller that it begs the question of influence. Did Colette ever see Fuller perform? I have not found any mention of Fuller in the abundant scholarship on Colette's life and writings. Yet Colette must have been aware of Fuller's artistic legacy as well as her reputation as an independent and enterprising woman, if only through her husband's circle of friends which included some of the most influential fin-de-siècle music and theatre critics. We know, for instance, that Colette and Willy frequented the 1900 Paris Exposition Universelle, which opened several months after the publication of *Claudine at School*.[15] It is likely that during this time Colette passed by (if she didn't attend) Fuller's theatre on the Rue de Paris. Although I am not really concerned with proving that Fuller had a direct influence on Colette, I find most intriguing a short review by Louis Delluc published in *Comoedia illustré* in January 1913 in which he describes Colette in a series of *poses plastiques*: 'She plays with a great white veil, in which she surrounds, drapes, and sculpts herself.'[16]

Playing with her veil/sail, Colette seems to incorporate Fuller's hieroglyphs-in-motion. In the above description of her dancing, Colette abandons the classic narrative and static gestures of pantomime for the improvisational challenge of moving with a large piece of fabric. Reading Delluc, I can imagine Colette tracing Fuller's figures. Yet the reflexive tone of the French verb 'se sculpter' shifts the emphasis from the object (what she sculpts) back to the subject (who is doing the sculpting). Using this 'great white sail', Colette thus sculpts herself. In *My Apprenticeships*, Colette recalls her growing awareness at this time of the interconnected poetics of gesture, rhythm, and language: 'The melodic and the written phrase both spring from the same elusive and immortal pair—sound and

---

[13] Colette (1984*a*), 994.   [14] Ibid. 997.
[15] Thurman (1999), 109.   [16] Colette (1984*b*), 114.

rhythm.'[17] As the rhythm becomes the word, my image of Colette doing Fuller dissolves, and I imagine, in turn, the white sail morphing into a blank page, the possibilities of which Colette has learned to explore through reclaiming her body. Moving from the stage back to the page (she would give up performing regularly with the birth of her daughter in 1913), Colette renders, as Nancy Miller notes, 'the rhythms of performance *in writing*'.[18]

Like Colette, Isadora Duncan also staged the psychosomatic implications of physical autonomy and then wrote about them in her manifestos. At the beginning of her book on Duncan, *Done Into Dance*, Ann Daly describes Duncan's amazing ability to make visible what she calls a 'narrative of force':

The general components of force are also those of Duncan's dancing: interaction, motion, directionality, and intensity. Duncan's solos—a single body struggling against, shrinking from, floating on, and thrusting into space—were enactments of agency, the self in the process of engagement with the external world, whether that meant love or fate, oppression or death.[19]

It is this concentrated unity of focus (her presence) that Abraham Walkowitz has captured so compellingly in his many drawings of Duncan's dancing. Reflecting Colette's remark that 'son corps parle plus que son visage' (her body speaks more than her face), Walkowitz leaves Duncan's face blank, allowing the viewer to focus instead on how her head follows the expressive motion of her torso. More importantly, Walkowitz's sketches and watercolours help us to comprehend how Duncan was able to transform her ideas about nature into a fleshy, weighty corporeality. In his work, Walkowitz blends watercolours (or shading) with ink lines to represent the hallmarks of Duncan's fame: the poetic tension of her stillness, her luxurious open reach to the sky, the lively skipping of her incarnation as a Bacchant, and the contracted anguish of loss. More than specific movements or gestures, however, Walkowitz's drawings evoke the vital spontaneity of Duncan's pleasure in dancing. For Duncan, the source of this pleasure was the interplay of forces, that 'central spring of movement' in the solar plexus, and its inspiration was Nature.

The first paragraph of Duncan's essay on 'The Dancer and Nature' establishes the marriage of beauty and wisdom through which Nature reveals herself as a woman dancing. Later in the same essay, Duncan declares:

Woman is not a thing apart and separate from all other life organic and inorganic. She is but a link in the chain, and her movement must be one with the great movement which runs through the universe; and therefore the fountain-head for the art of the dance will be the study of the movements of Nature.[20]

---

[17] Colette (1957), 110.   [18] Miller (1988), 232.
[19] Daly (1995), 6–7.   [20] Duncan (1928), 68.

As Ann Daly makes clear: ' "Nature" was Duncan's metaphorical shorthand for a loose package of aesthetic and social ideals: nudity, childhood, the idyllic past, flowing lines, health, nobility, ease, freedom, simplicity, order and harmony.'[21] Duncan's take on 'Nature' was connected to a nostalgic return to Greece. It was essentially an 'anti-modern impulse', one that shunned many technological advances of the early twentieth century. Even though she certainly took advantage of her historical position as a 'modern' woman, Isadora Duncan fetishized Greek culture. In her hybrid Hellenism, she wedded her notion of an eternal and inspiring 'Nature' to Platonic ideals of 'Beauty'.

In no country is the soul made so sensible of Beauty and of Wisdom as in Greece. Gazing at the sky one knows why Athene, the Goddess of Wisdom, was called 'the Blue-Eyed One', and why learning and beauty are always joined in her service. And one feels also why Greece has been the land of great philosophers, lovers of wisdom, and why the greatest of these has called the highest beauty, the highest wisdom.[22]

Eventually, of course, Duncan evolved choreographically from her early renditions of a sweet and gentle nature in her 'La Primavera' days, in which she enacted a number of figures in Botticelli's painting (complete with flowers circling the neck and waist), to representations of 'Nature' which included fierce and destructive energies as well as harmonious ones. Certainly by the time she was dancing her Greek vignettes such as *Orpheus* or *Iphigenia in Tauris*, Duncan's expressive palette had expanded to include both Apollonian and Dionysiac themes:

My idea of dancing is to leave my body free to the sunshine, to feel my sandaled feet on the earth, to be near and love the olive trees of Greece. These are my present ideas of dancing. Two thousand years ago a people lived here who had perfect sympathy and comprehension of the beautiful in Nature, and this knowledge and sympathy were perfectly expressed in their own forms and movement . . . I came to Greece to study these forms of ancient art, but above all, I came to live in the land which produced these wonders, and when I say 'to live' I mean to dance.[23]

Isadora Duncan spent much of 1903 in Greece with the whole Duncan clan. Led by Raymond Duncan's fierce desire to reinvent an archaic Greece (one not sullied by modern equipment or politics), the family crossed the Ionian Sea in a small fishing boat to make their first pilgrimage to this ancient land. The chapter in her autobiography, *My Life*, documenting this odyssey is filled with poetic quotations from Byron and Homer, as well as depictions of Isadora and Raymond gambolling about the Greek countryside, drunk with Plato.[24] Its euphoric tone is also inflected with wry comments about bedbugs, hard wooden planks for sleeping, the assorted perils of the countryside, not to mention the

---

[21] Daly (1995), 89.   [22] Duncan (1928), 66.
[23] Duncan (1927), quoted in Daly (1995), 101.   [24] Duncan (1927), 116–35.

astonishment of the modern Greeks to this band of foreigners who looked like ancient sculptures come alive. The rest of the story is well known, a testimony to the odd myopia of a radical American fundamentalism. Dressed in tunics and shod in sandals, the Duncans bought some land with a view of the Acropolis and proceeded to build their house, Kopanos. Eventually, it dawned on them that there was no water to be had in the area, and although Raymond would have deeper and deeper wells dug (at Isadora's expense), eventually they would give up the fantasy of living in Greece permanently, and Raymond would return to Paris to start a theatre school there.

While in Greece, the Duncans met the Sikelianos family: Philadelpheus, an archeologist; Angelos, who would become a renowned poet and later marry Eva Palmer; and Penelope, a singer, who became Raymond's wife. The alchemy between the Sikelianos family and the Americans was very interesting. Both Penelope and Angelos helped Raymond Duncan actualize his dreams of living like the ancients. But then again, the impulsive utopianism of the Americans (not to mention their financial assistance which, in the case of Eva Palmer, was considerable) also helped the Sikelianos family to dream of reaching back past the modern Greek state to reconstruct the simplicity of peasant life, as well as the humanitarian power of an ancient, popular theatre.

In 1927, and again in 1930, Angelos and Eva Palmer-Sikelianos produced two epic theatrical festivals at the ancient theatre in Delphi, which included events such as athletic games and exhibitions of folk art, and featured Eva Palmer's stagings of Aeschylus' *Prometheus Bound*, the first time in modern Greece that anyone had attempted to mount ancient Greek tragedy in an outdoor setting on that scale (see further Michelakis, this volume). Through her directorial work, Palmer managed to accomplish what Isadora Duncan loftily envisioned when she wrote her short essay on 'The Greek Theater':

Greek Tragedy sprang from the dancing and singing of the Greek Chorus. Dancing has gone a long way astray. She must return to her original place—hand in hand with the Muses encircling Apollo. She must become again the primitive Chorus, and the drama will be reborn from her inspiration.[25]

Born in 1874 to a well-to-do and well-placed New York City family, Palmer had all the advantages of money, connections, and liberal-thinking parents. Her father introduced her to some of the most radical thinkers of the late nineteenth century, Robert Ingersoll among them. Her mother developed both her fine musical sensibility and her interest in the arts, as well as sponsoring an awareness of social injustice and modelling a fervent belief in women's suffrage.[26] As she grew up, Palmer went to schools in America, France, and Germany, giving her a patchworkish education that was long on English literature and short on mathematics.

---

[25] Duncan (1928), 87.   [26] Palmer-Sikelianos (1993), 32.

Precocious, but undisciplined, Palmer took up the challenge posed by M. Carey Thomas, the legendary president of Bryn Mawr College, who flatly told Palmer it was unlikely she could pass the entrance exams. She studied hard ('eighteen hours a day for six months') and managed to gain admission to this bastion of women's education and classical studies, where she spent the next two years studying Greek for the first time and immersing herself in English literature. She also directed annual class plays and was pleased when Thomas suggested that she direct *Hamlet* the following year. In her memoirs, Palmer writes that Thomas 'had also a knack of sensing and encouraging one toward one's own strong but still unexpressed leanings'.[27] I suspect that it was her pleasure in the more practical, hands-on nature of theatre that compelled Palmer to abandon the scholarly cloistered setting of Bryn Mawr for the freedom of Europe, where she spent a year in Rome with her brother before settling in Paris, in a pavilion near Natalie Barney's place in Neuilly.

From the time she was first sent to school, Eva Palmer evinced a passion for recitation. Her autobiography recounts numerous occasions of standing on a chair performing Shakespeare, Swinburne, or Poe to a spellbound group of her schoolmates. They were witnesses to some of Palmer's first attempts to merge language and rhythm, and although she was told by a teacher to stop, as these events were considered 'too exciting' for the girls, Palmer's passion for 'melody in words' was ignited. In a chapter on 'The First Delphic Festival', Palmer connects these early experiences to her later work:

So this impetus toward the singing of words was for long obscured; and Mrs. Dowe's negative imperative was perhaps still working, while entirely new conceptions of Greek Choruses were building in my consciousness. But then I no longer was interested in either reciting or acting myself. I had come to long for many voices, for many women, or preferably many men, expressing in perfect individual freedom, and in perfect composite unity, the complete inner meaning of the word.[28]

In Paris, Palmer studied acting and performed in amateur theatricals such as those with Colette in Natalie Barney's garden. Her striking long red hair and beautiful eyes led both Sarah Bernhardt and Mrs Patrick Campbell (well-known actresses of the day) to invite her to play *Pélléas and Mélisande* with them. In both cases, her professional aspirations were thwarted; one because of Bernhardt's fear of being upstaged, and the other because Palmer refused to give up her friendship with Natalie Barney, an association that Mrs Campbell claimed was bad for her protégée's reputation. In any case, Palmer recounts: 'I had seen by that time a good deal of back-stage politics and meanness, and my ambition to go on the French stage, or any other stage, was not so ardent as it had been.'[29]

During the spring of 1905, while Palmer was trying to decide what to do with her life, she met Raymond Duncan and his wife, Penelope Sikelianos, and their

[27] Palmer-Sikelianos (1993), 25–6.   [28] Ibid. 105–6.   [29] Ibid. 57.

baby. Upon hearing Penelope sing Greek ecclesiastical melodies, Palmer had an epiphany: 'I felt that I had heard music for the first time; heard a human voice for the first time.'[30] Because of strikes by workers that threatened to become violent on the first of May, Palmer invited the Raymond Duncan family to move out to Neuilly with her. Soon the house was in the midst of a mini-Greek revival, with Raymond painting friezes on the walls, and the women sewing their own apparel. One afternoon while resting, Penelope explained the shifts in tone that Palmer found so compelling in her singing:

A mode...is not a scale; it has nothing to do with the piano. Each mode has special intervals of its own, which do not exist on the piano. A mode is a mood; and a Greek song uses the mode which suits its content: one mode if the words are gay, another if they are melancholy, another if they are martial, and so forth. We have many musical modes. We therefore have infinite melodic variety.[31]

Inspired by the sound and rhythm of the language and intrigued by a lifestyle that sought to capture the essence of ancient life, Palmer went to Greece with Raymond and Penelope, and there met Angelos Sikelianos, with whom she would find the focus for her life's work in the theatre.

Galvanized by Nietzsche's *Birth of Tragedy*, her husband's epic poetry, as well as her studies of Greek culture, Eva Palmer-Sikelianos set out in the mid-1920s to stage *Prometheus Bound* at Delphi. As her guiding mantra, she kept two lines in mind. The first was from Plato's *The Republic* and the second one was from Aristotle's *Poetics*: 'The tragic chorus is the union of poetry, music and gymnastics', and 'the tragic chorus expresses in movement the character, the sufferings, and the actions of the actors'.[32] What helped her transform these lofty ideas into a living, breathing, moving, theatrical unit, however, was her extraordinary facility at movement analysis.

It is unclear to me whether Palmer-Sikelianos ever had any specific movement training, either in some kind of Delsartesque living pictures during her youth in New York City (which is a good probability), or as part of her studies in acting in France. Maybe she was just naturally perceptive at distinguishing the physical dynamic of stance and gesture, both on and off the stage. In any case, her autobiography *Upward Panic* contains a number of compelling descriptions of people's physical personalities. One of her most perceptive movement descriptions comes in her chapter on Isadora Duncan. Even before Palmer met Raymond Duncan, she had seen Isadora dance several times: '[W]e all felt that the shackles of the world were loosened, that liberation was ahead of us.'[33] Indeed, at the beginning of her chapter on Duncan, Palmer-Sikelianos recalls how everyone originally thought of Isadora as the embodiment of Greece:

---

[30] Ibid. 46.   [31] Ibid. 50.   [32] Ibid. 106   [33] Ibid. 181.

What she did was always connected with Greek vases and Greek bas-reliefs; and only gradually, after a number of years of unquestioning gratitude for what she brought us, one began to date the vases which were evoked by her dancing.[34]

Palmer-Sikelianos's search for the movement forms of an ancient, archaic Greece led her to recognize the inconsistencies in Isadora's gloss on Greece, which Duncan herself points out in the end of *My Life* when she claims that: 'It has often made me smile—but somewhat ironically—when people have called my dancing Greek, for I myself count its origin in the stories which my Irish grandmother often told of crossing the plains with grandfather.'[35] Nonetheless, Palmer-Sikelianos's articulation of Duncan's movement style is very evocative:

Her arms were beautiful, and the soft undulations were infinitely charming to a world which knew only the tiresome stiffness of the ballet; but there is not a single example of any work of Greek art before the fourth century which resembles Isadora's dancing. It was always flowing. Even in powerful dances like her 'Marche Slave' and her Chopin 'Polonaise', the lines of her body went into curves. She always faced her audience frankly, head and chest in the same direction. There was never the powerful accent of a strong angle, and never the isolating effect of keeping the head in profile with the chest 'en face' which is characteristic of archaic Greek art. Even in moving around the outside circle of the stage, it was always straight ahead, more like a child running, with none of the pause and power which are added by what I have called the Apollonian movement in the dance.[36]

As we know, Isadora used her classical connections to legitimize her own dancing and distinguish her work as 'Art'. Eva Palmer-Sikelianos, on the other hand, was interested in using a more archaic movement vocabulary, not because she was dedicated to being strictly 'authentic' (she wasn't), but because she thought that this 'Apollonian' style best carried the dramatic power of the tragic chorus (see Figure 3.1). In his portrait of Eva Palmer-Sikelianos in the book *The Splendour of Greece*, Robert Payne recounts the comments of a modern Greek actress which reveal how Palmer-Sikelianos's skills at movement analysis created a foundation for her uncanny ability to animate history.

She was the only ancient Greek I ever knew . . . She had a strange power of entering the minds of the ancients and bringing them to life again. She knew everything about them— how they walked and talked in the marketplace, how they latched their shoes, how they arranged the folds of their gowns when they arose from the table, and what songs they sang, and how they danced, and how they went to bed. I don't know how she knew these things, but she did![37]

One of the tools that was available to Eva Palmer-Sikelianos in her search for the appropriate gestures and movements in reconstructing the role of the chorus

---

[34] Palmer-Sikelianos (1993), 181–2.   [35] Duncan (1927), 340.
[36] Palmer-Sikelianos (1993), 182.   [37] Payne (1960), 102.

Figure 3.1 Chorus of Oceanids for *Prometheus Bound,* directed by Eva Palmer, (1927).

in ancient Greek drama was a book called *The Antique Greek Dance* (English translation 1916), written by Maurice Emmanuel and originally published in French in 1896. In this massive tome, the author meticulously cross-referenced gestures and positions of the body found in Greek sculpture, bas-reliefs, and vase-paintings with passages from poetry and drama. He categorizes these designs into three basic groups: (*a*) gestures that are ritualized and symbolic, (*b*) gestures of everyday life, and (*c*) mostly decorative gestures (See Figure 3.2). Moving from poetic rhythms to music rhythms to dance rhythms, Emmanuel reconnects the visual and the written evidence, creating an encyclopaedic documentation of ancient Greek movement styles (see further Naerebout, this volume).

It is unclear whether Eva Palmer-Sikelianos ever consulted this exhaustive reference. In her autobiography, she speaks of going to museums to look for visual evidence and consulting archeological texts, but never directly mentions Emmanuel's book. There are, of course, some obvious similarities. For instance, in the group of ritual and symbolic gestures Emmanuel describes a gesture of

Figure 3.2 Chorus of Oceanids for *Prometheus Bound,* directed by Eva Palmer, (1927).

worship referenced in a sculpture from the Berlin Museum and described as a boy 'holding the arms out with the palms up'.[38] This is exactly the position that the Oceanids chorus takes in *Prometheus Bound.* In a photograph by the Greek artist Nelly of the 1930 production, we see a semicircle of women facing Prometheus in this supplicating pose.

Later in Emmanuel's book there is a section on the 'Chorus of the Dance', in which he analyses women's group movement, including the folk dance that Palmer-Sikelianos used in her choreography, as well as the Pyrrhic or warrior dances, which were also included in the Delphic festivals. In this section, Eva Palmer-Sikelianos would have found clear justification for her belief that the chorus moved as a rhythmical unit in circular patterns, using their whole bodies to create a wave-like ripple across the stage space. In any case, Palmer-Sikelianos was pointedly less interested in historical accuracy *per se,* than in reviving the spiritual aspects of Greek drama. In response to a compliment by a Mr Buschor,

---

[38] Emannuel (1916*a*), 25.

the Director of the German School of Archaeology concerning the 'archaeological correctness' of her 1927 production, Palmer-Sikelianos declares:

[T]he performance was bristling with archaeological mistakes; but even you did not detect them, and you are not conscious of them even now. And that is because the play was moving around its own pivot; it was emotionally true, or almost true—and that was sufficient to make even you feel that it was correct archaeologically. But there is no such thing as archaeological correctness. There is nothing in Greek drama except the emotional truth and consistency of the performers, and the immense responding emotion of those who are present. The faculties of the actors, the chorus and the audience in the great circular theatre become one, and form an overwhelming magnetic force. It is a tidal wave which nothing can resist; not even archaeological conscientiousness.[39]

The one place where Palmer-Sikelianos worked assiduously for historically accurate reproductions was in the area of costumes, weaving all the fabrics she used. Early on in their collaboration, Raymond and Eva had found that by combining a heavy warp with a thin weft, they could create a cloth that draped with the same kinds of folds they admired on ancient sculptures. Indeed, Palmer-Sikelianos was quite proud of the fact that later archaeologists found evidence that her method was exactly the same one used in ancient times. Although she used silk (which the Greeks did not use) for the chorus dresses, Palmer-Sikelianos believed that this artistic liberty was justified on the grounds that the silk 'would look like the folds on a Greek bas-relief', and would create the image of waves rippling across the ocean.[40]

In her autobiography, Palmer-Sikelianos devotes a whole chapter to weaving. Clearly weaving gave her a great deal of pleasure. It was the physical enactment of her creativity, one that merged individuality and sociability. She writes: 'There is something about the loom, something eminently sociable on one hand, because of the different stages in setting up a warp where several usually work together, and something restful and rhythmical in loneliness when the swift shuttle seems to clarify one's thoughts.'[41]

Eva Palmer-Sikelianos's theatrical genius lay in how she used the elements of costume, gesture, and movement to galvanize the theatrical space. Unlike the proscenium frame of most indoor theatres, the outdoor arena at Delphi emphasized the three-dimensionality of space, which Palmer-Sikelianos further animated through her choreography. This sense of moving with and through space is, as we have seen throughout this chapter, a mark of American modern dance. Eva Palmer-Sikelianos brought this sensibility with her to Greece, using it to help her reinvent the epic sensibility of Greek drama. In *Upward Panic*, she recalls how her chorus of young Athenian women had practised for two years, finally becoming 'word-perfect, melody-perfect, move-perfect'. But something was missing. They hadn't yet learned to animate the space. Then, they went out to

---

[39] Palmer-Sikelianos (1993), 113–14.   [40] Ibid. 109.   [41] Ibid. 78.

the ancient theatre. 'It was a revelation. The thing that none of us had been able to do in Athens happened by itself on the great mountain. Their voices were free and strong, their movements beautiful and powerful. They were inspired.'[42]

For Palmer-Sikelianos, the physical space was also a metaphysical arena, the 'orchestra' (literally meaning a 'dancing-place') held a spiritual energy, the potent possibility of creating a *communitas* among everyone present. The chorus moved in the central circle, which was ringed by an ascending and expanding circle of seats for the spectators. Like the ripples from a pebble thrown in the water, the lines of energy in the ancient theatre radiated outwards from the chorus and actors towards the audience. In her essay 'What is Great Theater?' Palmer-Sikelianos articulates how space and rhythm can create a spiritual connection. Palmer-Sikelianos's four physical 'laws' delineate how 'the attention of actors, chorus, and audience was centered on a point, the orchestra, and formed circling waves of power which increased in intensity as the drama unfolded'.[43] She describes this moment as the 'thrill' of great performances, the moment when the audience and actors experience a mutual sense of belonging, an awareness of their shared humanity. In an essay titled, 'The World's a Circular Stage: Aeschylean Tragedy through the Eyes of Eva Palmer-Sikelianou', Gonda Van Steen connects this focus in her directing to the Sikelianoi's larger project of creating a University:

Her choice of circular and centripetal choreographic movement within this 'sacred' setting of nature and ruins expressed her belief that a simple, primitive form could help to transmit the Delphic Idea. The Sikelianoi's ideal was to create a universal center of centers, a univers-ity, at Delphi, which would unite peoples around spirituality and Art.[44]

This ideal university proved to be elusive. After depleting her own fortune and after many attempts to secure state institutional support for the Delphic Festivals, Palmer-Sikelianos returned to the United States to try and interest Americans in her ideas and raise money. While in the States, she worked with Ted Shawn and his men's group at their dance retreat at Jacob's Pillow, and also staged *The Bacchae* at Bryn Mawr and Smith Colleges. Eventually, she returned to Greece, where she died after suffering a stroke at a performance held in her honour. As I am writing this, there are still a lot of gaps in Eva Palmer-Sikelianos's biography. I wonder, for instance, how much she was aware of the American dancers appearing in Greece in the 1910s and 1920s. In February 1914, Loïe Fuller and her troupe gave an outdoor performance at the Athens Stadium. It is possible that Palmer-Sikelianos saw or heard of Fuller's performances, but so far as I can tell, there is no documentation about any interaction between these two women artists.

---

[42] Palmer-Sikelianos (1993), 114–15.   [43] Palmer-Sikelianos (1967).
[44] Van Steen (2002), 379.

Interestingly enough, the last line of Anatole France's introduction to Loïe Fuller's autobiography (which was first published in French in 1908) reads:

There you have to the life this Loïe Fuller . . . who reanimates within herself and restores to us the lost wonders of Greek mimicry, the art of those motions, at once voluptuous and mystical, which interpret the phenomena of nature and the life history of living beings.[45]

For someone who was seen as the living embodiment of Art Nouveau, a woman who was acclaimed at the Paris Universal Exposition of 1900 as 'La Fée Électricité' and who played Salomé as recently as 1907, the rhetorical shift evident in France's language is rather remarkable. Indeed, this idealization of an eternal nature and universal humanity, with nods to Greek antiquity, attests to Fuller's amazing ability to reinvent herself. This last section of my chapter takes up Loïe Fuller's work with her dance group to analyse how she incorporated the contemporary cultural evocations of 'nature' and 'Greek' in her stagings of what were, essentially, Modernist theatrical landscapes.

Of course, it is important to remember that early on in her career Fuller had invoked the 'origins' of dancing in ancient cultures to distinguish her movement inspiration from the music-hall dancing which framed her first appearances in Paris. While she disassociated her movement style from that of academic dancing, Fuller had long connected her work to the ancient Greeks, who 'danced with their whole bodies—with their head and arms and trunk and feet'.[46] By 1908, however, the term 'Greek dancing' clearly referenced Duncan's dancing and that of her imitators. Fuller was thus careful to distinguish her school of dance from that of her early protégée:

By no means is my kind of dancing like Isadora Duncan's, although there are one or two points in common. The two kinds are as different as night and day. Miss Duncan's dancing is essentially a cultivated art—a learned kind of dancing that takes much practice—whereas mine is natural, inspirational, and spontaneous. Miss Duncan imitates the movements of dancers as represented on Greek vases and her pupils copy her. I and my pupils give the original natural expression and movements which inspired the Greeks when they made their vases.[47]

What Fuller meant by 'natural' dancing can be seen in the photographs taken by the American Harry C. Ellis of Fuller's young students rehearsing outdoors. This extraordinary series of action shots shows the group of long-limbed girls with turbans and tunics, skipping, swinging, and generally cavorting in a fairly chaotic manner. They are usually leaping in the air, sometimes with their faces open to the sky, sometimes curled over, with their arms continuing the C curve of their body. While they may be all doing the same thing (skipping, for instance), they are not all doing it in the same manner, or at the same time.

---

[45] Fuller (1913), x.   [46] Crawford Flitch (1912), 88.
[47] Fuller, quoted in Current and Current (1997), 196.

This makes for a random visual field, but also gives their movement a sense of spontaneity and individuality, two qualities that Fuller wanted to cultivate in her group. Unlike similar photographs of Elizabeth Duncan's pupils which portray young girls moving as a unit, all with the same leg forward and the same lifted chest, Fuller's students exude a sense of the wilder, less tamed side of nature. Rather than cultivating her dancers, Fuller seems to have simply let them loose.

Despite her strategic differences from Duncan, Fuller's 'Muses', as they were often called, wore the stylized tunics and bare legs made famous by Duncan. Although her movement vocabulary differed substantially from Duncan's, Fuller was savvy enough to cash in on the trend for 'aesthetic' or 'natural' dancing that was sweeping her home country at the time. Thus, on her 1909–10 North American tour, one of Fuller's troupe, a young German woman named Gertrud Von Axen, performed solos—both on Fuller's programmes and separately—that apparently were remarkably similar to Duncan's early work.[48] In the Fuller collection at Lincoln Center, there is a programme for a concert of solos by Von Axen to the music of Beethoven and Schubert given, the heading notes, 'By Special Arrangement with Loïe Fuller'. The cover photo shows Von Axen with her arms outstretched in front of her, her upper body leaning away, with the end of her wrapped tunic draped gracefully down her back. The inside carries Fuller's endorsement: 'Miss Fuller considers Gertrud Von Axen the most perfect and real Greek dancer before the public today,' and the back excerpts press comments from Fuller's recent tour. Von Axen's performance was predictably acclaimed as 'graceful', 'charming', and 'spontaneous'—exactly the descriptions used when Duncan was first dancing.

Alternately billed as 'Loïe Fuller's Ballet of Light', 'Loïe Fuller and her School of Dance', or 'Loïe Fuller and her Muses', the company usually presented an evening of dances that ranged from *Midsummer Night's Dream* set to Mendelssohn's music, or Scriabin's *Prometheus* (basically Fuller's *Fire Dance en masse*—see Figure 15.2 of an earlier version from 1897), to more abstract works set to modern, impressionistic music such as selections from Debussy's *Nocturnes*, Stravinsky's *Feu d'Artifice*, or *Orchestrations de Couleurs sur Deux Préludes* by Armande de Polignac, a piece that was composed expressly for Fuller's company. Works such as *Midsummer Night's Dream* sketched out a vague narrative—'In a forest, a Shepherd sleeps and dreams of fairies, gnomes, and elves...'—onto which Fuller would hang a series of atmospheric events that swept, like waves, cross the stage. There is a photograph of the company in a bucolic setting, perfectly arranged like a picture, with Loïe Fuller on the far right, draped in flowing fabric. Although it is more staid than the frolicking, action shots by Ellis, one can imagine the curtain rising on the tableau, with the lighting gradually growing brighter, like a rising sun, as the stage action begins.

---

[48] Current and Current (1997), 202.

The more abstract works were essentially music visualizations, in which Fuller's exquisite lighting effects were further enhanced by the manipulations of fabric (often with little mirrors sewn on it to reflect the lights) by the girls onstage. No longer a solo figure evoking fleeting images of a lily, clouds, or fire, Fuller was now working with a larger palette, allowing her to create an impressive series of theatrical landscapes. In the same way that Duncan's dancing realized 'a narrative of force', Fuller's choreography now depicted the forces of nature. Giovanni Lista describes Fuller's work at this time in terms that echo Emerson's notions of the transcendence of nature: 'She thinks, like Emerson, that human beings, to truly communicate with the universal aspects of nature, need to downplay their unique position in the world.'[49] Unfortunately, most of the visual documentation of these works by Fuller are still studio shots, with the young girls of her company posed in formal tableau. There are two outdoor photos, however, taken at dusk, that give us an idea of the kinds of atmospheric play of light and shadow that would become a trademark of her later work.

Fuller thought of her music visualizations as a 'new form of art'. In a 1914 interview, she describes her efforts to merge 'pictorial orchestration' with 'magical lighting'.

Specialists of the dance do not understand that I aim only to give an harmonious impression trying to express the spirit of the music. I intend to continue it, in some way, to continue it as the waves unfurling on the shore continue to obey the breath of the wind. I try to follow thus the musical waves in the movements of the body and in colors; I am trying to create a harmony between sound, light, and movement.[50]

While some music critics disparaged Fuller's dances for betraying the music, others claimed she had unified the different genres, creating a fusion of sound, movement and light. Léo Claretie calls her work a 'transposition'. Clearly refuting a previous commentary, he writes: 'Music is a joy for our ears, she gives us again a joy for our eyes. She renders the music pictorial. Claude Debussy is translated, he is not betrayed.'[51] Distinguishing Fuller's efforts from either ballet or what he dubs decorative spectacle, Lista also suggests that Fuller was onto something new: 'In fact, it was really about creating a new form of expression, neither ballet nor decorative spectacle, but rather a sort of tableau vivant which unfolded like a pure music visualization.'[52] I find his phrase, 'a living tableau unfolding through time' intriguing, for it points not only to the influence of Muybridge's and Marey's experiments in chronophotography but also to the future of cinema (see further Naerebout, this volume). Ironically, these works also recall the earlier nineteenth-century magic lantern shows that

---

[49] Lista (1994), 468.   [50] Harris (1979), 28.
[51] Quoted in the programme for 'Loie Fuller et son école de danse', Théâtre Municipal du Chatelet, May, 1914.
[52] Lista (1994), 489.

depicted landscapes changing dramatically from dawn to dusk, or with the arrival of a storm. Once again, Fuller was harnessing a variety of technologies to produce exquisite images of nature.

Occasionally, Fuller participated in these creations (playing in Prometheus, for instance), but mostly she served as choreographer/director for the company. One exception was her *La Danse des Mains*. This solo, inspired by Rodin's sculptures of hands and his observation that the soul can express itself through any part of the body, was performed in total darkness, with only her hands illuminated. Several of Fuller's programmes for 1914 contain a sketch entitled 'La Danse des Mains', which portrays four sets of hands in different expressive gestures: clawing the air, commanding attention, holding something, or simply reaching towards the sky. Writing in *Le Théâtre*, Jean D'Orliac echoes Rodin's aesthetic sensibility by claiming: 'The entire human being, with all his multiple emotions is evoked by these expressive fingers whose rhythms move her supple hands.'[53] If Fuller's music visualizations were changing landscapes that indicated her future directions in cinema, her *La Danse des Mains* pointed towards the expressive montage of light, shadow, and close-up that would mark her signature on this new medium of film.

In response to a question from an interviewer for the *Dramatic Mirror*, Fuller once declared: 'It is an American monopoly to combine stage dancing with self-respect.'[54] This chapter has explored very briefly the theatrical work of Colette, Eva Palmer, Isadora Duncan, and Loïe Fuller, and its invocations of ancient Greece, with an eye to understanding how self-respect was cultivated in the bodily practices of these women, and how they learned to stage that experience of physical subjectivity for the world to see. Through their embodied training, these women learned how to mobilize the space and enact force, creating a dynamic in which their bodies could effect change. True feminists as well as humanists, they were encouraged at the beginning of a new century by the potential for their own personal and professional realization, and they shared the fervent desire to communicate those possibilities to the world.

[53] D'Orliac (1914), n. 377.
[54] Fuller quoted in de Morrini (1978), 216.

4

Reception or Deception? Approaching Greek Dance through Vase-Painting

Tyler Jo Smith

Ancient Greek vase-painting has long interested both dancers and dance historians. The black- and red-figure vases of Athens, as well as those produced in other regions of Greece, are perhaps most often associated with the mythological lives of gods and heroes, pursuits of athletes and warriors, or extracts from symposia. Themes of performance do make their appearance as well. On a sizeable number of painted vases, we witness actors, acrobats, musicians, and dancers. While each of these areas has been given a certain amount of consideration by classicists and archaeologists, the relationship between art-form and image remains vague and enigmatic.[1]

The most abundant category of dancing figures on vases is the male figures often referred to as 'komasts'. Appearing on the sides of many black-figure cups, and sometimes joined by dancing women, these performers leave us with far more questions than answers. Is their dancing spontaneous or rehearsed? Ritualistic or sympotic? Does their signature bottom-slapping gesture (see Figure 4.1) encourage us to identify their routine with one known from antiquity, such as the *kordax*, the 'lewd, grotesque, and shameless dance' mentioned by Theophrastus in his *Characters* (6)?[2] While such an interpretation is indeed tempting, a certain amount of caution should be exercised when approaching the imagery. One need only consider A. D. Trendall and T. B. L. Webster's attempts to match vases with known and lost dramas, and with varying degrees of success.[3] It should go without saying that,

---

For assistance with the research and writing of this paper, I gratefully thank Ian Jenkins, Peter Kurth, Fiona Macintosh, Frederick Naerebout, Alkis Raftis, Dawn Setzer, and most of all Dimitris Plantzos who escorted me to the former Duncan home in Athens. Further thanks are owed to the Archive of Performances of Greek and Roman Drama (Oxford); and the Dora Stratou Greek Dances Theatre (Athens), where I was Visiting Research Fellow during spring 2008. The University of Iowa Libraries kindly provided much needed information about Lillian Lawler from the Iowa Women's Archive. During the academic year 2000–01, the Bizzell Library of the University of Oklahoma and Department of Classics and Letters generously assisted in the compilation of my own archive of Lawler's published writings.

[1] On music see recently Bundrick (2005).
[2] Schnabel (1910).
[3] Trendall and Webster (1971).

Figure 4.1 Komast figure.

despite our very limited knowledge about them, the vase-painters of Athens, Laconia, Corinth, and elsewhere were neither choreographers nor playwrights.

   This chapter is concerned with the relationship between dance and image, both ancient and modern. When vase-painters created dance iconography, their sources of inspiration must be considered. To what extent were painters portraying contemporary dancing events or, rather, bound by artistic convention? How difficult was it for painters, limited both by techniques and available space, to reveal a dynamic three-dimensional art-form on a curved two-dimensional surface? Once we turn to the modern picture, we confront further problems of translation. How does the modern dancer, historian, or student of the past comprehend and contextualize these ancient images? How and for what purpose should each of these groups use them? While some have attempted to re-create the dances as modern performance on the basis of viewing vases and other arts, others have voiced extreme scepticism regarding this approach.[4] Here we shall focus on each of these questions in an effort to clarify not only what was useful to the ancient artisan and/or modern viewer, but what was available to them as well. As a contribution to reception studies, it is hoped that we shall better understand early twentieth-century approaches to ancient Greek dance through the lens of vase-painting.[5] It should become obvious that, at least in some instances, we have been misled, even deceived, by incorrect interpretations of the iconographic evidence.

---

   [4] Naerebout (1997), 234–53.
   [5] There is remarkably little written on vase reception; see Nørskov (2002). Kurtz (2000) is primarily concerned with sculpture. See also Prettejohn (2006).

By the early twentieth century Greek vases had themselves become vital to the discussion of ancient dance. The careers of Isadora Duncan, a dancer, and Lillian Lawler, a classical scholar, may be cited in this regard. These two professional American women upheld a fascination with, and dependence, on vases in their work. Yet their selection process is what appears most striking. Despite the sizeable number and iconographic range of komast vases, such lively dancing figures seem never to have entered into the somewhat idealized conception of the ancient Greek dancer that Duncan and Lawler sought to perpetuate.

GREEK VASES IN THE MODERN WORLD

The history of the study of Greek vase-painting has been well documented by Cook and Sparkes, and is most recently treated by Nørskov.[6] Indeed it is the period of eighteenth-century neoclassicism, followed by nineteenth-century collecting and classification that have received the most scholarly attention, and for obvious reasons. Early discussion of vases focused on the question of origins and an ensuing 'Etruscophilia' or 'Etruscomania',[7] the natural result of the discovery of large numbers of such objects in Italian soil. J. J. Winckelmann, who visited Rome but never Athens, devoted a certain amount of attention in his writings on ancient art to sculpture; yet he has recently been recognized as the first to compare 'Greek' vases with the drawings of Renaissance masters, thus elevating their status as art somewhat.[8]

Similarly, Sir William Hamilton, though not the first collector of Greek vases, was no doubt instrumental in their contemporary rise to fame. His vases would eventually belong to the British Museum—where for the first time in their history these humble terracotta vessels would enjoy public display—but not before he had enlisted the Chevalier d'Hancarville to publish them in the form of text and more importantly drawings under the title *Collection of Etruscan, Greek and Roman Antiquities from the Cabinet of the Honble Wm Hamilton* (1766, 1777).[9] During the late 1780s, Hamilton's mistress, and later wife, Emma, developed and displayed her famous 'Attitudes' for guests attending his Naples home. This dancing of sorts was inspired by both pose and dress on ancient works of art, and to some extent by the Greek vases in Hamilton's own collection.[10] Vases also featured prominently in portraits beginning with

---

[6] Cook (1997), 275–311; Sparkes (1996), esp. ch. 2; Nørskov (2002).

[7] e.g. Sparkes (1996), 47; and Nørskov (2002), 35. On the question of Etruscan or Greek origins see Jenkins and Sloan (1996), 51–2.

[8] Nørskov (2002), 11. See also Cook (1997), 278 on Winckelmann's uncertainty; and Jenkins (2008), 120.

[9] Burn (2003), 143; and in general Jenkins and Sloan 1996.

[10] Naerebout (1997), 47–8. For another view see Touchette 2000, esp. 126–30.

Pompeo Batoni's *Ferdinand Duke of Brunswick and Lüneburg* of 1767, and more than once in Sir Joshua Reynolds's portrayals of Hamilton.[11]

The shapes and motifs of Greek vases, primarily red-figure, inspired the prolific potteries of Wedgwood and Spode and the classicizing style of Flaxman. Their general rise in appreciation throughout Europe was accompanied by a parallel rise in value. Like sculpture, vases became the property of the private gentleman-collector in Britain, and most notably those who had completed their Grand Tour, such as the designer Thomas Hope and the architect Sir John Soane.[12] Despite the ongoing debate about origins and confusion about chronology, 'the students of the eighteenth century did two services to vase-painting; they discovered it and they recognized it as Greek'.[13]

Excavation and discovery of large numbers of Greek vases, particularly in Etruscan tombs, throughout the nineteenth century resulted in the creation of both private and public collections, as well as the growth of existing ones.[14] Furthermore, the Greek War of Independence (1821–30) and the emergence of modern Greece stimulated interest in the eastern Mediterranean and, in the wake of these events, were many excavations and abundant archaeological discoveries. The Archaeological Society of Athens was established in 1837, and the founding of the great 'foreign' schools followed later in the century, beginning with the French School in 1846, the German Institute in 1874, the American School of Classical Studies in 1881, and the British School at Athens in 1886.[15] Not only did these institutes sponsor their own official excavations, many museums themselves, such as the British Museum and others on the Continent (i.e. Berlin), conducted their own field projects as well and 'received large quantities of finds'.[16] The resulting publications took the form of large-scale museum or excavation catalogues, attentive to the factual information about the artefacts as well as their formal artistic qualities. Similarly, vases and other finds were exhibited in the major museums, including the two recently opened in Boston and New York, by technique, shape and/or chronology; thus more as art objects, than as artefacts or archaeological assemblages.[17]

The introductions of programmes and professorships of Classical Archaeology, as at Oxford and Cambridge during the late nineteenth century, led to the inevitable conclusion that Greek vases and their companions, among them coins, gems, sculpture, and architecture, were on the road (albeit a slow one!) to

---

[11] Jenkins and Sloan (1996), 52, fig. 21, and 176–8.
[12] Jenkins (2008) on the former; Smith (2007*a*) on the latter.
[13] Cook (1997), 279.
[14] Nørskov (2002), 61–4.
[15] On these developments see Kurtz (2000), 223; Karamanolakis (2008). For the broader Greek perspective: Damaskos and Plantzos (2008).
[16] Nørskov (2002), 66.
[17] Nørskov (2002), is concerned with the issue throughout, and see 147–9 for the American museums.

becoming worthy of academic discourse in their own right.[18] Another development belonging to the late nineteenth century, and of particular relevance here, is the work of the French musicologist and composer Maurice Emmanuel. His 1895 thesis and slightly later book drew heavily on the images of dancers and dance portrayed on Greek vases, and to a lesser extent on sculpted reliefs (see also Naerebout, this volume).[19] Such overt reconstructionism, while innovative, would influence not only classical dance historians, but also, as we shall see, contemporary practitioners of dance, such as Isadora Duncan.

The twentieth century may be viewed in many respects as the most important, indeed the seminal, epoch in the modern history of Greek vase study. Though a detailed account of this period, or indeed earlier ones, is far beyond our present scope, twentieth-century vase scholarship may be summed up in terms of three areas: the contribution of Sir John Beazley, the creation of the *Corpus Vasorum Antiquorum*, and advances in archaeological science. The first two are of greater relevance here than the third, and it is to these we shall now turn.[20] John Davidson Beazley was Lincoln Professor of Classical Archaeology at Oxford from 1925 to 1956. Though best known as the grandfather of vase connoisseurship and attribution, as witnessed by his colossal 'lists' of Athenian painters (*Attic Red-figure Vase-painters* [*ARV*], 1942; and *Attic Black-figure Vase-painters* [*ABV*], 1956), his academic career was further consumed with the study of ancient gems, maintaining the Oxford Cast Collection, and the founding of the *Oxford Monographs on Classical Archaeology*.[21] His earlier publications on Greek vases were equally as authoritative and ground-breaking at the time, among them *Attic Red-figured Vases in American Museums* (1918) and *Greek Vases in Poland* (1928).

His life and work are well documented elsewhere and need not occupy us here.[22] However, there are several aspects of Beazley's influence worth mentioning. First, though not an avid collector of antiquities, Beazley's vases were deposited in the Ashmolean Museum. Today they comprise a small but significant percentage of the Oxford museum's vase holdings, where they have historically served the dual purpose of public education through display and hands-on study for current students of the University.[23] Secondly, Beazley's so-called 'method' of vase-painter attribution has received perhaps an unmerited level of

---

[18] See Boardman in Kurtz (1985), who details the evolution at Oxford, specifying that 'Greek Vases' was not established as a subject until Bernard Ashmole became Chair (1956–61). Ashmole himself had received tuition in the subject as a student under Beazley; see Kurtz (2000), 233–5, and 307. Cf. Stray (1999), 13, for Cambridge, whose Classical Archaeology chair was not founded until 1931.

[19] The book's title says it all: *La Danse grecque antique d'après les monuments figurés*. See Naerebout (1997), 61–4.

[20] Though on science see Boardman (2001), 290–3.

[21] Kurtz (2000), 291–301; and in general Kurtz (1985).

[22] Smith (2005), with previous bibliography. See in particular Kurtz (1985) and Rouet (2001).

[23] Nørskov (2002), 202–16, esp. 210 on the Beazley gift.

attention.[24] The substance of Beazley's contribution to the field is felt more readily in the weighty paper lists themselves and, more importantly today, in the existence of the massive Web-based archive that bears his name (http://www. beazley.ox.ac.uk).[25] Beazley's classification of Greek vases by painter, and to some extent by potter, while criticized widely in the twenty-first century in favour of more postmodern approaches, influenced not only contemporary and successive generations of scholars, who would go on to devote their learning to the output of individual named 'artists',[26] but perhaps also the art market itself, where an unprecedented value would come to be placed on arguably once inexpensive utilitarian objects.[27]

I would not wish to argue that Beazley was (or still is) single-handedly responsible for either of these trends to the exclusion of other key players (i.e. Furtwängler before, Pottier during, Boardman after). The increased interest in and monetary rise of Greek vases must be viewed in relation to broader cultural developments and phenomena, such as the response to the 'New Archaeology' by classical archaeologists on both sides of the Atlantic or the unbelievable rise in the value of art worldwide.[28] Yet, therein resides the problem. Beazley's creation of 'artists', such as the red-figure Berlin Painter, may well have augmented the status of Greek vases as objects or art rather than craft. Though hardly what the Oxford-trained classicist intended or pondered, we must pause to ask: did the archaic symposiast consider his mixing bowl and pouring jug, or the classical athlete his oil bottle, a work of art? Might the term 'pot', favoured by the few, as opposed to the long-used 'vase', preferred by the many, better serve these decorated vessels?[29] Regardless of terminology, there can be little doubt that Beazley's legendary scholarship on the topic heightened awareness of Greek vases in both esoteric academic circles and in fashionable social ones, both in England and beyond.

The first fascicule of the *Corpus Vasorum Antiquorum*, or *CVA*, that of the Louvre, appeared in 1922. The corpus of ancient vases was conceived by Edmund Pottier, at the time an assistant curator at the Louvre who, according to Rouet, was placing himself 'firmly in the footsteps of epigraphists and philologists of the nineteenth century'.[30] The international project aimed to publish in catalogue form the major vase collections according to the museums in which they were held, comprehensively, and thus including all fabrics (i.e. Corinthian, East Greek, South Italian, etc.). Such an undertaking, while massive in scale, would enable enthusiasts of the subject to compare multiple examples by

---

[24] Boardman (2001), 128–38.
[25] Smith (2005), 23–4.
[26] Whitley (1997); followed by Oakley (1998).
[27] As argued by Vickers and Gill (1994), esp. ch. 2. See also Nørskov (2002), 251–92.
[28] On the former see Dyson (1993).
[29] On terminology see Vickers and Gill (1994); Sparkes (1996) also prefers 'pots' or 'pottery'.
[30] Rouet (2001), 128.

form, style, iconography, distribution and provenance—in fact, the very same purpose the Beazley Archive would eventually serve for Athenian painted pottery.

The *CVA*, like Beazley's lists, was not without its critics, then as now, and 'Beazley's biographical approach' would effect the classification employed by fascicule authors dealing with Athenian material in particular.[31] Despite resistance, the *CVA*, like Beazley's *ABV* and *ARV*, would prove fundamental in shaping contemporary perspectives on Greek vase-painting in terms of collecting, display and publication. Both sets of scholarly tools were used regularly by both classicists and archaeologists, and would have been well known to any person educated in these or related disciplines. Equally, anyone working on, or seeking to rework, ancient Greek dance by the 1920s could have had recourse to a comprehensive catalogue of extant Greek vases. What is significant—and is not simply a result of the narrow reach of scholarship—is that only a fraction of this corpus was made known to the wider public.

ISADORA DUNCAN (1877–1927): STAGING THE IMAGE

> Dance, and let the pictured visions of the painters
> Move and speak and breathe and tear our quickened
> Heart-strings;
> Dance, and in the throbbing joy of rhythm and gesture,
> Music, poetry, and painting melt together.[32]

Isadora Duncan's passion for ancient Greek culture is well-known and much discussed. Not only in the area of dance performance did she look to the model of Greece generally, but also in the dress of the ancients that she, her family, her pupils and others of her generation donned.[33] The mania for ancient Greek fashion, décor and theme in performance was widespread and diverse, as documented in the major productions of Anna Pavlova, the Ballets Russes and later Martha Graham, to name but a few.[34] Even on the small stage we might have encountered young women performing a 'Summer Pageant' at the University of Virginia in August 1913 (at the time a single-sex male institution), in the 'classic' or 'natural' Greek guise of Isadora (Figure 4.2).[35]

The details of Isadora's life have been written and rewritten, and she has been described in recent years as 'an over-exposed subject'.[36] The fact that she was

---

[31] Rouet (2001), 136–7; and see Van de Put (1999).
[32] Extract from Joel Elias Springarn, 'Isadora Duncan Dancing'; Raftis (2004), 67.
[33] The best range of published photographs appears in Duncan et al. (1993).
[34] Doy (2002), 53–5. Terry (1963), 101 on imitators. On clothing: Daly (1995), 109; and Graham (1959), 107; Levinson (1929), 71 and 137.
[35] On this phenomenon in America see Daly (1995), 100–3.
[36] Daly (1994), 30; and see Needham (1996) for the state of scholarship to date.

Figure 4.2 Summer Pageant, University of Virginia, 1913.

inspired and influenced in the creation of her performance persona by Greek art is also well-documented. However, most scholarly writing dedicated to the subject has pointed to relief or free-standing sculpture as her primary artistic models, and Greek vases have received far less billing.[37] Here we shall attempt to redress the balance. In both the writings by and about Duncan, there is adequate evidence to suggest that vases were just as important in the formulation of her career as sculpture or other arts. That being said, it is impossible to say exactly what kind of vases she used, and it is safe to assume that she was less concerned with technique (i.e. black- or red-figure), provenance (i.e. Athens, Attica, South Italy, elsewhere), or chronology (i.e. Archaic, Classical, Hellenistic) than she was with the most helpful and, for her unique purposes, reproducible in terms of poses, gestures, or clothing. When she drew inspiration from vases, it seems she did so indiscriminately; though it is important to stress that she looked to the

[37] e.g. Jowitt (1987); Terry (1963), 114–18. On other sources see Levien (1977–78).

hand-holding line-dancers that adorn many vessels, and may well have been attracted to their female subject-matter.

At the turn of the twentieth century, Isadora Duncan and her family moved from the US to the UK. The Duncan children are said to have had an early interest in the arts and culture of the Greeks cultivated by their father.[38] In London she danced for 'London society' and began to make her name as a private (and later public) entertainer. It is known that during this time she read Nietzsche's *The Birth of Tragedy*, Winckelmann's *Journey to Athens*, and met the likes of none other than Jane Ellen Harrison, who read Greek verse during her programme at the New Gallery in March 1900.[39] It was also in London, where Isadora and her side-kick/brother, Raymond, were inspired in their dancing by viewing the art of Archaic and Classical Greece. Quoting from her autobiography entitled *My Life*:

We bought some cot beds for the studio and hired a piano, but we spent most of our time in the British Museum, where Raymond made sketches of all the Greek vases and bas-reliefs, and I tried to express them to whatever music seemed to me to be in harmony with the rhythms of the feet and Dionysiac set of the head, and the tossing of the thyrsis.[40]

Levinson, writing about Duncan some years later would echo the sentiment saying that vase-painting above all other ancient arts and monuments had developed and enriched her dancing.[41]

The Duncans proceeded to the Continent and eventually made their way to Greece itself. Both Isadora and Raymond were greatly enthralled by vase imagery and are known to have visited museums with substantial collections, such as the Louvre, the National Museum in Athens, and those in Berlin and Munich.[42] Throughout her life she made several visits to Russia, the first in 1905, and Stanislavsky is alleged to have possessed a Greek vase Isadora gave him personally.[43] Her stint in Paris, however, comprises the next important segment of our story. The hours and days supposedly spent studying the Greek vase displays in the Louvre have been described as the 'turning point' of her career as a dancer:

we...begin the day by dancing in the gardens of the Luxembourg, walking for miles all over Paris, and spend hours in the Louvre. Raymond had already got a portfolio of drawings of all the Greek vases, and we spent so much time in the Greek vase room that the guardian grew suspicious, and when I explained in pantomime that I had only come there to dance, he decided that he had to do with harmless lunatics, so he let us alone.[44]

---

[38] Blair (1986), 76. See also Jowitt (1988), 7; and Duncan et al. (1993), 26.
[39] Terry (1963), 26; Daly (1995), 93, and n. 17; Jowitt (1988), 87. According to Silverman (1977–78), Harrison 'guided the young dancer through the collections at the British Museum', 3.
[40] Duncan (1927), 54–5.
[41] Daly (1995), 146–7; and cited in Copeland and Cohen (1983), 439.
[42] See Magriel (1977), 28 (quoting C. van Vechten, 1917), and 71–2 for her chronology; Jowitt (1988), 84; and Naerebout (1997), 62–4.
[43] Setzer (2006).
[44] On the Louvre see Macdougall (1977), 38; see also Kurth (2002), 69. Duncan (1927), 52–3, for the quote.

The drawings of Raymond Duncan have proved impossible to trace and perhaps do not even survive. Thus, it is difficult to know exactly which objects he sketched ('all' of them?), which images were to prove the most useful for pose and costume, and how exactly vases were employed at this early stage by the sibling pair.

Undoubtedly the Duncan's passion for things Greek—for both ancient pots and performance—culminated in Athens, where they arrived in 1904. Isadora was famously photographed by the American fashion photographer, Edward Stiechen on the Acropolis and by her brother Raymond, 'dancing the dances of the Greeks' in the Theatre of Dionysus. It was also in Athens where the Clan Duncan, as they referred to themselves, built their family 'temple' (more a compound) four kilometres away on the slopes of Mt Hymettos at a place then known as Kopanos, today the home of the Centre de Recherche sur la Danse Isadora et Raymond Duncan. Their desire to walk wholeheartedly in ancient footsteps was further expressed in the 'Mycenaean' architecture chosen for their home, as well as in Raymond's attempts at amateur archaeology on the building site.[45] Again it would be the vase rooms, this time at the National Museum that captivated her attention. 'I came to study these forms of ancient art, but above all, I came to live in the land that produced these wonders, and when I say "to live" I mean to dance.'[46] Her studies wisely led her to the famous Eleftheroudakis bookshop in search of books on archaeology.[47]

Throughout her life and career Duncan repeatedly claimed not to be interested in the literal reconstruction of ancient Greek dance, and described her art as being 'far removed from the copying of Greek figures and forms'; rather she studied Tanagra figures and vases in order to unlock their hidden beauty or spirit or essence.[48] In a 1901 report from Paris, Isadora is quoted as saying: 'I drew my inspiration from Greek sources. Strictly speaking, I do not try to reconstruct Greek dances. This is practically impossible.'[49] However, an anonymous journalist in Athens would later quote her as saying: 'The ancient dancing of Greece, the liveliness pictured on the picturesque statues and the ornate representations on the preserved vases are the system on which I base my dances today.'[50] In her words: 'I do not mean to *copy* it, *imitate* it; but to *breathe its life, to recreate it in one's self with personal inspiration.*'[51] Or, put more potently: 'We are not Greeks, and therefore cannot dance Greek dances.'[52] At the same time, she openly envisioned her own young pupils as 'children dancing on Greek vases',

---

[45] Kurth (2002), 113–14.
[46] From the *New York Sunday World*; Daly (1995), 101 n. 38. And see Duncan et al. (1993), 51.
[47] Raftis (2004), 72.
[48] Terry (1963), 36, 100; and Kurth (2002), 58. Mary Fanton Roberts (1908) makes the point clearly at the time.
[49] Daly (1995), 101.
[50] Raftis (2004), 71.
[51] Preston (2005), 275, n. 17.
[52] Cited in Lawler (1964), 24, and n. 22.

and on more than one occasion was photographed, as in the well-known Genthe series, striking the exact poses of (not necessarily dancing) figures adorning dozens of Greek vases.[53]

Attempts to match Duncan's static forms with the images on Greek vases, even in the collections she is known to have encountered, seems a fruitless exercise.[54] As we shall learn in the final section of this chapter, Greek vase-painting even at its height was a highly conventionalized art-from, and its vision of dance hardly true to life. However, we do know that Raymond and Isadora ignored the fat-bottomed, fat-bellied, bottom-slapping komast dancers on vases because such figures in no way measured up to the by then well-established stereotypes of the classical ideal. Indeed, the Duncans viewed the Parthenon as 'the pinnacle of perfection', and had 'found in Athens everything which satisfied our aesthetic sense'.[55]

The reception of Duncan during her life indicates a public highly aware of her philhellenism, and she sparked the passions of numerous critics, poets, artists, and eventually scholars. After her death, Louis Séchan devoted a chapter of his *La Danse grecque antique* (Paris, 1930) to Isadora, complete with Auguste-François Gorguet's 1900 illustrations of her striking '*quelques pas et attitudes*'.[56] She has been compared with Wedgwood, Keats, and Phidias, labelled 'High Priestess', 'hetaira', 'Amazon', 'Baccante', and even represented by George Barbier in 1917 as a red-figure maenad.[57] Achilles Neis, a Greek journalist, observed in the Athenian press in 1903 that Greek art, and especially representations on vases, were visible in both her dance instruction and performance.[58] Eva Palmer–Sikelianos described her as 'a Southern Italian vase come to life', stating that her art belonged to 'Greece in a later decadent period'.[59] In a 1909 review for *Comoedia Illustré*, André Marty asked: 'have we seen her on one of those immortal paintings that adorned Greek vases?'[60] And in 1910, Ovion reviewing *Iphigénie* for the *Mercure de France*, on the subject of the gestures stated that 'one can point out by the hundreds the designs on vases where the poses of Isadora Duncan in this . . . can be traced'.[61]

Interestingly, however, it was Raymond Duncan rather than Isadora, who more obviously nodded in the direction of translating vase images into performance. The 'arrested motion' associated with human figures on vases was used by Raymond as actual dance steps and moves, as opposed to the mere photo

---

[53] Loewenthal (1993), 38; and Genthe (1929).

[54] Cf. Jowitt (1988), 85, and Daly (1995), 96–7, who juxtaposes her poses with sculptures.

[55] Duncan (1927), 123.

[56] Séchan (1930), 315–57, and pl. XVII.4.

[57] Daly (1995), 107; Raftis (2004), 22 (Bakst), 25 (Bourdelle, Bynner), 43 (Kanellos), 60–1 (Philadelpheus), 69 (Strindberg); and see *L'Oeuvre* 28.2 (1911). Raftis (2003) is an excellent collection of artistic renderings. For Barbier see Raftis (2003), 58 and 213.

[58] Raftis (2004), 51.

[59] Ibid. 53.

[60] Loewenthal (1993), 133.

[61] Ibid. 135. Cf. Stratton (1916), 261.

opportunities welcomed by Isadora.[62] His use of poses on vases is remembered by one of his students in New York in the 1920s as a literal translation of figures on Greek vases, and only marginally definable as dance, though this trend is certainly clear in photographs of Raymond from earlier in the century.[63] His 'two-dimensional, straight-off-the-vase stuff', as it has been described by one Duncan scholar, was not the spirit of Greek dance promoted by Isadora.[64] Already in 1908, Raymond had chosen vase motifs, including one of an artisan decorating a large *kantharos*, as the cover art on a brochure advertising his newly founded 'Fotodotera' commune.[65] His holistic approach to fitness with its Platonic overtones and generous dose of Greek vase-painting, known also as his theory of movement, was committed to print in a 1914 treatise entitled *La Danse et la gymnastique*, published in Paris.[66] But neither brother nor sister could have appreciated the complexity of the dance images or of the artefacts themselves in their own day.

While the Duncans may have been among the first practitioners of modern dance to attempt to recreate ancient Greek dance on the basis of surviving Greek vases, they were by no means the first nor last Greek dance reconstructionists. Maurice Emmanuel began with an interest in the ancient Greek 'vocabulary of dance', but would conclude 'that the movements portrayed in antique works of art are identical to the movements of contemporary French classical ballet'.[67] It has even been suggested that Isadora (and no doubt Raymond) was familiar with the work of Emmanuel, which may explain why vases were such a 'strong interest' for her.[68] Like Duncan, Emmanuel proved enormously influential, though in rather different circles. Several generations of French dancer-scholar-classicist-ethnographers persisted with the one-to-one approach—i.e. that ancient image equals ancient movement and thus may be translated accurately into modern movement,—the most recent being Marie-Hélène Delavaud-Roux, who has published three books on various aspects and types of Greek dance, among them pyrrhic and Dionysian.[69] It must be said that regardless of their field of training, each of their studies has one crucial and important common element—some level of misunderstanding (and in some cases ignorance) of first, vase-painting as an independent art-form, guided by its very own set of rules and conventions, and secondly, of vase iconography and its inherent limitations.

---

[62] Jowitt (1988), 84. See also Raftis (2004), 58 (Sikelianos).
[63] Loewenthal (1993), 173–4; and Duncan et al. (1993), 112–13, 172–3 (pupils).
[64] Jowitt (1988), 84–6. Roatcap (1991), 16–17.
[65] Duncan et al. (1993), 110.
[66] Cf. Watts (1914). The connection to the 'Delsartism' of the late 19th cent. has also been made: e.g. Jowitt (1988), 83–4; and Daly (1995), 123–8.
[67] Naerebout (1997), 61.
[68] Ibid. 63–4, and n. 189. See further Naerebout, this volume.
[69] On her contribution and approach see Naerebout (1997), 95–6.

Misunderstandings apart, it could be proposed that Isadora Duncan, and to an extent her family, did for Greek dance what Beazley did for Greek vases. She elevated Greek dance to a more noble art than it had been previously considered, and she was instrumental in the development that led to its being counted as amongst the hallmarks of women's education and refinement.[70] Her dependence on vases, in turn, must have encouraged a popular perception of the importance of their imagery as a window onto the world of Greek dance.

LILLIAN LAWLER (1898–1990): WRITING THE IMAGE

Lillian B. Lawler, an American classicist, is best known for her introductory book entitled *The Dance in Ancient Greece* (1964), and for her *The Dance of the Ancient Greek Theatre*, published in the same year. However, she wrote widely on the subject of Greek dance. A number of her articles are concerned with the named dances of ancient literature and are very much written from a textual perspective.[71] She also includes vase iconography and other arts in her writings, but often with demonstrably inadequate understanding of the visual evidence. Oddly enough, like Duncan, Lawler was not as discerning with vases as she might have been, and illustrates a wide range of techniques, iconography and dates (indeed she was even interested in the Bronze Age), according to her immediate needs. That being said, in the introduction to her handbook of dance, her tone is confident. Of archaeological sources she claims they are: 'of prime importance to the student, and serve to render the dance strikingly vivid', while 'a great many errors have been made by writers on the dance who have tried to interpret representations in Greek art without knowing how to do so'.[72] Of vase-painting specifically she states: 'the observer must use great caution'.[73] Certainly, she was no reconstructionist, and in her review of Séchan's 1930 book on Greek dance mentioned above, she takes the author to task for his defence of Emmanuel: 'one might point out a characteristic weakness of the two Frenchmen's stand: Both insist that since human bodies are the same now as they were in Greece, the dance must be essentially the same now as it was then. The absurdity of this assumption is, of course, self-evident.'[74]

Yet Lawler's own interpretations reveal more than once a desire to match an individual image or object with a known occasion or routine. Such overzealous treatment of the iconography, as with the dancing Duncans, is in its own way misleading. As a result, Lawler's publications, while fundamental in many

---

[70] Daly (1995), 16, 100, and 110–12.
[71] Ley (2003) devotes substantial attention to her research, esp. 476 on schemata; see also Naerebout (1997), 77–85, and 138–9.
[72] Lawler (1964), 17.
[73] Ibid. 21. Ley (2003), 477, describes her attitude to vases as 'guarded'.
[74] Lawler (1931), 222–3. See also Lawler (1927), 91.

regards, are best avoided for artistic material. The captions accompanying some vase illustrations in *The Dance in Ancient Greece* offer presumptions about the figures portrayed that seem unbelievable based on general knowledge of iconography at the time, and are motivated by a need to comprehend and categorize the art according to her own, contemporary terms: 'dancers rehearsing' (fig. 2), 'dancers in a circle' (fig. 3), 'nocturnal dancers in mountainous terrain' (fig. 4), 'burlesque of a "basket dance" by a phlyax dancer' (fig. 35). Elsewhere in the same book, she is a bit more tenuous: 'supposed kordax dancers' (fig. 34), or 'the figure may portray a dancer carrying a cake' (fig. 40). She refers to both vase-painter and vase without regard for region, technique, or time, or how such variables would no doubt have impacted on dance images. For Lawler, the vases are one of several varieties of archaeological evidence (i.e. mosaics, figurines, gems) to be considered alongside six other broad areas: literary, metrical, musical, epigraphical, linguistic, and anthropological.[75]

Despite the vase's value as a source, she remains concerned by its sometimes 'damaged condition', and provides advice to those pursuing such materials to 'confine himself to sure representations of the dance in the best period of the dance and of art'.[76] With literature ever her springboard, Lawler's Greek vases are expressions of Dionysian and Artemisian cult, animal routines, *kordax* and *geranos*, satyr play and snake-handling—and with very mixed, and not terribly impressive results.[77] At the same time, there are moments in her scholarship where vase imagery might have supplemented her case to great effect, and one wonders why she (*a*) avoided making more and better use of them, and (*b*) never acknowledges other scholars with more expert knowledge of such things.[78] For a start, Beazley's lists and the *CVA* would have proved useful, and she must have been aware of the existence of both, if not their intrinsic benefits.

Lawler's impact on classical and dance scholarship must not be ignored. Though well-peppered with references to ancient texts, her approach to Greek dance is highly pedagogical, at times even popularizing. She is described by Ley as 'by far the most impressive figure in the modern study of ancient Greek dancing', and Naerebout views her as a figure so dominant in the field that he has deemed her period of productivity 'the Lawler era'.[79] Like Isadora Duncan, Lawler visited Greece but was far less fazed by it all than Duncan had been. The unpublished travel journal she kept, labelled 'Trip to Greece in the summer of 1936', indicates a greater interest in meals and postcards than the material or visual culture of ancient peoples. Vases are mentioned only once (in Volos Museum!), along with a terracotta figurine of a dancer, while the sculpture and

---

[75] Lawler (1964), 15.
[76] Ibid. 21.
[77] Lawler (1941–2), 359–61; (1944), 60; (1947–8); (1948); (1952); (1957); and Lawler and Kober (1945), 104.
[78] e.g. Lawler (1942), an article on Aristophanes' *Birds*.
[79] Ley (2003), 473; Naerebout (1997), 77–8.

architecture experienced throughout the country seems to have captivated her more. But this was not Lawler's first trip to Europe for study purposes. During the academic year 1925–6 she was in residence as Fellow of the American Academy in Rome, but claims only to have spoken Italian 'haltingly.'[80]

Lawler returned to Greece in 1955, on this occasion as a participant in the summer programme of the American School of Classical Studies. This more directed and systematic exploration of sites and museums no doubt had a great impact on the pair of dance books she published almost a decade later. It is interesting to note that amongst the information in her archive at the University of Iowa, where she taught at both the beginning and end of her career, there is a good number of publication quality photographs of Greek vases, some of which did feature in her writings on dance. Also an obituary appearing in one Pittsburg newspaper declared 'she traveled on all continents observing dances'. It is undeniable that an ethnographic vein is present throughout many of her articles in the spirit of J. G. Frazer, but she was not the sort to 'go native' in the Duncan manner.

VASES AND DANCES: IMAGES AND READINGS

Dance imagery appears not only in Greek vase-painting, as we have seen, but also in other arts, such as sculpture, gems and even wall-painting. There is little doubt, however, that Greek vases are our richest source of visual information about Greek dance. In this section we shall take a cursory glance at the evolution of dance imagery on vases and its spread to several vase-producing areas of Greece. By doing so, we shall attempt to understand and contextualize better the visual evidence available to Duncan and Lawler, not to mention Emmanuel and his successors. It should become clear that ancient painters were not working exclusively from live or artistic models, but perhaps from some combination of both. Vase-painters were constantly challenged by the desire to depict figures in motion, be they athletes, animals, or dancers. Portraying rhythmic movement on vases was perhaps the most difficult task of all. Painters of dance manipulated the black- and red-figure techniques to achieve a reasonable end result. Space will not permit us to cover animal dances or choruses, or the dances of mythological figures such as satyrs.[81] What appears to have influenced both the modern dancer and the modern scholar, is the dance of mortals and the movement of the human body.

---

[80] The biographical information mentioned here is taken from her 'Biographical and Personal Data', State University of Iowa, dated 21 Feb. 1961; and from additional materials supplied by the Iowa Women's Archive, University of Iowa.
[81] See now Rothwell (2007) on each of these categories.

Two traditions of dance imagery emerge early on in Greek art.[82] The first, which I will only mention briefly, is initially found on late Geometric vases of the late eighth century, such as the *skyphos* fragment from Laconia, where dancers move in a repetitive manner with their hands joined.[83] In this case, the figures are male, but in many instances they are female. Chain dancers of this type, either male or female, performing in a single direction with hands joined, continue to be portrayed by vase-painters working in various techniques and locations. Perhaps the best documented group is the so-called 'Frauenfest' vases of Corinthian painting, where both shape and image allow for a cultic interpretation.[84] Throughout the history of both black- and red-figure painting these all-girl choruses continue to be depicted, and there is some evidence to suggest they were particularly appealing to Isadora Duncan (perhaps more in reference to dress than dance), and Lillian Lawler also illustrates them.[85]

The second type of dancing, occurring first on the black-figure vases of Corinth beginning in the late seventh century, reveals the figures as a solo or group performer (Figure 4.1); the routines vary and the dancers barely, if ever, touch each other.[86] These are the komast dancers, which both Duncan and Lawler seem to have eschewed, despite their relative prevalence. The reasons for this neglect merit some closer scrutiny, and we shall turn to this issue in due course. In the meantime, an examination of their variety will demonstrate how fruitful a source of inspiration they might also be to modern choreographers.

The komast dancer emerges in the black-figure vase-painting of Corinth, the first centre of artistic production for the decorative technique incorporating dark figures on a light background with incised details.[87] The word komast derives from the ancient Greek *kōmos*, meaning reveller or band of revellers, and is thus related to the English word comedy. For this reason generations of scholars, including those at work in the early twentieth century, desired to connect the figures with the origins of drama more readily than with the history of dance. It is on the basis of the large number of male dancers in short red chitons, decorating *aryballoi*, *kotylai* and other shapes, that the term 'padded dancer' has come into modern usage. It should be added that once the imagery travels to Athens, Laconia, and elsewhere, the dancer quickly sheds his short red *chiton* in favour of full nudity. Early on a few painters of the Komast Group, such as the KX Painter in Athens, paint rather confusing images, where dancers appear semi- or partially clothed.[88] We are left with the impression that the dancing figures, be

---

[82] These are discussed in more detail in Smith (2004), esp. 9–11.

[83] Athens, National Museum 234. Boardman (1998), fig. 131.

[84] Pemberton (2000).

[85] See articles pertaining to Duncan in *L'Oeuvre* 28.2 (1911), where vases are illustrated throughout; and Lawler (1964), e.g. figs. 19 and 48. On this style of dancing on vases see M.-H. Delavaud-Roux (1994).

[86] e.g. Boardman (1998), fig. 385 (Copenhagen NM 1631).

[87] For a general survey with previous bibliography see Smith (2007*b*).

[88] On the painters of the group Boardman (1974), 18.

they padded or not, draped or nude, may be more familiar to the painter from one art-form (i.e. other painted vases) than from another (i.e. live dancing).

The KY Painter in Athens is the first to paint a large number of vases with dancers as decoration, most notably on his so-called 'komast cup' shape, but also on a few *kraters*. Several hundred cups alone can be recognized by this hand and there is an incredible amount of repetition in the appearance of his figures. This painter is also the first to establish a set of dance steps and gestures and repeat them in numerous examples. His friend, the Falmouth Painter, enjoys the same routine, but in 100 per cent of his examples offers up unapologetic nude males. Other early Athenian black-figure artists, such as painters of Siana cups and Tyrrhenian amphorae, insert the komast dancers, by now mostly nude figures, into more complicated settings, such as the symposium and its erotic aftermath.[89]

As the komast dancer travels throughout the mid-sixth century beyond Corinth and Athens—to Laconia, Boeotia, East and West Greece—he continues to be defined by his familiar dance routine and tell-tale bottom-slapping gesture. In some instances he carries drink and occasionally music accompanies the dancing. That being said, regional variations come in other forms, the first being dress. Dancers in Laconia wear the short *chiton*, though very heavily ornamented; while in East Greece the dancers of Chios and Miletus prefer the local fashion of a short loincloth and in some cases a turban. Boeotian dancers for the most part resemble Athenian in their motions and costuming, and this is no great surprise in light of what we know about Boeotian black-figure in general.[90] In West Greece, yet another stylistic variation occurs on a Caeretan hydria from *c.*530 BCE, where a frieze of male and female dancers decorates the shoulder of the object.[91] The males are not surprisingly nude and dance energetically; the females, by contrast, sport short red *chiton*s that are rather too short for polite company.

The second iconographic category where regional variations are recognized is the context or setting of the dancing. As we have already noted, Athenian painters of the first quarter or so of the sixth century quickly adopt the komast figure and adapt his appearance. These changes—such as the nudity of dancers in the repertoire of the Falmouth Painter—are clear cases of painter/group preference. And such preferences can and should be recognized throughout the black-figure output of the rest of the sixth century. What happens once our dancers travel to Laconia, Beoetia, and elsewhere? How is this seemingly ubiquitous male dancer transformed from a Corinthian komast to a Laconian one, or from an Athenian komast to a Boeotian one? In much the same way, Siana-cup painters invited the dancer to the symposium, so he is received at other occasions elsewhere.

Laconian painters suggest a religious and/or sympotic setting in a number of scenes, such as the cup where the figure dances in front of what appears to be a

[89] Smith (2007*b*), 55–6; Boardman (1974), 31–3, 36–7.
[90] Beazley initially included the Boeotian komast vases in *ABV*; see Kilinski (1990), 14–15.
[91] Paris, Musée du Louvre 10.227. Smith (2002), 45, fig. 8.

temple.[92] The sympotic settings are more easily recognized by couches (*klinai*) and *kraters*, though interpretations become complicated by the other-worldly 'winged daemons' visible in several scenes.[93] Laconian painters sometimes place the dancers on either side of a giant musician, where the central figure has been considered by some to represent Dionysus or Apollo.[94] Another regional aspect of Laconian komasts is their representation in other artistic media, most notably lead figurines—small votives dedicated at the sanctuary of Artemis Orthia.[95] Boeotia also contributes a certain amount to the regional story. There we may observe the figure in much more complicated settings, especially as participants in religious festivals, or as decoration on what may only be interpreted as ritual vessels.

The interplay of decoration and form is comprised in a single example: a tripod-*kothon* now in Berlin.[96] On this rather unusual vase, the dancers decorate one of the main sides, while on the other two we see other stages of the festival: animal sacrifice and banquet. It should be noted that although this object is unique in many respects (size, number of figures, etc.), it seems to belong, along with the komasts, to a larger series of similar embellishment and form. Another Boeotian example worth mentioning is the *lekanis* (shallow bowl) in the British Museum.[97] The painter chooses the silhouette technique, rather than pure black-figure, and includes the figures in a rather involved festival of Athena around the exterior. Here is not the place to discuss which festival or indeed which dance may be represented on this or other vessels, yet it is worth noting that the place of manufacture of this object and related ones is not certain.

What if anything might we conclude as a result of this brief survey? In the interest of full disclosure, there is one crucial detail of the komast's biography that has been excluded up to now. As we have seen, the komast dancer is a subject chosen by vase-painters working in each of the centres manufacturing black-figure vases. What we have failed to mention is that in several instances, as has been appreciated by Karl Kilinksi in his work on Boeotia, the komast is the first human figure painted in the black-figure technique.[98] As the technique travelled round Greece, it would seem that so too did the dancing komast figure. In this light, the komast can and should be regarded as part of the repertoire of stock figures appearing throughout the sixth century BCE. He is the one and only dancing male figure of Archaic iconography, regardless of occasion or venue, dress or nudity, movement or medium. Recognizing the relationship between technology and iconography enables us to understand the limits of the evidence better, especially as applied to the practice of dance reconstruction. It is hoped that the

---

[92] Bonn, Private Collection. Pipili (1987), no. 208, 75, fig. 107 (once London Market).
[93] Pipili (1987), 71–2.
[94] Ibid. 118, no. 205a–e.
[95] Ibid. 119, no. 212.
[96] Inv. no. F1727. Boardman (1998), 225, fig. 441.
[97] London B80. Boardman (1998), 229, fig. 450.
[98] Kilinski (1990), 41.

komast of black-figure vases will now be envisioned as dancer-performer, on the one hand, and as a decorative-artistic motif, on the other.

Dancing scenes on red-figure vases also focus on images of *kōmos*, yet insert the revelling figures more obviously and systematically into sympotic settings. The earliest practitioners of the technique, such as the 'Pioneers', Euthymides and Euphronios, are interested in more accurate portrayals of human anatomy and especially in showing the body in motion. The red-figure technique, with its first outline drawn figures and 'relief line' details, allowed far better manipulation of the human body, such as foreshortening of limbs or the turning of the torso.[99] As a result, a certain amount of their imagery highlights the training athlete or the raucous reveller. The komast and other dancers of red-figure painting are less stiff and rigid than their black-figure predecessors, and the scenes and figures often more credible. These early red-figure painters, while at times portraying full nudity, other times reveal a rather lightly clad male dancer, complete with boots, cloak (*chlamys*) and stick. This trousseau of travelling attire is sporadically employed by Athenian black-figure painters from the mid-sixth century, but in red-figure such accessories become more regular features. The implication is of males, young and old, very likely aristocratic, *en route* to or from a symposium. With this in mind, we would expect the many red-figure cup painters active throughout the sixth and early fifth centuries, such as Onesimos and the Brygos Painter, to be particularly attracted to the subject of dance.[100] As in black-figure examples, the dancing figures are nude or lightly clad, and some hold drink or music. A special category of red-figure dancers have been labelled 'Anakreontics' in reference to a series of 'elderly komasts' sporting eastern (Lydian) attire and carrying parasols, one of whom is inscribed with the name Anakreon—the Ionian poet who arrived in Athens *c.*520 BCE.[101] Their effeminate dress has led to accusations of cross-dressing, yet the symposium is also their venue of choice. Much like their black-figure companions, the red-figure dance scenes may have as much or more to tell us about the ancient art of vase-painting than the ancient art of dancing.

DEFINITION, DISPLAY AND DECEPTION

Finally, it seems timely to ask why komast dancers, with their exaggerated anatomy and bottom-slapping routines have featured so little in modern studies of Greek dance. As we have seen, the komast figure was ubiquitous, yet both Duncan and Lawler focused their attentions on line-dancing figures or the more maenadic types; and it might even be argued that between them they helped

[99] Boardman (1988), 11–15.
[100] Ibid. 218–20.
[101] Ibid. 219; and Miller (1999).

popularize a rarefied image of Greek dance. The answer to our query, however, must be at least twofold, and involve issues of both definition and display.

The komast figures, whether appearing in groups, solos or pairs, nude or clothed, joined by women or others, have not always been counted under the broader heading of 'dance'. Most early studies of the *clothed* (allegedly 'padded') black-figure revellers discussed them in relation to Greek dramatic origins, and their similarities in appearance to later comic actors. Others, working from this premise, connected the figures with Dionysiac worship, considering the male reveller a mortal equivalent to the mythical satyr, and thus the male counterpart to the maenad.[102] Both approaches have pushed komast dancers, whether in their guise as formal performers or as informal revellers, away from the more general discussions of ancient dance and straight into the corpus of writings on dramatic origins and/or Dionysus. In Naerebout's *Attractive Performances* (1997), it is both appropriate and welcoming to find 'archaic komasts' credited with their own listing in his comprehensive bibliography.[103]

And what of the much larger group of *unclothed* or lightly clad komast of black- and later red-figure? It is arguable that many such dance images were omitted from earlier studies for reasons of their lewd content. It is not uncommon for nude komasts (and a few clothed ones) on vases, perhaps the sad victims of over-indulgence, to be shown vomiting, defecating, or urinating, and of course involved in explicit homosexual and heterosexual encounters. While such interruptions to the party are occurring, their dancing cohorts blissfully continue to entertain themselves and the others around them. Now enters the problem of display. In the past, major museums have at times rotated the komast scenes decorating one side of a vase towards the back of the display case, thus away from public view, while showing off a more palatable scene from mythology towards the front. Such was the case with the collection of black-figure Tyrrhenian amphorae in the Louvre until the recent reinstallation of the museum's vase rooms. This practice was very much in keeping with earlier generations of curators or dealers who 'repainted' vases in order to disguise a prominent erect phallus or overt sexual content. While not every male komast is either grossly phallic or coarsely behaved, it must be said that enough of them are and seem to have tainted the larger group. The pure lack of understanding of the figures (*who* are they?) and their actions (*what* are they doing?), combined with their mystery (*where* are they?), has led several generations of twentieth-century scholars to rely on well-worn explanations of ritual or myth. As for Duncan and Lawler, even with their documented exposure to major vase collections, these simple dance scenes either were not exhibited for them, or largely escaped their notice.

In the early twenty-first century, as we reflect on the contributions to the study of Greek dance of two modern American women, Duncan and Lawler, we no

---

[102] Smith (2007*b*), 61–72.
[103] Naerebout (1997), 122–3, and see 139–40 for *kōmos*.

Figure 4.3 Modern komasts.

longer underestimate the reliance of each on Greek vases, nor take it for granted. At the same time, we admit their unintentional deceptions in using the painted pots, as well as the complexity of ancient dance imagery in its own day. It may surprise some to learn just how much more Greek vases will have to offer classical reception studies. For both Lawler and Duncan, as we have heard, the most abundant category of dance iconography on vases, the komast figures, was largely ignored. Though komast vases were well-known to Beazley—the Komast Group featured in *ABV*, and he regularly used *kōmos* as a descriptive term—some earlier scholars described such dancing as grotesque, undignified or belonging to the untamed Bacchic realm, and thus most unsuited to either classical idealism or reconstruction.[104] The irony of this is very great. The black-figure komast has emerged in recent years as a modern icon of ancient Greek dance. From Swatch watches to bookmarks to wine-labels, the humble male reveller dances on, a most unlikely representative of ancient Greek *joie de vivre*.

Interestingly, as more recent scholarship increasingly draws attention to these figures, they are beginning to emerge not only in advertising, but in

[104] See n. 2 above; and Smith (2007*b*), 66–9.

contemporary choreography as well. There are others better equipped to analyse the degree of komastic influence on modern or even postmodern dance performance, and this question must be left to future studies. It would not be inappropriate, however, to conclude with mention of Tony Harrison's extraordinarily vibrant and exhilarating clog-dancing satyrs from *The Trackers of Oxyrhynchus* (with laktismography by Lawrence Evans)—creatures in every way reminiscent in their description of many komasts dancers on ancient vases.[105] Likewise, the 'twisted' and 'disharmonious' beauty of Jirí Kylián, and the image of performance chosen for the European Network for the Research of Contemporary Dance Production (Figure 4.3)—each exemplify how the 'lewd, grotesque and shameless' dancing figures of the past may serve as a source of enormous potential to present and future choreographers.[106]

---

[105] e.g. Chansky (1991), 523.

[106] Jirí Kylián, after being awarded a Golden Lion for Lifetime Achievement during the 6th International Festival of Contemporary Dance at La Biennale di Venezia, is quoted in an interview as saying: 'Certainly I believe in universal beauty, and I seek it continuously in every person, in every dancer . . . I believe it is my clear duty to identify that beauty, that positivity. But it should be clear that I do not regard this concept in terms of the "classical" Greek ideal, but rather in terms of the "Hellenistic" one, whereby beauty is not canonical perfection but is to be found in sometimes twisted and apparently disharmonious things'; and see n. 2 above.

5

A Pylades for the twentieth century: Fred Astaire and the aesthetic of bodily eloquence

Kathleen Riley

> You'd never know it,
> But buddy, I'm a kind of poet and I've gotta lotta things to say.
>
> Johnny Mercer, 'One for My Baby' (1943)

> Dancing is possessed of all of the advantages of a beautiful language, yet it is not sufficient to know the alphabet alone. But when a man of genius arranges the letters to form words and connects the words to form sentences, it will cease to be dumb; it will speak with both strength and energy; and then ballets will share with the best plays the merit of affecting and moving.
>
> Jean-Georges Noverre, *Letters on Dancing* (1760)

> The soul is wholly embodied, and the body is wholly ensouled.
>
> Ralph Waldo Emerson, 'Essay 5: Love' (1841)

In the same year that George Balanchine arrived in the United States,[1] Fred Astaire (1899–1987), whom Balanchine later cited as 'the most interesting, the most inventive, the most elegant dancer of our times',[2] had begun to revolutionize the movie dance musical. Former Balanchine protégé, Edward Villella called Astaire 'the personification of neo-classicism within a popular American art form',[3] and it is noteworthy that, prior to and alongside Balanchine's conscious development, with the New York City Ballet, of a genuine American neoclassicism, Astaire was unconsciously but no less effectively reinventing the art of the ancient pantomime.

---

[1] Balanchine arrived in New York aboard the *Olympic* on 18 Oct. 1933.
[2] Balanchine in Nabokov and Carmichael (1961), 44–56, at 48.
[3] Quoted by Alan M. Kriegsman in 'For Dancers, A Peerless Model', *Washington Post*, 23 June 1987.

Pantomime was a ballet-style entertainment in which a silent solo dancer (usually male and masked) enacted successively the various characters in a given pantomime plot (*fabula*) to the accompaniment of instrumental music and sung narrative. This entertainment flourished in the Greco-Roman world between the end of the first century BCE and the end of the sixth century CE. Its essential characteristic, that of bodily eloquence, is vividly delineated and vigorously defended in Lucian's dialogue *De Saltatione* (*On Dancing*), which was probably composed in Antioch around the middle of the second century CE. Ismene Lada-Richards describes this treatise as 'a boldly imaginative document, the first attempt in Western theatrical history to map the somatic and mental qualities required of a successful stage-performer'.[4] The dancer generally recognized as the greatest exponent of the genre of pantomime was the brilliant and charismatic Pylades of Cilicia (probably a *nom de théâtre*), who, we are told, burst upon the Roman scene around 22 BCE, and whose popularity Lillian B. Lawler in 1946 compared to that of 'the modern radio crooner or moving picture star'.[5] Pylades was a gestural virtuoso, a master of bodily eloquence, and it is my contention that, in his deliberate development and consummate realization of a radical aesthetic of bodily eloquence, Fred Astaire can rightfully be deemed his twentieth-century heir.

'I JUST DANCE'

When you come to the evolution of the dance, its history and philosophy, I know as much about that as I do about how a television tube produces a picture—which is absolutely nothing. I don't know how it all started and I don't want to know. I have no desire to prove anything by it. I have never used it as an outlet or as a means of expressing myself. I just dance.[6]

With this pointed disavowal and colossal understatement Astaire concluded his autobiography, which was published in 1959. It has been the recurrent complaint of film and dance historians that Astaire was 'notoriously sphinxlike about the nature of his art'.[7] He was, without question, a highly intuitive artist and one with a deep distrust of artistic pretension. Although he was an intelligent man and a creative genius, he never felt the need or the desire to dissect his creative impulses or to claim for his working methods the seal of artistic aspiration. By his own admission, he was not well versed in the history and philosophy of dance, and had probably no knowledge of Pylades or ancient pantomime. So, if Astaire himself made no conscious attempt to borrow from or reinvent this art form, is it legitimate to analyse his achievements in terms of classical reception? To answer this, we need to broaden our notion of what the act of reception constitutes or

---

[4] Lada-Richards (2007), 12.
[5] Lawler (1946), 241–7, at 241.
[6] Astaire (1959), 325.
[7] Harvey (1975), 10.

implies. In particular, we need to examine the question of intent, whether reception is always a controlled or premeditated creative enterprise.

In an essay on Shakespeare's reading and hybridization of the classics, Colin Burrow makes an important point:

Shakespeare's works exploit the slippage between the august ideals of humanist education and its practical shortcomings, between its ambitions and its unintended consequences. Misremembering and mishearing the classical tongues can be as much a response to 'the classics' as careful imitations and artful echoes.[8]

We can, I believe, expand Burrow's thesis of the 'unintended consequences' of reception to include instances of unconscious as well as misremembered appropriation. The act of reception should be conceived not merely as explicit or deliberate reworking, direct exploitation or self-declared inspiration, but also, and often more revealingly, as implicit, indirect, and even accidental (or perhaps inevitable) engagement with the classical past. Accordingly, reception scholarship should be directed towards the investigation of both the intended and unintended consequences of reception. The reception scholar should study the phenomenon of unwitting or unstudied reinvention as closely as the carefully selected epigraph or loaded linguistic borrowing. It is imperative to acknowledge the ability of classical material to penetrate the cultural consciousness by circuitous or subterranean means, yet no less profoundly. Such a line of enquiry can prove fascinating and fertile, even when it yields ultimately insoluble puzzles. 'One value of reception', Martindale argues, 'is to bring to consciousness the factors that may have contributed to our responses to the texts of the past, factors of which we may well be "ignorant" but are not therefore "innocent".'[9]

In the case of Fred Astaire, his ambitions, unlike those of Jean-Georges Noverre in the second half of the eighteenth century, did not extend to a conscious crusade to revive or reinvent ancient pantomime. They did, however, entail the conscious creation and frequent articulation of a corporeal methodology with precise and striking similarities to the art of ancient pantomime. Astaire's bodily eloquence and his cinematic translation of it were revolutionary in the 1930s, but the classically trained eye is able to detect in his revolutionary methods, and his intuitive self-development as a great dance stylist, a fortuitous continuation and reinvention of an ancient tradition. Moreover, the way in which Astaire was 'received' by audiences and critics at the time, and by dance analysts subsequently, underlines this process of continuation and reinvention. And it is surely significant that dancers and choreographers like Balanchine and Martha Graham, who consciously ransack the classics for ideas, had unbounded admiration for Astaire's gifts.

---

[8] Burrow (2004), 9–27, at 15.
[9] Martindale (2006), 1–13, at 5.

It is worth pointing out that Astaire was not always sphinxlike about the fact of his artistry. During the period in which he made his transition from Broadway to Hollywood, he proved himself a willing and articulate commentator on his evolving aesthetic of bodily eloquence. He was also, on occasion and in spite of his ambivalence about dance as a medium of self-expression, an outspoken defender of his professional motivations and objectives. A statement he made in late 1932, in response to the Boston and New York critics' scornful reception of *Gay Divorce* is illuminating:

> *Gay Divorce* wasn't written by Ibsen and I don't quite understand why so many reviewers insisted upon criticizing it as though it were meant to be a lofty essay into the field of ethics or esthetics. It's nothing of the sort. It's just plain romping around for the amusement of the people who pay to see it. Critics, it seems to me, too often refuse to approach a play in the spirit in which it is offered; they don't view shows with sufficient detachment. It's no great indictment of a reviewer's critical capacity to find that after he has razzed a show the audiences shriek with laughter at it. The audiences may be wrong, but I think that when by and large a drama or musical show gives a lot of people a lot of pleasure there must be something in it even if the critics have patronizingly passed it by as being only so-so stuff.[10]

What is fascinating about this measured outburst, apart from its eloquence, is the fact that it is simultaneously a denial of artistic intent ('just plain romping around') and a refutation of the charge that light musical fare is meaningless and something to be 'passed by'. It serves as a neat summation, therefore, of Astaire's attitude to his work and of his Pyladean feat in producing great art that was, at the same time, commercial and popular.

A PRIME MUSICAL AND NARRATIVE INSTRUMENT

One of the things that separated Astaire from his predecessors and contemporaries in the field of popular dance, and placed him in the Pyladean tradition, was the fact that, as dancer, choreographer, and craftsman of camera angles, he utilized and concentrated attention on his entire body, making it a prime musical and narrative instrument. In the first place, at 5 foot 9 inches (1.75 m) and 135 pounds (61.2 kg), he was blessed with an ideally proportioned dancer's physique. Margot Fonteyn observed in particular 'his slender build, long legs, shoulders neither too narrow nor too wide, head neither too large nor too small. It is not often that a dancer is proportioned so harmoniously from head to elegant foot. . . . With Astaire the balance is perfect'.[11] Leslie Caron, who danced with Astaire in the 1954 film *Daddy Long Legs*, has offered a similar appraisal:

[10] Quoted by Lucius Beebe in 'Fred Astaire Dances Without Adele', *New York Herald Tribune*, 1 Dec. 1932.
[11] Fonteyn (1980), 34.

He was perfectly formed for dancing. The sinews within were quick, he was just the right height, and there was the right metabolism, the right balance between his heartbeat and glands—which makes you fast or slow. He had this incredible speed and tremendous nervous energy, and a remarkable breathing capacity.[12]

Balanchine proposed that Astaire 'ought to have a statue. I mean that absolutely. The beauty of his body...the way he moves, his elegance, his dancing.'[13] In his *symmetria*, the perfect 'commensurability' of all parts of his body to one another and to the whole, Astaire conformed to the canon of Polyclitus[14] and thus to the ideal body shape for a pantomime dancer, as outlined by Lucian's Lycinus. The dancer's body, Lycinus insists, 'must be neither very tall and inordinately lanky, nor short and dwarfish in build, but exactly the right measure, without being either fat, which would be fatal to any illusion, or excessively thin, for that would suggest skeletons and corpses' (*De Salt.* 75).

Astaire's style of dancing, which was partly trained but largely self-taught, was notable for its eclecticism and unorthodoxy, and it defies straightforward categorization. He himself termed it 'a sort of outlaw style'.[15] It was essentially a fusion of ballet, ballroom, and tap, as evidenced by three of Astaire's acknowledged inspirations—Danish ballet star Adeline Genée, Edwardian ballroom sensations Vernon and Irene Castle, and rhythm tap pioneer John W. Bubbles (the stage name of John William Sublett).[16] The distinctive feature of this anarchic amalgam was its employment of the whole body. Ned Wayburn, whose New York school Astaire attended during his vaudevillean days, credited his former pupil with being 'the first American tap dancer consciously to employ the full resources of his arms, hands and torso for visual ornamentation'.[17] This singular freedom of movement was, in great part, attributable to Astaire's early ballet training, which 'helped him release the upper part of the body before elevation and showed him that a dancer could use much more than his feet'.[18] In an interview he gave to *Theatre Arts Monthly* in 1937, four years into his screen career, Astaire outlined his corporeal creed, as it were: 'In every kind of dancing, even tap, the movement of the upper part of the body is as important as that of the legs.'[19]

---

[12] Quoted in Giles (1988), 24.

[13] Balanchine in Nabokov and Carmichael (1961), 44–56, at 48.

[14] The *Canon* of Polyclitus is the first datable professional treatise on sculpture and was probably written during the third quarter of the 5th cent. BCE. In this work, Polyclitus laid down the guidelines for the ideal proportioning of the human body, founding them on precise numerical relationships borrowed from the Pythagorean doctrine. He held that the key to achieving the beautiful (*to kallos*) and the good (*to eu*) in art lay in the mastery of *symmetria*.

[15] Astaire (1959), 325.

[16] In his only blackface number on screen, 'Bojangles of Harlem' (*Swing Time*, 1936), ostensibly a tribute to Bill Robinson, Astaire is dressed in the style of the character Sportin' Life, whom Bubbles portrayed the year before in Gershwin's *Porgy and Bess*. Astaire's percussive style of dancing in this number also owes more to Bubbles than to Bojangles.

[17] Quoted in Barnett (1941), 72–85, at 78.

[18] Stearns (1994), 223.

[19] Quoted in Eustis (1937), 371–86, at 379.

SPEAKING WITH THE HANDS

In *De Saltatione*, Lycinus extols the pantomime dancer's superlative *cheironomia* (literally the measured motion of the hands), the art of talking with the hands, of gesturing with them rhythmically and captivatingly. He recounts the experience of the Cynic philosopher Demetrius, whose hostility to pantomime, and what he considered the superfluity and aimless nonsense of its exponents' gesticulations, turned to rapture when he was invited by the leading Neronian *pantomimus* to watch him perform, without orchestra, chorus, or libretto, the whole story of the loves of Ares and Aphrodite. Demetrius was spellbound by the spectacle and cried out: 'I hear the story that you are acting, man, I do not only see it; you seem to me to be speaking with your very hands' (*De Salt.* 63). The calculated eloquence of Astaire's hands is what chiefly distinguishes him as a legatee of the ancient *pantomimus*. He was what Lesbonax of Mytilene called *cheirisophos* (handiwise, *De Salt.* 69) and had at his command what Cassiodorus termed 'loquacissimae manus' (most talkative hands, *Variae* 4.51.8).

Always self-conscious about his unusually large hands, he often contrived while dancing to disguise their size by curling his middle fingers. Yet he also incorporated his hands into the dance, not merely as beautiful adornments but as meaningful narrative components. The expressive use of his hands was central to Astaire's entire aesthetic, as he indicated on several occasions. In a press interview during the run of his last stage show, he offered this advice to aspiring professional dancers: 'Another phase which I cannot stress too strongly is the proper use of the hands.' After his permanent move to Hollywood he repeated his advice: 'The novice in dancing should get the fundamental points first—he must know what to do with his hands, which are just as important as feet in dancing.'[20] Those who saw Astaire dance on stage, or who analysed his technique, repeatedly singled out the rhythmic movement of his eloquent hands. Shortly after the opening of Cole Porter's *Gay Divorce* at the Ethel Barrymore Theatre in New York, Noël Coward enthused to Robert Garland of the *Sun*: 'Fred dances with his hands, his eyebrows, his body, his brain. Fred dances all over.'[21] In a review of his performance in the London production of *Gay Divorce*, J. T. Grein described Astaire's speechless enactment of the love story in his duets with Claire Luce as 'something akin to the fingering language of the deaf and dumb'.[22] Interestingly, Lawler said of the masterly *cheironomia* practised by Pylades that it amounted 'almost to a sort of sign language'.[23]

---

[20] Quoted in Eustis (1937), 386.
[21] 12 Dec. 1932.
[22] J. T. Grein, 'An Up-to-Date Puck: Fred Astaire', *Illustrated London News*, 25 Nov. 1933, 840.
[23] Lawler (1946), 241–7, at 242.

Figure 5.1 Speaking with hands. 'Change Partners' from *Carefree*, RKO, 1938.

Marshall and Jean Stearns, in their authoritative history of jazz dance, declared: 'Astaire's use of his arms and hands, and indeed his entire body, was one of his greatest contributions to American vernacular dance.'[24] Some of the best examples of Astaire's *cheironomia* are found in his duets with Ginger Rogers. At one point in 'Night and Day' (*The Gay Divorcée*, 1934) he has his left hand firmly around Rogers's waist and, as he senses the weakening of her resistance, he flutters his free right hand in mischievous anticipation of his imminent conquest. By contrast, in the early moments of 'Smoke Gets in Your Eyes' (*Roberta*, 1935), he forms his right hand into a clenched fist in an attitude of intense longing. In *Carefree* (1938) Astaire plays the part of a psychoanalyst and in the dance 'Change Partners' his hands become tools of hypnosis as well as emblems of restrained yearning (see Figure 5.1). Astaire's hypnotic hands also feature in the Guardian Angel duet, which is part of the daydream sequence in *Daddy Long Legs*. Here, however, they are emblematic of paternal solicitude rather than romantic yearning, and they create a charming marionette effect. Throughout the dance Astaire makes less of an attempt to conceal his oversized hands and, indeed, their largeness seems choreographically and narratively apposite. The strong, graceful hands hover protectively, beguile playfully, and guide their ward (Leslie Caron) gently. What is also interesting about this dance is that Astaire uses his hands far more expressively and affectingly than the ballet-trained Caron uses hers.

Astaire the soloist is an equally fine *cheironomos*. The dramatic dance monologue, 'One for My Baby' from *The Sky's the Limit* (1943), in which a drunken, self-pitying Astaire proclaims himself 'a kind of poet', begins with 'a ballet of hand gestures, . . . a legible pantomime accompaniment to the lyrics'.[25] In *Yolanda and the Thief* (1945) Astaire serenades Lucille Bremer while playing the harp, plucking and caressing the strings in mesmerizing fashion and with such apparent mastery that it is hard to believe his playing was, in fact, dubbed by jazz harpist, Bobby Maxwell.

A MASTER DRAMATIST

The legacy of the ancient pantomime is also apparent in the strong storyline and psychological content of Astaire's dance creations, in what Lycinus defines as 'display of mind' (*De Salt.* 69). Astaire held that 'to attain a high peak, the dancer must be capable in "head-work" as well as in foot-work'.[26] His dances were never, or very rarely, mere exhibitions of technical virtuosity. To paraphrase Edward Villella, you don't see his technique; you see his mind during his technique.[27]

---

[24] Stearns (1994), 223.
[25] Barnes (1994), 179.
[26] 'In the Dance World: Fred Astaire Airs His Views', unidentified newspaper from 1933 in the Astaire scrapbooks in the Howard Gotlieb Archival Research Center, Mugar Library, Boston University.
[27] Villella in Roseman (2001), 16.

What is so compelling about Astaire is his extraordinary physicalization of the abstract, the way in which his body communicates with such fluency musical and narrative intricacies. Michael Kidd, who collaborated with Astaire on the 1953 film *The Band Wagon*, said: 'Astaire is like the embodiment of a thought and the whole dance is like a conversation—he even thinks in dance steps.'[28] In 'I'll Be Hard to Handle' (*Roberta*, 1935) and 'Isn't This a Lovely Day' (*Top Hat*, 1935) we see Astaire and Ginger Rogers quite literally conversing through dance, bantering and sparring their way towards the discovery of a glorious rapport. Ordinary speech is made redundant by the semantic precision and lexical interplay of their feet, by the seemingly improvisatory wit of their somatic phrasing. A later, though less sophisticated, example of a conversation in syncopated tap occurs in 'Mr and Mrs Hoofer at Home', a raucous vaudeville routine from the musical biopic *Three Little Words* (1950). Here Astaire and Vera-Ellen simulate a domestic quarrel, which they tap out with greater fury than wit. The quarrel is sparked by a mysterious phone call Astaire receives in the course of the dance. Placing the receiver of the candlestick telephone on the floor, he taps furtively and somewhat suggestively into it, thereby hinting at the extra-marital nature of the call.

Dance critic Arlene Croce proclaimed of Astaire: 'Above everything else, he was a master dramatist. Drama clings to every move he makes.'[29] Astaire's powers as a terpsichorean bard were evident from the time of his celebrated partnership with his sister Adele in musical comedies on Broadway and in London's West End. In a review of *Apple Blossoms*, the Astaires' third Broadway appearance, Alexander Woollcott of the *New York Times* identified Fred as 'one of those extraordinary persons whose senses of rhythm and humour have been all mixed up, whose very muscles of which he seems to have an extra supply are downright facetious'.[30] In September 1921, during the tryout in Philadelphia of their next show, a flop called *The Love Letter*, the critic for the *Sunday Ledger* mused: 'But those Astaires! Why is it that they, who really have nothing essential to do with the unfolding of the romantic story, should have their little singing and dancing duets stand out as the acting part of *The Love Letter* that probably will linger longest in the memory?' Critiquing the same show, the *Boston Globe* applauded Fred's emergence as 'a pantomimic comedian'.

When the Astaires made their London debut in *Stop Flirting*, their unusual corporeal eloquence was duly noted. Francis Birrell, writing in the *Nation and Athenaeum*, said they 'uttered the least important word with every inch of their bodies, never being content with the employment of the essential extremities—tongue, hand, or foot'.[31] Of Fred, the *Birmingham Post* reported, 'he has not only winged heels, but winged arms and winged back' and, of Adele, 'hers is not only

---

[28] Quoted by Michael Freedland in an obituary of Michael Kidd, *Guardian*, 7 Jan. 2008.
[29] Croce (1972), 6.   [30] 7 Oct. 1919.   [31] 16 June 1923.

the poetry of motion but its wit, its malice, its humour'.[32] The *Birmingham Dispatch* provided an account of the mesmeric, transporting quality of the siblings' richly nuanced somatic vocabulary: 'Their humour lies in gesture, their attraction in the power to set us dancing with them, to send us in spirit, twirling and striding and frolicking in glorious abandon.'[33] In response to their second London success with the Gershwins' *Lady, Be Good!*, R. De Cordova commented in *The Sphere*: 'In all their dances they aim at doing something with a meaning or a story.'[34]

London's critics were also impressed with the bodily eloquence of Astaire the individual artist, perceiving hitherto untapped depths to his acting within and outside of the dance. In *Gay Divorce* they identified an intensification or maturing of his storytelling powers, which they deemed revelatory. What they were witnessing was a consummate actor, one who could articulate through his movements ecstasy or despair, who could make aphorisms with his ankles, and who could render incarnate the wit of a Noël Coward or a Gertrude Lawrence and the ethereal enchantment of Shakespeare's Ariel or Oberon. J. T. Grein, essaying an explanation of 'the uncanny eloquence of his feet', said:

There is something in those feet that means more than a *tour de force*. Those nimble, graceful, volatile feet are voluble in their evolutions. They convey something; they accentuate, as it were, the dialogue, render it more apt and telling.[35]

Most incisively, a review in London's *Illustrated Sporting and Dramatic News* isolated two key components of Fred's corporeal eloquence, which we particularly associate with the cinematic Astaire—the hypnotic and protean exposition of character achieved apparently without artifice or self-consciousness:

The limbs of Fred Astaire are, like W. S. Gilbert's lover's professions, 'eloquent everywhere'. What in the private is an ugly jerk, in Captain Astaire is a mood index, for he cannot kick a footstool without expressing character.... He can suggest instant changes of mood and all seems so unpremeditated that you feel you have stolen unawares on a dancer who thinks he is alone.[36]

By this time, such was the dramatic impact of his dancing that critics and producers began to speculate in more general terms about Astaire's histrionic potential. His performance in the groundbreaking revue *The Band Wagon*, his penultimate show on Broadway, had established him as an actor in his own right, one whose greatest asset was his bodily eloquence (see Figure 5.2). In one of the show's sketches, a burlesque of the Good Old South entitled 'The Pride of the Claghornes', Robert Garland noted that 'within a few short minutes, [Astaire] presents a complete characterization with scarcely any words at all'.[37] Astaire won

---

[32] 23 Dec. 1923.   [33] 19 Jan. 1924.   [34] 27 March 1926.
[35] J. T. Grein, 'An Up-to-Date Puck: Fred Astaire', *Illustrated London News*, 25 Nov. 1933, 840.
[36] 18 Nov. 1933.   [37] *World Telegram*, Nov. 1931.

Figure 5.2 Fred Astaire and Tilly Losch in 'The Beggar Waltz' from *The Band Wagon* New Amsterdam Theatre, New York 1931.

unanimous acclaim for his aptitude as both comedian and tragedian, one critic going so far as to declare: 'The American theatre could produce a far worse Hamlet.'[38]

Upon entering the Lambs Theatre Club the day after the triumphant opening of *The Band Wagon*, he was greeted by one of his fellow members with the exclamation: 'Boy, I hear you're an actor!' As confirmation of his increasing acceptance as a straight actor, he received several offers to appear in original plays in the legitimate theatre, for example from producer and director Guthrie McClintic, the husband of Katharine Cornell. A further endorsement of his acting abilities came on 9 April 1932, when Florenz Ziegfeld cabled him to ask whether he would be interested in playing in an all-star revival of Kern and Hammerstein's *Show Boat*,[39] generally regarded as the first true American 'musical play' or 'book musical'. However, it was to Hollywood that Astaire soon made his way and in talking pictures that his silent eloquence would leave its most lasting impression.

Prior to his transition from the stage to motion pictures, Astaire had given a great deal of thought to the notion of integrating dance into a story and of using it to advance and penetrate the deeper meaning of the verbal narrative. During the post-Broadway tour of *The Band Wagon*, he told Carmen Crocker:

What I like about dancing is when there is a thought behind it—an idea. You go to a lot of these theatres and you see dancers dance their feet off, and it doesn't mean a thing.[40]

He was concerned not only with communicating a story through dance but also with allowing the dance to arise naturally and logically from the plot, however slight the dramatic framework might be. In conversation with Samuel S. Modell in 1933, he said:

If I may say it, the success of the majority of my dances has been due in great measure to the fact that I have introduced my numbers not only at the psychological moment but in a manner that would logically blend with the ideas of the play.[41]

To Morton Eustis in 1937, he explained: 'It is extremely important for a dance cue to flow naturally in and out of the story.... Each dance ought to spring somehow out of character or situation, otherwise it is simply a vaudeville act.'[42]

In Stephen Harvey's opinion, Astaire's achievement in translating his dumb eloquence on to celluloid, and in propelling the film narrative forward through dance, was nothing short of revolutionary:

---

[38] For a synopsis of the critical reaction to Astaire's acting performance in *The Band Wagon*, see 'The Private Life of Fred Astaire', *Photoplay*, Jan. 1936, 34.

[39] The original production premiered at the Ziegfeld Theatre in New York on 27 Dec. 1927 and was immediately acknowledged as a classic.

[40] *St Louis Times*, 1 April 1932.

[41] 'In the Dance World: Fred Astaire Airs His Views', unidentified newspaper from 1933 in the Astaire scrapbooks in the Howard Gotlieb Archival Research Center, Mugar Library, Boston University.

[42] Quoted in Eustis (1937), 371–86, at 381.

Incredibly, he was the first to realize that dance could convey and even deepen any given emotion onscreen. Astaire introduced the heretical notion that the human body could express the deepest of feelings even without the benefit of words.[43]

John Mueller has demonstrated persuasively that, years before Balanchine's 'Slaughter on Tenth Avenue' (*On Your Toes*, 1936) or Agnes de Mille's 'Laurey Makes Up Her Mind' (*Oklahoma!*, 1943), 'Fred Astaire was choreographing dances that were profoundly integrated into the plot—or, to put it another way, he was crafting dramatically eventful dances whose movement vocabulary was carefully related to, and developed from the plot situation.'[44]

Astaire wrought a similar revolution when, in the late 1950s, he made the transition to television. Between 1958 and 1968 he created four one-hour dance specials for NBC, in all of which he was partnered by an exciting young dancer named Barrie Chase. The first of these, the landmark *An Evening with Fred Astaire*, contained no less than three memorable dance-dramas, 'Change Partners', 'Man with the Blues', and 'St James Infirmary' (each like a distinct play in itself), and a solo routine in which Astaire displayed his pantomimic gifts to good effect by dancing with a series of imaginary props. In a prelude to 'St James Infirmary', Astaire introduced jazz trumpeter Jonah Jones as 'a man who, I consider, plays a most eloquent trumpet'. Expanding the theme of non-verbal eloquence, he added, 'I like to think that my feet tell a story in dance.' What ensued was a short, humorous dialogue conducted almost entirely in trumpet and tap.

'I DON'T MAKE LOVE BY KISSING, I MAKE LOVE BY DANCING'

Lucian's Lycinus marvels at the ability of the ancient dancer to 'imitate Proteus himself' (*De Salt.* 19), to make incarnate in a single form a whole cast of characters: 'In general the dancer undertakes to present and enact characters and emotions, introducing now a lover and now an angry person, one man afflicted with madness, another with grief . . . yet they are all but a single man' (*De Salt.* 67). He quotes a barbarian spectator who was astonished to learn that all the roles in a five-act pantomime drama were to be performed by the one dancer: 'I did not realize, my friend, that though you have only this one body, you have many souls' (*De Salt.* 66).

In both his solo and partnered routines Astaire combined the contrasting versatility of tragedian Pylades and his comic rival Bathyllus. With sister Adele the dances he performed were typically conceived and executed in a comedic vein. The signature piece in their comedic repertoire was the 'run-around', or

---

[43] Harvey (1975), 12.
[44] Mueller (1985), 23.

'The Oompah Trot' as it was nicknamed in London, a novelty routine devised for them in 1921 by director Edward Royce and used in five different shows over the next decade. The concept was simple but ingenious: Fred and Adele would jog, shoulder to shoulder, around the stage in a widening circle, with their arms extended as though they were grasping the handlebars of a bicycle. As the music quickened, so would the pace of their run-around. They would sustain several circuits before exiting into the wings to wild applause.[45] 'The Oompah Trot' made such an impression on the young Frederick Ashton, when he saw the Astaires in *Funny Face* in 1928, that twenty years later he borrowed it for his ballet *Cinderella* in which he and Robert Helpmann played the Ugly Sisters.[46] As the Sisters made their exit from the ballroom, they circled the stage in an increasingly high-stepping, trotting movement, with heads and ostrich feathers bobbing. Sadly there is no footage of the Astaires performing this popular piece of pantomimic whimsy, but Fred did reprise 'The Oompah Trot' with Gracie Allen in 1937 as part of the Academy Award-winning 'Fun House' sequence choreographed by Hermes Pan for *A Damsel in Distress*.

With 'The Beggar Waltz' in *The Band Wagon*, a new dimension to Astaire's dancing began to evolve. This was a *pas de deux* of pathos and romance, choreographed by Albertina Rasch, in which Astaire was partnered by Austrian ballerina, Tilly Losch (see Fig. 5.2). It was also, according to Ethan Mordden, 'the earliest Dream Ballet...in the musical's history'.[47] The unfolding of its action was significantly aided by the show's revolutionary scenics, in particular the double revolve (or turntable) designed by Albert R. Johnson and used here for the first time in a theatre revue. The dance drama begins with the vagrant Astaire on the steps of the Vienna State Opera. Losch, the company's star ballerina, upon entering the stage door, sees the beggar and drops a few coins in his outstretched hand. Astaire falls asleep and the stage revolves to reveal the sumptuous interior of the opera house and the lustrous substance of the beggar's dream. Astaire has exchanged his rags for a costume of rich cloth and is dancing on stage, with Losch and the chorus, to Arthur Schwartz's ballet music with its soaring crescendos dissolving into a lilting waltz. As the duet ends, the set again revolves, returning to the opera house exterior. The beggar awakes and Losch re-emerges from the stage door. Meeting his gaze, she pauses and tosses him her small purse. As she departs, he sinks back forlornly onto the steps. 'The Beggar Waltz' presented Astaire with a sizeable acting challenge and was an indication of his ripening narrative powers. As the beggar, his body skilfully and movingly portrayed supplication, exclusion, and dejection; as the imagined star of the corps de ballet, it assumed impressive and jubilant command of the stage.

---

[45] For a detailed description of the run-around 'stunt' and its genesis, see Astaire (1959), 82–4.
[46] Ashton's *Cinderella* was launched by London's Sadler's Wells Ballet (now The Royal Ballet) on 23 Dec. 1948.
[47] Mordden (2005), 29.

The dance that definitively signalled Astaire's metamorphosis into a romantic leading man and actor-dancer was 'Night and Day' in *Gay Divorce*. This extraordinary plot-advancing number was 'the first genuinely romantic adagio dance of his career'.[48] Fred and Adele's real-life relationship had necessarily precluded duets of an intensely romantic nature. However, with Adele's retirement in 1932, that prohibition was lifted and Fred acquired a new leading lady in the voluptuous Claire Luce. With her style in mind, he applied himself purposefully to the creation of 'an entirely new dancing approach'.[49] The result was an acknowledged masterpiece, a highly dramatic, highly sensual dance, splendidly evocative of the ardency of Cole Porter's lyrics.

For his first starring vehicle with Ginger Rogers (*The Gay Divorcée*, 1934), Astaire reprised in adapted form his stage choreography for 'Night and Day', and this version Croce designates 'a movie in itself'.[50] At no point do Astaire and Rogers depart from the idiom of dance as they disclose the deepest, most intimate of feelings. The dance therefore transcends any contrivances, campery, or inconsequentiality for which the scripted story is culpable. It is essentially a dance of seduction, a fact which illustrates yet another element common to both the Pyladean aesthetic of corporeal eloquence and the artistry of Astaire—the sublimated projection of physical desire. 'No tragic plot', Lada-Richards affirms, 'would have centred . . . on the act of making love on stage. Pantomime, on the other hand, can represent in dance . . . the amorous adventures of the gods, the sexual act even giving the impression of being performed on the stage.'[51] Similarly, as Frank Cullen indicates, 'what the public willingly witnessed on the silver screen was Fred Astaire making love to a woman through the symbols of dance. That was unusual. Dick Powell sang to Ruby Keeler while she danced; he was pleading his love. Fred Astaire took Ginger and pulled her close to him, guiding her through a series of intimate physical moves.'[52] At the conclusion of 'Night and Day', Astaire gently deposits Rogers on a low circular bench. From her semi-horizontal position, she bestows on him a look of ravished wonder as he, taking her surrender coolly in his stride, offers her a cigarette. Astaire's wordless eloquence in this regard not only circumvented the stringent Production Code (also known as the Hays code),[53] which came into effect in July 1934, but also made conventional expressions of romantic love superfluous.

---

[48] Croce (1972), 13.
[49] Astaire (1959), 176.
[50] Croce (1972), 33.
[51] Lada-Richards (2007), 35.
[52] Cullen (2006), 38.
[53] The Production Code was the set of industry censorship guidelines governing the production of American motion pictures. The Code was adopted in March 1930 but included no provisions for its effective enforcement. An amendment to the Code, implemented in June 1934, established the Production Code Administration and required all films released after 1 July 1934 to obtain a certificate of approval before being released. In practice the Code was enforced through a system of self-regulation adhered to by the motion picture studios.

On the screen the stories Astaire told in dance were mostly love stories, but their emotional range and psychological complexity were considerable. For example, as a soloist he embodied the childlike *joie de vivre* of 'I've Got My Eyes on You' (*Broadway Melody of 1940*) and the very adult despair and nihilistic rage of 'One for My Baby' (*The Sky's the Limit*, 1943). The earlier dance contains a delightful and brilliantly executed mimed dialogue. Having found two mementos of the woman he secretly worships (Eleanor Powell), a piece of sheet music with her picture on the cover and a powder-puff ball inscribed with her name, Astaire proceeds to show off for the picture, tossing and juggling the ball with carefree precision.[54] Taking up the picture, he swirls it about joyfully and into a deep backbend. With the picture propped up on a table, he tries to inveigle his imaginary partner into a further dance, his body and facial expressions making clear his actions and her reactions. He entreats, she declines; he teases, she rebukes; finally he is penitent and she succumbs. He sweeps the picture into his arms where it remains for the rest of the dance. So convincing is Astaire in the way he tenderly mimes his love for Eleanor Powell by dancing for and with her image, that this number represents the film's most romantic 'duet'. Mueller wryly designates it 'a kind of courtship dance in absentia'.[55]

With Ginger Rogers Astaire danced a thrilling duet of fatalistic abandon and daring solemnity to Irving Berlin's 'Let's Face the Music and Dance' (*Follow the Fleet*, 1936) and, to Jerome Kern and Dorothy Fields's 'Never Gonna Dance' (*Swing Time*, 1936), a heartbreaking valediction to love, a sequence that simultaneously recapitulates and elegizes the characters' entire relationship. The latter is a monumental creation, operatic in its structure and dimension, the culmination of several musical and choreographic motifs deployed throughout the film. Croce calls it 'the supreme dramatic event of the [Astaire–Rogers] series'.[56] Part of its emotional power lies in the fact that, unlike previous films in the series, in which the pair's happy ending is delayed by inane misunderstandings and contrived instances of mistaken identity, *Swing Time* focuses on a grown-up relationship between two characters who are well aware of their love for one another but who are forced apart by more plausible complications and the constraints of honour, much like Alec and Laura in Noël Coward's *Brief Encounter*. The dialogue which precedes the number is beautifully spare, deriving its potency from what is left unexpressed. The song 'Never Gonna Dance', with its references to the discreet wolf and 'the la belle / La perfectly swell romance', is almost incomprehensible outside the context of the film; its strange, plaintive lyrics are integral to the story of the dance, which is also the story of the film retold.

---

[54] Astaire's dextrous tossing of the powder-puff ball recalls part of a sequence he performed on stage in *Gay Divorce* with the aid of a similar sentimental souvenir, in this case a lipstick. This fact is gleaned from the only known footage of Astaire on stage, which was shot by Fred Stone at the Shubert Theatre in 1933.

[55] Mueller (1985), 169.

[56] Croce (1972), 108.

At the song's conclusion, the lovers walk side by side in silence, with Astaire turning intermittently to face Rogers in wordless despondency. Every inflection and intonation of their bodies is redolent of pain and longing. From this exquisitely eloquent perambulation they glide into a dance which dramatizes successively helpless despair, desperate desire, brief exultant abandon, and finally, desolation. In this and other Astaire–Rogers duets, the dancing forms are wonderfully sculpted against stunning monochromatic Art Deco sets, designed under the direction of Van Nest Polglase, like a classical frieze come to life.

ELEVATING THE EVERYDAY

One of the most remarkable things about Astaire was his corporeal eloquence outside the dance, a corollary of his innate *eurythmia*. Claire Luce thought he had 'a beat in his heart that's like music. His rhythm was sensational. He becomes an instrument in an orchestra'.[57] Stephen Harvey observed: 'Even when his feet were rooted to the sound-stage floor, every gesture or vocal inflection was orchestrated to some internal dance rhythm only he could hear.'[58] The most idiosyncratic element in Astaire's bodily eloquence outside the dance was his unaffected, eurythmic walk, which his close friend and most frequent collaborator, Hermes Pan, defined as 'a loose rhythmic saunter that looks as if it's, in a way, dancing. I remember Gershwin wrote music especially for that'.[59]

When Astaire played nuclear scientist Julian Osborn in Stanley Kramer's *On the Beach* (1959), his first dramatic screen role, there was talk of having to weight his legs to impede his natural gait. What is also striking is that Astaire's body, in stillness and in motion, often suggested the classical contrapposto pose, projecting a lithe nonchalance but also a coiled readiness for dance reminiscent of the principle expounded at chapter 77 of Lucian's treatise: 'the dancer must by all means be agile and at once loose-jointed and well-knit, so as to bend like a withe as occasion arises and to be stubbornly firm if that should be requisite.'

The fact of Astaire's 'extraneous' corporeal eloquence obscures or renders irrelevant the distinction between his dancing and non-dancing self. Even the way he rolls dice or straightens his tie is dancelike. As Harvey explains:

[57] Interviewed for *The Fred Astaire Story*, BBC Radio 2, 1975 (Episode 1: 'Curtain Up', 22 March).

[58] Harvey (1975), 14.

[59] Interviewed for *The Fred Astaire Story*, BBC Radio 2, 1975 (Episode 1: 'Curtain Up', 22 March). The music Gershwin wrote especially for Astaire's walk was a delightful and jaunty chamber piece entitled 'Walking the Dog', which was used in the 1937 film *Shall We Dance* to accompany two pantomimic routines for Astaire and Rogers. These routines involved no formal dancing but simply showed Astaire and Rogers walking back and forth along the promenade deck of a ship.

Practically no other actor expends so much physical energy just to deliver dialogue as Astaire does. . . . Every motion Astaire makes on screen, however prosaic, seems just a beat away from becoming a dance cue. . . . This is what makes the usually difficult transition from story into song look so spontaneous in Astaire's musicals. At some point the kinetic energy barely suppressed behind every Astaire gesture can no longer be contained—it has to be vented in an outburst of dance.[60]

This spontaneity, and the apparent effortlessness with which it is achieved, is incredible when one considers how premeditated and finely rehearsed each of Astaire's movements was.

Harvey's description of Astaire's transformation of the most prosaic motion into a dance cue relates to another distinguishing feature of Astaire's corporeal eloquence, his elevation, through dance, of the everyday. Just as George Eliot aroused in her readers an awareness of the tragic and epic dimensions of ordinary human existence, Astaire instilled in his audiences a belief in the sublime excitement latent in commonplace activities such as having one's shoes shined or driving golf balls off a tee. He also brought wondrously to life the most unremarkable of props such as canes, chairs, metal ashtrays, a powder puff, a hat rack, and a raincoat, thus 'animating the inanimate, making the mundane magical'.[61] This accomplishment underscores Astaire's Pyladean ability to make something that is technically complex and artistically imposing relatable to a mass audience.

An excellent early example of Astaire's transfiguration of the ordinary through the medium of dance is 'A Needle in a Haystack' from *The Gay Divorcée*. This dance soliloquy discovers Astaire in the sitting room of his London flat, changing from a dressing gown into street wear and, in the process, tap-dancing upon the hearth, vaulting a sofa, executing a breathtaking series of cabrioles, and leaping aloft a chair before offhandedly donning his hat and making his exit.[62] It is easy to forget just how revolutionary the simple interior setting and psychological significance of this dazzling sequence must have appeared to cinema audiences in 1934.

The dance is effectively an exposition of character. In less than two minutes and twenty seconds, it tells the story of Guy Holden, American in London, a new type of hero for a new world order. Guy is, recognizably yet atypically, the boy next door, an engaging amalgam of Midwestern candour and Continental carelessness. Outfitted by Savile Row and Jermyn Street, this twentieth-century knight-errant also sports anarchic sartorial insignia such as a necktie around his waist. In short, he is the very embodiment of brash refinement. That Guy epitomizes a modern, democratic ideal of heroism is cleverly communicated through the dance's subtle but meaningful juxtaposition of tradition and innovation.

---

[60] Harvey (1975), 14.
[61] Beth Genné, obituary of Fred Astaire, *Dancing Times*, Sept. 1987.
[62] Here, Arlene Croce (1972, 33) emphasizes, Astaire 'demonstrates that screen choreography could consist of a man dancing alone in his living rom'. Astaire had performed a similar 'getting-dressed' dance on stage in *The Band Wagon* to the Dietz-Schwartz number 'New Sun in the Sky'.

The first such juxtaposition occurs in the interaction between the youthful Holden, raffish, omnipotent emblem of proto-Cool and his imperturbable, middle-aged English valet. Patiently and impassively the valet catches, in fairly rapid succession, Guy's cravat, dressing gown (which Guy backhands to him), and discarded choice of necktie before proffering, with an air of ceremonial solemnity, a looking glass and tie bar. The second juxtaposition can be observed as Guy, in his shirtsleeves, leans contemplatively against the mantelpiece on which is placed a Roman bust, possibly of a young Augustus, under whose watchful imperial gaze Guy begins spontaneously to rap out rhythms with his hands and feet. His clownish Chaplinesque waddle across the hearth amusingly undercuts the sculpture's Roman *gravitas* and *dignitas*. This particular juxtaposition also indicates that Astaire's Guy Holden is a reinvention of Roman *urbanitas*, an indefinable metropolitan sophistication. As the dance progresses, Guy's restless form is juxtaposed with another Roman statue, this time of Mercury, the god with winged heels and, among other things, patron of invention, wit, persuasion, and chance. At the end of the sequence, the valet tosses hat and umbrella to Guy, who is poised contrapposto atop a chair. The bowler and tightly furled umbrella—supreme symbols of stolid Englishness—are contrasted with the rakish angle at which Guy sets his hat and his nonchalant parting salute.

SEEING MUSIC

Astaire's bodily eloquence was greatly enhanced by his exceptional musicianship. At Lucian 74, Lycinus maintains that, in addition to a retentive memory, keen intelligence, faultless sense of timing, and poetic discernment, a dancer should have in his mental armoury the ability 'to select the best songs and melodies, and to reject worthless compositions'. Astaire was a dancer with an enviable capacity for recognizing and exploiting good music. His collaboration with the finest popular composers of the day was one of mutual creative advantage. Among those who wrote songs especially for him were George and Ira Gershwin, Vincent Youmans, Howard Dietz and Arthur Schwartz, Cole Porter, Jerome Kern, Irving Berlin, Harold Arlen, Harry Warren, Johnny Mercer, and Burton Lane and Alan Jay Lerner. Astaire was himself a lifelong, semi-professional songwriter and skilled at several instruments. As Beth Genné points out, he was equipped with a rare appreciation of the inner workings of music:

Like Ashton and Balanchine, Astaire also instinctively understood the shape of the music to which he danced, its inherent logic, how the individual parts came together to create a unified whole. His dances to American popular song thus never seemed additive—superimposed on a musical structure. Because he so well understood the music and because the arrangements and orchestrations of the songs to which he danced were worked out in collaboration with him (often written with him in mind), his movements and the staccato sound of his feet interacted with music as an integral, a *necessary* component of the whole.[63]

Lycinus complains that some dancers 'make senseless movements that have nothing to do with the harpstring, as the saying goes; for the foot says one thing and the music another' (*De Salt.* 80). Astaire's understanding of the inherent logic of the music to which he danced largely accounts for the articulacy and pertinence of his every gesture and movement. He could produce fresh and unexpected effects while ensuring choreographic, musical, and narrative congruence. Even at its most unpredictable, his inventive use of the off-beat is never irrational. On the contrary, as Bob Fosse commented (with particular reference to the number 'Let's Say It with Firecrackers' in *Holiday Inn*, 1942): 'With Fred you could never know where the rhythm was going to go. It was always a surprise. It never exactly turned out the way you thought it was going to go and yet, when you heard it, you said, "Well, that's right. It can't be any other way." '[64] Like the *pantomimus*, Astaire's musicality enabled him to translate vision into hearing. This act of translation has two facets. The first is that Astaire lets his audience *see* the music; it is as though he is melody and rhythm incarnate. Villella called him 'the most immaculate musical mover I had ever seen'.[65] The second is that, if you watch Astaire dancing, without the soundtrack, you can almost hear the music by means of seeing his movements.

'EITHER THE CAMERA WILL DANCE, OR I WILL'

Astaire's bodily eloquence was also enhanced by an instinctive understanding of how best to present the dancer on film. While *Gay Divorce* was playing at New York's Shubert Theatre, Astaire spoke to Nanette Kutner about the possibility of his going to Hollywood: 'I hope to create something entirely new. There ought to be a photographic medium of developing and putting across rhythm on the screen.'[66] When he was established in Hollywood as the movie musical's most innovative exponent he said:

I have always tried to run a dance straight in the movies, keeping the full figure of the dancer, or dancers, in view and retaining the flow of the movement intact. . . . Keeping the

---

[63] Beth Genné, obituary of Fred Astaire, *Dancing Times*, Sept. 1987. Similarly, John Winge (1949), 7–9, at 8 observed of Astaire: 'He does not just accept a tune and turn it over to the Music Department for arranging. Being deeply concerned about anything and everything related to his picture, he will tell the arranger accurately how he wants his dances to be executed—where he wants orchestral accents, and what kind, where off-beats, where the dance will run parallel with the music, where it will be independent or running against it.'

[64] Fosse interviewed for the PBS television documentary *Fred Astaire: Change Partners and Dance*, directed by David Heeley, 1980.

[65] Villella in Roseman (2001), 21.

[66] *Gotham Life*, 1932.

whole body always in action before the camera, there are certain obvious advantages that the screen has over the stage. You can concentrate your action on the dancer; the audience can follow intricate steps that were all but lost behind the footlights, and each person in the audience sees the dance from the same perspective. . . . In consequence, I think that the audience . . . get a larger, clearer and better-focused view, and so, derive a larger emotional response.[67]

Astaire's insistence on keeping the full figure of the dancer always in view of the camera, his removal of meaningless inserts and editing effects, and his limited or judicious use of cuts preserved the choreographic integrity of the dance, focusing attention on the dancer's body and investing the story he told with a compelling fluidity and coherence. Even in his pioneering use of special effects (e.g. slow motion, split screens) and certain choreographic gimmicks (e.g. dancing on the ceiling), he tended more to showcase than distract from his corporeal eloquence. As Stanley Crouch has stated:

[He] wanted the camera to serve the dancer so that all the complexity, nuance, and expression would be the dancer's responsibility . . . Novelty shots and startling setups were replaced with a luminescent individual power held in place by an overwhelming ease. Astaire gave the impression that the way he was moving at any moment was three things plaited together: the only, the most natural, and the *best* choice.[68]

Fred Astaire's achieved refinement of his learned and intuitive skills (aided by his dancer's physique and innate grace) bears a demonstrable and intriguing relationship to the tenets expounded by Lucian and exemplified by Pylades. Despite his self-deprecatory profession of ignorance of the history of dance, it is apparent that Astaire brought to the expression of his art a keenly informed, cosmopolitan intelligence and a natural, but educated, musicianship, which complemented his intuitive genius and ensured it did not work alone or unin-fluenced. Astaire's methods and standards of execution reflect, to a significant degree, those attributed to Pylades. In the expression of bodily eloquence through compelling narrative in dance, Pylades could have had no more worthy successor in the twentieth century than Fred Astaire.

---

[67] Quoted in Eustis (1937), 371–86, at 379.
[68] Stanley Crouch, 'Brothers-in-Arts: The Unique Talent That Links Fred Astaire and Louis Armstrong', *Slate Magazine*, 23 Feb. 2006.

II

DANCE AND DECADENCE

6

'Where there is Dance there is the Devil': Ancient and Modern Representations of Salome

Ruth Webb

Of all the individual dancers of antiquity, the one who has enjoyed the richest and the most enduring afterlife is without doubt the daughter of Herodias, wife of Herod Antipas, whose dance secured the head of John the Baptist. The princess, who is nameless in the Gospel and in many late antique sources, appears in early Christian sermons, in medieval churches in East and West, in manuscript illumination, in the literature and visual arts of the late nineteenth century as well as on the twentieth-century stage and screen. The reworkings of her story associate her, and thus dance, with death, destruction, and a dangerous female sexuality, this last being particularly evident in the late nineteenth and early twentieth-century versions. All the versions of her story also provide the space for meditation on artistry and the relationship of viewer to viewed.

Here I will focus on two phases of the depiction of Salome: her treatment in late antiquity, in the writings of the Church Fathers, and in the late nineteenth and early twentieth centuries. There are some notable similarities—especially in the (often ambiguous) associations of dance with sexuality, the feminine, and the non-, the un-, or the anti-Christian. It was the dance of Salome, for example, that prompted the declaration by John Chrysostom that 'where there is dance, there is the devil', part of a rejection of dance, both sacred and profane, that has had a long-standing influence on western culture.[1] But there are also significant differences as authors and other artists use and adapt the figure of Salome, and the idea of dance, as a means of discussing cultural tensions and problems within their own society. Most strikingly, the ethnic and cultural identity of Salome becomes

---

[1] See Jungmann (2002) on the associations of dance in 15th- and 16th-cent. Germany, for example; Jane Cowan (1990), 23 quotes a revealing remark by a relative about 'Methodist feet', summing up the internalized prohibition against dancing. As I completed work on this article in March 2009, the Swiss canton of Lucerne overturned a ban on dancing on religious holidays that had been in place since 1428.

a major problem in many sources, particularly as nineteenth-century theories of the racial determination of cultural characteristics came to the fore.

It is a sign of those debates that her presence in a study of 'the Ancient dancer' needs some justification. There is no doubt about her inclusion on chronological grounds: the dramatic date of her performance is the early first century CE, the Gospels that first mention her dance belong later in the same century. But in terms of geography and culture she is part of a different antiquity. If the artists of the Middle Ages and Renaissance treated her as they treated all figures from the past, dressing her in contemporary fashions with or without a hint of classicizing drapery,[2] it has become common since the nineteenth century to see her as the epitome of the oriental dancer, a figure with very different associations from those of the classical ideal of calm and reason, far removed from any hint of sexuality, that was current in the late-nineteenth and early twentieth centuries.[3] This vision of Hellenism affected the construction of 'Greek dance' at the same period, as is clear from the careful distinction made by Ruby Ginner between 'undulating movements' (such as in oriental dance) described as sensuous, and the 'speed . . . athleticism, and the cultivation of fine restraint' that, according to her, characterized the products of Greek culture.[4]

In what follows I will first give an overview of the main sources in this study, from the Gospel account to the 1930 novel *Salome* by George Sylvester Viereck and Paul Eldridge, then present an analysis of the treatment of the dancer and the themes of vision, artistic creation and cultural identity as they appear in the various versions of Salome's story, beginning with the Gospel version.

SALOME THROUGH THE AGES: AN OVERVIEW

The contrast between the fantasies inspired by the figure of Salome over the centuries and the plain Gospel narrative that was the ultimate source for the story could hardly be greater. Matthew 14:6–11 simply tells us (in the King James translation):

But when Herod's birthday was kept, the daughter of Herodias danced before them, and pleased Herod. Whereupon he promised with an oath to give her whatsoever she would ask. And she, being before instructed of her mother, said, Give me here John the Baptist's head in a charger. And the king was sorry: nevertheless for the oath's sake, and them which sat with him at meat, he commanded it to be given her. And he sent, and beheaded John in the prison. And his head was brought in a charger and given to the damsel: and she brought it to her mother.

---

[2] See e.g. Filippo Lippi's *Feast of Herod*, in Prato Cathedral. For further examples, see Hausamann (1980).

[3] See the analysis of early 20th-cent. responses to Strauss's *Elektra* in Goldhill (2002), 137–77.

[4] Ginner (1933), 33.

Mark 6:23 adds the detail of Herod's offer of half the kingdom and makes Herodias' role slightly more prominent by having the nameless daughter go to her to ask for advice. Both Gospels add the further information that Herod feared John and that Herodias' anger was roused by John's condemnation of her marriage to Herod, brother of her first husband, Philip (Matthew 14:4; Mark 6:17–18). Neither Gospel describes the dance.

For early Christian writers the daughter of Herodias, as the cause of the death of John the Baptist, provided a convenient symbol of dance as an anti-Christian activity, reinforcing the widespread opposition to dance and secular music and song in the early Church. The only exceptions to this rejection of dance were the abstract, heavenly dance evoked by Clement of Alexandria,[5] the choral dance of Miriam, treated as an image of the Church[6] and the dance of David before the Ark recounted in 2 Samuel 6. 'If you must dance', says Gregory Nazianzenus (Or. V *Contra Julianum* 2.35), 'dance like David and not like Salome' (see further Hall, this volume). As this suggests, the daughter of Herodias provided the perfect illustration of the dangers of dance.

Two writers, or rather orators, who focus on the dance are John Chrysostom and Basil of Seleucia, though they do so in very different ways.[7] John's sermon on the Gospel of Matthew is a close reading of the text that lingers on each word in a manner that adapts techniques of scholarship to the pulpit.[8] Basil, by contrast, represents the events leading to the Baptist's death in a rhetorical performance that combines imagined direct speech (*ethopoiia*) and the vivid evocation of the scene (*ekphrasis*), both techniques that were used in rhetoric to involve the spectators in a scene and make them feel as if they were present themselves. Both of these sermons are of interest for the way in which they focus on the dance. Basil describes it and makes it live in his audience's imagination, telling succinctly how she undulated her body, raised her hands and feet in the air.[9] John dissects the passage to reveal its meaning. In John, in particular, the treatment of Salome (I will use the name for convenience, although it does not appear in either source) can be compared with his many utterances about the theatre and dance of his day. In fact both develop the assimilation of the princess to the performer in ways that bring out the transgressive nature of the act, and tap into the rich vein of polemics about the theatre, in general, and the dance, in particular, in early Christian writing.

[5] Clement of Alexandria, *Protrepticus*, 12.119.1–2. See McKinnon (1987), 31–2.
[6] Ambrose, *De virginibus ad Marcellinam, sororem* 1.3.12. See McKinnon (1987), 133.
[7] John Chrysostom, *In Matthaeum Hom.* 48, *PG* 58.487–96; Basil of Seleucia, *In Herodiadem*, *PG* 85.225–36.
[8] On Chrysostom's pedagogical techniques see Maxwell (2006), 88–117.
[9] Basil of Seleucia, *In Herodiadem*, *PG* 85.228. For a translation of the passage with Greek text see Webb (1997), 136.

NINETEENTH AND TWENTIETH CENTURIES

The interest in representing Salome intensified in the later nineteenth century with Flaubert's *Herodias* (1877), the work of Symbolist writers and painters, and Oscar Wilde's *Salome* (1893) which followed in the Symbolist tradition.[10] Flaubert's tale (one of three short stories) centres on the figure of Herod as he struggles to retain power in the face of the challenges posed by Roman hegemony and various local rivalries. At the opening of the tale, Herod is waiting anxiously for the arrival of the Roman Proconsul, Vitellius, and John the Baptist (Iaokanaan) is immured deep in the palace dungeons. Salome herself remains a shadowy figure, a nameless girl who has only just been brought to the court by her mother in the hope of increasing her faltering hold over her husband. Until her dramatic entrance at the feast to celebrate Herod's birthday, narrated at the very end of the story, Herodias' daughter is an enigmatic presence who is glimpsed by her stepfather, and thus the reader, on a distant rooftop or as a disembodied arm reaching for a tunic from behind a curtain.

It is in the account of the dance at the climax of the story that the young girl comes to the fore. Her sudden appearance, still unidentified, interrupts the sumptuous, and fractious, feast celebrating Herod's birthday. After a description of the details of the mysterious stranger's costume, the narrator's attention moves first to the movements of feet and arms—'her feet slipped back and forth, to the rhythm of the flute and a pair of castanets' (101). This first evocation of the body in movement gives way to the interpretation of that movement as the expression of changing emotions: 'Her arms curved round in invitation to someone who always eluded her ... The mournful sound of the gingras [flute] replaced the castanets. Despair had followed hope' (101). Flaubert describes the movements that accompany the sound of the flute in terms typical of the oriental dance: 'With eyes half closed, she twisted her waist, made her belly ripple like the swell of the sea, made her breasts quiver, while her expression remained fixed, and her feet never stood still' (101). From this moment of 'languor' comes renewed energy in movement, treated as an expression of passion. The narrator compares her to the 'priestesses of India', 'the Nubian women from the cataracts', 'the Bacchantes of Lydia' and 'invisible sparks' fire the male spectators with excitement. At the acrobatic climax she opens her legs wide (in the splits) and turns 'like the sorceresses' spinning top' (102).

It is at this moment that Herod makes his offer. Salome at first responds wordlessly, balancing on her hands, gazing at him but then she runs to her mother and returns to make her request 'lisping slightly ... with a childlike

---

[10] Flaubert's *Herodias* is quoted in the translation by A. J. Krailsheimer in the Oxford edition (1991) and Wilde's *Salome* from the Oxford edition, in a translation by I. Murray (1989). References to these editions appear in brackets after the citation.

expression' (102) and nearly forgets Iaokanann's name. So, despite his elaborations on the basic plot, Flaubert follows the Gospel version quite closely, presenting Salome, for all her art, as the instrument of her mother's will. No thoughts or feelings are ascribed to the girl. She has been instructed in dance by her mother (as in Basil); and once she receives the head from Herod she takes it to Herodias in the gallery, where she is waiting and observing the scene, and then promptly disappears from the text.

Oscar Wilde's *Salome*, by contrast, developed the role of its cruel and sensual central character in ways that depart from the Gospel and scandalized contemporary audiences and readers. Wilde's princess manipulates and teases, toying with one admirer, 'The Young Syrian', whose despairing suicide she hardly notices. When she dances, it is in the blood of the rejected lover. Wilde innovates by attributing the choice of Iokanaan's death to Salome herself, rather than to her mother, and by providing her with a very personal reason for her wish: she demands Iokanaan's head in response to his rejection of her. In this version, moreover, the death of Iokanaan is not the end, indeed it cannot be once Salome is individualized to such an extent. Instead, Salome goes on to make an impassioned speech to Iokanaan's decapitated head, in which her mood changes from exultation to sorrow at the death of the man she loved, as she enumerates the qualities of his body in sensual imagery reminiscent of the *Song of Songs* before finally kissing his dead lips. Outraged by her behaviour, Herod orders her death and the play ends with Salome crushed beneath the soldiers' shields (a punishment that Iokanaan had earlier called to be visited upon Herodias (317)).

Read as a text, Wilde's *Salome* is most striking for its hieratic and portentous language and for the association of thwarted sexual desire, dance, and death, themes which all meet in the central character of Salome. As a playwright, Wilde was able to leave the representation of the dance to the director and actress, or to the reader's imagination. The only indications contained in his text are given when Salome herself calls for her 'seven veils' just before her dance and when Herod expresses his pleasure on seeing that she will perform barefoot: 'Ah thou art to dance with naked feet. 'Tis well! 'Tis well! Thy little feet will be like white doves' (322), a pleasure that turns to horror as he realizes that she is about to dance in the blood of her dead admirer.[11] These suggestions were, famously, developed into an independent dance piece by Maud Allan.

Wilde even plays with the possibility that the dance, the defining action of the traditional Salome, might not take place. His Herod, rather than being surprised by the performance as in Flaubert's story, repeatedly asks his stepdaughter to dance for him, a request that she at first refuses with the support of her mother. As Herod offers half his kingdom, Salome gradually shows interest, then accepts,

[11] Wilde (1989), 322. Tydeman and Price (1996), 19–20 note that Wilde is said to have wanted to cast a Romanian dancer he had seen performing on her hands, suggesting that he wished to stage something very like Flaubert's account.

though her mother, perturbed by Iokanaan's voice rising from his prison, remains opposed. The text then jumps to Herod's approval of the dance (and his hubristic expression of victory over Herodias, 'Ah! Wonderful! Wonderful! You see that she has danced for me, your daughter') which soon turns to horror as Salome names her reward (323).

To the reader of the script, therefore, the dance is a lacuna in the middle of the text. In the absence of description, all that bridges Herodias' last attempt to stop her daughter and Herod's triumphant exclamation is Salome's statement that she is ready and the stage direction 'Salome dances the dance of the seven veils' (323). When the play was staged, however, the dance that filled the verbal lacuna took on an altogether different role. The dance itself appears to have been Wilde's own invention and its exact nature depends in each case on the director and actress. (Only in Strauss's operatic version is there any fixed score for the dance.) Most importantly, by staging the dance, Wilde's version, like Strauss's opera, potentially placed every spectator in the role of Herod watching the dance more fully than do the literary descriptions like that of Flaubert (or the brief account by Basil of Caesarea). Or rather, as Lawrence Kramer has observed, they place the audience in the situation of the unobserved observer, a privileged position which is not available to Herod himself.[12] Moreover, by depicting the audience of the performance within the play, these works perform their own metatheatrical commentary on the act of viewing.

One further, little known, literary version of the Salome story was published by a German American writer, George Sylvester Viereck, in collaboration with Paul Eldridge in 1930. *Salome: The Wandering Jewess* is a pendant to his first novel with Eldridge, *My First Two Thousand Years: The Autobiography of the Wandering Jew*, published in 1928. Like the hero of the first novel, Viereck's Salome is condemned to eternal life and, like that novel, *Salome* is written in the first person as if it were a personal memoir. Although Viereck seems to have known Wilde's work and to have aspired to imitate it, this *Salome* is by no means comparable in terms of complexity of theme or characterization.[13] Its very crudeness, however, makes it worthy of attention because of the way in which the story is used to explore various cultural concerns, particularly concerning gender and race.[14]

The heroine recounts how, after her childhood and young adulthood in first-century Jerusalem, she wandered the world in search of knowledge. Rather like the hero(ine) of Virginia Woolf's *Orlando* (published in 1928), she travels through different times and places—ancient Arabia, India, Africa, medieval France and Spain, Tibet—acquiring a learned tortoise (sic) named Lakshmi

---

[12] Kramer (1990), 284–5.

[13] Louis Untermeyer discussed the frequent comparisons made between Viereck's poetry and Wilde in the *New York Times* of 13 July 1907 (consulted online 24/03/09).

[14] For further examples of this use of the Salome story, see Gilman (1995).

along the way. An androgynous figure from the start, she appears in both male and female guise, consorts with Pope Joan and Catherine the Great and joins in the Crusades as a male knight. The story of Cartaphilus, the Wandering Jew of Viereck and Eldridge's first novel, is carefully intertwined as he and Salome cross each other's paths in first-century Jerusalem and then at various points throughout the novel, the close of which finds Salome and Cartaphilus together in late nineteenth-century London. The further implication is that they are still, somewhere, in the world of the reader just as Woolf's Orlando is portrayed as still alive in 1928.

Salome's eternal youth is by no means the only departure from the traditional version of the story. The novel opens with the birth of the nine-year-old Salome's brother and her first dance is performed shortly afterwards for her dying grandfather, Herod the Great, whom she visits in secret, disguised as a boy. By the time of John the Baptist's death, this Salome has been twice married, twice widowed and has borne one child (a deformed boy who dies shortly after his birth). She is also, as in Wilde, in love with John (Jokanaan), whom she has encountered in the desert before his capture, and at first protects him from her mother, persuading her stepfather, Herod Antipater, to imprison rather than execute him. She then steps aside after Jokanaan has spurned her in his prison and allows her mother to bring about his execution.

The canonical dance is split into several different events: Salome tells Jokanaan in his cell that it was her dance that persuaded Antipater to stay his execution,[15] the added information that Herod offered half his kingdom as a reward, shows that we are to think of this dance as the one recounted in the Gospel, though it is not described. In the scene in Jokanaan's prison cell, Salome undresses and dances before the prisoner who averts his eyes.[16] Once she has decided to allow Herodias to kill Jokanaan, Herod requests another dance which is, however, forestalled by Salome's vision of Jokanaan. Running out of the banqueting chamber, Salome sees Jokanaan's head lying on the platter. The dead lips speak, cursing her with the eternal life that is the subject of the rest of the novel.

Despite their differences in context and form, it is possible to trace some themes and concerns that are present, to varying degrees, in all of these representations of Salome. In what follows, I will focus on the portrayal of the dance and on the constructions of vision and the gaze, gender and cultural dynamics. The daughter of Herodias proves to be remarkably resistant to any simple categorization in any of these perspectives, and this very difficulty may help

---

[15] Tydeman and Price (1996), 166 note a similar twist in the 1953 film starring Rita Hayworth which they describe as 'either audaciously inventive or simply ludicrous'. In fact Viereck's novel may have provided the inspiration for this innovation.

[16] Viereck and Eldridge (1930), 78. This detail may have been suggested by Salome's statement in her final monologue addressed to the head of Iokanaan in Wilde's play 'me thou didst never see' (Wilde (1989), 328).

explain why she finds a place within many different cultural conflicts from antiquity to the modern world.

SALOME IN THE GOSPEL

Despite its spare narrative, the Gospel account contains powerful themes.[17] The basic association of dance and death lies at the core of the tradition as dance is firmly aligned with what is Other from the perspective of the narrator. The dance itself introduces the theme of vision, and of captivation through vision, that is reworked and emphasized in later accounts. Herod is forced to act against his will by the effects of visual pleasure, a fact that is stressed in the Greek account at the level of the language. For whereas most of the actions are simply linked by various forms of 'and' (*kai* or *de*) the direct causal relationship between the dance and Herod's oath is underlined by the use of the adverb *hothen* ('whence', 'whereupon').

It is also important to note that it is not simple sexual desire that works this effect but the impact of the dance, an art form and a product of culture. The story thus contains the germ of a meditation on the dangers of sight, as in the classical myths of Actaeon and Tiresias, and, more importantly, on theatricality and the impact of bodily presence in performance. This is emphasized in the Gospel version, despite its brevity, by the vocabulary used. The words translated 'before them' in the King James translation are '*en mesōi*', literally, 'in the middle', a term that can also mean 'in public', assimilating the daughter of Herodias to a public entertainer. More strikingly, when she 'pleased' Herod, the verb used, '*areskō*', also belongs to the vocabulary of theatrical entertainment used in inscriptions of particularly successful performances that pleased their audiences.[18]

All this is explored against the background of a twofold conflict. One part of this conflict takes place between the female world of artful entrapment and danger and the male domain represented by John and the hapless Herod. The Gospel accounts make clear that Herodias wanted John dead to stop his criticisms of her second marriage to Herod. The fact that Herod finds himself caught in a trap of Herodias' making is underlined by the mention of his grief on discovering that he is obliged either to kill John or to break his oath.[19] The other aspect of the conflict involves tensions between the proto-Christian culture represented by John and the dominant Jewish culture of Herod and his court. The grid of associations thus produced leaves Herod in an ambiguous, and highly

---

[17] See also the comments in Garber (1992), 340 who notes the presence of 'parents and willful child; incestuous desire; taboo; and a gap.' (Though the willfulness of Salome is scarcely present, if at all, in the Gospel.)

[18] See e.g. *IK* 31.17 (Stephanis 2639); *IK* 31.83 (Stephanis 2225a).

[19] The rash oath or prayer that has unintended consequences is itself a familiar motif in myth and folklore.

vulnerable, position, a quality that is further developed in Flaubert's *Herodias* where he is caught in the multiple conflicts of domestic and foreign affairs that form the background to Herodias' scheming. In the Gospel, he is allied to John—and the authorial voice—by gender but alienated from them by his culture and this ambiguity finds expression in later versions in the weakness and effeminacy of Herod.

It is significant that Herod is faced not by one female figure but by two and that in Herodias and her daughter we have a divided representation of the feminine into the younger, sexually attractive woman and the older, manipulating woman. This doubling of the female figure has multiple consequences. Garber draws attention to its impact on the construction of the gaze: 'Herodias gazes on Herod gazing on Salome.'[20] But it also serves to stress the vulnerability of Herod, outnumbered by the women of the family. Paradoxically though, the division of the female roles also serves to dilute to some extent the power of the figure of the dancer. The daughter dances, but she is merely the instrument: the intention and understanding of her act are not hers but her mother's. The figure of the knowing dancer using her art to bewitch and enslave the viewer may lie behind the story but it is eclipsed in its telling, as if the combination of female sexuality with intelligence were too dangerous to contemplate.

However, one further consequence is that Salome in fact emerges as a richer and more intriguing figure: the dancer here, uniquely, has a familial identity beyond (and in conflict with) that of the performer. In addition to the intimations of incest that colour Herod's relationship with both women (Herodias being his brother's former wife), the maternal relationship in which Salome is so firmly placed may militate against her being seen in purely sexual terms: we are constantly reminded of her familial context and of her potential role as mother herself, as well as lover.

EARLY CHRISTIAN SALOMES

From a Christian perspective, the actions of Herodias and her daughter could only be seen in negative terms. Both Basil's and John's readings of the passage are structured around the central contrast between Christ, represented by John the Baptist, and the devil who works through Herodias and her daughter. Basil makes the dichotomy clear in his opening sentences in which he claims (using the name of Herodias for the daughter, too) that 'the voice of the Evangelists today condemns the dance of Herodias and brings out into public the godless madness of those women. . . . the devil worked out the drama, Herod collaborated, Herodias danced'.[21] John, for his part, exclaims when he first comes to the mention

---

[20] Garber (1992), 340.
[21] Basil of Seleucia, *In Herodiadem*, *PG* 85.226D–228A.

of the dance: 'O banquet of the devil, satanic theatre, unlawful dance and a reward (*misthos*) more unlawful still!' (*PG* 58.489). Further on he thunders: 'Where there is dance, there is the devil.' The authors of both sermons treat Herod as an example of the man who falls victim to his own weakness and sensuality, becoming a slave to pleasure. (Though Basil's Herod only makes a show of grief and is secretly relieved to be able to rid himself of his troublesome prisoner.) The ultimate responsibility, however, is placed squarely on the shoulders of Herodias: John explains 'But though he (Herod) was so lawless, the woman (Herodias) was more lawless still' (*PG* 58.491), and goes on to describe her as 'the architect' who 'wove the whole drama' to avenge herself upon John for his freedom of speech (*parrhēsia*). Basil similarly emphasizes the mother's agency when he describes her as her daughter's teacher and makes her express her desire for the Baptist's death in direct speech.[22]

In his treatment of the dance and the feast John Chrysostom assimilates Salome's performance to the practices of his own age. By emphasizing the corruption and drunkenness of the event (both elements that are not mentioned in the Gospel), he is able to criticize the practices of his congregation and their contemporaries, as he does so often in his sermons.[23] Also, unusually, he addresses himself directly to the women in the audience: 'Listen you unmarried girls, and even more so you married women, who are willing to behave in such an ugly manner at other people's weddings, leaping and jumping, bringing shame on your whole sex' (*PG* 58.490). He goes on to warn the men that they risk falling into the same trap as Herod. His listeners are thus invited to think themselves into the story and to see Herod and his family as all too close to their lives.

Salome is also assimilated on several different levels to the professional performers of the late antique stage who were both despised and adulated in society. In particular, both John and Basil identify the reward offered by Herod with the payment given to artists. John uses the term *misthos* ('fee') and Basil refers to it both as a *misthos* and as an *athlon* ('prize'). They link Salome's dance to the economic and social realities of dance in their own day. There may have been a fine distinction between performers who were hired for a fee and those who competed freely for a prize, but to appear publicly and to receive either was thoroughly shaming, particularly for a woman and even more so for a member of a royal family.[24]

---

[22] Basil of Seleucia, *In Herodiadem*, *PG* 85.232c and 233b.

[23] John Chrysostom, *In Matthaeum Hom.* 48, *PG* 58.490, 493; cf. *In Illud, Propter fornicationes uxorem* I *PG* 51.211; cf. *In Cap XXIX Genes. Hom.* 56, *PG* 54.486 (against the practice of hiring professional entertainers for weddings).

[24] Elsewhere, *In Pentecostem*, *PG* 52.808, Chrysostom claims that even a maidservant would be ashamed to dance in public as the daughter of Herodias did.

Both John and Basil also elaborate on the causal connection between the stepdaughter's dance and Herod's offer that is hinted at by the single word *hothen* in the Gospel account. Basil's narrative account gives a few details of the movements he imagines her performing—raising her hands and her feet—and culminates in the effect on the audience: 'she drew everyone's gaze as she danced and Herod was overcome with wonder at the dance.' The verb Basil uses here is a strong one (*helkein*—to drag) and betrays an idea of the vulnerability of the viewer to visual sensation. John Chrysostom frequently attributes power of this sort to performers who make their spectators into 'prisoners', 'set them ablaze' or 'wound' them.[25] In this sermon he draws an explicit parallel between the impact of Salome's dance and the influence of the professional performers of his day: the story of Herod is confirmed by the experiences of his contemporaries who are made prisoner by (male pantomime) dancers (*PG* 58.490). The moral is made clear later in the sermon: 'today's dancers do not ask for the head of John the Baptist but for the viewers' soul' he says, adding that it is impossible to be in the middle of a drunken feast and not to be moved by the sight of a woman dancing (*PG* 58.493).

The sermons of both John and Basil thus emphasize the idea of the dance as a form of captivation and malign enchantment of the viewer by the dancer in which the gaze is a source of vulnerability rather than dominance. This power of the dance is identified clearly by Chrysostom as the work of the devil ('where there is dance, there is the devil'; *PG* 58.491). He returns to this theme later, when he elaborates on the dangers of feasts, telling his listeners that he works through Salome to give her dance its power: 'even if the daughter of Herodias is not present, the devil who danced through her is dancing through them [dancers] now and leaves taking with him the souls of the participants as his prisoners' (*PG* 58.493). The image of the malign, degraded Salome being 'danced' by the devil is haunting, as is Chrysostom's statement that all dancers partake of the same demonic essence: the devil who danced through the daughter of Herodias is present each and every time there is dance: every dancer is, in a sense, a simulacrum of Salome.

These two sermons simultaneously insist on the dancer's power—on the persuasive quality of the dance—and on the dance's status as commodity in a manner that reveals clearly the complex responses to dance and other theatrical performance at the time. Furthermore, dance, as in Chrysostom's warning to the women of his congregation cited above, is presented as an aberration, a perversion of the natural god-given state in which the ideal Christian should live: 'This is how camels dance,' John Chrysostom exclaims, 'it was not for this that God gave us feet, but so that we might walk in an orderly manner (*eutakta*); not so that we could behave disgracefully (*aschemonein*), not so that we could leap like camels . . . but so that we could dance with angels. If the body is ugly when it behaves so disgracefully, what about the soul?' (*PG* 58.491). Basil's account of

---

[25] See Webb (2008), 170–1.

Salome's dance likewise draws attention to the 'ugliness' and 'disorder' *akosmia* involved in her movements (raising her hands and feet), relating physical to moral *akosmia* (*PG* 85.232c). Such charges of moral disorder and perversion are most often associated with the male pantomime dancers, particularly because of their embodiment of female roles.[26] But the treatment of Salome shows how they could be elicited by any form of dance.

MODERN VERSIONS

In this section I will look at the modern depictions of Salome against the background of the Gospel and early Christian versions to try to see which themes recur and in what ways. We have already seen how the Gospel portrayal of Herod is echoed and magnified in Flaubert's tale. The triangular relationship between Herod, Herodias, and her daughter is dealt with differently in different works as is the division of attributes between the two female characters. I will pay particular attention to the portrayal of the dance and its effect (or lack of it) on the viewer and to questions of cultural identity. As we shall see, just as for the early Christians, the story continued to be an important way of addressing cultural concerns.

One characteristic that all the nineteenth- and twentieth-century versions share is the exoticism of Salome and her culture. Flaubert creates a foreign world in his short story by his use of detail and vocabulary. The omniscient narrator stands outside the story, but speaks in terms of the ancient orient as when he cites the Indian, Nubian and Lydian women as comparisons for Salome, as if they were familiar sights, or refers casually to the sound of the *gingras*, using an ancient Greek term for a type of oriental flute. The result is a certain tension for the reader between the narrator's voice and the *persona* of the author—a nineteenth-century Frenchman. Elements of the dance itself (particularly the reference to the soft movements of the torso banished from 'Greek dance' by Ginner) recall accounts of oriental dance. As has often been noted, Flaubert saw, and slept with, the famous dancer Kuchuk Hanem during his visit to Egypt and may have based at least some elements of Salome's dance on her performances.[27]

Wilde's orientalism is of a different nature, taking the form of a generally exotic atmosphere created by the poetic language and the sense that the characters share a culture that is different from that of the reader/spectator, a feeling that becomes particularly acute when Salome asks for her veils before dancing. It is clear from photographs and written accounts that Maud Allan's portrayal of Salome used costume, movement and gesture (note the arms in Figure 6.1) to

---

[26] See Lada-Richards (2007), 146–50; Webb (2008), 147–8.
[27] Said (2003) 187; Garber (1992), 341. Karayianni (2004), 49–55 gives a critique of Flaubert's encounter with Kuchuk Hanem and of Said's treatment of it.

4946 C ROTARY PHOTO, E.C   MISS MAUD ALLAN, AS " SALOME."   FOULSHAM & BANFIELD.

May 25th '09.

Figure 6.1 Maud Allan as Salome.

create a composite vision of the exotic. Viereck's Salome inhabits a similarly exotic world at the beginning of her life in first-century Jerusalem. Unlike Flaubert and Wilde, however, Viereck takes care to identify his Salome as specifically Jewish rather than exotic or oriental: the novel begins with the nine-year old princess witnessing the preparations for her baby brother's circumcision, complete with accounts of the knife and the prayers (in transliterated Hebrew for added colour).[28]

One consequence of the orientalization of Salome was to allow certain aspects of her story—sexuality, dance, desire, and the interconnections between them—to be developed and explored at a safe distance. As Rana Kabbani has pointed out of nineteenth-century harem fantasies—in which the figure of the female dancer played a particularly important role—the idea of the Orient allowed Europeans to place themselves outside the moral and economic constraints of their daily lives and to explore ideas of unbridled sexuality.[29] It is interesting to compare this distancing of Salome with the approach of the Church Fathers, for in one sense they, too, orientalize the dancer and the dance, just as they do all the other aspects of their contemporary culture. They invite their audiences to look again at familiar practices like dance and secular celebrations and to see them as strange and as incompatible with the new identity and culture of the Christian. The practices themselves are, however, close to the audience's experience; it is the metaphors and imagery that make them appear strange and frightening, as in the image of the rapacious devil dancing through Salome and every dancer ever since. The dynamic is therefore very different from that involved in nineteenth-century orientalism; and one sign of this difference is the willingness of the Church Fathers to refer to, even insist upon, the economic aspects of dance, precisely the type of sordid reality that was excised from the orientalists' fantasies.[30]

Vision and the Orient

The role played by vision, particularly the dominating classifying vision of the western visitor, in orientalism has been made clear by Edward Said and emerges with particular clarity in his analysis of Flaubert's orientalist writings, including *Herodias*. Said's discussion of this text draws attention to the place of this tale within a tradition in which the Orient is conceived as spectacle portrayed through the omniscient narrator's gaze. The depiction of Salome displays Flaubert's characteristic evocation of sensual details, here binding together the ancient and the oriental with associations of wealth, luxury and excess.

---

[28] Viereck and Eldridge (1930), 17–18. It is noticeable that when Viereck has his characters quote from the Old Testament, a part of Jewish literature that has been adopted by Christianity, they use the Latin, not the Hebrew version (see ibid. 60).

[29] Kabbani (1988), 67–85; Karayianni (2004), 47 similarly notes how the oriental dancer embodied what the European body was not.

[30] See the comments of Karayianni (2004), 54 on Flaubert's encounter with Kuchuk Hanem.

When Salome appears at Herod's feast she is reduced to a catalogue of shimmering details—the silk veil over her head and shoulders, her jewels, the embroidered trousers, the slippers on her feet.[31] As she removes her veil to dance, Flaubert's Salome partakes in the further association of the oriental with the interplay between exhibitionism and concealment that is so characteristic of depictions of the harem and that characterized the tantalizing glimpses of the unknown stranger earlier on in the tale. At the climax of the dance, Herodias' daughter stands on her hands, allowing the fabric that had covered her legs to fall down on either side of her face and implicitly (though it is not stated) revealing the rest of her body. Maud Allan's Salome costume (see Figure 6.1) went further by showing her bare torso (not a feature of actual Middle Eastern dance costume at this period), other photographs show that the skirt was also transparent (see e.g. Tydeman and Price (1996), plate 8). The act of unveiling reaches its apogee in Wilde's imaginary 'Dance of the Seven Veils', which is interpreted by performers as a gradual removal of one veil after another to the point of nudity, in some more recent performances of the Strauss version.

The Gaze Disrupted

In Flaubert's text, however, things become more complicated between the moment of unveiling that begins the dance and the inverted posture at its end. In the description of the dance itself Salome moves gradually from being a collection of costume and body parts (feet, arms, waist, belly, breasts) open to reading by the narrator,[32] to a composite of ancient oriental womanhood as she is compared to 'the priestesses of India', 'Nubian women', the Bacchantes of Lydia'.[33] Then, at the climax of the dance she becomes a mass of shimmering objects in motion, sending out the 'invisible sparks' that captivate Herod. Lawrence Kramer (1990) has shown how, in this way, Flaubert's dancer defies categorization as a simple object of the male gaze. Instead she defeats his ability to look, particularly at the end of the dance, after Herod's offer, when she turns around him and, while standing on her hands, returns his gaze in her inverted pose, usurping the power of the gaze and turning it back on the viewer.

What is particularly interesting in the present context is the way in which Flaubert's text echoes the ideas about the vulnerability of the viewer that are found in the Church Fathers and that are a central feature of the biblical narrative. The difference is that whereas Chrysostom and Basil presented the captivation

---

[31] Kabbani (1988), 73 quotes a comparable passage from an account by Flaubert of his own encounter with an Arab courtesan, noting the detachment with which the European observer creates his version of the Orient.

[32] Flaubert (1991), 101: 'Her arms curved round *in invitation . . . one could not tell* whether she was mourning . . . or swooning' (my italics).

[33] Ibid. 102. See also Kabbani (1988), 72–3 on the Queen of Sheba in Flaubert's *Temptation of St Antony.*

exercised by Salome as the norm in performance situations and as an urgent warning of what might happen to their contemporaries, Flaubert's disrupted gaze is located in a time and a place that exist at a safe distance from the reader—an orientalized antiquity (or an antiqued Orient)—that allows the reader to observe both Salome's written dance and Herod's reaction potentially—but only potentially—undisturbed.

If Flaubert's dancing girl cannot be firmly placed within the 'harem fantasy' tradition, in which the supine bodies of naked women are displayed for the male voyeuristic gaze, it is precisely because she is a dancer, an active participant in the relationship between viewing and viewed. Flaubert may develop to the extreme the Gospel insistence on her secondary function as the instrument of the mother figure but, in dancing, she becomes an agent in her own right. There is thus a sense in which every dancer upsets the model of the dominating gaze by refusing to present the body as object, even as he or she invites it through public performance.[34] In fact, the dancer's necessary awareness of her role as the object of the gaze both distinguishes her from the model of the harem woman, typically depicted as unaware of the presence of the viewer, and enables her to return, or to dominate, the viewer's gaze. And in the case of Salome in particular, the earning of the reward is a constant reminder of the economic aspects of dance as work.

Wilde and the Art of Dance

Wilde's Salome raises rather different questions. In performance, the metatheatricality noted above makes her both aware that she is watched (by Herod) but unaware of the theatre audience in the darkened auditorium. Most remarkably, the order of events in the play deprives the dance of the persuasive power it so successfully deploys from the Gospel to Flaubert. For Wilde's most significant innovation, which seems to have gone largely unnoticed, is his inversion of the order of Herod's promise and Salome's dance. Rather than being prompted by the dance's visual power, the promise in Wilde's play precedes the dance and is Herod's inducement to Salome to dance for him.

The reasons Herod gives for this uncanonical request are varied and contradictory, which may reflect the innovative nature of the ordering of events. At one moment Herod is made to cite his happiness at friendly overtures from Caesar ('I am happy tonight,' 319); immediately afterwards he evokes his need to dispel the feeling of dread that bears down upon him:

Salome, Salome, dance for me. I pray thee dance for me. I am sad to-night. Yes, I am passing sad to-night. When I came hither I slipped in blood, which is an ill omen; also

---

[34] Kabbani (1988), 70 quotes Norman Bryson's claims that 'for its erotic content to be fully yielded . . . all signs that the body has other purposes, another history, are to be suppressed'.

I heard in the air a beating of wings, a beating of giant wings. I cannot tell what that may mean . . . I am sad to-night. Therefore dance for me. (320)

In addition there are strong hints of Herod's incestuous desire for his step-daughter, particularly in Herodias' repeated attempts to dissuade Salome. In this version, then, it is Salome who is slowly and inevitably persuaded by Herod's insistence and by his increasing offers:

Dance for me, Salome, I beseech thee. If thou dancest for me thou mayest ask of me what thou wilt, and I will give it thee. Yes, dance for me, Salome, and whatsoever thou shalt ask of me I will give it thee, even unto the half of my kingdom' (320).

This Herod plays the part of the patron, purchasing the entertainer's services. But Herod is not entirely in control of the situation as Salome—the first example of a speaking Salome—puts words into his mouth asking, 'You swear it, Tetrarch', to which he replies 'I swear it, Salome', and then stating, 'You have sworn an oath, Tetrarch' which brings the response, 'I have sworn an oath.' She thus publicly and ineluctably binds him to a promise whose consequences he cannot foresee. The dance, however, changes nothing in Herod, as is suggested in the language he uses after it ends which echoes the terms of his promise: 'I will pay thee royally. I will give thee whatsoever thy soul desireth. What wouldst thou have? Speak.' It is by speaking to name her price that Salome confounds this Herod who tries in vain to dissuade her and then to escape from his obligation. The entrapment is thus transferred from the dance to the language.

As all this suggests, Salome's dance plays a very different role in Wilde's play. It is freed from any persuasive function and simply allows Salome to fulfil her part of the bargain and to oblige Herod to do the same (as well as having the practical advantage of freeing the performer from the need to produce a dance that could plausibly have induced Herod to make his offer). In the absence of any detailed directions from the author himself it is difficult to know what Wilde saw as the dance's character or function, but several possibilities suggest themselves. One is that it served as an expression of Salome's thoughts and desires and was the gestural counterpart of the speech that follows. Strauss's music certainly runs through a range of contrasting and often dissonant sounds and moods in his interpretation of the dance scene.[35] From an act of performed persuasion it becomes a form of expression, even an example of art for the sake of art. In this way, Salome comes to stand for Wilde's own artistic ideals and perhaps for Wilde himself.

Salome thus gains a certain status as an artist within the play. Kramer's observation that, in kissing the head of Iokanaan she incorporates the power of speech that he embodies is borne out by the way, noted above, in which she

---

[35] On the score, which was shocking to contemporaries, see Kramer (1990) and Tydeman and Price (1996), 133. On dance conceived as a form of pure expression in this period see Scanlon and Kerridge (1988).

controls her stepfather's discourse, dictating to him the words which he echoes.[36] In fact this episode shows that this usurpation of male power takes place before the kiss. Most importantly, she controls the field of artistic creation through her dance and, in Strauss, through her song and music (Kramer notes that it is the Salome motif that plays as the curtain falls).[37] This Salome, who threatens to take control of artistic communication, is not permitted to survive in the world of the play and is crushed on Herod's orders. Her transgression is therefore not merely a sexual one—her desire for Iokanaan—but an artistic one.

Wilde's Salome may therefore seem far from its Gospel origins (though it was its placing of biblical characters on stage that earned it its first ban in Britain)[38] particularly in its treatment of the dance as the result, not the cause, of Herod's promise. It does however reflect several of the themes that are latent in the biblical account. In particular, Wilde's articulate, desiring Salome merges aspects of the biblical Herodias with the figure of her daughter to create the dangerous mixture of intelligence, sexuality and artistic control that was deftly avoided in the Gospel version. It is no wonder that this Salome is kept so firmly within the frame of the play that she dies as it ends. However, the idea of the dance as instrument of captivation and persuasion is denied in favour of the dance as expression of emotion and desires and as an art form freed from any purpose.

As noted above, the strange and exotic setting allowed the exploration of themes that were shocking to contemporary mores such as the active sexual desire of Salome. It is noticeable that reviewers of early performances expected such distance to be maintained: more than one criticized actresses for being 'too English' in their portrayal of the dancing princess.[39] Their complaints may well have had a sound technical basis, but the subtext is clear: the passions that Wilde put on stage were incompatible with ideals of Britishness and could only be countenanced in other peoples. One can compare the contemporary reactions to the 1910 staging of Strauss's *Elektra* analysed by Simon Goldhill, which associated perceived national characteristics with certain visions of classical antiquity.[40]

Salome in Viereck and Eldridge

Viereck and Eldridge's novel brings together the themes of dance, death, the exotic (here in the form of Judaism) and gender problems in the figure of the undying Salome. Dance itself is not a major theme in the novel, only surfacing in the early scenes in Jerusalem and giving rise to minimal description. In fact, the dance is partially obscured in different ways: Salome's dance before her stepfather is only mentioned by her to John (Jokanaan) (78); her dance in Jokanaan's cell is

---

[36] Kramer (1990), 280.   [37] Ibid. 293.
[38] Tydeman and Price (1996), 22. For its possible association with the taboo of incest, see Macintosh (2009), 118, 12.
[39] Tydeman and Price (1996) 42 and 55.   [40] Goldhill (2002), 137–77.

not seen by him (ibid.); her final dance is interrupted by the vision that signals his death (80). The first dance, performed by the prepubescent Salome before Herod the Great, is evoked in a little more detail. Yet, despite the sparse presence of dance in the novel as a whole, the *idea* of dance permeates the work from beginning to end through the choice of a heroine who is known almost entirely for her dance.

Dance, here is strongly associated with death: Herod the Great expires at the climax of Salome's first dance (32); the death of John the Baptist interrupts the last one. It is also a form of self-expression for Salome, who twice dances naked and unseen in the desert (64, 101). It is part of her thwarted attempt to seduce Jokanaan as well as serving as the bargaining tool that at first saves Jokanaan's life. The first dance before Herod the Great also brings to the fore the question of the gender of the dancer, the pre-pubescent Salome begins to dance in her boy's disguise but removes the clothes to dance naked at Herod's request (32). The naked dance, hidden from the view of the musicians (who are behind a screen in the novel) and requested by the male spectator, recalls Flaubert's description of the 'Bee dance' performed for him by Kuchuk Hanem. But, as Garber emphasizes, Flaubert was also impressed by the 'Bee dance' of the male dancer, Hassan el-Belbeissi and there was a strong strain of homoeroticism in his response to the Orient.[41]

In Viereck's portrayal of Salome, the hint of male homosexuality is evoked in the young girl's disguise only to be thrust aside immediately by the grandfather's demand that she dance 'like a woman' (i.e. naked). The element of gender ambiguity is present throughout, however, in Salome's androgynous appearance, established early on in the novel (38), and in her own adoption of male disguise. Though it is rarely as blatant as in the 1930 novel, this theme is present in many other versions of *Salome*: in Flaubert's text, the disembodied arm of the mysterious stranger is compared to a work by Polycleitus (93), best known for his statues of youths, and the dancing girl is compared by Vitellius at the feast to the male pantomime dancer, Mnester (101). Wilde's heroine usurps masculine attributes and, most strikingly, in the hallucinatory film version by Ken Russell, also analysed by Garber, the dancing Salome is played by a male and a female performer in alternation.[42]

In Viereck and Eldridge's novel, the ambiguity of Salome is closely associated with Judaism. Their Salome is desperate to escape the restraints imposed upon her by her patriarchal culture (this is what inspires her secret and lethal visit to Herod the Great). In her later adventures this desire is shown in her constant search for knowledge and in her apparent changes of gender. These might at first sight appear to be positive qualities to the twenty-first century reader, and to reflect other avant-garde treatments of the Salome story in the early twentieth

---

[41] Garber (1992), 341.   [42] Ibid. 343.

century.[43] However, within the novel, Salome's ambitions are given strongly negative associations: Salome is unable to bear a healthy child and is forced to use her prodigious knowledge to create a simulacrum of a daughter, an unnatural monster. Moreover, we are constantly reminded of the constraints of biology: this Salome is at the mercy of the moon, a powerful abstract symbol in Wilde's play, that here serves as an allusion to the painful menstruation that (literally) brings Salome to her knees at several points in the book (e.g. 41, 78).

She is thus made to embody a thoroughly negative vision of the independent, creative and intellectual woman. What is more, Viereck and Eldridge's Salome brings together several stereotypes of the Jewish woman in her combination of sensuality and barrenness (also a quality of the 'oriental' woman) and of Judaism in general, in her attempts to create a Golem-like daughter.[44] The antisemitism of the novel becomes blatant in the scenes in which Salome crosses paths with Cartaphilus, the Wandering Jew. As she is made to remark to Cartaphilus on one of their encounters: 'a Jew always recognizes his own. However straight the nose, however perfect the tongue, whatever the uniform or the name a Jew cannot hide his identity from a Jew. The soul, too, bears the scar of circumcision.' In the final scene of the novel, Salome is reunited with Cartaphilus and his familiar (a gorilla-like creature who has learned to 'pass' as a human). Cartaphilus is portrayed as a close friend of Disraeli 'the true Oriental' (431) whom he is busy manipulating, for his own ends (the 1874 purchase of the Suez canal shares with the help of Rothschild is mentioned).[45]

CONCLUSIONS

Despite the diversity in genre and period, these versions of the Salome legend, beginning with the Gospel, share many themes in common. Vision, and the impact of a sight on the viewer is one: the captivating power of Salome's performance, present in the Gospel and remarked upon by the Church Fathers, emerges clearly in Flaubert's version of the dance, its avoidance provokes the elisions and rearrangements of both Wilde's and Viereck's versions. Dance emerges in all the versions as a form of transgression, as has often been noted, but the transgression takes different forms. In the ancient versions Salome transgresses socially and, in dancing at all, breaks the laws of nature in John

---

[43] See Tydeman and Price (1996), 159–65 on Alla Nazimova. Studlar (1997) argues that identification with Salome allowed women in the early 20th cent. to explore ideas of assertiveness and independence associated with the New Woman.

[44] Gilman (1995) traces the complex and contradictory characterizations of Jewish womanhood in late 19th- and early 20th-cent. German culture.

[45] It is no surprise to learn after reading his *Salome* that Viereck was an apologist for Nazi Germany and, as such, was imprisoned in the US from 1942 until 1947. http://www.lib.uiowa.edu/spec-coll/Bai/johnson2.htm (consulted 24/11/08).

Chrysostom's interpretation. In the later versions this transgression emerges in Salome's ambiguous gender.

Her art is present throughout but in rather different forms: in the Gospel and the Church Fathers it is represented in terms of her (socially degrading) assimilation to the professional performer. In Flaubert's *Herodias* it is the only quality attributed to the young girl and is the cause of Herod's captivation, while in Wilde it is forcibly removed from this idea of dominance by the reordering of events that enables the dance to exist for its own sake, only for the dancer to be obliterated. In Viereck's novel, Salome's dance seems devoid of art. But the idea is far from absent from the work: it is transferred instead to Salome's quest for an artificial daughter, associating the theme of artistic creation with that of thwarted maternity that produces monstrous offspring. This Salome therefore becomes a perverted version of Herodias, the woman who moulds her own daughter in order to achieve her own ends.

All these versions, in their different ways, use the Salome story to reflect upon cultural tensions within their own societies. For John Chrysostom, she serves as the epitome of non-Christian culture and this characterization, present within the Gospel version itself, permeated later visions of her. It emerges most strongly in Viereck's presentation of the eternal, Jewish Salome whose hidden presence throughout world history bears an uncanny resemblance to Chrysostom's hidden devil working through each and every dancer. There is, however, a radical difference between John Chrysostom's category of the un-Christian and the understanding of racial difference that underpinned Viereck's work. For John Chrysostom it was a matter of choice and of culture. For Viereck, Salome's Jewishness was a matter of race not choice and was therefore inescapable. The very invisibility of Salome, her ability to blend into each and every context reflects the deep anxiety provoked by the possibility of Jewish assimilation.[46]

Viereck's novel simultaneously expresses anxieties about the emancipation of women, as well as Jews. This theme is present in Wilde's *Salome* in the princess's usurpation of male speech and was a perceived threat in the performances of Maud Allan, expressed in accusations of lesbianism and anti-British sedition.[47] Yet the furore about Allan suggests one of the uses of Salome in a culture, like that of early twentieth-century Britain, that felt deep ambivalence towards the dancing female body. Salome and the Salome dancer represented a zone of exotic and morally dubious dance from which the newly emerging discipline of 'Greek' dance could be distinguished. In fact both types of dance, as practised in the early twentieth century, had a great deal in common: bare feet, freedom of the torso, light clothing, the use of fabric as veils (see further Macintosh, this volume). Maud Allan danced both forms; Flaubert the traveller, on seeing Kuchuk Hanem's dance, likened her to an image on a Greek vase (in addition to

---

[46] See the remarks of Nochlin (1997), 10–11.
[47] Tydeman and Price (1996), 80–2; and further Macintosh, this volume.

imagining her as Judith to his Holofernes).[48] The existence of the Salome figure allowed Greek dance to present itself as the rational and respectable form by rejecting all the negative associations (female sexuality) onto the other. The strategy is clear in Ginner's characterization of 'Greek dance' as distinct from the 'Mediterranean' and the 'primitive', a distinction which is underpinned by Karl Ottfried Müller's theories of the Nordic origins of Greek culture via the 'Dorian invasions'.[49] Imaginary ideals of Greekness thus played a major part in the construction of the modern vision of the exotic Salome, whether, as in Flaubert's case, they shaped his perception of the Orient he visited in ways that are reflected in the classicizing orientalism of his *Herodias*, or whether they contributed to her construction as a negative image of classicism.

Salome thus emerges as an extraordinarily rich figure in both ancient and modern thought. Not only are the themes first evoked in the Gospel version subject to constant shifting, reorganization and re-evaluation but each new version is underpinned by the previous traditions, in particular the opposition to dance that is so unambiguously articulated by John Chrysostom. In bringing together ideas of visual pleasure and the vulnerability of the viewer, the spectre of the scheming woman, female sexuality and the conscious use of dance to seduce, while portraying the body as an active instrument, a source of economic reward and of reproductive power, the story portrays the inherent tensions and contra-dictions that could be elicited by the idea of dance in antiquity. The ways in which each later version foregrounds certain of these aspects of dance, while simultaneously occluding others, reveals the long and varied afterlife of these perceptions of dance.

---

[48] Karayianni (2004), 50 and 106.
[49] Ginner (1933), 10, 33, and 55. On Müller (1824) see Goldhill (2002), 149–50.

7

'Heroes of the Dance Floor': The Missing Exemplary Male Dancer in Ancient Sources

Edith Hall

'Why, after the reign of the dancing Sun King, was dance no longer an appropriate occupation for men?' This is the question with which Ann Daly opened an influential intervention in the feminist debate on dance. She argued, with the support of revealing quotations from the Romantic dance critic Théophile Gautier, that in the Romantic era dance became 'less a moral paradigm and more a spectacle'; the ballerina became a reified object for scrutiny, she says, by the male gaze:

Because the connotative passivity of such overt display was anathema to the virile, strong, action-oriented control of the masculine ideology, dance came to be identified as 'effeminate'.

She argues that men's effective prohibition from engaging in this self-display during high Romanticism indicates, furthermore, 'an attempt to maintain the male's virile image—his dominance—untainted by the "feminine"'.[1]

In a nutshell, ever since Louis XIV, dance has been seen as fundamentally effeminate; since we live under patriarchy, in which the female body is the principal bearer for society of erotic signification, the perceived effeminacy of dance inevitably results in it becoming conceptually sexualized and vulnerable to charges of moral depravity and aesthetic decline. These connotations add up to what we understand by 'decadence' in the widest sense of that term, incorporating also a sense of a lapsarian fall from Edenic innocence.[2] To dance was and still is to run the risk of relinquishing autonomous control over the meaning created by one's own body, and thus to relinquish all that is signified by masculinity in culture.

Daly points out that return of men to prominence in ballet in the 1970s and 1980s, with the marketing of Rudolf Nureyev, Mikhail Baryshnikov, and

[1] Daly (1987), 22.

[2] In exploring the wider semantic as well as historically specific later nineteenth-century resonances of the term 'decadence', I have found particularly helpful the analyses of Joad (1948), 55–117 and Gilman (1975).

Edward Villella, required a good deal of 'dancing is masculine' propaganda in the press, and a spate of books that hyped these performers as strong, virile, heterosexual, and athletic. In the third millennium, the necessity of making the character of the outstanding dancer, Troy Bolton in the *High School Musical* movies, a star basket-ball player, with a particular penchant for noisy break-dancing in masculine settings like used car dumps, merely underlines how little has changed. Troy Bolton is played by Zac Efron, whose indeed dazzling grace and skill are far more authentically displayed in the early 1960s dances of the movie *Hairspray* (2007). But his packaging as the new icon of the strongman dancer provides just another occasional and prodigious exception that only proves Ann Daly's rule. The dangerous associations of dancing 'will never be truly destigmatized for men (and women) as long as the oppositions of masculine–feminine are maintained, because it is due to those polarities that dance is dubbed "effeminate" in the first place'.[3]

It is incontrovertible that men who dance are inviting uneasy responses because they relinquish control over the way their body is consumed and bears meanings that are mediated by gender hierarchies. Daly's view can, however, be given historical depth and amplification by referring the argument back to antiquity, and in particular, in the second half of this chapter, to Homer. This procedure not only allows the reader who is interested in the cultural presence of the ancient dancer in the modern world to review some of the earliest and most influential passages on dance in ancient literature, but also emphasizes that the perceived effeminacy of dance is a strand in thinking that was not by any means a new phenomenon in the late eighteenth century.

The thoroughgoing liberation of men, and women, from the effeminate associations of dance would need the overhaul of those constitutive constructions of gender (and the power structures underpinning them), which happen to have been dominant not only for the last two centuries but since the earliest stages in the making of the western cultural tradition. Although, as we shall see, apologists for dance both in antiquity and from the Renaissance onwards have seized on the two ancient exemplary figures—the Greek Socrates and the biblical David—who offered them a small amount of ideological ammunition, dance has been defined as potentially effeminizing and dangerously related to sexual arousal for the entire period that comprises European cultural history. It began no more with Théophile Gautier than with the Puritans, the early Church Fathers, or with the late pagan opponents of Roman pantomime against whom Lucian's polemic is aimed in his treatise *On Dancing*. The contentious issue of dance's threat to compromise masculinity has fluctuated in intensity and has taken different forms at different periods and in different cultural contexts. Yet we risk underestimating the importance of the perceived threat, and the difficulty in countering it, if we

---

[3] Daly (1987), 24.

ignore the extent to which it informs the entire debate from antiquity through the Renaissance and beyond.

Advocates of dance as an art-form, whether ancient or modern, Lucian or Ménestrier, seem at first sight to have had rich pickings in the Mediterranean sources to which they appealed. For texts in ancient Greek and Latin are the products of a civilization where dance by men as well as women, free as well as slave, was central to numerous dimensions of public life. These included military training and state ceremonial, religious ritual, theatrical entertainment, and symposia. Ancient Greek and Roman authors make many thousands of references to dancing nymphs and maidens, and to ritual dances for either (and occasionally both) sexes, but also to properly masculine martial dances for men such as the Pyrrhic. Such references could usefully supplement the ancient discussions of the imperial era's pantomime dancer, because these discussions reveal that pantomime, which had arrived late on the ancient scene, had always been controversial and perceived by some as a sign of social degeneracy. It was therefore polemically less useful than it might have been.

The industry even of the ancient anthologists of references to dance—Plutarch and Athenaeus as well as Lucian and Libanius—is astonishing; even more so was the cherry-picking fervour of the campaigners for (and against) the social utility of dance in the Italian Renaissance, and subsequently in the seventeenth and earlier eighteenth centuries, who leapt on their ancient forerunners. The work of some of the most industrious of them was linked closely to the intensely religious form that international politics took while the Netherlands consolidated its position as a Protestant world power opposed to France:[4] a helpful example is constituted by the more than one hundred classical authors (including, inevitably Xenophon on Socrates and some passages of Homer) collected by Ioannes Meursius in *Orchestra. Sive, de saltationibus veterum* (1618); another is the anonymous pamphlet of 1683, the Dutch title of which translates as *A French Dancing Master Heckled and Helped* (*Dansmeester van Franequer geheekelt ende geholpen*).

Yet when the repertoire of standard examples from ancient texts are scrutinized more closely, what begins to become apparent is the severe shortage of the type of evidence that the proponents of dance so desperately needed—exemplary male dancers whose morals and masculinity were equally admirable. From the seminal sections on dance (bk. 3 chs. 3–4) in Ludovici Ricchieri's *Lectionum Antiquarum Libri XVI* (Venice, 1516) and Thoinot Arbeau's *Orchésographie* (Langres, 1588) onwards,[5] the Renaissance and Early Modern treatises tried to address this dearth by developing a canonical catalogue of dancing men in Greek, Roman, and indeed Old Testament sources. But it is the main purpose of this chapter to demonstrate that the material they had to work with was inherently inadequate.

---

[4] See Brinson (1966) 146–7.
[5] On the seminal nature of Ricchieri's (also known as Caelius Rhodignius') compilation of ancient testimonia on dance, see Naerebout (1997), with n. 29.

Unease with male dancing is built into the foundations of western discourse, where it has always a tendency to activate associations with erotic licence, effeminacy, and aesthetic and moral degeneracy, from Archaic Greece onwards.

The first group of ancient male dancers who are repeatedly mentioned consists of historical individuals whose fondness and aptitude for dancing were features of the manner in which they were presented in ancient sources. But almost all of these were inherently problematic as exemplars. Some were professional dancers of whom nobody knew anything beyond the fact that they were briefly named in one of the ancient treatises, which did not help advance the argument much: Telestes, a Greek theatrical dancer associated with the famously martial play *Seven against Thebes* (Athenaeus 1.22a), proudly cited, for example, in one of the dedications to Juan de Esquivel Navarro in his *Discursos sobre el arte del danzado* (1642),[6] was scarcely a household name. Another problem was that often all the promoter of dance could find was a brief reference to this dimension of the ancient figure, with no further elaboration of where, what, with whom, or why they danced (this was the case with, for example, Alexander the Great).

Much worse was the problem that several of them, if closely scrutinized, easily provided ammunition for the other side; most of the dancing Roman emperors, for example, were themselves construed as decadent and tyrannical in the ancient sources: the emperor Nero, whose cultural antics are so memorably described in Suetonius' biography, was indeed sometimes adduced by desperate dance apologists, even though he was likely to do their case more harm than good. A more respectable figure who surfaces from time to time, for example in Thoinot Arbeau's *Orchesography* (1589),[7] is the republican Roman politician Appius Claudius. He was said by Macrobius (*Saturnalia* 3.14) to have ordered dances to celebrate a triumph, but was an unsatisfactory exemplar since he was not a dancer himself.

Dance advocates also had to deal with the infamous link between drink, insanity and dancing drawn by Cicero in his announcement, when defending Lucius Murena against the accusation that he danced when drunk, that '*nemo fere saltat sobrius, nisi forte insanit*' ('hardly anyone dances sober, unless he happens to be mad' (*Pro Murena* 6). This text was quoted widely by Renaissance writers, especially opponents of dancing, although even dance apologists managed to turn it to their advantage by simply saying that this fairly familiar ancient Roman had been known to dance![8]

Yet to obscure professionals, notorious tyrants, and drunkards, the apologists could at least add Socrates, singled out as a crucial example in Lucian's *On Dancing* 25. The dedicatory sonnet by Rodrigo Martínez de Consuegra, printed at the beginning of Esquivel's treatise,[9] is typical of the genre of pro-dance

---

[6] Esquivel (1642), 4 verso, trans. Brooks (2003), 257.   [7] Arbeau (1967), 13.

[8] Arcangeli (1994), 147; for a later, satirical example see Mclaine (1711).

[9] 4v, trans. Brooks (2003), 256.

polemic in affirming that 'Socrates would have considered himself lucky in antiquity, if he could have carried out his eager desire to learn to dance, in your school.' Since Socrates provided a glimmer of hope, all the Renaissance dance historians of necessity made a great deal of him: a typical reference is Thomas Elyot's brief account in the historical section of his defence of dancing, 'Of the first begynnyng of daunsing and the old estimation therof' in section 20 of his *Boke named the Governour* (London, 1531):

Also the auncient philosophers commended daunsing; in so moche as Socrates, the wysest of all the grekes in his time, and from whom all the sectes of philosophers, as from a fountaine, were deriuied, was nat ashamed to account daunsinge amonge the seriouse disciplines, for the commendable beautie, for the apte and proportionate meuinge, and for the craftie disposition and facionyng of the body.

Elyot here recycles what had already become the standard fare in such *apologiae*, a passage in Xenophon's *Symposium*. Socrates, at a dinner party held by Callias, has partaken of gymnastic exercises before the commencement of the festivities (1.19), eaten, and enjoyed a performance organized by a Syracusan dancing-teacher, who has brought with him three youthful performers: a female pipe-player, an acrobatic female dancer, and a male harpist who can also dance (2.1–13). Socrates is particularly impressed by the beautiful body of the young man, and comments (2.27–8), 'while he danced no portion of his body remained idle; neck and legs and hands together, one and all were exercised. That is how a man should dance, who wants to keep his body light and healthy.' At this point Socrates surprises his companions by asking the Syracusan dancing master to teach him some steps. Everyone bursts out laughing.

In response, Socrates delivers the speech that was repeatedly ransacked in treatises defending the dance (2.31–3):

Well, do you find it so laughable that I desire to improve my health by exercise, to enjoy my food more, or to sleep better? Or is it, rather, that what makes you laugh is the *type* of exercise that I have chosen? But I don't want, like long-distance runners, to have my legs grow muscular and my shoulders leaner in proportion; nor, like a boxer, a broad chest and shoulders at the expense of my legs. What I want is a distribution of exertion through all my limbs, in order to give an even balance to my body.

Socrates then dismisses the possible objection that he is too old to strip in public, since he can 'do gymnastics' under cover; he imagines that they think it funny that a man with a pot-belly should dance, but he has, indeed, already been practising, and was discovered in the process by Charmides only a day or two ago (2.33–9).

This complex scene sets up the idea of dance as ridiculous in a dignified man, but excusable if it is construed as a form of physical exercise, akin to and overlapping with gymnastics, performed discreetly in pursuit of muscle tone, bodily symmetry, a good appetite, and sound sleep. The laughter arises as a result of the juxtaposition on the one hand of the dancing by three young, unnamed, and certainly non-citizen performers (two of them female), where beauty and eroticized pleasure for the audience are clearly the purpose, and on the other hand the vision of the elderly, free citizen Socrates, pot-belly and all, taking dancing lessons. The dance regimen he recommends has a very different purpose from the recreational, sexualized dancing with the purpose of providing the spectators with pleasure that concluded some symposia; this is underscored by the famous danced enactment at the end of the dialogue, in which the Syracusans' beautiful slaves perform again, this time, in an erotically charged manner, the seduction of Ariadne by Dionysus (9.3–7). Even here the aphrodisiac effect on the spectators is carefully defused by containing its physical expression within marital relations: we are told that the result is that the married symposiasts leap on their horses to go back to their wives, and the unmarried ones swear to get married.

Socrates' advocacy of dance in pursuit of health, given the dearth of male exemplars of dancing in classical sources, proved vital to all subsequent apologists of dance (see Figure 7.1), however much the actual passage, read fully in its context, itself points to the inherent eroticism of mixed-sex dancing by beautiful bodies. This was noted by William Prynne in *Histrio-Mastix*, who shrewdly pointed out that dance advocates who cited Socrates as their exemplar had deliberately neglected 'Zenophons dancing Trull, who enamoured Socrates and

Figure 7.1 Socrates Dancing (Paris 1790).

the other Spectators, with her dancing and Player-like action'.[10] Most references to Socratic dancing did carefully distort or trim what is actually said in Xenophon, for example John Weaver's *An Essay towards the History of Dancing* (1712), which simply said that 'the best of Philosophers Socrates, and the best of Men among the Heathens learn'd to dance'.[11] Xenophon's rhetorical thrust was actually better suited to the rather different writings of the sixteenth-century medical humanists, such as Girolamo Mercuriale's *De Arte gymnastica* (1569), whose discussions of diet and exercise drew on ancient treatments of gymnastics in the context of the cultivation of health to a degree that virtually excluded references to contemporary practices.[12] Socrates was also adduced by the Protestant dietician, Joseph Duchesne, who encouraged men to dance.[13] But the example of Socrates actually lent itself all too easily to undermining the case for dance as an art form. A fine expression of the tension underlying this difficult distinction can be found in the works of Claudius Deodatus, a seventeenth-century court physician at Basel, who was very worried about dancing because he could see its health benefits but on no account must it be performed *for pleasure.* It must be for bodily exercise, before, not after dinner, and not indecent. Dancing for pleasure is something that barbarians and pagans invented.[14]

When the promoters of dance turned to the Bible, especially the Old Testament, the picture looked just a little more promising. Although critics of dancing had strong support in the incident of the Golden Calf (Exodus 32), which was by far the most frequent example cited by Christians as evidence of the pagan and diabolical nature of the dance,[15] there were available for citation several exemplary female dancers in the Old Testament. They included Miriam, the sister of Moses and Aaron (Exodus 15: 20), Jephthah's daughter (Judges 11:34), the women of Israel who danced to greet Saul (1 Samuel 18:6), and Judith who led the women in the dance (Judith 15:12, 13). These model sisters, daughters, wives and mothers are routinely offered up by dance apologists as counter-ballast to the Salome archetype (see Webb, this volume). But it is much more important that there is one *man* who dances in the Old Testament. Not only did he dance, but he possessed unquestionable, indeed talismanic moral status and authority. This biblical dancer is David, the most important king of Israel, God's chosen and anointed leader, the ancestor of Jesus Christ, who dances when introducing the Ark of the Covenant (see Figure 7.2).

In these third-millennial days, when close knowledge of the Old Testament can be no more assumed in any cultural historian than close knowledge of Homer, it is worth fully citing the story in the version that English-language readers will have heard it from the date of its publication by King James I in

[10] Prynne (1633), 249.   [11] Weaver (1712), 27.
[12] Archangeli (2000), 11.   [13] Duchesne (1606), 294–5, 300–10.
[14] Deodatus (1628).   [15] Arcangeli (1994), 145.

Figure 7.2 David dancing and playing his harp before the Ark (1678–1743).

1611. David has the Ark of the Covenant brought into the city with gladness (2 Samuel 6:13–17, 20–1):

13: And it was so, that when they that bare the ark of the LORD had gone six paces, he sacrificed oxen and fatlings.

14: And David danced before the LORD with all his might; and David was girded with a linen ephod.

15: So David and all the house of Israel brought up the ark of the LORD with shouting, and with the sound of the trumpet.

16: And as the ark of the LORD came into the city of David, Michal Saul's daughter looked through a window, and saw king David leaping and dancing before the LORD; and she despised him in her heart.

17: And they brought in the ark of the LORD, and set it in his place, in the midst of the tabernacle that David had pitched for it: and David offered burnt offerings and peace offerings before the LORD.

20: Then David returned to bless his household. And Michal the daughter of Saul came out to meet David, and said, How glorious was the king of Israel to day, who uncovered himself to day in the eyes of the handmaids of his servants, as one of the vain fellows shamelessly uncovereth himself!

21: And David said unto Michal, It was before the LORD, which chose me before thy father, and before all his house, to appoint me ruler over the people of the LORD, over Israel: therefore will I play before the LORD.

David, dressed in the priestly garb of the linen *ephod*, danced before the Lord with all his might.[16] He danced because he was God's appointed leader of Israel. The passage has always been cited in defences of dancing, as the singular *locus classicus* for the good Jewish male dance.[17] It confronted the ancient Christian anti-dance polemicists with a challenge, as can be seen from the austere third-century Roman presbyter Novatian's uncharacteristically pallid and evasive insistence that David's dance was not comparable to the pagan dances Novatian so disliked, since it was performed in a respectable manner during the worship of God (*de Spectaculis* 3.2–3):

That David led dancing in the sight of God is no excuse for the Christian faithful to sit in the theatre, for he did not distort his limbs in obscene gestures while dancing to a tale of Grecian lust. The nablas, kinuras. tibias, tympana and citharas played for God, not an idol. It is not thereby permitted that unlawful things be seen. By a trick of the devil sacred things have been transferred into illicit ones.

St Ambrose insisted that David's singing and dancing was '*non pro lasciuia, sed pro religione*', and consequently it was obvious that he cannot have used the types of motion that are associated with professional performers (*Apology for the Prophet David* 58.5). The Puritan John Northbrooke in his 1577 polemic against dancing and other pleasures goes further, and insists that what David actually danced was obviously warlike and indeed 'may be called *Saltatio pyrrhica*'.[18] But the reason why David, like Socrates, was ultimately difficult to develop into a full-scale model of the exemplary male dancer lies in the way that the biblical text

---

[16] David's dance is vigorous: he 'rotated' or 'whirled' (from the verb *karar*) with all his might and 'leapt' or 'jumped' (from *pzz*). Thanks to my father, Stuart Hall, for help with the Hebrew and with biblical sources, and for pointing out that the strength of this language, and therefore the vigour of the dance, is, interestingly, already softened in the Greek of the early Church Fathers.

[17] Andresen (1974), 350–1.   [18] Northbrooke (1577), 119.

itself develops. Any dance apologist working within Christian culture and seeking to find support in the details of the text would almost certainly be dismayed by what he found there. John Weaver was surely sensible to keep his summary of the passage to a minimalist single sentence, 'And *David* danc'd before the Ark; his pious Zeal transporting him to this Corporeal Exultation.'[19] For the biblical narrative acknowledges within its embedded differential perspectives the strong possibility that such dancing, especially in revealing clothes before people of the opposite sex, could be construed as a shameless act of a 'vain fellow'. Indeed, it was construed as such by the kingly dancer's own legitimate wife, Michal, even if she was firmly put in the wrong.[20]

A few pro-dance writers somewhat nervously quote Jesus rebuking the Pharisees in the gospel of Matthew (11:17), saying, 'We have piped unto you and you have not danced',[21] which compares Jesus' festive life-style to a children's dance-game, but does not literally commend dancing. It is, indeed, possible to feel sorry for the pro-dance writers during the whole discussion between the first Renaissance treatises and the late eighteenth century, on the ground that they were completely unfamiliar with the apocryphal *Acts of John*, which includes the startling story of Jesus' own dance with his disciples (chs. 94–6). According to this work of what is almost certainly early Christian proto-monastic fiction (perhaps as early as 200 CE), the night before his arrest, Jesus told the disciples to stand, hand-in-hand, forming a ring about him. He stood in the middle, and instructed them in a call-and-response hymn which includes the lines 'Grace danceth. I would pipe; dance ye all', 'The Whole on high hath part in our dancing', and 'Whoso danceth not, knoweth not what cometh to pass'. Jesus concluded by telling the disciples to respond in like kind to his dancing: he went on, mysteriously, to say 'thou that dancest, perceive what I do, for thine is this passion of the manhood, which I am about to suffer'.[22] This may be evidence that the early Christians who enjoyed the *Acts of John* danced, although in any case their solemn bishops were within decades to put a stop to it. Yet it is revealing for us because it is such a striking example of the kind of text on which the Renaissance writers would certainly have seized had it been accessible to them.[23]

The third group of exemplary ancient males cited in the treatises consists of mythical figures, divine or heroic, connected with dancing. Several of these were mythical bards such as Orpheus and Musaeus, whose figuring as dancers was

[19] Weaver (1712), 63.
[20] Arcangeli (2000), 13 offers a collection of passages where David is cited in support of dancing for the promotion of health, for example in a 1550 commentary on dietetics, by the Lyon physician Jérôme de Monteux.
[21] *ēulēsamen humin kai ouk ōrchēsasthe*, e.g. Arbeau (1967), 13.
[22] Translation by James (1924).
[23] For further sources and bibliography on Jesus' dance with his disciples, see Elliott (1993), 307, 309. I am very grateful to Stuart Hall for drawing my attention to this fascinating text.

tendentious at best, or the ethically problematic Proteus, the shape-shifting god who seemed to anticipate the art of the pantomime dancer. Even more unfortunately for the dance apologists, the divinity most associated with dancing was Dionsyus/Bacchus, whose other connections with madness and intoxication severely compromised his usefulness, as noticed already by Rinaldo Corso in 1555.[24]

Euripides' *Bacchae*, indeed, provided easy cannon fodder for Prynne in *Histrio-mastix*.[25] But Apollo was considerably more promising. One of the most influential pictures of dancing of all time is drawn at the opening of the Pythian section of the Homeric *Hymn to Apollo*, where the archer god very nearly becomes a divine prototype for the male dancer, but not quite (195–206). While his parents Zeus and Leto watch with pleasure, the Muses sing, the Graces, Seasons, Harmonia, Hebe, and Aphrodite dance an archetypal women's chorus, 'holding each other by the wrist'. Apollo's sister sings along, Ares and Hermes 'sport' (*paizous'*) amongst them, 'while Apollo plays his lyre stepping high and beautifully and a radiance shines around him as his feet and close-woven chiton flash'. But even this passage does not really offer the exemplary role model the dance apologist so desired. Apollo steps high as he plays his instrument, while the gods Ares and Hermes (often depicted as rather immature) are larking around, but the only real dancers are female.

The third group of potential exemplars were the mythical founding fathers of different types of military dance, especially the Pyrrhic and en(h)oplic, performed with spear and shield. There are several ancient (but non-Homeric) aetiologies for these hyper-male dances, which variously link them with Achilles, or Neoptolemus (also known as Pyrrhus), the Spartans Castor and Pollux, the semi-legendary Spartan lawgiver Lycurgus, the Theban Epaminondas, the Cretan Pyrrhichus, leader of the legendary warrior guild of the Curetes, and also with ceremonies at warriors' funeral pyres and at Athens with the chaste, intelligent goddess of war, Athena herself.[26] The Curetes were seen as equivalent to the Roman dancing priests of Mars, the Salii, and often coupled with them in argumentation. Some apologists for dancing try to develop the Pyrrhic dance into a legitimate forerunner of dancing recreationally or as an art-form, even though as a model for artistic dancing, since it insisted on a universal link between dance and militarism, it had obvious limitations.

The mythical founding fathers were in turn associated, in many treatises on dance, with the ethnic groups whose dancing activities were stressed in ancient sources, and who had already been seized on by pro-dance polemicists such as Lucian in antiquity: the Spartans, Cretans, and Thessalians dominate these discussions. The information about these communities that is documented in

---

[24] Corso (1555), 8 verso. I am very grateful to Frederick Naerebout for taking the time to discuss Corso with me, and for letting me use his unpublished translation of the dialogue.
[25] Prynne (1633), 236.   [26] Borthwick (1970).

ancient sources provided a masculine, warlike model of dancing in the context of military training, in company with other men, which overlapped with public ceremonial and ritual dancing in these warlike societies.[27] Such sources were only marginally useful for anyone wanting to advocate dancing by men for artistic reasons geared to the generation of aesthetic pleasure in the viewer. Other ethnic groups appear from time to time, especially the Etruscans, who were used to avoid the (correct) impression that pantomime was a relatively late invention in terms of pagan antiquity and associated with the empire. To ensure that pantomime was provided with the desired antiquity, reaching far back into the mists of time, rather than being a true 'decadence' as a sign of deterioration from more manly Roman Republican dancing, dance apologists often claimed that it had originated much earlier in indigenous Italian dances of one kind and another.[28]

The final important category of ancient authoritative figure cited in treatises in support of dancing consists of 'Homer' and some characters in his epics. The Homeric epics present dance in an ambiguous way which is nevertheless of crucial importance to dance history and cultural history. The poems were very early identified as foundational texts that offered paradigms of moral behaviour and a shared psychological currency that circulated throughout the Greek world. But they also formed the basis of the education of everyone in ancient Mediterranean society from at least the seventh century BCE. For a thousand years, countless schoolboys living under the Macedonian or Roman empires, whose first languages were Syrian, Nubian, or Gallic as well as Latin or Greek, studied Homeric epic intensively, and had committed large swathes to memory by early manhood, when they learned to be statesman, soldiers, lawyers, historians, philosophers, biographers, poets, dramatists, novelists, painters, or sculptors.[29] All the genres and media these men produced were formed in response to the great epic *Ur*-works in the Greek language. No later author could ever again make a fresh start when shaping a narrative or a visual representation of single combat, a voyage, a funeral, or indeed a dance. It was surely partly their psychological internalization of what we shall now see was the highly ambivalent Homeric picture of the male dancer that held respectable ancient Greek and Roman men back from recreational dancing for pleasure and outside the strictly defined arenas of military training, and, increasingly, health care.

When Homer was once again placed at the heart of the curriculum, by the Renaissance humanists, the process was continued into modern western culture.

---

[27] Perhaps the polarity between fighting and dancing originated not in an opposition but in the close similarity between training for the steps in military drill and in dance. This, at any rate, is the argument of William MacNeill in *Keeping Together in Time* (1995). The dance/drill connection may be personified in the earlier, Sumerian tradition in the figure of the Sargonic divine she-warrior Inanna, who made her mortal troops 'dance' on the battlefield. Battle, indeed, was called 'the dance of Inanna'.

[28] e.g. L'Aulnaye (1790), 62–3.

[29] See, with further bibliography, Hall (2008*a*), ch. 1.

John Ruskin was absolutely correct when he stressed that it does not matter whether or not Homer is actually read, since 'All Greek gentlemen were educated under Homer. All Roman gentlemen, by Greek literature. All Italian, and French, and English gentlemen, by Roman literature, and by its principles.'[30] The Homeric poems became widely available in accessible modern languages as well as easy Latin not long after the first printed Greek edition was published in Florence by the Cretan Antonios Damilas, in two volumes (1488). Translations made the Homeric epic dance scenes available to all who wished to consult them. Moreover, the translated vehicles which brought Homeric epics to the public often elaborated what they found in ways that interpreted quite as much as they translated. With Poliziano's Latin hexameter translation of *Iliad* books 2–5 (1472–5), composed under the patronage of Lorenzo di Medici, for example, we can see how the bedroom scene between the Homeric dancer Paris and Helen was read by the earliest Renaissance readers who encountered it; Poliziano thoroughly augmented the glamour of Alexander's personal appearance, and the erotic intensity of the episode. Where much of Poliziano's version is atmospherically Virgilian, these sequences are distinctly like the much more 'decadent' Roman love elegists in their diction and tone.[31]

Through translation, adaptation, or more indirectly, Homer has shaped all our ethical and aesthetic categories. In the case of the ethics and aesthetics of *dance*, the genealogical stemma through which Homer has exerted that influence is particularly clear, even though one important branch of the tree—Aelius Aristides—is missing. As I have outlined briefly in a previous book published by the APGRD,[32] and as Lada-Richards explores in more detail in the present volume, the text that proved most conspicuous—indeed ubiquitous—in the discussions surrounding the emergence and rise of ballet in the seventeenth and eighteenth centuries was the canonical defence of pantomime dating from the Roman imperial era, Lucian's sparkling apologetic treatise *On Dancing*, addressed to a Cynic philosopher named Crato.

Lucian was answering, indirectly, a then still recent oration that is most unfortunately lost to posterity, an attack on the triviality and moral injuriousness of pantomime composed by the brilliant orator Aelius Aristides. Aristides' oration was perhaps composed in response to moves to include pantomime dancing in the programme of competition events at sacred festivals, a privilege previously jealously guarded by performers of recited drama and of citharody, who looked down and also envied the popularity of their new, athletic rivals.[33]

---

[30] Ruskin (1869).   [31] Rubinstein (1983), 55–61.   [32] Hall (2008*b*).
[33] See Hall (2008*c*) 16–17 with n. 47, written with the help of information from Professor Glen Bowersock, who argued this position in a paper delivered at a symposium on Aelius Aristides held at Columbia University, New York, on 13 April 2007 (the organizer was William Harris). The paper will be published as part of the conference proceedings.

The loss of Aelius Aristides' polemic is unfortunate, because it laid down the parameters within which all later antique authors, whether Christian or pagan, discussed the admissibility of the pantomime dancers in a respectable community. It is, however, possible to recover many of his arguments from those who tried to refute him, above all Libanius, who quotes him and answers him directly in his oration (no. 64) *Reply to Aristides on Behalf of the Dancers*, although it dates from more than two centuries later.[34] Even though this oration did not itself inform the post-Renaissance dance treatises until much later than Lucian,[35] it shows how the terms of the debate in the Roman empire had always been deeply informed by images from the Homeric poems.

Lucian's treatise may also be responding, less explicitly, to Aristides in its profusion of references not only to Lotus-Eaters, Sirens, Proteus, Circe, and *Odyssey* 5 (*On Dancing*, 3, 4, 8, 19, 85), but to the seminal passages that allude to dancing in the *Iliad* which we are about to consider in more detail.[36] The type of material and issue Aelius Aristides used was also still being rehashed by the patristic critics of dance (Novatian, Tatian, Tertullian, and Arnobius as well as John Chrysostom) writing in Latin and Greek up to several centuries later. And it is clear from these sources—themselves, of course, endlessly recycled by the anti-dance controversialists of more recent times—that the Homeric poems were fundamental to the ways in which the argument had been formulated.

It is important, therefore, to look in detail at what the Homeric poems have to say about dancing, and some of the results suggest that they must have been less than wholly encouraging to people interested in *promoting* dance, at least for men. At the climax of the *Iliad*, for example, the elderly Priam has finally decided to embark, at great personal risk, on the dangerous mission into the enemy camp to attempt to recover Hector's corpse from the tent of Achilles. He launches a devastating rhetorical attack on his surviving sons (24.248–64),

> rebuking Helenus, Paris, noble Agathon, Pammon, Antiphonus,
> Polites of the loud battle-cry, Deiphobus, Hippothous, and Dius.
> The old man summoned the nine of them and gave them orders:
> 'Come to me at once, you worthless sons who cause me grief. How I wish
> You had all been killed at the ships rather than Hector . . . I have had
> The bravest (*aristous*) sons in wide Troy . . . yet Ares has slain them
> And those of whom I am ashamed are alone left me—frauds,
> Dancers (*orchēstai*), bravest (*aristoi*) at beating the ground with your feet,
> Stealers of lambs and kids from your own people,
> Why do you not get a wagon ready for me at once,
> And stow all these things upon it so I can get on the road?

---

[34] See Mesk (1908).

[35] The crucial event in Libanius studies was the relatively late appearance of Johann Reiske's complete *Orationes and Declamationes*, published in Altenburg between 1791 and 1797.

[36] *On Dancing* 8 (Meriones as dancer), 13 (the Cretan dancing scene on Achilles' shield), 85 (Menelaus' speech in *Iliad* 13).

The sons who are bravest and excel on the battlefield are explicitly contrasted with the sons who are scathingly said to be bravest at their dance-steps, a contrast underlined by the repeated term *aristous/aristoi*.[37] There is a clear polarization in Priam's rebuke of the figure who dies on the battlefield to save his fatherland from a foreign enemy, and the irresponsible 'hero of the dance' who commits crimes against his own people. Dance is linked with social degeneracy. Dancing is the key trope in this most primal and definitive expression of the difference between good and bad masculinity, and around it are organized a series of other associations. The scholiasts on the *Iliad* were quite clear that the term showed that these sons of Priam were certainly not heroes where it mattered, 'in wars' and that it had connotations of softness.[38] No wonder it is not cited in Lucian's defence of dancing.

Yet Aristides may well have quoted it, and even if he did not, its very absence may have spoken loud to Lucian's audience. The passage was famous in antiquity and almost certainly inspired the orientalized dance movements of the Trojan chorus in the third play of Aeschylus' Iliadic trilogy *Phrygians*, remembered by a character in Aristophanes as 'making many gestures, in one direction, and another, and another'.[39] This is important because it suggests that later Greeks heard the rebuke as somehow connected with the Trojan ethnicity of the 'heroes of the dance floor'; this in turn suggests that the text offers one of the very few indications of a cultural difference between the Achaeans and the Trojans in the *Iliad*, or at least of an ethnocentric agenda that implies that the Trojans, doomed to defeat, were over-inclined to the pursuit of pleasure. More recently, the striking image has certainly encouraged translators to adapt and extend the connotations of effeminacy and eroticization, for example in Pope's loose paraphrase, where Priam complains that Mars had taken all his valorous sons:

> And left me these, a soft and servile crew,
> Whose days the feast and wanton dance employ
> Gluttons and flatterers, the contempt of Troy.[40]

The Trojans are not, as in Priam's rhetoric, just heroes of the dance floor, but over-eat, are soft and servile, and their dance is unambivalently presented as wanton!

Unlike all his brothers, Paris/Alexander has once before in the poem been explicitly imagined as a dancer, and attentive listeners, when they heard Priam's rebuke, will have remembered the earlier passage: ancient commentators on the poem certainly did. When considering the third book of the *Iliad*, which is the part of the poem where all the key players on the Trojan side are introduced they

---

[37] The use of the term *orchēstai*, moreover, may have activated ironic associations by contrast with the Homeric phrase *orchamos andrōn*, 'leader of men' (*Iliad* 2.837 etc.).

[38] See Erbse (1969–77), 5. 568.   [39] Fragment 696B.3 *KA*; see Hall (1989), 133.

[40] Pope (1783), 2. 338.

cross-referred their readers to Priam's rebuke.[41] Alexander has already shown himself to be less than a perfect warrior by shrinking from facing Menelaus—whose wife he has stolen—in single combat. In consequence, Alexander's brother Hector has already chided him for cowardice. Paris has eventually agreed to fight, but has been worsted by Menelaus, who despite interventions by Aphrodite is about to kill him. So Aphrodite rescues her favourite, and whisks him away to his bedroom in the palace. She now needs to make Helen keep him from death on the battlefield, and so she disguises herself as an old slave, who grabs Helen by her fragrant robe, and speaks to her (3.390–4):

> Come with me; Alexander is calling you to go home.
> He is there in his chamber, on his inlaid bed, radiating beauty
> And gorgeously dressed. You wouldn't think he had just arrived from fighting
> With a man (*andri*), but that he was off to the dance,
> Or had just stopped dancing to sit down there.

The archetypal male lover is here visualized as a dancer, dressed for a dance or relaxing just after dancing. He reclines on his inlaid bed where he waits for his fragrant wife, rather than standing upright on the battlefield and grappling with a man. The antithesis of the warrior and the dancer/lover is crystallized and consolidated in the uneasy sex scene that follows immediately afterwards. Paris is full of desire, and despite chiding him for cowardice, Helen allows him to make love to her while his comrades suffer on the battlefield. One of the ancient *scholia* here comments, interestingly, that dancing is for young men 'who are not yet married', leading one late twentieth-century commentator to remark approvingly that in looking as though he were off to a dance, Homer implies 'just the right hint of possible decadence'.[42]

One of the few other passages that reference male dancing in the *Iliad* works with a similar duality between war and the dance. The one occasion where the warrior figured as a dancer is on the Achaean side, he is a Cretan, and his dancing is associated with his particular prowess as a warrior. Aeneas taunts Meriones, who has nimbly dodged his spear, boasting that if he *had* managed to hit him, he would have made an end of him, 'even though' he is a dancer (*orchēstēn*, 16.617). The possibility is fleetingly envisaged here of a type of dance, with Cretan connections, which does not impugn but enhances a warrior's ability. In antiquity and subsequently it has sometimes been read as a solitary Homeric reference to the Pyrrhic dance. In Dio Chrysostom's *Second Discourse on Kingship*, for example, Alexander lectures his father Philip on the type of dancing which should be allowed by a good king (60):

our king should institute dance movements and measures that are not marked by reeling or violent motions, but are as virile and sober as may be, composed in a sedate rhythm;

---

[41] Erbse (1969–77), 1. 428.   [42] Ibid.; Kirk (1985), 322.

the dance should be the 'enhoplic,' the execution of which is not only a tribute to the gods but a drill in warfare as well—the dance in which the poet says Meriones was skilful.

The dance-conscious reader of the *Iliad* could only find two other enigmatic references to dance with potentially positive connotations, and they both occur in book 13. When Menelaus kills Peisander, during the long period of the Trojans' ascendancy, he addresses them in the plural: this is how they will, he threatens, be driven back from the ships (13.623–5): 'You cowardly she-dogs! (*kakai kunes*), you did not fear the terrible anger of Zeus, avenger of violated hospitality, who will one day destroy your lofty town.' But then Menelaus turns from addressing the Trojans to apostrophizing Zeus (13.631–9):

How can you favour the Trojans, these wrongdoers, who are so presumptuous
About their prowess that they can't get enough of the din of war?
It is possible to have too much of anything, whether sleep, sex, sweet singing or
Blameless dancing (*amumonos orchēthmoio*),[43] although most people
Would rather have too much of these than of war. But the Trojans
Can't get enough of battle!

Here dance is yet again rhetorically opposed to war and associated with sex, and in the mouth of Paris' rival, the unerotic warrior Menelaus (who is nevertheless not always as brave as he might be and is by no means a fighter of the first rank). But the flexibility and rhetorical versatility of the topic of dance in epic discourse shine here through Menelaus' inversion of expectation. The very Trojans whose masculinity is impugned—they are cowardly she-dogs—are here also criticized for being too keen to fight, when there are things that a sensible man would rather be doing, which include dancing and sex. This is, effectively, the only passage in Homer where dance seems to be approved by a masculine hero who is also emphatically a Greek, which rather puzzled at least one ancient scholiast, who commented on the epithet 'blameless', that it showed that some dancing was blameworthy, or 'low' (*phaulon*).[44] Menelaus' speech was nevertheless noticed by dance advocates, but needed to be misquoted somewhat, since the notion embedded in the rhetorical context, that you could have too much dance, like too much sleep and sex, scarcely supported their arguments!

Toward the end of the same book it is the Trojan Polydamas who says to Hector that he should listen to good advice, because god has distributed gifts among men so that some are, like Hector, good at war, while others excel at dancing (*orchēstun*), some at singing, and some at thinking strategically (13.730–4). It is interesting, however, that already in antiquity the lines that include dancing and singing as manly gifts, to be counted alongside fighting and thinking, were

---

[43] On the epithet 'blameless' see further below, n. 54.
[44] Erbse (1969–77), 3. 521.

deleted by assiduous scholars as inappropriate to the tone of the poem; the line was actually omitted from most of the best ancient manuscripts. Even in Leaf and Bayfield's late Victorian commentary on the *Iliad* the line was described as 'a tasteless interpolation'.[45]

This leaves the most famous Iliadic passage of obvious interest to dance historians. It is difficult to decode because it is not set in the 'here and now' of Priam's Troy and the battlefield outside it, but in a remote time depicted by a divinity on a priceless artwork. Thoinot Arbeau was followed by many when he defended dance by saying, simply, 'Vulcan engraved a dance upon a shield as a symbol of beauty',[46] referring to the last, nostalgic scene at Knossos which Hephaestus hammers onto the shield that he makes for Achilles (18.590–606):

> And the famous strong-armed smith decorated it with a dance floor (*choron*)
> Like the one which Daedalus once fashioned for lovely-haired Ariadne
> In the wide spaces of Knossos. There youths and maidens worth many cattle
> Were dancing (*orcheunt*), holding each other by the wrists.
> The girls were clothed in light linen dresses, the boys in fine-spun chitons,
> Shimmering with a touch of olive oil. The maidens wore exquisite garlands
> And the youths wore golden daggers hanging from silver sword-belts.
> Some of the time they would run fluently on their responsive feet,
> Like a potter bending to try out his wheel in his hands, to see if it will run
> Smoothly. At other times they would run in rows athwart each other.
> And around the lovely dancing a great crowd watched with pleasure,
> While in the middle two acrobats (*kubistēres*) revolved, leading
> The rhythm of the performance.

This passage represents a thoroughly glamorized picture, formed in the eighth or seventh century BCE, of what dancing had looked like long ago in the bygone age of glorious heroes in which the *Iliad* was imagined to be set. It is an Archaic Greek picture of how a god might have portrayed a human courtship dance in the already distant Mycenean or Minoan times.

Not only is it set in the remote past, when gorgeous brides were still bought with expensive gifts rather than sold off with dowries, but it is specifically set in Knossos. 'The picture these lines create is as vivid as if the frescoes of the Minoan palace had suddenly come to life', is a typical scholar's response.[47] Another way of putting it is that it was clearly one of the texts inside Arthur Evans's head when he presented the frescoes of Knossos, especially the 'Miniature Fresco of the Sacred Grove and the Dance' to the world.[48] The most striking feature of the dance from the perspective of a historian of ancient performance practice, however, is the intermixing, or alternating, of male and female performers. The dancers on the miniature fresco are actually female. Geometric and classical Greek art shows a great number of single-sex choruses, and occasionally a female

---

[45] Leaf and Bayfield (1898), 2. 326.   [46] Arbeau (1967), 13.
[47] Burns (1974–5), 2.   [48] Evans (1930), plate 18.

chorus led by a single man, but there is hardly a single secure instance of dancing together in what is probably meant to be understood as an alternating girl/boy pattern.[49]

The physical contact between marriageable young people of opposite sexes is one of the features of the dance that can easily be construed as part of a fantasy, not of anything debauched or decadent, since the erotic overtones are carefully positioned within the context of the intention to marry, but certainly of sensuousness and luxury. The passage's effect is created through its accumulation of details—the garlands, the fine costumes, the glistening oil, the gold and silver accoutrements, the light-footed running. But this scene of fantasy-embroidered nostalgia for a beautiful lost past does prudently locate these desirable young dancers, their minds fixed on mating, in a public, open-air place where they are supervised by a happy multitude.

Hephaestus' Knossos scene encodes an Archaic Greek's imaginative responses to whatever traces Minoan and Mycenaean culture had left in the visible world or the cultural imagination several hundred years after they had disappeared. If the past is another country, most of the other great Homeric dance scenes, those in the *Odyssey*, are set in similarly liminal imagined spaces. The suitors in Ithaca are said to spend the whole evening taking pleasure in dance and song at the precise moment when the poem introduces the painful contrast between their hedonism and Telemachus' increasing seriousness of purpose (1.421). This certainly inspired Sir John Davies to frame his poetic advocacy of 'the authenticall and laudable use of dauncing' in his *Orchestra* (1496), published soon after the *Odyssey* had entered the cultural imagination, as a dialogue held in Odysseus' absence between Penelope and her courtly lover, the suitor Antinous.

However, the most famous and most discussed Homeric dance scene is the one that takes place in Phaeacia, on the marginal island of Scherie that forms the threshold between the supernatural world of Odysseus' wanderings and the 'real' world of Ithaca. After leaving the wholly super-mortal world of Calypso's island, Odysseus is shipwrecked on the Phaeacians' beach, and they are eventually able to transport him physically in their ship from Scherie to Ithaca. Yet Scherie is not part of the ordinary human world; it is a utopia where food grows automatically and people live in endless pursuit of pleasure through recreational activities. Its ontological and indeed its 'ethical' status was a prominent matter for discussion by ancient philosophers from Plato onwards. Arete, its Queen, had for ancient readers an uncomfortable degree of status: Odysseus is instructed by Athena herself as well as Nausicaa that he must supplicate her before Alcinous (which he does at 8.146–50). This suggests that Scherie, in comparison with the 'proper' patriarchal order prescriptively described in Ithaca, has an 'inverted-world'

---

[49] Lonsdale (1995), 283 n. 27, however, argues that the lack of evidence for mixed-sex dancing in the ancient Greek world may be purely accidental.

matriarchal flavour in company with the islands inhabited by Calpyso, Circe, the Sirens and of course the Laestrygonians with their enormous royal females.

The young Phaeacian men are figured as dancers before Homer's audience has met even one of them directly, in the scene where Nausicaa tells her father that she wants to do the laundry. She explains that she is anxious to ensure that her brothers are properly dressed 'when they go to council or the dance' (6.63–5). In Phaeacia, young men's clothing is something to be looked upon with approval or disapproval, by women as well as men, when they are engaged in the public activities of council-chamber deliberation, or dancing. King Alcinous subsequently confirms to Odysseus that the Phaeacians are naturally gifted at certain activities (8.246–65):

> 'We are not particularly remarkable boxers, nor yet wrestlers,
> But we are very fast on our feet and incomparable sailors.
> We love to feast incessantly, we love music and dancing
> Newly washed linen, warm baths and beds. So come now, you
> Phaeacians who are the best at dancing, begin the fun, so
> Our guest may tell his friends, when he returns home,
> How much we excel all other peoples at sailing, running,
> Dancing and minstrelsy. One of you, go and fetch the sweet-sounding
> Lyre of Demodocus, which I think is lying in my house.'
> Godlike Alcinous finished speaking. A herald arose to retrieve
> The hollow lyre from the royal household, and the nine men
> Chosen to be umpires, responsible for managing the sporting events,
> Presented themselves. They smoothed out the dance-floor,
> Making a fine broad space, and soon the herald returned with
> The lyre for Demodocus, who took his place at the centre.
> And the young men in the bloom of youth who were skilled at dancing
> Began to tread the sacred ground with their feet, and the sight of their
> Feet flashing amazed Odysseus in his heart.

This passage is repeatedly adduced by Homeric scholars in the unceasing debates over the manner in which ancient Greek epic poetry was originally performed. The Greek does not make clear whether the dance of the young men continues while Demodocus sings his song of Olympian adultery—a dance which as late as 1947 one estimable scholar still believed could only have taken the form of 'a kind of farcical cabaret show'[50]—or whether they dance a separate choral prelude or hymn of some kind. Despite its ambiguity, the passage, naturally, figures large in the studies by the scholars, most recently A. P. David, who from time to time argue that hexameter Homeric poetry was indeed originally accompanied throughout by dancing.[51]

The passage is also of profound importance in cultural history because, whatever the truth of David's claim, dancers have always been prompted by it

---

[50] Stanford (1947), 338.   [51] David (2006); see also Georgiades (1956).

to stage danced versions of the 'Lay of Ares and Aphrodite'. One of the most significant of them was John Weaver's *The Loves of Mars and Venus* at Drury Lane in 1717, now generally held to have been 'the first *ballet d'action* in Europe'.[52] Weaver described the work in his subtitle as 'a dramatick entertainment of dancing attempted in imitation of the pantomimes of the ancient Greeks and Romans', and he knew that in the ancient world the theme was often danced, indeed it was one of the few pantomimes that Lucian had described in any detail (*On Dancing* 63). But it is important to see how Weaver's updated revival took care to keep his star male dancer, the enormously tall and dignified Louis Dupré, appropriately masculine and warlike. Although Mars seduces Venus in the fourth Act, he is introduced in the first scene of all, performing a Pyrrhic dance in a military camp.

In the original scene in the *Odyssey*, whether or not we are to understand that there was dancing throughout Demodocus' performance of his sexy song about the adultery of Aphrodite and Ares, a new dance commences at its conclusion (8.370–80):

> Then Alcinous told Laodamas and Halius to dance by themselves,
> For no one was their equal. So they took a fine red ball in their hands
> Made for them by the skill of Polybus, and one of them took to bending
> Himself backwards and throwing it skywards, while the other
> Leapt off the ground and caught it easily before it fell again to the floor.
> When they had completed their vertical ball feat
> They began dancing on the fertile earth, changing their positions
> Frequently, while the other youths stood by the dance-floor beating time,
> And applauding loudly.

Odysseus is awestruck by these acrobatic Phaeacian dancers (8.384), but in antiquity, they attracted a good deal of criticism from the censorious. The Christian readers of the *Odyssey* such as St Basil (*Homily* 22, 5.25–42) actually went to considerable lengths to prove that the point of the Phaeacia episode was to show that Odysseus taught a previously decadent society how to behave with more restraint!

Stoics and other moralists saw Alcinous' manifesto of the Phaeacian way of life as indicating an *excessive* love of pleasure and recreation in Phaeacia; critics include Heraclides Ponticus (quoted by a scholiast on *Od*. 13.119) and Horace, *Epistles* 1.2.28–9. It is fascinating to find Brian Hainsworth, in his late twentieth-century commentary on the passage, still defending the Phaeacians from such charges by insisting that the dancing is a decorous sign of a peaceful and well-ordered society that contrasts with the 'disorderly licence of the suitors' Ithaca'.[53] Plutarch argued that the point of the inclusion in the *Odyssey* of the ribald tale of

---

[52] Brinson (1966), 164.
[53] Hainsworth in Heubeck, West, and Hainsworth (1988), 1. 361.

Aphrodite and Ares was that if you paid attention to stories of this type you will
end up as coarse and decadent as the Phaeacians themselves (*On How Young Men
Should Listen to Poetry*, 19e–20a). Even the more liberal ancient Epicureans, who
saw pleasure as the legitimate goal of life in the man who had engaged in
philosophical reflection, were uneasy about the Phaeacians: Philodemus seems
to have been concerned that the luxuriousness of the Phaeacian court, with its
dancing to songs about adultery, needed a good deal of defending.[54]

Lonsdale has argued that since the Phaeacian feast is the result of Nausicaa's
urge to find herself a husband, dancing in the *Odyssey* 'always occurs in the
context of a wedding, real or imagined'.[55] This may be to downplay the
importance of dancing on the magical, luxurious island, since there is no actual
wedding in the offing, and the song to which the Phaeacians dance is about
adulterous rather than conjugal sex. But perhaps the *Odyssey* taken as a whole
should be seen as advocating a model of socially acceptable dancing with an
erotic overtone, but exclusively in relation to marriage, just as Hephaestus' young
people in the *Iliad* practice mixed dancing in relation to publicly endorsed and
supervised courtship rituals. When Telemachus arrives at the court of Menelaus,
for example, the Peloponnesian king is celebrating the wedding of his two
children, and 'two acrobats led the measures of song and dance, revolving
among them' (*Od.* 4.17–19). Yet, once again, it needs to be remembered that
Menelaus' Spartan palace in the *Odyssey* is a place of fabulous wealth and
opulence, and the residence of the lovely Helen, from which she once eloped
with her gorgeous eastern lover.

The final references to dancing are also wedding-related. Just after the slaying
of the suitors, Odysseus orders Telemachus and the loyal slaves to wash, dress and
put on their tunics, and asks that the women dress as well. The bard is to play
music for a festive dance (*orchēthmoio*, 145), so that people will assume 'that we
are holding a wedding' (23.130–6). When Phemius obeys (144–51),

> He stirred up in them a longing for sweet singing and blameless dance.[56]
> The great house echoed and re-echoed to the steps of the prancing men
> And fair-girdled women, and people who heard them from outside would say,
> 'It seems that someone has finally married the much-courted queen!
> Shame on her that she did not carry on looking after her wedded husband's
> Household property until he himself came home.'

---

[54] Asmis (1991), 36–7.   [55] Lonsdale (1995), 277.

[56] The Greek adjective for dance here, as in the speech of Menelaus at *Iliad* 13.631–9, is
amumōn, a fairly common word, with positive connotations, often translated as 'excellent'. It is
formed from a root meaning 'blame' or 'criticize', but with a privative alpha. It was therefore seen by
some authors of dance treatises, following the discussion of the term in Lucian *On Dancing* 23, as an
important adjective which could be used to argue that the Greeks saw this type of dance, at any rate,
as harm*less*.

Both sexes are therefore dancing here, but the dancing is a charade, and interpreted by its internal audience as somehow indicative of an inappropriate mating. The dance is laden with even more sinister overtones as an activity designed to conceal what are actually thoroughly corrupt and perfunctory funeral rites. But the dance is, in another sense, a joyful accompaniment to a symbolic re-enactment of Odysseus and Penelope's wedding night, for it leads into their final reunion in their marriage bed.

The Greek epic poems' own dance-consciousness certainly goes some way towards explaining why choreographers have found them, especially the *Odyssey*, so attractive as the basis for performance texts. Ballet has had a strong relationship with the *Odyssey* from at least as early as the interludes in Badoaro and Sacrati's opera *L'Ulisse errante* (1644), and Antoine Bandieri de Lava's 1729 ballet *Les aventures d'Ulysse* (performed in Paris in 1729) inaugurated a long-standing tradition of danced realizations of the epic that continues to this day.[57] An important example is the Czech ballet company Latérna Magika's epoch-making *Odysseus* (with music by Michael Kocáb), which has been revived repeatedly since 1987. The *Iliad* has also been adapted into dance theatre, notably in Salvatore Taglioni's choreography for a Neapolitan *L'ira d'Achille* (1826). Yet Homeric poetry's commentary on dancing at the same time made too close an enquiry into the relevant passages a dangerous game for anyone seeking to advocate male dancing, at least outside the context of socially regulated sexual desire (aimed at reproduction of the household and community), which was permissible at weddings because sanctioned by the whole community.

The Homeric poems and hymns provide scarcely any model for, or legitimization of, dancing for pleasure by exemplary mature males. Beautiful recreational dancing is virtually confined to Olympus (where it is performed by females accompanied by male singers and acrobats), Troy (an eastern palace culture doomed to destruction, where it is rhetorically contrasted with masculinity and martial excellence), the suitors' decadent Ithacan banquets, and the magical isle of Phaeacia, which is a luxurious antitype to the real world of hardworking Greek peasant farmers.

If Homer was a problematic authority for advocates of male dancing, the *Aeneid* was even worse. There is one passage where Aeneas is, through a simile likening him to Apollo, mentally associated with dance at least of a ritual kind, in *Aeneid* 4.143–50. Yet here, as the gorgeous lover of the African queen, he is at his most like Mark Antony, and least like Augustus.[58] Taking the hazard of decadence out of the dance and the dancer would, it seems, mean having to rewrite the entire history of the western curriculum. This is not to deny that some Archaic and Classical Greek authors certainly support the view that dancing by men is acceptable, but they are always uneasy about male dancing that is not

---

[57] See Reid (1993), 2. 726–52.   [58] See Weber (2002).

performed as part of a masculine education for appropriate reasons, such as physical health, the cultivation of self-discipline, and the consolidation of social cohesion in the community in a way that also prepared young men for war.

The ancient authors did also provide a few positive images that are often developed into elaborate arguments in defence of the dance, such as that dancing originated in imitation of the movements of the heavenly bodies, a Platonic and Pythagorean aetiology. It had become familiar to the Renaissance even before the translation of Plutarch's *De musica* into French in 1572 and was made much of by, for example, Corso, Esquivel, and Weaver (see further Ravelhofer, this volume). Indeed, the dance advocates would have been well advised to look harder in Plato and Aristotle than they did;[59] they do not seem to have been fully aware of the considerable philosophical interest expressed by these foundational thinkers in dance, as opposed to the more colourful and familiar concrete descriptions of dancing and dancers, discussed above, which they constantly recycled. Unlike Homeric epic and Roman biography, many philosophical works remained untranslated into modern languages until relatively late, and therefore inaccessible to all but the highly educated and studious.

In conclusion, dance has been associated with decadent pleasure-seeking, unmanliness, and the arousal of sexual desire from its very first appearances in western cultural history. These associations resulted from an early symbolic opposition of dancing and fighting, an opposition which paradoxically may have been partly a result of the intimate relationship and parallelism between dancing and drill-training in educational practice. The result, in any case, was that dancing for pleasure, especially for men, was an activity under a moral question mark from the moment that discourse on the dance begins.

Dance apologists seeking ammunition from classical and biblical sources needed to ignore many famous passages altogether, rewrite or misrepresent others, and highlight emphatically the two exemplary male non-military dancers—the Greek Socrates and the Jewish David—who seemed to support their case. But the dancing of these culture heroes, even if it was not part of directly military training, was locked into the discourses of medicine and ritual respectively, rather than pleasure, recreation, entertainment, the performance arts, or aesthetics. The ancient sources have played an important role in maintaining a situation in which, right up to the present day, the man who would dance for pleasure, his own or his audience's, is challenging some fundamental elements in society's calibration of masculinity. He still runs the risk of being accused, as Priam accused his surviving sons, of being a hero of nothing but the dance floor.

---

[59] Scott (2005), 1.

8

Servile bodies? The Status of the Professional Dancer in the Late Seventeenth and Early Eighteenth Centuries

Jennifer Thorp

> Take Bathyllus: where would you find . . . among the players one who rises
> so high in dancing . . . Around Bathyllus the crowd is excessive, and he
> refuses more women than he condescends to please.[1]

This was not a description of the ancient Greek pantomimic performer of that
name, but Jean de la Bruyère's comment, in 1688, on the noted Parisian dancer
and star of the Paris Opéra, Guillaume-Louis Pécour (see Fig. 8.1). The choice of
pseudonym reveals an interesting conceptual link between the two worlds of
ancient and baroque theatre dance which would not have been lost on de la
Bruyère's readers: Bathyllus of Alexandria was the freed slave and favourite of
Maecenas, and was considered to be the foremost pantomime dancer of his day,
while Pécour was one of the 'gilded youths' at the court of Louis XIV, a dancer of
remarkable beauty and ability who was trained by and subsequently succeeded
Pierre Beauchamps as the leading dancer and choreographer at the Académie
Royale de Musique (the Paris Opéra).

The quotation also sums up one aspect of what this chapter sets out to discuss:
the ambivalent social and moral status of dancers and the equally ambivalent
attitude of polite society towards them, within the context of baroque performance
culture in late seventeenth- and early eighteenth-century Paris and London. It is
noteworthy that such responses to the dancer at this time also reflect, albeit
sometimes indirectly, a similar discourse surrounding the dancer in Greco-Roman
antiquity.

The original Bathyllus, like his contemporary Pylades, was performing in the late
first century BCE; and together with some of their most successful female counterparts in later centuries, such as Basilla (third century CE) and Theodora (sixth
century CE), they produced an art form described by Lucian as 'diversified, wholly

---

[1] Bruyère (1962), 119–20.

Figure 8.1 Guillaume-Louis Pécour, the modern Bathyllus.

harmonious and richly musical' and in a recent study as 'emotionally absorbing as well as technically staggering and hauntingly beautiful in the eyes of its admirers'.[2] Although their art was to survive all the shifting cultural priorities and values of the age, there was also lengthy debate, often fuelled by the hostility of the Christian Church, over the extent to which the dancer's ability to imitate characters and passions educated or corrupted their audiences.[3] The presence of female dancers caused considerable anxiety, and particularly if (as Theodora apparently did at one stage) they turned from narrative mime to the lewdest forms of comic buffoonery, which was considered not even appropriate for slaves to perform.[4]

All dancers by definition were regarded as infamous, despite their popularity and their central role in culture; and because they were thought of as morally suspect, all but a few of them found themselves barred from respectable society. The situation was perpetuated by the nature of their training and work, which encouraged generations of dancers within the same family to work in the same carefully organized troupes, functioning inside an artistic world of their own. Although one cannot invoke any of this as the direct heritage of early modern dancers in France or England, it is intriguing to see the many parallels between the two ages and the two cultures. The Church Fathers' polemics against the ancient dancer cast a long shadow, which extended to the dance culture of the early modern period. Not surprisingly, these polemics acquire new significance at a time when the sphere of the male professional dancer broadened beyond the relatively narrow confines of the court to include public theatres; now, moreover, the male dancer was accompanied on the stage by professional female dancers.

ANCIENTS AND MODERNS

Many dance apologists went out of their way to quote ancient sources as a means of giving respectability to their art and to show that they were well enough educated to be familiar with the writings of Greco-Roman antiquity as well as *au fait* with contemporary writings on all aspects of the arts. In France, despite the new structures they advocated for theatrical dance, the dance theorists drew heavily on classical sources for inspiration and justification of their art. By the late 1650s Claude-François Ménestrier was clearly influenced by the writings of Lucian and Aristotle in his rationale for ballet: that it encompasses all the arts, that its subject must be agreeable, and its entrées reveal variety and diversity of character; and thirty years later he expanded these thoughts to discuss ancient spectacles and modern ballets from the perspective of dance being common to both.[5] Michel de Pure

---

[2] Lada-Richards (2007), 13.
[3] Webb (2005), 9; Webb (2008).
[4] Webb (2002), 288.
[5] Ménestrier (1658), 50–6; Ménestrier (1984), preface.

described the spectacles of antiquity—circuses, gladiatorial contests, games, plays, and triumphal marches—as having inspired the plays, carousels, jousts, fireworks, balls, and mascarades of his own day; and Jacques Bonnet was to echo the same sentiments a generation later.[6] By this date Jean-Baptiste Du Bos had also published his highly influential *Réflexions critiques sur la poésie et sur la peinture*, including a long discourse on theatrical dance, drawing on sources from antiquity, *commedia dell'arte* traditions, and his astute observations of operatic dance in his own day (see further Lada-Richards, this volume).[7]

In England, William King's lampooning in 1709 of the pretentious use by some 'learned dancing masters' of Ioannes Meursius's catalogue of ancient dances did not so much attack the idea of antiquarianism as question its relevance to dance in his own day when cited by ignorant practitioners.[8] But he was up against the tide, because invoking ancient precedent was very soon to become part of the mainstream. A few years later John Weaver was to draw heavily on a wide range of ancient and patristic sources in his *Essay Towards an History of Dancing*, published in 1712 as the first extended apology for dance in the English language.[9] It was also a means of establishing Weaver's own *bona fides* both as a scholar and as a choreographer; thus, although his pantomimes included danced scenes both of dramatic nobility and comic *commedia dell'arte* style buffoonery, he also took inspiration directly from ancient sources in his *Loves of Mars and Venus* (1717), 'a Dramatick Entertainment of Dancing attempted in Imitation of the Pantomimes of the Ancient Greeks and Romans'. Its opening scenes included a Pyrrhic dance, which was well described in sources available to Weaver at the time (see further Hall, this volume).[10] It also included a solo *passacaille* for Venus, and a duet for Venus and Vulcan in which the two dancers expressed a range of emotions inspired by the protean performances of ancient pantomimes.

Ancient precedent was not simply invoked to grant intellectual and aesthetic respectability, it was also in part a necessary antidote to opponents who were regularly recycling arguments against dance that date back to late antiquity. Dance played an essential role within cultural life in both Paris and London. The royal court had long included dance within its private entertainments, be they the court ballets in and around Paris or the masques of Stuart London, in

---

[6] De Pure (1668), 46–52; Bonnet (1723), 19–30.

[7] Du Bos (1719), 1. 492–535.

[8] William King, *Useful Transactions in Philosophy*, Jan. & Feb. 1709. Meursius's original catalogue had been published as *Orchestra sive de Saltationibus Veterum* (Leyden, 1618). For a discussion of the late 17th- and early 18th-cent.'s general interest, and John Weaver's specific interest, in the antiquity of dancing, see Ralph (1985), 128–38.

[9] Ralph (1985), 116–21.

[10] Weaver would have had access to relevant sources for this: John Hudson's edition of the *Opera Omnia* of Dionysius of Halicarnassus, which included descriptions of the Pyrrhic dance, had been published in Oxford in 1704, and Thoinot Arbeau's *Orchesography* (Langres, 1588), which also included its basic steps as reflected in the later dance known as Buffens or Mattachins, must have been well known to him also since he borrowed its title for his own translation of a later French dance treatise.

which courtiers, members of the royal family and professionals all danced. There was also a flourishing dance culture within the public theatres of both capitals, with the additional attraction of professional female dancers who were seen on stage in Paris from the 1680s onwards, and in London from a generation earlier. Their arrival came at the height of long-standing animosity by some elements of society to the acceptance of women in previously male-dominated professions.

The Church, already hostile to the stage and all who performed upon it, seized upon the question of women performing in public as a useful additional weapon against what they saw as the innate corruption of theatrical performances and the resultant collapse of morality. In France the *querelle du théâtre* was waged with increasing vehemence during the second half of the seventeenth century, and indeed was part of a larger spiritual debate sparked off by the Jansenists. As Henry Phillips has noted, 'The *querelle du théâtre* is . . . a good illustration of a particular spiritual mentality applied to a specific area of social life.'[11] In their writings on the theatre, both sides invoked lengthy discussions of Roman law and of the writings of Lucian, Tertullian, and others, as well as appealing to the writings of the Church Fathers; each side also threw up new champions, setting perceptions of religious morality as voiced by Bossuet and Voisin against perceptions of theatrical life as voiced by d'Aubignac, Chappuzeau, and Caffaro.[12]

That both sides were predominantly concerned with actors rather than dancers did not detract from the inclusion of dancers at the edges of the debate, whether dancers by association with actors, or female dancers by association with male dancers. In the polemical exchanges, for example, between the theologian Thomas Caffaro and the Abbé Pégurier on St Cyprian's attitude to dance, Caffaro averred that St Cyprian's acceptance of David singing and dancing before the Ark of the Covenant indicated that he did not condemn outright dancing and singing (and so by extension operas and plays), but only 'those spectacles which represent fables in the lascivious manner of the Greeks and Romans, and in celebration of false gods'. Pégurier responded that by condemning lascivious dancing, St Cyprian by definition was condemning opera and other forms of drama.[13]

In England the animosity between puritans and traditionalists was no less harsh than the *querelle du théâtre* in making moral judgements of the theatre.[14] But opinions were also enflamed by the ongoing love-hate relationship with French

---

[11] Phillips (1980), 11.

[12] Ibid., ch. 9 *passim.*

[13] Ibid. 75. I am grateful to Fiona Macintosh for bringing this reference to my attention, and for her guidance on the sources for many other aspects of dance in Greco-Roman antiquity.

[14] A major polemical debate which had a great influence on the functioning of the London theatres in the opening years of the eighteenth century was sparked off by Jeremy Collier's *A Short View of the Immorality and Profaneness of the English Stage* (London, 1702); interestingly however, he was less concerned with dance as profanity than with the spoken word, and in general the London critics' animosity towards dance tended to be overshadowed by their indignation about spoken drama.

culture, and particularly French dance culture, that dominated English theatrical life in the late Stuart era. That London audiences in 1702 could flock to see Mademoiselle Subligny of the Paris Opéra dance at Lincoln's Inn Fields theatre, while one critic referred to her as 'that surprizing Monster . . . [a] French Adventure' and his colleague simply longed 'to be ogling' her feet, perhaps, says it all.[15]

THE CULTURE OF DANCE PERFORMANCE IN THE THEATRICAL WORLDS OF PARIS AND LONDON C.1680–1730

Despite the polemics of the religious moralists, however, the appearance of female dancers on the public stage brought changes to the aesthetic and appeal of theatrical dance, particularly in French opera. The presence of female professional dancers encouraged new choreographies in the form of duets for a man and woman, and expressive solos for women; and many of the extant theatre dances from the early 1700s reveal this heightened art form.[16] Otherwise, the genres of dance remained as they had existed for a century or more: serious or comic, noble or grotesque, ordinary or imitative (that is, expressing emotions or activities of specific characters); and the aesthetic of dance continued to juxtapose the graceful and elegant with the rougher and more naturalistic forms of movement.

Another important difference to emerge within the dance world, and particularly in the French *ballets de cour* of the seventeenth century, was its own concept of unity. While the dramatists adopted the neo-Aristotelian unities of time, place and action on stage, the apologists for dance imposed their own views of unity. Led by Claude-François Ménestrier, who saw the unities as irrelevant to ballet, these writers insisted on the need for overall coherence in the structure of the ballet, linked themes within its various groups of entrées, and appropriate representation (through costumes, music, dance steps, and imitative gesture) of those themes and characters.[17] It seems likely that their views were less a formal reaction against the dramatic unities than a reaction against the outlook of their predecessors, typified by the writings of Monsieur de St Hubert (1641). St Hubert's main concerns were for the categorization of ballets according to the number of entrées, and the inclusion of subjects which would translate well

---

[15] Anon. (1702), 67.

[16] One might note here particularly the expressive solos of Marie-Thérèse de Subligny, or the duets created for herself and Claude (Jean) Balon, which survive from the opening years of the century. They exhibit sustained balances and pirouettes, interspersed with lively ornamented steps, and extend across many dance types and time signatures: loures, gigues, passacailles, even a menuet rondeau: Little & Marsh (1992), 156–7.

[17] Ménestrier (1682), 137; Ménestrier (1658), n.p.; de Pure (1668), 215–91.

into dance and spectacle on stage without necessarily bearing much relation to each other.[18]

According to the Abbé Du Bos, writing in 1719, the work of Jean-Baptiste Lully in France had brought a closer relationship between dance and music as well as a greater expressiveness in dancing: 'Sixty years ago' (i.e. in the time of St Hubert), according to Du Bos, 'fauns, shepherds, peasants, Cyclops and Tritons danced almost uniformly, but nowadays dance is divided into different characters, even the female dancers adopting characterisation as the men do'.[19] Any study of Lully's *tragédies-en-musique* reveals the special relationship between dancers and chorus on stage, as the dancers depicted through physical movement the mood or emotion which the chorus expressed in song. In England too, the operas staged in the late seventeenth century by Purcell and Blow, in particular, revealed dance as an integral part of the performance in which speech, song, and dance might all work together towards the same end. That phenomenon was to recur in a quite different way a generation later, in English pantomime, while entr'acte dancing within and after plays provided purely danced entertainment throughout the era under discussion. None of these developments would have been possible if the dance profession had not operated inside some sort of regulated environment. But whereas in France the system was dominated by the authority of the king and the royal academies, in London any system was more haphazard, a prey to market forces and opportunistic personalities.

The Académie Royale de Danse was set up by letters patent issued in the name of Louis XIV in 1661. The ostensible reason for its foundation (given in clause 11) was that the king wanted higher standards of dancing in his court ballets, but the impetus for setting up this new body more likely came from the younger dancing-masters who found the existing supervision by the Guild of Ménétriers oppressive.[20] The new Academy consisted of thirteen members, most of whom had worked with the king in creating and performing court ballets, and in the name of the Academy they now set standards, trained and examined other dance teachers, and supervised the profession of dancing within the city and suburbs of Paris, and (in theory) throughout the whole of France also.

In the face of such well-planned regulation the Guild of Ménétriers soon found itself seriously undermined. Under the aegis of the new Academy the notion of *la belle danse* as a particular genre of dancing, with its own performance aesthetic based on notions of beauty, grace and propriety, developed and encouraged the codification of dance steps and methods of recording them in notation. Public performance by professional dancers also came to be regulated, by the establishment of the Académie Royale de Musique in 1672, and in

---

[18] He and his contemporaries regarded a ballet of thirty entrées to be 'un Grand Ballet', up to twenty entrées 'un Beau Ballet', and ten or twelve entrées 'un petit Ballet': St Hubert (1641), 5.

[19] Du Bos (1719), 1. 495.

[20] Needham (1997), 187; Pruiksma (2003), 173.

later years when it had become the Paris Opéra it ran its own school, the École Royale de Danse (founded in 1713), to train up dancers for the stage. The result was creativity within the hands of a small number of dancing-masters working within the confines of the academies, and excellent technical standards from dancers who nevertheless were not encouraged to show any initiative or independence. French opera and ballet flourished, but an inevitable (and culturally very rich) antidote also took hold in the parodies and experimental works in the fairs, private salons, and even at the Comédie Française itself.

In London the situation was quite different. Attempts to regulate the dance profession were never wholly successful, and the absence of any meaningful financial or artistic support from the Crown also encouraged entrepreneurism both as a commercial necessity and as a philosophy within the performing world. Dancing-masters were supposed to be licensed by the Sessions Courts and to register their apprentices, but the records indicate that adherence to such regulations was at best sporadic. In the City of London, bye-laws and ordinances dating back to the sixteenth century, which confined the performance and teaching of music and dancing to Freemen of the City, were repealed in 1700 in favour of confining such activities just to members of the Worshipful Company of Musicians, but there was widespread evasion.[21]

Theatrical dance suffered no regulation at all beyond the edicts of the Lord Chamberlain (which however were rarely directed against the dancers themselves, but rather against the management and repertoire of individual theatres) and the contracts awarded to dancers by the theatre managers. One result seems to have been more creative freedom than was possible in France at that time, and there are many instances of French dancers coming to work in London, presumably for artistic reasons since Paris Opéra dancers already enjoyed better wages and privileges than their English counterparts. While the technical standards of English dancers benefited from the influx of French dancers and dance styles, there was also much adaptation to existing English traditions—a phenomenon seen most clearly at the Court of Queen Anne in the extant dances of Mr Isaac, some of which were also performed on stage. Yet despite the encouragement of independent-minded dancers in London, particularly in entr'acte dancing and English pantomime, most dancers still had little say in what they were required to do or the conditions under which they worked.

There is much evidence in both Paris and London that entire families were involved in music and dance performance, with the result that generations of dancers were 'locked in' to a particular cultural context and mindset. Intermarriage between dancing families, which was not uncommon, simply strengthened those ties. Thus in Paris, the Favier family were regular performers, all of great merit and versatility, at Court and in the Paris Opéra over many years.

---

[21] Crewdson (2000), 270–2.

The dancer and choreographer Jean Favier came from a family of violinists and dancing-masters, and made his own stage debut in 1660, dancing as a monkey in the ballet staged between the acts of Cavalli's opera *Xerxes*. He performed regularly throughout the 1670s, taking on roles which included serious, comic, mythological, pastoral, and (before 1681) he also danced women's roles. His younger brothers Henri and Jean-Jacques also performed, but it was probably Jean who was the most successful, becoming dancing-master to the Dauphine at Court in the 1680s, and creating the comic mascarade, *Le Mariage de la Grosse Cathos* in 1688. He married into a family which had connections with the Comédie Française and with whom Favier had performed in Molière's *comé-die-ballets*; and his son Jean (born in 1694) continued the family tradition of a career in dancing, in Paris and Dresden.[22]

In London too there is evidence of similar dynastic networks of dancers working in the theatres, supplementing their income with teaching, and strengthening what social position they had by intermarriage: for example, the Priest family of dancing-masters active over several generations, or the linking by marriage of the Gahory, Thorp, Fourcade, and Isaac families of recusant danc-ing-masters and musicians.[23]

AMBIGUITY OF DANCERS' SOCIAL AND MORAL STATUS

In both Paris and London, theatrical dancers of both sexes could inspire great adulation onstage, yet their social and moral status remained anomalous. Al-though in France actors (and by extension, dancers) had been absolved from the automatic status of infamy by the Edict of 1641, many bishops continued to refuse to give the sacraments to them unless they publicly renounced their profession, and it is tempting to see here a parallel with ancient Roman law by which performers of servile status could not convert to Christianity (and thereby become free) unless they revoked their career on the stage.[24] De la Bruyère in his *Jugements* makes those parallels explicit:

The condition of actors was infamous according to the Romans and honourable according to the Greeks; what it is for us? We think of it like the Romans, but live with it like the Greeks.[25]

Plato's account of the duality of dance—both as a divine gift from the Muses to enable expression of the state of the soul, and as the base or vulgar dancing appropriate only for performance by slaves and hired foreigners who would never

---

[22] Harris-Warrick and Marsh (1994), 21–7.
[23] Thorp (1998), 198–210; Thorp (2007), 439–43.
[24] Phillips (1980), 10; Webb (2002), 297.
[25] Bruyère (1688), 352.

be permitted to teach freemen or women (Plato, *Laws*, 1.2.93 and 2.7.97)—was echoed in early modern attitudes to the dancer. Even those hostile to dance in the seventeenth and early eighteenth centuries recognized its spirituality in certain circumstances, usually by reference to the biblical evidence of David dancing before the Ark of the Covenant (see Hall, this volume), but the old moral ambivalence towards base pantomimic and vulgar dancing was as strong in the early modern era as it was in antiquity. It is possible to detect traces of Tertullian, for whom men performing women's parts was considered at best unmanly and at worst (for example in adultery scenes) sinful, since the actor could confuse and contaminate the audience by identifying himself too closely with the role; and also to detect the counter arguments of Lucian and Libanius, who averred that performance is merely imitation and that the audience realized that, even while applauding the apparent conviction with which it was presented.[26]

Such arguments are found during the eighteenth century in the popular press around the subject of the deleterious effects of pantomimic dancing: the *Grub Street Journal* of 8 April 1731 for instance sardonically noted, of the female members of the audience, that far from being

recreated with carnal and sexual diversions . . . the simplicity and innocence of our women was at such a pitch that they could appear for threescore nights together at bawdy entertainment, in which the most lascivious acts, nearly tending to copulation itself, were repeatedly represented; and of which they were so entirely ignorant and inexperienced that they could not guess what it meant, nor were so much as put to the expence of a blush.[27]

The main cause of all this outcry seems to have been a salacious dance in John Rich's pantomime *Perseus and Andromeda*, which was immortalized in John Miller's *Harlequin Horace*, and which clearly represented a crossing of boundaries in acceptable taste. Richard Steele had published a complaint concerning the sexually explicit gestures of *commedia dell'arte* characters on the London stage over a decade earlier, but the reaction to this latest affront to decency was different in that it was directed against dancers rather than actors. As such, it simply compounded the insuperable problem common to both eras (and even today), that while many respectable audiences rejected blatant lasciviousness on stage, many more felt drawn as much to the base and comic-vulgar as they did to the noble and spiritual. For them, the performing arts were a mixture of edification, entertainment, and the vicarious enjoyment of skills which they themselves did not possess or of thrills of which they could only dream; and the better the performance the more it drew the audiences.

The double standards applied even to the best dancers may be seen in the comments of their contemporaries. Pierre Beauchamps, for example, clearly made a great impression in his role as the dancing-master in the *Ballet des plaisirs*

---

[26] For ancient discussions, see Webb (2005), 8–9; Slater (1994), n.p.
[27] O'Brien (2004), 13–16.

troublés. Not only did Jean Loret, in a letter dated 17 February 1657, comment that 'The incomparable Beauchamps, for his marvellous suppleness and elevation, his precision and his high beaten jumps . . . was proclaimed by the noble audience as the best dancer in France today'; but the verses assigned to his character in that ballet also noted of him that:

> Fortune smiles at me
> And I am cherished by everyone. I live in opulence,
> After the ballet, there is no difference
> Between master and valet.[28]

Beauchamps was the son of a court violinist and distantly related to Molière, so what he lacked in social standing was compensated by influential contacts and his own considerable abilities.[29] His fame became matched by his wealth, acquired from his fees as a performer and from numerous gifts from Louis XIV, who took daily dance classes from him. He became a respected collector of fine art, even selling two Guido Reni paintings to the king. But he died in obscurity long after his retirement from court and theatre in the 1680s and the deaths of his champions and friends Molière, Lully, and, in 1715, Louis XIV himself. The essentially ephemeral nature of the dancer's status, both on stage in performance and offstage as a private individual, was a recurring characteristic of the dancer's life: acclaimed one day and forgotten the next.

Of the modern Bathyllus, Guillaume-Louis Pécour (the son of another Court official), one eyewitness commented in 1695: 'Many people came to see the *Ballet des Saisons* and simply cannot wait to come again . . . and all because Pécour danced a Spanish Saraband.'[30] Five years later, another spectator, having watched his parody of the chaconne from *Amadis*, which he danced in the character of Harlequin in *Arlequin Jason ou la Toison d'or comique*, noted that 'No one has been able to rival his style, his speed of foot, the variety of steps and the accuracy of his ear. He has a wonderfully inventive imagination, and no character has been invented that he cannot bring alive.' And yet another addressed him with the plaudit: 'Everyone knows that you are the model of the perfect dancer, and that others are praised only in so far as they imitate you.'

The roles Pécour danced during his performing career (which lasted from 1671 to at least 1702) ranged from comic, character and allegorical roles to heroic, noble and 'serious' roles, and hardly a season passed without his appearance on stage either at court or in the public theatre or at the Jesuit colleges of Paris; he was constantly in the public eye. His wealth became fabulous, and for years his loans to the Paris Opéra kept the company afloat. Outside France,

---

[28] Loret (1877), 2. 30; Kunzle [Astier] (1974/5), 32.

[29] For other references to Beauchamps's dance skills see also Powell (1995), 169 n. 9, 10.

[30] All the following descriptions of Pécour are quoted in Gorce (1990), 3–26, together with a list of his dance roles.

however, away from royal patronage and the support of the Academies, he had been less successful and much more vulnerable: when he had come to London as a young dancer in 1674 with his dance colleagues Dumiraile and Lestang, they quickly ran foul of the authorities for agreeing to additional performances by which, allegedly, they broke their contract with the theatre company that had hired them. Pécour fled back to Paris as soon as he could, and never ventured to London again.[31]

In France, the status of the dancers employed at the Paris Opéra was one of rare privilege and freedom, and those privileges also extended to the women dancers.[32] Under the constitution of, and levels of pay within, the Académie Royale de Musique as set down in the regulations of 1713, the female singers and dancers, even if underage or married, could if they so wished live wherever they chose in Paris, free from all parental or marital tutelage, protected from police harassment, deportation, or imprisonment.[33] This very independence in early eighteenth-century Paris, however, brought its own social ambivalence, for few female dancers were able to establish their independence without being perceived as sexually 'available'; and even after their performing days were over and their audiences had turned elsewhere, their only hope was to marry well, take wealthy lovers, or retire into seclusion.

Marie-Cathérine Guiot, for example, for whom some outstanding choreographies by Pécour still survive, enjoyed a meteoric stage career at the Paris Opéra from 1705 onwards, and apparently led a blameless private life before retiring to a convent twenty years later on a pension of 1000 *livres* paid by the opera house because she had been an active member of the company for over fifteen years.[34] In every other respect, however, she was ignored by her contemporaries after she retired, apart from unkind comments in the press that she had been forced off stage by increasing obesity which made it impossible for her to dance with the 'unforgettable' and 'unsurpassable' grace and vigour for which she had been so highly praised throughout her career. Such an attack, revealing as it does such double standards by her audiences and critics, may have been an indicator that, once she stopped dancing, she was no longer interesting enough in an age when sexual promiscuity (real or rumoured) was what enhanced the allure and fame of a performer. Quite different were contemporary reactions to Guiot's colleague, Françoise Prévost, described by her recent biographer as a 'theatre urchin' and renowned in adulthood as much for her dancing as for her love affairs with the Ambassador to Malta and the Comte de Middelbourg.[35] Indeed the Opéra

---

[31] LC 5/140 p.472. Dumiraile and Lestang stayed on to dance in the Court masque *Calisto* at Whitehall the following spring: LC 5/190 fol. 84r; LC 5/141 p.197.

[32] Lecomte (2007), 106.

[33] The regulations of 1713 are set out in Durey de Noinville (1757), 1. 114.

[34] Durey de Noinville (1757), 2.143. Guiot's career and dance qualities are discussed in Whitley-Bauguess (1988), 32–67, and in Thorp (2005), 91–106.

[35] Astier (2007), 123–59.

dancers were expected to take lovers; those who did not, such as Marie-Thérèse de Subligny, Marie Sallé, or Marie-Cathérine Guiot herself, were dubbed 'Vestals' and deviant.

In England there was little security for dancers of either sex. The Crown showed little effective interest in the theatre, and nothing like the Paris Opéra system of protection and privileges existed for performers in London. Only a few theatrical dancers came from wealthy enough families to be able to undertake formal apprenticeships which would offer at least a few years of security. One such was John Evans whose family paid a fee of £105 in 1725 for his apprenticeship to John Thurmond junior, the pantomime dancer-choreographer of Drury Lane theatre, and another was John Dennison whose family paid the same amount in 1749 to have him trained by the Covent Garden dancer Charles Lalauze.[36] From the master's point of view these apprenticeships were lucrative, if highly taxed, for he was entitled to all the income earned by the apprentice from any performances. From the apprentice's point of view, he acquired training within a network of professional contacts, performance experience, and parish settlement which meant access to poor relief in hard times. For under the English Poor Laws, any unlicensed performer (that is, anyone not formally apprenticed, not under contract to a patent theatre, or not the owner or main occupier of rateable property) was technically a vagrant, liable to be hounded out of the parish in times of sickness, injury, unemployment, or eviction from lodgings.

The result for many dancers was a self-perpetuating circle of social and economic inferiority, made worse by the need to keep up appearances in order to attract any teaching work outside the theatre. No wonder that the highest social aspirations of many male dancers in London was to be categorized as a 'gentleman' and to acquire either property which would give them rights of settlement, or a sinecure post which would provide status and an assured income. When it went wrong—in times of unemployment or sickness, and particularly in old age—there might be nothing apart from charity left to help them. One poignant case is that of Jean Boisleau of Soho, recorded in the archives of La Providence, the French Protestant Hospital set up in London by the Huguenots. The registers record his application for assistance from the hospital on 3 July 1742: 'Boisleau, Jean: of Orléans. 70 years old, formerly a dancing-master but now with no profession and no means of livelihood. Recommended by Master Justell.' The hospital gave him regular assistance for several months, and on 28 January 1744 admitted him to the hospital itself. There he stayed until April 1751, when the hospital paid a bill for 'Jean Boisleau. Coffin 5s., wool shroud 1s., Ground etc. 9s. 4d., Total 15s. 4d.'[37]

---

[36] Milhous (1991), 13–25; Inglehearn (2008), 50–1; Thorp (2008), 62–4.
[37] Marmoy (1977), 52, entry for Boi(s)leau.

For women also, at all levels of society, the long-term options seem to have been marriage into a moneyed family, living with relatives or in charitable institutions, or prostitution. The ancient association between dancers, particularly female, and immorality was never far from the surface,[38] and the celebrated actress-dancer sisters Margaret and Elizabeth Younger of London provide an example within the early eighteenth-century dance world.

Margaret danced at Drury Lane theatre under her married name Bicknell from 1702 onwards, and attracted much ambiguous praise for her agreeable looks and winning expressiveness. Audiences warmed to the ways in which she

could in all proper gesture and motion represent all the decent characters of female life. An amiable modesty in one aspect of a dance, and assumed confidence in another, a sudden joy in another, a falling off with an impatience of being beheld, a return towards the audience with an unsteady resolution to approach them, and a well-acted solicitude to please, would revive in the company all the fine touches of mind raised in observing all the objects of affection or passion they had before beheld . . . Mrs Bicknell has the only capacity for this sort of dancing of any on the stage.[39]

Her sister Elizabeth also performed at Drury Lane theatre before moving to John Rich's company at Lincoln's Inn Fields theatre and Covent Garden. Both sisters gained some notoriety for their private lives, but whereas Margaret found her career an increasing struggle (perhaps due to ill health: she died of consumption in 1723), Elizabeth went from strength to strength in pantomimic roles and retired in 1734 to marry the Hon. John Finch, a younger son of the Earl of Nottingham.[40]

For dancers lower down the status ladder, never able to achieve stardom or attract wealthy patrons, life could be very uncertain. It is a sign of the milieu in which they worked that even if few of them resorted to crime when times were bad, there does seem to have been a willingness to accuse theatrical dancers wrongfully of criminality simply because they were not from 'respectable' sections of society. In this sense, the Church Fathers' anxieties about the boundary-breaking nature of the performer's art and the consequent belief that he/she acts as the conduit for moral pollution had wide repercussions.[41] Fairground performers were particularly vulnerable in this respect, as may be seen in a lawsuit of September 1732, when one Richard Coats accused Thomas Mills, a piper, and John Henly, a dancer at the Tottenham Court Road Fair, of attacking him in Marylebone Fields and stealing 2s. 2½d. from him. The Court however ruled mistaken identity after alibis were provided by other players and a Music Booth keeper at the Fair ('They were both in my Booth, one playing, and the other dancing, from before seven in the evening till past ten, and were never out except

---

[38] Webb (2002), 289, 293–5.
[39] *Spectator*, 5 May 1712. Admittedly this piece was a puff for her performance the following night.
[40] Highfill et al. (1973–93), 16. 362–4.
[41] Phillips (1980), ch. 9 *passim*.

they might step to the door to piss, but no further'), and both men were acquitted.[42]

While the evidence for actual law-breaking is sparse, one dancer at least seemed to justify his reputation for criminality. This was Daniel Phillips, who appeared at the Old Bailey in April 1694 accused of stealing a silver tankard, but was acquitted, having averred that his employment as a dancing-master was worth £300 a year so he had no need to steal, and that the sole witness was acting out of malice since he had recently had her arrested for spreading scandal. However, just over a year later Phillips was committed to Newgate Gaol for his part in the theft of costumes from the theatre where he worked, namely a purple velvet coat, a red cloth suit, and 'divers other goods to a great value'.[43] Even though most of the costumes were recovered (after having been 'plundered for their silver and gold lace, fringes, etc.'), Phillips had threatened a witness with murder, and had also jumped bail and fled. The jury sentenced him to death.[44]

Many dancers would have regarded themselves as servile to their employers. John Essex, who was later to become better known as a translator of French dance treatises and country dance collections, and a writer on etiquette, was a dancer employed at Drury Lane theatre by Christopher Rich, a tyrannical manager who was described by the character Critick in *A Comparison Between the Two Stages* (1702), as 'an old snarling Lawyer, [and] waspish, ignorant pettyfogger'. Essex complained to the Lord Chamberlain in February 1703 that Rich had stopped thirty-two days of his salary for 'not performing a Dance when I was so lame I had not the power to do it'.[45] Apparently he should have received payment even if injured, and now either wanted his money or a discharge from the company. That same year, even a dancer of the stature of Anthony L'Abbé, who was to go on to become the leading choreographer of his day in London and dancing-master to the Hanoverian royal family, was so incensed by Thomas Betterton's failure to renew his contract at Lincoln's Inn Fields theatre that he too complained to the Lord Chamberlain.[46]

Whatever the relationship with their employers, there is no doubt that many dancers saw themselves as servile to their audiences, who could be very quick to point out the shortcomings of those who failed to please because they did not perform as promised. Such criticisms, however, sometimes savoured of hypocrisy and veiled quite different reasons for the hostility. *The London Daily Post*, for

---

[42] POB: T17320906–32.

[43] Probably Dorset Garden theatre. The Old Bailey case papers describe it as 'the Play-house in Salisbury Court', but that theatre had been burned down in the Great Fire and the name may be in error for Dorset Garden which lay nearby and was managed by Christopher Rich, to whom the case papers also refer.

[44] The case is well documented in official papers, private comment, and press reports: POB: T16940418–38, T16961209–55, S16961209–1; Luttrell (1857), 3.488; Wilson (1961), 82 (a letter dated 25 June 1695); *Intelligence Domestick and Foreign*, 21–25 June 1695; *Post Man*, 15–17 Dec. 1696.

[45] LC 7/3 fol. 81.

[46] LC 7/3 fols. 29–30.

instance, published on 7 December 1734 an apology by the Drury Lane theatre manager Charles Fleetwood, responding to the Drury Lane audience being 'incens'd at their Disappointment' that Michael Poitier and Catherine Roland failed to dance 'as their names were on the Bills for that Day'. But the real reason may have been that the audience felt cheated of its voyeuristic fascination with two dancers known to be indulging in a well-publicized love affair offstage. Things could only get worse: just over a year later the *Grub Street Journal* slated them for indecent dancing: 'at the end of the dance, she is lifted by Poitier, that she may cut the higher and represent to the whole house as immodest a sight as the most abandoned women.'[47]

Many dancers who bore the brunt of audience hostility, however, did so through no fault of their own. The riot at the Little Theatre in the Haymarket on 9 October 1738 reflected the twofold nature of the audience's anger: hostility towards the Licensing Act (which had recently closed this theatre and all others in London apart from Covent Garden, Drury Lane, and the King's Theatre in the Haymarket, leaving many performers unemployed, destitute, or in prison for debt), and hostility towards the troupe of players brought in specially from Paris, by royal command, to entertain visiting French and Spanish Ambassadors. As *The Daily Advertiser* had commented a few days earlier (on 4 October): 'It seems to be a little unnatural that French Strollers should have a Superior Privilege to those of our Country.' Violence was expected, and when the curtain rose on 9 October the French actors were seen standing between two rows of Grenadiers who had bayonets fixed: 'At this the whole Pit rose and unanimously turned' to Justice Deveil who was sitting in the Pit, and he ordered the soldiers off the stage. The opening Serenade was drowned out by catcalls from the audience, so the actors went offstage and the dancers were sent on: 'they opened with a Grand Dance of Twelve Men and Twelve Women, but even that was prepared for and they were directly saluted with a Bushel or two of Peas, which made their Capering very unsafe.'[48] The uproar continued and Justice Deveil had the sense to terminate the performance.

Indeed, dancing on stage could be a dangerous business, particularly in pantomimes where the dancers were expected to bring off all sorts of acrobatic feats as well as dancing. For example, the actor-dancer Francis Leigh 'a young lad belonging to . . . Drury Lane' had a nasty accident on 16 Nov 1728, as described in the *Universal Spectator*: he was 'descending in a machine at a rehearsal of . . . *Perseus & Andromeda*, when the same was let down with such force that the poor boy broke both his arms'. Fortunately he survived, but the real exploitation lay not just in the intrinsic danger of his work, but also the fact that at that time he could not have been more than ten years old.[49]

---

[47] *Grub Street Journal* 8 Jan. 1736, quoted in Milhous and Hume (1991), 2. 869.
[48] Victor (1761), 1. 43.
[49] He came of age (that is, reached his 14th birthday) in about 1732.

An even worse disaster occurred during a performance, at Covent Garden on 1 October 1736, of John Rich's pantomime *The Necromancer or Harlequin Dr Faustus*, in which performers were killed. At the end of scene 6, in which Faustus, having seduced the Miller's wife and stolen a sack of grain, 'appears above, in the air, seated in an open chariot drawn by the Miller and his Man, with the Miller's Wife by his side and the sack of corn behind him; he whips 'em along, and drives across'. This was the flying chariot which on that evening tipped up in mid-flight as its fly-wires broke one after the other, throwing all four occupants down onto the stage far below and then crashing down on top of them; two of the unfortunate occupants died of their injuries a few days later.

Despite rapid assertions that the leading performers (who included Rich himself and the dancer Francis Nivelon, as Faustus and the Miller respectively) were not involved and that substitutes had been used, the disaster provoked correspondence in the press about the status and expectations of stage performers generally. One letter from 'A Reader', who had witnessed the accident and subsequently discussed it with 'two gentlemen in the legal profession', reported their reactions: one thought that in such cases the manager of the theatre was culpable and should be tried, but the other thought that such accidents went with the job. The first responded that this could not apply in this case because 'an Actor or a Player of a Common Interlude, in the eye of the Law, is no Vocation at all; and for they that are only licensed their Master is not answerable'. He went on to aver that the performers volunteer for what they do and know what is entailed; the manager therefore, in any fatal accident, should be within the sense though not the letter of the law, and added that this concept 'relates equally to operas, rope-dancing, prize-fighting, tumbling etc., viz. all that cannot properly be called a legal Vocation'.[50] Here we start to see, perhaps articulated for the first time, the notion that individual performers could choose whether to undertake certain roles or not, alongside the older view that it was the profession rather than the individual which could denigrate status. Of course it ignores the pressures and inducements which would have been applied to persuade the performer to take on such a role, but it is nevertheless interesting that by this date, in some quarters at least, a performer should be acknowledged as a free-thinking individual.

CONCLUSION

Literary allusions to classical antiquity gave early eighteenth-century dance treatises a cachet which blended in with the salon culture of the time and also allowed the commentary to move away from the ambivalent world of theatrical dance into the apparently more respectable world of social manners. Ancient

---

[50] *Daily Journal* 5809: 6 Oct. 1736, p. 1.

sources thus were invoked not just to counter old prejudices inspired by dance, but also to give it a new respectability as a social activity, removed from the vulgarities of the theatre. A capacity to poke gentle fun at this genteel world was an added bonus and encouraged such flights of fancy as Soame Jenyns's poem, *The Art of Dancing* (London, 1729):

> Then poetry was too the dancer's friend,
> And all the muses did his steps attend:
> With equal grace, in Hesiod's sacred lines,
> Ev'n yet the hero and the dancer shines:
> 'Valour to some' he says, 'the Gods impart;
> To some a genius for the dancing art.'
> Ev'n yet, in Homer's lofty verse, is seen
> Merion's engaging step and graceful mien:
> Still in the dance he charms our wond'ring eyes,
> And Greeks and Trojans yield to him the prize.

It is nevertheless noteworthy that, in this world, when the criticisms became more cruel they were directed at the dancing-masters rather than at their clientele. The anonymous poem *The Dancing-master, a Satyr* (London, 1722), for example, is full of scurrilous descriptions of unmusical, clumsy, drunken, bullying, greedy, ill-educated and foppish dancing-masters of the day; and Henry Fielding was similarly caustic on the vice of snobbery: 'The lowest and meanest of our species are the most strongly addicted to this vice . . . it visits alehouses and gin shops, and whistles in the empty heads of fiddlers, mountebanks, and dancing-masters.'[51] Few apart from the clergy, who in any case had their own agenda to pursue, seem to have dared to make the observation that such 'vices' only flourished because 'polite society' facilitated and directly encouraged them.

While it can be misleading to draw direct parallels between the cultures of the two quite different worlds of Greco-Roman antiquity and the (in dance terms) baroque era of France and England, two common themes which cannot fail to make an impression are the ambiguous status of the professional dancer, and the double standards which society applied to their treatment. Many troupes of dancers in antiquity were literally slaves, with no legal rights and of no significance as human beings, regarded simply as commodities to be exploited; their servile status was imposed from outside and perpetuated down the generations. Most dancers in seventeenth- and eighteenth-century France and England, on the other hand, while for the most part not able to control their own destinies to much avail, were servile only in the sense that they had sold their souls to the profession of dancing; their servile status was imposed from within and perpetuated by the close artistic communities in which they lived and worked. In that sense, the dancers themselves colluded with the double standards applied towards

---

[51] Rawson (1972), 26 n. 76.

the life they led. This becomes particularly apparent in the life-styles of those dancers who were successful and could make their way in the world: despite their riches, their fame, and their influence, they were still dominated by the need to please their public and gratify their patrons, as failure to do so would end their material well-being.

The mixed signals that such a lifestyle sent out must have further blurred the already ambivalent attitude of society towards theatrical dancers, and allowed deep-rooted prejudices and suspicions to continue and flourish. That dancers throughout the whole of history have tended to be suspected of vice and immorality is perhaps more a characteristic of the rarified artistic world that they represent than a true reflection of their own beliefs and morality. Part of their fascination for audiences is simply that they are 'different', specialists in physical movement whose relationship with music and stage spaces is not like that of other performers, and who can move and think in a way that many in their audiences are unable. That most of their demeanour was open to misinterpretation, either in antiquity, or in baroque western Europe, or at any other time and place, was also understood on one level by their audiences. But, since those audiences had bought into the cultural context, they were willing to accept the blurring between dancer as the embodiment of transformation and dancer as imitator or reflection of life. Any sense of genuine individualism was limited and very slow to gain ground. Perhaps all that really mattered was that the dancers should dance meaningfully and the audience should watch intelligently in a partnership of performance which, when all went well, placed each at the service of the other.

9

Dancing Maenads in Early Twentieth-Century Britain

Fiona Macintosh

In Gilbert and Sullivan's operetta, *The Grand Duke* (1896), Ludwig, the leading man of a theatre troupe with more than a smattering of classical knowledge, finds himself in charge of the corrupt state of Pfennig Halbpfennig. Ludwig announces his plan to institute an Athenian-style court: with *Troilus and Cressida* in the company's repertoire, they, at least, possess the appropriate costumes. But in Pfennig Halbpfenning's new-fangled court, it isn't simply about dressing the part: the plan is to 'act' the part too. In addition to adopting the conventions of the Attic stage, the courtiers will also ape the customs of the Greek symposium, reclining, drinking, and watching

> rather risky dances (under certain circumstances)
> Which would shock that worthy gentleman, the Licenser of Plays,
> Corybantian maniac kick, Dionysiac or Bacchic,
> And the Dithyramb revels of those undecorous days.
> *(Confidentially to the Audience)*
> And perhaps I'd better mention,
> Lest alarming you I am,
> That it isn't our intention
> To perform a Dithyramb
> It displays a lot of stocking,
> Which is always very shocking,
> And of course I'm only mocking
> At the prevalence of 'cram'!
> *(Chorus—It displays a lot of stocking, etc.)*
> Yes, on reconsideration, there are customs of that nation
> Which are not in strict accordance with the habits of our day,
> And when I come to codify, their rules I mean to modify,
> Or Mrs Grundy, p'r'aps, may have a word or two to say...
> They wore little underclothing, scarcely anything or nothing,
> And their dress of Coan silk was quite transparent in design -
> Well in fact, in summer weather, something like the 'altogether'
> And it's there, I rather fancy, I shall have to draw the line.[1]

---

[1] W. S. Gilbert and A. Sullivan, *The Grand Duke; or, The Statutory Duel* (1896), first performed at the Savoy Theatre, 7 March 1896.

In many ways this scene may be said to satirize the Hellenizing craze that had swept London since at least the early 1880s, when the newly opened department store Liberty's began selling 'Greek' gowns, and the revivals of Greek plays in private drawing rooms and minor theatres attracted luminary participants and equally stellar audiences.[2] Additionally, Ludwig's commentary conveys a prurient excitement about the scantily clad performers that is never far from the surface in reviews of the theatricals of the previous decade.[3] What is different, however, is his emphasis on dance—something that was conspicuously absent from the commentaries on the 1880s Greek choruses, whose members were barely distinguishable from the neoclassical columns around which they were decorously draped. But always beneath the marmoreal surface of those sculptural descendants of Emma Hamilton, and central to their appeal, was their Galatea-like potential for active physical response. The Apolline surface, there as elsewhere, merely served to veil the Dionysiac murky depths, which Nietzsche had recently designated in his *The Birth of Tragedy* (1872) and which were to prove so intriguing over the next few decades.

Retrospective in many ways, then, *The Grand Duke* was nonetheless much of the moment. There was plenty of 'stocking' on display at the Alhambra during the 1890s, when high-kicking was all the rage; and there was equally plenty of what Ludwig calls 'cram' to inform anyone interested that Greek dance had got there first. The ancient Greeks, moreover, were being praised for being even more daring than contemporary risqué practice: they didn't use body stockings, neither did they resort to the body make-up now favoured by the women who appeared in the *poses plastiques* at the Palace Theatre.[4] What marked the Greeks as different and Greece as an enviable paradigm to Ludwig and others in the 1890s was the total absence of the censorious Mrs Grundys from its orbit. As the poet and critic, John Addington Symonds, who was very shortly to become the first British public advocate of homosexuality, had explained: 'the themes of celibacy and aestheticism, and of the sinfulness of carnal pleasure . . . are wholly alien to Greek moral and religious notions.'[5]

However much *The Grand Duke* satirizes the 1880s' male gaze and the supposed 'naturalness' of the ancient Greeks much vaunted by *fin de siècle* 'decadents', it also anticipates the anxieties that were to come to the fore during the Edwardian era when the 'Corybantian maniac kick, Dionysiac or Bacchic' became fashionable and women were regularly labelled 'maenads' after the

---

[2] Hall and Macintosh (2005), 462–87.
[3] Ibid. 485.
[4] Hindson (2007).
[5] Symonds (1880), 179. Cf. Urlin (1914), 20, who insists that ancient Greek 'women wore tights, or very scanty clothing, as professional dancers . . . and their attitudes and postures were almost exactly those of the modern ballet'. For the influence of Emmanuel, which is clearly felt in the modern parallels made here, see Naerebout, this volume.

ancient devotees of the Greek god, Dionysus.[6] The Symbolist poet, Arthur
Symons had affectionately dubbed the Alhambra dancer of the 1890s a 'Maenad
of the decadence',[7] but by the beginning of the twentieth century the maenad
had regained the terrifying superabundance of amoral energy that Euripides
documents so graphically in his second messenger speech in the *Bacchae* (1043
ff.). When Hugo von Hofmannsthal's maniacal Elektra dragged herself off the
ground for her final, fatal dance at the end of her eponymous play at the Kleines
Theater, Berlin in October 1903, it was the maenad who was to inform her
performance. The stage direction reads: '*She comes striding down from the doorsill.
She has thrown back her head like a maenad. She flings her knees up high, she
stretches her arms out wide, it is a nameless dance in which she strides forward.*'[8]

This chapter explores the various maenadic incarnations of the Edwardian
period—those 'aestheticized' objects who were felt to have danced off vases, heads
thrown back with their long hair tossed and tussled wildly behind (Figure 9.1),
as well as those who resisted and challenged the aestheticization of the male gaze.
Most significantly, it charts their surprising trajectory from 'mad' maenads to
exemplary models of Anglo-Saxon social decorum. The First World War was a
watershed in Britain in relation to what came to be seen as German corporeal and
decadent culture; and in the post-war period there were numerous attempts to
rehabilitate the Greek dancer and to redefine her in sharp contradistinction to the
pre-war dangerous transgressors.

The pioneering schools of Margaret Morris and Ruby Ginner—both in their
own way transgressive maenads in the pre-war period—'cleaned' up the tainted
image of the Maenad and guaranteed her a place in the education of young
women well into the 1950s.[9] For some this sanitized maenad was a relief; for
others, she was merely a charade. A 'Dionysian Festival' at the Savoy Theatre,
organized by the Ginner-Mawer School, in 1922 was hailed as a 'beautiful and
effective spectacle', which 'fortunately avoid[ed] any attempt at a realistic reproduction of the Bacchantic orgies of the Dionysia'.[10] However, the absence of the

---

[6] On the differences between *fin de siècle* 'decadence' and the so-called 'degeneration' of the
Edwardian period, see Blom (2008). For useful discussions of 'decadence', Potolsky (2004).
[7] Symonds, 'Intermezzo': 'Fart lewd, aesthetical in part, / and fin de siècle essentially. / The
Maenad of the Decadence / Collectedly extravagant, / Her learned fury wakes the sense / That,
fainting, needs for excitant. / This science of concupiscence.'
[8] Hofmannsthal (1964), 77. Trans. A. Schwarz.
[9] The Classical Greek Dance Faculty (from 1923 the Association of Teachers of the Revived
Greek Dance, which grew out of the Ginner–Mawer School—see further below—and from 1937
known as the Greek Dance Association) has been affiliated to the ISTD since 1951. In the 1950s it
was on the curriculum of many girls schools, but once it ceased being taught in teacher training
institutions, most of the teaching (as today) took place in private studios in Britain, the
Commonwealth and Europe. For details of its current activities, examinations, Annual Festival
and Summer Schools, see http://www.istd.org/classicalgreek. For details of classes, teacher training
and Summer Schools for the Margaret Morris Method, which is still practised world-wide,
see http://www.margaretmorrismovement.com.
[10] *The Telegraph*, 5 July 1922.

Figure 9.1 Maud Allan 'dancing off a vase' (1908).

Dionysiac at the Albert Hall during the 1934 Greek Dance Festival to mark the twenty-fifth anniversary of Ruby Ginner's involvement in Greek dance was a cause for lament. Yet the reviewer went on to highlight the paradoxical nature of post-war maenadism: 'it has always been a mystery to me why this essentially educational form of dancing should attempt to copy the Bacchic orgies with their unpleasant hidden meanings.'[11] Indeed, the incorporation of Greek dance within the school curriculum of necessity entailed a process of radical domestication, with the result that there was ultimately very little recognizably 'Bacchic' about the post-war maenads' performances.

MAENADS AND SISTERHOOD

The privileging of the dancer in literary discourse at this time was as much to do with the impact of Nietzsche's *The Birth of Tragedy* (1872) as it was with developments in comparative anthropology. Nietzsche had identified the singing, dancing chorus as the wellspring from which tragic drama originally developed; and from the beginning of the new century a group of classical scholars—shortly to be known as the Cambridge Ritualists—designated dance as a form of primitive prayer and maintained that Greek tragedy had grown out of the ritual dances in honour of the god Dionysus.[12] If the essence of tragedy could be located in the hitherto neglected ancient chorus, the paradigmatic chorus became those maenadic dancers who danced in honour of Greek tragedy's patron god, Dionysus.

Euripides' *Bacchae* received relatively little serious critical or popular attention before *The Birth of Tragedy*, despite its curious and notable absence from Nietzsche's schema. This earlier neglect was inextricably bound up with the wider negative reception of Euripides throughout most of the nineteenth century, when he was held to be uneven, decadent, irreligious and the destroyer of high tragedy.[13] Writing very much within the nineteenth-century tradition of the *damnatio* of Euripides, Nietzsche nonetheless succeeded in focusing attention on the *Bacchae* in the wider cultural sphere during the last few years of the century.

In Germany and Russia there were followers of Dionysus, who shunned the modern world altogether and lived in quasi-Bacchic settings and practised Dionysiac rituals.[14] In Britain, however, it was the maenad herself who proved alluring; and this fascination manifested itself initially in the aesthetic and

---

[11] *The Dancing Times*, April 1936.

[12] Harrison (1912) with Gilbert Murray's Appendix, 'An Excursus on the Ritual forms Preserved in Greek Tragedy', 341–63; Harrison (1913).

[13] On Euripidean reception in the nineteenth century, see Michelini (1987).

[14] Blom (2008), 200–2. In Russia, for example, Vyachelsav Ivanov (1866–1949), classical scholar and author of *The Hellenic Religion of the Suffering God* (1904), lived in 'The Tower' believing he was Dionysus from 1905 onwards. In Germany, there were numerous bearded and naturist followers of Dionysus, including the young Hermann Hesse.

political spheres, notably in the paintings of Alma Tadema and in the discourse surrounding the emergent New Woman.[15] Gilbert Murray prefaced his 1902 translation of the *Bacchae* with an essay in which he linked the ecstatic nature of the Dionysiac to the idea of political liberation.[16] 'Maenads' of early Modernism were very often broadly conversant with such a politicized reading of Euripides' tragedy, and for them liberation had a decidedly urgent, feminist emphasis. Murray's close colleague, the prominent Cambridge Ritualist, Jane Harrison found that her advocacy of the Dionysiac led to comparisons between herself and a maenad. Commenting on a London lecture given by Harrison, one reviewer saw her 'throwing back her head [as] she burst into a chorus of Euripides in Greek'.[17] Some years later, Harrison and Murray were both taken to task for having unleashed 'in the minds of an entire generation . . . the corybantic Helle-nism . . . of Isadora Duncan . . . the irrational semi-sentimental free-verse and sex-freedom Hellenism of all the gushful geysers of "rapturous rubbish" about the Greek spirit'.[18]

The maenad merged in the male, establishment imaginary in the first decade of the new century with the deviant, educated, independent spirits who were enacting and promoting new, alternative lifestyles within their midst. Pentheus' nightmare vision in the *Bacchae* of women wielding phallic *thyrsi*, hunting and nurturing their young independently of the male guardians of the community, was unfolding before their eyes. Dancing maenads, in particular, became synonymous with the anxieties surrounding the self-sufficiency of the New Woman— not only did these women resist male supervision, they also led lifestyles that were contributing to the declining birthrate and the emasculation of the populace. During the *fin de siècle*, the 'decadent' had been focused on lush, erotic, and deviant male homosexuality; now in the wake of Max Nordau's *Degeneration* (translated into English in 1895), the anxieties shifted to the New Woman, and especially the Sapphic New Woman in the early twentieth century. One German reviewer of Strauss's operatic version of Hofmannsthal's *Elektra* commented that the tragic heroine's feminine strength at the end of the opera made her 'almost a lesbian'.[19] The suffragette was deemed sex-crazed, mannish, bi-sexual, a lesbian, or a monstrous hermaphrodite; and by June 1908 when the Hyde Park demonstration of the Women's Social and Political Union attracted between 300,000 and 500,000 supporters, she was dangerous in number as well as in conduct.[20]

Numerous incarnations of dancing maenads appeared on the London stage during the course of 1908. In a particularly static production of Gilbert Murray's translation of Euripides' *Bacchae* directed by William Poel in November at the

[15] Prins (1999).
[16] Macintosh (2007).
[17] Cited by Peacock (1988), 62.
[18] Paul Shorey in Payne (1978), 187.
[19] Blom (2008), 302.
[20] Ibid. 226ff, 246, 248.

Royal Court Theatre, the chorus consisted of four 'stately' maenads, who moved only once from the sides of the proscenium during the two-hour production, and whose function was to chant the 'more solemn passages and to strike the note of inevitable fate'. They were matched by three other chorus members, who danced and sang 'the gayer chorus speeches',[21] but whose performances bore little resemblance to intoxicated followers of Dionysus. This was in marked contrast to the regular appearances of the Canadian dancer, Maud Allan at the Palace Theatre from March 1908 as a 'reeling Bacchante', whose entire body (including her skin) danced with 'thrills and shivers such as are produced with the sudden contact with cold water'.[22]

Allan was deemed by reviewers to have danced straight off a Greek vase;[23] and with the imprimatur of no lesser luminary than King Edward VII himself, whose admiration for her performances at Marienbad in September 1907 had secured her London contract. Allan's billing at the Palace was an attempt on the part of the management to introduce a high cultural act into the theatre's programme. Although renowned for her alluring appearance as Salome (see Webb, this volume), Allan was regularly billed in London as the leading exponent of Greek dance during the Edwardian period. In fact, there were sufficient similarities between Salome and the maenad to make Allan's seemingly divergent repertoire teasingly coherent: for not only did Greek myth link the maenads to the beheading of Orpheus, Salome's frenzied caressing of John the Baptist's head bears some hideous resemblance to Agave's tragic and unwitting parading of Pentheus' head in the final scene of the *Bacchae* (1165 ff.). Artists of the period exploited those affinities and often made the connections between Salome and maenad explicit.[24]

So prominent was Allan in London in 1908 that Isadora Duncan could be trailed merely as 'Another Classic Dancer', when she came to London in July to perform at the Duke of York's Theatre after some five years' absence on the Continent.[25] Allan and Duncan were equally adept at managing the popular press, which reported their rivalry with considerable rapaciousness on both sides of the Atlantic. But Allan had already enjoyed five months' media attention in Britain before Duncan's arrival; and she had established a much wider fan base than Duncan, whose early career performing in the salons of the aristocracy of Europe had earned her an elitist image in Britain. The *Daily Mail* did much to promote Allan's populist reputation and took especial interest in her significant contribution, through sell-out Special

---

[21] Poel to Murray, 25 Oct. 1908 [Gilbert Murray Papers, Bodleian Library: GM 14.212–13].

[22] *The Daily Mail*, 7 March 1908. Cf. *The Observer*, 8 March 1908 of her dance to Rubinstein's *Valse Caprice* as a 'wild Bacchantic intoxication of joy'.

[23] See eg. Ralph Renaud (San Francisco) cited in Allan (1910), but regularly too of others—e.g. Hofmannsthal said it of Ruth St Denis when he first saw her in Berlin 1907 (Segel (1998)).

[24] See e.g. the painting by Joseph-Emile Millocheau 'A Maenad Weeping over the Head of Orpheus' in which a naked repentant maenad caresses the head of the dead Orpheus as she lies on the beach (reproduced in Vicars (1902), 74).

[25] *The Weekly Despatch*, mentioned in *The Daily Mail*, 23 July 1908. Allan is billed as 'The Greatest Living Exponent of Greek Art' see *The Daily Mail*, 7 July 1908, cited in Allan (1908), 104.

Matinées, to the hard-strapped Fund that the editor had set up for the London Olympics of that year.[26] Allan's other altruistic acts—genuine and/or stage-managed—met with equally close attention from the press: a visit to hospital to see an ailing fan occasioned a front-page story as well as an inside picture of the dancer solicitously attending the patient's bedside.[27]

If Allan was felt to have danced straight off a Greek vase, she was also taking her audiences into unchartered territory. It was her 1908 London season that introduced audiences to uninhibited, even ecstatic, dancing that had previously either been deemed unaccountably alien or confined to scholarly discussion of ancient Dionysiac ritual. As the former Oxford classical scholar and now drama critic of the *The Telegraph*, W. L. Courtney observed:

> for the first time probably, Miss Allan gave us a suggestion of the wild, chaotic dancing of the Dervish, something mad and tempestuous, and exhausting, after which the dancer falls inert, breathless, nerveless on the ground.[28]

Reports elsewhere of Allan's performances comment on 'the growing intoxication of the music . . . [she is] reeling, but still rhythmically moving until she collapses with the same grace with which she was just spinning round the stage'.[29]

Such observations anticipate, by just over a decade, Socrates' comments on ecstatic dance in Paul Valéry's Xenophon-inspired dialogue *L'âme et la danse* (1923), in which the dancer, Althikte, ends the symposium with a dance 'with her whole being', during which 'her head, flung back, sweeps the ground with her loosened hair'. Althikte's maenadic dance transports her into another world, where 'swelling and resounding joy tends to get beyond all bounds, and is shaking like a battering ram the walls that separate beings from another'. At the culminating point of supreme ecstasy, Althikte falls lifeless to the floor before reviving herself some minutes later. As Socrates notes, for some this would be 'coldly looked at' as pure madness; but for the initiated, Althikte's dance, just like Allan's, demonstrates unequivocally the boundary-breaking Dionysiac and its consequent loss of individuation.[30]

---

[26] For the rivalry between Allan and Duncan, see *The Daily Express*, 8 July 1908 and *New York Times*, 8 Aug. 1908; for the Olympics, see adverts in *The Daily Mail*, which undertook to raise the £10,000 when London took the Olympic Games over at short notice from Naples, after the earthquake of 1906. For a fictionalized account of this and other episodes of Allan's colourful life, see the novel by James (2008), and the earlier (anonymous) pornographic novel, *Maudie: Revelations of Life in London and an Unforeseen Denouement* (London 1909).

[27] *The Daily Express*, 31 July 1908.

[28] *The Daily Telegraph*, 13 Feb. 1909. Cited in Allan (1910). Cf. *The Academy*, 2 March 1908: 'We have the largest Eastern Empire the world has ever seen . . . We have to thank Miss Allan for beginning our education in a branch of art which we have persistently neglected.'

[29] *The Mail*, 7 March 1908.

[30] Valéry (1951), 53–4, 85–7, 53–4. The dialogue is based on Xenophon's *Symposium* and has a whole chapter devoted to it in Séchan (1930). Cf. Nora's tarantella at the end of Act II of Ibsen's *The Doll's House* (1879) and the folk dance of release in Strindberg's *Miss Julie* (1888). For ecstatic dance in Duncan and HD [Hilda Doolittle], see Anderson (2008); for Xenophon's *Symposium*, see further Hall, this volume, 149.

Even if the discerning eye was able to see beyond the seemingly frenzy-struck dancer, there were further reasons why Allan was 'coldly looked at'. Although she was no political feminist,[31] her matinée audience was predominantly female and socially diverse and 'might have been [attending] a suffragist meeting', according to the *Daily Chronicle* (13 June 1908). Her popularity was reflected and fuelled by massive postcard sales and all-female, 'Allan-parties' where women dressed and danced like Salome. To the Pentheus-like male establishment, she was the catalyst for covert, subversive gatherings of women. Moreover, her close relationship with the Prime Minister's wife, Margot Asquith, led to lurid speculation; and just as she was rumoured to have secured her contract in London after having danced naked in Marienbad before the king, many now inferred that she was enjoying a *ménage à trois* with the Asquiths or, more likely, a lesbian affair with Margot Asquith.[32] Bisexuality was no less a threat in these politically sensitive years; in many ways it posed an even greater one because it fuelled anxieties about the menace to the family/society originating from within rather than without.

Although maenads were spotted everywhere during this period when London opened up to European ideas and codes of behaviour from which it had remained isolated during much of Victoria's reign,[33] Greek-style dancers, in particular, were regularly imputed (or imagined) to have had Sapphic relations. This was true no less of Fuller, Duncan, and St Denis than it was of Allan, and her lesser known imitator, Lady Constance Stewart Richardson;[34] it was just that in Allan's case, her sexuality was to be used against her in the future.

Allan's strength, and what was to become Allan's weakness, was that her dances—be they Greek or her Salome dance—were highly erotically charged. Commenting upon her performance in 1908 as a Nymph/Tanagra Statuette to Chopin's *Valse in A Minor* (op.34 no.2), *The Times Literary Supplement* reviewer notes:

She wears light classic drapery that seems not so much to clothe her as to serve an ambient air wherein she floats. Her limbs and feet are bare: slender and supple limbs, feet that seem rather to caress the ground than to be supported by it. When her arms wave it is a wave in the true sense that they form; a ripple runs along them, slowly dying out at the finger tips.[35]

The reviewer is no passive spectator—he is caught up in the diaphanous tunic; he becomes metonymically identified with the ground which her bare feet 'caress'; and finally he vicariously participates in the 'dying' fall that is enacted by the undulations of her arms. The review concludes with an account of her 'master-stroke', her Salome dance, in which 'our dream is sensuous, decadent, macabre'; and Allan is able, the reviewer insists, to achieve the 'nice' distinction 'between the lascivious and

[31] See her comments in Allan (1908), 113–17.
[32] Walkowitz (2003).
[33] Hynes (1968), 254–306.
[34] See Blom (2008), 248. For Natalie Barney's lesbian salon in Paris, see especially Dorf (2007*a*), (2007*b*), and further Cooper Albright, this volume.
[35] *The Times Literary Supplement*, 26 March 1908, 102.

the voluptuous'; she is 'Our Lady of Dreams' who 'gives you beautiful dreams'.[36] As Walkowitz points out, Allan was not just an 'iconic figure of fantasy', she 'was also an active agent in the production of this fantasy'; and by combining Greek dance and the Salome dance within the same programme, she confounded conventional morality and the traditional polarity of virtue and vice.[37]

Eventually, however, both the ambivalent range of Allan's programme and the ambiguous nature of her venue—the Palace never quite escaped its previous incarnation as the venue for *poses plastiques* on the edge of Soho—meant that she found herself increasingly on the fringes of what was deemed to be cosmopolitan, and more particularly German/Jewish, decadent voluptuary.[38] Her earlier musical training in Germany, together with her association with J. T. Grein's planned touring production of Oscar Wilde's *Salome*, directed by his wife and starring Allan in the title role, led to a vehement right-wing and antisemitic backlash. The production, which opened at the Royal Court, was mounted to serve as a propaganda exercise sponsored by the Ministry of Information designed to promote British culture, and the fact that what was deemed a 'Jewish' production should be seeking to represent 'British' culture during the war caused outrage in certain circles.

In 1918 Allan ill-advisedly appeared in court seeking to defend herself against the accusation of being the enemy within—treacherous and (Sapphically) pleasure-seeking rather than gainfully employed in the war effort—who had precipitated, and was now undermining, the war itself. Her case was against a latterday Pentheus, an independent right-wing, antisemitic Member of Parliament, Noel Pemberton Billing, who had accused her of leading 'The Cult of the Clitoris'. The defence maintained, amongst other things, that Allan's *Vision of Salome* fostered a cult amongst transvestites; and with the testimony of the now married and 'respectable' forty-year-old former lover of Oscar Wilde, Lord Alfred Douglas, Wilde's play was proclaimed immoral. For continuing to enact such immoral subject matter and for her own alleged personal misconduct—notwithstanding the scandal of her brother's homicide and subsequent execution many years earlier in San Francisco—Allan was damned by association and lost her claim against Billing.[39] She failed in many ways to win her libel case because, like the other 'maenads' of her generation, she 'possessed too much knowledge'—in this case about the female anatomy by admitting she knew what a clitoris was.[40] But she was also being punished for having danced like a maenad, just as Pentheus had sought to punish those devotees of Dionysus upon whom he longed to gaze on Mount Cithaeron in Euripides' *Bacchae*.

---

[36] Ibid. 102.
[37] Walkowitz (2003), 345.
[38] Ibid.; and generally Hynes (1968).
[39] On the trial, see Hoare (1997).
[40] Walkowitz (2003), 373.

MAENADS AND MOTHERHOOD

Although Allan was no political activist, she came to embody all the worst fears surrounding the politically and sexually liberated New Woman of the Edwardian era. Following the trial, she was fixed in the public mind as a member of a subversive sisterhood, which was not only undermining the war effort, but also actively seeking to resist and overturn the institution of marriage. For Allan was not just unmarried and childless, she was also linked (through her brother's crimes) with infanticide and (through her role as Salome) with necrophilia. As a solo-performer too, she could be said to have been guilty of anti-generative acts: the autoerotic nature of her performance as Salome was matched by a sense of radical disengagement from her audience that was detectable in her Greek dances as well.[41]

Even if the press coverage from 1908 sought to promote Allan as a major fundraiser for worthy causes and someone who cared for the welfare of her fans, there was in other respects a decidedly self-regarding streak to her comments from the outset. Revealing and significant in retrospect is her statement in 1908 about the reason behind her decision not to open a school:

I have always steadfastly refused the many tempting offers to found a school of dancing. I have not the time to spare, for one thing, and secondly I do not believe the academies can turn out the real classical dancer.[42]

There are two points of note here: first, the absolute refusal (because 'I have not the time to spare') to teach, which flies in the face of the practice of all the other principal exponents of Greek dance, as we will see; and second and equally significant is her suggestion that Greek dance does not require training, but is in some way a product of innate 'genius'.

In marked contrast to her contemporaries—notably Duncan who began her first school in Grünewald in Berlin in 1904—Allan did not found a school until 1930, when she opened The West Wing in London with the avowed aim of teaching children from the slums to dance. In 1937 the school's name was changed to The West Wing School of Movement, over which she presided with the musicologist Dr Curt Sachs and which was closed in 1940 following eviction for rent arrears. Even though Allan's notebook jottings from the late 1930s suggest that she was planning a serious curriculum for her pupils,[43] it is hard not to see this belated venture into pedagogy as anything other than a financially driven necessity rather than any ideologically shaped project. In many respects, even as a sad, ageing dancer Allan continued to resemble the negative

---

[41] Walkowitz (2003), 359–60.
[42] *The Weekly Despatch*, July 1908 cited in Cherniavsky (1998), 57.
[43] Cherniavsky (1998), 157–60.

aspects of the ancient maenad—albeit now only in her self-absorption and her utter disengagement from society and its normative framework.

There were numerous attempts by women writers in the immediate post-war period to resist the derogatory associations of the maenad. Vera Brittain was especially incensed by a leading article in *The Times*, which argued that female undergraduates needed stricter discipline if they were to be admitted to full membership of Oxford University. For Brittain, it was vital to put the record straight:

Is it generally presumed outside the precincts of this university that . . . women students are free to wander withersoever they will from darkness to dawn? . . . Or are we pictured as Maenads dancing before the Martyrs' Memorial, or as Bacchantes revelling in the open spaces of Carfax or the High?[44]

A poem by N. M. Haldane (later Naomi Mitchison) rewrites the 'mad' maenad against the background of the outbreak of the war and presents her as a newly awoken, creative, and wise Bacchant.[45] There is a real sense in which the war years mark the watershed for the dancing maenad as well, especially following Allan's libel case in 1918, when there was a new urgent need to find an alternative Greek dancer to the maenad typified by Allan and her imitators.

In many ways, it was not difficult to find the alternative in Duncan herself, because she had been presented in Britain, as we have seen, as Allan's rival from 1908 onwards. Moreover, however chaotic and unorthodox, Duncan's lifestyle had the distinct advantage of having been largely conducted outside of Britain. As tragic mother, and then surrogate mother of the six 'Isadorables' who took her surname, she was readily assimilated in the popular consciousness as the Founding Mother of Greek Dance. As early as 1913, Constance Stewart Richardson placed Duncan at the beginning of a tradition; and this was later endorsed, amongst others, by Ruby Ginner, Margaret Morris, Ninette de Valois, and Marie Rambert, all of whom widely acknowledged their debt to her example.[46] Even the leading Russian/French dance critic, André Levinson, who was openly hostile to Duncan in the early years of her career, proclaimed in 1928 following her death that she would head the chapter of any attempt to document the developments in modern dance from the beginning of the twentieth century.[47]

Both Margaret Morris and Ruby Ginner, who came to represent the two major strands in the development of Greek dance in Britain in the inter-war years, grew up in the south of France in artistic families and lived in Bohemian

---

[44] *Testament of Youth* (1933), 505, cited by Hurst (2006), 200–1.

[45] Hurst (2006), 201.

[46] Stewart Richardson (1913), 55; Ginner, *The Dancing Times*, Oct. 1917 and *The Link* 2 (Oct. 1927), 73; Morris (1969); for de Valois, *The Dancing Times* Feb. 1926. Rambert, like Morris, studied in Paris under Raymond Duncan in 1909 before going to the Dalcroze Summer School, see Genné (1996), 32–3.

[47] Levinson (1929), 147.

circles in London in the pre-war years. Morris had discovered Greek dance through lessons with Raymond Duncan in Paris in 1909; and Raymond Duncan's six 'Greek positions' provided the staple of the Margaret Morris Method that was eventually to extend beyond the theatre to include general educational and remedial dance training. Morris's accounts of her School's first few months in 1913 bear witness to her fears lest prospective parents should get to hear of her unorthodox private life. At the time she was enjoying a passionate affair with the Scottish artist J. D. Fergusson, who was to become her partner for life, but who was then living in Antibes in a world far removed from the upper-middle class milieu in Chelsea, upon whose patronage she depended.[48]

During the First World War with Fergusson she set up the Margaret Morris Club in Chelsea, which sought to promote egalitarian (proto-Labour Party) politics; and under her influence, the aesthetic corollary of Labour politics within the Greek chorus was also hotly debated in neighbouring circles.[49] In the post-war period, Morris's school rather than her career as a performer became the focus for her creative energies; and she advocated Greek dance as a branch of education and part of the personal development of adult amateurs rather than something for solo performers. Morris was one of the first to recognize what Levinson was to articulate some years later—namely that Duncan had democratized dance.[50]

Although Ginner never worked with Raymond Duncan, she shared many formative experiences with Morris in addition to having been brought up in the south of France. As was the case with Morris, parental disapproval meant that theatre rather than dance provided her early training. Like Morris, she began her professional career in Frank Benson's Company before working for Mme Brema's Operatic Company at the Savoy. Both Morris and Ginner were principal dancers and choreographed choruses for Brema's operatic productions. Morris choreographed the choruses for Gluck's *Orfeo et Eurydice* (1910), in which Ginner danced; and later that year Ginner was invited by Brema to choreograph the choruses for Handel's *Allegro*, which proved to be the turning point in her career.[51]

Ginner's introduction to Greek dance had come through her training with the pioneer of speech and elocution training, Elsie Fogerty, in whose productions of *Alkestis* (1902) and *Antigone* (1904) at Crystal Palace Ginner had appeared as a member of the chorus. Fogerty acted as both model and facilitator in Ginner's teaching career by taking her on as a teacher of movement in her School of Training, Drama, and Dancing at the Albert Hall (shortly to become the Central School of Speech Training and Dramatic Art and now known as the Central School of Speech and Drama). Increasingly recognized as a specialist in

---

[48] Morris (1974), 72.
[49] See Blondel (2002), 72: 5 November 1916, for the Clarissa Club (from 1914 the Choric Club) set up by two of Morris's students, Kathleen Dillon and Hester Sainsbury.
[50] Morris (1926), Introduction; and Levinson (1929), 148.
[51] See press cuttings amongst the Ginner Papers in the NRCD (BB/N/3 1910–1913) for her widely acknowledged success as choreographer and dancer in *L'Allegro*.

choreographing Greek choruses, in 1912 Ginner formed her own company of 'Grecian Dancers', which went on to perform in numerous venues over the next couple of years.

Like Morris, and in marked contrast to Allan, Ginner was a political radical in the pre-war years as an active member of the Womens' Freedom League, a splinter group from the Women's Social and Political Union formed in protest against the Pankhursts' autocratic leadership. In September 1912, Ginner appeared at Beckenham Town Hall as the innovative eighteenth-century dancer Marie Camargo in the avowedly feminist 'The Pageant of Great Women' written by Ciceley Hamilton and produced by Edith Craig. In November that year her 'Selection of Dances of all Nations' was the highlight of the International Suffrage Fair at the Chelsea Town Hall, organized by the Women's Freedom League. According to the League's newspaper, *The Vote*: 'Miss Ruby Ginner's name . . . will stand out with prominence in the historic record of the International Suffrage Fair. Her own remarkable dancing, and the enthusiasm she inspires in her admirable band of dancers, emphasizing the outstanding feature of the Fair—Internationalism.'[52]

The war years marked the end of Ginner's career as a professional performer and the beginning of her career as a leading teacher of Greek dance. Some years later she describes her evening classes for war workers as being pivotal: 'under the calming joyous influence of the Greek dance, gradually one saw the terrible tension relax, the nerve wracked bodies rest, and for a while the tired eyes were at peace.' Greek dance, according to one of her students, was 'one of the sanest influences at work in a war-tortured world'.[53] That Greek dance was perceived to afford some escape from pressing realities was recognized by at least one reviewer, who commented on how whilst drama reflected the war, 'the art of dance [was] untouched; . . . a sure refuge from anxiety and gloom. [Ginner's Company] took the mind clean away into the happy realms of pure art and beauty.'[54]

Ginner's evening classes during the war led her to realize 'the community' implications of her practice and to appreciate the value of dance beyond the theatre. It was during this period that she founded, together with the mime and voice specialist, Irene Mawer, the Ginner–Mawer School of Dance and Drama, which provided the focus of Ginner's attention for the rest of her career.[55] During the war years, the Ginner–Mawer School followed the Margaret Morris School in inaugurating a Summer School, which was to prove a notable feature in their calendar—for Morris, these began in 1917 in Devon before moving to

---

[52] See cuttings in the Ginner Papers, NRCD (BB/N/3 1910–13).
[53] Ginner, *The Link*, vol. 2 March 1936 (=Special Issue 'The Greek Dance Festival'), 5.
[54] *Observer*, June 1917.
[55] For information about Mawer, I am indebted to one of her former students, Dr Rosemary Poutney. Mawer arranged and performed in the choruses, for example, for Lewis Casson and Bruce Winston's *The Trojan Women* at the Holborn Empire in December 1919, when Sybil Thorndike played Hecuba.

Figure 9.2 Margaret Morris Summer School (*c.*1926), Antibes.

Antibes in 1922 (see Figure 9.2); for the Ginner–Mawer School, they began in
1918 and were to occupy an increasingly important slot in Benson's Shakespeare
Summer Season Festival in Stratford. It was here that work on the Greek chorus
was explored and developed.[56] When Eva Palmer-Sikelianos, the most renowned
specialist on Greek choral dance in the late 1920s (see Cooper Albright and
Michelakis, this volume), visited the Ginner–Mawer School in London in 1929,
she claimed she had found 'the true spirit of the Greek school' and promptly
issued an invitation for the students to perform at the second Delphic Festival in
1930. The Ginner–Mawer School had the unique distinction of being the only
foreign company to be invited to participate in the Festival; and they gave two

[56] It was here in 1919 that the choruses for *The Trojan Women* were developed (see n. 55), and 1
July 1920 at the Prince of Wales Theatre and at the 1921 Shakespeare Summer Festival the choruses
for *Iphigenia in Tauris* (see BB/N/10—Scrapbook 1921–31 and *The Dancing Times*, Aug. 1921)
with Ruby Ginner as Iphigenia and Irene Mawer as Chorus Leader, and music by Eve S. Russell
were performed. Other chorus work by Ginner and Mawer include: 1920 *Medea* (8 March at the
Holborn), with Thorndike in the title role and Ginner in the chorus; 4 July 1922 at the Savoy
Theatre, the 'Dionysian Festival' included choreographed choruses from Euripides' *Bacchae*. See the
Ginner Papers, NRCD [BB/N/10].

performances in Athens, one in the indoor Olympia Theatre and the other in the Herodus Atticus in the days leading up to the Festival.[57]

If the dancing maenad under the tutelage of Allan had been a solo-performer, for Morris and Ginner she was a member of a chorus. As we have heard, it was their respective interest in the ancient chorus that had led them to Greek dance in the first place: the collective rather than the individual was their preferred model. If neither Morris nor Ginner appears to have had their own children, they took enormous pride in their surrogate families—their pupils—who, as had literally been the case with Duncan, became their adopted families. An event at the New Scala Theatre on 9 July 1925 organized by the Ginner–Mawer School was described as being like a 'family party'; and Ginner speaks passionately in the 1930s of the need to protect 'our children from harm'.[58]

The Representation of the People Act 1918 granted the vote to women over the age of 30, who were themselves householders or married to householders. The Judge who presided over the Maud Allan trial that year was clearly appealing in his judgment to those newly enfranchised 'mature' women to 'police' the younger wayward women who formed Allan's constituency.[59] The mature maenads of the dance similarly set out in the post-war period to nurture the members of the younger generation who were under their tutelage in such a way as to 'tame' any maenadic deviations.

TAMING THE MAENAD

In 1908, as we have heard, Allan proudly resisted the idea of running a school on the grounds that this was an unlikely milieu for the emergence of the innately talented, 'classical dancer'. But unnurtured talent can, of course, very often result in dilettante-ism; and it was this anxiety that led to a heated debate that very year, at the International Dance Federation Meeting in Berlin, when the German delegate refused to accept that 'Salome dancing' constituted dance proper.[60] However, it was not only Allan's *Vision of Salome* that besmirched the image of Greek dance, it was also the content of many Greek dances in the Edwardian period that caused offence. In 1921, the *The Dancing Times* bemoaned the frequently substandard work of many of Duncan's imitators 'who thought that "Greek Dancing" consisted in the casting off of as many garments as possible, and skipping about the stage'.[61] This lamentable absence of technique led cynics

---

[57] See the scrap book of the tour in the Ginner Papers, NRCD (BB/F/2).
[58] *The Birmingham Post*, 10 July 1925.
[59] Walkowitz (2003), 374 includes the following words from Justice Darling's speech: 'in a short time women will be able to have their influence upon legislation, and . . . I hope they will make it their business to see that much more purity is introduced into public representations than is the case at present.'
[60] *The Daily Mail*, 24 July 1908.
[61] *The Dancing Times*, Dec. 1921.

and would-be supporters alike to concur that the popular perception of Greek dance was that it was simply about donning the appropriate costume and 'appear [ing] in a few more or less graceful poses or run[ning] about and pick[ing] up flowers to the accompaniment of some really good Chopin or Rubinstein music'.[62]

That the Greeks were dubious allies in the cause for what was termed 'Natural Movement'[63] was pertinently pointed out by André Levinson in 1922. According to Levinson, the notion that the Greek revival was about the expression of 'natural'—as opposed to stylized—movement had to be seen against the background of the dominance of the dictates of theatrical Naturalism at the turn of the century. Greek dance, according to Levinson, no less than any other dance form, was subject to a set of strict conventions;[64] and Greek dance, as it was practised in the early 20s, was urgently in need of a set of readily identifiable and measurable conventions in order to enhance its credibility.

The appeal of Greek dance was that, in marked contrast to classical ballet, it was equally accessible to the 'average' as well as to the highly talented child; and it provided an 'outlet and aid to the child's imagination today'.[65] In 1924 the Association of Teachers of the Revived Greek Dance introduced exams, under the auspices of The Association of Operatic Dancing of Great Britain (later the Royal Academy of Dancing) to standardize practice within this relatively new area of dance. Not only did the curriculum include dance, it involved in the more advanced stages the study of the visual arts, literature and myth as well. If 'Ladies' Greek' in the Victorian period meant Greek without accents and the need to struggle with a parallel translation,[66] there is a real sense in which the 'Ladies' Greek' of the early twentieth century became 'The Revived Greek Dance' in which dance classes and Greek civilization were now afforded to the sisters of those young men who learned the classical languages at school. The pupils at the Ginner–Mawer School were being offered genuine insights into what was formerly forbidden territory. Although Greek Dance was always more 'respectable' than other kinds of dance for young ladies—and in Margaret Morris's Summer Schools in Antibes seems to have acquired considerable upper-middle class cachet—through the Ginner–Mawer School, at least, it increasingly widened its social base. Indeed, in marked contrast to the Greek language, which remained broadly an elitist subject within the curriculum, Greek Dance brought classical antiquity to sections of society normally excluded from its orbit.[67]

---

[62] *The Dancing Times*, January 1919.

[63] On Madge Atkinson's 'Natural Movement', see the NRCD collection of her papers.

[64] Levinson (1991), 29, 31.

[65] For a report of Ruby Ginner's lecture, under the auspices of the Bedford Froebel Society, see *The Bedfordshire Standard*, 26 October 1923.

[66] Hurst (2006).

[67] For its social cachet, see Genée (1996), 31; Classics within the British education system, see Stray (1999); Classics and the British class system, see Hall (2007), 386–97.

In addition to providing a rounded 'education', The Revived Greek Dance also acquired respectability through its supposedly 'health'-promoting qualities. From the outset, the revival of Greek dance was inextricably linked to other 'health' movements in Britain and Europe at the end of the nineteenth century (see Naerebout, this volume). The year that witnessed the Allan–Duncan rivalry in London also saw the foundation of Baden Powell's anti-urban Boy Scout Movement and the world's top athletes on display in the Olympic Stadium in West Ham. The Greeks were deemed the best guides in the promotion of healthy living because their early training in physical education and dance was said to have developed their ideal physiques. In a manual entitled *The Renaissance of the Greek Ideal* (1914), Diane Watts identifies the ways in which the modern body falls short of the ancient ideal. Watts systematizes a series of movements (largely based on Greek sculptures), which allegedly enables the reader to recover the Greek 'ideal'.[68]

Watts's exercise programme was considered no marginal, cranky venture but received wide endorsement in medical circles, including amongst opthalmologists, who maintained that failing eyesight could be stemmed by an improvement in posture in accordance with Watts's method.[69] Ginner's 1960 study *A Gateway to the Dance* similarly receives medical endorsement with a preface by Professor A. P. Cawadias, Professor of General Practice, who proclaims Greek dance as a way to counteract 'the general restlessness, exaggeration and neurosis of the world today'.[70] Like Watts, Ginner maintained that Greek dance led to a 'healthy and beautiful physique, to a perfectly controlled expression of mind and soul', which the modern world with its 'rush and hurry', its 'too much mechanism' and 'loss of mental and physical control' denies. In a world in which 'jerk and loss of rhythm' has become the norm, there is a consequent 'loss of healthy vitality and joy'.[71]

A note of caution was sounded against Ginner's emphasis on physical beauty as the goal to which all should aspire. It came from the Christian Socialist and close friend of Arthur Symons, the Reverend Stewart Headlam who reminded Ginner and the members of the 'Dancers' Circle' at her lecture in 1922 that reverence for the Greeks needed slightly less romanticism: Christianity, he averred, had gone one important step further in pointing out that bodily deformity did not necessarily preclude beauty.[72] As a fierce champion of the theatre generally and dance in particular (against its opponents in the Church) and a staunch and unorthodox Anglican supporter of the pilloried (it was Headlam who had raised bail for Oscar Wilde), Headlam's voice was one not

---

[68] Watts (1914).

[69] See e.g. Bates (1920).

[70] Ginner (1960), p. vi. Cf. the health-promoting exercises of the Margaret Morris Method and even Stewart Richardson (1913) on the importance of outdoor exercise for good health.

[71] Ginner's Lecture in Leamington 17 Dec. 1922, 'The Position of Dancing in the Education of Ancient Greece. An Address read by Miss Ruby Ginner at the last Dancers' Circle Dinner' (BB/N/10).

[72] *The Morning Post*, 18 Dec. 1922; *The Telegraph*, 18 Dec. 1922; *The Era*, 24 Dec. 1922.

easily dismissed.[73] Moreover, his important intervention serves to highlight the interconnections at this time between 'The Revived Greek Dance' and the theory of Eugenics.

For Ginner, Greek dance was the perfect 'admixture' of two racial groups, one the indigenous, Pelasgians: 'a short, dark-haired race, with all the passionate, superstitious, imaginative, and artistic qualities of the Southerner.' The other from the North: 'fair-haired, tall and warlike, with the stern repression of passion peculiar to the Northerner'; one sub-group of which, the Achaeans, were 'blue-eyed . . . of a magnificent physique . . . brave, chaste, self-controlled and law-abiding'.[74] Not only does this sound remarkably like contemporary racial theory—with the 'Southerners' sounding identical to Matthew Arnold's Celt as well as widely held stereotypes of the so-called 'Jewish character', and the Northerners becoming synonymous with the Aryan ideal of Nazi ideology;[75] it also draws much of its detail from Ginner and her colleagues's reading of Nietzsche's *The Birth of Tragedy*. In the Introduction to her study of 1960, Professor Cawadias praises Ginner for 'insisting on pure Greek dancing' and having thereby 'stopped it deviating towards Dionysiac disorder and gymnastics.'[76]

Greek dance was the 'most beautiful, the sanest type of movement', Ginner insisted, and a necessary antidote to 'the neurotic movements that monopolise theatres and ballroom dances to the hideous and nerve-tearing din of jazz bands'.[77] Indeed, jazz is regularly cited in the 1920s by Ginner and other exponents of the art of Greek dance (notably Duncan) as the decadent 'other' against which their own art form is being routinely defined.[78] Jazz with its roots in African American culture is deemed primitive and exotic—a kind of drug which caught the war-torn western world when it was at its most vulnerable and which induces 'imbecilic' movement and often promotes immorality.[79] According to Mark Perugini, husband of Irene Mawer, what is necessary in the post-war period is for the western world 'which has known the exalted calm of classic Greek art, the orderly logical, yet virile mentality of Latin culture and Anglo-Saxon progress' to recapture the 'idyllic classic days, for inspiration . . . beauty, joy and—sanity'.[80]

If Allan had made Greek dance appear perilously German and/or Jewish, it was essential in the post-war period that it be aligned with 'healthy' Anglo-Saxon

---

[73] Foulkes (1997), 166–86.

[74] Ginner (1933), 1, 3.

[75] On the ubiquity of the theory of Eugenics at this point, see Blom (2008), 338–52. For Arnold's Celt as a counter to the Greek, see Macintosh (1994). Cf. *Lady's Pictorial* 20 Oct. 1917, where Ginner and Morris are praised for teaching 'the eugenics of joy in the fullest meaning of the term'. On Ginner's emphasis on the racial characteristics of dance, see further Webb, this volume.

[76] Ginner (1960), p. vi.

[77] Lecture at Leamington, see n. 69 (BB/N/10).

[78] Duncan (1928), 244.

[79] See e.g. *The Stratford-upon-Avon Herald*, 10 Aug. 1923; *The Bedfordshire Standard*, 26 Oct. 1923.

[80] Perugini (1928), 9.

culture. In the 1920s Greek dance is regularly invoked as a model for the embryonic British Dance movement on account of its 'open-air and athletic' character.[81] The Greeks and the British routinely become one in their alleged shared love of games and the great outdoors; and the Greeks' athletic dances are appropriated readily and effortlessly, we are told, by the English-speaking peoples of the twentieth century.

Throughout the late 1920s The Ginner–Mawer School consolidated its reputation, both within Britain and across the empire. The School organized numerous large-scale, spectacular events—notably outdoors in Hyde Park;[82] and after their performances in Athens in association with the Delphic Festival in 1930, they went on in 1936 to stage a vast spectacular day's event in the Albert Hall with some 500 performers and were making plans to perform in Wembley Stadium in 1937 with 800 dancers as part of the National Festival of Youth.[83] But these performances did not always meet with commendation. By the second part of the 1920s, reviewers frequently detect a note of tiredness about 'The Revived Greek Dance'—as if it were at the end of a long tradition that began with Duncan. Veritable praise for Ginner's performances apart, there is a suggestion that outside influence is vital for the creativity of Greek dance, even if there is an equally strong realization that its survival is guaranteed owing to its pedagogical value.[84]

No doubt the critics of Greek dance were right—it needed outside influences in order to survive aesthetically in comparison with the vibrant, intercultural mode of classicizing that was the norm in 1920s Paris, where Jazz wasn't shunned as 'barbaric' but was being eclectically adopted by Cocteau and Diaghilev's company. Ninette de Valois and Marie Rambert knew this all too well and showed what could be done by combining the strengths of the new Russian ballet with aspects of Greek dance.[85]

Just as Ginner and Duncan begin to sound outmoded by the 1920s, so too in many ways does the writing in the journal of the 'Revived Greek Dance', *The Link* (now under the editorship of Mark Perugini). In 1929, the year after women had acquired equal voting rights with men, an editorial strikes a decidedly avuncular note:

Modern civilisation has conferred on women a new duty—the public duty of registering her vote; but she must not overlook that greater duty, known to women of all times past, of being beautiful, in mind and body.[86]

---

[81] Colebrook (1925), 45; Ginner (1926), 14.

[82] The Ginner–Mawer School performed outdoors as part of the League of Arts Hyde Park Entertainments in 1927, 1929, 1930. In 1933 they gave two performances (captured on film, a copy of which is in the NRCD) and the combined audience figures were a staggering 12,000.

[83] Ginner (1936), 7.

[84] See *The Birmingham Post*, 10 July 1925; *The Dancing Times*, Aug. 1925; *The Dancing Times* Aug. 1926.

[85] Genné (1996).

[86] 'On Inspiration, and the Future' by 'Aristodemus', *The Link*, vol. 3 no. 8, Oct. 1929.

Greek dance is designated the key to fulfilling this 'greater duty': the maenad, once in the vanguard of the campaign for political suffrage, is now urged to remember her place within an avowedly patriarchal system.

But however 'tamed', however 'muted', the dancing maenads (as had been the case during the First World War) still had a significant function in the dark and ominous days leading up to 1939. In 1936, against the background of the Berlin Olympics and the same year that the Ginner–Mawer 'family' of 500 dancers gathered together for the Dionysian Festival in the Albert Hall, one of Ginner's supporters advocates most presciently and poignantly the urgent need to sustain the ideals behind Greek dance:

Very far away in the past our lives began in the beauty of truth of those who lived before, very far away into the future we intend to hand on this torch to the generations that will come; that whatever may happen in the future, wars and rumours of war, there shall yet be a vision of beauty, truth, and sanity, to hold before the world.[87]

With more than a passing nod to Clytemnestra's famous speech in Aeschylus' *Agamemnon* (281–350), the writer is boldly, if not precariously, holding up the ideals of 'beauty, truth, and sanity' as beacons in a lugubrious and morally fragile world. The maenads' message and motives may have been radically refashioned, but their mission now, albeit briefly, had acquired a new urgent significance.

[87] Helga Burgess, 'Lessons from the Greek', *The Era*, 29 Jan. 1936.

III

DANCE AND MYTH

10

Ancient Greece, Dance, and the English Masque

Barbara Ravelhofer

I say, a moving grove.
Macbeth, V.v.38

English masques flourished in the sixteenth and seventeenth centuries. A distinctive kind of dramatic entertainment, they involved music, dancing, fanciful costumes and settings, and were staged in country houses, at schools and universities, and at court. Continental fashions in ballet and staging technique had a huge impact on London productions, and likewise, the Renaissance enthusiasm for ancient cultures was shared by many English poets and designers. So, on occasion, on a masquing night, the horizon of theatrical illusion opened towards mainland Europe and the classical past.

How can you capture the past in fleeting movements? In western Europe, attempts to theorize dance and revive the customs of ancient Greece reach back to at least the fifteenth century, when Domenico da Piacenza, a celebrated Lombard choreographer of Jewish background, rediscovered Aristotle. Domenico developed a technical terminology which distinguished between 'natural' and 'accidental' movements.[1] Subsequently, early modern scholars explained classical dance based on Greek and Latin literary sources; in this way, Ioannes Meursius wrote *De ludis graecorum* (Leiden, 1625), a study of Greek pastimes and sports with a survey of pyrrhic dancing. Meursius's other work on the topic, *Orchestra. Sive, de Saltationibus Veterum* (Leiden, 1618), an exhaustive dictionary of ancient dance steps and genres, is still noted for its bibliographical rigour (an *Index saltationum* includes entries on *daktylos, cordax, emmeleia* and so on, with copious Greek and Latin cross-references to Pollux, Lucian, Aristotle, Cicero, Quintilian, and many other authorities). Meursius was convinced that dances

---

[1] At the very least, Domenico da Piacenza was familiar with the *Nicomachean Ethics* and *Poetics*. See Smith (1995), 1. 11 and chs. 8–9; and Naerebout (1997) includes a broad survey of early modern attempts to re-create Greek dance, English masques excepted.

had not only been watched but performed by the philosophers of the ancient world.[2]

Others sought a more practical and contemporary approach. Fabritio Caroso, one of the most celebrated Italian choreographers of the sixteenth century, drew comparisons between choreography and Ovidian versification.[3] In Caroso's view, a performance was a mute dialogue ('pedalogo' or 'pedalogue', as Caroso joked because he believed that both poets and dancers relied on 'feet').[4] His richly illustrated dance manual *Nobiltà di dame* (1600) demonstrated the compatibility of courtly dance with ancient metre as it included a particular circular choreography, *Contrapasso Nuovo*, which applied Greek versification (transmitted via Ovid) to the performance of three dancing couples.[5] Caroso tried to express ancient rhythm with particular steps, specially invented for the occasion: the *spondeo* step (– –) imitated the spondee and consisted of two simple steps, while the *dattile* (– ∪∪) was performed as a triple step with a possible emphasis on the first. In its creative engagement with the past, Caroso's work was typical of the period, and similar to that of English artists concerned with spectacle.

With regard to English masques, designers, poets and performers often turned to Greece and Rome: between 1604 and 1640, the ancient muses were yet again invoked on the English stage with complicated choreographies, sumptuous costumes and extravagant settings. George Chapman, who first translated the *Iliad* and *Odyssey* into English, was among the luminaries of anglo-hellenic illusionistic theatre, writing a *Memorable Masque* (1612) inspired by Menander, Lucian, and Aristophanes for performance at the Inns of Court.[6] Ben Jonson, who liked to think of himself as an English Horace, composed, with *Sejanus*, a tragedy famous for its faithful use of Roman sources. The same preference for classical subject-matter emerged in Jonson's masques: a revived Penthesilea, Queen of Amazons, danced on stage in his *Masque of Queens* (1609), and *Love's Triumph through Callipolis* (1631) imagined Charles I as the ruler of a London which had turned into a Greek 'Citty of *Beauty* or *Goodnes*'.[7] One of the most elaborate descriptions of a neo-classical masque choreography derives from Jonson's *Pleasure Reconciled to Virtue* (1618), where a singing Daedalus directed labyrinthine dances:

---

[2] Meursius (1618), in particular, sig. 2ʳ, '*saltationem apud veteres inter honesta habitam esse, & heroas illos priscos, philosophosque, non se tantum in spectandâ oblectasse, sed saltasse etiam ipsos*'.

[3] Fabritio Caroso composed *Il Ballarino* (Venice: Ziletti, 1581) and a revised sequel, *Nobiltà di dame* (Venice: Il Muschio, 1600); *Raccolta di varij Balli* (Rome: G. Facciotti, 1630) is a reprint of *Nobiltà di dame*. As Caroso described Ovid's pentameter lines, 'the immortal poet Ovid demonstrated this well in his verse (for one calls that joining of feet a *caesura*)'. See Caroso (1995), 102, 'Passo Puntato Semigrave'.

[4] For 'pedalogo [pedalogue]' see Caroso (1600), *Laura Suave*, 115.

[5] Caroso (1600), 240–4, *Contrapasso Nuovo*. For a full discussion of this dance, see Ravelhofer (2010), in press.

[6] Chapman (1613), sig. a3ʳ, [a4]ʳ.

[7] Jonson (1925–52), 7. 736, l. 18.

Come on, come on; and where you goe,
so enter-weave the curious knot,
As ev'n th'observer scarce may know
which lines are Pleasures, and which not.

   .   .   .   .   .

Then, as all actions of mankind
are but a Laborinth, or maze,
so let your Daunces be entwin'd,
yet not perplex men, unto gaze.
But measur'd, and so numerous too,
as men may read each act they doo.
And when they see the Graces meet,
admire the wisdom of your feet.
For Dauncing is an exercise,
not only shews the movers wit,
But maketh the beholder wise,
as he hath power to rise to it

   .   .   .   .   .

and now put all the aptnes on
of figure, that proportion
or colour can disclose.
That if those silent arts were lost,
Designe, & Picture: they might boast
from you a newer ground.[8]

Subtle formations which traced letters or multiple geometric patterns were in great demand in masque productions. Unfortunately their precise nature is now lost to us, as not one of the choreographies for the great court masques has survived (if indeed they were ever put to paper in the first place). Movement is one of the most elusive aspects of drama, and Jonson, like so many other poets, reaches the limits of language when seeking to verbalize the ephemeral for posterity. Readers may struggle to infer the complex geometries of Daedalus' playful crew; even so, Jonson's lines express great trust in the power of dance. In the words of Jonson's mouthpiece Daedalus, ballet is capable of reconciling contradictory aesthetic signals. The curious knots and interweavings seem at first chaotic because they represent the unpredictability of human existence. Yet they have a logic of their own, for they are measurable, 'numerous' (in the early modern sense of 'number-ous', regular and countable), and their 'figure', 'proportion', and 'colour' (in the early modern sense of poetic rhythm) speak to those who are capable of reading the signs. Dance may illuminate the past but this joyful knowledge is a hard-earned privilege, requiring effort on the part of both dancers and beholders.

The masques by Thomas Campion offer another intriguing example of how classical antiquity materialized on stage in word, image, and movement.

---

[8] Ibid. 7. pp. 488–9, ll. 253–84; abbreviations silently expanded, u/v spelling normalized.

Campion was a great champion of the classical past. In a funeral elegy upon Anna of Denmark he compared the death of the Queen to the fall of Troy.[9] In particular, Campion regarded the tried and tested forms of classical poetry as models for the present: 'Old customes, if they be better, why should they not be recald, as the yet florishing custome of numerous poesy used among the *Romanes* and *Grecians?*' But, as Campion knew, adaptation to the needs of another language required discipline, for which reason many poets resorted to simpler English rhymes ('the unaptness of our toongs and the difficultie of imitation dishartens us; againe, the facilitie and popularitie of Rime creates as many Poets as a hot sommer flies').[10] This sense of discipline and proportion in rhyme—or rhythm—informed Campion's approach to poetry, music, and dance, as the following discussion will show.

Campion may never have seen Caroso's books, whose circulation in Jacobean England is not proven.[11] Yet he too was deeply interested in making lost rhythms audible—and visible. Written in 1607 to celebrate the wedding of the Scottish courtier James Hay and Lady Honora Denny, Campion's *The Lord Hay's Masque* represents a striking fusion of anglo-classical elements. A parvenu and royal favourite, the 27-year-old bridegroom had, against all expectation, wed a lady from rich and well-respected old English stock. Apparently, Hay was not graced with an excessively handsome complexion (Princess Elizabeth addressed him in her letters as 'Camel-face'), but he compensated these defects with a cosmopolitan background, suave manners, and considerable diplomatic skills. Above all, Hay knew how to show off his refined tastes at banquets and entertainments, inventing the 'antesupper' (laid out for visual display only and thrown out before the supper proper was served) and sponsoring masques with over a thousand different dishes.[12] An apt early example of Hay's delight in ostentation, the *Lord Hay's Masque* honoured King James, present at the performance, while several members of the aristocracy danced disguised as 'knights of Apollo' to entertain Hay and his bride.

To commemorate the social success of Hay's illustrious wedding and perpetuate the impact of the masque beyond its performance night, Campion published a masque booklet (or libretto), which described in detail plot, scenes, lyrics, and performers.[13] The publication even included scores of the songs which could be played by musically gifted readers, so that Campion's art could be re-enacted by a

---

[9] 'O singing wayle a fate more truely funerall / Then when with all his sonnes the sire of Troy did fall.' The poem, 'To the Most Sacred Queen Anne', was included in a 1613 collection of songs of mourning. In Campion (1967), 121, ll. 9–10.

[10] *Observations in the Art of English Poesie* (1602), in Campion (1967), 294.

[11] Some studies have proposed that Henry Prince of Wales learnt Italian dancing from such books but without conclusive evidence. See Smith and Gatiss (1986), 198–207.

[12] Schreiber (1984) and his 'Hay, James, First Earl of Carlisle (*c.*1580–1636)', in *Oxford Dictionary of National Biography*. For a longer discussion of Hay's conspicuous consumption see Raylor (2000); and Ravelhofer (2007), 144–55.

[13] Campion (1607).

Figure 10.1 A Knight of Apollo from *The Lord Hay's Masque* (1607).

wider public in private. Extra costs were incurred not only with regard to music (more complicated and hence expensive to print) but also illustration. Among early modern publications of masques, the 1607 imprint of *The Lord Hay's Masque* is singular in depicting a dancer. The woodcut of a noble masquer, or 'knight of Apollo' (see Figure 10.1), was placed opposite a poem dedicated to the king: for the first and last time in the seventeenth century, readers learned from a design what a masque performer looked like. Sparing no expense in performance and subsequent publication, *The Lord Hay's Masque* represented a striking, lasting document of the patron's and poet's newly gained importance.

When invited to a masque, Jacobean spectactors paid close attention to the appearance of performers and often commented on fashion and even footwear. Costume, like stage design, belonged to a well-defined theatrical vocabulary which complemented spoken or sung information and gave audiences additional clues as to the meaning of the action evolving before them. Masque accounts responded to sartorial interest with minute observations: it is not uncommon to find page-length descriptions of performers' costumes which digress on fabrics, colours, jewellery, plumes, and other accessories. What may seem trivial to modern readers would have been of great significance to seventeenth-century ones, and it is therefore necessary to inspect Hay's Apollonian knight carefully from head to toe.

The headgear recalls pseudo-classical Italian or French entertainment fashion, with jewels and, possibly, heron's feathers indicating expense and high mainten-ance. A mantle covers a more tight-fitting doublet with narrow sleeves and a knee-length garment after the ancient military fashion; this must be the kind of costume an older Hay had in mind, reminiscing years later about his masquing days ('the mode was to appear very small in the wast, I remember I was drawne up from the ground by both hands whilst the tayler with all his strength buttoned on my doublet').[14]

We do not know who created this particular costume but the designer and architect Inigo Jones, who was responsible for such matters in most court productions of the period, might have stepped in here as well. Jones gleaned many ideas for fashion from Cesare Vecellio's *Habiti antichi* (1590) and various French and Italian festival books.[15] In Jonesian masques, Turkish, Polish, Hungarian, or Persian characters were often dressed up in a style similar to Hay's noble dancers. To English observers, Hay's troupe might therefore have looked eastern European or oriental, had not the sleeves harked back to northern fashions of the early sixteenth century. Altdorfer, Cranach, or the *landsknechts* of Dürer and Burgkmair come to mind—perhaps the costume designer intended a martial effect? For colours, carnation had been chosen, a kind of flesh-colour which at the time varied from light pink to deep crimson. Apparently carnation showed off very well under artificial lighting (Francis Bacon wrote an essay on this topic[16]); and for this reason the colour was frequently selected for noble masquers who had to dance under the adverse conditions of candle- or torch-light.[17] The seventeenth-century English 'buskin', a tight-fitting boot with a fairly flexible sole as worn by Hay's knights, was the balletic equivalent of the ancient *cothurnus*, and denoted soldiers and heroes.[18] Campion's contemporaries readily drew such cross-connections: in Shakespeare's *A Midsummer Night's Dream*, Titania famously scorns Oberon for fancying Hippolyta, 'the bouncing Amazon, | Your buskin'd mistress and your warrior love', a twofold taunt which

---

[14] Raymond (1917), 25; cited in Schreiber (1984), 10.

[15] Peacock (1995). Jones's designs are reproduced in Jones (1973).

[16] 'Of Masques and Triumphs', *The Essays or Counsels Civil and Moral* (1625), in Bacon (1996), 416–17.

[17] Ravelhofer (2006), ch. 7.

[18] Leloir (1951), 47, 110, for a short history of the buskin. Shakespeare (1983), II.i. 70–1.

insults Titania's rival as loose (because of her un-ladylike 'bouncing') and unfemi-
nine (because wearing masculine footwear). In comparison, Hay's masquer
appears morally unimpeachable, greeting us with a confident and socially acceptable classical posture, the *contrapposto*; yet Apollonian as the costume itself
purports to be, it has been assembled in a Dionysiac mélange of styles.

Masque designers did on occasion attempt historical accuracy. One of the
most sustained efforts was made in Ben Jonson's *Albion's Triumph* (1631): here
Inigo Jones assembled gladiators and pugilists (copied after Onofrio Panvinio),
turning the Banqueting House temporarily into a modest early Stuart Colosse-
um. Yet as often many other pseudo-classical masque costumes of the period
appear joyfully eclectic, such as that for Charles's French consort, Henrietta
Maria, in Jonson's *Chloridia* (1631). The queen took the stage disguised as the
nymph Chloris with contemporary pumps and puffed sleeves. It is not clear to
what extent an early modern English audience would have been familiar with
Greek art and iconography; indeed, one wonders whether spectators enjoying
Hay's masque would have identified someone dressed up as, say, Socrates or
Clytemnestra, as being Greek. Access to Greek art and iconography was limited,
especially during the first decades of the seventeenth century; Lord Arundel's
famous collection of classical statues, groundbreaking for disseminating an
understanding of ancient sculpture in Jacobean England, was not yet available.[19]
Whoever designed the costume for Lord Hay's aristocratic dancers thought
it sufficient to make them look vaguely exotic and oriental—in short,
non-English—to achieve the desired effect.

The foreign conceit of the costume responded very well to the origins of the
person who had commissioned the entertainment. After all, Hay was not English
but had a Scottish background. In the masque booklet, a dedicatory poem faces
the illustration of the masquer. This poem dwells on the fraught history of
Scythia before it addresses King James as a peacemaker:

> The disunited Scithians, when they sought
> To gather strength by parties, and combine
> That perfect league of freends which, once beeing wrought,
> No turne of time or fortune could untwine,
> This rite they held: a massie bowle was brought,
> And ev'ry right arme shot his severall blood
> Into the mazar till 'twas fully fraught.
> Then having stird it to an equall floud
> They quaft to th' union, which till death should last,
> In spite of private foe, or forraine feare;
> And this blood sacrament being knowne t'have past,

---

[19] Arundel's collection started with statues excavated in the Roman Forum which he brought
home on his return to England in 1615. In the 1620s he employed agents such as Gervase Markham
and William Petty to travel in Asia Minor in search of antiquities. Smuts (2004–9).

> Their names grew dreadfull to all far and neere.
> O then, great Monarch, with how wise a care
> Do you these bloods devided mixe in one,
> And with like consanguinities prepare
> The high, and everliving Union
> Tweene Scots and English: who can wonder then
> If he that marries kingdomes, marries men?   (sig. A²)

In the early modern English imagination, Scythians were proverbially uncivilized (in Shakespeare's *Titus Andronicus* and *King Lear*, they attract the byword 'barbarous'). Campion takes us on a rough ride back to the archaic past, alluding to the ancient sacrament of blood-drinking by which Scythians supposedly pledged friendship and loyalty. While proudly dwelling on historical precedent, the poem counterpoints past with present rites of demonstrating unity, and lauds the more civilized custom of dancing and banqueting. 'Scythian' is, in writing, close to 'Scot', and a classically tutored early modern speaker might well have pronounced the word with a velar /k/. Exotic dancers gesture at a distant past yet practise orderly formations which honour a present king in the audience. The poem promotes James's pet project, the Union of Scotland and England, of which Hay's Anglo-Scottish marriage is an individual's example at a domestic level.[20] A Scythian subtext and Apollonian dancers serve to underline the Scottish courtier's faithful allegiance to a king who has unified England and Scotland.

The importance of the theme of 'transformation' in Jacobean masques has long been recognized. Frequently stage devices or variety in costume indicated change: thus, lovers were turned into men, humans into animals, trees into dancers, or statues into ladies. A masque protagonist is usually on the way to becoming someone else.[21] The plot of Lord Hay's masque hinged upon transformation: the Knights of Apollo had profaned Diana's holy forests and frightened her nymphs. ('Diana' was also called 'Cynthia' in the masque—yet another example of Campion's Helleno-Roman syncretism.) For their crimes, Diana turned the knights into golden trees. Eventually, however, she relented, mollified by Apollo; the trees began to dance with joy, and then transformed back into men again. Thus restored and chastened, the knights of Apollo vowed to live orderly thereafter. As a visual proof of their reformation they offered their old coats, which were decorated with green leaves of satin, to the Tree of Chastity. The rich costume represented in the illustration reflects the masquers' final garments, which they received with Diana's blessing. In this masque, therefore, the change of costume—from golden tree and green man to carnation-coloured knight—signalled the masquers' moral growth towards temperance and self-control. Sartorial (and moral) developments were underscored by movement. A choreography in which trees were set in motion to turn into actual dancers

---

[20] For a nuanced study of this aspect see Lindley (1979), 1–11.
[21] David Lindley and Timothy Raylor have stressed this; see also Ravelhofer, (2007).

represented a pivotal moment of the masque. Let's examine this most mobile classical grove as it was presented in performance:

the foure *silvans* played on their instruments the first straine of this song following: & at the repetition thereof the voices fell in with the instrumentes which were thus devided[:] a treble and a base were placed neere his Majestie, and an other treble and base neere the grove, that the words of the song might be heard of all, because the trees of gould instantly at the first sound of their voices began to move, and dance according to the measure of the time which the musitians kept in singing, and the nature of the wordes which they delivered.

> [Song] Move now with measured sound,
>   You charmed grove of gould,
> Trace forth the sacred ground
>   That shall your formes unfold.
>
> Diana, and the starry night for your Apollos sake
> Endue your Silvan shapes with powre this strange delight to make.
> Much joy must needs the place betide where trees for gladnes move,
> A fairer sight was ne[']re beheld, or more expressing love.
>
> Yet neerer Phoebus throne
>   Mete on your winding waies,
> Your Brydall mirth make knowne
>   In your high-graced Hayes.
>
> Let Hymen lead your sliding rounds, & guide them with his light,
> While we do Io Hymen sing in honour of this night[.]
> Joyne three by three, for so the night by triple spel decrees
> Now to release Apollos knights from these enchanted trees.

This dancing song being ended, the goulden trees stood in rankes three by three, and Night ascended to the grove, . . . touching [them] severally with her wand. . . . That part of the stage whereon the first trees stoode began to yeeld, and the three formost trees gently to sincke, and this was effected by an Ingin plac't under the stage. When the trees had sunke a yarde they cleft in three parts, and the Maskers appeared out of the tops of them, the trees were sodainly convayed away, and the first three Maskers were raysed again by the Ingin. They appeared then in a false habit . . . of greene taffatie cut into leaves, and layed upon cloth of silver, and their hats were sutable to the same.   (sig. C2^{r–v}, i/j and u/v spelling normalized)

The masque booklet gives us important clues as to performance conditions, describing in great detail how four sylvans, or wood sprites, played music while a set of golden trees started moving to a sung chorus.

On the performance night there must have been a significant amount of noise, probably caused by the audience. This required dividing the musicians into two groups, one ensemble of instrumentalists being positioned next to the king's ear, the other close to the performers. In each case high- and low-pitch sounds were carefully balanced. The description also hints at a lighting issue, indicated by the colour of the dancing trees and the fact that the trees had to be accompanied by a torchbearer (stanza 4, 'Let Hymen lead your sliding rounds, and guide them with his light'); the golden colour was no doubt chosen to show off in a dark environment.

In terms of choreography, Campion's lyrics reveal much useful information. The shorter stanzas might have accompanied a forward marching of the trees in pairs of three. The longer stanzas could have been sung to balletic variations executed on the spot or sidewards. There was a clear front-stage focus, as we find in European theatre dances of the period; in this particular case, the trees inched ever closer to the throne of King James, nicely addressed as Apollo ('yet neerer *Phoebus* throne'). The choreography seems to have been short on jumping (not advisable in light of what must have been a cumbersome costume); instead the text mentions 'sliding rounds'. At the end of the dance, the trees executed 'hayes': this serpentine figure was frequently practised in Italian social and theatrical dancing of the late sixteenth and early seventeenth centuries but also very popular in seventeenth-century English country dances. The 'hay' alluded, of course, to the name of the bridegroom (indeed the printed version of the masque capitalizes the word as if it were a name), and thus the tree choreography became emblematic theatrical dancing.

Finally, it is important to consider the rhythm of dance and song. The song sets out in straighforward iambic metre; its rhythm appears almost monotonous, especially in the shorter stanzas. This might have been a concession to the dancers. A score emphasizing clear cadences and caesurae would have prompted performers when to start or finish a dance phrase, thus enabling them to catch breath and gather themselves for the next formation. Incidentally, equestrian ballet of the period was characterized by obtrusively regular music scores for that very reason; and even though Campion did not have to deal with performing horses, the over-explicit rhythm of his lyrics would seem to betray a certain lack of trust in the capacities of his ballet dancers.

But we should also not neglect other, more charitable reasons which might have informed Campion's choice of regular iambic metre. To begin with, the triple stress in each line of the shorter stanzas may have been intended to underscore the words' 'triple spel'; triple devices often served as markers of enchantment in English Renaissance poetry. Were the audience prompted to *hear* the magic of the trees' transformation? At this point it seems worthwhile to return to Campion's sense of poetic discipline and rhythmical proportion. *Observations in the Art of English Poesie* (1602), Campion's treatise on English versification, investigated what the author called 'measures'—a resonant word: 'measure' evoked restraint and control; at the same time it also meant 'dance', 'verse feet', 'number', and 'rhythm', thus beautifully embracing the arts of choreography and poetry alike.[22] Campion identified some suitable 'measures' or 'numbers' which could be used in Greek and English poetry with equal

---

[22] In addition they could also allude to certain Elizabethan dances. See Ward (1988), and Mullally (1998).

success. David Lindley has described his remarkable work as 'the last, and subtlest, of the forlorn Elizabethan attempts to regulate English verse by the rule of classical metrics'.[23] In particular, Campion extolled the iambic dimeter because the '*Iambick*' was 'our most naturall and auncient English verse'. He termed the iambic dimeter 'our English march, because the verse answers our warlick forme of march in similitude of number'.[24] An example (my under-linings of stressed vowels):

> Greatest in thy wars,
> Greater in thy peace,
> Dread *Elizabeth.*[25]

Stanzas 1 and 3 of the song in Hay's masque follow this pattern, each line containing an equal number of three stressed syllables ('Move now with measured sound' etc.). Campion may have tried to re-create some kind of ancient, warlike, English mode inspired by classical rhythm.

One could, of course, object to the extra syllable at the beginning of each line in stanzas 1 and 3, which mars the neat appearance of the dimeter. This might, however, simply be a concession to the dancers. The lyrics were written for a theatre choreography in which a group of nine had to move synchronously. It is much more difficult to dance in time as a group if performers must start without a cue. The additional initial syllables gave Campion's dancing trees a short extra moment in which they could prepare their first step. They served as an upbeat, a clear signal when to start. Indeed, looking at the corresponding music score, we find that the first words in stanzas 1 and 3 coincide with an upbeat, and the last words of each line hold three beats each (Figure 10.2). Such long pauses allow dancers to finish whatever they happen to be doing. Lindley has shown how Campion's masques responded to Continental ideas of *musique mesurée*, analogous to the poet's experiments in *A Booke of Ayres*.[26] While Campion certainly had a clear interest in French musical theory, other concerns too may have informed metrical choices, such as Campion's desire to harness classical authority or practical considerations of performance.

Unfortunately, despite such rhythmical precautions, in performance this moment did not work out so smoothly. A margin, possibly added after the text had already been prepared, added sourly that 'either by the simplicity, negligence, or conspiracy of the painter, the passing away of the trees was somewhat hazarded the patterene [*sic*] of them the same day having bene showne with much admiration, and the 9 trees beeing left unsett' (sig. [C2]ᵛ). Apparently some high-ranking members of the audience had been privileged with a preview of the

---

[23] Lindley (2004–9).

[24] *Observations in the Art of English Poesie* (1602) in Campion (1967), 301.

[25] Ibid. 302.

[26] Lindley (1986), ch. 4. In particular, Campion's air 'Come let us sound' 'united the quantitative scansion of the verse to music exactly reproducing the metre, after the fashion of French *musique mesurée*'.

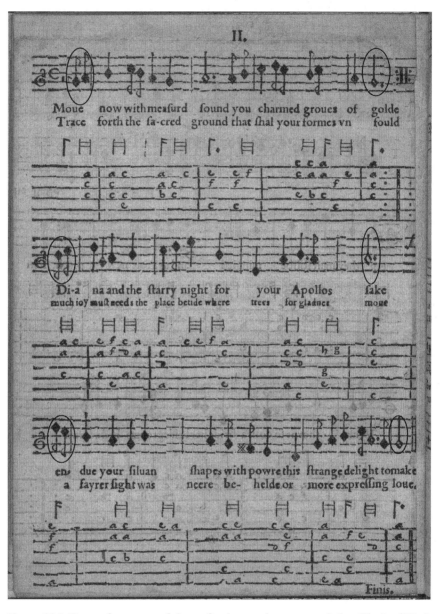

Figure 10.2 Extract from score of chorus for the tree dance, appended to *The Lord Hay's Masque*. Upbeat and cadences marked. Spread on a table, the layout with lute tablature enables several singers and musicians to play from the score at the same time.

transformation scene. As a consequence, a stagehand forgot to readjust the machines which moved the trees, and the masquers must have emerged from the contraption less ceremoniously.

What can we conclude from the joint effect of dance and song, poetry and costume in *The Lord Hay's Masque*? This entertainment was prepared for a Scottish courtier anxious about bloodlines and pedigree. The masque did everything to create a history for Hay in a catch-all spanning the classical and the ancient Scottish world. Was the conceit of the dancing Greek grove a reaction to that other— Scottish—moving grove, the trees of Birnam Wood in *Macbeth*, written in 1606? At the end of Shakespeare's play King Malcolm, contemplating his predecessor's severed head, promises to restore order in 'measure, time, and place'.[27] The king is, as it were, the state's tragic choreographer. In the less sanguine masque, blood is shed only in the archaeological preface, while the performance itself results in a peaceful marriage of kingdoms. In European literature, forests and groves are traditionally places of danger and temptation; Victor Hugo still knew that 'Parnassus is a mountain . . . the forest is barbarous'.[28] Birnam Wood heralds carnage, but numinous nature can also be benevolent: Hay's moving grove illustrated the power of transformation and showed the way towards civilization.

Campion and his collaborators made no purist attempt to revive a dancing Greek chorus. Instead, they were much more interested in conveying a continuity of history in word, sound, and image. The dances followed a classical rhythm, but at the same time their figures served for very topical references. Such eclecticism was not always appreciated by contemporaries, as we know from reactions to Jonson's historicizing masques. Jonson was criticized for mixing up mythical figures from different countries and periods and making Penthesilea dance with Boudicca. Unperturbed, the poet dismissed such pedantry with utter contempt:

I discerne a possible Objection, arising agaynst mee, to which I must turne: As, How I can bring Persons, of so different Ages, to appeare, properly, together? Or, Why . . . I joyne the living, with the dead? I answere to both these, at once, Nothing is more proper; Nothing more naturall: For these all live; and together, in theyr Fame.[29]

The magnificent monster that was the masque mingled classical with northern cultures and creatures. Campion's and Jonson's Greece owed much to the early modern imagination, and Inigo Jones was no Berthel Thorwaldsen. Nonetheless, the artists and poets who created masques pursued ancient history and literature with enthusiasm and often mentioned their sources with gratitude. When Lord Hay splashed out for an exuberant night's delight, antiquity gave a past to the Scottish *homo novus*. In exchange, Hay's masque offered a new lease of life to old gods and temple groves. May they all live together in their fame.

---

[27] Shakespeare (1994), V.vii.103.
[28] 'Le Parnasse est un mont. . . . La forêt est barbare.' Hugo (1979), 248.
[29] *The Masque of Queenes*, in Jonson (1925–52), 7. 313, ll. 670–6.

11

Dancing with Prometheus: Performance and Spectacle in the 1920s

Pantelis Michelakis

Prometheus, the Titan chained to a rock in punishment for giving fire to human beings, may seem an unlikely subject for modern performances of Greek tragedy based on movement and rhythm. For one thing, the tragic play *Prometheus Bound* attributed to Aeschylus is markedly static. However, even a brief glance at the position of Prometheus in the history of dance suggests otherwise. *The Creatures of Prometheus*, for instance, choreographed by Salvatore Viganò to Ludwig van Beethoven's only balletic score in 1801 was performed in various versions throughout the nineteenth and early twentieth centuries, with music by Mozart, Haydn, Beethoven, Gluck, Weigl, and Viganò himself. The aim of this chapter is not to provide a survey of Prometheus in modern dance but to focus on two of the earliest productions on the subject to have been recorded on film, in which dancing by the bound protagonist himself or the Chorus of the Daughters of Oceanus takes centre stage: the theatrical production of *Prometheus Bound* by Eva Palmer, which was performed in Delphi in 1927 and again in 1930, in the context of the first dramatic festivals to take place in modern Greece; and the solo dance *Prometheus Bound* which was choreographed and performed by Ted Shawn, the self-styled father of modern dance in America,[1] which had its debut in the Lewisohn Stadium in New York, in 1929.[2]

Earlier versions of this paper were delivered in Chicago and Oxford. For generous help and advice I am particularly grateful to Helene Foley, Ioulia Pipinia, Kathleen Riley, Vanda Zajko, and Fiona Macintosh. For their assistance with source material I am also thankful to the staff in the following museums, libraries, and archives: the Dance Division of the New York Public Library for the Performing Arts, the Historical Archives of the Benaki Museum, the Greek Broadcasting Corporation Film Archive, and the Film Archive of the Greek Foreign Affairs Ministry in Athens. Research for this article could not have been undertaken without the generous financial and institutional support of the British Academy, the University of Bristol, and the Archive of Performances of Greek and Roman Drama in Oxford.

[1] For instance, Shawn (1979), 276: 'I was long Papa Shawn to those men, and to generations of dance students, and I am now Grandpapa Shawn to a host of youngsters'.

[2] The solo dance was first performed on 6–8 Aug. 1929 in Lewisohn Stadium, New York and on 15 March 1930 in Bachsaalm, Berlin: Schlundt (1962), 70 and 73.

Palmer's *Prometheus Bound* has been influential and has received extensive critical attention (see too Cooper Albright, this volume). Shawn's dance on the other hand has been largely ignored, despite the fact that it is still occasionally revived at the Dance Festival of Jacob's Pillow in Massachusetts, where Ted Shawn founded his dance school in the 1930s.[3] Looking at Palmer's and Shawn's choreographic work side by side is interesting for various reasons: because of the subsequent collaboration between the two, which was short-lived but close;[4] because of the various aesthetic and artistic preoccupations they shared; and also because of the wider issues their work on Prometheus raises about choreography and cinema and the ways in which they can be understood as metaphors for the encounter of modernity with antiquity in the 1920s. The fact that both their productions are based on dance and that both have been recorded on film is not a mere coincidence but a manifestation of an aesthetic of movement which blends and juxtaposes ancient and modern rhythms in search of a utopian social order.

This chapter seeks to make three interrelated arguments: first, that a discussion of Palmer's and Shawn's interest in Prometheus is not possible without a close look at the issue of dance movement; second, that the dance forms Palmer and Shawn developed cannot be examined independently of their attitude towards the processes of documentation and archivization of their art; and third, that the political and ideological work their dances sought to perform cannot be adequately understood unless situated within and against the wider social and cultural history of dance and the reception of Prometheus in the 1920s.

I

Like other early twentieth-century pioneers of modern dance, Palmer and Shawn drew on a number of dance techniques inspired by ancient Greece as a reaction against what they dismissed as the pretentiousness and elitism of classical ballet. These techniques included the system of rhythmic gymnastics associated with the Swiss Émile Jaques-Dalcroze, the system of exercises 'to improve the emotional depth of actor's gestures'[5] associated with the French musicologist François Delsarte, and the pioneering dance techniques developed by the American dancers Loïe Fuller and Isadora Duncan (see further Cooper Albright, this volume). Inspired by a range of dance techniques, Palmer's and Shawn's dances attempted to piece together into a coherent whole an eclectic mixture of gestures and movements derived from different sources. Palmer's sources included not

---

[3] On Palmer's *Prometheus Bound*, see Palmer (1993); the contributions in Papageorgiou (1998) as well as Sideris (1976); Mavromatis (1983); Jacquin (1988); Glytzouris (1998); Papadaki (1998); Wiles (2000), 183–9; and Van Steen (2002). Brief references to Shawn's *Prometheus* can be found in Shawn (1979), 221–2; Terry (1956), 75–6.

[4] Palmer (1993), 199–214.

[5] Alter (1994), 55.

only ancient vase-paintings but also Plato's views on education (especially his emphasis on the combination of poetry, music, and gymnastics), Nietzsche's interest in music and the tragic chorus, modern Greek folk dances, and the musical notation of the Greek Orthodox church.[6] Similarly Shawn's sources of inspiration included not only Greco-Roman iconography and sculpture but also athletics, acrobatics, a Modernist symphony on Prometheus by the Russian composer Alexander Scriabin (first performed in 1911) on which his dance was choreographed, and probably an earlier dance on Prometheus with the same musical score by Loïe Fuller (see Figure 15.2).[7]

Palmer's and Shawn's dances differ from one another in a number of ways. However, both of them are largely based on mimetic principles. Shawn's *Prometheus* follows a principle that he and his wife and dance partner, Ruth St Denis often referred to as 'music visualization', the translation 'into bodily action [of] the rhythmic, melodic, and harmonic structure[s] of musical composition[s]'.[8] The Prometheus dance visualizes the moods and emotions conveyed by Scriabin's symphony through simple and dramatic movements and gestures embedded into a basic spatial frame: Shawn's Prometheus looks up towards Zeus in defiance, down towards mankind in compassion and love, left and right towards freedom and hope in longing and anticipation. Similarly, the choreography of Palmer's Chorus provides a visual commentary on the narrative of their songs. According to the notes of the production, it included more than 250 poses inspired by sketches of figures drawn from classical vase-paintings:[9] for instance, the phrase at the beginning of the first *stasimon* (lines 398–401) that Griffith translates literally as 'Pouring a tear-dripping flow from my soft eyes, I soaked my cheek with wet streams'[10] was rendered with a sequence of movements which involved the placing of the hands of the Chorus on their head, cheeks, eyes, and heart.[11]

The easy identification of the sources of inspiration of the two dances and the mimetic principles on which they are based creates a sense of transparency and authenticity. The two dances suggest an investment in a cultural discourse 'that imagines dance as archaic and pre-discursive' and allows it to claim 'for itself a more direct and unmediated form of documentation' than language-based art

[6] Plato: Palmer (1993), 49–50, 158; Nietzsche: Palmer (1993), 171–2; music: Palmer (1993), 93–101; modern Greek folk dance: Veloudios (1998).

[7] On Prometheus in music, see Antcliffe (1926). On Scriabin's *Prometheus: Poem of Fire*, see Bowers (1996) and Eaglefield Hull (1916); the score can be found in Scriabin (1995). On Loïe Fuller's 'Fire Dance', see Cooper Albright (2007), 175–6 and her ch. in this volume. It is not inconceivable that Shawn attended, or at least heard of, the American debut of Scriabin's *Prometheus: Poem of Fire* in New York in 1915.

[8] Ruth St Denis, quoted in Jordan (1984), 35, on the concept of 'music visualizations' which she and Ted Shawn adopted in the late 1910s and the 1920s.

[9] Bella Raftopoulou's sketches are reproduced in Mavromatis (1983), and some of Palmer's choreographic notes in Glytzouris (1998).

[10] Griffith (1983), 159.

[11] Glytzouris (1998), 154.

forms such as poetry and conventional theatre.[12] However, and despite the fact that both dances single-out ancient iconography and sculpture as privileged interlocutors, neither of the two can be reduced to an engagement with ancient Greek art and culture to the exclusion of modern influences. And neither of the two dances can be reduced to issues related to gait and gesticulation alone. In both of them the structure and clarity of a meticulously scripted notation of poses are combined with an imaginative refiguration of their sources of influence. More importantly, their choreography is animated by the fluidity and energy of bodily movement. What gives the dances their distinctive character is not only the poses they draw our attention to, but also their ability to make invisible the organizing principles that bring these poses to life and set them in motion: rhythm, pace, periodicity, the ebb and flow of movement, the body of the dancer, which are all downplayed in favour of foregrounding 'a mythical and fictional origin of . . . symbols of Greek thought'.[13]

II

Moving from the two dances to their recording on film, we find a similar preoccupation with authenticity and a comparable concealment of organizing principles. The films of the two dances promise a faithful reproduction of the stage spectacle they record, the ability to fragment, store, and retrieve accurately the reality of the live performance. Their sole aim appears to be to record as objectively and exhaustively as possible a reality which includes not only the spectacle itself but also its context: the audience and the imposing natural landscape of Palmer's *Prometheus*, and even details such as the smile on the face of Ted Shawn as he steps out of his role at the end of his dance. The cameras filming the two performances are static and invisible, and the cameramen behind them have left almost no traces on or off screen.[14]

In the case of the Delphic film, its documentary value was further enhanced by its original screening as news footage, accompanied by live singing of the songs of the Chorus.[15] It is not difficult to imagine that screenings of Shawn's dance would also have had musical accompaniment—perhaps in the manner of the live dance itself which must have made use of sound recordings of Scriabin's symphony. Yet for all their strategies of documentary authenticity, the two films are

---

[12] Pearson (2002), 109.

[13] Ibid. 113.

[14] I have not been able to identify the producers of Shawn's film. Palmer's film was shot by Dimitris Gaziadis, one of the better known directors of early Greek cinema whose participation nevertheless in this particular project appears to have left no traces in Eva Palmer's and Angelos Sikelianos's rich correspondence around the Delphic Festivals held in the Benaki Museum. On the film of the Delphi *Prometheus*, see Lambrinos (1997) and Sideris (1976), 362–3.

[15] The relevant sources can be found in Sideris (1976), 362–3 and Eliadis (1960), 25.

not unmediated records of stage spectacles. They are compositions and reconfi-
gurations of individual segments of those spectacles. They bring together frozen
images, taken from different camera angles, to form filmic narratives which,
however continuous and self-effacing they might appear, are marked by the
ruptures and discontinuities of point of view, framing, and editing. Both films
are preoccupied with authenticity but at the same time they have their own,
filmic, narrative logic and grammar: they are condensed versions of longer stage
events, and they are filmed from different angles. The film of Palmer's *Prometheus* also features post-production close-ups of the performers, quick succession
of different shots, title cards introducing the characters and summarizing the
plot, and other devices which strengthen the visual attraction of its individual
frames and the causal consistency of its narrative.

The body of the actor and the eye of the camera, the physical and the
mechanical, are not only closely interwoven in the *Prometheus* productions
under examination; they are also homologous, combining as they do movement
and stasis, freedom and control, aesthetics and ideology. The implications of this
linkage between performance and spectacle in the revival of Greek tragedy in the
1920s embrace not only choreographers and dancers but also viewers; not only
the processes of encoding, through dance and cinema, but also the processes
of decoding, through spectatorship.[16] As one of the spectators of Palmer's
Prometheus points out with disarming directness, the Chorus was like 'an archaic
frieze which moved in front of our surprised eyes with the slow unwinding of a
movie'.[17] The film of the production was similarly praised by the press for the
vividness of its picture and its live music which gave its spectators 'almost the
same shiver felt by those attending the festival'.[18] Another spectator of Palmer's
stage production, the poet Kostas Karyotakis, describes, probably not without
irony, how cameras and film crews 'gave a special, / most graphic, tone to
Prometheus' pain'.[19]

Between the genuine endorsement of cinema's documentary power by many
spectators and the press and its ironic exposure by a neo-romantic and symbolist
poet, the relation between film and dance emerges with greater clarity.[20] Choreography downplays the modernity of its movement, rhythmicization, and the
body of the dancer to elevate dance to a privileged position in relation to its
classical pictorial sources and subject-matter. In a similar way, film editing
performs an act of concealment in relation to the eye of the camera in order to

---

[16] Cf. Abel (1999), 6.

[17] Miliadis (1998), 99; quoted also in Sideris (1976), 355.

[18] From the article 'The Impact of the Delphic Festival—The Movie—The Revival of
Ancient Tragedies in the Outdoors', newspaper *Empros*, 27 May 1927 (in Greek).

[19] 'Delphic Festival', ll. 3–4, published in Savidis (1992), 169.

[20] While a more comprehensive study might consider the different types of gaze that the two
dances and their films mobilized and the different communities of spectators they reached, my
interest here is in the role of spectatorship in the conceptual linkage between film and dance.

celebrate the film's privileged relation to the reality it records. Dance claims to be more authentic than other modern art forms in representing Greek tragedy, and film more efficient than other technological media in recording dance. In this competition between different art forms and media, dance and cinema flirt with each other in more than one way. Dance flirts with the cinematic principle of 'still images in motion' not only because of a desire to be documented and archived, but also because of the conflicting desire to develop techniques that will enable it to operate outside the linguistic frameworks of other art forms.[21] If dance can reconcile artistic freedom and discipline, movement and stillness, to produce animation from heterogeneous elements it embodies and performs, film, in its turn, is marked by a similar paradox. Still frames give the illusion of movement, and the vital role of the camera is downplayed as an unwelcome presence which needs to be concealed or ignored.

Both Shawn and Palmer coordinated and inspired the archivization of their work. Even a quick look at the Ted Shawn collection in the New York Public Library for the Performing Arts or the Angelos and Eva Sikelianos collection at the Benaki Museum in Athens testifies to the wealth of material on and by the two figures: autobiographies, books, articles, newspaper interviews, notes, correspondence, photographs, film reels. Both of them were interested in the institutionalization of their art through the training of dancers, the foundation of dance schools, and the dissemination of their ideas through public lectures and other events. Archivization, the drive to keep under control the ephemeral nature of dance as a living art and the contingent nature of reality at large, informed not only their systematic documentation of their work but also the very way in which they conceptualized it as a succession of static pictures, rather than fluid movement, and as a point of entry into a different, archaic world.

What their meticulous and intense engagement with the archive does *not* spell out, however, is how heavily it was conditioned by practices of viewing inextricably linked with the emergence of modern visual media. Palmer's and Shawn's preoccupation with authenticity and their search for inspiration in the material remains of ancient Greece were based on assumptions about the still image informed by photography as a direct imprint of reality and as a basic component part of larger, profoundly modern, visual narratives, of pictures in motion. They were also built on similarly modern assumptions about movement as a quantifiable and linear concept which can be broken down to its constituent parts for analysis, storage, and retrieval (cf. Naerebout, this volume).

The way in which the conceptualization of 'classical' dances was permeated by the promises of modern technologies of viewing is evident not only in the work of Palmer and Shawn but also in the work of other pioneers of early modern dance, most notably the so-called 'magician of light' Loïe Fuller.[22] Similarly, in critical

---

[21] Pearson (2002), 110.
[22] Cooper Albright (2007).

writings about dance the instrumental role of moving pictures in the connection between ancient iconography and modern dance was identified as such at least as early as 1914, when Raymond Duncan, brother of Isadora Duncan and brother-in-law of Eva Palmer's future husband, gave a speech about dance and gymnastics: in it he spoke of how he worked for years making sketches after Greek vases until the day that he had in front of his own eyes 'the vision of movement of all those vases synthesized in a single, grand, cinematographic movement. I had then,' he continues, 'a vision of ancient Greece in movement'.[23] Shawn and Palmer did not embrace modern technologies of the visual in the celebratory manner of some of their contemporaries, but they nevertheless exploited, internalized, and creatively applied them to all aspects of their work.

III

The profound implication of such technologies in the documentation and conceptualization of Shawn's and Palmer's dances does not exhaust the ways in which the two performances can be circumscribed within the larger cultural framework of the late 1920s. As vehicles of culture, Shawn's and Palmer's dances on Prometheus did not simply store and reproduce cultural practices and disciplines; they also played an active role in their shaping. Through the choreography and display of his male body, Shawn provided a new take on nineteenth-century associations of Prometheus with punishment, defiance, and resistance to authority. Associating them with the performance of masculinity, in a solo dance that he himself identified as 'a study in limitation',[24] Shawn enabled the politicization of Prometheus along bold and provocative lines. In this, he was not alone.

Shawn's Prometheus must be situated in an interpretative context which emerges at least as early as 1900, with the display of an almost naked Prometheus in the arena of Béziers in southern France, performed by the extravagant Édouard de Max in the stage production of Jean Lorrain's *Prométhée*, with music by Gabriel Fauré (which surpassed in daring the roles of decadent Roman emperors for which the actor had previously earned his fame). It must also be set against other representations of Prometheus such as the now lost film adaptation of his myth directed by Louis Feuillade in 1908, whose poster of an almost naked Prometheus capitalized on the notoriety of Édouard de Max's performance (revived in Paris only a few months before the film's release). This strand in the reception history of Prometheus

---

[23] Duncan (1914): 'J'ai travaillé des années et des années en faisant des dessins d'après ces vases jusqu'au jour ou j'ai eu devant les yeux la vision des mouvements de tous ces vases synthétisée en un seul grand mouvement cinématographique. Alors j'ai eu la vision de la Grèce Ancienne en mouvement.' Duncan, like his sister, was influenced, at the very least indirectly, by the work of Maurice Emmanuel whose study of ancient dance was contemporaneous with and heavily dependent upon developments in chronophotography (see further Naerebout, this volume).

[24] Dreier (1933), 16.

continues well into the 1960s and may be seen most clearly in Gregory Markopoulos's film adaptation of Prometheus entitled *Illiac Passion* (1967).

Shawn's Prometheus represents neither the scandalous and transgressive masculinity of Édouard de Max's early twentieth-century Prometheus, nor the enigmatic celebration of homosexuality of Markopoulos's avant-garde film. Shawn's Prometheus poses not so much a threat to the 'condition of the male as a rational . . . subject'[25] as a provocative affirmation. Shawn used Prometheus, alongside other archetypal figures such as Greek heroes, Olympic athletes, Asian divinities, and Indian warriors, for the legitimization of a masculinity which he himself identified as 'natural'[26] and 'universal' but which dance historians have found distinctively western and American in its roughness and aggression. If Shawn turned to male mythological figures such as Prometheus, he did so not only 'to dispel the popular link of dancing and effeminacy and to counter the dominance of women in the concert dance field' (see further, Hall this volume).[27] He turned to the past to go a step further, seeking to rehabilitate dance as a public art which had historically been the prerogative of men.[28] Seeking to challenge prejudices against dance as an art for 'sissies', as many newspaper reviews of his time put it,[29] he developed a performance identity which was hypermasculine. The visual display of his almost naked body was accompanied by the systematic and free use 'of his upper body and limbs to reach, punch, and strain, and a good measure of stamping [and] rapid stepping turns'[30] (see Figure 11.1).

Shawn was a dancer but his choreography was based on movements reminiscent of athletics and boxing. As a pioneer of dance and a closet homosexual exploring the limits of both his art and culture, Shawn sought a precarious balance between two extremes: the conformity with, and even celebration of, normative models of masculinity and the detachment of masculinity from heterosexuality. Film historians are divided on his legacy,[31] perhaps not unlike Palmer herself who was initially attracted by his pioneering spirit but who was later frustrated by his flirting with patriarchal, patriotic, and colonial mentalities.[32] Shawn's solo as Prometheus provides a self-dramatized tale of triumphant suffering and defiance which the history of

---

[25] Hewitt (2005), 157.

[26] Burt (1995), 102–8. Shawn embodied numerous heroes, gods, and other archetypal figures: see Schlundt (1962) and (1967). Among them, Adonis (*Death of Adonis*, 1923) was performed only with a fig leaf G-string, as noted by Foulkes (2002), 92. The *Dance of the Ages* (1938) alone included a series of archetypal figures performed by Shawn: the Shaman ('a nameless Prometheus' as the programme puts it), the High Priest, the Poet-Philosopher, the Ward Heeler, the Politician-Demagogue, the Liberated Soul, and the Creative Artist: Schlundt (1967), 57.

[27] Foulkes (2002), 88.

[28] Ibid. 90.

[29] See the review extracts collected in Schlundt (1967).

[30] Jordan (1984), 44 drawing on Siegel (1979), 307.

[31] Foulkes (2002), 94–5; Burt (1998), 132–3.

[32] Palmer (1993), 212–14.

Figure 11.1 Ted Shawn as Prometheus (1931).

his reception allows us to cast not only in the heroic terms that he himself opted for,[33] but also in more ambivalent and complex terms than he could have anticipated.

If Shawn focused on the training and display of his own body, the body of a male, professional actor in cosmopolitan New York, Palmer concentrated on the training and exhibition of a collective body of amateur dancers, a group of school girls from provincial Athens, almost to the complete exclusion of all other aspects of the production which she left to others. To be sure, Palmer's Daughters of Oceanus were neither the first modern chorus of the *Prometheus* to dance, nor the first modern chorus of Greek tragedy to consist of female students. In 1925, just two years before Palmer's original production of the *Prometheus*, Adolphe

---

[33] On Prometheus as the solo which best describes Shawn's 'style, his attitude and his mission', see the brief but suggestive comments by Terry (1956), 75–6.

Appia's production of the same play in the Swiss town of Basel featured female students of eurhythmics. But, whereas the female chorus of Appia's production attracted the hostile criticism of reviewers who saw it as '"ten delicate girls" weakly gesticulating "blossomlike" around the rock',[34] Palmer's chorus was unanimously considered the highlight of a very successful production.

Her preoccupation with the collective, female chorus, rather than with the male protagonist, needs to be situated within, and against, a strand in the reception of Prometheus different from Shawn's. Her approach to the play and the myth draws on nineteenth- and early twentieth-century associations of the Titan with group dynamics and identities rather than with individualism, and with the dispossessed and marginalized rather than with the heroic. But if previous representations of the myth and the play along the lines favoured by Palmer focused on Prometheus *himself* as symbol of human labour, creativity, and defiance, Palmer projected these values onto the female chorus. Sometimes perceived as lacking character development and narrative integration,[35] the Chorus of the Daughters of Oceanus was transformed by Palmer into the protagonist of her production. What Palmer did, then, was to politicize the female and the collective as a double assault on associations of Prometheus with the dominance of the male, white individual.

Palmer choreographed female bodies in a way that challenged not only 'the separation of public and private spheres that immured women in the confines of domesticity',[36] but also the separation between professional and amateur dancing that made dance the prerogative of small élites. Her experimentation with group dance rather than solo dance and with femininity rather than masculinity must be set in a wider context of interplay between the agency of dance, the politics of gender, and the issue of labour organization. Despite the Nietzschean language she often used for the chorus's Dionysiac spirit and for the loss of individuality in the collective,[37] Palmer displayed an interest in the collective informed by visions of the community associated with utopian socialist thinking. One of the theorists she quotes with approval in her correspondence with Shawn in the late 1930s is the English novelist and essayist Aldous Huxley who, in his *Ends and Means*, published in 1937, condemns the darkness of 'panic animality' of the masses exploited by dictators and the dehumanization brought about by industrialization and modern life. Palmer is rather dismissive of Huxley's proposed solution of an 'ideal factory' based on the work of small groups of ten or twenty people, which she calls 'characteristically Anglo-Saxon, timid and bloodless';[38] but the similarities of his solution with her own views on the Greek chorus are difficult to miss.

---

[34] From *Basler Nachrichten*, 12 Feb. 1925, quoted in Volbach (1961), 9–10. On this production, see further Beacham (1994), 211–12.

[35] The relevant literature is reviewed in Scott (1987) and Sienkewicz (1984).

[36] Franko (1995), 2.

[37] Palmer (1998) and (1993), 171–4.

[38] Palmer's letter to Ted Shawn, written probably in 1939, in Anton (1997), 230.

Palmer's preoccupation with the training of amateur groups provided a theoretical alternative not only to the exploitation of workers in factories and of citizens
in totalitarian states but also to the commodification of the chorus girls of the
entertainment industries of Broadway and Hollywood. Like them, the Greek
chorus reproduced and acted out, through choreography and performance, structures of labour organization.[39] It offered bodily gestures and movements which
were not mechanical and repetitive but which were nevertheless coordinated
under the precise control of Palmer's choreography. Even the diversification of
the movements and gestures of the chorus leaders was based on principles of
economy and efficiency which presented themselves as a model for the functioning
of larger organizational structures. Palmer's chorus can be said to be the performative embodiment of both the industrial workers in Palmer's ideal factory and
the citizens in her ideal community (see Figures 3.1 and 3.2).

Unlike Isadora Duncan who, for all her interest in the Greek chorus established herself as a dancer and choreographer through solo performances,[40]
Palmer used her female chorus to assert a view of female agency at the service
of a 'social organization of cooperative movement'.[41] Individual voices and
bodies (including her own) were subjected to a larger vision, in which the dancers
and their personal gender, or ethnic identities mattered less than the dance itself.
The stage productions of the Delphic Festivals of 1927 and 1930 are often
considered as the culmination of Palmer's life and career, not least because of the
artistic impact they have had and the critical attention they have received. For
Palmer herself, however, and this is what I would offer as a corrective to the
way in which her contribution to the revival of Greek drama has often been
emplotted, they were only a first step towards the ambitious revival of Delphi as a
spiritual centre and for the foundation of the Delphic University of Human
Understanding.[42]

Even when that utopian vision failed to materialize and Palmer was forced to
return to America to raise more funds for her ambitious plans, her training of
female, amateur choruses provided the necessary preparation for another goal,
the training of professional male dancers: 'I had succeeded in making my
Oceanides and my Suppliants the vital centre of the play, in fact the protagonist',
she says in her autobiography. 'This inevitably led me beyond itself toward a
greater possibility.... The beauty and magnificence of men's voices, the power
and dignity of their gestures, became an obsession. I felt that with a chorus of
men I could really produce a Greek play.'[43] Like her work with amateur female

---

[39] On the chorus girls of the entertainment industry and the early theoretical interest they
generated among cultural theorists, see Burt (1998), 84–100.

[40] On Duncan and her interest in the Chorus, see Franko (1995), 17–20.

[41] Franko (2002), 21. For parallels with Ginner and Morris, see Macintosh, this volume.

[42] Palmer (1993), 122.

[43] Ibid. 147. The most productive experiences that Palmer had with professional male dancers
were with Ted Shawn and his Men Dancers, with whom she experimented with 'dances', as she puts

choruses, her devotion to Greece was placed at the service of higher goals: on the one hand she considered Greece her spiritual home and wanted to return to it as soon as she could; on the other hand, she found the professionalism and cultural tolerance of America liberating—even if only temporarily. What Palmer discovered through the dance training of amateur schoolgirls from Greece was a way of acting out her belief in progressive aesthetics and politics. Distancing herself from solo dance and its associations with individualism, she was able to materialize for the first time a vision which was stimulated, but not constrained, by the Promethean liminality of the collective, the female, the non-American, and the archaic.

By way of conclusion, I should reiterate the point which has informed my analysis throughout this chapter: Shawn's and Palmer's work on Prometheus did not collapse the differences between performer and spectator, between human and mechanical movement, and between dance and film in the way that the work on acting of some of their contemporaries tried to do.[44] Nor did it seek to radicalize such differences. Rather, Shawn's and Palmer's preoccupation with the training and filming of human bodies was based on the belief that the differences between their 'age of the machine' and the 'classical man' can be embodied and displayed. To focus on a mythological character bound to the rock to explore an aesthetics and politics of masculinity, as Shawn did, and to turn an onstage group of female spectators into the acting protagonist of a tragic spectacle, as Palmer did, are not paradoxical. On the contrary, they illustrate the tensions and dilemmas inherent in a Modernist project in which motion and stasis, personal and collective identities, art and technology, past and present coexist in dynamic tension. Palmer's and Shawn's work on Prometheus raises questions not only about the complex relation between dance and the processes of its archivization, but also about dance and the social history of its production and conceptualization.

it, from Aristophanes, Aeschylus' *Persians*, and Shelley's *Prometheus Unbound*: 'at last, my material and my floating embroideries were responding to noble movement in the way I had imagined': Ibid. 206.

[44] See e.g. the discussion of the Russian theorists on acting Lev Kuleshov and Ippolit Sokolov in Yampolsky (1999), 63.

12

From Duncan to Bausch with Iphigenia

Alessandra Zanobi

The mythical story of Iphigenia, which was dramatized by Euripides in the two plays *Iphigenia at Aulis* and *Iphigenia amongst the Taurians*, stands as a telling link between the work of two of the most important dance innovators in twentieth-century dance: Isadora Duncan and Pina Bausch. These two artists are credited with the development of a new dance language, which expresses emotion through the body rather than narrating action. Interestingly, Pina Bausch's work seems to start where Duncan's stopped, namely with the choreography of Gluck's *Iphigénie en Tauride*. In fact, Duncan worked for more than a decade on different aspects of *Iphigénie*, but could never create a full-length choreography with the original musical scores (Figure 12.1). *Iphigenie auf Tauris* was instead the first large-scale choreography by Bausch. In order to understand these affinities and interconnections, it is important to ask why the regularly dubbed 'conservative' composer Gluck and, more importantly, why the mythological figure of Iphigenia proved pivotal to the innovations of these two pioneers of modern dance.[1]

THE CHOICE OF GLUCK

Isadora Duncan's fascination with the story of Iphigenia lasted for her entire artistic career. In the thirteen-year period from 1903 to 1916, Duncan kept working on selected parts of Gluck's *Iphigénie en Aulide* and *Iphigénie en Tauride* and choreographed twenty dances; these constitute the only composite choreographical work in the form of a dance-drama that she ever attempted.[2] Ann Daly has remarked that 'the Gluck tragedies were successful transitional work for Duncan bridging her early, predominantly musical works with the later, primarily dramatic works.'[3] Bausch choreographed her *Iphigenie auf Tauris* set to music

---

[1] For Gluck as 'radical', see Goldhill (2010).
[2] Layson (1983), 43.
[3] Daly (1995), 148.

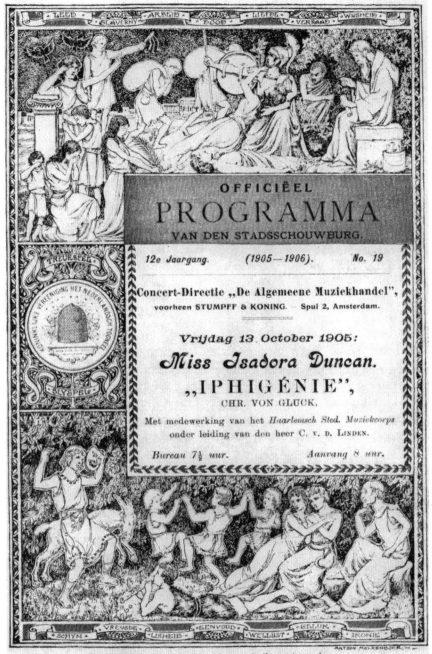

Figure 12.1 Programme for Duncan's *Iphigénie* (1905).

by Gluck as a dance drama in 1974; this was her first large-scale choreography, which can be considered the starting point of a new and original way of dance-making, and also a transitional piece displaying *in nuce* typical features of Bausch's early works and anticipating her mature modes.

Duncan's and Bausch's choice of Gluck was primarily motivated by the fact that Gluck's operas contained extensive sections suitable for dance; in fact, his operatic reform developed in parallel with the dance reforms promoted by Gasparo Angiolini (1731–1803) and Jean-Georges Noverre (1727–1810), each of whom collaborated with Gluck.[4] This parallel reformative impetus in music and dance is attested by Noverre's statement that his work achieved 'a revolution in dance as striking and as lasting as that achieved by Gluck in music'.[5] In the same preface to his *Lettres sur la Danse*, Noverre explains the close relationship between choreography and musical composition that the *ballet d'action* required:

In place of writing steps to written airs, as couplets are set to known melodies, I composed, if I may so express myself, the dialogue of my ballet, and I had the music written for each phrase or idea. Thus I dictated to Gluck the characteristic manner of the Ballet of the Savages in *Iphigénie en Tauride*. The steps, the gestures, attitudes, and expressions of the different characters which I outlined to him gave to this celebrated composer the theme for that fine piece of music.[6]

A revival of Gluck's music was actually prompted by modern dance towards the end of the nineteenth century. The first to promote Gluck's revival was the French theorist of expression, François Delsarte (1811–71), who fully appreciated the emotional quality of Gluck's music and credited him with the invention of what Delsarte called the 'aesthetic orchestra'.[7] According to Delsarte, Gluck assigned each instrument to a specific emotion and was thus able to codify a scientific grammar through which his music could express emotions. Delsarte's system, which was written down by Genevieve Stebbins in 'The Delsarte system of expression' (1885), conspicuously influenced Duncan and other dance reformers at this time.[8] Indeed, several modern-dance choreographers deeply involved in the creation of a new aesthetics and language of dance have given full-length

---

[4] Gasparo Angiolini (1723–96) signed the choreography of *Don Juan* (1761) and *Orfeo ed Euridice* (1762), while Noverre that of *Iphigénie en Aulide* (1777) and that of *Iphigénie en Tauride* (1779).

[5] Noverre (1807), Preface, vii: 'j'ai fait dans la Danse une révolution aussi frappante et aussi durable que Gluck a opérée depuis dans la musique'.

[6] Ibid. i, viii: 'Au lieu d'écrire des pas sur des airs notés, comme on fait des couplets sur des airs connus, je composois, si je puis m'exprimer ainsi, le dialogue de mon Ballet, et je faisois faire la musique pour chaque phrase et chaque idée. Ce fuit ainsi que je dictai à Gluck l'air caractéristique du Ballet des Sauvages dans Iphigénie en Tauride; les pas, les gestes, les attitudes, les expressions des différens personnages que je lui dessinai, donnèrent à ce célébre compositeur le caractère de la composition de ce beau morceau de musique.'

[7] The adjective 'aesthetic' is used by Delsarte in the sense of being able to produce emotion, feeling, sensation.

[8] e.g. Ruth St Denis, Ted Shawn, and Rudolf von Laban.

performances of Gluck's operas, among which *Orfeo ed Euridice* and *Don Juan* have been largely favoured. In this respect, Duncan's and Bausch's choice to choreograph the Iphigenia operas stands out from the general trend of modern dance.[9]

Duncan's and Bausch's preference for Gluck's Iphigenia operas seems to have been motivated by the relevance of the emotional content of the Iphigenia myth, which Gluck had been able to match in his music.[10] The two Euripidean dramatic treatments of the Iphigenia myth are more concerned with the display of thoughts, fears, dreams, and childhood memories rather than action. Indeed, the focus on a variety of human feelings and dispositions, such as the sense of loss, loneliness, fear, madness, longing, love, and friendship, clearly accounts for the appeal of Iphigenia to Duncan's and Bausch's modern sensibilities. But their choice of Gluck's operas is motivated by a further reason: the two choreographers shared the composer's aim of creating a 'total theatre'. This idea is implicit in Gluck's operatic reforms, which had the intention of reviving the spirit of ancient Greek drama where verbal poetry, non-verbal music, and dance had their own proper roles, but none overwhelmed the other. Greek tragedy was exemplary in this respect because of its achievement of this perfect balance.

In a similar fashion to Gluck, Duncan also explicitly aimed at reviving the totality of ancient Greek drama, whose powerful expressive qualities combined with the elevated spiritual and educative function she appreciated. Duncan wanted dance 'to take its legitimate place in tragedy with music and poetry, to be the intermediary between the tragedy and the audience'.[11] In her understanding of the significance of Greek drama she was strongly influenced by Nietzsche in his *Birth of Tragedy* (1872), especially in his understanding of the pivotal function of the chorus as embodying the spirit of music itself.[12]

Duncan repeatedly claimed that in her dance she aimed at impersonating what was the chorus in Greek tragedy: 'When I have danced, I have tried always to be

---

[9] Choreography for *Orfeo ed Euridice* by: Dalcroze (1912–13); Fokine (1911); Laban (1927); Balanchine (1936); Wigman (1947); Mark Morris (1996). For *Don Juan*: Laban (1925); Fokine (1936). Both Duncan (1900–15) and Bausch (1975) choreographed *Orfeo ed Euridice*. See further Meisner, this volume.

[10] The libretto of the *Iphigénie en Aulide* was written by Marie François Louis Grand Bailli du Roullet after Racine's *Iphigénie* (1674); the libretto of the *Iphigénie en Tauride* was written by Nicolas-François Guillard after the play *Iphigénie en Tauride* (1757) by Claude Guymond De La Touche. Gluck's choice of the Iphigenia story is in keeping with the peak of popularity that the myth enjoyed in the eighteenth century, during which it became the subject of several dramatic and operatic adaptations. For a list of dramatic and operatic versions of the Iphigenia myth see: Glliksohn (1985), 228–32; Heitner (1964); Matthiessen (2000), 364 n. 3; Ewans (2007), 31–53. For comment on the libretti, see Philippo (2005), 77–106.

[11] Duncan (1928), 84.

[12] LaMothe (2005), 248 has claimed that Duncan meant 'her dancing to deliver the kind of experience, both aesthetic and religious, that Nietzsche uses Attic tragedy to elucidate: an encounter with Dionysian energies of nature from which a person emerges with an affirmed sense of his or her bodily self as participating in the creation of values, religious ideals in particular'.

the Chorus ... I have never once danced a solo. The dance, again joined with poetry and music, must become once more the tragic chorus.'[13] By assuming a function similar to that of the chorus in Greek tragedy, Duncan aimed thus at embodying the spirit of the music, which she conceived as 'the great, impersonal, eternal and divine well-spring' of all art. In Duncan's opinion, Gluck was one of the composers who better understood the function and very essence of the Greek chorus, that is its impersonality; this is why Duncan chose to choreograph the movements and dances of Gluck's choruses, among which the dance of the maidens of Chalcis and that of the Scythian warriors remained central to her repertoire (the former from *Iphigénie en Aulide* and the latter from *Iphigénie en Tauride*).[14]

The inclusion of a long quotation of Gluck's words on his operatic reforms in the programme of the 2004 performance of Bausch's *Iphigenie auf Tauris* may stand as her own manifesto of artistic and reforming purposes:

I tried to lead the music back to its genuine purpose, which is: to support poetry, to emphasize the expression of the feelings and the interest of the situation, and to avoid holding up the action with useless ornaments. Furthermore I have believed that my greatest effort should consist of seeking a beautiful simplicity; and I have avoided making a display of difficulties at the expense of clarity.

Gluck's strong opposition to the virtuoso aria displays of the singers, which arrested dramatic time and were not appropriate for the expression (*Ausdruck*) of powerful and elevated feelings, echoes Duncan's and Bausch's opposition to a mere display of dance technique. Like Gluck and Duncan, even Bausch was looking for a 'total theatre', which, like Greek tragedy, makes a balanced use of different expressive media; indeed, in her pieces she employed a fusion of various art forms.

Even for Bausch, then, classical drama is the archetype of a theatre which expresses its existential meaning in a highly appropriate form, and her engagement with it can be interpreted as a will to create a dance which not only deals with existential meaning, but also strives to find a form suitable to express that meaning. In addition to this, Greek drama's portrayal of familial, social, and political conflicts

---

[13] Duncan (1928), 96.
[14] See Daly (1995), 146–8. A critic of the *Münchener Neueste Nachrichten* (1906) praised Duncan's dances to Gluck's music that she performed in the Volkstheater in Munich as follows (quoted in Jeschke and Vettermann (1995), 222–3): 'Miss Isadora Duncan danced *Iphigenia* by Gluck last night in the almost overcrowded Volkstheater. As strange as these words may sound to many, whoever saw the elegant artist again yesterday moving about majestically, virginally pure, and devoted as Iphigenia, or wholly abandoned to rhythm as one of *The Maidens of Chalkis* and in a portrayal of dancing Scythians, would have to admit that, to a certain degree, *Iphigenia* by Gluck was truly danced: in any event, that Isadora Duncan's dancing to the music of Gluck has to be recognized as simply perfect. As usual, the actual ballet pieces, particularly the dance of the maidens of Chalkis, expressing joy at seeing the Greek troops, and the precious musette, all nicely played by the orchestra as well, evoked greater interest than the pantomime scenes. The harmony, grace and fluid beauty of her every movement and pose, as well as the easy, fascinating purity of this barely clad artist, seem as much as ever unequalled and no doubt difficult to equal.'

as well as its existential, emotional, and psychological content have offered fertile ground for appropriation and adaptation through the filter of contemporary sensibilities. Like Duncan, Bausch thought that dance needs to be an expression of life, an existential journey, a way to discover the most basic drives within oneself:

Very few people know what happens within themselves, why they have certain feelings, why they suddenly feel unhappy or content with themselves, why they go through periods of depression etc. Can we afford to waste our time with melodramatic diversions?[15]

In this sense, Bausch's theatre can be defined, maybe even paradoxically, as 'classical'; and in this sense Odenthal's statement that Bausch 'created a new, contemporary form of the antique tragedy: dance theatre' can be understood.[16]

IPHIGENIA: A RITE OF PASSAGE

Both Duncan's and Bausch's sensibilities were drawn to the Iphigenia myth. The reasons for this may be various, but no doubt the most relevant is that the figure of Iphigenia can be said to stand as the symbol or archetype of woman subject to various forms of patriarchal authority and searching for a measure of autonomy.[17] Undoubtedly, both Duncan and Bausch in their unconventional and revolutionary artistic pursuits sought to promote a type of woman able to express herself freely and uncompromisingly, especially in relation to the male-dominated establishment. Duncan explicitly and repeatedly promoted the emancipation of women; and in her assumption of the role of Iphigenia, she was able to enact the generation of a higher creative and distinctly feminine ideal (thus interpreting the figure of Iphigenia more from a Goethean than Euripidean perspective and maybe suggesting a sharing of Goethe's concept of the eternal feminine).[18]

In Bausch's case, we can infer that a similar perspective was at play: Iphigenia's sacrifice could metaphorically represent the sacrifice of womanly values to a set of dogmatically, and male, codified ones.[19] This theme appears again and even

---

[15] In Climenhaga (2009), 63.

[16] Odenthal (1994), 35.

[17] Edith Hall informs me that in a forthcoming study she will propose that the Tauric Iphigenia is a rare example of a female figure involved in a quest plot, which is far more commonly a typical male endeavour. Heilbrun (1990) convincingly argues that female figures have been restricted to the marriage or erotic plot, but never to the quest plot. In this respect, Iphigenia stands out from her fellow female characters by being a quest heroine. Most probably, it is this outstanding aspect of her story which made Iphigenia a suitable figure to be appropriated by Duncan and Bausch as the archetypal representative of the female existential quest.

[18] For a discussion of this aspect of Goethe's *Iphigenie auf Tauris* see Torrance (2007), 177–206.

[19] Climenhaga (2009), 11 rightly states that 'Bausch is very aware of the plight of women in contemporary society, and the imagery she chooses reflects this concern. In other words, the metaphor of a woman chosen as a sacrifice to the power and control of men is not lost on Bausch, but she is able to extend the metaphor . . . and, therefore, avoid falling into didacticism.'

more forcefully in the *Le Sacre du Printemps* (1975), where Bausch seems to question why 'a woman invariably serves as the victim of social violence'.[20] However, this is not to suggest that Bausch's work is characterized by an overtly feminist approach: she herself asserted that her theatre was shaped by the fact that she was a woman ('it certainly has to do with myself—with the fact that I am a woman'), but she denied her involvement with feminism *per se* ('Feminism— perhaps because it has become such a fashionable word—and I retreat into my snail-shell. Perhaps also because they very often draw such a funny borderline there that I don't really like it. Sometimes it sounds like against each other instead of together').[21] More importantly, if at the beginning of Bausch's career as a choreographer, the theme of sacrifice was possibly more concerned with the situation of women, later on the theme extended to both genders; to use Schmidt's words 'we all, men as well as women, are sacrifices at the altar of society'.[22]

Furthermore, both Duncan's and Bausch's engagement with the Iphigenia story is due to the pivotal role played by the theme of sacrifice and ritual in both the Euripidean plays.[23] The theme of ritual is crucial for modern choreographers and dancers at large and must be briefly considered as a constituting phenomenon of modern dance's aesthetics.[24] The aspiration to a return to the condition of ritual together with the concept that dance sprang out of it has been, in fact, the stronghold of modern dance. As Copeland has remarked: 'originality in modern dance was typically conceived of as a return to origins'; and a return to ritual was sought as a means for dance to go back to its primeval source.[25] This primitivist notion of dance was prompted by the development of anthropological studies at the beginning of the century. Among the scholarly investigations of the so-called Cambridge Ritualists, Jane Harrison's theory of the origin of dance in ritual especially exerted a pivotal influence.[26] Harrison maintained that 'almost everywhere, all over the world, it is found that primitive ritual consists, not in prayer and praise and sacrifice, but in mimetic dancing'.[27] She thus established that dance was the most primitive art and that it developed as a necessity to represent

---

[20] Manning (1991), 146 has noted the difference in this respect between Wigman's 1957 version and Bausch's interpretations of the final sacrificial dance in the *Sacre*; for Wigman the sacrificial dance represents a 'heroic act' celebrating 'women's capability of self-endurance and self-sacrifice'.

[21] Cited in Hoghe and Tree (1980), 73–4.

[22] Schmidt (1982), 2.

[23] See Goff (1999), 109–25.

[24] Copeland (2004), 132. Modern dancers' engagement with ritual is all pervasive from at least Ballets Russes' *Le Sacre du Printemps* (1913) and includes Ruth St Denis's oriental choreographies, Graham's *Primitive Mysteries* (1931) and Laban's movement choirs, whose origins he explained as follows: 'the lay dance choir is a rediscovery of a much earlier artistic community in which mysterious ritual was the foundation of social unity and the spectator played a secondary role' (quoted in Toepfer (1997), 301).

[25] Copeland (2004), 123.

[26] For a discussion of Harrison's influence on modern theatre see Peters (2008), 1–41.

[27] Harrison (1913), 168.

a feeling collectively felt and expressed into action.[28] Moreover, Harrison claimed that ritual constituted 'a bridge between real life and art' since ritual and art developed from the same impulse and need to recreate an emotion, more precisely, an unfulfilled emotion or an unsatisfied desire. Thus art, according to Harrison, 'springs by way of ritual out of keen emotion towards life'.[29]

Harrison concluded her study of the relation of art and ritual with the claim that ritual is not an 'obsolete' practice, but 'a perennial need'; and that the present seems particularly suited for a revival of ritual since 'a first-hand emotion and expression' is needed and looked for:

> Some of the strenuous, exciting, self-expressive dances of today are of the soil and some exotic, but based as they mostly are on very primitive ritual, they stand as singular evidence of this real recurrent need. Art in these latter days goes back as it were on her own steps, recrossing the ritual bridge back to life.[30]

Harrison's concept seems to have been fully embraced by Isadora Duncan, who similarly claimed that dance has to become once again an 'expression of life'.[31] In order to transform dance into an expression of life again and thus into a religious endeavour, Duncan chose the Dionysian ritual out of which Greek drama sprang as paradigm of such an art: 'The dance of the future will have to become again a high religious art as it was with the Greeks. For art which is not religious is not art, is mere merchandise.'[32] She implied that dance had to return to its ritual roots, and thus a new 'liturgy' apt to express life had to be created.[33]

Duncan was on friendly terms with the Cambridge Ritualists, especially Gilbert Murray and Jane Harrison; and Harrison provided a reading of the *Idylls* of Theocritus during one of Duncan's performances.[34] Duncan's idea of the return to ritual and thus to the primitive origins of dance became, indeed, the foundational myth of modern dance. It is, then, no coincidence that the

---

[28] Ibid. 171: 'But historically and also genetically or logically the dance in its inchoateness, its undifferentiatedness, comes first. It has in it a larger element of emotion, and less of representation.'

[29] Ibid. 215.

[30] Ibid. 207.

[31] Duncan (1928) 141: 'The dance is not a diversion but a religion, an expression of life.'

[32] Duncan (1903), 24.

[33] LaMothe (2006), 89 has convincingly argued that Duncan adopted the Nietzschean 'vision of dance as a theopraxis', which the German philosopher especially developed in *Thus spake Zarathustra.* It is important to stress that Duncan (1928), 139 did not intend to revive the dances of the Greeks archaeologically, but she envisaged Greek theatre as the most accomplished example of an art which was rooted in life: 'To revive the antique dances would be a task as impossible as it would be useless. The dance, to be an art for us, must be born out of ourselves, out of the emotions and the life of our times, just as the old dances were born of the life and emotions of the ancient Greeks.' As LaMothe (2006), 113 has remarked Greek culture is for Duncan 'an ideal of an alternative mode of valuation'. See further Naerebout and Cooper Albright, this volume.

[34] The performance was reviewed in *The Times* (16 March 1900) by the musicologist, J. Fuller-Maitland: 'Miss Duncan's exceptional beauty of face and figure fits her for the self-appointed task of illustrating in dance such passages as were chosen from the Homeric Hymn to Demeter and the Idylls of Theocritus; these were read with much effect by Miss Jane Harrison.'

founding choreography of modern dance, Vaslav Nijinsky's *Le Sacre du Prin-temps* (1913), actually depicts a pagan ritual of the Rite of Spring; in this ground-breaking piece, Nijinsky was able to create 'a coherent system of ritual dance . . . and to bring back through the theatre, dormant techniques of ritual dance'.[35] In *Sacre*, Nijinsky shared Duncan's idea of the necessity of returning to ritual in order 'to start again at the beginning, and to discover the movements that would trigger psychic release'.[36] Not surprisingly, Nijinsky's *Sacre* has become, in turn, the 'rite of passage' for modern dance choreographers in assessing the originality of their artistic works.[37]

As to Pina Bausch's engagement with ritual, it seems that this very concept stood as the foundational narrative of her artistic creations. According to Mulrooney, 'Bausch's work is, in itself, practically a ritual Rite of Spring', more precisely a 'ritual burning' of set and conventional structures of feeling; such ritual destruction is enacted in order to trigger a 'renovation of perception' as well as a 'perennial reinvention of identity'.[38] In this sense, Bausch's work is in line with the instances of early modern dance in their aspiration to bring dance back to the condition of ritual.

However, Bausch's concept of ritual is ambivalent: in fact the positive regen-erative function of ritual can find its dead end precisely at the point where ritual becomes crystallized in a system of institutionalized norms of behaviour or social rituals.[39] Early works such as *Iphigenie* and *Sacre* are already concerned to show how violence is embedded in the religious and social rituals of any given community, even more importantly, how such violence is somehow sanctioned by institutionalized rituals.[40] The same theme occurs over and over again in her later productions, where ritual became the metaphor *par excellence* to describe engendered social attitudes and stereotyped behaviour which are imposed upon the body of the dancers by different cultures and societies.[41] Her numerous city-

---

[35] Hodson (1985), 42.

[36] Ibid. 46. In an interview in 1910 Nijinsky proclaimed his admiration for Duncan as a revolutionary artist (quoted in Hodson (1986), 67–8): 'Among the dancers whom I admire I must name Isadora Duncan, Thamar Karsavina, Pavlova, my sister Nijinska, and Fokine. Isadora Duncan is a very great artist. Her influence on modern dancing is very important. Before her time dancing was under the restraint of an exacting technique. Isadora has danced to give freedom to movement, and has broadened the dancer's horizon. Fokine, too, has done this. Before these two the imagination and temperament of a dancer were bridled.'

[37] Leonide Massine (1920); Mary Wigman (1957); Maurice Béjart (1959); Kenneth MacMillan (1962); Pina Bausch (1975); Martha Graham (1984). For a comprehensive catalogue of choreographies on the *Sacre du Printemps* see Acocella et al. (1992); they list forty-four choreographies of the *Rite*. For the popularity of the *Rite* in German modern dance see Manning (1991), 129–58.

[38] Mulrooney (2002), 22 and 338.

[39] See Burns (1972) and Goffman (1974).

[40] Birringer (1986) 92: 'In her choreographic treatment of Stravinsky's *Rite of Spring*, the ritual dance was constantly repeated—to the point of total exhaustion—as a central metaphor for the well-rehearsed behavior of men following the rules of society and selecting women as sacrificial victims, even as the women themselves envision and anticipate the selection.'

[41] Craine (2008) claims that 'there has always been a sense of ritual about Bausch's work'.

inspired pieces basically depict the social rituals enacted by different countries and cultures.[42] As for *Iphigenie* in particular, the rite of passage embedded in the myth seems indeed of pivotal significance in Bausch's work.

According to the myth-ritualist theory, Greek drama sprang out of ritual, more specifically from an annual ritual enacting the death and renewal of the god of vegetation (Dionysus). This rite of passage, involving a change of condition in nature, was associated with the rite of passage from one stage of life to another within the social community; thus, in Greek drama the rite of passage of vegetation interfaced with that of initiation into society.[43] In the Iphigenia myth, the rite of passage in question is one of coming of age, more specifically the passage from maidenhood to adulthood.[44] The puberty rite entailed a passage from the condition of maiden to that of adult woman and on its integration into the social fabric through marriage. In the Iphigenia myth the transition from one condition to the other is not accomplished, since Agamemnon's daughter does not get married, but becomes the high priestess in the temple of Artemis.[45] Iphigenia does not, as it were, abandon that liminal and possibly sacred state which is characteristic of the transitional period.[46] That she is only partially, and undoubtedly not conventionally, reintegrated into the social community is stressed by the fact that Artemis brings her to the marginal region of the Tauric Chersonnese.

Indeed, it is the condition of sacred liminality embedded in the myth of Iphigenia, which seems very suitable to Bausch's idea not only of where artistic creation lies, but also, perhaps, of where authentic life is possible. It is the liminal condition of being which, in its positive aspect, allows a creative, unstructured, and even ludic approach to life. It is this state which permits the flux of life not to crystallize but to remain open; the negative side is that liminality requires, to a great degree, non-integration, separation, and, possibly, loneliness. The Iphigenia story contains an additional theme which is central for Bausch, 'the conflict between social regimentation and self-expression, the need to belong and the impulse to be free'.[47] In Bausch's *Iphigenie auf Tauris* the issue of belonging plays a prominent role: the protagonist lives in a foreign country to whose 'customs'

---

[42] *Bandoneon* (1980, Argentina); *Viktor* (1986, Rome); *Palermo, Palermo* (1989, Sicily); *Tanzabend II* (1991, Madrid); *Ein Trauerspiel* (1994, Vienna); *Nur Du* (1996, America); *Der Fensterputzer* (1997, Hong Kong); *Masurca Fogo* (1998, Portugal and Brazil); *O Dido* (1999, Rome); *Wiesenland* (2000, Budapest); *Agua* (2001, Brazil); *Rough cut* (2005, Korea); *Nefés* (2003, Istanbul); *Ten Chi* (2004, Japan); *Bamboo Blues* (2007, India).

[43] Dowden (1989), 7 defines this process as the 'interface between fertility and initiation'.

[44] See Dowden (1989), 9–47.

[45] Lyons (1997), 137 states: 'Iphigenia remains blocked at the moment of transition, and instead of undergoing the changes by which women's lives are usually marked, becomes a stand-in for the goddess herself.'

[46] Van Gennep (1909) postulated that ancient rites of passage entailed three stages: separation, liminality, incorporation; Turner (1967), 93–111 defined liminality as the state 'betwixt and between'.

[47] Holden (1989).

she does not adhere; and she longs for her lost homeland towards which she has, nonetheless, ambivalent feelings because of the sacrifice she had to undergo in order for the Greek fleet to set sail for Troy. A similar sense of displacement is experienced by her brother Orestes, who is an outsider even in his own country because of the matricide he has perpetrated and which sets him aside from the social community.

Liminality is a key feature in Bausch's work in many respects.[48] For instance, the absence of a prearranged storyline and musical score, the lack of closure which all her pieces present, and, most of all, her very method of constructing dance through the questioning approach are all devices meant to avoid any kind of static or given framework to her pieces. In relation to the devices adopted to maintain this liminal condition, Bausch's refusal to work within the boundaries of a given dance technique and to create one of her own vividly recalls Duncan's similar intention. It thus seems no coincidence that the myth of Iphigenia was befitting to both Duncan and Bausch in their striving to create a dance which was an expression of life, where life is intended as a constant and continuous flux of being, which, by its very nature, requires a non-dogmatic, unstructured, and ultimately Dionysiac approach.

DUNCAN'S IMPRINT ON BAUSCH

The unique dance-making style elaborated by Bausch, which might appear to be totally unrelated to any previous ones, actually has deep roots in the tradition of modern dance. It should be seen as the last step in an evolutionary process which can be traced back to the very first impulse from which modern dance developed at the beginning of the twentieth century: that is the need to free the body from the constraints of traditional ballet, whose physicality was felt to be artificial, impersonal and, although well suited for telling fairy-tales, deemed totally inappropriate to portray the human condition and mature subjectivity, with its conflicts, feelings, and existential problems, which had become a central theme in western art.

As Sondra Fraleigh rightly points out: 'Modern dance opened the expressive ground to a fuller range of subjectivity by opening up a new range of movement-possibilities and felt (or psychic) states intrinsic to movement.'[49] What set in motion the search for a wider dance vocabulary was the correspondence between movement and meaning as formulated by Delsarte in his 'Law of Correspondence'.[50] As Ruyter has remarked, the idea of correspondence between

---

[48] Already Jane Harrison (1913), 41 postulated that 'Art and religion . . . spring from the incomplete cycle, from unsatisfied desire'; Auslander (2003), 130 has maintained that 'liminality . . . contains the potentiality for cultural innovation'.

[49] Fraleigh (1987), 103.

[50] Delsarte's 'Law of Correspondence' states that 'To each spiritual function responds a function of the body; to each grand function of the body corresponds a spiritual act' (in Stebbins (1885), 67).

movement and meaning could stimulate and encourage 'the development of individualized movement vocabularies and choreographic structures in relation to what was to be expressed'.[51]

The search for an appropriate and enriched dance vocabulary capable of new expressive accomplishments, which can be considered the distinctive feature of modern dance, was pioneered at the start of the last century by many but Duncan was perhaps the figure who most prominently influenced the course of the renovation of dance language. In the formulation of her principles, Nietzsche's arguments against the validity of the Cartesian split between soul and body were perhaps most keenly felt. Nietzsche set in motion the premise of the birth of the body's autonomy as a pre-rational medium for the knowledge of the self.[52] The language the body speaks is regarded by Nietzsche as the purer and more honest because it comes directly from experience (the body does not say 'I' but performs 'I').[53] The emphasis Nietzsche puts on the value of the non-intellectual knowledge achieved through the body and the fact that this intuitive faculty has an important role in the process of understanding, is strictly connected with his appreciation of dance as the preferred medium to convey it. Dance made a seminal step on the way to becoming an autonomous art with a cognitive and not just pleasure-inducing function.

Duncan's specific contribution is centred on what she called 'the return to the natural body' and the exploration of the movement possibilities associated with it. Duncan's concept of the natural body is a pivotal one in her philosophy of dancing and one which has been often misunderstood or simply dismissed as a Romantic residue. On the contrary, Duncan's idea of the natural body was revolutionary and deeply influential for the subsequent generation of choreographers and dancers. Duncan claimed that 'all true dance movements possible to the human body exist primarily in Nature' and that 'the fountain-head for the art of the dance will be the study of the movements of Nature'.[54] The concept of 'Nature' is indeed a central one in Duncan's dance theory. She saw 'Nature' as a creative universal force or energy, from the observation of which she developed the fundamental principle intrinsic to human movements. The principle was that 'all free natural movements conform to the law of wave movement'.[55] Duncan

---

[51] Ruyter (1996a), 64.

[52] For a discussion of Nietzsche's influence on Duncan see LaMothe (2005), 241–66 and (2006).

[53] Nietzsche (1883–5). Trans. Hollindale (1961), 62: Zarathustra warns the despisers of the body not to value their intellect over their body since in the body 'there is more reason' than in the 'best wisdom'.

[54] Duncan (1928), 68. Daly (1995), 33 has argued that 'Duncan challenged the paradigm of technique with that of the Natural'.

[55] Duncan (1981), 45: 'All energy expresses itself through this wave movement, for does not sound travel in waves, and light also, and when we come to the movements of organic nature it would seem that all free natural movements conform to the law of wave movement. The flight of birds, for instance, or the bounding of animals.' See further Cooper Albright, this volume.

claimed that she developed her 'theory of wave movements' from the observation of Greek art (see Figure 12.2).[56] Thus Greek art, by reflecting and complying with the natural law of wave movement, attains harmony, or more precisely, conformity of form and movement to Nature, which, in Duncan's opinion, is what creates Beauty.[57] The correspondence between form and movement had the inherent corollary that, since body forms differ greatly from individual to individual, each individual has to find the type of movement apt to express the uniqueness of his/her body form.

According to Jowitt, 'Duncan left to choreographers of the next generation the idea that the body itself, and not just the choreographic scenario, ought to reflect the dancer's response to the world'.[58] Indeed, in this respect Duncan's influence on modern performance has not always been fully recognized; for instance, Ann Daly has maintained that:

as new as Duncan's dancing had been, it had been built upon romantic ideas about morality and spirituality that could not accommodate the more secular interests of modern art...Duncan may have helped to negotiate the transition from late nine-teenth-century Victorianism to early-twentieth-century modernism, but she never did emerge fully into the new aesthetic order.[59]

However, Preston has claimed that Duncan's work has to be placed in the context of Modernist performance; her influence on key figures of Modernism such as the theatre reformers Stanislavsky (1863–1938), Gordon Craig (1872–1966), or the dance reformer Rudolf von Laban clearly attests to the innovative character of her dance theory.[60]

Stanislavsky, who saw Duncan dancing in Moscow in 1907 while he was working on his new Method of acting, was struck by her performance in which he recognized 'the truth of the inner creative urge' he sought in acting.[61] Laban saw Duncan dancing in Paris in 1901 and, several years later, acknowledged her pivotal role in the development of modern dance:

The main achievement of Duncan was, however, that she reawakened a form of dance-expression, which could be called dance-lyrics, in contrast to the mainly dramatic dance forms of ballet. There was no story behind her dances, which were, as she herself termed

---

[56] Duncan (1928), 90: 'In the thousand and thousands of figures which I have studied on these vases, I have always found an undulating line as the point of departure.'

[57] Duncan (1981), 36: 'Two thousand years ago a people lived here who had perfect sympathy and comprehension of the Beautiful in Nature, and this knowledge and sympathy were perfectly expressed in their own forms and movement. Of all the thousands of figures of Greek sculpture, bas reliefs, and vases there is not one but is in exquisite bodily proportion and harmony of movement.'

[58] Jowitt (1985), 28.

[59] Daly (1995), 209. According to Mazo (2000), 52 'the famous Stanislavski Method of acting is nothing more than a device for switching on at will what Isadora called the *motor in my soul*'.

[60] Preston (2005), 273–89. For her influence in Britain see Macintosh, this volume.

[61] For a discussion of the encounter between Duncan and Stanislavsky see: Rene (1963), 40–3 and Roslavleva (1965).

LES DANSES D'ISADORA DUNCAN
PAGE D'ALBUM PAR A.-F. GORGUET

Figure 12.2 'Les Danses d'Isadora' (1909).

it, the expression of the life of her soul. She reawakened the sense of poetry of movement in modern man. At a time when science, and especially psychology, endeavored to abolish radically any notion of a 'soul', this dancer had the courage to demonstrate successfully that there exists in the flow of man's movement some ordering principle which cannot be explained in the usual rationalistic manner.[62]

The seminal concept of the free body, that modern dance pioneers established, was further developed by later generations of twentieth-century choreographers such as Doris Humphrey (1895–1958), Martha Graham (1894–1991), and Merce Cunningham (1919–2009).[63] The elaboration of 'the free body' language by individual choreographers generally resulted in the invention of a wide variety of new movement patterns, which, although broadening the expressive ability of dance over the traditional ballet vocabulary, nonetheless tended eventually to crystallize in fixed prearranged frames.

Placed in this historical background, Pina Bausch's artistic research stems from and continued the most advanced research in dance techniques, especially those established by German *Ausdruckstanz*. But, as a distinctive feature, her major accomplishment was a faithful return to Duncan's idea of 'freedom of the body' in its primary sense, namely an individual vocabulary of movement generated by the dancers themselves.[64] In terms of conceptual legacy, it seems that Bausch's work was much indebted (no matter how consciously) to the position of Isadora Duncan, who never had the intention of creating her own dance technique or vocabulary, as her words well show: 'My intention is to build a school . . . In this school I shall not teach the children to imitate my movements, I shall help them to develop those movements which are natural to them.'[65] Duncan's statement about the necessity to develop a personal vocabulary is echoed by Pina Bausch's famous claim: 'I'm not interested in how people move, but what moves them.'[66] Moreover, Duncan's aversion to the artificiality of ballet's prearranged set of steps is echoed by Bausch's statement

---

[62] Laban (1948),5.

[63] Garaudy (1972) and LaMothe (2005), 241 have rightly argued that it is necessary to distinguish between the pioneers of modern dance such as Isadora Duncan and Ruth St Denis who 'cultivated the visions, movement principles, and audiences for modern dance' and the founders such as Martha Graham and Doris Humphrey who 'built on their work in codifying enduring techniques of dance training'.

[64] Toepfer (1997), 146 has claimed that 'the whole idea of *Ausdruckstanz*, of the body as a powerful instrument of expressivity, seemed to emanate from her [Isadora Duncan]'. See also Mulrooney (2002), 100: 'Bausch's work was to evidence a reaction against the prevailing postwar aesthetic which was the formalism of German Ballet . . . and American dance. Instead it reached back to Isadora Duncan.'

[65] In relation to this, it is interesting to quote Vaslav Nijinsky's comment on Isadora's dancing after a performance in Russia (in Nijinska (1981), 224): 'her performance is spontaneous and is not based on any school of dancing and so cannot be taught . . . It is not art'; similarly, as Jowitt (1985), 28 has remarked, Ted Shawn claimed that 'Duncan's art was a dead end, a matter of individual genius'.

[66] Cited in Climenhaga (1997), 97.

that 'it does not mean anything to teach steps. You cannot teach steps. You have to reach in and change the entire body.'[67] In relation to this, it is worth comparing the most outstanding feature of Bausch's choreographic work which is, as rightly stated by Norbert Servos, the role played in it by the body of the dancer: according to Bausch, the body is not an object or an instrument any more but becomes the subject of the dance. As a consequence, the story of the dance is told as history of the body and not as danced literature; this very fact is opposed to the idea of a previously dictated musical, thematic, or dance pattern.

For this reason, her very experimental and creative method of dance-making was based on the so-called question-and-answer approach and on preliminary improvisation which gave the dancers an active role in the process of creation. The very first step of the dance-making process started simply with some questions posed by Bausch to her dancers about different issues; the dancers then replied to her questioning with an improvisation which could be danced, spoken, sung, or expressed in any way they felt most appropriate. Through this process, the dancers were not simply executors of previously arranged steps and sequences, but had the chance to bring on stage fragments of their own individuality and personal story, which interested Bausch most.

All the tools of her dance-making were clearly meant to achieve an open performance without a narrative plot, without a homogeneous musical frame (she mainly made a collage of classical and modern music); a montage device (borrowed from the cinematic tradition) provided the final structural frame. Her performances, then, do not have a linear development (as in classical ballet, for example, where a story is described through dance), but are rather a collection of fragments of different individual experiences suggesting specific emotions. Her dance language is neither descriptive nor narrative, but rather a poetic one expressed by the body. Since in her work the story is told as history of the body, which is a source of subjectivity, and the actions of the dancers are the body's reflections upon reality, her theatre has often been defined as theatre of the experience. This dance theatre of the experience led her to abandon any previous tradition either literary (for the themes) or connected with the dance repertoire and to produce works which are totally new creations. Nonetheless, her pieces are not abstract; they tend to show instead dramatic situations charged with intense emotional conflicts which are presented in a non-literal manner.[68] This particular choreographical method and the abandonment of a narrative structure can be seen as the outcome of a progressive evolution. This is clearly shown by the presence in her repertoire of pieces where a narrative plot is still present, as well as in the use of a ready-made score rather than a patchwork of different musical tones.

[67] Cited in Riding (1997).
[68] Anderson (1984).

Bausch's movement vocabulary, which employs extensive use of torso and arms, seems to be connected with Duncan's idea that the solar plexus and the torso are the generating source of the movement (she designed the solar plexus as the physical location of the soul and the centre of emotion).[69] The stemming of the movement from the solar plexus frees the lower body and places emphasis on the flow of the movement from the upper chest and the arms. Bausch's statement that 'the steps always come from somewhere else, never from the legs' can, in my opinion, be interpreted in this light.[70] In 1997 Bausch agreed to repeat her *Le Sacre du Printemps* with the dancers of the Paris Opera Ballet and explained the difficulties in teaching them the piece since they were not used to feeling the movement stemming from the chest: 'even running is difficult at first because you have to think of running from here [i.e. the chest].'[71]

Moreover, one of the tenets of Duncan's dance theory prescribed that movements ought to be successive, as she herself explained:

The primary . . . movements . . . must have within them the seeds from which will evolve all other movements, each in turn to give birth to others in unending sequence of still higher and greater expression.[72]

Anderson has argued that Duncan's theory of successive movements is directly linked to the interpretation of 'subjectivity as a dynamic, on-going activity demonstrated in the body' and that 'the quality characterising her technique was fluidity'.[73] Even in the case of Bausch, the quality of the movement is fluid, not fragmented but a continuous emotional flow from one movement to the other which could resemble an ongoing interior monologue, a sort of danced stream of consciousness. Thus, the dance vocabulary is a technical tool aptly devised to express the emotional content of dance.

Another further point of contact between Duncan and Bausch resides in what we can call the search for impersonality. I discussed above how Duncan aimed at

---

[69] Duncan (1927), 75: 'I spent long days and nights in the studio seeking that dance which might be the divine expression of the human spirit through the medium of the body's movement. For hours I would stand quite still, my two hands folded between my breasts, covering the solar plexus . . . I was seeking and finally discovered the central spring of all movement.' Duncan's belief that all motion stems from the solar plexus echoes Delsarte's focus on the origin of movement from a central anatomical location. Duncan acknowledged her admiration for Delsarte in an interview in 1898 (quoted in Jowitt (1985), 24): 'Delsarte, the master of all principles of flexibility, and lightness of body, should receive universal thanks for the bonds he has removed from our constrained members.'

[70] Cited in Servos (1984), 235.

[71] Riding (1997).

[72] Duncan was possibly influenced by Delsarte's formulation about the three types of movements: oppositions, parallelisms, and successions. Succession is the fluid and wavelike movement which Delsarte claimed to be the most powerful of the three for emotional expression. Similarly, Laban (1950) links the 'motion factors' of flow to the 'power of feeling'.

[73] Anderson (2008), 358.

embodying the impersonal nature of the chorus; as Jowitt has remarked, in her avoidance of impersonation, Duncan 'presaged the abstractions of early modern dance, in which the dancer eschewed impersonation and equated her own persona with universal human feelings and drives'.[74] Bausch seemed to have a similar intention; the fact that in Bausch's pieces there are no protagonists or soloists, but rather single personalities who emerge at times from the group and then merge into it again, seems to point to Duncan's avoidance of impersonation. Furthermore, the implication embedded in Bausch's approach is that it is possible to transform a subjective content into a universal one since human beings are capable of empathizing kinetically with emotions and pain 'suffered by others' as her words seem to imply:

It is never how it really happened; it always transforms itself many and many times, into something that ends up belonging to all of us. If something is true in one person, and he or she tells something about his or her feelings, I think we end up recognizing the feeling, it is not a private history. We talk about something that we all have. We all know these feelings and have them together.[75]

Even in the case of *Iphigenie*, where the presence of a fixed storyline prevents dancers from performing their own personal experience, nonetheless the dancer's emotional commitment is achieved by the fact that the subject of the piece is not the story itself but the feelings in it.[76] In fact, in *Iphigenie*, Bausch was not much concerned with giving a danced narration of the original plot, as she clearly states: 'Of course it is a story, but that's not important. It is about what happened to them and the feelings they had. What I try is to find the pictures, or the images that can best express the feeling I want to convey.'[77]

According to Norbert Servos, in the choreographing process of *Iphigenie*, 'Pina Bausch already went beyond any previous concept of the interpretation of librettos. She did not choreograph material, but took instead individual elements from the plot as a point of departure for her own wealth of associations.'[78] It is this wealth of associations and search for images apt to convey feelings and meaning which are characteristic traits of Pina Bausch's choreography in *Iphigenie*. I think that the fundamental and pivotal one is the association of the idea of the Greek man (Orestes) with the image of the naked body, and the association of the idea of the barbarian man (Thoas), with the image of the dressed and

---

[74] Jowitt (1985), 27.

[75] Durán (1994).

[76] In an interview after a revival of the 1974 performance of *Iphigenie* in Wuppertal in 2002, Bausch herself recognized that *Iphigenie* requires a different engagement for the dancers in this piece who are, instead, used to perform themselves. In relation to this she said: 'Each of them is such an individual personality. It is difficult for them to dance in a piece like *Iphigenie*. I love everybody in the company and everybody is so special, that I wanted to find something different for each one to do. It is necessary to see what they can do in the other works, where everyone is just themselves.'

[77] Pina Bausch at Turin Academic Symposium 1992.

[78] Servos (1984), 19.

constrained body. While Orestes and Pylades wear just skin-coloured shorts and are bare-footed (see Figure 14.1), Thoas wears a black suit, shoes, and a long black leather coat, which will hang on stage with its threatening presence throughout the performance. The visual contrast between the naked body of the Greek man, which possesses this interior and spiritual freedom, and the heavily dressed body of the barbarian man, blindly subjected to oppressive rules, expresses the emotional contrast between, on the one hand, the interior need for freedom of choice and the quest for a personal truth, and on the other, the dogmatic constraints which deny and annihilate their attainments.

Finally, Bausch's idea that the Greek man can represent and symbolize the fundamental interior search for freedom, which becomes increasingly difficult to achieve as civilization proceeds and develops, seems also to be strictly connected to the political, social, and religious involvement of the Greek in the society in which s/he lives. The symbol of this involvement, which is the polar opposite of the alienation felt by the contemporary individual, is represented by the very nature of ancient Greek theatre. Bausch's Greek turns out to be surprisingly close to Duncan's idea of the natural and free Greek body: indeed, for both these choreographers, working upon Iphigenia led to complex explorations of alternative aesthetic, personal, and political freedoms.

13

Ancient Myths and Modern Moves: The Greek-Inspired Dance Theatre of Martha Graham

Henrietta Bannerman

Martha Graham, dancer, choreographer, and pioneer of American modern dance is renowned for the canon of Greek-inspired dances she created; in fact so highly regarded did Graham become for her staging of Greek plays and myths that the British classicist, Oliver Taplin has called her, 'the most articulate proponent of Greek tragedy in dance'.[1] Taplin's view is shared by the Israeli scholar, Nurit Yaari, who refers to Graham as one of modern theatre's 'great interpreters of Greek myth and tragedy' ranking her amongst the early twentieth-century's most important playwrights, such as Eugene O'Neill, Jean Cocteau, William Butler Yeats, Albert Camus, and Jean Anouilh.[2]

From the late 1940s to the end of the 1980s, Graham constantly revisited the Greek myths reinterpreting them through the medium of her ground-breaking dance theatre. Amongst the twelve dance dramas that Graham produced are some that stand out as masterworks: these include *Cave of the Heart* (1946), *Errand into the Maze* (1947), *Night Journey* (1947), and *Clytemnestra* (1958).[3] Even in the very first years of her career, Graham was steeped in Greek theatre, so much so that her development as a dancer and choreographer grew largely from her journey into the world of antiquity. These early and sometimes flawed experiments were not carried out in a vacuum; nor indeed did they pass without trace, as I will show later in this chapter.

Graham's work is rarely performed in current times, especially in Britain. It may also be considered of some concern that in keeping her dances alive and accessible for contemporary American audiences, the Martha Graham Company is compelled to provide a considerable amount of background information or contextualization. Despite the perceived necessity for such tactics in conserving

---

[1] Taplin (1989), 52.
[2] Yaari (2003), 224.
[3] For a list of Graham's Greek dances, see the listing at the beginning of this volume.

Graham's work, the recent opportunity I had to see the Martha Graham Company perform a range of dances, including *Errand into the Maze* (1947),[4] disabused any impression that they might be considered to have become museum pieces. On the contrary, they remain vital and potent theatrical works that resist any possibility of fossilization. In this chapter, I hope to demonstrate that Graham's Greek-inspired dances continue to be relevant and that they chime with our own era. I shall explore both the 'Greekness' of the contemporary context as well as the long shadow of her legacy, cast often in unexpected places—notably in the work of the British ballet choreographer Frederick Ashton.

Whilst much attention has rightly been placed on the impact of the 'Grecian' aesthetic of Isadora Duncan, and in fact on Greekness in general in the early years of the development of modern dance, it is equally important to stress the ways in which Graham's contemporaries were also experimenting with Greek themes and how these experiments were often very different to her own. For Balanchine it was a preoccupation with formal questions that led him to Greek culture; and for Anthony Tudor and Hanya Holm, to whom I shall return later, it was the burlesque or even comic vein of Greek antiquity that they found alluring and pertinent. Their approach might be regarded as refreshing in a world of ballet, where seriousness and classicism are often equated with a layering on or patina of Greekness. However, for artists such as Graham and Doris Humphrey, Graham's peer in the evolution and promotion of American modern dance, it was a deep exploration of ancient Greek culture which spurred them on. In Humphrey's case it was her preoccupation with choral dancing and therefore with the Greek chorus that led her to explore tragedy. For Graham, however, it is Eliot's 'mythical method' that she appears to have followed.[5] Like Eliot and other Modernist writers of the era, Graham reformulated ancient myth and used it as an organizing principle for her dances, created within the modern, inchoate world. In this chapter I shall reveal that what makes Graham's work powerful and different is her radical recastings of the Greek myths, where the content provides the key to archetypal patterns that can illuminate twentieth-century preoccupations.

MYTH AS STOREHOUSE

From the very earliest years of her independent career, Graham had been involved in the creation of the new art of American modern dance and it might seem strange that she should have conceived the idea later that she could

---

[4] The Martha Graham Company performed at the Saratoga Performing Arts Center in Saratoga Springs, New York on Friday, 13 June 2008 in partnership with the Office of the Dean of Special Programs at Skidmore College.
[5] Eliot (1923), 483.

turn to the ancient Greek myths and to a culture altogether other than to her own. But Graham was the direct descendant of the two mothers of American dance, Isadora Duncan and Ruth St Denis. Duncan explored the old world of Europe in pursuit of her Greek ideal and St Denis, as Graham put it, 'turned her head and her heart across a continent to the Orient'.[6] By registering this dual heritage, Graham acknowledged her own interest in the 'old' and 'exotic' worlds of art and theatre despite having announced in the early years of her career: 'Of things American the American dance must be made'.[7] From the late 1920s and until the 1940s, Graham took mainly American themes as subjects for her dances, although even such works as *American Provincials* (1934) bore witness to her potential for Greek theatre as the critic John Martin pointed out. He agreed that the dance was 'an American study' but he saw too that it expressed 'something larger'. 'It is indeed', he wrote, 'that concept without time or place which the Greeks called Medea' and, proclaimed Martin, 'what a Medea Miss Graham could play if she put her mind to it!'[8]

Martin foresaw that Graham had the potential to produce powerful incarnations of the classical heroines, and she would indeed go on to dramatize these legendary figures on the dance stage. However, in the 1930s, another celebrated pioneer of American modern dance, Doris Humphrey was also embarking on a journey into Greek mythology. In 1931 Humphrey conceived an ambitious project—to create a danced version of *The Oresteia*.[9] Like the later Graham, Humphrey was inspired by the Greek myths, but unlike Graham she did not use them to probe the psychology of their 'heroes and villains'. Rather, she wanted to 're-create Greek theatre itself, with themes appropriate to modern life',[10] an idea she attempted to realize with *Dionysiaques* (1932), the first of two big works Humphrey made in the early 1930s. Inspired by her readings of Nietzsche and by a book on the Minoan excavations in Crete, Humphrey drew on the bull-god cult of ancient Crete for a section in *Dionysiaques*. This was described in a programme note as a 'ritualistic bacchanale' which celebrated 'the ancient practice of sacrificing a chosen one for the good of the many'.[11] For Humphrey, this prehistoric act as mythologized in Cretan culture became a metaphor for the rebuilding or renewal of society, a theme which often underpinned her dances.

In order to realize *Orestes*, the second of the major works created in the early 1930s, Humphrey turned to Darius Milhaud's *Les Choéphores* (1915–17), the second in his trilogy of short opera oratorios based on the *Oresteia* with a text by

---

[6] Graham cited in Terry (1963), 156.   [7] Graham cited in Barretto (1999), 54.

[8] Martin cited in Jowitt (1988), 202.

[9] It is also interesting to point out that in 1926, the British choreographer and one of the founders of the Royal Ballet, Ninette de Valois, produced her *Oresteiad* at the Cambridge Arts Theatre.

[10] Siegel (1979), 133.

[11] Ibid. 134. On sacrifice and Modern Dance see Zanobi, this volume.

Milhaud's 'favourite' poet, Paul Claudel.[12] This was a project which Humphrey
continued to pursue for three years (1931–3) during which time she created a
dance with seven scenes focusing on the plot hatched by Electra and Orestes to
kill their mother, Clytemnestra. Although Humphrey planned to set the other
two sections of Milhaud's trilogy—*Agamemnon* and *Eumenides*—she was unable
to find sufficient sponsorship to stage this work fully and had to be satisfied with
only studio performances of *Orestes*.[13] *Orestes* has survived under the title *The
Libation Bearers* (1933) and is described by the Doris Humphrey Institute as

[a] powerful dance rendition . . . told in bold choric patterns, with shuddering details. The
chorus races through the space in a frenzy, throwing their bodies back and forth, and
wildly twisting from side to side in their lament for the murdered King Agamemnon.
There is much use of 'xzeronomia' (ancient Greek for 'hand gestures'), which deploy
the emotions they feel. Clawing at their cheeks and gnawing the dirt beneath their feet,
they all sink to exhaustion and wait for Orestes to appear to avenge the murder of his
father. The chorus rejoices in his appearance with spiralling movements and wild,
abandoned leaps.[14]

Others too were working with Greek themes in the 1930s, especially those
choreographers who had come to the States from Europe. The British choreographer, Antony Tudor also made several Greek ballets in the earlier stages of his
career. Like Balanchine, he emigrated to America but not before producing
masterworks such as *Dark Elegies* (1937) and *Lilac Garden* (1936). Tudor was
a protégé of Marie Rambert (who had many years earlier danced in Nathalie
Barney's play about Sappho to Raymond Duncan's choreography in Paris), and
when still under her tutelage he created two Greek-inspired ballets, neither of
which has survived. The first of these was a witty version of Aristophanes'
comedy, *Lysistrata* (1932), in which Tudor made 'good fun' of the Athenian
wives' intrigues against their warfaring husbands.[15] *The Descent of Hebe* (1935)
was the second of Tudor's ballets based on Greek antiquity and was particularly
satisfying in the way in which Tudor followed the structure of the Ernest Bloch
music to which the ballet was set. Aside from its musical achievement, *The Descent
of Hebe* was relatively straightforward in dealing with the story concentrating on
Hebe's penance for 'stumbling and spilling the nectar'.[16] By the time Tudor
created his third ballet inspired by Greek antiquity—*Judgment of Paris* (1938)—
he had broken away from Rambert and embarked on an independent career.

Judgment of Paris has withstood the test of time probably because Tudor recast
the myth as a contemporary satire with a strong element of black humour. Set in
a sleazy dance hall or café at the turn of the twentieth century, the beautiful
muses of the legend become a trio of 'faded prostitutes',[17] who half-heartedly

---

[12] Reynolds (2005).   [13] Siegel (1979), 135.
[14] http://dorishumphreyinstitute.org (last accessed 18/06/2007).
[15] See Perlmutter (1991), 35.   [16] Ibid. 51–2.
[17] Chamberlain Duerden (2003), 42.

parade their tawdry charms. With tottering struts and musical-hall bumps and grinds—movements far removed from the refinement of ballet—these run-down strippers compete, not for a golden apple, but rather to win the business of Paris who, already drunk, becomes ever more intoxicated and increasingly oblivious to the temptresses' gyrations.

Balanchine and Tudor spent the best part of their careers working in the fresh and dynamic culture of a young America, yet they emerged as artists from an older European tradition. It is not altogether surprising, therefore, that for some of their ballets they drew from an ancient civilization with its rich store of myths and legends. The same might be said for the German dancer, Hanya Holm, who left her native country for New York in 1931 to open an American branch of the Mary Wigman School. Holm was to engage wholeheartedly with the burgeoning American modern dance movement establishing herself as a major choreographer with the group dance *Trend* (1937) described as a 'kind of heroic choric drama'.[18] Holm's European heritage also bequeathed her a leaning towards mythological dances prompting her to create works such as *The Golden Fleece* (1941) based on a story which concerned 'an alchemist's prophetic dream of turning base metals into gold'. The idea came from the surrealist artist Kurt Seligmann but his 'fantastic' and 'imaginative' designs hampered Holm's choreography because the costumes were so cumbersome that the dancers could barely move.[19]

Holm went on in the post-war period to rework other classical themes and was more successful with the dance sections that she mounted for the Vancouver Festival's 1959 production of *Orpheus and Eurydice*. For this venture she was also faced with several challenges since her cast of students from Vancouver ballet schools had received no modern dance training. Nevertheless, Holm found the young dancers 'extremely eager'[20] and ready to embrace a 'whole new vocabulary of movement'.[21] But she also had to cope with a mammoth and ambitious structure which towered almost 'eighteen feet above stage level.' Its sweep of wide, spiralling steps set at 'varying heights and at different angles' dominated the stage space and left little room for dancing. The restricted space led Holm to choreograph a series of 'difficult lifts, making dramatic use of the various stage elevations for the placing of the couples'.[22] For the infernal dance for the Furies, she whipped up 'a wild orgy' of demonic creatures all of whom jumped head first into an open hatch set half-way up the flight of curving stairs.[23] In complete contrast to this evocation of hell was the *Dance of the Elysian Fields* with movements that were 'light and lively, airy and soaring'.[24]

Perhaps the most intriguing of Holm's Greek productions was a Broadway musical, which like Tudor's *Judgment of Paris* was based on the myths

---

[18] Martin (1961), n.p.

[20] Holm cited in Windreich (1979), 10.

[22] Ibid.   [23] Sorrell cited Ibid.

[19] Mason Hauser (1983), 371.

[21] Windreich (1979), 11.

[24] Ibid.

surrounding the Trojan War. *The Golden Apple* (1954) was written by John Latouche with music by Jerome Moross, and set the mythological figures in small-town America at the turn of the twentieth century.[25] Innovative in every way, *The Golden Apple* did away with spoken language replacing it instead with a sung libretto and Holm's 'fresh' and 'amusing' dances.[26] As the American dance critic Walter Terry noted:

> The full-scale dance numbers, the Judgment of Paris scene, the dance fragments, the exuberant actions and striking stage designs all contributed richly to the dramatic purpose and pace ... My own favourite dance moment came with By Goona-Goona Lagoon in which Bibi Osterwald, as Lovely Mars, and her colleagues indulged in some pseudo-Polynesian activities which would cause the ethnic dance expert (and the Polynesian) and everyone else to howl with delight.[27]

Others agreed that *By Goona-Goona Lagoon* was 'the most hilarious dance number of recent seasons';[28] but Holm made serious dances as well for *The Golden Apple*. These included *Come Along Boys*, 'a dance of returning soldiers, [which filled] the stage with a wonderful series of movement inventions, the chief being a circular formation resembling a carousel'.[29] For Terry, *The Golden Apple* was a Broadway show that was 'as deserving of the same attention accorded the dance theatre itself'.[30]

The dance theatre of the 1950s was very much the province of Graham; and although she was yet to embark on her full-length *Clytemnestra* (see Figure 13.1), works such as *Cave of the Heart* (1946), a distillation of Euripides' *Medea*, and *Night Journey* (1947), inspired by Sophocles' *Oedipus Tyrannus*, had already been recognized as powerful evocations of the classical theatre. The American theatre critic, Eric Bentley, for example, wrote about them as 'the fullest realization ... of that magical theater of which Craig and Yeats and so many others have dreamed'.[31]

Humphrey's *Orestes* may have predated Graham's *Clytemnestra* (1958) by some fifteen years, but Graham's fascination with Greek myth was longstanding. It was inculcated in Graham from earliest childhood and consequently formed her *habitus* as Graham tells us in her autobiography *Blood Memory* (1991; first published 1959). Her father, whom she admired and who taught her a great deal, fired her imagination when he recited stories from the ancient legends and myths. She recalls that 'he told the story of Achilles and how his mother dipped him in water, as if it were a baptism'. Graham continues:

> I remember thinking about the error of the foot, how it was his heel, some small part of the body, that became his undoing. I wanted to redip him into the water to protect him.[32]

[25] Mason Hauser (1983), 372.   [26] Anon. (1954*b*).   [27] Terry (1954).
[28] Anon. (1954*a*).   [29] Ibid.   [30] Anon. (1954*b*).
[31] Bentley (1983), 198.   [32] Graham (1991), 27.

Figure 13.1 Bertram Ross as Orestes in Martha Graham's *Clytemnestra* (1958).

It is interesting to note from Graham's words that not only was she enthralled by ancient myth, but that she already wanted to reinvent or retell the stories in her own way. She was to spend much of her creative energy as a dancer and choreographer pouring new life into the legendary figures of Greek mythology and dramatizing the mythical realm of their existence.

TOWARDS THE DEVELOPMENT OF A GREEK-INSPIRED DANCE THEATRE

There is no specific point in time when Graham's personal journey into the world of Greek myth began. As I noted earlier, this is because the spirit of ancient Greek culture was present in practically all Graham's dances, even in those works which were made in response to the socio-political issues at the forefront of the era. *Immediate Tragedy* (1937), for example, was about the Spanish Civil War and had little to do with Greek theatre. However, Graham produced a dance so imbued with the spirit of ancient Greek drama that it retained the capacity to move audiences 'long after the tragic situation in Spain [was] brought to a conclusion'.[33] Certainly throughout her years with Denishawn—the company run by her mentors Ruth St Denis and Ted Shawn[34]—Graham was still immersed in ancient legends although these were not always aligned with Hellenic culture. For their spectacular productions, Denishawn drew most often from the mythic and mystical domain of the orient, a world of rich and exotic images far removed from everyday American experience (see further Michelakis, this volume).

When Graham presented her first concert as an independent artist in 1926,[35] the majority of her dances continued to resonate strongly with oriental themes. Nonetheless, a photograph of her in the solo *Désir*, reveals that she was beginning to strip her dances of the decorative excesses of Denishawn developing instead a stark, austere style. Standing in profile, she arches backwards, her body making a dramatic curve in space as her arms are raised in a strong vertical line, hands clasped to accentuate the shape. This movement is rendered all the more effective by her figure-hugging dress, the plainness of which is relieved only by a full-length two-tone scarf draped across and hanging from her shoulders.[36] Graham's radical movement was inspired to some extent by her German counterpart Mary Wigman, but it was fed by her own uncompromising determination to forge a new

---

[33] Martin cited in de Mille (1991), 222–3.

[34] Graham joined the Denishawn School in 1916 and danced with the company until 1923.

[35] For a list of all the works Graham presented at her first concert in 1926 see, for example, de Mille (1991), 434–5.

[36] Graham (1991), 115.

aesthetic—one that would express the surging vitality, hard edge, and revolutionary spirit of the American dancer.

As Yaari points out, it was also during these very early years in her independent career that Graham first turned to classical themes in solos such as *Fragments: Tragedy and Comedy* (1928). Stodelle paints a picture of Graham in *Tragedy* as 'gravely processional, pictorially like the draped terra-cotta figurines of Tanagra. Clad in sculptured folds of bright red jersey, she moved slowly with a sense of profound resignation.'[37] This dance seems to presage *Lamentation* (1930), Graham's iconic and deeply moving dance of anguish. A sorrowful figure shrouded in purple fabric writhes and twists stretching the tube of material this way and that. At one moment, both arms are thrust dramatically into the air, at another the torso folds forwards and arches backwards in an arc of despair. Spare and austere, sculptural rather than kinetic, *Lamentation* is a bold Modernist statement, but it also demonstrates Graham's innate capacity to express human suffering, the most salient and affecting facet of Greek tragedy.

Graham took another step on the journey towards her Greek dance dramas when in 1931 she appeared in Sophocles' *Electra*. For this production by the University of Michigan, she created and performed three solos which conveyed a 'dance impression of the shifting moods of the play'.[38] These early indications that she could fruitfully combine classical Greek theatre with her own emerging style of modern dance prompted Graham to produce solos such as *Dithyrambic* (1931), named after the ancient Greek hymn sung to Dionysus and performed to the 'eccentric and broken' rhythms of Aaron Copland's *Piano Variations*. In this fifteen-minute marathon, Graham transformed the dithyrambs of the pre-classical satyrs sometimes into 'flicks' and 'touches' of dance,[39] and at others into heroic phrases of movement such as a 'stunning' series of falls, in which she repeatedly hinged backwards from the knees until she was almost horizontal against the floor.[40]

There were other dances inspired by Greek themes in the early years of Graham's career including *Choric Dance for an Antique Greek Tragedy* (1932), later reworked and presented as *Tragic Patterns* (1933). Under its original title, the work received a rather unusual première as it was part of a very long bill presented at the opening of the Radio City Music Hall in 1932. Graham and her all-female group were a curiosity amongst the motley array of comedians, acrobats, singers, and even a horse-act, that made up the evening's programme. In their long dark costumes and holding themselves aloof from the other music-hall turns, the women of Graham's Group were thought to be 'foreigners—

---

[37] Stodelle (1984), 49.   [38] Anon. cited in McDonagh (1974), 84.
[39] McDonagh (1974), 86.   [40] De Mille (1991) 184.

possibly Greek',[41] an impression which may have been compounded by the 'very two-dimensional' choreography that they performed.[42]

In 1938, Graham produced *American Document*, her first fully-staged dance drama for which she integrated movement with spoken text and a specially-commissioned score in order to tell the story of the American people. *American Document* also introduced the ballet-trained Erick Hawkins into the all-female Group, and with the arrival of Hawkins there was an entirely new element in Graham's movement vocabulary—the male/female duet. Graham could now express the full range of human emotion and above all, appear as a feminine and sensual woman. With *American Document*, Graham broadened her choreographic palette leaving behind the plainly staged concert dances and moving confidently towards the realization of her psychologically charged dance dramas.

The early 1940s saw Graham's turn towards psychologically oriented reworkings of ancient myths. This new departure was fuelled in some respects by the surrealist preoccupation with the theories of Sigmund Freud and Carl Jung, which swept like wildfire through the artistic community of New York.[43] But these ideas were not necessarily new for Graham. During her childhood she had discovered the structures of the mind and how they found expression in movement from the research that her father carried out into mental disorders.[44] As an alienist or early form of psychiatrist, he had become particularly adept at reading hand and foot gestures, telling Graham that he knew when people were lying by the way they held their hands. It was from her father that Graham learnt that 'movement never lies' [45] and understood early in life that it is the behaviour of the individual rather than their words that reveals whatever is going on in the mind.

Graham's introduction to the idea that the Greek myths were passageways to the unconscious mind arose in part from her intimate conversations with the Jungian analyst, Frances Wickes, author of books such as *The Inner World of Man* (1938). As trusted friend and confidant,[46] Wickes helped Graham to fight the internal demons which plagued her personal life, but she also provided the spiritual and philosophical ground on which Graham built several of her dances.[47] Her knowledge and understanding of Greek literature was bolstered

---

[41] McDonagh (1974), 91.
[42] Marchowsky cited in Helpern (1999*a*), 26. According to Marie Marchowsky, Graham sent the dancers to study the Greek figures displayed in the Metropolitan Museum in New York.
[43] Shelton (1983), 121.   [44] De Mille (1991), 22.
[45] Graham (1991), 20; de Mille (1991), 16 and 97.
[46] There are varying views as to whether or not Graham submitted herself to psychoanalysis with Wickes. See Graham (1991), 186 where she refers to Wickes as her 'analyst'. See also de Mille (1991), 78 for the view that Graham was 'never analyzed'.
[47] Stodelle (1984), 133.

by Hawkins, Graham's partner both in dance and in life;[48] but it was the guidance that she received from the mythologist Joseph Campbell that best prepared Graham for her psychological interpretations of the Greek myths. Renowned for books such as *The Hero with a Thousand Faces* (1949), Campbell 'worked with Graham on Jung's theories and discoveries'[49] and shared with her his idea of mythology as the underlying support for all human belief and action.[50] The *Notebooks* that Graham kept between the 1940s and 1960s were published in 1973; and even the most cursory leaf through them reveals how voraciously Graham read and the extent to which she researched into psychology and Greek drama.[51]

The shift towards classical myth took place in 1944 with the enigmatic *Herodiade*, a dance for two women based on the biblical story of Herodias (see Webb, this volume). Created in the same year as *Appalachian Spring*, the last work that Graham made inspired by her American heritage, *Herodiade* signalled the new direction she was about to take.[52] Based on Stéphane Mallarmé's lyric poem *Hérodiade* (begun in 1864 but unfinished at the poet's death), Graham's riveting, psychological portrayal of the mysterious composite Herodias/Salome figure culminates in a solemn ritual, in which the heroine fatefully prepares herself for some unknown ordeal. Undoubtedly *Herodiade* contained the seeds of the Greek dance dramas that were to come, as the critic Robert Sabin noted: 'like the plays of Aeschylus and the great trilogy of Eugene O'Neill, [*Herodiade* purges] the spectator with pity and terror.'[53]

With *Herodiade* paving the way, Graham created three major Greek works beginning in 1946 with *Cave of the Heart;* then in 1947 came *Errand into the Maze*, a retelling of the myth of Theseus and the Minotaur, and also in 1947, *Night Journey*, dances to which I shall return later. In 1958, her growing reputation for mounting Greek tragedy on the dance stage was sealed by the evening-long *Clytemnestra*, an impressive adaptation of Aeschylus' *Oresteia*. It is clear from the copious notes that Graham made when writing her script for this work that she consulted Richard Lattimore's and George Thomson's translations of Aeschylus.[54] However, Graham departs from the chronological sequence of the story in order to present the dance drama largely as a replay in Clytemnestra's mind of the key moments in her life. In a series of scenes, we witness the brutal murder of Agamemnon, suffer with the beleaguered members of Clytemnestra's

---

[48] Hawkins had been a Harvard scholar in classics before turning to dance in the 1930s, and his enduring interest in the Greek plays had an impact on Graham's choreography. See de Mille (1991), 279; Hawkins cited in Helpern (1999*b*), 38.

[49] de Mille (1991), 277.   [50] Erdman cited in Helpern (1999*b*), 38–9.

[51] See Yaari (2003) for a detailed analysis of Graham's reinterpretation of Greek mythology from the point of view of modern psychology and her recasting of the myths as narratives of the feminine.

[52] *Herodiade* was first given in 1944 as *Mirror Before Me*. The name was changed to *Herodiade* at the request of its composer, Paul Hindemith. See Bannerman (2006).

[53] Sabin (1944), 20.   [54] Graham (1973), 245.

Figure 13.2 *Phaedra* (1962).

family, and encounter meddlesome gods, prophetic seers, and a set of demented Furies, all of whom torment Clytemnestra's thoughts and memories. Hailed as a triumph by the critics, *Clytemnestra* was to be Graham's only full-length work and it has not been seen on stage in its entirety since 1995. In 2008 the Martha Graham Company performed a new production of *Clytemnestra* in Athens (23–25 October), Beijing and in Paris (April 2009) and at Skirball Centre, New York (12–16 May 2009).[55]

Another of Graham's outstanding Greek-inspired dance dramas is her controversial *Phaedra* (1962), based on Euripides' *Hippolytus* and Racine's *Phèdre* (see Figure 13.2). Already in her 60s and with her physical powers declining, Graham wisely gave herself a role in which she mainly acted, shaping the work in such a way that most of the dancing was performed by others.[56] As with her other adaptations of the Greek legends, Graham reinterpreted several aspects of

[55] See http://clytemnestraproject.com (last accessed 15/10/09).   [56] McDonagh (1974), 263.

Euripides' drama. For example, rather than have Theseus read the suicide note in which Phaedra falsely accuses Hippolytus of raping her, she physically acts out this scene which is described by Stodelle as a 'tour de force of histrionics that sets the spectator's nerves on edge, the lie serves a double purpose: as it stirs up uncontrollable fury in Theseus, it permits Phaedra to live out—as in a wishful dream—the sexual gratification she so desires'.[57]

Much has been made of the eroticism and sexuality of *Phaedra*, not the least in respect to Noguchi's designs for the work as de Mille explains:

The set consisted of symbols, and the little figure of Venus as a butterfly pinned to the wall, which at the moment of consummation opened two very large and pretty wings and revealed a tiny female in its center in a split, both legs extended in midair, straight out to the sides, constituted probably the most explicit and graphic sexual symbol that had been revealed on a decent stage.[58]

Clearly the work shocked many including two American Congressmen. They complained that Graham was compromising her role as a cultural ambassador, although one of these two dissenters was mainly affronted by the sight of a dance 'with a lot of couches and young men in loincloths'.[59] Graham herself in the title role of *Phaedra* ruffled British sensibilities. As an older woman kicking her legs suddenly into the air and revealing the red tights worn under her gown, she prompted some women in a London audience to mutter 'oh dear'.[60] Despite *Phaedra's* 'erotic extravagances', as Stodelle points out, the dance is 'essentially moral' since it highlights the villainous acts of the gods with Phaedra, cursed by Aphrodite with an unnatural lust for Hippolytus. Phaedra emerges as the victim who is almost blameless: 'Hating herself for incestuous desires, she took her own life.'[61]

For Bertram Ross who created the role of Hippolytus, many aspects of *Phaedra* were aimed towards 'the glorification of the male anatomy and chastity. Life without women'.[62] Ross points out that most of the men in the company were physically desirable but unattainable to women since they were homosexual. He proposes that Graham, who never made a secret of her sexual appetite, created *Phaedra* (at least in part) as a metaphor for the desire she harboured for her male dancers but which had to go unfulfilled.[63] Ross may well have provided additional insight for Graham's interpretation of the Hippolytus myth in *Phaedra*, since she went on eventually to revisit the theme of male homosexuality in *Phaedra's Dream* (1983).

The action for this dance takes the form of a nightmare in which Phaedra witnesses Hippolytus' seduction by another man, identified only as The Stranger.[64] In her review of this work performed a year after its première, Kisselgoff's words

---

[57] Stodelle (1984), 231.   [58] De Mille (1991), 354.

[59] P. J. Freylinghuysen cited in Graham (1991), 210.

[60] Paul Taylor, in Tracy (1997), 235.   [61] Stodelle (1984), 233.

[62] Bertram Ross, in Tracy (1997), 165.   [63] Ibid.   [64] Kisselgoff (1984).

about *Phaedra's Dream* resonate with Ross's views regarding the implicit reference to male homosexuality in *Phaedra*:

> How Miss Graham arrives at the male love duet that is the center of her current piece perhaps only she can fully explain. And yet nothing in her work is ever arbitrary and, as usual, the original source gives her all the justification she needs. For one of the crucial aspects of the original myth is that Hippolytus angers Aphrodite, the goddess of love, precisely for his 'scorn of women'. Euripides suggested he was primarily asexual, beholden to Artemis, the rival goddess of chastity.[65]

Kisselgoff argues that in treating Hippolytus' sexual orientation as ambiguous, Graham remains faithful to Euripides; certainly the scholar Richard Grene had already identified what he termed 'the perversity of Hippolytus' ostentatious purity' and had indentified Hippolytus as a 'very monk of continence'.[66] If in both *Phaedra* and *Phaedra's Dream* Graham used the story of Phaedra's guilty lust in order to express her own unfulfilled longing for the young homosexual men in her company, it could be argued that her rewriting anticipates many subsequent rereadings of Euripides' text.[67]

PRINCIPLES AND PRACTICE IN GRAHAM'S GREEK DANCES

Having registered the major stages through which Graham passed in formulating her approach to the Greek-inspired dance dramas, I turn now to the principles that underpin these works. First and foremost, Graham tackled universal aspects of human experience. As a twentieth-century artist, however, she followed the modern Jungian principle that the myths are analogous to mental structures or motifs lodged within the brain and which recur through time as they are passed from generation to generation. These schematic mind patterns are Jungian archetypes which, according to Anthony Storr, are 'the organising influence on images and ideas'.[68] Embedded in the collective unconscious as ancestral chains of feeling and behaviour, they link the antique and modern worlds. Graham addressed these archetypes and in so doing exposed unruly and irrational passions ingrained within the subsoil of human consciousness.

Graham's movement system was designed to be kinaesthetically powerful and visceral. She had always taught that it was the torso—'heart, lungs, stomach, viscera, and above all, spine—which expresses'.[69] Centring her work in the upper body, Graham built on the natural act of breathing to initiate the flow of energy from the torso outwards towards the rest of the body and limbs. Through the contraction controlled from deep in the pelvis, and the spiral, where the upper

---

[65] Kisselgoff (1984)   [66] Grene (1955), 159.   [67] McKee (2007).
[68] Storr (1998), 16.   [69] De Mille (1991), 97.

body rotates around the axis of the spine, the torso became the central force and principal medium through which to express the sensations of pleasure or pain and to convey the joys, and sorrows of the archetypal heroines.

The solo for Ariadne which opens *Errand into the Maze* is a good example of how Graham's movement language conveys the heroine's internal struggle. Arms interlocked across abdomen and pelvis as though to shield herself from an impending danger, her torso convulses in electrifying contractions sending tremors through every nerve and muscle. The impetus of the contraction extends to throat, head, and hands and skews her body in such a way that she becomes the incarnation of an 'indescribable anxiety' that possesses her.[70] *Errand into the Maze* is essentially a duet which converts the myth of Theseus and the Minotaur into a study of a woman's deep-rooted psychological trauma. The terrifying bull that Ariadne confronts is little more than a projection of her own fear and when finally she succeeds in vanquishing this monster, she gains control over the tumult of dark emotions which threaten to overpower her. Integral to the drama of Graham's works are the symbolic sculptures fashioned for the dances by her long-term collaborator Isamu Noguchi. For *Errand into the Maze*, he provided an abstract structure described by de Mille as a 'door frame like whitened bones'[71] and by Stodelle as a 'forked tree trunk'.[72] According to Graham, Noguchi's sculpture was 'molded after a woman's pelvic bone' and for her, it perfectly symbolized the idea behind *Errand*—the driving force of sexuality, 'or the fear of it'.[73]

Like the majority of Graham's dances, *Errand into the Maze* was created as a dramatic vehicle for herself, and it is a facet of her Modernism that she placed the heroines of classical myth that she embodied centre stage. The men are banished to the sidelines, or, as in *Errand*, their role is altogether usurped. Graham took another Modernist approach in the way that she structured her dances. Since she dealt most often with the internal lives of her heroines, often forcing them to relive the pain of past events and experiences, she borrowed techniques from the art of cinema by using the devices of flashback and 'poetic montage'.[74]

On another level, Graham followed American Indian and eastern philosophies in her belief that life exists in 'recurring cycles of death and renewal', often presenting time in her dances as cyclical, although above all, it was the present that mattered most to her: 'the only thing we have is the now' she declared.[75] This emphasis on the now or the instant is very clear in *Cave of the Heart* created the year before *Errand into the Maze*. As already noted, this work is a distillation of Euripides' play and is defined by Medea's dance of vengeance. In this extraordinary solo, the evil sorceress gloats over her murderous act, the poisoning of the young princess who had replaced her as Jason's wife. Her savage movement

---

[70] Stodelle (1984), 135.   [71] Graham (1991), 281.
[72] Stodelle (1984), 281; for a full description of this dance, see Ibid. 134–6.
[73] Graham (1991), 232.   [74] Oswald (1983), 43.   [75] Graham (1991), 14.

and violent gestures are chilling to behold, but there is little to compare with the way she consumes, Kabuki-like, her own intestines, symbolized by a glittering thread which sparkles and quivers in her hands. With this snake-like cloth in her mouth, she shuffles sideways on her knees in a cataclysmic frenzy of jealousy. It is as though in this single instance, Graham encapsulates Medea's past crime as well as foreseeing her ultimate act of revenge, the slaughter of her children.[76] Medea's unquenchable thirst for revenge is also expressed through a choreographic device specially designed for this work and which has come to be known as the *Cave turn.*[77] This is a spectacular dive forwards into a pivot on one leg as the other shoots upwards in a split *arabesque.* Travelling across the stage with five of these vertiginous *pirouettes*, Medea slices into the surrounding space, her leg like the tail of some venomous creature thrashing the very air she breathes.

Graham understood the relationship between Greek myth and the innermost reaches of the mind and heart, but even more importantly, she grasped the principles that underpin Greek tragic theatre. Perhaps the most familiar of the characteristics that Aristotle stipulated for tragic drama is the arousal of 'pity' and 'fear' and the subsequent purging of these emotions through *catharsis.*[78] The poetic and artistic treatment of affliction makes us aware, on the one hand of human frailty, and on the other of human spirituality. In the words of R. P. Draper:

No tragedy is simply a cry of pain. It is an apprehension of pain in relation to a sense—perhaps bleak, perhaps consolatory—of what it is to be human and therefore to belong to a species which must not only endure suffering, but also give voice to its awareness of suffering as its destiny.[79]

Draper's definition of tragedy as a poetic expression of human suffering is particularly appropriate for Graham's *Night Journey*, which served as the model for her later dance tragedies.[80]

Night Journey is not a literal reading of Sophocles' play. The dance foregrounds the plight of Jocasta and skilfully condenses the complex plot of the drama, highlighting its main events (see Figure 17.1). The opening images feature Jocasta as she prepares to die, and in the closing moments the audience witnesses her suicide. Within this cycle of time, the dance retraces Oedipus' triumphant entry into Thebes, his courtship of Jocasta, the consummation of their marriage and the

---

[76] In Graham's dance, this event takes place only in Medea's mind as symbolized in the dance of vengeance. For the Kabuki-motif (also used in Ninagawa's *Medea*), see Smethurst (2000).

[77] Bannerman (1998), 238.

[78] On these controversial terms, see Halliwell (1998).

[79] Draper (1980), 12.

[80] The version of *Night Journey* used for analysis is the black and white film specially made for cinema by Nathan Kroll in 1960 (released 1961 available on DVD, Martha Graham in Performance, Kultur, USA) with Martha Graham as Jocasta, Bertram Ross as Oedipus, and Paul Taylor as Tiresias. Bannerman (1998), 182–9.

moment when Tiresias reveals the incestuous relationship. After Oedipus' act of self-blinding, the dance returns to its starting-point as Jocasta is on the verge of suicide. For the final moment she sheds her dark outer robe revealing a simple light-coloured shift. It is as though she casts off the veneer of her worldly existence and in so doing cleanses herself of the pollution that has debased her.

Night Journey conforms in the main to the conditions that Aristotle stipulates for tragedy. Some of these conditions hinge on the notion of a 'complex' plot, with phases through which the drama must pass if it is to constitute a genuine tragedy. These phases are *peripeteia*, or reversal in fortune, for example, from happiness to misery, and *anagnorisis*, or discovery—'a change from ignorance to knowledge'.[81] According to Aristotle, one or other, or both, of these actions must be present since they provoke the depth of emotional response integral to the genre of tragedy.[82]

Although Graham does not follow Sophocles in setting up the intricacies of plot established throughout the play, I would claim that towards the end of *Night Journey*, there are instances of both *reversal* and *discovery*. These devices combine at a strategic moment in the dance when Jocasta and Oedipus are entwined as man and wife within a length of cord. As the women of the chorus finish their prophetic dance of doom around the couple, the seer Tiresias crosses the stage, his staff thudding ominously against the ground. He places himself behind Oedipus and Jocasta and inserts one leg with his foot flexed between them as though reminding the pair of the injuries that Oedipus received after birth. This dramatic leg gesture is the device through which the truth of Oedipus' parentage is revealed; and as Tiresias touches the supporting rope with his staff, it falls away leaving Jocasta and Oedipus to collapse to the ground in a sudden reversal of fortune. As a consequence of this double action of discovery and reversal the relationship dramatically changes key; emotional tension mounts as events become ever more nerve-wracking culminating in the final disaster of Jocasta's suicide.

No reference to *Night Journey* is complete without mentioning Graham's powerful dances for the six Daughters of the Night. Stodelle likens the chorus to figures on ancient Greek vases 'brought suddenly to life',[83] an apt description of the women as they begin the main choral dance. Arranged in profile to the audience, they lunge forwards in a series of deep strides, shielding their eyes with claw-line hands as though to warn the audience of the self-blinding that Oedipus must commit. Stricken with horror at Jocasta's and Oedipus' polluted act their bodies contort in deep contractions, arms held in angular and twisted shapes as though broken by the weight of the suffering that is to come. Their gestures, sharp, elemental, percussive make them seem like birds of prey hovering over a scene of destruction, tearing at the rotten flesh of the incestuous union they witness.

---

[81] Aristotle, *Poetics*, chs. 11, 16.   [82] Ibid.   [83] Stodelle (1984), 149.

The doom-ridden choral dance for the Daughters of the Night represents Graham at the height of her choreographic powers, a viewpoint expressed by many critics over the years and exemplified in a review by the American critic, Anna Kissellgoff:

If one had to choose any fragment of Graham choreography to preserve for posterity, the sensational choral passages for these Daughters of the Night would top the list. Every movement was once worked out on Miss Graham's own body as she choreographed the work. To see the angular contractions in which breath is so visibly expelled, or to be stunned by the distortions of the human body for expressive purposes in these passages is to see choreography that remains incomparable.[84]

Graham's sense of Greek theatre did not always depend on her capacities as a high tragedienne—she could also work with comedy, an aspect of her choreography and performance that is often overlooked.[85] *Satyric Festival Song* takes us back to the early years of Graham's career. Created in 1932 as part of a suite of dances called *Dance Songs*, the solo unites Graham's American heritage and her deep-seated love of Greek myth. Inspired by her trips to the pueblos of southwest America and the clowns she saw painted in white, green, and black, the dance draws also on the ancient satyr figures, the half-human, debunkers of Greek tragedy. In an absurd, tight-fitting dress with broad stripes of black and green, she tosses her hair about, skitters off-balance, topples over sideways and lands with a neat roll on the floor. Her capering gestures are just as much those of a Dionysian goat-creature,[86] as they are the antics of a clown.

GRAHAM'S INFLUENCE ON THE
WIDER DANCE COMMUNITY

At the beginning of this chapter, I referred briefly to the major British ballet choreographer, Frederick Ashton, who like Tudor, trained with Marie Rambert, but who clearly also benefited from Graham's style. I have previously focused on works such as *Mephisto Waltz* (1934) and *Le Baiser de la Fée* (1935) created shortly after Ashton first saw Graham perform in New York in 1934.[87] For the purposes of this chapter, I want to draw attention to Ashton's version of Stravinsky's *Persephone* made for the Royal Ballet Company in 1961.[88] I am interested in this ballet because the choreography with its angular movements, use of stasis and sharply defined body designs, bears similarities to the movement vocabulary that Graham used in her Greek dances.

---

[84] Kissellgoff (1989).   [85] Bannerman (2001).
[86] Beiswanger cited in Morgan (1980), 146.   [87] Bannerman (2007).
[88] For an excellent description and analysis of this ballet, see Morris (2006), 21–6.

Stravinsky's *Persephone* was composed in 1933[89] as 'a musical realization of André Gide's poem', which in turn was based on the *Homeric Hymn to Demeter*.[90] Conceived as a hybrid work to showcase the talents of the actor/dancer, Ida Rubinstein, the score featured portions of spoken text declaimed by Rubinstein, material for a tenor who as Eumolpus narrated the story and passages for a large chorus placed on stage. Stravinsky himself did not consider the work to be successful and after its première at the Paris Opéra in 1934, with choreography by Kurt Jooss and décor and costumes by André Barsacq, this unwieldy production received only a further three performances although other choreographers have since been drawn to the score.[91] The composer himself did not regard *Persephone* favourably and when asked about his views on the use of music as an accompaniment to recitation, Stravinsky replied, 'Do not ask. Sins cannot be undone, only forgiven.'[92]

A principal reason as to why Ashton was drawn to the difficult Stravinsky score was its suitability as a vehicle for one of his muses, the Russian-born ballerina, Svetlana Beriosova. Amongst Beriosova's many attributes was a melodious speaking voice in which she could deliver the French text. According to the critic Clive Barnes, in his staging of Stravinsky's melodrama, Ashton managed to iron out some of the flaws in a flawed masterpiece. By unifying the disparate elements of the score or what Barnes has described as 'those disconcerting grinds of gear changes as the score slips from speech to song and then to orchestra', Ashton 'swept away' these inconsistencies. Barnes describes some of the most satisfying moments in the ballet:

The small things of fluttering hands, and arms bent just so in instinctively correct Grecian angles; the larger things of completely untroubled craftsmanship in the big ensembles, as the huge cast walk and dance through their interweaving patterns with a joyful certainty.[93]

The ballet was also notable for its décor by the Greek painter Nico Ghika who avoided the conventional ideas of a 'Grecian' setting (for example cypresses and Doric columns) by providing 'brilliantly coloured, sunlit landscapes with spiky rocks',[94] which gave the impression of a 'mountainous Greek landscape'.[95] In closely following Gide's text, Ashton echoes the poet's 'Christian interpretation of the myth in which Persephone returns to the underworld at the end of her own free will, out of the compassion for its denizens'.[96] But he respected too the syncopated rhythms of Stravinsky's music, although the acrobatic and erotic *pas*

---

[89] This score was commissioned by the actress and dancer Ida Rubinstein and was premiered in 1934. Ashton's restaging of *Persephone* was the first of its kind since the 1934 production.
[90] Kavanagh (1996), 458 and 461.   [91] Morris (2006), 21.
[92] Stravinsky cited in Vaughan (1977), 325.   [93] Barnes cited ibid. 324.
[94] Vaughan (1977), 326.   [95] Morris (2006), 26.   [96] Vaughan (1997), 325–326.

de deux Ashton created for Persephone and Pluto was, according to Barnes, 'a shade too lush for the music'.[97] Overall the ballet was an ambitious venture since it integrated movement with a chorus of singers placed in the orchestra pit, and the role for Beriosova as Persephone in which she both spoke and danced.[98]

Like Graham, Ashton had already made a number of ballets that were based on ancient Greek mythology; and chief amongst these was *Daphnis and Chloe* (1951) for which the two-dimensional, flattened shapes held in the dancers's torsos enhanced the ballet's Greek imagery.[99] Whilst Graham evolved an entirely new vocabulary of choreographic devices to develop the tragic themes of her dances, Ashton modelled his choreography for *Daphnis and Chloe* on the research into Greek dance that he found in Maurice Emmanuel's treatise, *The Antique Greek Dance* (English translation 1916—see further Naerebout, this volume).[100]

In his preparation for *Persephone*, Ashton again drew on Emmanuel's illustrations but fusing them this time with a 'modern, angular idiom' in a style which was markedly 'free' and 'unclassical'.[101] But after viewing film clips and photographs, it is difficult not to infer that Ashton's modern idiom in *Persephone* reflected Graham's Greek movement vocabulary, which he probably saw again in 1954 when the Martha Graham Company performed in London for the first time. The audiences were notoriously small for the company's two-week season, but Ashton was surely amongst the British dance intelligentsia who went to the Saville Theatre to see a repertory of works such as *Errand into the Maze* (1947) and *Night Journey* (1947).[102]

Certainly there is something of Graham's style in the percussive and uncharacteristically jagged choreography that Ashton produced for *Persephone*. For example, phrases of movement performed by Persephone's friends feature a sharp twist of the torso against legs moving in exaggerated opposition to the upper body. [103] These strongly accented walks accompanied by an extreme spiral in the upper body are similar to walking and striding actions in Graham's movement language. In terms of her Greek works, these stylized walks are versions of the ancient Greek iconography of vase-paintings and bas reliefs but performed to the sharper rhythms and accents of a modern age.

---

[97] Vaughan writing about Barnes (1977), 326.
[98] 'In the first performances Beriosova wore a Japanese transistor microphone concealed in her costume, but in a revival six years later her speaking part was pre-recorded': Vaughan (1997), 324.
[99] Morris (2006), 22. He had also made *Judgment of Paris* (1938), the same year as Tudor's ballet by the same name.
[100] Ibid.   [101] Kavanagh (1996), 462.
[102] There is little evidence to prove that Ashton was at these performances or that he saw Graham perform after 1934. However, many of his fellow Royal Ballet choreographers went to see Graham as did all the dance critics of the era, and Ashton was present at a party given for the Martha Graham Company, probably during their first London season in 1954 (see Wood (1999), 86). It is also possible and quite likely that over the years he saw Graham perform in Europe and America.
[103] See Monica Mason coaching dances from *Persephone* in Jordan and Morris (2004).

Equally striking in Ashton's *Persephone* is a two-dimensional and uncharacter-istically modern pose for Alexander Grant as Mercury.[104] The flex and thrust of the leg gestures, the arm bent sharply at elbow and wrist, and the hand held to the forehead as it grips the *caduceus* or serpent-entwined wand, are reminiscent of the chiselled body designs which Graham repeatedly used, especially in her Greek dance dramas. Ashton may have attempted to expand the range of expression available to him in ballet by superimposing on it the harsher shapes found in Graham's movement vocabulary, because the jazzy Stravinsky music with its motoric beat demanded a harder-edged style of dancing than is available through ballet. As a production that calls not only for a large cast of dancers but also a singer, a chorus, and a leading dancer who can speak French verse, *Persephone* could not retain its place within the Royal Ballet's repertory. Although it is now a lost work, *Persephone* is still regarded as a major achievement within Ashton's canon.[105]

If Graham's Greek movements infiltrated the dance language of Britain's most revered ballet choreographer, then her influence also fed back into Greece particularly through the work of Rallou Manou, credited as the first teacher and choreographer to bring Graham's system to Greece.[106] Manou formed a school in Athens in 1941 which became established as a leading centre for training generations of lay and professional dancers. In 1951 with the composer Manos Hadjidakis,[107] she founded and directed Hellenic Chorodrama (Greek Dance-Drama), a company in which the dancers were encouraged to follow their individual artistic impulses whilst remaining within the framework of the tradi-tions of their Greek culture.[108] During her studies of modern dance, Manou spent some time with Graham in New York and as a choreographer followed her in creating works based on the ancient Greek myths and legends. In 1956, for example Manou produced a version of *Medea* to music by Hadjidakis and performed in the amphitheatre at Epidauros. Manou went beyond Graham's range, however, by also making dances that looked at contemporary Greek themes.[109] Such a production was the composer Mikis Theodorakis's *The Dead Brother's Song* (1960), a version of Sophocles' *Antigone*, first performed in choreographic form in 1962 and described as a mix of 'ancient Greek tragedy, the myths and symbols of modern Greek history and the structural elements of folk and popular songs'.[110]

---

[104] Crickmay courtesy of the Victoria and Albert Museum, Morris (2006), 27.

[105] Morris (2006), 33.

[106] Author's conversation with Wendy Wasserman (2007).

[107] The other two founders of Hellenic Chorodrama were the painters Spyros Vassiliou and Nikos Hatzikyriakos-Ghikas. See http://www.iovhellas.gr/english/article.php? (last accessed 01/03/06).

[108] Cohen (1965), 57.   [109] Ibid.

[110] Theodorakis provided the music for Ashton's fellow Royal Ballet choreographer, John Cranko's production of *Antigone* (1959). Theodorakis (2007).

Graham's dramatic sensibility and her sure sense of Greek tragic theatre placed her at the forefront of twentieth-century dance ensuring that she became a giant amongst choreographers of her own generation and a constant source of inspiration to artists working in several fields of the arts. Graham died in 1991 but she continues to be held in high esteem in many branches of the theatrical arts providing endless fascination not only for dance students and professional dancers but also for actors, theatre directors, designers and academics. Childhood stories prompted Graham's imagination to roam amongst the goddesses, the gods and the flawed mortals of ancient Greek mythology setting her on a creative journey—to reinterpret the 'high drama of mythological Greece' for a modern age.[111] After a lifetime of recreating the archetypal heroines and staging them as vivid personalities within her theatrically rich and timeless dance dramas, Graham surely earns her reputation as 'the most articulate proponent of Greek Tragedy in dance'.

---

[111] Stodelle (1984), 251.

14

Iphigenia, Orpheus, and Eurydice in the Human Narrative of Pina Bausch

Nadine Meisner

In considering the perpetuation of classical theatre and myth on the modern dance stage, the name of Pina Bausch does not immediately spring to mind. Her myths, when she chose to summon them, are those propagated by the popular culture of her wartime generation. Or they are those belonging to the national traditions of foreign co-producing cities.[1] Or they are all those other ideals that are pedalled daily to us, as we search for hope to make our passage through life easier. But, actually, more often, Pina Bausch didn't deal with myths at all. She dealt with human life as it is: our childhood memories, our adult anguishes, our courage and despair, our tenderness and cruelty.

There are, though, two major exceptions in her oeuvre to all this; two pieces closely linked to classical theatre and myth. They are her early stagings of Gluck's *Iphigenie auf Tauris* (1974) and *Orpheus und Eurydike* (1975). And they are the only two 'conventional' opera productions she ever created. The epithet 'conventional' is problematic here because both productions, for all their early positioning in her career, have a clear Bauschian imprint. Even so, 'conventional' can, *faute de mieux*, be applied to differentiate these productions from other Bausch stagings. With the Gluck operas, the music, the libretti, remain more or less intact, whereas with Bausch's 1977 treatment of Bartók's *Bluebeard's Castle* it is her vision that dominates, using the opera as a springboard, as indicated by the

---

Bibliographical note. The material directly about Bausch and her work for this chapter came from a diverse range of sources, chief among which was an interview conducted by the author in Wuppertal in May 2006 with Dominique Mercy, long-serving member of Pina Bausch Tanztheater Wuppertal, who created the roles of Orestes in *Iphigenie auf Tauris* and Orpheus in *Orpheus und Eurydike.* In addition to their live performances much use was made of Pina Bausch Tanztheater Wuppertal's video recordings of the two productions. The printed sources used were mostly reviews and features by the author, as well as an interview conducted by her with Bausch, which were published in *The Sunday Times, The Times, The Independent, Dance and Dancers* and *Dance Now.*

[1] Bausch (1940–2009) made a large number of pieces co-produced and created in capital cities, starting with *Victor*, which premiered in Rome in 1986.

title *Pina Bausch's Bluebeard—On listening to a tape recording of Bela Bartók's opera 'Duke Bluebeard's Castle'*.[2]

Before examining *Iphigenie auf Tauris* and *Orpheus und Eurydike*, it would be useful to provide an overview of her work, since this is not necessarily widely known. Her company is in great demand all over the world; it spreads itself thin and British audiences, in particular, have only had intermittent access to Bausch's work. She came, moreover, from a tradition that is not shared by British dance and she transmuted that tradition into something unique.

In modern dance individual creativity occupies a central space, contrary to the codified, hierarchical, and rigidly conformist system perpetuated by classical ballet. Put crudely, modern dance encourages personal expression; whereas classical ballet does not. Modern dance, with its emphasis on solo work or small ensembles, provides a democratic environment where everyone (almost) can choreograph; classical ballet, with its elaborate infrastructures and large numbers, demands obedience and authority, with the corps de ballet at one end of the spectrum, the choreographer or ballet master at the other. It is no wonder, then, that most ballet choreographers have been men.

Modern dance, on the other hand, has been the congruous setting for female creative control. Bausch was one in a line of major women modern-dance creators, starting with Isadora Duncan, Mary Wigman, and Martha Graham. Like these women, Bausch started choreographing not so much because she wanted to be a professional choreographer, but because she wanted to dance. 'I never had the thought or the wish to be a choreographer,' she once said. 'I was a dancer, I loved to dance. There was a certain time when there was not enough work for me to dance and I felt so much the need to express myself, I thought maybe I'll make a little piece, something for myself.'[3] The irony was, her talent was so immediately apparent that many other dancers wanted to be in her pieces and she effectively ended up choreographing herself out of her work: 'I'm on the waiting list for many years, my own waiting list!'[4] So apart from her central role in *Café Müller* and her solo dance in *Danzon*, she never appeared in her mature work, which is the opposite of how Graham organized her career.

Like Graham, though, she *invented* her language. This is not only a fundamental thing to do, it is also supremely difficult. You have to abandon what you have learnt: 'I worked with many different teachers, many different styles. And for me, it was always a problem. I never wanted to copy anyone. I did not want to do something I had learnt. And it was very difficult . . . The steps I already knew, I did not want to use.'[5]

---

[2] In 1976 Bausch also created a distinctive version of *The Seven Deadly Sins*, but this Weill–Brecht sung work was conceived as a *ballet chanté*, according the choreographer's individual vision a large place in the overall staging.

[3] Interview with the author, July 1992.

[4] Interview July 1992.

[5] Interview July 1992.

So what were the different styles of her training? Philippine Bausch was born in Solingen, West Germany and her first roots were German modern dance. As such, her predecessors were Kurt Jooss, Mary Wigman, Rudolf von Laban. German modern dance, variously called *Ausdruckstanz* (expressive dance), *Neue Künstlerische Tanz* (new artistic dance) and *Freier Tanz* (free dance), flowered in the first decades of the twentieth century, around the same time as American modern dance, but was mostly separate, although Wigman did set up a school in the USA. Bausch was a student of the Folkwang School in nearby Essen, whose dance department was directed by Kurt Jooss and whose curriculum included many forms of dance, including ballet. (Jooss, in his own choreography, fused his modern-dance foundations with balletic forms.) After that, Bausch's other formative influences came from American dance, because in 1958 she won a scholarship to study in New York (see further Zanobi, this volume). She went to the distinguished Juilliard School where her teachers included big pioneering names in ballet such as Antony Tudor and in modern dance such as Jose Limón. She danced with several companies, among them the Paul Taylor Dance Company. At that time appeared the first manifestations of American minimalist art which were to lead to American postmodern dance, but on the whole she seems to have been more attracted to those strands closer to expressive European dance.

Back in Germany, in 1962 she joined her teacher Kurt Jooss's new Folkwang Ballett. It was there that she started choreographing. Some of her earliest work had, briefly, a balletic aesthetic: its uplifted, gravity-defying shapes the opposite of earth-rooted modern dance. She quickly attracted attention and, in 1973, after choreographing the Bacchanale in Wagner's *Tannhäuser* for the Wuppertal Stadttheater—an all-dance sequence—she was offered the directorship of its ballet company. In this way she became the first modern-dance director of a post-war German opera house. The company was eventually named Tanztheater Wuppertal (later Pina Bausch Tanztheater Wuppertal): the term 'Tanztheater' an indication of her intent, shared by certain other German choreographers of the time, such as Johann Kresnik, to create 'dance theatre'. This would contain a range of theatrical components other than dance, underpinned by a psychological dimension.

With this agenda, she ruffled feathers among the Wuppertal audience, accustomed to their dance company in its previous classical ballet guise. Bausch's launch piece, *Fritz* (1973), already displayed dance-theatre credentials and, although it had no spoken text, it had Bausch revue-style personages. Dominique Mercy, who had by then joined the company as a dancer, recalls: 'It was about the fantasies of a boy. And there was a parade of strange guests: a bearded woman, twins, a sick man in a nightgown—that was me.'[6] The auditorium was only half-full at the start, but then people started leaving, slamming doors behind them. With *The Seven Deadly Sins* (1976), three years later, even the dancers rebelled,

---

[6] Interview with the author, Jan. 1999.

enraged at what they saw as the absence of dance. And after its première Bausch fled, vowing never to return. But, eventually, of course, she did.

In searching to define the Bausch aesthetic of the dance sequences, whenever they occur, Bausch herself might have answered that her movement language varied according to its context. The spectator, on the other hand, would rightly argue that there are common denominators giving all her dance a characteristic identity. Equally, it is true that her choreography has been subject to the natural process of evolution, always recognizable, but subtly changing. Her two Gluck productions belong to the same period as her celebrated *Le Sacre du Printemps* (1975), brought to London not long ago (2008) and one of her last all-dance pieces. And there is certainly a common aesthetic in these works, even if the Stravinsky score and scenario provokes an entirely different, viscerally violent dynamic, at odds with the lyricism of the operas. There is in all three productions the same incorporation of gesture into the dance, so that the result is a mix of dancerly and demotic movement. There is the use of repetition to build vibrant patterns. Indeed, in Bausch's dance-theatre pieces repetition can be taken to an obsessive, shocking extreme, at times psychologically revelatory, at times surreal. And finally there are the premises of modern dance itself, best defined in contrast with ballet: the acceptance of gravity, contrary to ballet's defiance; and the shaping of movement from an internal, psychological impetus, contrary to ballet's focus on external appearance, which is learnt through imitation. This last premise means that the reason for a movement and how it feels is, largely, more important in modern dance than in ballet. There is a famous quote, frequently used to describe Bausch's work. She said: 'I am not interested in how people move, but in what moves them.'[7] Equally, however, it needs to be emphasized that, although she may not be interested in dance for the sake of dance, she is the sublime choreographer of limpidly beautiful, startlingly vivid dances.

For the Wuppertal opera house audience the Gluck stagings represented the more acceptable and conventional face of Bausch's art. The idea for *Iphigenie auf Tauris*, staged one year (1974) before *Orpheus und Eurydike*, came from the Wuppertal opera house's Intendant. Bausch herself was hesitant, frightened at the scale of the undertaking, far bigger than anything she had ever done.

For Christoph Willibald Gluck (1714–87), however, *Iphigenie auf Tauris* was the culmination of a long career.[8] He had already made a much-publicized Paris

---

[7] 'Nicht wie sich Menschen bewegen, sondern was sie bewegt' from an interview with Pina Bausch (9 Nov. 1978), cited in Climenhaga (1997), 97.

[8] Gluck made his debut as an opera composer in Milan in 1742 with a setting of Metastasio's *Artaserse* which was successful enough to be followed by other operas in Milan and neighbouring Italian cities. For a large part of his subsequent career he was in Vienna, under Hapsburg patronage. His entry in *The New Grove Dictionary of Music and Musicians*, ed. Stanley Sadie (Oxford, 2001) says: 'More successfully than any of his contemporaries, he translated the widespread agitation for reform of opera and theatrical dance on the part of European intellectuals into actual works for the stage, first in pantomime ballets and Italian serious operas for Vienna and then in operas of various sorts for Paris' (10. 48.).

debut in 1774, with a companion piece, *Iphigénie en Aulide*, its libretto by M. F. L. G. L. Roullet based, via Racine, on Euripides' play of the same name. Gluck composed his opera version of *Iphigenia amongst the Taurians* in 1779. Like his earlier *Iphigénie en Aulide*, he created it in Paris under the patronage of his former singing pupil, the then *dauphine* Marie Antoinette. He used a French libretto by Nicolas-François Guillard (whose youth and inexperience made him a malleable collaborator) and recycled (as he often did) much of his music from *Semiramis*, a ballet created in Vienna in 1765, based on Voltaire's play. Achieving great success, *Iphigénie en Tauride* was the penultimate of Gluck's operas, although he revised it for a German-language production (*Iphigenie auf Tauris*) in Vienna in 1781. For this, Guillard's libretto was translated and adapted by Johann Baptist von Alxinger in collaboration with the composer, who moulded the music and vocal line to the German words.[9]

Also in Paris, the same year as *Iphigénie en Aulide*, Gluck staged, to great acclaim, *Orphée et Euridice*, another opera with numerous precedents based on the same myth. This *Orphée* was an enlarged French version, adapted to Parisian tastes, of the *Orfeo ed Euridice* that Gluck had composed in 1762 in Vienna with an Italian libretto by Ranieri de' Calzabigi. The original Calzabigi staging was highly significant in opera history. It was the first of three so-called reform operas in which Calzabigi and Gluck, under the aegis of the Intendant of Viennese theatre, Count Durazzo, reacted against what they saw as the fossilized form of *opera seria*. They were crystallizing what was already in the air of the Age of Enlightenment. The threads of similar notions can be detected in other composers; but it took a talent like Gluck's to formulate them with such force and over such a long period. Joined by the ballet master Gasparo Angiolini,[10] who choreographed the dance passages of *Orfeo ed Euridice*, Gluck and Calzabigi brought a fresh dramatic realism to the musical stage, not just in opera but also in dance.

In fact, Gluck had turned his attention first to dance: he had, at the time of *Orfeo*, already arranged and composed several ballet scores and with Calzabigi and Angiolini had, in 1761, collaborated on a three-act ballet-pantomime, *Don Juan*. This work made a big impression on the public, embracing the innovatory, associated premise of the *ballet d'action*, a through-drama using only dance and gesture, the opposite of the previous notion of dancing as a divertissement

---

[9] For the sources of the libretto, see Philippo (2005).

[10] Gasparo Angiolini (1731–1803) was born in Florence in a family of theatre artists. After working in Italy, he moved to Vienna where he became a pupil of the ballet master Hilverding and was influenced by his ideas of the *ballet d'action*. His choreography for Gluck's *Don Juan* ballet and *Orfeo ed Euridice* was the start of a busy and successful career, which included further Gluck collaborations and a dozen years or so spent in Russia creating many new works. He was also a composer, writing the music for some of his ballets. See further Lada-Richards, this volume.

sandwiched between speech or song. The seeds of a new ballet genre had been circulating for some time, pioneered by Franz Anton Christoph Hilverding,[11] ballet master in Vienna, and propounded also, *mutatis mutandis*, by the famous French innovator Jean-Georges Noverre (see further Lada-Richards, this volume). These ideas were to determine the future direction of ballet.[12] For its part, the Gluck-Angiolini *Don Juan* was quickly and widely imitated.

Orfeo ed Euridice was also a big success. Its happy ending, in which, contrary to the myth, the lovers are ultimately reunited in life, might strike today's audiences as jarring, but was very much in keeping with audience expectations of the time. More importantly, Gluck and Calzabigi showed, in early form, a modernizing spirit that shifted the focus of attention away from the star singer's disruptive bravura displays back to the musical drama. In their staging, the singer was subordinate to a drama articulated with simplicity and coherence; the recitatives that broke up the action were also discarded. Gluck and Calzabigi pushed their reforms further with *Alceste* (1767)—in which the dances were choreographed by Noverre—and *Paride ed Elena* (1770). The published edition of *Alceste* (1769) included a famous preface, signed by Gluck, that was, in essence, a Gluck-Calzabigi manifesto:

I have sought to restrict music to its true purpose of serving the poetry, as regards the expression, and the situation of the fable, without interrupting the action or chilling it with useless and superfluous ornaments . . . Thus I have wanted neither to stop an actor in the greatest heat of the dialogue in order to wait for a tiresome *ritornello*, nor to stop in the middle of a word on a favourable vowel, nor to show off the agility of his beautiful voice in a long *passagio*, nor to wait for the orchestra to give him time to recover his breath for a cadenza . . . In short I have sought to ban all those abuses against which good sense and reason have for some time cried out in vain.

Furthermore I have believed that my greatest effort should consist of seeking a beautiful simplicity; and I have avoided making display of difficulties at the expense of

---

[11] F. A. C Hilverding (also Franz Hilferding van Wewen; 1710–68) came from a famous acting family in Vienna. He probably studied in Brno and Paris, after which he was appointed court dancer and later court dancing master in Vienna. A prolific choreographer from 1744 onwards, he worked mostly in Vienna before taking charge of the ballet in Moscow and St Petersburg (1758–64), then returning to Vienna in 1765.

[12] The British dancing master John Weaver (1673–1760) had formulated similar ballet theories, long before Hilverding, Angiolini, and Noverre, but did not receive the same opportunities for developing his ideas on stage. See further Lada-Richards, this volume.

clarity; I have not judged it to be praiseworthy to invent some novelty that did not naturally arise from the situation and the expression.[13]

Just as Gluck achieved immediate success with his *Orfeo* and *Iphigenia* operas, so Bausch won approval from a hitherto recalcitrant audience. She used, with adaptations, the Viennese versions of *Iphigenie auf Tauris* and *Orfeo ed Euridice*, but with the latter's Italian translated into German. She also supressed *Orfeo*'s happy *deus ex machina* ending, thereby remaining faithful to the original myth but forgoing the celebratory dances designated by the score.

As opera productions, her stagings certainly stand out from most of her work; but they also represent stepping stones to the dance-theatre of her mature style. It would be wrong to go to the extent of claiming they were pivotal: they did not mark a sudden turning point. They were, as already said, part of a continuum that would lead to defining works such as *Arien* (1979) and *1980* (named after the year it was created). How are they part of a continuum? They are not, ultimately, so far from dance theatre: Gluck's libretti and the singers expand Bausch's means, adding the verbal dimension of her later works. Then, there is a strong emphasis on visual imagery, which from *Orpheus* onwards would be due to the imprint of the designer Rolf Borzik, Bausch's partner in private life, until he died prematurely in 1980.

Another characteristic factor allying these productions to her dance theatre is their distinctive psychological focus. Bausch's work does not paint the powerful archetypes of Martha Graham, but the ordinary people, the humble majority. She shows how each of us, so different, so complex, is extraordinary. The main protagonists of the two operas are, of course, the opposite: heroic, archetypal characters. But even if the lives of these protagonists are exceptional, Bausch presents them with the humane simplicity she accords to the protagonists of her other works. She shows us the human dimension behind larger-than-life deeds: even Orestes' matricide is drawn in domestic terms, full of mother–son pathos.[14] You could almost say she cuts these superhumans down to normal size. This equalizing approach features prominently in her later work and her creative method.

It is this naturalism which brings her close to Gluck and to the Euripides of *Iphigenia amongst the Taurians*. Bausch, Gluck, Euripides: all are innovators; they reach into the human heart to tell their stories and seek a new, more appropriate language.[15] Aristotle reported Sophocles as saying that he, Sophocles, portrayed men as they ought to be, and Euripides as they were.[16] The probable shifts between speech and singing or chanting by the (all-male) actors were a theatrical stylization, but within this convention Euripides still revolutionized tragedy by making his characters speak in a human way. According to Aristotle, it wasn't until Euripides wrote roles using everyday language that natural dialogue was

---

[13] This translation is taken from *The New Grove Dictionary of Music and Musicians*, 10. 48.
[14] See further below for a fuller description of this scene.
[15] Much of the following material in this paragraph is derived from Hall (1999), ix–xxxix.
[16] Aristotle, *Poetics*, ch. 25.

discovered.[17] He also had a wonderful gift for vivid narrative, as demonstrated in the 'messenger speeches', such as the herdsman's bemused description of Orestes' fit of madness near the start of *Iphigenia amongst the Taurians*. He saw that human actions were the external result of human motivation, not divine determinism. Iphigenia argues that humans, in committing evil deeds, use the concept of divine duty as a justificatory shield, when in fact the gods don't want blood. And Euripides had a gift for simile and metaphor, often traced thematically, exactly the way that Bausch creates her evolving chains of emblematic movement images.

In preparing *Iphigénie* Bausch and her company read not only Euripides and the Gluck libretto by Guillard, but also Goethe's *Iphigenie auf Tauris*, written in 1787, six years after the opera's German revision. The three versions present important differences: Guillard's opera libretto, particularly, departs from Euripides, influenced by seven earlier operas and, especially, by Guymond de la Touche's successful 1757 play *Iphigénie en Tauride*.[18] Bausch, of course, followed the opera libretto, but as with most opera producers, she also had the freedom to make cuts, modifications and additions. As related by Dominique Mercy,[19] these amendments came less from Euripides or Goethe (if at all), than from the imaginations of Bausch and her designers Jürgen Dreier and Rolf Borzik. (Figure 14.1)

Like Euripides, Gluck–Bausch start with Iphigenia alone, but the context is different: Gluck–Bausch pitch us dramatically into the midst of a violent storm. Iphigenia lies face down on the ground in a supplicant's posture; the music's *sforzando*, like a clap of thunder, brings on the chorus of her priestesses. They enter in plaiting lines, their vehement, multi-directional movements echoing not only the turmoil of the storm, but also the turmoil in Iphigenia's heart. Even after the storm abates she is still tormented—'deep in my heart, alas, the storm still rages,' she sings. She has had a horrifying dream, enacted by Bausch's dancers, in which she saw her father Agammenon:

> bleeding, pierced with wounds, and fleeing
> the murderous rage of an inhuman spectre.
> This dreadful spectre was my mother!
> She armed me with a sword and disappeared at once,
> I wanted to fly, but heard a cry, 'Stop! It is Orestes!'
> I saw an unhappy wretch and held out to him my hand;
> I wanted to help him, but a fatal power
> Forced me to pierce his breast![20]

---

[17] Aristotle, *Rhetoric* 3.2.5.
[18] Philippo (2005).
[19] Interview with the author in Wuppertal, May 2006.
[20] Act I, scene i, trans. Lionel Salter (1983 and 1986).

Figure 14.1 Bernd Marszan and Dominique Mercy in *Iphigenie auf Tauris* (1998).

Although Euripides does not provide a storm, he too makes Iphigenia sing about her dream in the first scene. However, in this dream, Iphigenia only intuits that Orestes is dead; she does not see how he dies. Gluck–Guillard's greater detail here, and its further elaboration in the scenes (also enacted by Bausch's dancers) of Orestes' dream and his dialogue with Iphigenia, point to a deliberate intention to evoke the full homicidal history of Iphigenia's family. Moreover, by having Clytemnestra press the sword into Iphigenia's hand, Gluck–Guillard not only take pains to portray Clytemnestra as an implacable avenger, more deadly than in other versions (as Phillippo suggests[21]), but they also delineate the terrible legacy which is being handed on to Iphigenia: a murderous inheritance which she almost fulfils but (as in Euripides) ultimately refuses.

Otherwise, the opera libretto preserves Euripides' opening premises: that Iphigenia was rescued by Artemis from Agamemnon's sacrificial altar and taken to Tauris; that, as priestess, she has the bitterly ironic duty of performing similar sacrificial killings on any strangers arriving in Tauris; that her brother Orestes and his friend Pylades arrive and are taken captive. In the Gluck staging, however, brother and sister recognize each other much later than in Euripides— not until Orestes is about to have his throat cut, in fact, when he utters a few chance words. This scene, near the opera's end, is followed by an unseemly scrum pitting the barbaric king of Tauris, Thoas, against Orestes and Pylades, the latter arriving with Greek reinforcements. The fighting is halted by a *deus ex machina*, in the shape of Diana, demanding peace. Euripides had given this role to Athena, as a probable homage to his Athenian audience. The opera's choice of Diana, the Roman version of Artemis, is dramatically more coherent, since it was Artemis who saved Iphigenia and it is in the temple of Artemis (or her Taurian equivalent) that Iphigenia reluctantly practises as high priestess.

This means that Euripides' inclusion of Iphigenia's wily plot to trick Thoas and escape doesn't figure. Euripides' Iphigenia is a strong figure with a streak of steel; Gluck–Bausch's is more passive and reactive.[22] Gluck–Bausch also make much of the brotherly relationship between Orestes and Pylades, each wanting to die for the other. This is translated by Bausch into extended duets full of mirror symmetries and unison.

Bausch introduces two new characters, a man and a woman, listed in the printed programme as Medien—German, for mediums or oracles. They are vivid, quintessentially Bauschian figures, dressed in a timeless mix of styles: the woman in a shapeless shift, the man in modern black tails. They accompany Thoas, because Thoas, profoundly anxious, never goes anywhere without his oracles. So this pair first appears when Thoas enters the Temple of Diana to inform Iphigenia of two new captives (Orestes and Pylades) and to remind her of her duty. He is panic-stricken because the oracles have predicted his death if, as he sings,

---

[21] Phillippo (2005), 92–6.
[22] Ibid. 99–100 suggests that this is under the influence of Guimond's play *Iphigénie en Tauride*.

the blood of a single stranger
sent among us escapes their wrath![23]

Thoas and his companions form an extraordinary trio. Thoas, played by Lutz Förster, a tall, rangy dancer, is in a fascistic green leather coat with exaggeratedly wide shoulders—National Socialism allied to antiquity. When he removes his coat, he reveals a long black dress and chiffon scarf: cross-dressing, the incongruity of which has a sinister disorienting effect, accentuated by his dancing which rampages about the stage with blustering, undignified hysteria. The oracle couple are bizarre and repellent: ancient mustiness made flesh in what might be the travesty of a stately ballroom dance. The woman carries a box containing soil: her material, maybe, for divination. The man is perhaps there to give intelligible form to her prophecies. He supports her as they walk or sits her on his shoulder or lowers her to the ground, holding her arm up and seemingly feeling her pulse. The woman's eyes are blackened, her legs bent and misshapen.[24] She is clearly in bad shape—but then, as Dominique Mercy joked, that's how you would be if you had been divining for centuries.[25]

There is something ludicrous, as well as grisly about this trio. And because of the physical intensity or directness of her language Bausch can be very grisly. The spare Modernist designs of *Iphigenie* contribute to this, using a few, contemporary every-day objects in a quasi-metaphorical way. So a roll-top enamel bath is the place where Agamemnon's naked corpse lies slumped in the dreams of Iphigenia and Orestes. It is also the vessel intended to catch the blood of Orestes as he waits for Iphigenia's knife.

The ritual devised by Bausch for Orestes' sacrifice is particularly effective. Whereas the opera directions specify that Orestes be adorned with garlands and purified with libations while the priestesses sing their hymn, Bausch chooses to halt the music for three and a half minutes, the total silence producing a peculiar hallucinatory suspension. The stage is bare except for the bath and a table, which here serves as the altar, and a white wall across the back at a slight diagonal. A procession travels from one end of the wall to the other, starting with a priestess who lays flowers on the altar. Orestes follows, and behind him come other priestesses. Orestes is carrying a ladder which will serve as steps to the altar, an echo perhaps of Christ who also carried the apparatus for his death.

Another Bausch invention is the sudden paralysis during the closing battle. When Diana intercedes with an aria, the fighting on the altar halts and Pylades' hand freezes in mid-air, about to strike Thoas a second time. Bausch, like Euripides, chooses to let Thoas live, which contradicts the opera—although

---

[23] Act I, scene ii, trans. Lionel Salter.

[24] Or did Bausch have in mind the Cumean Sibyl, the famous prophetess in Campania, Italy? According to Ovid (*Metamorphoses* 14. 132–53), Phoebus Apollo wanted to seduce her and, to this end, he granted her as many birthdays as the grains of sand she had scooped up in her hand. She didn't, though, think to ask him also for eternal youth. As described by Petronius (*Satyricon* 48.8) she became so shrivelled as the centuries passed, she ended up looking like a cicada. She hung in her cave, in a bottle, and when boys asked her 'Sibyl, what do you want?', she would reply 'I want to die.'

[25] Interview May 2006.

the libretto gives room for ambiguity—where Thoas' death confirms the pro-
phecy that had so terrified him.[26]

There are, of course, certain things that dance does better than words: certain
gestures, certain postures that are particularly resonant. For example, because
Bausch is a remarkably vivid choreographer, the enactments of the history of
Iphigenia and Orestes in their dreams and dialogue are particularly shocking.
During Orestes' dream (Act II, scene iv), where he is plagued by the Furies and
Clytemnestra, we see Clytemnestra bending towards Orestes as he lies asleep; and
as she does this, Orestes turns toward her like a small child, cradled in her skirt.
This tender moment makes his matricide seconds later all the more jarring.
Similarly, straight after (scene v), when Iphigenia questions Orestes, Bausch
has the absent or dead members of the family—Agamemnon, Clytemnestra,
Electra—stand in a silent group: a resonant image of ghosts or consciences. And
when Bausch echoes Orestes' answer about who murdered Agamemnon—'This
abominable monster was . . . His wife!'—she has Clytemnestra enact the murder
over and over in a typical Bausch sequence of stylized repetition.

Effective as they are, these scenes are mime, rather than dance. With real
dance, Bausch is at her best with the ensembles, especially those for Iphigenia's
priestesses whose patterns vividly match the music. According to Dominique
Mercy, Bausch conceived the priestesses not as replications of Euripides' chorus,
but as individuals who are Iphigenia's companions.[27] This is borne out at times
by the staging, which singles out particular priestesses.

The extensive length of the danced duets for Orestes and Pylades are a weakness,
becoming mired in the mirror symmetries and agonized poses. Iphigenia's solos
are, according to the dictates of the music, cast in the same melancholic tonality
and because these mine a narrow range of lyrical movement motifs, they are also in
danger of becoming monotonous. But one solo stands out as different. It comes
after Orestes, concealing his identity, tells Iphigenia (in the opera libretto) not
only that her parents have been murdered, but that her brother Orestes is also
dead. The solo depicts Iphigenia's attempt to absorb this terrible news and bring
herself to conduct a funeral ceremony in honour of Orestes. Its choreography,
built of simple, naturalistic gestures—a characteristic Bausch procedure—vividly
suggests the inner turmoil within a body, semi-immobilized by shock. The movements, delicate and understated, therefore have a domestic ordinariness, as does
the chair and table at which she must sit, the whole effect forming a poignant
contrast with Iphigenia's extraordinary circumstances. The obsessive repetition of
these movements—laying her hands on the edge of the table, getting up, turning

---

[26] In Euripides, Orestes, Pylades, and Iphigenia escape—thanks to Iphigenia's ruse—in Orestes'
boat, along with the effigy of Artemis. Adverse winds drive them back towards Tauris, but before
Thoas can seize them Athena appears and instructs him to let them go. In this way Orestes and
Iphigenia return to Greece. Another version by Sophocles has Thoas pursuing the fugitives to the
coast of the Troad, where Chryses, a priest of Apollo, kills Thoas.

[27] Interview May 2006.

away, returning—affectingly convey her total distraction, as she tries to absorb what she has learnt and what she must do.

Orpheus und Eurydike, staged a year later (1975), is the more accomplished and powerful of Bausch's productions, revived, like *Iphigenie*, in the 1990s after a long gap.[28] The story is largely as recounted by Virgil[29] and Ovid,[30] except for the happy ending (which Bausch rejects). There is also the introduction of a new character, Amor, who acts as go-between advising Orpheus on how to retrieve Eurydice.

The theme that love is so powerful it can even conquer death is in itself poetic and inspiring; and Amor, in assisting Orpheus, incarnates this theme, which in the opera is sustained to the end.[31] Amor appears before the grieving Orpheus and, as well as telling him to use his beautiful voice to appease the Furies and enter Hades, instructs him what condition the gods have imposed:[32]

> Thou art forbidden to look upon Eurydice,
> till emerged from the caverns of the Styx;
> nor art though to tell her of that mysterious prohibition;
> otherwise thou shalt lose her again for ever.   (Act I, scene ii)[33]

In this way the libretto provides a valid reason for Orpheus' crucial backward glance, which is another departure from the accounts by Virgil[34] or Ovid,[35] but has the virtue of providing the opera with extra dialogue for the two protagonists. Orpheus looks back because Eurydice, distraught at his inexplicable coldness, is half-fainting and refusing to follow.

With *Orpheus* Bausch is one step closer to the dance-theatre of her mature career because, contrary to *Iphigenie*, she actually puts the solo singers on stage

---

[28] *Iphigenie auf Tauris* was revived in 1991; *Orpheus und Eurydike* in 1992. Bausch used the dancers's memories and video recordings and cast Dominique Mercy (Orestes, Orpheus) and Malou Airaudo (Iphigenia, Eurydice) in the central roles they had created for the original stagings. In 2005 Bausch's *Orpheus and Eurydice* entered the repertoire of the Paris Opéra Ballet, one of only two Bausch productions to be performed by an external company. (The other, *Le Sacre du Printemps* also entered the Paris Opéra Ballet repertoire.)

[29] *Georgics* 4. 452–526.

[30] *Metamorphoses* 10. 1–85; 11. 1–66.

[31] Equally, Amor, associated in mythology with Cupid and Eros, has his own, not dissimilar love-story, *Cupid and Psyche*, in which Psyche is eventually rescued from Hades by Cupid.

[32] Hermes was the traditional guide who led the dead into Hades. A 5th-cent. BCE panel, part of a parapet around the Altar of the Twelve Gods in the Agora at Athens, showed Eurydice, Hermes and Orpheus at the moment Orpheus fatally looked back. An ancient copy of this panel can be seen at the Museo Archeologico Nazionale in Naples.

[33] English translation of Calzabigi by G. G. Bottarelli, London 1773, revised by Charles Johnston.

[34] '[A] sudden frenzy seized the unwary lover—worthy of pardon, except by the pitiless Underworld—he stopped, and unmindful, alas, and overcome in spirit, looked back at his own Eurydice. Then and there all his labour was spent in vain' (*Georgics* 4. 486–92).

[35] 'They were not far from the border of the world above; here frightened that she might not be well and yearning to see her with his own eyes, through love he turned and looked, and with his gaze she slipped away and down' (*Metamorphoses*, 10. 53–63).

Figure 14.2 Pina Bausch's *Orphée et Eurydice*, Paris Opéra (2004–5).

with the dancers. This makes for a radically original staging, truly an integration of dance and opera (Figure 14.2). And because of that, the sense of the dance as mere decorative visualization doesn't appear in *Orpheus*, the way it occasionally does in *Iphigenie*. With *Iphigenie*, where the singer is not physically enmeshed in the stage action, the attachment of dancer to singer, solo to aria, sometimes feels schematic, the movement sometimes close to a dumb-show.[36] But in *Orpheus* the dancers and singers, in confronting and mixing with each other, spark extra resonances. The only drawback with this duplication is the confusion it might initially cause an unprepared spectator, especially as the singing Orpheus is a contralto—the modern equivalent of the castrato who featured in the 1762 première. (Eurydice is a soprano, as is Amor.)

The *Orpheus* staging is also tauter and intensely gripping, aided no doubt by the extraordinary musical structure at Bausch's disposal. Calzabigi, the librettist, produced a short, spare scenario, with a minimum of protagonists. This is classical unity at its most excitingly concentrated, full of suspense and emotional verisimilitude. A single loss of impetus in Bausch's staging comes with the second

---

[36] However, according to Dominique Mercy (during the author's interview with him in May 2006), Bausch did, whenever permitted by a theatre's architecture, bring the singers in *Iphigenie auf Tauris* physically closer to the action by positioning them in the auditorium, at the side of the stage.

ballet sequence, the Dance of the Blessed Spirits. By its very musical nature, though, this section appears as a lull, describing as it does an expanse of serenity, much admired by musicologists. But it is difficult to make extended serenity choreographically interesting and Bausch does not solve that problem. Blessed Spirits apart, however, Bausch's graphic, pared-down movement, mixing the demotic with the dancerly, has an eloquent directness that goes straight to the heart. Orpheus's opening solo in the first tableau has an abandon that comes from extreme distress, his arms slamming against the floor as the singer cries 'Eurydike! Eurydike!'

The memoirs of Johann Christian von Mannlich (1741–1822), a friend of Gluck in Paris, record an amusing anecdote about this particular sequence during the 1774 rehearsals for the French version. It suggests how close Bausch's demotic concept of choreography is to Gluck's desire for naturalistic means. Apparently, Gluck wanted the singer Joseph Le Gros, to shout 'Eurydike! Eurydike!', not artfully sing it. Despite many attempts, however, the singer couldn't oblige. 'It's incredible,' Gluck said, 'you always shout when you should sing, and, when for once, you need to shout, you can't do it . . . shout with the pain you would feel if your leg was being cut off.'[37] After that, Le Gros managed to follow Gluck's instructions. For Mannlich the result was uniquely effective: 'That isolated cry, slicing through everything, as if outside the music, meant that the soft and beautiful harmony of the chorus had an even greater impact and touched even the hardest heart.'[38]

Bausch's production is divided into four highly contrasted tableaux, which follow the opera's changes of setting rather than its three-act divisions. To these tableaux she gives the titles Mourning, Violence, Peace, and Death. The designer Rolf Borzik develops further the emblematic potential of ordinary objects already present in *Iphigenie*. They become metaphorical components, arranged like an art installation: rows of high chairs, for example, lined along one side of the stage in the second tableau become an evocation of the labyrinthine hinterland of the Underworld.

Evoking antiquity, Borzik also makes much of nature, juxtaposing organic with man-made materials. The result is a poetic visual experience that is both ancient and contemporary. The first tableau is the most complex, a version of the opera's stage directions which specify 'a delightful grove of laurel and cypress-trees, surrounding a little plain, upon which stands the tomb of Eurydike'. Borzik's interpretation is a vision of total desolation: the 'delightful grove' reduced to a single dead tree, sprawling uprooted across the stage. Eerily,

---

[37] 'Cela est inconçevable, Monsieur, vous criez toujours quant vous devez chanter, et quand une seul fois il est question de crier vous n'en pouvez venir à bout. Ne pensez pas dans ce moment ni à la musique ni au Choeur qui chante, mais criez au moment indiqué avec de la douleur, comme si on vous coupoit une jambe' (in Mannlich (*c*.1989–93), 119).

[38] Ibid. 119–20. 'Ce cri isolé, coupant, comme etranger à la musique, la douce et belle harmonie du choeur fut du plus grand effet et toucha l'âme la moins sensible.'

Eurydice is also there; she is a memorial, a figment of the past, and of the present, filling Orpheus' mind. Poised on a high pedestal, she wears an unnaturally long white wedding dress and holds a blood-red bouquet that is the only splash of colour in a monochrome world. The unnatural proportions are unnerving, signposting her status as a lifeless icon.[39] At the back is her grave, a glass coffin containing a mound of earth. Before her are mourners; while on the other side stands Orpheus, quasi-naked in flesh-coloured briefs. He is locked in grieving immobility and staring through a glass screen, as if through the transparent, obstructive nothingness of death.

In an act of shocking directness, he then prostrates himself, forehead touching twigs and leaves arranged in a circle on the ground. There is also a hopscotch, drawn in chalk, the children's game which contains, in some versions, resonances of a journey from earth to heaven. Like the other singer–dancer pairings, the two Orpheus figures relate to each other as though joined by an invisible thread, linked in their emotions, yet physically independent. Although they are often fairly close to each other, just as often they are apart; and although the dancer obviously moves more than the singer, there are periods when it is the other way round.

The chorus, in Gluck's conception, is both a reference to Greek tragedy and a fundamental element of the action. In the first tableau, the chorus become the mourners, supporting Orpheus in his grief; in the second, they are the Furies, first aggressive, then yielding to Orpheus' entreaties. This means that Bausch's own group dancers move to both the choral and ballet passages, creating a profusion of imagery that echoes or supplements the libretto. Swaying lines of dancers give external form to Orpheus' turmoil; women replicate Eurydice's death and frozen icon-pose, or spill out from the wings pulling out bolts of white cloth that now seem like bridal veils, now like shrouds as they corkscrew the material round them. Bausch was a canny theatrical craftsman who understood the need for surprise, navigating with great sureness between the obvious and contrived, and knowing the value of stillness amid movement.

The appearance of Amor, played by a female dancer and a soprano, introduces a new note, fleet and alluring. The dancing Amor carries a crow (of enigmatic significance) and places it in the glass coffin. Amor moves almost playfully around Orpheus and draws a long line with a piece of chalk that is the route they must follow. The chalk line continues into the second tableau, Violence, where three-headed Cerberus is vividly represented by a gruesome male trio in leather aprons, half-refuse collectors, half-abattoir workers. They dance with curious sideways steps and unceremoniously manhandle new arrivals, as if transporting beef carcasses for storage. Gluck's Dance of the Furies and Spectres (which recycles the most sombre part of his *Don Juan* ballet score) overlaps with the choral music and Orpheus' singing and lyre.

---

[39] From the auditorium, it is impossible to be sure whether she is played by a live woman or a doll!

The Furies—Orestes' tormentors whose recriminations drive him to the brink of insanity—live in Tartarus, the deepest part of Hades, where the wicked are punished. Some of the dancers, though, are more like Fates, pulling the threads of human destinies. There are also women, stumbling with outstretched arms, brides who died before they could be married.[40] Or are they the Danaids who, blindly obeying their father, killed their husbands on their wedding night, and after death were punished by being made eternally to fill a leaking jar with water? There are other ambiguous images: Amor reappears with the crow, but there is also a woman carrying bread or cake; and a third, trying to reach an apple hanging from the ceiling.[41] Visual ambiguity is typical of Bausch's work. She doesn't tell you what to think; you have to interpret; you see her work the way you can.

As the opera progresses, so the staging gets simpler. The third tableau, Peace, interprets Gluck's Elysian Fields with glass screens (echoing the glass of the first tableau), rocks (shaped rather like sofas) and eerily pale, sun-deprived, flowers. The Blessed Spirits, men and women, dance and it is here that Eurydice first appears, in her dual singer-dancer form. But it is only at the end of this that Orpheus, who has watched the dancing, finds her. The final tableau, Death, is a vast, frightening emptiness, devoid of anything save for a small heap of dead leaves and pale grey walls. (As such, it is a minimalist interpretation of the cavern and rocks described in the opera's stage directions.) Here, the interplay between the singing and dancing performers is a tour de force. It is the singer who physically shows Eurydice's despair, singing crouched on all fours, and first falling to the ground when Eurydice is reclaimed by death. Orpheus the dancer reacts by retreating into devastated solitude, kneeling in one corner of the stage, his back to the audience, while the singing Orpheus kneels by the two dead Eurydices. The visual simplicity and emotional power of this scene is almost palpable. It is unsurprising that Bausch, with her sense of extreme theatre, should choose a tragic ending. And so the curtain comes down on the group of three dead women and the male dancing Orpheus, alone, now also dead, and tilted on to his side by Cerberus.

Although these two productions belong to Bausch's early career, they contain all the humanity of her mature style. She sought the ordinary in the extraordinary, because her prime interest was life, the everyday life as we all live it. And in training her attention on the ordinary, it was a logical development that from the late 1970s onwards, after her two Gluck productions, she should create her pieces through structured improvisations, setting tasks and questions for her dancers to

---

[40] The reference to brides is in Servos (2005), 55–8.

[41] Psyche, entering Hades, placated Cerberus and Charon the boatman with two obols (coins) and two cakes; in front of Persephone she refused the meal offered, wisely eating only bread. Tantalus, for his offences, was punished in Tartarus by being kept perpetually famished and parched, unable to reach the abundant water around him and the fruit-laden boughs above his head.

prepare and perform in the studio. Emerging from this methodology, her mature, signature pieces are a polyphonic fresco of sketches, songs and dances, carefully sifted and woven, in which the performers tell us about themselves, their joys and sorrows and hopes. In this way, Bausch holds a prismatic mirror up to the audience. She makes us see ourselves. And she makes us realize that each of us is wonderfully unique and fascinating, as extraordinary in fact as the heroes and heroines of Greek myth.

IV

ANCIENT DANCE AND THE
MODERN MIND

15

Knowing the Dancer, Knowing the Dance: The Dancer as Décor

Daniel Albright

Opera, as we know, began with a thought-experiment: how can we reimagine the lost music of Greek tragedy? Among the varied sources of classical ballet is a similar thought-experiment: how can we reimagine what Terpsichore herself danced, in classical antiquity? But whereas the Florentine camerata had to think up Greek music almost from scratch, the reconstructors of old dance could work with many visual clues, especially the suggestions of movement that could be inferred from the unstable postures of many Greek statues. In the 1790s Emma Hamilton danced her 'Greek' attitudes in her husband's salon in Naples, with Goethe, among others, in the audience. As Horace Walpole commented: 'Sir William Hamilton has actually married his gallery of statues.'[1] Hamilton wasn't alone; the German dancer/actress Henriette Henel-Schutz and the Danish actress Ida Braun both copied her example—there were many Galateas around 1800 striking odd poses in the hope of finding a plausible Pygmalion.[2] In this chapter I try to indicate some of the ways in which the dream of breathing life into a Greek statue became part of a larger project of animating the whole dance-stage.

What is the origin of dance? According to one distinguished authority, dance precedes speech, precedes thinking, precedes feeling itself—dance is the very first art of being human. The distinguished authority I have in mind is Ludwig van Beethoven, who described the beginning of his ballet, *The Creatures of Prometheus* as follows:

The two [statues] move slowly across the stage from the background.—P[rometheus] . . . is pleased when he sees that his plan is such a success; he is inexpressibly delighted, stands up and beckons to the children to stop—They turn slowly towards him in an expressionless manner. . . . he explains to them that they are his work, that they belong to him, that they must be thankful to him, kisses and caresses them.—However, still in an emotionless

---

[1] Cited in Tours (1963), 90.
[2] Marshall (1998).

manner, they sometimes merely shake their heads, are completely indifferent, and stand there, groping in all directions.[3]

Prometheus has shaped clay into a man and a woman, and animated them with the fire that he stole from heaven; but he is disappointed that they are just zombies, brainless creatures capable only of blank uncertain movement.

The music that Beethoven wrote to accompany their coming-to-life is startling: first, we hear a vague rhythmless preluding, then Prometheus' temporary pleasure in his new creation. How are these half-baked gingerbread figures to be turned into a man and a woman capable of reason and affection? Prometheus ponders the problem, and decides to take them to Parnassus where Apollo and the Muses will instruct them how to be human by means of music and dance—as the scenario puts it:

Euterpe, assisted by Amphion, starts to play music, and at the sound of their harmonies the two young people start to show signs of understanding, of the power of reflection, of an appreciation of the beauties of nature and of human feeling.[4]

By means of various dances from Terpsichore, the Graces, and Bacchus, the new man and woman learn the arts of pleasure and the arts of war.

So far the ballet seems to have little drama, little conflict; but Beethoven and Viganò have a surprise. Melpomene, the Muse of tragedy, takes a dagger and mimes the act of dying; overcome by her own art, she denounces Prometheus for having created a new race born but to die—and she kills Prometheus with her dagger. But the ballet will end happily: Pan and his fauns dance a grotesque dance that brings the dead Titan back to life. At the beginning Prometheus gives life to the human race; and at the end the life-giver is himself in need of resurrection. Beethoven described the resurrection with a theme that came to obsess him: the theme we know from the final of the third symphony, the *Eroica* (1804, three years after *The Creatures of Prometheus*). Beethoven also used this theme as *contradanse*, and in a set of piano variations from 1802: the piano piece begins with the theme's naked bass line, then slowly outfits it first with its true melody, and then with countermelodies; the drama is like that of a statue that gradually comes to life, as if the variations were a miniature version of the preceding year's ballet. In the third symphony, the theme appears after a funeral march, another suggestion of resurrection—the simple melody seems to represent for Beethoven some cosmic vivacity, some primal dance that catches up trees and rocks and men in its irresistible toils of grace. The theme begins delicately, but soon moves toward three heavy clumps—in the *Eroica* finale these clonks undergo a remarkable development, that could be called the apotheosis of the stomp.

---

[3] Beethoven's holograph of choreographic notes for the scenario for #1, from the Berlin 'Landsberg 7' sketchbook, as cited in Cadenbach (1995), 4.

[4] Ibid. 7. The intelligent and moving scenario was devised by the great choreographer Salvatore Viganò, who commissioned the music from Beethoven and danced the role of the male *Urmensch*.

One of the minor characters in *The Creatures of Prometheus* is Amphion, who sang the city of Thebes into being through the sheer force of music. Amphion might be called the patron saint of ballet décor, since every set designer and stage carpenter must hope to be the proper instrument through which music and dance can summon up an appropriate environment. On the other hand, dancers have little need of décor, since they *are* the space in which they move—just like the statue once it has come to life; and now I arrive at the main theme of this chapter. A dance is a kind of art in which the performer's physical presence constitutes the surround in which the dance takes place—as Yeats put it, 'How can we know the dancer from the dance?'[5]

The increasing realization towards the end of the nineteenth and beginning of the twentieth centuries that the dancer *constitutes* his/her own décor, and indeed potentially his/her own language décor, proves central to the development of theatrical Modernism. This realization comes about in part through shifts in aesthetics and philosophy, which enable Winckelmann's privileged Greek statue to be toppled as Schopenhauer restores music as pinnacle of the arts. This philosophical valorization of music leads, in turn, to the aspiration in theatre practice to reintroduce what the ancient Greeks termed *mousikē*—music, drama and dance.[6]

For Nietzsche, this all-encompassing art form achieved perfection in Greek tragedy, where the singing/dancing Dionysiac chorus enact the oneness (that Yeats articulates) between the artist and their art. If Wagnerian practice precluded the moving body within its ideal of the *Gesamtkunstwerk*, the Modernist dancers, such as Loïe Fuller, appeared to effect that unity in their performances. So alluring was the intermingling of dancer and décor, that certain experiments led to the submergence of the performer by the décor absolutely. Equally, however, if the animation of the Greek statue led ultimately to Modernism's often exhilarating symbiosis between dancer and décor, the dancer often overwhelms the denigrated stage design and proves its superfluity. Finally, if the ideal Modernist dancer constitutes her own visual décor, modern dance has equally attempted to recover its art form's early function in ritual as a mode of discourse. Dance in this sense is not just décor; it is language décor as well.

The action of Beethoven's ballet opens with two statues—'Prometheus comes running through the wood towards his statues of clay, to whose hearts he hastily draws the divine torch' as the scenario puts it.[7] Statues are aspects of décor; but once they come to life they are actors inside the décor. This equivocation between character and place, person and thing, is quite typical of ballet. Indeed ballet is founded on this equivocation: on the one hand, dance is humane, intensely

---

[5] 'Among School Children' (1926) in Yeats (1977), 446.
[6] On *mousikē*, see essays in Murray and Wilson (2004).
[7] Cadenbach (1995), 7.

expressive, a leaping for joy or a drooping with sorrow; on the other hand, dance is soulless, virtuosic, a mobile made up of pendula in the form of arms and legs, naked movement for movement's sake, prior to all thinking and feeling. From one point of view, a ballerina is a woman in a state of perfect emotional volatility; from another she's simply a marionette tugged and jerked by someone else's obsession—by Coppélius', by the fairground charlatan's, by the demon Rothbart's.

The statue that moves is a kind of totem, not just for ballet, but for all experiments at the boundaries between one artistic medium and another—what might be called *Zwischenkunst*, or inter-art. Marie Sallé was the first dancer to effect that transition in London in her 1734 ballet pantomime *Pygmalion*, with music of her own composition, when she dazzled audiences as a Greek statue, which breathed into life, clad only in a diaphanous shift. The following decade Sallé's close collaborator, Jean-Philippe Rameau, made his first experiment in what he called an *acte de ballet* with the wildly successful *Pygmalion* (1748), in which musical gesture is quite specific—in the overture the hammering of Pygmalion's chisel is clearly heard, and the statue comes to life in a wonderfully spare, hesitant, unsure manner.

In 1770 Jean-Jacques Rousseau, no admirer of Rameau, wrote a kind of riposte in the form of another *Pygmalion*, devised in a completely original form, the melodrama: a spoken text interrupted by or glossed with music. English speakers can experience something of the wonder of Rousseau's melodrama from a piece of incidental music that William Boyce composed in 1756 for a version of Shakespeare's *Winter's Tale* called *Florizel and Perdita*. Leontes, the jealous raging king, considers that his wife Hermione has been dead for sixteen years, but in fact she has been in hiding; and just like resurrected Alcestis, to whom she is often compared, Hermione reveals herself by pretending to be a statue that thaws into human flesh as music plays—just as in Rameau, there is a wonderful tentativeness to the music as the statue gropes towards life.

A statue that feels, speaks, dances, dwells in a threshold state between life and death—between the arts of space and the arts of time. The Greek word *mousikē*, though it is the source of the word *music* in all western languages, does not mean music; it means anything pertaining to the Muses; the breathing statue is as close to an entity of pure uninflected *mousikē* as can be imagined. The formal study of the comparative arts begins, to some extent, with Gotthold Lessing's 1766 book, *Laokoon*—a study that begins with a meditation on the problem of the too-expressive statue.

Of course the Beethoven–Viganò *Creatures of Prometheus* isn't, and can never be, part of the standard repertory—too little of its choreography survives—but by 1801 we are not far from the artistic milieu of *La sylphide* (1832) and *Giselle* (1841). In both these early favourites, dance at its highest pitch seems to belong in some domain beyond human life: in *La sylphide* in the ether of discarnate winged beings who seem to learn emotion from contact with men; in *Giselle* in the world of the dead, who inflict human beings with the compulsion to dance as a sort of infernal punishment. The large rhythm of the Romantic ballet of

Taglioni, de Bournonville, Gautier, Adam, is the large rhythm of *The Creatures of Prometheus* or *Pygmalion*: a descent from inexpressive superhuman dancing to a sort of dancing fevered and fretted with passion. The sylphide first learns to mime human tears by putting her index fingers to her eyes and tracing down her cheek the outline of a fall, and finally learns spasms of human pain when the poisoned scarf is placed on her shoulders; the Wilis first dance with cool spectral aplomb, then grow excited by Hilarion's agony as he dances himself to death. The Romantic ballet is a ghost's dream of human life, a statue's fantasy of frenzy.

This curriculum for Romantic ballet was anticipated by Heinrich von Kleist, whose 1810 essay on the marionette theatre argues that no human dancer can approach the grace of a certain kind of dancing puppet:

I wanted to know how it is possible, without having a maze of strings attached to one's fingers, to move the separate limbs and extremities in the rhythm of the dance. His answer was that I must not imagine each limb as being individually positioned and moved by the operator in the various phases of the dance. Each movement, he told me, has its centre of gravity; it is enough to control this within the puppet. The limbs, which are only pendulums, then follow mechanically of their own accord, without further help.... Often shaken in a purely haphazard way, the puppet falls into a kind of rhythmic movement which resembles dance...

'And what is the advantage your puppets would have over living dancers?'

'The advantage? First of all a negative one, my friend: it would never be guilty of affectation. For affectation is seen, as you know, when the soul, or moving force, appears at some point other than the centre of gravity of the movement. Because the operator controls with his wire or thread only this centre, the attached limbs are just what they should be ... lifeless, pure pendulums, governed only by the law of gravity. This is an excellent quality. You'll look for it in vain in most of our dancers ... take that young fellow who dances Paris when he's standing among the three goddesses and offering the apple to Venus. His soul is in fact located (and it's a frightful thing to see) in his elbow ... Grace appears most purely in that human form which either has no consciousness or an infinite consciousness. That is, in the puppet or in the god.'[8]

The enhaloed puppet, the puppet as god, would have a considerable role to play in the theatre of the future: both Gordon Craig and Antonin Artaud would try to devise a theatre in which human actors aspired to the devastating impassivity of dolls. But ballet was the venue in which Kleist's piecemeal statues would triumph: in, say, *Coppélia* (1870) and de Falla's *El retableo de Maese Pedro* (*Master Pedro's Puppet Show*, 1923). And what is most remarkable is the fact that, once you admit a puppet as protagonist in a ballet, the puppet starts to take over—the whole stage, the whole action, puppetizes. The puppet's status as décor as well as actor asserts itself: puppetness is hard to confine to the body of the dancer; it infects the whole theatre with its clockwork elegance.

---

[8] Kleist (1810).

By the time we reach the stage dances of the twentieth century, the statue and the puppet are more eager to assert their status as god. When we think of modern dance, as opposed to ballet, we probably first think of the hyper-expressivity of Martha Graham—poses of hysteria, ecstasy, dismemberment, the whole repertoire of Dionysus. But in the early years of modern dance there was a strong classicizing component: Isadora Duncan based her work on the postures of Greek statues; and Ted Shawn liked to play the roles of Adonis and Prometheus—there are film clips of Shawn, powdered white, naked except for a discreet loincloth, going through a series of postures, somewhat in the manner of a bodybuilder showing off his noble musculature (see Michelakis, this volume). I like to think that the opening of *The Creatures of Prometheus* might have looked something like Shawn's Prometheus: here we have the primary act of dance, inert matter heaving itself into motion by means of music.

Most of the living statues of twentieth-century dance, however, turned out, superficially at least, to be not 'Greek' but Asiatic—Ted Shawn can still be seen, in other old movies, dancing the role of Shiva. Shawn's wife, Ruth St Denis, confessed that her career was inspired by an advertisement she saw in Buffalo New York, for Egyptian Deities cigarettes—this made her want to become Isis. The gestures of the modern dancer are sometimes hotly expressionistic, sometimes hieratic, simple, cold, Egyptian—or Greek in the Winckelmannesque sense of the general and serene. But most importantly, perhaps, is that these 'statuesque' figures are truly composite: after Frazer and early anthropology, Shiva informs perceptions of the Greek at this time, no less than St Denis's Isis intermingles in her practice with contemporary ideas about, say, Athene.

So far we have studied the problem of places that turn into people, and people that turn into places, by means of statues. But the strange reciprocity of dancers and décor manifests itself in other ways as well. The intimacy of ballet and architecture has always been clear.[9] Dancers can shape themselves into bizarre stage constructs—as Balanchine's tempters, for example, become a merry-go-round in *The Prodigal Son* (1929); but it is also true that stage constructs can dance. Sometimes a stage prop will discreetly partner a lead dancer—in the movie *Royal Wedding* (1951) a hatrack obliges Fred Astaire with the favour of her company, and in *The Red Shoes* (1948) Moira Shearer discovers a newspaper that transfigures into a real man, a suave dance partner. As we know from Michael Powell's and Emeric Pressburger's 1978 novelization of their filmscript, this scene represents the heroine's lust for fame—she seems to be enjoying a little pressburger of her own. In fact one can dispense with the human dancers entirely,

---

[9] e.g. in Taglioni's 1832 *La sylphide* the minor sylphides form themselves into a sort of gated gazebo into which the main sylphide enters, as contemporary drawings show; in Balanchine's *The Prodigal Son* (1929), the prodigal is about to be taken for a ride in the tempters' merry-go-round, as the bad men fleece him out of everything he has: the vehicular form of this section of the ballet is that of a centrifuge, a mad whirl that goes nowhere.

and simply let the props do the work. The locus classicus of this theme is Giacomo Balla's 1917 Futurist ballet *Fireworks*, based on Stravinsky's four-minute orchestral razzle, which is a ballet without dancers. In fact it is a ballet without movement, except insofar as clever variations in the lighting exposed new angles in the odd assemblage of star-shaped and tent-shaped contraptions that occupied the stage. Balla programmed forty-nine different lighting moves—some of the lights were hidden inside small translucent stage objects in the fashion of Chinese lanterns.

But ultimately the architecture of dance depends not on the ingenuity of set designers, or even on the ingenuity of choreographers, but on the architecture of the human body itself. In a kind of manifesto written for a dance-architecture workshop at the Isadora and Raymond Duncan Centre for Dance, 29 September–5 October 2003, the choreographer Carol Brown wrote:

Dance and Architecture have much in common. Both are concerned with practices of space. For a dancer the act of choreography as a writing of place occurs through the unfolding of spatial dimensions through gesture and embodied movement. For the architect space is the medium through which form emerges and habitation is constructed. For both, the first space we experience is the space of the body. . . . We became space through stillness. In tracking the interior shifts of attention and awareness and inhibiting a desire to move we could feel the voids and solids, cavities and densities of our corporeal selves.

She goes on to speak of 'The dancer's kinesphere or personal envelope of space.' I find the notion of a kinesphere (the term is Laban's) illuminating. Like everybody else, I have a certain sense that my body-space isn't strictly delimited by my skin, but extends in an irregular manner on all sides, and I feel uncomfortable when my territorial limit is invaded. As W. H. Auden put it:

> Some thirty inches from my nose
> The frontier of my Person goes,
> And all the untilled air between
> Is private *pagus* or demesne.
> Stranger, unless with bedroom eyes
> I beckon you to fraternize,
> Beware of rudely crossing it:
> I have no gun, but I can spit.[10]

I think of my kinesphere as extending to every point that I can reach with my arms or legs. Since I'm not a very limber person, there's a sort of ozone hole in my kinesphere, somewhere between my shoulder-blades; but for the spry the kinesphere is more or less the sphere traced by a full rotation of the circle in which Leonardo inscribed Vitruvian man. A dancer's kinesphere, of course, is much larger than this—in fact, enormous. In a solo dance we sense not only the

---

[10] Auden (1976), 519.

dancer's actual movement, but the modulations of the kinesphere in which the dancer is enveloped: at full run the kinesphere thins out in front while gusty tatters trail behind the body in a sort of wake of air; and the famous Futurist sculpture by Umberto Boccioni 'Unique Forms of Continuity in Space' (1913), albeit not necessarily pertaining to dance, nonetheless seems a good representation of the quivering tunnels in the atmosphere that a dancer's body creates.[11]

A great many aspects of ballet costume and stage movement pay homage to the kinesphere. For example, tutus come in many shapes and sizes, but the standard tutu is pretty close to the circumference of the circle that represents the full extension of a ballerina's hip-swivel—a tutu is a way of visualizing one aspect of the kinesphere. Certain Modernist costume experiments go far in visualizing other aspects of the kinesphere; the costumes designed by Oskar Schlemmer for his *Triadic Ballet* (1921) are interesting in this respect (see Figure 15.1). Note the figure in front: her knob-head represents, more or less, the kine-cylinder that a dancer's head would make in the course of jumping straight up; and the balls at the end of her arms represent the lesser kinespheres that her hands would make if rotated in every direction. To her right we see costumes that represent different forms of twirls and swirls, sometimes eccentric, sometimes perfectly centred. The motion-trace of the dance is imprinted on the costumes themselves—even as static architectural elements in a photograph the costumes prescribe choreography. The costumes constitute a stage set, but are nevertheless icons of rotation and gesture, icons of pure dance; the line between dance and décor has rarely been so thoroughly erased. The music for the *Triadic Ballet* was written for mechanical organ by Paul Hindemith (who was to collaborate some years later with Martha Graham on *Herodiade*—see Bannerman, this volume). Nothing of the music survives except a few minutes' worth of recordings, which go nicely with the puppetoid costumes of Schlemmer, with their suggestions of sproing and whomp and the huffing of bellows.

So we see that costume can be a means for elucidating the kinesphere. But choreographers have found other means as well. Streamers tied to the wrist, or cloths dangled in air, are potent markers of the slipstream of the dancer's body. The expansion of the radius of the kinesphere by means of fans and fabric became one of the projects of early Modern Dance. Isadora Duncan liked scarves—as everyone knows, she died when her long iridescent silk scarf got tangled in the tyre of an automobile. But the most important experiments with lengths of cloth were performed by Loïe Fuller, who inspired more symbolist painting and poetry than any other native of Chicago, Illinois (see Figure 15.2).

---

[11] The sculpture is on display at the Museo de Arte Contemporânea, São Paulo. There are casts in the Museum of Modern Art and Metropolitan Museum of Art, New York and in the Tate Modern, London.

Figure 15.1 Costumes for Oskar Schlemmer's *Triadic Ballet* (1922).

Fuller used sticks to manipulate fabric, continuously reshaping her kinesphere into various cloud-forms—a giant butterfly in Moser's painting or, as Isadora Duncan wrote:

Before our very eyes she turned to many coloured, shining orchids, to a wavering, flowing sea flower, and at length to a spiral-like lily . . . she became fluid; she became light; she became every colour and flame, and finally she resolved into miraculous spirals of flames wafted toward the Infinite.[12]

She occupied so much of the stage that she became, more than a dancer, a sort of weather. Duncan was the least of the poets preoccupied with Fuller's genius: W. B. Yeats wrote:

> When Loie Fuller's Chinese dancers enwound
> A shining web, a floating ribbon of cloth,
> It seemed that a dragon of air
> Had fallen among dancers, had whirled them round
> Or hurried them off on its own furious path;
> So the Platonic Year
> Whirls out new right and wrong,

---

[12] Duncan (1927), 95.

Figure 15.2 Loïe Fuller's *La Danse du Feu* (1897).

Whirls in the old instead;
All men are dancers and their tread
Goes to the barbarous clangour of a gong.[13]

Stéphane Mallarmé went still further. He called Loïe Fuller 'an inexhaustible fountain of herself', and spoke of her 'vertigo of soul', 'her quick nuances sloughing off their limelight phantasmagoria of twilight and grotto, such speed of passion, delight, grief, anger'.[14] But of primary interest for our purposes is Mallarmé's meditation from 1893 on the relation of dance to décor:

This transition from sonority to pieces of cloth . . . is, uniquely, the spell that Loie Fuller puts into effect, instinctively, with a thrusting-forward or a withdrawing of a skirt or a wing, constituting a place. The enchantress makes the ambiance, pulling it out of herself and drawing it back into herself, through a silence pulsating with crêpes de Chine. Instantly there vanishes an imbecility: the traditional planting of permanent or stable décor, as opposed to the mobile choreography. . . . The pure result is a free stage . . . exhaled in the play of a veil, with poses and gestures.[15]

A dancer that constitutes a place: this is the ideal fusion that we've been tracing throughout this chapter. Those sceptical that this is truly possible should watch a 1903 film, not of Loïe Fuller herself, but of an imitator named Ameta: she describes a kinesphere at least twelve feet in diameter; but perhaps most impressive of all is the kine-tornado of cloth she creates at the end. Around 1914 Wyndham Lewis and Ezra Pound would create an artistic movement called Vorticism—as Pound wrote:

The image is not an idea. It is a radiant node or cluster; it is what I can, and must perforce, call a VORTEX, from which, and through which, and into which, ideas are constantly rushing. In decency one can only call it a VORTEX.[16]

Ten years before Vorticism came into being, Ameta's dance clearly shows how a storm of movement can focus itself into a burning tip of energy. In the fixed stage set of the old ballet—the décor that Mallarmé deplores—the painted perspective lines lead the spectator's eye to some vanishing-point of no particular interest. But in Ameta's dance the role of the perspective lines is taken by the two sticks she manipulates, and their line of sight leads us directly to the dancer herself. The stage set is in the dancer's hands, and swells, deflates, spins, erects itself, in exact response to the music.

The search for larger and larger kinespheres eventually led to truly vast dance objects. In 1942 Balanchine choreographed a polka for circus elephants, and

---

[13] 'Nineteen Hundred and Nineteen' (1923) in Yeats (1977), 428.
[14] Mallarmé (1945), 311, 308.
[15] Ibid. 308–9.
[16] Pound (1980), 207.

commissioned Stravinsky to write the music.[17] But the apotheosis of the dance elephant occurred in Walt Disney's *Fantasia* (1940), where Ponchielli's *Dance of the Hours* is choreographed for ostriches, hippos, elephants, and crocodiles. In a cartoon ballet the dance and the décor really are one, since there are no static elements at all: the décor transmogrifies as effortlessly as the personages—indeed ever since the early days of *Steamboat Willie* a certain orphic pan-psychism was part of Disney's stock in trade, as buildings lifted their foundations, trees lifted their roots, and danced. In *Fantasia*, the kinesphere attains a visible presence at once ponderous and ethereal, as an elephant floats off in a bubble—the Doric columns of Disney's stage architecture remind us, once again, that behind even this absurd dance-fantasy there lies some dream of classical Greece. At the end of the sequence, the pachyderm thump becomes too great, and the stage itself collapses.

There are precedents for this general crash of the theatre: Disney's animators may have been thinking of the Marx Brothers' *A Night at the Opera* (1935), but long before that there was Saint-Saëns's *Samson et Dalila* (1877), in which Samson pulls down the pillars of the Temple of Dagon and exterminates the Philistines, along with himself. Through the centuries many clerics have used this story from the book of Judges as an example of the inherent corruption of the theatre itself: for example, in Ben Jonson's *Bartholomew Fair* (1614), a Puritan named Zeal-of-the-land Busy gets into a shouting match with a puppet at a puppet show, and finally becomes so angry that he shouts 'Downe with Dagon . . . I will remoue . . . that heathenish Idoll' (5.5). However, I'd like to propose a different sort of allegorical reading for Disney's *Dance of the Hours*. In many ways the film provides an ideal specimen of that dance theatre advocated by Mallarmé and Loïe Fuller: and if the stage set crashes down on the heads of the very large dancers, it is a sign that external décor is unnecessary: the dancers themselves have to constitute the place in which they dance. There is a line of Balanchine's used in advertising a video documentary of his career: 'It's like a fish goes through the water. The music is the aquarium and the dancer is a fish.' But sometimes, you might say, the dancer is the aquarium and the music is the fish.

Strange inversions of actor and environment are a striking aspect of recent stage productions. Richard Strauss's opera *Salome* is a puzzle for stage directors: it's often difficult or impossible to find a soprano—a sixteen-year-old with an Isolde voice, Strauss called her—who can sing the role and dance a convincingly seductive Dance of the Seven Veils (see Webb, this volume). Since the opera's première in 1905, a dancer double has often taken over the choreographic chores; but in an imaginative 1989 version from Barcelona, the director employed Montserrat Caballe—a very large, rather elderly woman with an almost ideal

---

[17] NB. This was not the first elephant that had attracted a choreographer's attention: in 1877, at the première of Petipa's *La bayadère*, a live elephant appeared on the Mariinsky stage; modern productions rarely include actual elephants, but Nureyev's staging made do with a fine elephant simulation.

voice for the part—as a human stage set. Caballe is perched on top of a pedestal, with much of the stage concealed by a curtain that dangles down from her: soon a dancing Salome emerges from the vast skirt of the singing Salome—Caballe's womb seems to give birth to the entire production. In Samuel Beckett's *Happy Days*, the lead character is a woman buried in a great mound of earth, first up to her waist, then up to her neck; place and person are eerily confused. In the Barcelona *Salome*, the singer is the aquarium and the dance and the music and the drama are all fish. Indeed, in one scene, the dancers seem in danger of drowning in the crests and troughs of the stage-filling skirt.

I'll conclude by talking about another aspect of décor. Dancers glide across a stage that may be adorned with a painted backdrop and various sorts of props; but they also glide across a stage that may be filled, in some sense, with words, mute words. Just as Beethoven's statue comes to life, nineteenth-century ballet as a whole grows out of the pantomime spectacle: as Marian Smith has shown, the Parisian pantomime tried every conceivable means to find surrogates for language: 'composers, choreographers, and designers at the Opéra introduced words into ballet performances in every way but actually having performers intone them.'[18] These ways included on-stage placards and orchestral quotations of familiar tunes whose lyrics were relevant to the action. We've looked at some of the elisions between dancer and visual décor; but there are elisions between dance and language décor as well.

In ballet as we know it, there are pantomime scenes full of encoded words: I [pointing to self] you [pointing to someone else] love [hands over heart]; and *Coppélia* is more easily understood by an audience that knows that the word for *doll* in terpsichorese consists of outlining an hourglass shape with your hands, followed by sharp up-and-down gestures with rigidly crooked elbows. But these incarnations of language in gesture are considered slightly sub-balletic: no ballerina ever became a *danseuse-étoile* on the basis of her elegant pantomime. Is it possible to find a language in the grand solos and duets that make up the highlight reel of ballet—a language with words more specific than *sad* and *glad*?

One way to approach this problem is through the study of choreographic notation. Dance and dance notation have always been twins, but in 1928, when Rudolf von Laban published his book on kinetography, dance notation attained a new precision. It might be interesting to record in labanotation a speech in American Sign Language: the notation could give an exact description of every aspect of the performance except what it means. The spectator of a ballet sees all sorts of emphatic diagonals and thrusts and flingings-out, but these vectors rarely terminate in paraphrasable meanings; ballet, with its eternal array of outstretched limbs in a ecstasy of pointing—pointing with arms, with elbows, with index

---

[18] Smith (2000), 97.

fingers, with index toes—is a perfect demonstration of the Poststructuralist linguistics in which every signifier points to another signifier without ever quite becoming a sign.

In this sense a book of labanotation is a text just as meaningful or unmeaningful as the text of *David Copperfield*. I suspect that there has been a certain tendency in recent dance to construct ballets that deliberately resemble labanotation, as if ballet's status as an art form could be heightened by making it approximate the look of a text. For example, we might take note of Edouard Lock's suite of dances for a 2003 production of Rameau's *Les Boréades*. Lock's dance company goes by the whimsical name of La La La Human Steps, but the dancers step less in the manner of human beings than of letters in an alphabet of arms and legs. There are many old demonstrations that dancers can shape themselves into the letters of the Roman alphabet—see, for example, this finely salacious alphabet from 1534 devised by Peter Flötner (see Figure 15.3). Indeed contemporaneously with Laban, we find the notion of making an alphabet out of dance, in the publicity for the Delphic Festivals in 1927 and 1930, in which Eva Palmer's Greek-style chorus (as if they had danced off a Greek vase) pose in the shapes of letters from the Greek alphabet.

Mallarmé remarked, in his meditation on Loïe Fuller, that 'The theatre always alters its component arts according to a special or literary point of view...in

Figure 15.3 Flötner's anthropomorphic alphabet (1534).

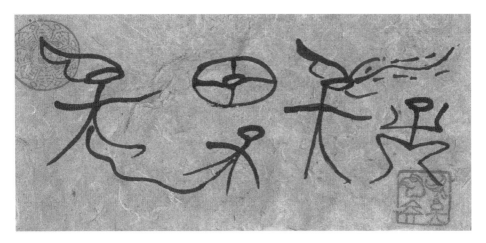

Figure 15.4 Naxi 'Happy Birthday'.

Ballet one could not recognize the name of Dance; it is, if you wish, hiero-glyph.'[19] In Lock's dances for the 2003 *Les Boréades*, the hieroglyphs whirl past with incredible speed, like an instantaneous scan of the whole Egyptian Book of the Dead. Could dance attain a language of such urgency and precision that it could step out of the theatre and become a mode of discourse?

Dance in ancient Greece on account of its role in ritual practice was indeed a mode of discourse. And we can see traces of this too not so much in ritual practice, as in discourse about ritual practice in southwestern China today. The Naxi minority of Yannan province speak a Tibeto-Burman dialect, and their script is the only pictographic language in use today—although it may be not in use much longer, since the number of fluent Naxi readers is estimated to be between ten and two hundred. Happy birthday! (see Figure 15.4)—birth is represented by an obvious picture of a woman giving birth; day is the sun; and happy is a couple singing and dancing—note the little streamer proceeding from the singer's mouth, a symbol of vocal emission. As in Chinese, there is no clear boundary between noun, verb, and adjective; even Naxi nouns often imply a great deal of motion.

The Naxi script is also said to constitute the earliest form of dance notation known anywhere in the world. The script is, of course, a sacred language—the Naxi always used a much simplified script for daily use, and now write to one another in Mandarin—and the sacred books of their shamanistic religion contain exact prescriptions for dance rites. These notations differ from labanotation in that they are true sentences—you can read a Naxi dance out loud, just as you can read any sentence. And, as you can see from the Naxi happy birthday sign, many

[19] Mallarmé (1945), 312.

ordinary Naxi sentences read like gestural inscription—dance notation. I'm charmed by the notion of speaking dance, as if dance isn't reserved for special theatrical occasions, but might be a regular feature of our conversation. I talk not only with my larynx, but with my hands, with my whole body. I want to learn how to speak dance. Perhaps, as Michael Ventris discovered with the Minoan alphabet, it will turn out to be an occluded form of Greek.

16

Modernism and Dance:
Apolline or Dionysiac?

Susan Jones

In 1948, the Russian choreographer George Balanchine argued for the preservation of the original version of his works: 'Each piece is unique in itself; nothing is replaceable.'[1] Yet in a famous exception, he failed to follow his own pronouncement. One of his most renowned ballets, *Apollon Musagète*, had been created in 1928 for the Diaghilev Ballets Russes, with music by Igor Stravinsky.[2] Balanchine began revising this piece in 1937 for a Stravinsky-Balanchine gala in New York, renaming it simply *Apollo*. Throughout his career he made extensive changes to its choreography and setting, and in 1979 he eliminated the prologue for a New York City Ballet revival, cutting nearly one third of the Stravinsky score.[3] When speaking about his initial restaging of the ballet he emended his previous claim about fidelity to the 'original version': '"Apollo" I look back on as the turning point of my life . . . It seemed to tell me that I could dare not to use everything, that I, too, could eliminate.'[4]

This discussion explores the significance of Balanchine's revisions to *Apollo* in the light of the pervasive influence of the narratives and drama of ancient Greece on twentieth-century modern performance dance. The title and theme of the ballet draws on the classical legend, in which, according to the Greek poet Hesiod (*Theogony* 918–20), Apollo was the son of the Olympian Zeus, the Titan Leto, and brother of the goddess Artemis. In the *Homeric Hymn to Apollo*, he is depicted ascending to Olympus, where he delighted the gods and goddesses with his music. Balanchine does not recreate literally the myths associated with Apollo in any version of his ballet, but instead suggests a situation that broadly outlines Apollo's birth, adolescence, and growth in creative power, showing how he acquired his trade from the muses, Caliope, Polyhymnia, and Terpsichore

---

[1] Balanchine (1948), quoted in Lederman (1975), 81.
[2] For an account of Balanchine's collaborations with Stravinsky, see Jordan (2007).
[3] See Garafola (2004), 20. Balanchine became director of Lincoln Kirstein's New York City Ballet in 1948.
[4] Balanchine (1948), quoted in Lederman (1975), 81.

(Balanchine used only three Muses), before finally ascending Mount Olympus to take his place among the gods. Nevertheless the distinctiveness between the versions of *Apollo* is pronounced, and it is easy to identify in them the choreographer's sense of his own apprenticeship. The revisions show us his artistic development as he reduced the narrative and representational function of dance and increased his mastery of pure form, celebrating dance for dance's sake in line with American innovations in abstract expressionism in painting, such as those by Robert Rauschenberg or Jackson Pollock.

We might ask, what significance do these revisions provide for a discussion of the survival of the ancient dancer in the modern world? And why should the twentieth-century choreographer's emendations to his original work be relevant to this context? I argue that we need to examine Balanchine's revisions in a wider account of Modernist aesthetics. In doing so, we find that his cuts are supported by a long history associated with the influence of Greek art and culture on Modernism, one that can be traced to *fin de siècle* discussions of Hellenism and early twentieth-century assumptions about what constituted 'the Greek' in dance.

Certain philosophical issues have been neglected in accounts of Balanchine's *Apollo* so that most critical responses to the two versions rely on a matter of personal taste. I propose that Balanchine's cuts provide a paradigmatic shift in aesthetics of the sort we identify in Modernism in other art forms. Broadly speaking, I place the versions of this ultimately neoclassical ballet between two aesthetic polarities associated with the writings of Friedrich Nietzsche. Taking my lead from the mood of 'tragic joy' expressed in the closing chords of Stravinsky's score for *Apollo*, I associate Balanchine's choreographic development with Nietzsche's account in *The Birth of Tragedy out of the Spirit of Music* (1872) of his engagement with Greek tragedy and his descriptions of the Apolline and the Dionysiac.[5] I argue that during the process of revision, Balanchine negotiates between the elegance of an Apolline aesthetics emphasizing the beauty of the dancing figure,[6] with a tougher, more masculinist account of creative struggle associated with Nietzsche's Dionysiac.

First, I outline Nietzsche's propositions in this text, showing how they contribute to his later thinking about *der Wille zur Macht* (the Will to Power) in *Also Sprach Zarathustra* (1884). I show how radical developments in twentieth-century dance emerged from his aesthetics, in part initiating the vogue for reconstructions of Greek dance in the early decades of the century which often rejected the constraints of classical ballet in favour of the liberating embodiment of Dionysiac energy. Finally, I discuss Balanchine's neoclassical revisionism in

---

[5] On the 'originality' of the Nietzschean polarities see Silk and Stern (1981). I follow Silk and Stern's translation of 'das Apollinische' and 'das Dionysische' rather than the 'Apollonian' and 'Dionysian', more frequently used in English literary critical studies.

[6] See Mallarmé (2003), 20. Mallarmé's account of the dancer who writes 'avec une écriture corporelle' suggests the economy of gesture and form associated with the Apolline.

the light of these early twentieth-century shifts in dance aesthetics, arguing that Balanchine's later versions of *Apollo* reversed the trend by moving away from Nietzsche's 'Dionysiac' mode with its emphasis on the rigorous struggles of the artist, towards a more assured 'Apolline' aesthetics of beauty.[7]

I

Nietzsche's influence on Modernist literature and music is well documented, but he introduces a space for dance, and indeed all art forms, suggesting an authority that exists outside language and that is rooted in the body rather than in the intellect. Although Nietzsche ultimately rejected the kind of physical abandonment associated with the Dionysiac dancer who subsumes his/her individuality to the powerful expression of the chorus, the activity of dancing nevertheless constituted a fundamental ingredient of his aesthetics.

In part, we can identify in certain forms of dance in this period a Nietzschean interest in the primitive and a search for an 'original unity'. Several examples from early twentieth-century dance spring to mind: Isadora Duncan's expressivism; Vaslav Nijinsky's choreography for *The Rite of Spring* (1913); Fokine's interest in folk dance and ritual; and Mary Wigman's *Witch Dance* (1914), all suggest a Dionysiac energy that turns against the Apolline symmetry of classical ballet forms. On the other hand, Nietzsche's language of Dionysiac forces retains a Romantic suggestion of the sublime, a striving for the 'noumenal' realm that Kant indicated was unreachable. In performance dance, we can identify this enduring Romanticism combined with an athletic Dionysiac element in a work like Fokine's *Spectre de la Rose* (1911), where, in spite of the predominantly *fin de siècle* mood of Romantic nostalgia, the animal force of Nijinsky's famous leap through the window at the close of the ballet arguably illustrates Nietzsche's references to an 'embodied' expression of the sublime in 'the full gestures of dance, the rhythmic movement of all the limbs'.[8]

We can best explore this development in aesthetics by first looking at the way in which dance contributes to, but is strangely elided from, Nietzsche's thinking in the early *The Birth of Tragedy*. Nietzsche's argument in this text is complex. He advocates the autonomy of art from outside forces, pushing for the primacy of the aesthetic over moral criteria. In short, he claims that existence can only be justified as an aesthetic phenomenon: humanity itself ultimately constitutes the aesthetic.

---

[7] See Stravinsky (1947). Even though this work is generally held to have been ghost-written, Stravinsky's remark that the Dionysiac must 'finally be made to submit to the law: Apollo demands it' (80–1) is reflected in Balanchine's revisions to the choreography.

[8] Nietzsche (2000), 26. All references in this chapter to *The Birth of Tragedy* are taken from this translation and page numbers quoted in the text.

Partly as a result of Richard Wagner's theories, the aesthetics of music occupied a central place in the European cultural practices of the mid to late nineteenth century. As a non-representational art form, music also offered artists in all fields formal examples of ways in which art might resist the confines of mid-nineteenth-century realism.[9] Music's status was celebrated of course by the Symbolist movement, partly through Pater's famous declaration: 'All art constantly aspires towards the condition of music.'[10] But Nietzsche achieves something very different from an elegant Paterian aesthetics, with its emphasis on beauty. To borrow the terms of the dialectic of the sublime and the beautiful invoked by Edmund Burke in the eighteenth century, Nietzsche shifts music from the realm of the beautiful towards a Modernist sublime.[11] He uses the Wagnerian model to show the tendency of contemporary music to move away from harmony through chromaticism (where notes in a melodic progression are raised or lowered by accidentals, without changing the key of the passage), towards dissonance. This shift in the treatment of melody offered to artists in other media the example of an art freed from traditional notions of the beautiful, opening up the possibility of an aesthetics premised on a jarring dynamic in style and content.

Nietzsche's inspiration arose from the example of Greek drama. As a classical scholar who developed radical textual readings, Nietzsche identified in *The Birth of Tragedy* what he claimed were the origins of Greek tragedy. The Apolline he associated with the restraint of rationalism, and with individuality. The Dionysiac he associated with the will of the unconscious, the life force, and in this context, with the origins of tragedy in the Dionysiac dithyramb, the hymn to the gods which constantly draws the individual back into the communal body of the chorus.

According to Nietzsche, Attic tragedy of the fifth century BCE represents a fusion of Apolline and Dionysiac impulses, or, as Douglas Smith puts it, 'a combination of the plastic art of sculpture with the formless art of music which produces a powerful visible representation of a spiritual state'.[12] In literary terms it represents the combination of two major currents of Greek poetry—on the one hand, the Homeric epic art, where language is used to imitate the visible physical world, the world of phenomena, and on the other hand, the lyric poetry of Archilochus and the odes of Pindar.[13]

Nietzsche found these origins not merely in a single source—music—but in that source's combination of Apolline and Dionysiac creative drives, the two forces on which the central opposition of the book focuses. But these drives are

---

[9] Of course, one might argue that we can identify realist tendencies in music—as in Beethoven's *Pastoral Symphony.*

[10] Pater (1986), 86.

[11] Edmund Burke, *A Philosophical Enquiry into the Origin of our Ideas of the Sublime and Beautiful* was published in 1757.

[12] Smith (2000), xvii.

[13] Music was always subservient to poetry until the late 5th cent. BCE when the so-called New Music led to virtuoso musical display. See the essays in Murray and Wilson ((2004).

not simply complementary. Nietzsche tended to see Greek civilization as the product of a struggle between the Apolline and the Dionysiac, which in parts three, four, and nine of *The Birth of Tragedy* he finds expression in the myths relating the conflict between the Olympians and the Titans. According to these myths, the new Olympian gods usurp the power of the Titanic demigods, although Titans such as Prometheus continue to defy their authority and eventually force a compromise: this struggle of the Titans is a common motif of Romantic poetry, of Goethe, Keats, Shelley; and it is interesting that in his dedication to Richard Wagner, Nietzsche identified himself with the unbound Prometheus, a Dionysiac figure rebelling against the rule of the Olympian gods. Of course in its contemporary context, Nietzsche's exhortation to renew what he saw as a stagnant German culture must surely be read into the political thrust of this text.

Yet out of this theory we can also detect the emergence of a twentieth-century Modernist concept of selfhood rooted in pain and conflict. The pain of individuation constitutes the pain experienced by the individual's desire to return to the communal and unconscious drives of the Dionysiac. But for Nietzsche (who acknowledged his debt to Schiller and especially to Schopenhauer's privileging of the aesthetic), the Dionysiac force constitutes the 'real', the original 'unity'. Interestingly, Nietzsche clearly associates the aesthetic with a pre-linguistic form of embodied expression, in the dance. Gesturing here to the realm of the aesthetic, he writes:

Now the world of nature is to be expressed in symbols; a new world of symbols is necessary, a symbolism of the body for once, not just the symbolism of the mouth, but the full gestures of dance, the rhythmic movement of all the limbs. Then the other symbolic forces will develop, particularly those of music, suddenly impetuous in rhythm, dynamism, and harmony.[14]

Nietzsche anticipates a number of features we encounter in aspects of literary Modernism: the notion of aggressive struggle, its ambivalent attitude to the body, which appears to privilege the body over the word yet ultimately turns away from the dance towards the predominance of the spirit of music. Nietzsche's failure to sustain a fuller discussion of dance at this point may result from his reliance on Schopenhauer. Schopenhauer expressly associates the action of the body with the will: 'Every true act of his will is also at once and without exception a movement of his body.'[15] Here Schopenhauer creates a problem, since the will constitutes for him desire and bodily needs leading to misery. He claims that you should be in touch with the will but not give in to it in order to reach a point of restraint, escaping the cycle of misery and desire. Schopenhauer's key to the will is provided by action, but our inner *awareness* of our own will manifesting itself in the body supposedly points us towards what exists beyond

---

[14] Nietzsche (2000), 26.
[15] Schopenhauer (1969), 2. 130.

the realm of representations altogether. Thus he privileges the aesthetic (and especially music), placing the creative artist, in relation to the aesthetic experience, in a state of will-lessness.

Nietzsche's *Wille*, however, is turned to positive effect in his advocacy of a degree of access to the Dionysiac. He is quite clear that dance, as it encapsulates the Dionysiac force, precedes that of music as a non-linguistic form of expression, where rhythmic movement creates its own music. This account is important for Jane Harrison, whose *Ancient Art and Ritual* (1913) was widely associated in the early twentieth century with the Cambridge Ritualists, anthropologists including F. M. Cornford, Gilbert Murray, and A. B. Cook. Harrison drew on Nietzsche when she emphasized the choral dance of the dithyramb, the idea of Dionysus arising out of the rite (*dromenon*) of tribal initiation; and, according to Martha Carpentier, Harrison also influenced Modernist writers including Virginia Woolf, T. S. Eliot, and James Joyce.[16] Other areas of high Modernism reflected Nietzsche's tone in their dynamic 'revolutionary' exhortations, as in Wyndham Lewis's *Blast*, Pound's hard-edged Imagist aesthetics, or Apollinaire's experimentations with layout in *Calligrammes*, which required of the reader a rigorous and energetic input. Of all the Modernist manifesti, Filippo Marinetti's least well known, 'The Futurist Dance' (1917), advocates for dance a tough, Nietzschean aesthetics, where the aggressive actions of 'The Machine Gun Dance' privilege the body as technological instrument engaging in struggle and conflict.

In Nietzsche's account, the characteristics of dance have moved far from the feminized aesthetics of the romantic sylph of the nineteenth century. Yet already we get a sense of the oppositional force of Nietzsche's aesthetics, the 'tragic joy' present in the spirit of music, that in this passage leads to the word 'harmony'. The Dionysiac is the real; the Apolline only has access to the illusion. For Nietzsche, Apollo's art is accessed in dreams (a move that anticipates Freud): and at the end of *The Birth of Tragedy* he claims that ultimately the two forces, the Apolline and the Dionysiac need to be resolved in order to produce great art. The seemingly harmonious rhythms of Apollo only occur through the incorporation of the forces of Dionysus—great harmony achieved through suffering and conflict, as in music the dissonant chord of the famous overture to *Tristan and Isolde* leads ultimately to a form of resolution. Nietzsche sums up thus, speaking of the Apolline beauty of Athenian art having been achieved by a harnessing of the Dionysiac principle: 'How much must this people have suffered in order to become so beautiful! But now follow me to the tragedy and let us perform a sacrifice in the temple of both deities!'[17]

So how do Nietzsche's theories about the origins of Greek tragedy find their way into the choreography of the early twentieth century? In fact, we see

---

[16] Carpentier (1998), 63: 'Harrison traced the evolution of *dromenon* (literally "things done", or rituals) into Greek drama using archaeological, as well as literary and historical evidence.'

[17] Nietzsche (2000), 131.

examples of Nietzsche's influence everywhere: in Émile Jaques-Dalcroze's famous staging of Gluck's *Orpheus und Eurydike* at Hellerau in 1913, where his practice of Eurhythmics ensured that the chorus expressed through their physical movements an internalized rhythm. Mary Wigman, having worked with both Dalcroze and Rudolph Laban (renowned for his creation of an influential dance notation) developed a practice of German expressionism in dance, paying homage to the Dionysiac when she had a reader recite passages of Nietzsche during her 1917 Dadaist performances.[18] Bronislawa Nijinska's bleak evocation of choral dynamics, in her choreography for *Les Noces* (1923), set to Stravinsky's music for piano and choir, offers a strident critique of any positive view of the community. One could argue, however, that Isadora Duncan was one of the earliest choreographers to encompass Nietzsche's return to the origins of Greek drama, and we can detect something of her own Apolline/Dionysiac struggle in the development of her thinking about dance.

In the early work of Duncan we see a more general appropriation of a 'Greek style' akin to any number of early twentieth-century exponents of 'Greek dance' (in Britain these included Madge Atkinson, Ruby Ginner, and Margaret Morris, who all acknowledged Isadora's influence—see Macintosh, this volume). When in 1901 an American journalist, reporting on Duncan's European performances, gave his article the headline: 'Like an Ancient Greek Bas-relief Come to Life She Astonishes Paris', we sense the fashionable imitation of a so-called 'Greek style'. As Duncan's biographer points out, Duncan herself, in a byline to the article, acknowledged an essential distinction between the impulse of reconstruction and that of interpretation: 'I drew my inspiration from Greek sources. Strictly speaking, I do not try to reconstruct Greek dances. This is practically impossible.'[19]

Duncan expresses here the spirit of a pervasive *fin de siècle* 'Hellenism' arising from a preoccupation with a Greek ideal of the body, partly fuelled by the renewal of the Olympic Games in 1896. She did attempt in part to emulate the poses of Greek dance, reconstructed from her observation of Attic vases and, as she wrote to the poet Douglas Ainslie, 'impersonal little friezes of figures . . . with an exquisite aloofness from human beings' (see further Smith, this volume).[20] This kind of imitation is akin to her motivation for a neoclassical refinement associated with the *tableau vivant* in her enactment of a number of gestures and figures from Botticelli's *Primavera*. Yet in her 'researches' of Greek dance at the British Museum she also encountered the Elgin marbles, which may indeed have suggested to her something very different to a Botticellian elegance. The Pheidian sculptures are robust, massive, forceful as well as reposeful. The reclining and lunging of several figures on the East Pediment of the Parthenon soon found

---

[18] Howe (1996), 100–1.
[19] Quoted in Daly (1995), 101.
[20] Ibid. 102.

their way into Duncan's dance vocabulary. In this brief illustration we may already recognize two distinctive impulses emerging in Duncan's 'borrowing' from the idea of Greek dance: a lightweight, feminized elegance associated with the representation of purity; and a more dynamic, weightier form altogether.

In fact Duncan was moving here towards the inspiration she drew, by her own admission, from the example of Nietzsche's *The Birth of Tragedy*. By 1905 she was claiming that 'dancing is the Dionysiac ecstasy which carries all away',[21] but more importantly for this discussion, in *The Art of the Dance* (1928) she wrote that dancing 'must become again the primitive Chorus, and the drama will be reborn from her inspiration. Then she will again take her place as the sister art of tragedy, she will spring from music'.[22] And in her own interpretations of *Orphée* (which began in 1900 and were repeated in various stagings through to the 1920s), she echoes Jaques-Dalcroze in her emphasis on the importance of the chorus: 'I do not try to represent Orpheus or Euridice but only the plastic movements of the Chorus.'[23] In the year of her death in 1927 she wrote: 'From the beginning I conceived of the dance as a chorus or community expression.'[24] This is a significant move for Duncan, in that, contrary to received evocations of her dancing as a highly subjective emotional outpouring, she frequently looked to the chorus as a vehicle for impersonality in an Eliotian sense.

One further point of interest regarding Duncan is that, although we have no concrete evidence, we might have expected her to have read Jane Harrison, especially since 'Harrison was listed as the reader on Duncan's 16th March 1900 program at the New Gallery'.[25] Harrison took inspiration from Nietzsche, but she pursued more vigorously than he the study of Hellenic matriarchal goddesses. Carpentier observes that for Nietzsche, both the Apolline and Dionysiac principles were dominated by male archetypes and that his attitude reveals a prejudice against Euripides, whose plays are dominated by female archetypes. This is especially odd because Euripides's *Bacchae* had always been the primary source of information about Dionysiac rites. But nor did Nietzsche discuss Aeschylus' *Oresteia* trilogy, also a strange omission because, beginning with Clytemnestra's murder of Agamemnon and culminating in the matriarchal Eumenides' demand for revenge, it tells the story of the penultimate confrontation between the old Dionysiac religion and the new Olympian or Apolline religion.[26] Nietzsche instead focuses on Prometheus—presenting a view of Greek religion as dominated by male archetypes.

Harrison, who otherwise takes her lead from Nietzsche, recovers the Greek matriarchal roles, and her impact on Virginia Woolf may well have emerged

---

[21] Quoted in Franko (1995), 17.
[22] Daly (1995), 148.
[23] Ibid.
[24] Franko (1995), 17.
[25] Daly (1995), 93.
[26] Carpentier (1998), 4–5.

from this aspect of her work. Female choreographers such as Martha Graham also followed in this tradition. Graham's interest in Greek dramatic forms began with her ballet *Dithyrambic* (1931), and she notably chose to explore characters such as Medea (*Cave of the Heart*, 1946), Jocasta (*Night Journey*, 1947), and Clytemnestra (*Clytemnestra*, 1958), in her innovative dance dramas (see further Bannerman and Zajko, this volume).[27]

We can trace an association between Nietzsche, Duncan, Harrison, and Graham through their ideological relationships to Greek drama, yet the issue of reconstruction of actual Greek dance in the twentieth century deserves momentary attention for its impact on choreography of the period. We have seen that Duncan acknowledged the impossibility of accurate historical reconstruction of Greek dance, yet many of her followers took a more academic approach to the Greek revival.

In 1923 Ruby Ginner founded the Greek Dance Association to promote and sustain the practice of her research (see further Macintosh, this volume). Ginner is of interest here because of the depth and scope of her research and for her explanation of method, which helps to illuminate the endurance of the 'idea' of the Greek in Modernist choreography through to Balanchine. In a retrospective study of 1960, Ginner explains that, like Duncan, she was in the 1920s 'primarily inspired by the choruses in Greek drama', realizing that 'the art of the dance was capable of a dramatic intensity not to be seen in the form of dancing at that time'.[28] Like Duncan, Ginner studied visual sources in the figures of dancers, athletes, and warriors represented in Greek sculpture and painting, but she articulates her method in greater detail:

My studies led me to discover that certain dance poses constantly recurred in these arts from early Dorian times throughout Greek history. This suggested that these movements had been definite technical positions in the Hellenic dance, and from these I formed a basis from which to reconstruct the ancient art.[29]

From this foundation, Ginner goes on to describe the complex reconstruction of movement from these 'snapshot' poses of movements in transition, of how she approximated 'what preceded and what followed the action, and what degree of force and speed were necessary to the rhythmic flow and continuity of the whole movement'.[30]

Using a range of visual, anthropological, and archaeological sources she recovered information on forms, including gymnopeaedic, ceremonial, and ritual dances, Phyrric war dances, choral, and social dances throughout the history of

---

[27] On Harrison and matriarchal roles, see also Beard (2000). For a full account of the impact of Nietzsche on Duncan and Graham, see LaMothe (2006).

[28] Ginner (1960), 18.

[29] Ibid. 18.

[30] Ibid. See further Naerebout, this volume for the source of this kind of reconstruction in the work of the French musicologist, Maurice Emmanuel.

ancient Greece. Yet Ginner was also interested in 'the close relationship between speech and movement',[31] and she gives particular emphasis to the intentionality behind gesture, the translation of gesture into words. She claimed that 'Hellenic dance was speech made visible',[32] finding this idea in the works of dramatists, poets, and philosophers. She consulted, among others, Plato, Pindar, Euripides, Lucian, Xenophon, Harrison, and Murray, her researches suggesting to her the survival of a highly mimetic strain in dance which did not necessarily accord with twentieth-century Modernism's emphasis on abstraction (of the sort later championed by Balanchine).

Nevertheless, such reconstructions inevitably rely on an act of imagination, and, as Ginner admits, even if she could imitate perfectly the 'physical movements as shown in the plastic arts', it required a knowledge of what '*ideas* lay behind the actions of the dancers' causing them to move as they did.[33] In this respect, Ginner tends broadly to divide her discussions into two categories falling between those dances associated with the 'ideal of the body beautiful' in the worship of Apollo, and those including the riotous Dionysiac dances, which she describes, drawing on Pindar, as the most 'tempestuous', 'passionate', 'emotionally exciting'.[34] Yet again we hear the pervasive influence of Nietzsche (probably gleaned from Harrison, whose *Ancient Art* Ginner cites in her chapter on 'Dionysiac Dances').[35]

Ginner's emphasis on historical reconstruction stemmed from a different impetus to the one prompting the individualist creations of modern dance choreographers like Wigman or Graham, who aimed to develop their own distinctive styles of movement. Nevertheless, a common interest in liberating the body from the strictures of classical ballet can be found in all these modern movements, and was perceived by most contemporary choreographers as consistent with a 'Hellenic' style, which Ginner identifies in the 'three fates of the Parthenon pediment' as representing 'a litheness of limb which can only come from complete freedom of movement'.[36] The vogue for Greek revival initiated by Duncan and sustained by Ginner and others played an important role in the development of modern dance, not least because these new forms inevitably turned towards a Nietzschean idea of the Dionysiac as a foundation for a more energetic, athletic style of movement. Balanchine's physically exuberant neoclassicism, a style of choreography based on traditional classical ballet technique where movements were liberated from the confines of a strictly symmetrical form, could be included here (as could the work of twentieth-century exponents

---

[31] Ginner (1960), 19.
[32] Ibid.
[33] Ibid.
[34] Ibid. 34, 55.
[35] Ibid., 55–61, esp. 57.
[36] Ibid. 20.

of 'Modernist' ballet such as Kenneth Macmillan, Jiří Kylián, and William Forsythe—see further Stanger, this volume).

Nietzsche's theories certainly contribute to the adoption of a high Modernist dance aesthetics in the twentieth century in the United States, where modern dance flourished in association with the universities. American modern dance was institutionalized through its close links to educational dance programmes and physical education degrees from the 1920s onwards, with the help of such figures such as Ted Shawn, Martha Graham, Doris Humphrey, and Charles Weidman, and later Merce Cunningham and José Limon. The musician and composer Louis Horst, Martha Graham's partner and collaborator, gave a central place to a 'Dance Study in Dissonance,' claiming that 'strongly dissonant movement . . . is a state of physical being throughout the body—a complete physical awareness which furnishes the dance with a new texture: tense, full of potential action, one part pulling against another'.[37] Here Horst advocates for the dance aesthetic the agonistic forces initiated in Nietzsche's *The Birth of Tragedy*. As a distinctive alternative to classical ballet's anti-gravitational dynamic, its emphasis on refined, symmetrical form, line and elevation, we may discern Horst's characterization of 'dissonance' in a work like Martha Graham's 1935 solo, *Frontier*. Her body extends itself with outstretched arms, the working leg in a high second position thrust into a series of aggressive jumps, while her leaps exist in tension with the body's earthward gravitational pull each time she lands. Graham's style bears a relationship to 'dissonant' dance arising from European expressionism in Mary Wigman's *Witch Dance*, or in Wigman's associate Hanya Holm's American production of *Trend* (1937), which likewise exhibit a tension between the body's embrace of the floor and a reaching away from it.

Innovations in European and American modern dance reflect the representation of dance in *The Birth of Tragedy*, but Nietzsche's later position on dance shifts from the idea of participation in the Dionysiac abandonment towards a greater sense of detachment on the part of the observer. In *Also Sprach Zarathustra* (1884), Nietzsche identifies to a much greater degree with the self-consciousness we associate with Modernism in the arts. The figure of Zarathustra is the creator or the man of wisdom, but in the second part of *Zarathustra*, 'The Dancing Song', where Zarathustra's self-consciousness prevents him from joining a group of dancing girls, he contemplates the dancer, transforming her into a symbol of dancing life. As Rüdiger Safranski interprets this moment, those who stand apart from life and do not participate in the dancing are the ones who register its significance: 'Wisdom, which seeks to apprehend life, also insists on distance.'[38]

---

[37] Horst and Russell (1961), 50. Horst sees in the idea of dissonant dance a phenomenon close to Adorno's privileging of the dissonance of Schöenberg and Stravinsky.

[38] Safranski (2003), 280.

Nietzsche's text anticipates the kind of narrative self-consciousness often predicated on distancing narrators or speakers in Modernist literary texts, as in T. S. Eliot's emphasis on detachment and 'escape from emotion', which left the poet in the position of one who mediated rather than participated in the Dionysiac fury.[39] To some extent Nietzsche also removes the autographic function of the dancer by placing creative wisdom in the mind of the distanced observer rather than in the dancer herself.[40] In effect, he offers a role for the critic of dance, as in Wyndham Lewis's condemnation of Diaghilev's blatant oriental-ism.[41] But Nietzsche's 'man of wisdom' also paves the way for the position of the 'master choreographer', who, like Balanchine, adopts a position of distance, judgment, and authority over his work. At the same time, Balanchine's choreog-raphy brought to classical ballet the very athleticism and liberation from academ-ic restraint that Ginner so approved in her descriptions of Greek dance.

II

Balanchine's revisions for *Apollo*, in which he eliminated the narrative elements, replacing them with a greater choreographic economy, established his authority in relation to his own dance traditions. The emergence of Balanchine's strong neoclassical formalism (which in works like *Apollo*, *Orpheus* (1948), and *Agon* (1957), also draw on classical Greek subjects) emphasizes his debt to the balletic purism of Marius Petipa, the chief choreographer of the Imperial Russian Ballet, St Petersburg, in the nineteenth century. As Tim Scholl has observed, Petipa's highly formal balletic choreography for the *divertissements* and interludes of *corps de ballet* work of the otherwise predominantly narrative nineteenth-century classics (such as *The Sleeping Beauty* or *La Bayadère*) offered Balanchine a model for his own experiments in formalism.[42]

Balanchine's amalgamation of the traditional and the modern is unsurprising, since he began his career with the Imperial Ballet, joining Diaghilev's Ballet Russes in 1924 before going to the US in 1933. Balanchine's interrogation of the workings of the body in relation to the stage space seems most effectively to reflect and respond to the construction of Petipa's grand ballet designs, where the massed movement of the *corps de ballet* functioned almost as building blocks of

---

[39] Eliot (1922), 787.

[40] Abbott (1996), 4. Porter Abbot described Samuel Beckett's writing as 'an author doing something in the present at every point in the text'.

[41] Lewis (1969), 155.

[42] See Scholl (1994). Scholl shows the importance of the founding of *Apollon* (1909), the Russian journal that replaced *Mir iskusstva* (associated with Diaghilev), for the development of the Russian Modernist movement as a whole (82). The significance of the title for Balanchine cannot be ignored.

an architectural plan, a technology of the body that emerges as part of a more general European post-war constructivism.

Yet Balanchine's aesthetic practice, which exploits and subverts the conventions of his predecessors, is unreservedly 'Modernist' in its formalism and attention to the abstraction of the dancing body as creative medium. When he became Director of the New York City Ballet he began to hire predominantly tall dancers whose elongated musculature accommodated what eventually must have seemed like the choreography of skyscrapers (the ultimate neoclassical form in architecture), displaying high extensions of the leg, their fleet footwork and graceful physique combining poise with a suggestion of geometric angularity. These dancers exhibited an athleticism that enabled them to distort the conventional symmetry of classical ballet while retaining its elegance. A typical 'Balanchine' pose, for example, subverts the usual symmetry of a high classical *developé devant en pointe*, in which the working leg is extended forward at a strict ninety-degree angle to the supporting leg. Instead the dancer thrusts the supporting hip out to push the line of the body off balance, creating a higher extension of the working leg and a far more athletic, kick-like effect to the movement.

But in 1928, when Balanchine created *Apollon Musagète*, he was still working for the Ballets Russes. His ballet demonstrated many of Nietzsche's propositions in *The Birth of Tragedy*—particularly in his conclusions about the aesthetic:

In the process, only precisely as much of that foundation of all existence, of the Dionysia[c] substratum of the world, may enter into the consciousness of the human individual as can be overcome again by the Apollon[ine] power of transfiguration, so that both of these artistic drives are compelled to develop their forces in strict proportion to one another.[43]

As we have seen, Nietzsche finally resolves this conflict by suggesting that we must 'perform a sacrifice in the temple of both deities!'[44] Balanchine's 1928 version underlines in a number of respects the conflict of artistic drives outlined by Nietzsche. This version gives us an explicit sense of the narrative. It has a much stronger element of setting, such as the slope suggesting Mount Olympus, and by implication, Apollo's striving to attain its heights (see Figure 16.1). The costumes are elaborate, including wigs to denote classical hairstyles, a tunic for the male soloist to show explicitly the Hellenic context, and the action is well documented—beginning with a graphic account of Apollo's birth and finishing with the climb to Mount Olympus.

The 1928 version included a prologue in which the birth of Apollo is enacted as a struggle of creativity, followed by Apollo's first tentative solo. The final sublime moment had Apollo dragging the muses, reaching literally for the heights. In the New York City Ballet version of 1979 the costumes are spare and the piece is danced on a bare stage without sets and without the prologue. In this later version, where the scenery has been cut and there is no slope representing Mount Olympus, the dancers

---

[43] Nietzsche (2000), 130–1.
[44] Ibid. 131.

Figure 16.1 *Apollon Musagète* (1928).

merely move off stage on the same horizontal plane (see Figure 16.2). In consequence both the dramatic power of the piece and its narrative quality are substantially eroded. Moreover, Stravinsky's strident opening musical accompaniment to
the original prologue is subsequently lost, which in itself anticipated, in its dissonant
passages, the agonistic conflict engendered in Apollo's reaching for mastery. The
1928 version in some respects expresses the musical score more accurately, especially
as the final chords suggest an appropriate lack of closure, fading incrementally into
silence as we watch Apollo reaching for but never quite attaining the summit before
the curtain comes down.[45]

While Balanchine revised this ballet on many different occasions throughout his
career, ultimately we have two major versions of *Apollos*. The 1928 version, with the
presence of the slope and the dancers' progress upwards, expresses an aspiration for
the sublime that illustrates both the Apolline/Dionysiac conflict and the conver-
gence of these forces as described by Nietzsche at the conclusion of *The Birth of*

[45] American Ballet Theater's current version remains closer to the original. Costumes and décor
are less elaborate but it includes the prologue showing Apollo's birth, and uses a minimalist
representation of the slope of Mount Olympus.

Figure 16.2 Balanchine's *Apollo* (1979).

Tragedy. But inherent in that move towards transcendence is the image of physical struggle, present in the haunting dissonance of the music and expressed choreographically through Apollo's effort in his first tentative solo to attain perfect balance, his momentary losses and recoveries of equilibrium expressing the precarious nature of his striving for artistic perfection. The upward struggle to lead the muses to the heights at the end likewise suggests the suffering of the creator.

In the second *Apollo*, the conclusion is in fact more Apolline. In the symmetry of Apollo's final pose, in which he calmly leads the muses along a horizontal plane, we perceive a Socratic, perfected picture of beauty. The narrative function of the piece, emphasizing the teleological movement of upward struggle has been subsumed in the expression of the beauty of the dance in its bodily forms. We still perceive, throughout the revised version of the ballet, traces of the mimetic function of much of the gesture and expression. In Calliope's solo (the muse of poetry), for example, where Balanchine uses a series of *sissones ouvertes*, the body accompanies them with open, presentational arm movements and the face mouthing 'speech' to express linguistic communication. Polyhymnia (the muse of mime) holds a mask and shows the power of gesture. For Terpsichore, representing dance and song, Balanchine created a *pas de deux* with Apollo that repeats an image of the bird in flight (Apollo kneels while she assumes the pose of a 'bluebird' lift on his shoulder—this is Balanchine's deliberate manipulation of a famous pose from Act III of Petipa's *Sleeping Beauty*).

However, it is more difficult, in the context of the later version, where the narrative framework is missing, to interpret these movements as having a purely representational significance. Without the explanatory scene of Apollo's birth, these mimetic traces hold fewer literal meanings. Instead, the final tableau of Apollo dragging the muses creates an abstract 'chariot' shape (the extended legs of the muses fanning out behind his body like the rays of the sun). We may be reminded of a passage in *To The Lighthouse*, when Lily Briscoe's use of 'the triangular purple shape' in her painting suggests, in its abstract formalism, the iconography of 'mother and child',[46] her aesthetics privileging symbolic form over literal representation. In the later version of *Apollo*, Balanchine retains traces of the myth, but prompts the viewer to appreciate the form for itself, the choreography eliciting her/his individual interpretation.

I believe Balanchine deliberately cut many of the framing narrative elements because in the first version he was uneasy about his own choreographic authority, and he was telling us the story of his conflict as burgeoning choreographer within the context of the aesthetics of dance at that period. Balanchine wanted to privilege the authority of dance as an art form, whose formal qualities could be appreciated for their own sake, and that displayed its own internal logic, its own inner dynamic (rather in the way that Eliot had reservations about his 'explanatory notes' to *The Waste Land*). By the time Balanchine made the final cuts to the 1979 version he was confident in presenting the dance as that thing in itself, having produced the visually and choreographically spare works of his high Modernist period, including *Concerto Barocco* (1941, to music by Bach), *The Four Temperaments* (1946, to Hindemith), *Agon* (1957, to Stravinsky). But the question arises: could *Apollo* ever be interpreted as pure form? Even in naming the piece, Balanchine introduces an intertextual element; in Julia Kristeva's terms, he opens a discursive field that gestures to literature and myth.

The example of *Apollo* provides a convenient *Künstlerroman* of a twentieth-century choreographer's struggle to find mastery of the form. It may be compared to early twentieth-century writers' uneasy engagement with problems of authority in other areas of Modernism (such as Joyce's *Portrait of the Artist As a Young Man* or of Woolf's Lily Briscoe, finally drawing the line through her painting at the end of *To the Lighthouse*). The case of Balanchine's *Apollo* helps us to understand the influence of a common aesthetics across a variety of art forms in the period. The first version of *Apollon Musagète*, with its more literal telling of the story of the struggle of the birth of the creator returned Balanchine constantly to the issue of the autographic function of dance. Who is the master—the creator

---

[46] Woolf (1992), 72.

of the myth? Apollo, watching his muses? The dancers themselves? The Ballet Russes, whose style Balanchine accommodates? What is the position of the choreographer here? The assured master choreographer of the later version leaves little room for doubt. In the second *Apollo* the stamp is Balanchine's. The style carries with it *his* autographic function irrespective of the dancer who interprets his work; he assumes the cool distance of the Zarathustran figure. But while *Apollo* has today become a modern classic of twentieth-century dance, I believe that in the process of revision Balanchine lost the drama of the initial debate about creativity, associating his Modernism with an Apolline rather than a Dionysiac aesthetics, emphasizing the beauty of the form, rather than the sublime struggle for it.

III

In conclusion, the versions of *Apollo* illustrate a distinctive shift between aesthetic polarities that we frequently identify in Modernism. Modern dance, liberating itself from the Apolline grace of classical ballet, tended to privilege the sublime power of agonistic forces released by the Dionysiac energy in the dance, rather in the way that D. H. Lawrence's short story the 'Woman Who Rode Away' (1925) illustrates the seduction and brutal energy of the Dionysiac will, expressed in a communal dance that echoes the situation of the *Rite of Spring*.

By contrast, Balanchine rejects the forceful resonances of a Nietzschean perspective on creative struggle in his ballet, leaving us in his final version of *Apollo* with a more elegant aesthetics associated with formal economy and harmonious beauty. Perhaps Balanchine's revisions give us a sense of what Jean-François Lyotard observed, that 'the artist and the writer, then, are working without rules in order to formulate the rules of *what will have been done*'.[47] But they also remind us that, with these two versions of *Apollo*, Balanchine sustained a dialogue with twentieth-century traditions of what it meant to 'borrow' from the Greek. In his later versions, where the remaining narrative element resides in Apollo's indication of a preference for Terpsichore over Calliope and Polyhymnia, Balanchine privileges the dance as an art form that stands in its own right. Rejecting the purely mimetic connection between words and gesture implied by Ginner's version of Greek dance, his emphasis on form and abstraction nevertheless expresses what she articulated as the worship of Apollo, when 'the human body was regarded as the finest instrument that could be used in the service of god and state'.[48] Leaving behind the Nietzschean struggle for creativity, Balanchine made sure his second *Apollo* marked his arrival in the vanguard of American Modernism and neo-classical style.

---

[47] Lyotard (1984), 81.
[48] Ginner (1960), 20.

17

Dance, Psychoanalysis, and Modernist Aesthetics: Martha Graham's *Night Journey*

Vanda Zajko

In his recently published book *The Dance of the Muses*, A. P. David articulates a vision of the origins of language-based art forms such as poetry and theatre that positions dance squarely in the centre of the cultural frame. Received myth may be seen as linear narrative, and dance as circling, speechless rhythm and yet, David argues:

in the highly stylised and independent medium of the round dance—where the human animal may come to feel, in his erratic sinews, as he joins hands with his community, his measure of participation in the awesome circling of divinity—the dance becomes revelatory of its object . . . the choral form gives shape to myth.[1]

The idea that dance is the earliest form of creative expression and that it establishes a sense of the collective is similarly conveyed by the influential theorist and critic of modern dance, John Martin, in the first of the four lectures he gave at the New School for Social Research in New York in 1931–2 to introduce his audience to what was at the time a largely unknown phenomenon.[2] For Martin, the connection in the modern popular mind between dance and 'the expression of gaiety and exuberance and nothing else' obscures the importance of movement, the 'substance' of modern dance, as 'the most elementary experience of human life'.[3] Martin's alignment of dance with movement (as opposed to with

I would like to thank Pantelis Michelakis and Tom Sapsford for their help with this piece. I would also like to thank participants in the seminar series 'Blood for Ghosts: Modernism and the Classics' at Corpus Christi College Oxford for their thought-provoking discussion, in particular Fiona Macintosh and Kathleen Riley.

[1] David (2006), 30.

[2] These lectures were originally published in book form as *The Modern Dance* in 1933 by A. S. Barnes & Co., Inc., New York and were reprinted without revision in 1965.

[3] Martin (1933), 7–8. He goes on to argue thus (8–9): 'In earlier civilizations, and even today among primitive people, dancing is involved in practically every important experience in the lives both of individuals and of the people as a whole. There are dances of birth, of death, of coming of age, of courtship and marriage, of fertility, of war and pestilence, of casting out devils, of curing the sick. Whenever the primitive mind came into contact with something that happened without his having had anything to do with it, something with the element of mystery and supernaturalism, he danced.' See also the exposition of the term 'metakinesis' at 13–16 where movement is described as 'a medium for the transference of an aesthetic and emotional concept from the consciousness of one individual to that of another'.

design, narrative or music) has been described as 'the logical outcome of his modernist ideology';[4] and he is certainly at pains to forge links between modern dance and anti-representational movements within other art forms in the early part of the twentieth century. The aim of this chapter is to examine whether it is viable to use the term 'Modernist' of modern dance in a manner analogous to its use elsewhere and to survey the part played by the reinvigoration of the classical tradition, so familiar from literary Modernism, in the development of modern dance and in particular in the work of Martha Graham.

The reason there is scope for this project is that dance, as an art form, has tended to be excluded from cultural histories of Modernism, despite the fact that arguably it shares many of the preoccupations of texts that have been included in the modernist canons of the better known fields of literature, music, and the visual arts.[5] *The Cambridge Companion to Modernism*, to take just one example, contains no essay on dance. There are all sorts of possible reasons for this: modern dance began quickly to regard itself as an American creation which was altogether uncompromising in its rejection of the aesthetic values of its European progenitor—classical ballet. Rather than work through its relationship with tradition by sustaining a creative tension with what had gone before, its practitioners were openly and actively hostile and sought to clear a space for themselves that was defiantly contemporary and American.[6] The loathing between the two groups was mutual. Agnes de Mille describes how the practitioners of modern dance were

---

[4] Lepecki (2006), 4.

[5] Louis Horst and Carroll Russell (1961), 15 argue for the similarities between Modernism in dance and in other art forms and give an explanation for why dance lagged behind: 'Because of the inferior status of dance in the culture of the Nineteenth Century, the rebellion against outmoded forms in the dance world didn't appear until the other modern arts were somewhat established. The manner and the reasons for the rebellion are strikingly similar, however, to what occurred with painters, sculptors, musicians and poets. Although there are scores of books about the visions and values in the other modern art fields, little has been written to explain the techniques of dance as a means of aesthetic communication.' However, there is no consensus about this and Sally Banes, for example, argues that 'historical modern dance was never really *modernist*' and that 'in many respects it is post-modern dance that functions as *modernist* art'. For the full discussion see Banes (1977), xiii ff.

[6] It should not, however, be imagined that Europeans played no part in the evolution of modern dance. In their magisterial history of dance in the twentieth-century Nancy Reynolds and Malcolm McCormick establish a genealogy which begins with its North American 'precursors'—Duncan, Fuller, St Denis, and Allan—but which then moves to Germany and the practitioners of *Ausdruckstanz*—most notably Laban and Wigman—before focusing again on artists in the USA and in particular on the developing dance scene in New York. The point here is rather that very quickly, and certainly in the 1930s and 1940s, American dancers began to lay claim to modern dance as their own invention. As Reynolds and McCormick put it (2003), 141–2: 'Throughout this period, when most Americans were still uneasy in the presence of Progressive art movements that were largely European in origin, they were at the same time unaware of their own culture as a source of artistic expression. Dance was associated with the decorativeness and aristocratic implications of the ballet; it seemed unlikely that it could ever mirror the robustness of the American scene. Choreographers in the modern field, dominated by those who became known as the Big Four—Martha Graham, Doris Humphrey, Charles Weidman, and Hanya Holm—were nonetheless insisting that it could. In spite of ideological differences, all concurred on the importance of developing recognizable American idioms.'

disdained by the traditional ballet dancers, who viewed modern dancers as amateur technicians who could not turn pirouettes and were therefore unskilled and deserving of scorn. Although, she adds wryly, 'the scorners did not always bother to go see what it was they were mocking'.[7]

In terms of its self-positioning modern dance does not fit easily into the established narratives of the gestation of Modernism which so often include themes of exile, deliberate displacement from home and quirky engagement with, and complicated deference to, western European classics. Classical ballet's own Modernist texts, most famously *The Rite of Spring* (*Le Sacre du Printemps*) and the three artists associated most prominently with it—Roerich, Nijinsky, and Stravinsky—fit much more comfortably within these established narratives.

This brings us to the second point worth consideration in this context which is that in its formative years modern dance was overwhelmingly, although not exclusively, the province of women. Julia Foulkes has discussed how although female modern dancers did not necessarily embrace specific goals about changing the status of women, they did have leading roles as choreographers, performers, teachers, and directors of companies and this placed them in the middle of ongoing debates about what women were capable of, the differences and similarities between men and women, and the role of women as creators of and commentators on American culture.[8] It may be that this predominance of women has played a part in the neglect of modern dance by theorists of Modernism, particularly given the way that as a loosely defined movement it has traditionally been regarded as masculinist, preferring 'firm, hard, dry, terse, classical masculinity, over against the messy, soft, vague, flowery, effusive, adjectival femininity of the late Victorians'.[9]

The third factor to consider is the position of modern dance in relation to the institutional and public contexts of review and scholarship that from the first did so much to promote Modernist agendas. Like those of psychoanalysis, the professional training organizations of modern dance have always been situated outside of universities and have never been considered mainstream: in addition, there were fewer journals devoted to new forms of dance than to innovative writing and visual art and the relation between the two. The journal *Dance Observer* founded by Louis Horst in 1934 and edited by him until his death in 1964 was dedicated to the task of persuading its readership that modern dance was an improvement on all other forms; and John Martin, the aforementioned dance critic of the *New York Times* from 1927 onwards did much to introduce and elucidate the new forms to his readers. Nonetheless, the absence of public intellectuals with a mission to articulate a Modernist dance agenda *in words* probably contributed to the lack of recognition afforded the discipline both at

---

[7] De Mille (1991), 161.
[8] Foulkes (2002), 29.
[9] Dekoven (1999), 176.

the time, and in more recent wide-ranging surveys of innovation in the arts in the early twentieth century.

Of course, dance has its own historians who write about its specific genealogies, and their accounts vary in terms of their emphasis on either continuity or rupture in ways that are reminiscent of literary history: depending on the argument being pursued, particular practitioners may be grouped together by virtue of thematic or political similarities or separated from each other because an element found in the work of one but absent in that of another is deemed crucial for defining a significant aesthetic moment. And if the aim is to stress the originality of the choreography of later periods, say the 1960s and 1970s, the innovation of dancers in the 1920s and 1930s is downplayed.[10] Within the context of dance history, debates over the definition of Modernism, its limits and scope, its relation to modernity, its status as, for example, oppositional aesthetic practice or inert periodizing term, are largely coterminous with those within the field of literary Modernism. There are also similar debates about the relative status of terms such as primitivism and classicism and their relation to the overall modernist project.[11] We shall now evaluate the status of this project as it took shape in dance with particular reference to the work of Martha Graham, and even more particularly, to her dance-dramatization of the Oedipus myth *Night Journey*. Compelling questions arising from this material will be how the relation between ancient myth and modern art form is configured by Graham, and the extent to which her mytho-poietic practice contributes to her position as a theorist of Modernism.

I

Martha Graham's oeuvre spans some 60 years—her first piece as an independent choreographer was staged in 1926 and her last in 1990—and so the options when it comes to categorizing her work are various. She was trained, in as much as that word does justice to the unorthodox and multifaceted programme experienced by its students, at Denishawn, the famous Californian school run by Ted Shawn and Ruth St Denis. Some of the intellectual ideas that later manifested themselves in her work seem to have had their origin there, in particular, perhaps, her sense of having access to the world as resource, both in terms of time and of

---

[10] An interesting example of this phenomenon comes from a recent 'revisionist' account of the work of Loïe Fuller (Garelick 2007). Fuller's work has tended to be portrayed as evidencing the sentimental kind of classicizing against which Graham rebelled. This book, however, describes her as 'exhibiting a typically modernist Hellenism' (176) and traces connections between Fuller's 'giant veil technique' and Graham's harnessing of breath to create 'her signature motions of contraction and release' (187–94).

[11] See Burt (1998), ch. 8, where 'the artistic ideologies of primitivism and Modernism' are discussed in relation to the choreography of Mary Wigman, Katherine Dunham, and Martha Graham.

space. It was at Denishawn that she first came into contact with Mayan, Aztec, and Toltec cultures, Kabuki and Nō theatre and the traditional dances of East India, Greece, and Spain. It was there too that she first developed an interest in the theatrical accoutrements of dance—costume, make-up, set design, and lighting—all elements that contributed to the innovation of her productions throughout her long career. And there that she met and first worked with her life-long collaborator the musician and composer, Louis Horst.[12]

Her aesthetic predilections, however, are generally considered to have developed as part of a revolt against those of the Denishawn school and Graham is often characterized as being part of the 'second generation' of American dancers, distancing herself from the ethos of the first generation which included Isadora Duncan, Loïe Fuller, and Ruth St Denis herself. All of these dancers were renowned for their expressivism: their bodies, unfettered by corsets and petti-coats, typified the liberated American New Woman who had emerged at the turn of the century and derided the artificiality of the *habitus* of the classically trained dancer. Duncan adopted a stylized Grecian drapery and became according to one commentator 'a paradigm of the new eroticism in American dance'.[13] St Denis's preference was for a wild variety of 'authentic' native costumes derived from the East, particularly from Egypt and India.

Graham's austerity in all aspects of her work can plausibly be read as a reaction against the exoticism of her predecessors.[14] It may also perhaps be seen as the pursuit of a kind of classicism where classicism connotes what is pared down, stark, disciplined, and without illusion.[15] The emplotment of dance history as a series of inter-generational conflicts is reinforced by the characterization of Merce Cunningham, for a time a member of the Graham company, as a rebel son who

---

[12] Horst is an extremely significant figure in his own right who is credited with establishing an innovative relationship between dance and music by separating out the two and composing his scores after the choreography was complete. His impact on Graham was overwhelmingly positive and it is surprising, and disappointing, therefore, that in her study of creative partnerships, *Creative Collaboration*, Vera John-Steiner cites Graham's collaboration with her sometime husband Erick Hawkins as the more significant relationship. For an evaluation of Horst see Reynolds and McCormick (2003), 144–5; Mazo (2000), 160–1; and Horst's own account of his intellectual influences and work process in Horst & Russell (1961), *passim*. In the foreword to the latter, Graham states that without Horst 'modern dance in America would not be what it is today and modern dance in any style all over the world would be without the magic of his imagination, his cruelty, his demonic will, and his skill'.

[13] Hanna (1988), 5.

[14] That said, Garelick (2007), 190 makes a convincing connection between Graham's experiments with costume, and in particular the lilac tube of jersey in which she performed her 1930 piece *Lamentation*, and Fuller's practice of obscuring her body in voluminous swathes of material.

[15] We should bear in mind, after all, that classicism has always been a site of contestation and was so within Modernist discourse more generally. James Porter (2005), 308 has recently argued that the ideology of classicism 'seeks to instill a feeling, the feeling of proximity to or identity with what is classical'. For Graham, as I shall argue, the classical was to be found primarily in the stark and unflinching narratives of myth that spoke to her so directly and powerfully across centuries and cultures.

in his turn reacted against his mentor's intellectualism and single-mindedness.[16] But the use of generational metaphors to describe ideological differences in this case, as so often, works to suppress some of the continuities between practitioners and evens out into a bland difference some of the most interesting points of contestation between them. So the debate about the extent of Graham's own expressivism is often undertaken in the shadow of Cunningham's own rejection of the idea of the body as a vehicle for conveying emotion. This has the result that the tension between expressivism and abstraction in Graham is underplayed and her work becomes caricatured as an oppressively long shadow that younger dancers fought to escape from.

Graham's extensive output has led to the partition of her work into different periods or stages. As with all progressivist narratives a continuous sense of development can be misleading, but it is inevitable that commentators should struggle for some sense of coherence when confronted with such a diverse and extensive body of work. Graham's extraordinary productivity does distinguish her from some other modernist icons whose celebrity and impact tends to be associated with one or two seminal texts, but within the dance world she is heralded as having made the same kind of indelible impression as a Joyce or a Pound. One survey, *Prime Movers* by Joseph Mazo, begins the chapter on Martha Graham with the assertion that when future lists of those who devised and organized the twentieth century's modes of perception are compiled, the name of Martha Graham will be enrolled amongst them and she will take her rightful place as 'one of the moulders of the age' alongside Darwin, Marx, Freud, Lenin, Einstein, Picasso, Stravinsky, Joyce, and the rest.[17] And Graham's status as a major creative figure has also been asserted by feminist writers who, since the 1990s, have worked hard to address the issues at stake in the construction of a Modernist canon that has privileged 'the European metropolitan (in particular, Paris and London) over the regional, the formally experimental over the realist and the popular' and centred its attention on a few dominant white male figures.[18] Their alternative roll call ranks Graham amongst other American women such as Gertrude Stein, H.D., and, perhaps most pertinently, Georgia O'Keefe.[19]

---

[16] See e.g. the account in Mazo (2000), 201–40. Mazo comments (211) that one of Cunningham's favourite words was 'multiplicity'.

[17] Mazo (2000), 153.

[18] See e.g. the discussion in the introduction of Stevens and Howlett (2000).

[19] The sense of space and light in O'Keefe's work is comparable to that conveyed, for example, by Graham's *Primitive Mysteries* (1931) and *Frontier* (1935). There is also a similarity in the quality of 'Americanness' evoked by both artists. Horst and Russell (1961), 122, 124, try to conjure up a sense of this quality as follows: 'The typical American has a lust to move, to go, to look for new frontiers...The "100% American" is direct and homely and proud of his simpleness, his straightforwardness. In revolt against the effete artificiality of Europe, the early settlers worshipped the honest, the open, the plain.... Walt Whitman was probably the first to stir America to the realization of her own indigenous beauty and spirit. The Regional Painters—Curry, Benton and Wood—and the novelist, Sinclair Lewis, emphasized a new ideal of subject matter. Now artists in every field have ceased to consider study in Europe a necessity. Frank Lloyd

II

Let us turn now to *Night Journey*, first performed by Graham and Company at the Cambridge High and Latin School in Massachusetts on 3 May 1947 and captured on video in a production from 1976 directed by Merrrill Brockway.[20] In the opening sequence, a woman's body, arms outstretched, sways slightly as if dangling from a noose; a twisted bed-like structure that looks as though it might be constructed from giant bones imbues the space of the stage with a sense both of intimacy and of death; to the left a sequence of small geometric shapes, to the right an oversize circular boulder and inverted L-shaped structure simultaneously evoke the architecture of a generalized antiquity and the pared-down abstraction of modern sculpture. The juxtaposition of these miniaturized and gigantic shapes disconcertingly distorts the spatial perspective and the landscape does not quite seem to fit the human form. Agnes de Mille describes *Night Journey* as 'a ballet dealing with unrelieved misery', performed 'on props and contrivances of the most uncomfortable nature that Noguchi could assemble' (see Figure 17.1). She imagines the bed he created to represent the abstract figures of a man and a woman lying facing each other and suggests that 'Jocasta and Oedipus rolling on top of this couple presented the appearance of stacked cadavers in a concentration camp'.[21]

Even before there is movement, then, the opening scene of *Night Journey* provides some clues as to the kind of rendering of the Oedipus myth it will be— set within a densely symbolic terrain, the classical and the modern are held together in a mutually defining embrace. Of the mountainside, the crossroads, and the Sphinx there is no sign and the story will begin near the end of Sophocles' version at the moment of the suicide of Jocasta. The dance begins with the entrance of Tiresias whose progression across the stage is made more portentous by the banging of his staff on the ground: he uses his staff to break the circle of the noose and the poised moment of Jocasta's reverie. From this point onwards the events portrayed are taking place within her memory as she revisits her relationship with Oedipus, recalling the moment of their meeting, their potent mutual seduction, and so the events that precipitate her decision to take her own life. The chorus is made up of young women and not, as in Sophocles' play, of august Theban elders.

Wright, with the smell of the Wisconsin farm land (where he worked as a boy) in his nostrils, wanted his buildings " . . . to come out of the ground into the light—the ground itself held always as a component part of the building itself." His designs were shaped by the Western plains and the political climate of the democracy to which he belonged.'

[20] This production sees Martha Graham recreating her role of Jocasta, music is by William Schuman, stage design by the sculptor Isamu Noguchi, lighting by Jean Rosenthal, and costume design is by Graham herself.

[21] De Mille (1991), 281.

Figure 17.1 Martha Graham as Jocasta in *Night Journey* (1947).

The dramatic technique of telling a story retrospectively, figuring its events as the internal vision of a figure in crisis looking back upon the crucial events of a life, is one that Graham used elsewhere, most pertinently for this discussion in her 1958 *Clytemnestra*. Her use of this technique might be considered to reveal that her principal concern was with the internal life of individuals, especially of women. Horst and Russell certainly recognize it as characteristic of her work and comment that her 'typical dramatic scene is laid within the mind or heart of a woman faced with an urgency for decision or action'.[22]

Graham's retrospective tellings might also be identified with the kind of self-consciously revisionist myth-making that takes as its starting point the idea that retelling a story from the perspective of a previously under- or mis-represented voice or figure from *within* an ancient text will validate a contemporary

---

[22] Horst and Russell (1961), 92.

reading.[23] I want to argue, however, that above and beyond these factors, the sense of individuality that pervaded Graham's work was one that owed much to its expansion within psychoanalytic writing, and that her choice to engage with mythic texts was bound up with her conviction that they allowed both the dancer and the observer to connect with atavistic instincts of profound significance beyond the merely individual.

Graham's conviction is clearly bound up with her sense of the classical that seems to equate, as I mentioned earlier, with a conviction of the potential of myth to speak to the modern condition. The following comments of James Porter about 'feeling classical' could almost serve as a comment on Graham's encounter with myth and an explanation for her preoccupation with it:

But while the feeling that accompanies the appropriate stance and attitude towards the classical past is one that can be learned or put on and affected, there is another way in which the feeling of being classical comes to be assumed. For above all it happens, as it were, before one knows it: it takes place in the very presupposition of a classical past, of a past that can address itself to the present and make its values felt and heard. For this reason, feeling classical is both an inarticulate experience of the highest order (it is felt, but not named) and the source of seemingly endless articulation (it asks to be named and described, to be put into language).[24]

The 'language' that Graham utilizes to articulate her vision of the classical is, of course, the language of movement and this might be said to mediate between the positions of articulacy and inarticulacy described here by Porter by allowing for a kind of 'physical stimulation and emotional release through action'[25] that by-passes the intellect or is somehow prior to it. We might recall here how Freud describes the work of analysis using the metaphor of translation, urging 'the translation of what is unconscious into what is conscious'.[26] The inarticulate experience of feeling classical is translated by Graham into the 'target language' of dance, but dance itself is an intermediary discourse that allows for the expression of a greater degree of unconscious material than language-based art forms. This somewhat clumsy formulation aims to convey the idea of the special relationship dance was perceived to have in this period with the unconscious primal instincts and energies of human beings, an idea which underpinned the creative choices of dance practitioners and which is also implicitly conveyed by the statements of David and Martin which began this chapter.

The engagement of Graham with psychoanalytic ideas is well known, at least in so far as the title of her autobiography *Blood Memory* has been identified as

---

[23] For a discussion of this kind of myth-making in the context of feminist strategy see Zajko (2008).

[24] Porter (2005), 308.

[25] Horst and Russell (1961), 15.

[26] 'Transference' in Penguin Freud Library 1.486. See also the final chapter of Bowlby (2007), 'Retranslations, Reproduction, Recapitulations'.

referring to Jung's notion of the collective unconscious, in the words of Graham herself to 'the point where your body is something else and it takes on a world of cultures from the past, an idea that is very hard to express in words'.[27] Her relationship with her 'alienist' father is generally held in part accountable for her early and continuing interest in psychology and in the relationship between body and mind—in her autobiography she recounts how as a child she witnessed the fidgety, nervous actions of one of her father's patients and enquired of him why the young woman behaved in this way. He replied that she was not well and that was what her body was expressing, offering the additional gnomic explanation that 'movement never lies'. We might think here of a comment made by Freud in the 'Fragment of an Analysis of a Case of Hysteria':

> When I set myself the task of bringing to light what human beings keep hidden within them, not by the compelling power of hypnosis, but by observing what they say and what they show, I thought the task was a harder one than it really is. He that has eyes to see and ears to hear may convince himself that no mortal can keep a secret. If his lips are silent, he chatters with his fingertips; betrayal oozes out of him at every pore.[28]

Graham's friendship and correspondence with the Jungian analyst, Frances Wickes has been documented by her biographers; and her encounter with the mythographer, Joseph Campbell (Campbell's wife, Jean Erdman, was for a time a member of Graham's company) has also been cited as a context for Graham's exploration of psychoanalytic ideas (see further Bannerman, this volume). These factors can certainly be considered when evaluating Graham's oeuvre; and yet the claim that her work is psychoanalytically informed need not depend on reconstructions of her personal relationships: the New York City of the 1930s and 1940s, the context for Graham's most innovative productions, was saturated with the insights and theories of the early psychoanalysts to the extent that it became inevitable that artists working there in a whole variety of media became fascinated with and influenced by them.

In her book *Terrible Honesty: Mongrel Manhattan in the 1920s*, Ann Douglas argues that 'no metropolis anywhere took up psychoanalysis so eagerly as New York', recalling how The International Psychoanalytic Society established its main American headquarters there within a few years of Freud's own visit to the city in 1909 and that over the decades its members proved more loyal to Freud and his teachings than any other group.[29] By the early 1920s there were about 500 Freudian or quasi-Freudian analysts practising there and translations of Freud and articles popularizing his ideas were being published in sufficient quantities to ensure that the culturally literate public were familiar with them. We have only to think of the two famous Barrymore productions of Shakespeare,

---

[27] Graham (1991), 13.
[28] 'Fragment of an Analysis of a Case of Hysteria' in Penguin Freud Library 8. 114.
[29] Douglas (1995), 123.

Macbeth and *Hamlet* in 1920 and 1922 for examples of theatrical performances which were avowedly Freudian and recognised by critics and audiences as such.[30]

Graham's notebooks and autobiography show that she was a voracious and eclectic reader and highly aware of her artistic environment and she was certainly excited by the experimentation taking place in other media. Recalling her reaction to her first exposure to modern paintings, she forges links between the creativity of Matisse and Gauguin and her own: 'I had never seen such glory. I realized then that I wasn't mad, not crazy, but I had "ancestors" who had walked this way before me. It has to do with, I would say, the explosion of a spirit and the defiance of a tradition.' And McCandlish Phillips of *The New York Times* quotes Graham's reaction to a painting by Kandinsky—a slash of red on a blue background—which again shows her making connections between her work and experiments with form in the visual arts: 'Perhaps you might call [my work] painting with movement. It has color, it has continuance of line, it has shock, and it should have vibrancy.'[31] Attuned to the upheavals in the world around her and the rejection of mimetic practices in other art forms, Graham figures herself as working within an alternative tradition of creative innovators whose inspiration comes not only from contemporary stimuli but also from a shared sense of the past, a past which connects with the present in non-linear, non-rational, non-linguistic ways.

Exploring the traces of the past in the present is of course a key concern of psychoanalysis because for Freud, famously, 'nothing that has once come into existence will have passed away'.[32] Whether one veers towards a reading of his work that emphasizes its positivistic use of the archaeological metaphor of recovery, or one that emphasizes the provisionality and performativity of the narrative constructed by the dialogue of the analyst and analysand, the past has a central role in making sense of the present. But a sense of the analytic encounter which allows for the dynamics of transference perhaps comes closest to capturing Graham's own sense of the revelation of the truth of the historical in the present. At the end of her life she expressed it thus:

I think you only find the past from yourself, from what you're experiencing now, what enters your life at the present moment. We don't know about the past, except as we discover it. And we discover it from the now.[33]

On the one hand, Graham considers that the dancer must draw on the experiences of her own life to discover whatever it is she has to say, and in this sense she is focused very much on the particularity of the present. On the other hand, there are times when she performs with such magnetism and power and expresses something of such wide-spread significance that 'the sweep of life

---

[30] Morrison (1997), 129–32.
[31] Both these passages are from De Mille's biography (1991), 84.
[32] 'Civilization and its Discontents', in Penguin Freud Library 12. 257.
[33] Graham (1991), 11.

catches up with the mere personality of the performer, and while the individual becomes greater, the personal becomes less personal'.[34] This redefinition of the personal calls to mind its status within the psychoanalytic project as a whole where, rather than being restricted to the discrete realm of private experience, it is positioned instead in dynamic relation to the social. The following quote from Armstrong describes the category of the personal within Freud's writings:

the category itself fits into a larger project where individual analysis and macrohistorical analysis stand in a strangely complementary relation much of the time. This latter move effectively deconstructs the discursive category of the personal in relation to the discrete realm of private experience, putting it instead in dynamic relation to the social, the public, the pre-personal . . . Such a deconstruction is inevitable from within psychoanalysis's own investigative logic, if we consider that Freud's over-all project might be termed an attempt to create a science of the personal, or the incursion of a universalizing discourse of human psychology into the radical specificity of individual experience and sexual object choice.[35]

There is no doubt that for Graham the significance of myth transcends its relevance for any one individual life and *The Notebooks* make clear that Jungian concepts such as the collective unconscious, the existence of race memory, and the psychological potency of archetypal figures also shaped her vision of the creative process. The repressed unconscious ideas made accessible to the artist via dream and myth, fascinated and disturbed her and provoked some of her most discomforting dance-dramas; they also play an important role in mediating the distance between the solitude of the dancer and the collectivity of her audience and allowed the meaning of particular dance-gestures to be inferred, or perhaps better, to be viscerally experienced. De Mille puts it thus:

Primitive (and basic) human relationships assume, therefore, almost mystic power. The simple maneuver of turning the face away, for example, removes personality, presence, the force of attention, relationship. Not only that, it seems to alter the relation of the individual to present time and present place, to mask here-and-now other-where and other-time. It also shifts the particular personalized to the general and the symbolic.

. . . Is it not also likely, then, that certain space relations, rhythms, and stresses have psychological significance, that some of these patterns are universal and the key to emotional response, that their deviations and modifications can be meaningful to the artist in terms of his own life experience and that these overtones are grasped by the spectator without conscious analysis.[36]

Despite the obvious cogencies between this eclectic range of psychoanalytic ideas and the themes emerging in Graham's work, Katherine Power has argued that we should beware of interpreting the work as 'a direct (and uncritical) translation of

---

[34] Ibid. 5.
[35] Armstrong (2005), 38.
[36] De Mille (1991), 141, 142.

psychoanalytic theory into theatrical terms'.[37] For her, Graham's appropriation of the theory is confrontational rather than respectful and particularly takes issue with its male-centred bias and the story of who owns desire, the story 'at the heart of both psychoanalytic theory and the western humanist tradition'.[38] For Power, Graham might call forth the Jungian archetype of the Terrible Mother and represent her as Medea, Clytemnestra, or Jocasta, but she ignores the Jungian project of achieving psychic balance through the encounter of these figures with their opposing forces, and instead allows them to run amok and 'conquer the landscape of the dance (read mind) utterly unopposed'.[39] If we turn now to the consideration of Graham's stance on gender, we shall see that it too is defiantly complex and evades any easy characterization as 'pro-women' or feminist.

III

Graham's particular brand of gendered mythopoiesis has recently been discussed by Nurit Yaari within the context of the works she terms the 'Greek Cycle'. These works that draw upon ancient Greek myth and drama for part of their inspiration span the whole period of Graham's creative life as a choreographer from 1928 to 1987. Nurit argues that Graham rereads ancient myths 'from a modern woman's point of view', and utilizes the ancient narratives to express 'her own quest for self-definition as a modern twentieth-century woman and artist'.[40]

There is no doubt that Graham was indeed interested in the conceptual entailments of what we would now call gender, and it is not accidental that for many years her company consisted only of women. But from the dance vocabulary she evolved throughout her career to the long one-piece costumes she made for her performers, which allowed the body the freedom to move whilst understating the distinctiveness of the female body, she down-played the associations of dance with traditional notions of female sexuality and beauty and with the stylized air-borne movement-scheme of ballet. Her aesthetic preference was for movement that utilized the ground as its inspiration and centre and presented 'strength and virility bordering on ugliness'.[41] She used 'stunning, sharp and percussive patterns of torso contraction and release (movements corresponding to life's breathing, sexual tension, agony and ecstasy, twisting and spiralling spinal movements . . . parallel and inwardly rotated positions of the legs . . . flexed feet' and 'an Egyptian-inspired walk in which feet move in one direction while the upper body twists open against that base, pelvic isolation and falls to the floor'.[42]

[37] Power (1999), 67.
[38] Ibid.
[39] Power (1999), 70.
[40] Yaari (2003), 225.
[41] Franko (1995), 56.
[42] Hanna (1988), 134.

One of the tensions in Graham's work, commented on by contemporary reviewers, is that between expressivity and abstraction. In this regard she shares with other artists of the period a concern with the relation between form and content and between unconscious drives and their manifestation in the body. The idea of the body as symptom, as bypassing language and expressing what is repressed is, of course, central to the discourse of the hysteric, and the contorted bodies of Graham's dancers bear more than a passing resemblance to the bodies of the young women photographed in La Salpêtrière. But in her work, technique is not intended to service the emotions but rather to work towards the perfection of form. In this way, according to Mark Franko, 'emotion entered her choreographic theory as a by-product of subjectivity rather than as a goal of technique'.[43]

Technique, Graham said, 'is a joy and a terror, a bore at times and a necessity always. Those who do not have order and discipline can never be dancers'. At the same time, she also demanded the cultivation of a childlike instinct which she claimed is 'what lets us feel the common pulse of humanity and of history'.[44] Her most famous movement-gesture, the contraction, a scooping movement rendering the spine concave manifests a perfect ambiguity about the expression of emotion and emotionlessness to the extent that it could be interpreted as suggesting sorrow or joy, 'but could also remain fundamentally obscure and even thoroughly abstract'.[45] Graham's commitment to such ambiguity can be seen as representing a struggle to undermine prevailing models of masculinity and femininity and to utilize psychoanalytically informed conceptions of gender to liberate dance from associations with 'the natural'. In this respect we might compare her project with that of Virginia Woolf, when at various times the author experiments with the idea of androgyny as a third term that might be pressed into service to undo the oppressive formations of femininity.[46]

The need for Graham to try to escape the natural associations of women's bodies is illustrated by a story she told in an article in *The New York Times* recalling a comment made by the New York theatre critic, Stark Young when invited to one of her performances: 'Oh must I go? I'm so afraid she is going to give birth to a cube on stage?' This comment does implicitly connect Graham's pioneering choreography with the innovations of cubist painting and so could conceivably be seen as complimentary; but it also shows how as a *woman* dancer her body was inevitably associated with certain biological processes. Graham was not interested in reinforcing the expectations of her audiences but in setting up a

---

[43] Franko (1995), 62.
[44] Mazo (2000), 199.
[45] Franko (1995), 39.
[46] Franko (1995) 56 comments thus: 'Graham's revolt against the classical tradition seemed to be a revolt against an artificial "feminine" in the name of an essential "masculine". Yet, her rhetoric allows a third term to show through in which the feminine is recuperated: an imaginary feminine masculinity. There is thus a double consciousness through which Graham articulates her own experience in male terms, but also reintroduces the feminine.'

potential confrontation between performer and audience and also within the dancers and audience members themselves.[47] She carried on dancing until well into her seventies, and when she did eventually retire from playing the lead roles she had devised, she often expressed her dissatisfaction that the dancers who took her place did not have the stomach for the confrontation that she herself had had.

Her own description of a scene from *Night Journey* where the king and queen consummate their relationship demonstrates the self-conscious provocation of her performance:

Oedipus then enters her life and she finally receives him. He carries her to the stool where she becomes the queen. He dances for her and she rises. Now it is here that I would take three or four steps to encircle the stool, make a wide extension forward, and then three little steps back in hesitancy. She does that but on the third time she falls to her feet.

She has in her hands the branches that Oedipus had given her when he carried her from the bed onto her small stool where she became the queen. She drops into a wide split fall and puts one flower out tentatively toward him, sits back and crosses her knees, opening and closing, opening and closing. It is this that a dancer sometimes avoids, hesitating to realize that she is inviting him into the privacy of her body. He comes forward, takes his cloak, and puts it around her. He picks up the flower and the two proceed to the bed. It is this moment of invitation that is sometimes lacking in the dance. Not every dancer can master this moment. It is not only a movement, but rather a gesture of invitation for him to come between her legs.[48]

One male student coached briefly by Graham is said to have commented uncomfortably that the Martha Graham Dance Company was the one dance company in America where the men suffered from vagina envy, and it is clear that Graham's version of the Oedipus myth is one where the pleasurable and mutual eroticism of the relationship between Oedipus and Jocasta is central and, indeed, where the sexual appetite of the queen is graphically represented both by Graham herself and by the mimetic gestures of the female chorus.[49] Graham emphasizes the active role of the woman in drawing the man into her body and so refocuses the sexual act around the image of incorporation rather than penetration. The chorus, who function throughout as a kind of collective externalization of Jocasta's memory and desire, shore up this image and Oedipus becomes an isolated male presence in a tidal current of contracting female corporeality.[50]

---

[47] See discussion in Foulkes (2002), 41.

[48] Graham (1991), 214–15.

[49] I am reliably informed by Tom Sapsford that the male pelvis is not designed to move in the way that Graham has her dancers move: vagina envy may be less metaphorical in this context than we might assume!

[50] Horst and Russell (1961), 92, describe the dramatis personae of the chorus as performing 'as symbols of her [the queen's] complex emotional reactions'.

IV

In common with many Modernist practitioners in the fields of literature and art, Graham contextualized Greek myth within a broader cultural perspective.[51] It has long been recognized that artists in various media turned towards some notion of the primitive in a search for a simplicity and honesty deemed at times to be chiefly lacking in the modern urbanized world. Simultaneously they turned outwards towards cultures not easily assimilable that offered an alternative vision of collective identity, and inwards towards the hidden depths of a multilayered self that came to signify the radical alterity at the heart of the familiar. In the US there was an additional impetus in that the celebration of cultural forms and artefacts from the New World helped to undermine the cultural hegemony of Europe and to shore up the sense of a specifically North American identity. The trajectory of Graham's work follows these interests, from her early experiences with the Denishawn School where, as I have mentioned, she first came into contact with a variety of dance and theatre traditions from around the world, via the ritualistic pieces in the 1930s such as *Lamentation* (1930) and *Primitive Mysteries* (1931), to the explicitly nationalistic triumph of *Appalachian Spring* (1944), to the myth-inspired dances from the later part of her career.

Dance historians often want to draw a distinction between the dances of Graham's earlier 'primitivist period' and the works she based on classical myths,[52] but for Graham herself they existed on an easy continuum since her claim to the past as her cultural inheritance was not contaminated by any sense of hierarchy. She drew on a range of Penitente Indian and Spanish American ceremonial practices, alongside an eclectic range of Catholic images, as the inspiration for some of her dances, but these rituals were not simply imitated but expanded upon, generalized, and abstracted in order to express both an ambivalence about and commitment to modernity itself. Her sense of 'the primitive' too was a complex and psychoanalytically inflected one. For Freud, establishing a psychoanalytic concept—repression—as the motor of cultural development, ancient Greece was the childhood of civilization and contrasted favourably in terms of its ingenuity and creativity with the over-repressed modern world.[53] And he saw in the mental life of primitive peoples 'a well-

---

[51] So Annes Brown (2007), 441: 'The tendency of Modernist classicism was to emphasise the place of Greek myth within a wider cultural perspective. Through the study of anthropology, the singularity of Greek myth was in a sense diluted by research which linked its core narratives to those of other cultures and existing primitive traditions.'

[52] See e.g. Mazo (2000), 163.

[53] This relational model is set up in the famous comparative analysis of *Hamlet* and Sophocles' *Oedipus Rex* in the *Interpretation of Dreams*, 366: 'Another of the great creations of tragic poetry, Shakespeare's Hamlet, has its roots in the same soil as Oedipus Rex. But the changed treatment of the same material reveals the whole difference in the mental life of these two widely separated epochs of civilisation: the secular advance of repression in the emotional life of mankind. In the Oedipus

preserved picture of an early stage of our own development'.[54] Modern subjects, then, could be conceived as descendants both of ancient Greece and of the other primitive societies whose cultural artifacts and customs were only just beginning to be explored.

Graham's sense of otherness was distinctive to her time and place, as was her lack of self-consciousness at drawing on whatever inspired her. She recalls how during her formative years at Denishawn, Ruth St Denis, dressed in a beautiful Japanese kimono, would speak to the students in gibberish and encourage the students to do likewise. Graham comments:

We were creating our own area of something Japanese, our own vocabulary. We were learning to improvise. . . . While Denishawn used foreign techniques, we were not re-strained by them when necessity called for individuality.[55]

The pressing urge towards creativity was greater than any consideration of what we might today term 'cultural imperialism', and Graham did not feel herself to be restricted by having to make a choice in her improvisations between Modernist abstraction and culturally eclectic primitivism or between European 'high culture' and the traditions of the new world. In this regard her artistic vision was very like that of the other Modernist pioneers who refused to be intimi-dated by prevailing orthodoxies of value and whose radical juxtapositions reshaped the boundaries of their various art forms.[56] Graham's reworking of the myth of Oedipus that had become, via Freud's interpretation, a canonical text of twentieth-century intellectual history, demonstrates how the intimate space of the performer's body became a public space for configuring her distinctive version of modernity.

---

the child's wishful fantasy that underlies it is brought into the open and realised as it would be in a dream. In Hamlet it remains repressed; and—just as in the case of a neurosis—we only learn of its existence from its inhibiting consequences.' The critique of over-repressed modernity continues in the 1908 essay '"Civilized" Sexual Morality and Modern Nervous Illness'.

[54] Penguin Freud Library 13. 53.

[55] Graham (1991), 65.

[56] The comments of Kirk Varnedoe (1998), 254–5 are extremely pertinent here: 'Modern artistic primitivism has, in its broadest implications, a lot to say about the way humans can use their cultural conventions to change themselves and to understand new things . . . It's too simple to say Picasso suddenly saw tribal objects as art. A changing definition of art readied him to see how something formerly excluded could be included—and would further transform the category in the process. . . . This creative use of existing forms as a way of gaining knowledge about the new and unfamiliar, and this way of then using that knowledge to reorder one's own tradition so as to make new meanings expressible, are central to the compelling character of twentieth-century Western art—as central as is its uncommon openness to the art of radically different societies, or to change in general.'

18

Striking a Balance: The Apolline and Dionysiac in Contemporary Classical Choreography

Arabella Stanger

if I appreciate so highly the value of classical ballet, it is . . . because I see exactly in it the perfect expression of the Apollonian principle.[1]

these models that the Greeks provide, the ordered Apollonian and the brilliant chaotic aspect of the Dionysian are both extremely valuable concepts. Finding or striking a balance between the two is a challenge for everyone in their lives.[2]

With the landmark neoclassical ballet *Apollon Musagète* (1928), George Balanchine and Igor Stravinsky re-shaped the field of modernist dance around a composition of classicism in its most pristine order. Viewed through the classical paradigm provided in *Apollo*, the cultural programme of high Modernism may be characterized as an effort to suppress the destructive spirit of the Dionysiac, in favour of choreographing a supreme classical order of Apolline forms.[3] Terry Eagleton, in *Sweet Violence, The Idea of The Tragic* (2003), proposes a later return of the Dionysiac in the cultural logic of the late twentieth century. Eagleton draws out the significance of the idea of 'the tragic' particularly in the intellectual culture of postmodernism, citing 'Dionysian madness *contra* Apollonian social order'[4] as a sensibility that underpins areas of late modern discourse. That which Eagleton describes as 'a syndrome which has re-emerged . . . in the shape of

I would like to extend my sincerest thanks to Fiona Macintosh and Maria Shevtsova for their invaluable support during this project. I would also like to thank Ingo Gildenhard, who supervised, and Ismene Lada-Richards, who examined, the original dissertation on which this chapter is based.

[1] Stravinsky (1975), 100.

[2] Forsythe and Copeland (2001).

[3] *Apollon Musagète* is the work's original 1928 title. It has been known simply as *Apollo* since 1957. See Jones, this volume for a framing of Modernist dance in the context of both its Apolline and Dionysiac associations and of *Apollo*'s significance in terms of early twentieth-century shifts in Modernist thought and culture.

[4] Eagleton (2003), 53.

some postmodern theorizing . . . Nietzschean without fully knowing it',[5] is observable also in the choreography of the late twentieth century where there has been the re-emergence of a Dionysiac sensibility.

In viewing the 1990s oeuvre of two western European-based practitioners who compose in the classical idiom, we may observe a very Nietzschean delivery of obscure Dionysiac spirit, through the architecture of radiant Apolline form. This chapter will consider how choreographers, Michael Clark and William Forsythe, both contemporary artists who display a compositional debt to Balanchine's paradigm of Apolline Modernism, frame through the idiom of a pointedly contemporary classicism, the meeting of Dionysiac madness not only *contra*, but also in tandem with, Apolline order.

The two epigraphs to this chapter express the views of two twentieth-century artists whose work originates within the field of classical ballet. Stravinsky here refers to his and Balanchine's *Apollo*, while Forsythe makes reference to a ballet choreographed over half a century later, his *Eidos: Telos* (1995), a work that demonstrates his self-defined compositional style, 'post classical analysis'.[6] Both Forsythe and Clark, standing as heirs to Balanchine's legacy of a redesigned classicism, pick up narratives and themes from the mythology of ancient Greece to reinvigorate the fundamentally Apolline idiom of classical ballet with a Dionysiac impulse for structural and social abandon. Nietzsche's depiction in *The Birth of Tragedy* (1872) of a generative tension between the creative drives of Apolline and Dionysiac energies, can certainly be traced in the work of Balanchine.[7] In light of Balanchine's legacy, Nietzsche's agonistic impulse is discernible also in some key works created by Clark and Forsythe.

Two pieces from Clark's *Stravinsky Project* trilogy are particularly rich in expressing the Nietzschean duality. *O* (1994, revised 2005) is set to Stravinsky's monumental *Apollon Musagète*, and *Mmm . . .* (1992, revised 2006) is set to the composer's modernist masterpiece, *Le Sacre du Printemps* (1913).[8] Clark's works are composed from a basis of sharp classical precision, but infuse Apolline forms with the performance of both eroticism and ecstasy. *Eidos: Telos* will be taken as the case study from Forsythe's oeuvre. *Eidos*, set to music by Thom Willems inspired by Stravinsky's *Apollon*, uses the myth of Persephone as one of its thematic foundations and presents a programme by which an Apolline classicism may be redefined through a Dionysiac impulse for idiomatic disorder.

It is important to note at this stage that Clark's and Forsythe's engagement with the Apolline/Dionysiac duality is rarely stated as an intentional artistic

---

[5] Eagleton (2003), 53.

[6] Forsythe and Saup (2004).

[7] See Jones, this volume for an analysis of *Apollo* as a work that negotiates the shift from the Dionysiac to Apolline in the context of a wider Modernist aesthetics.

[8] Clark's title *Mmm . . .* makes reference to Stravinsky's *Sacre* by standing, during the work's initial stages of production, as an acronym for 'Michael Clark's modern masterpiece'.

motivation. As such the works analysed here are pieces that both demonstrate intrinsically, rather than proclaim explicitly, the Nietzschean polarity and that make a significant thematic engagement with ancient Greece. If Nietzsche's proposal in *The Birth of Tragedy* provides an aesthetic conception of ancient Greece that proves particularly useful in assessing the modern artistic reception of the ancient world, it has proved especially helpful in analysis of developments in modern ballet.[9] Furthermore, if Eagleton is right in identifying the resurgence of the Dionysiac in the cultural discourse of the late twentieth century, that impulse is no better illustrated than in the choreographies of Clark and Forsythe whose work displays an acute tension in opposing creative energies, as a path to the conceptual incorporation of ancient Greece in contemporary classical choreography.

CLASSICAL BALLET: AN APOLLINE DESIGN

Clark and Forsythe share an initial schema for their respective choreographies: the technique of classical ballet, a form that throughout its historical development has been associated with distinctly Apolline approaches to artistic and social organization. Ballet's institutional formalization within the seventeenth-century French court of Louis XIV, makes alignment to the absolutist principles of order and harmony, where the performances of the *ballet de cour* demonstrate both the delineated social structure and civilized bodily etiquette that configure society at the royal court of the *ancient régime*.[10] Louis XIV forged further Apolline associations by choosing the god Apollo as his personal emblem: the 'Sun King' even embodied his namesake the sun god during, among other spectacles, a performance of *Le ballet de la nuit* (1653) within the gardens of his pleasure palace at Versailles.[11]

An Apolline sensibility can be detected also in the professionalization of ballet in this period (at the foundation of the Académie Royale de Danse in 1661), which heralds both the first systematic designation of the fundamentals of classical technique and the advent of ballet as a form consecrated for individual, non-amateur practice. Through the placement of the classical form in the bodies of individual, trained professionals, and its consequent termination as a primarily amateur practice for performing groups made up of royal courtiers and aristocrats, classical ballet becomes, very early on in its development, distanced from

---

[9] See Silk and Stern (1981), 185, on the 'archetypes' that Nietzsche crafts from Apollo and Dionysus which, they argue, in many ways sit more happily in 'the modern world', than in ancient Greece.

[10] See Franko (1993) for discussion of the development of the French *ballet de cour* as part of a wider cultural imperative for maintaining the structures of absolutist rule.

[11] As detailed in Scholl (1994), 96.

the non-regulated communal practice of the chorus (the realm of the Dionysiac) and dedicated instead to the systematic individualistic practice of the professional (the realm of the Apolline).[12]

Theatrical ballet and its formal classical technique were further crystallized within the Imperial Theatres of nineteenth-century Russia, where Marius Petipa, Director of the Imperial Ballet from 1869–1903, and creator of significant monuments of the classical canon, developed vocabulary according to the ideals of classical proportion, social orderliness, and distilled beauty in form.[13] In mid-twentieth-century New York another Russian choreographer, George Balanchine, executed the most Apolline refinement of classical ballet to date.[14] Balanchine's economy of form composes human geometry through a radicalized technique that embodies the edicts of personal limitation, sculptural simplicity, and schematic purity of craft. However Balanchine's neoclassical expression of the Apolline 'ideal' does not altogether blockade the Dionysiac; and as we shall see through the work of Clark and Forsythe, the choreographic premise of an Apolline classicism becomes a structure through which Dionysiac impulses may thrive.

Ancient Greece has been a popular subject for Modernist innovators in the field of dance, all of whom engage with this world through a variety of methods very distinct from Balanchine's structural presentation of Apolline principles. Methods include the invoking of an ancient philosophical and behavioural ideal through unfettered dance performance as the enactment of social emancipation (Isadora Duncan); the staging of a stylized Greek aesthetic through evocative stage design and passionate, expressive bodies (Michel Fokine's work with Léon Bakst for the Ballets Russes); the lustful, anti-academic creatures of mythology presented as animated friezes (Vaslav Nijinsky's *L'Après-midi d'un Faune*, 1912), or the replotting of Athenian narratives through dance that performs the drama of psychology as much as it does a technique of the body (Martha Graham—see further Bannerman and Zjako, this volume).

Late twentieth-century choreographers have also turned to the ancient world by largely building on the templates left to them by their Modernist progenitors. The 'emotion made movement'[15] of one of Pina Bausch's earliest works, *Orpheus und Eurydike* (1975), locates her as an inheritor not only of the German *Ausdruckstanz* movement, but also, as a modern interpreter of mythological narrative, of Graham's choreographic psycho-dramas. Mark Morris's *Dido and Aeneas* (1989) stages a narrative as choreographically dark and sumptuous as

---

[12] For Nietzsche's discussion of the individual, and in particular the notion of individuation *vis à vis* the Apolline, see Nietzsche, (1999), 26–7. All references to *The Birth of Tragedy* in this chapter are taken from this English edition. For Nietzsche's discussion of the chorus as associated with communality and the Dionysiac see 36–46.

[13] Petipa's defining *grands ballets* of the classical canon include *The Sleeping Beauty* (1890), and, with Lev Ivanov, *Swan Lake* (1895).

[14] For details of Balanchine's background, see Jones in this volume.

[15] Boccadoro (2005).

Purcell's operatic score. The choice of Morris to cast himself as the original Dido both complicates this tragedy of desire and loss and recalls Graham's own reassignment of traditional gendered roles within mythology, in works such as *Night Journey* (1947). Another North American choreographer, Twyla Tharp continues to extend the legacy of Graham and Greek mythology, in her work choreographed for the Martha Graham Company in 1993, *Demeter and Persephone*; while Lucinda Childs in 2003 turns to a work from the Ballets Russes canon, *Daphnis et Chloe*, set to Ravel's score, choreographed originally by Fokine in 1912.

Clark and Forsythe differ from the various routes forged by many of their contemporaries, whose works largely pick up threads left by Graham and Diaghilev's stable of artists. Instead they follow clearly in the footsteps of Balanchine, in that they craft and incorporate a philosophical understanding of ancient Greece (Nietzsche's identification of the Apolline/Dionysiac tension) through the primarily idiomatic tools of the classical technique. It is through the legacy of Balanchine—particularly directed through two of his 'Greek' works *Apollo* and *Agon* (1957)—that the works of Clark and Forsythe, both as radical restagings of the classical form and contemporary restagings of ancient Greece, engage with the Apolline/Dionysiac question.

Balanchine's *Apollo* is a choreographic realization of ancient Greece that diverges from the exotic, erotic, and Dionysiac world of Diaghilev's Ballets Russes for whom the work was originally created, and finds form instead in the idiomatic and narrative crystallization of the Apolline ideal.[16] The ballet maps a biography of the young god Apollo presenting his evolution from uncultured, Dionysiac youth, toward civilized Apolline divinity: in movement, music and structure the piece plots Apollo's journey as he moves towards refinement, self-control and divine maturity. The ultimate and literal embodiment of the Apolline principle occurs at the end of the work, when Apollo and the muses make their ascent to Mount Parnassus as a performance of Apollo's apotheosis: Stravinsky's score here plots a steady tempo and forbidding diminuendo that leads to the summit of orchestral and melodic harmony. *Apollo* marked both the turning point in Balanchine's own career and the zenith of Apolline classicism in choreography for the stage.[17]

The Apolline imperative to clarify was sustained throughout Balanchine's oeuvre, particularly in his 'leotard ballets' where the arch legibility of his dancers' bodies were exposed through sleek practice clothes and an empty, starkly lit stage. One such ballet is *Agon*, whose première on 1 December 1957 in New York's City Center of Music and Drama was the result of almost ten years' gestation.

[16] Scholl (1994), 79–104, views *Apollo* in terms of a movement away from the values of the earlier Diaghilev period and asserts: 'the ballet supplants the Dionysian sensuality of Nijinsky's work with a classical apollonian purity', 98.

[17] Balanchine (1982), 17, says of the work: '*Apollon* I look back on as the turning point of my life. In its discipline and restraint, in its sustained oneness of tone and feelings, the score was a revelation. It seemed to me that I could dare not to use everything, that I, too, could eliminate.'

Lincoln Kirstein had first suggested the ballet to Stravinsky in 1948, after the success of Stravinsky and Balanchine's second 'Greek' collaboration *Orpheus* (1948). *Agon* went through many Greek-themed titles including *Terpischore* and *Nausicaa*,—the latter especially anticipating a narrative engagement with Greek mythology—before its more abstract incarnation as simply a 'competition before the gods'; hence *Agon* ('contest'), was decided upon.[18]

Once this official commission for *Agon* had been agreed in around 1953, Kirstein sent Stravinsky a seventeenth-century dance composition manual by F. De Lauze; the ballet academy and legacy of Louis XIV thus imprinting *Agon* with a distinctly Apolline ancestry. *Agon*'s structure, a suite of boldly modernized 'historical' dances such as a *courante*, *branle*, and *passepied*, presents the Sun King's *danse d'école* within the angular bodies and geometrical framework of a modern Apolline craftsman.[19] Classicism (both Greek and ballet-academic) and the driving force of a stark Apolline economy, are presented clearly in this work, and while *Agon*'s title is the most explicit thematic reference to ancient Greece, the ballet's idiom stages a contemporary classicism where not only Apollo but also Dionysus provide driving choreographic principles. The neoclassical works of Balanchine's career, as Susan Jones detects in the choreographer's revisions of *Apollo* in this volume, move increasingly toward, 'a more assured "Apolline" aesthetics of beauty'.[20] However, what is striking about *Agon* is the extent to which the Apolline exists in taut relation to the Dionysiac. This tension can be observed in the celebrated *Pas de Deux* that closes the second section of the work.

The *Pas de Deux* is itself a demonstration of the athleticism and technical finesse that Balanchine had refined at this point in both his choreography and the dancers produced through his training system.[21] However, despite the Apolline constructions of Balanchine's idiom on which the work is hinged (clean geometrical lines, bodies used to plot classical scaffolding), the work demands a dangerous disregard of gravity and exhibits an explicit sexuality.

Toward the end of the work, the two dancers break from a fiendishly fast sequence of supported *allegro*, rapid *pirouettes* and high leg extensions, and emerge, at Stravinsky's bold change of pace, into a slow and sensuous *adagio*. The female dancer manoeuvres herself into a languid *arabesque* behind the male dancer who has dropped at this point to his knees to face the audience, offering his shoulders as her support. She continues to fold into a deep *arabesque penché* over his shoulder (as the working leg extends up behind the body, the torso hinges forward toward the floor, enabling a 180 degree line from toe to toe), so

---

[18] For a more detailed account of the events that lead to *Agon*'s creation see Hodgins (1992), 38, 99–100.
[19] Hodgins (1992), 91 details the social dance forms from which Stravinsky and Balanchine draw.
[20] Jones, this volume.
[21] The work was choreographed on Diana Adams and Arthur Mitchell; two dancers whose technical flair underlines the style that was typically produced through Balanchine's training.

that her head hovers face-first just by his groin and her working leg extends high and straight above them both. This suggestive image is typical of what Sally Banes terms the 'imaginative and extreme sexual acrobatics'[22] of *Agon*, and demonstrates a transmission of the more Dionysiac stirrings of human experience through the clean Apolline architecture of modern classical virtuosity.

CLARK'S *STRAVINSKY PROJECT*

This presentation of Dionysiac instinct through Apolline form, particularly through the use of the classical body to reference the sexual act, is a trope that comes to define the classical technique as used by a younger admirer of Balanchine, Michael Clark, who in 1994 revealed his attitude to Balanchine and his classical inheritance generally: 'Balanchine's *Apollo* is an amazing piece of work, but I hate that idea that you can't create anything new . . . You have to redefine classicism . . . you have to add new words to the language or it dies out.'[23]

Clark was born in Aberdeen, Scotland in 1962 and as a youth was successful in Scottish Dancing before joining the Royal Ballet's London-based lower school, White Lodge, in 1975. Clark's natural ability was quickly noticed during training and he was proposed as one of the most outstanding classical dancers the School had produced in recent years.[24] At this time Clark received his classical training in the *Cecchetti* system. Enrico Cecchetti, Italian born and trained, was *Maître de Ballet* with the Imperial Ballet in St Petersburg and teacher at the Imperial Ballet School from 1887 to 1902. Cecchetti is an important founding father of academic ballet technique; and the formal purity of his technique and fluid quality of its style are qualities for which Clark would be lauded as a dancer, and which craft a distinctly Apolline approach to dancing classical ballet.[25]

At the time of his formal training, Clark also began to explore the cultural life of 1980s London, in particular experiencing the punk and New Wave music scene surrounding bands such as *Throbbing Gristle* and *Wire* and joining the underground clubbing scene unfolding around performance artists such as Leigh Bowery and Trojan. These contemporary influences would be incorporated as major defining characteristics of Clark's work: indeed the early pieces produced by Clark's dance troupe (formed in 1984 when Clark was just 22 years old) would become key to defining the aesthetic and stylistic concerns of this multi-generic artistic group itself. Just as Clark's academic training provides a base for

---

[22] Banes (1998), 204.

[23] Watson (1994).

[24] Don Macpherson (1984), in a review of *New Puritans* (1984) at Riverside Studios, describes Clark as 'the most gifted classical dancer of his generation'.

[25] In an early review Alistair Macaulay (1981) praises Clark's 'insouciant command . . . fleet elegance . . . and seamless phrasing' as a dancer with Ballet Rambert.

his exploration of Apolline features in choreography, so many of these influences from his own cultural environment—for example the raw driving energy of punk music, the erotic overtones of flesh-baring fashion design and the perceived 'excess' of an ecstatic clubbing culture—combine to signify the invasion of a contemporary Dionysiac experience in the aesthetic, choreography, and performance of classical dance.

Clark's *Stravinsky Project*, a three year project made from 2005–8 in partnership with London's Barbican Centre, features the re-workings of earlier pieces: 2005's *O* and 2006's *Mmm…*, as well as a new work *I do* (2007) set to Stravinsky's *Les Noces* (1923). Thematically *O* engages with explicitly Apolline principles while *Mmm…* explores explicitly Dionysiac urges; and through theme and form both works present the most acute meeting of Apolline classicism and Dionysiac excess that we find in all of Clark's oeuvre.

The Apolline clarity of Stravinsky's *Apollon* is taken as the momentum for *O*, which narrates a simple plot close to that of Balanchine's original version (Figure 18.1). First, we are shown the birth of Apollo who emerges after a solo of self-exploration from within a large mirrored cube structure, followed by the solos of three muses.[26] Next comes a *pas de deux* for Apollo and Terpischore and the final 'apotheosis' in which (as performed in November 2007) the muses sink to the floor on their backs, facing the heavens and earthbound, while Apollo slowly dives into an *arabesque penché* (providing, like the *penché* in *Agon*, phallic imagery through classical exercise), his working leg hinging up toward the heavens, his torso and gaze fixed below.

Mmm… presents an even simpler plot driven by a Dionysiac progression toward ecstatic transcendence in sacrifice. The work is made up of a series of dances with varying numbers of bodies (a total of twelve dancers make up the 2006 version) and performed to varying levels of orgiastic fervour, with a token 'blessing of the earth' scene by The Sage (played originally by Bowery). The ballet closes with the Chosen Maiden's sacrificial solo: as danced by soloists of both gender, this final rite becomes a study in a violent yet meticulous hysteria.

In movement vocabulary Clark demonstrates a clear concern with the confrontation of an Apolline structure in classical technique and Dionysiac urges of the human body. As Catherine Wood observes, Clark is 'engaged in a process of trying to … reconcile connections between the contradictory states of the body's personalities: … the natural impulses and drives of the body versus the repressed abstraction of formal training'.[27] We can detect this particularly in the idiom Clark has developed: a skewed and sensuous mutation of classical positioning where the centre of gravity is lowered and an erotic body is sculpted through movement initiating from the centre of the pelvis. A demonstration of this

---

[26] Clark follows Stravinsky and Balanchine's libretto which incorporates solos for Calliope, Polyphymnia and Terpischore.
[27] Wood (2004), 38.

Figure 18.1 Michael Clark's *O* (2005).

lascivious posture opens the prologues to *O* and *Mmm*...where a tense and contorted dragging walk is performed from the corners of the stage with dancers extending perfectly academic legs and feet to follow the pelvis, which is thrust forward to lead all movement. This formalized prowl is performed in slow motion by various dancers to the song *Theme* (1978), a dirge by British post-punk band, Public Image Ltd (PiL).

The prologues to *O* and *Mmm*...may be defined as Dionysiac in being set, typically for Clark, to a soundtrack of punk: a musical form that grew out of late 1970s western youth cultures. Punk is characterized by short discordant compositions of extreme volume and tempo; high octane public performances leading to chaotic and sometimes violent audience participation; and on occasion political dissent in the use of goading anti-establishment lyrics. This is certainly the case with British groups who emerged from pre-Thatcher Britain, such as the Sex Pistols whose song *Submission* (1977) is also used in these prologues.

In rejecting radically individualist social politics such as those espoused by Thatcherism and turning instead to the experiential extremes offered through drug use and the ear-splitting rapture of musical discordance, the space of 1980s punk culture offers a modern experience of Dionysiac intoxication and self-oblivion. Mckenzie Wark cites Nietzsche in order to propose punk as a contemporary form of Dionysiac music:

What punk discovered was...some of the neglected Dionysian territories of western aesthetics...They took simple musical forms and ground them down until they liquefied, often dissolving into chaos. And they took their audience with them. The punk aesthetic had a Nietzschian impulse to show a public that 'their entire existence, with all its beauty and moderation, was based on a veiled substratum of suffering and knowledge, revealed to them once again by the Dionysiac.'[28]

In marked discord with the music of Apollo, which Nietzsche describes as 'Doric architectonics in sound',[29] the sound of punk finds its ancient precursor in the dithyramb. Both these forms draw closer to Dionysiac intoxication through sonic frenzy where 'music alone allows us to understand the delight felt at the annihilation of the individual'.[30] In this way the use of a punk soundtrack, whether in preparation for the ecstatic dissonance of Stravinsky's *Sacre* or for the harmonious strains of his *Apollon*, forms a sonic and experiential prologue to Clark's exploration of the Dionysiac in classical choreography.[31]

---

[28] Wark (1999), 154. Compare Wark's location of the Dionysiac in 1980s' punk culture, with the discussion by Hall (2004), 9, and Zeitlin (2004), 51–2, of a slightly earlier 'Dionysiac' cult in the psychedelic music and drug culture of the late 1960s' and early 1970s' North American hippie movement.

[29] Nietzsche (1999), 21.

[30] Ibid. 101–2.

[31] Silk and Stern (1981), 378, discuss musical dissonance as characteristically Dionysiac.

A major route through which Clark introduces a Dionysiac impulse to the Apolline structures of classical ballet is through a choreography of eroticism. Clark has observed that 'sex is at the heart of [his] work';[32] and the Apolline and Dionysiac are placed in direct conflict within *O* and *Mmm . . .* through the themes of birth and death and their entwining with a potent sensuality. *O*'s birth sequence, for example, in which Apollo (played originally by Clark) grows within and emerges from the mirrored cube, imbues the Apolline sculptures of primary classical vocabulary with the erotic self-worship of a Dionysiac youth. Apollo, clothed in white lycra, begins his self-exploratory solo upside down by walking his feet up one side of the cube and extending one leg over his head into a deep inverse split, recalling Leto's split at the original labour scene of Balanchine's *Apollo*. Apollo slowly finds his feet within the cube and progresses to one of the cardinal positions of classical ballet: he takes a hypnotic series of *battements tendus* (where one foot points to the floor, extending the leg in a straight diagonal from the hip) on all alignments whilst constantly measuring his appearance in the reflective surface of his cube. The academic precision of this sequence, illuminated in a white lighting design, radiates a sculptural beauty evocative of Michelangelo's *David*, casting Apollo in marble as a young god. Dionysiac energies, however, still prevail: the sequence is blissful and trance-like in its pacing and Apollo's self-regard communicates a sensuous and potentially transgressive desire.

This is not the contemplative self-measure of an individual drawing up boundaries of self-knowing, but is the trance of a creature seduced by his own image and drawn, beyond the beauty of Apolline forms, towards Dionysiac rapture. The sequence performs the Dionysiac's engulfing of Apolline individuation where '[t]he individual, with all his limits and measure, became submerged . . . in the self-oblivion of the Dionysiac condition and forgot the statues of Apollo'.[33] In this way Clark's version of *La Naissance D'Apollon* performs a visually explicit presentation of Schopenhauer's *principum individuationis*, the principle of extreme measure through self-contemplation that Nietzsche proposes as deified in the Apolline,[34] which in this setting gives way to the blissful Dionysiac state of self-forgetting. The moment of individuation is taken to such extremes (Fiona Burnside proposes Narcissus as Clark's mythological reference[35]) that the boundaries of self-knowledge belonging to Apollo are broken through by a tide of self-eroticism driven by Dionysus. It is in this scene that we may observe the emergence, through the contemplative sculptural forms of Apolline classicism, of Nietzsche's understanding of Dionysiac oblivion as it 'discharges itself over and over again in an Apolline world of images'.[36]

---

[32] Clark and Henderson (2007).
[33] Nietzsche (1999), 27.
[34] Ibid. 26.
[35] Burnside (1994), 30.
[36] Nietzsche (1999), 44.

Clark's performance of self-eroticism inherits a tradition of staging Apollo with Dionysus in classical dance by referencing the opening choreographic sequence of Balanchine's *Apollo*, where Apollo begins his first solo by strumming his lyre to a suggestive crescendo. What is termed by Tim Scholl as *Apollo*'s 'auto-erotic' opening, itself re-stages the faun's self-induced orgasm at the close of Nijinsky's *L'Après-midi d'un faune*.[37] Nijinsky's faun is the embodiment of those 'wilder impulses' that the Apolline so carefully blockades.[38] It is the faun's transgressive sexuality, especially his final act of auto-eroticism, which met with such outrage when displayed within the public spaces of Europe in 1912.[39] The response of Nijinsky's critics is similar to the outrage levelled at many of Clark's early works, whose graphic references to an impish sexuality (for example the 'bottomless' costumes for 1984's *New Puritans*) incensed the conservative critics of 1980s Britain as much as Nijinsky's *L'Après-midi* insulted the audience of 1912 Paris. For example, in one review for Clark's *our caca phoney H our caca phoney H* (1985), the work is defined as 'a parade of barbarism, high-octane vulgarity and cross-dressing' and Clark himself as 'no more than a hooligan'.[40] In both these contexts, a provocative sexuality performed through the bodies of highly trained and highly regarded classical dancers (as is the case with both Nijinsky and Clark) translates into transgression, excess, and loss of self-control: all features of Dionysiac intoxication.

Further traditions of staging Dionysus in contemporary theatre are evoked in the original 1990s prologue sections to both *O* and *Mmm*... These sections, now removed altogether, present Clark being 'given birth to' on stage by his own mother and performer, Bessie Clark [Hassall]. This explicit rendering of birth recalls the late 1960s counter-cultural energy of Richard Schechner and *The Performance Group*'s work *Dionysus in 69* (1970). Schechner's reworking of Euripides' *Bacchae* displays a concern with the infusion of the Dionysiac in the birth/death circuit. The work includes both a birth ritual (for Dionysus) and death ritual (for Pentheus), where characters are passed underneath a human 'canal' composed of the legs of nine naked performers.[41] *The Performance Group* frame their work with the rendering of these sensual rituals, and likewise Clark frames his two Stravinsky ballets in a similar way: the half naked Apollo's sensual birth ritual at the start of *O* is balanced by the half-naked Chosen Maiden's frenzied death ritual at the close of *Mmm*....

Clark's own emergence from a youth-led counter-culture in 1980s' Britain draws further parallels between these earlier receptions of Greek tragedy and his own work, particularly their discernibly anti-institutional and arguably

---

[37] Scholl (1994), 79.
[38] Nietzsche (1999), 16.
[39] Eksteins (1989).
[40] Crisp (1985).
[41] Zeitlin (2004), 61.

Dionysiac values. For example, the appearance of the Chosen Maiden in *Mmm* . . . , naked except for over-sized knickers and a 'Hitler' moustache—reminiscent of Klaus Michael Grüber's g-string-clad Dionysus who makes his entrance in the *Berliner Schaubühne's Bacchae* of 1974 to a recording of Stravinsky's *Apollon*— reclothes the radical nudity of a late 1960s sexual revolution in the pastiche design of a 1980s trash fashion culture.[42] Like the experimental groups of the 1960s, the social context of Clark's artistic production informs a Dionysiac experience in his works. The 'modern ecstatic cult'[43] that Pat Easterling detects in 1960s/1970s counter-culture is present also in the punk and underground clubbing culture that produced the collaborations for Clark's early work.

This drive to ecstasy is certainly present formally in the movement towards 'self-oblivion' glimpsed through the bodies of *Mmm*. . . . The Dionysiac condition is choreographed into the final solo, where, amid contortions of the torso and limbs which form a grotesque body unrecognizable from the Apolline statues of *O*, the dancer intermittently throws herself or himself onto the floor in a violent performance of encroaching possession. Like Apollo, the Chosen Maiden treads a fine line between the Apolline, demonstrating supreme technical control in this fiendishly difficult solo, and the Dionysiac, charging towards her/his death in an exhausting and ecstatic performance of sexually charged transcendence. What Clark inherits from Nijinsky, Schechner and Grüber here is a staging of ancient Greece that enshrouds a treatment of birth and death in a fatal eroticism. This treatment does appear to an extent in Balanchine's *Apollo*, in the eventually deleted labour scene played out with Leto's legs in a wide split displayed to the audience.[44] However, Balanchine's Apollo never dies; and unlike the final moments of Clark's *O*, he makes an ascent to his place among the Olympians, circumventing the ultimate Dionysiac descent altogether. It is precisely this relationship of the Dionysiac to death and descent within the ancient world that is significant with regard to Forsythe's *Eidos: Telos*, where, as with Clark's *Stravinsky Project*, stagecraft, movement idiom, and allusion to Greek mythology combine to introduce Dionysiac chaos to the Apolline structure of classical dance.

FORSYTHE'S *EIDOS: TELOS*

William Forsythe was born in 1949 in New York City and grew up in Long Island. He trained at Jacksonville University, Florida with an ex-dancer of Balanchine's and at The Joffrey Ballet School, New York, dancing briefly with

---

[42] See Fischer-Lichte (2004), 337. The *Schaubühne's Antiquity Project*, of which Grüber's *Bacchae* is part, was, according to Cartledge (cited in Easterling (1997*b*), 36 n. 3), 'presented as a hymn of counter-cultural liberationist rebellion'. For discussion of the *Antiquity Project* in these terms see Erica Fischer-Lichte (2004), 332.

[43] Easterling (1997*b*), 36.

[44] See Jones, this volume.

the company before leaving America for Germany in 1973 to work under John Cranko at the Stuttgart Ballet.[45] After making pieces in the early 1980s for Stuttgart and as a freelance choreographer in Europe and North America, Forsythe was invited in 1984 to become Artistic Director of The Ballett Frankfurt, where he set about transforming the company into a major force in the international dance scene. In 2002, due to the withdrawal of municipal investment, the company was terminated; but by January 2005 Forsythe had regained financial backing and established a smaller troupe, The Forsythe Company, which performs internationally today. Like Clark, Forsythe comes from an academic background in terms of his dance training, and this background remains firmly imprinted in his choreographic style. Forsythe says of his relationship to classical ballet: '[I]t is in my body and I live with it . . . Ballet was my mother tongue in dance . . . you can't erase it from your consciousness.'[46] However, Forsythe has built a distinctive choreographic style upon working with the basis of an advanced classical technique, but unsettling this highly ordered framework with a logic of disorder and the dynamism of a ferocious movement impulse.

Although traces of an organized formal economy indicative of Balanchine's style remain in Forsythe's choreography (particularly the early oeuvre of the 1980s), his work demonstrates evolutions in anatomical and theatrical composition that reflect a new cultural philosophy aligned with the principles of instability, fragmentation, and chaos. As a choreographer Forsythe is openly influenced by the texts of poststructuralist thinkers. He has discussed his early work as 'deconstruction' in relation to the theories of Paul de Man;[47] and the programme for *Impressing the Czar* (1988) includes a section from Roland Barthes's *S/Z* (1970) that asserts the 'plurality of . . . systems' and the 'infinite structure' of text.[48]

The chaotic formalisms that we find in Forsythe's work embody the values that delineate a decidedly non-Apolline mistrust of reason and rationality, as espoused by postmodern cultural theorists whom Eagleton labels 'Nietzschean without fully knowing it'.[49] In light of Eagleton's characterization of such philosophies as 'Dionysiac',[50] the fractured grammar of movement that Forsythe presents through the scaffolding of an athletic classical body (the type of body sculpted through Balanchine's style) can be thought of as introducing a contemporary Dionysiac chaos to Balanchine's post-war world of Apolline rationality.

Work started on *Eidos* in 1994 after the death of Forsythe's wife Tracy-Kai Maier, who was also a dancer in The Ballett Frankfurt. Forsythe explains how *Eidos* is a response to his and the company's loss, and how Greek mythology—particularly the myth of Demeter and Persephone—enters the work as a vehicle

---

[45] See Forsythe and Tusa (2003) where Forsythe discusses his relationship to Balanchine's style.
[46] Forsythe and Tusa (2003).
[47] Ibid.
[48] Brandstetter (1998), 44–5.
[49] Eagleton (2003), 53.
[50] 'The latest wave of this Dionysian current is poststructuralism' (Eagleton (2003), 226).

for the treatment of death ('the cast and myself . . . filtered that event, through [Roberto] Calasso's work, "The Marriage of Cadmus and Harmony [1988]"'[51]). While in Balanchine's *Apollo* and Clark's *O*, the story of Apollo's birth, ascent, and Apolline civilization provides the narrative framework, the thematic impetus of the Persephone myth announces *Eidos* as a piece that deals, albeit through the beauty of classical form, with death, descent, and Dionysiac chaos. Julie Copeland describes the work in these terms:

there's great beauty, there's great chaos, there's death and rebirth, it goes back to the classical Greek myths, the Apollonian and the Dionysian.[52]

Through *Eidos'* treatment of death and rebirth, its engagement with the work of Balanchine, Stravinsky, and Calasso, and through its presentation of classically constructed yet chaotic dancing bodies, the tension between an Apolline and a Dionysiac creative impulse becomes heightened.

Eidos is a work of three parts: Part I, entitled *Self Meant to Govern*, is a pure dance section choreographed around an on-stage violin solo composed by Thom Willems based on Stravinsky's *Apollon*; Part II is built around a spoken monologue written and performed by Dana Caspersen, based on Calasso's Persephone; Part III is a performance of virtuoso choreography and vocal and sonic hysteria, in which the full company take the stage to draw the work to a dark and frenzied close. *Self Meant To Govern* (choreographed in 1994 as an independent work) prepares for the evocation of Greek myth that we shall see in Part II, but also for the pervading tension between Apolline/Dionysiac drives through referencing Balanchine's *Apollo*. Ann Nugent observes Forsythe's allusion to Balanchine:

Part I of *Eidos : Telos* pays homage to . . . *Apollo* [which] haunts [the work] like the ghost of a memory that can be experienced but never quite recaptured. It emerges variously . . . in fragments of sound and movement that seem familiar.[53]

Live music composed by Willems and inspired by Stravinsky's score, sets this ultimate Apolline composition in Dionysiac turmoil as a solo violinist plays the screeching, fragmented score on a darkened stage whilst the dancers contort around his body. The music here is not the celestial and abstracted 'architectonics'[54] of Apolline sound but takes on human form and Dionysiac sensuality, as the bodily presence of the musician becomes the focus for the movement of the spatially unhinged cohort of dancers. The bodily focus of the musician is heightened as one female dancer uses the violinist as a support for her 'high-extension adagio', a movement reminiscent of the opening moments in

[51] Forsythe cited in Forsythe and Copeland (2001).
[52] Forsythe and Copeland (2001).
[53] Nugent (1998), 29.
[54] Nietzsche (1999), 21.

Balanchine's *pas de deux* for Apollo and Terpischore, causing Nugent to view this figure as 'the new Terpischore'.[55]

It is in Part II, however, that we can observe traces of the ancient world and the Dionysiac condition being played at full force, where voice, lighting, and Greek mythology combine to express a delirium and despair induced at the approach of death. Caspersen-as-Persephone begins her monologue dressed in a heavy full-length skirt and in some versions naked from the waist up. Hers is a violent Persephone, delivering a deranged indictment of a coexistence between the realms of light (earth) and dark (Hades), in a half-spoken, half-wailing performance of female fury. There are traces of Calasso's text here, particularly in an expression of the condemned through the imagery of flowers. For example, his words are employed to relate the sensuous horror of entering Hades: '[I]t was a place where dogs would lose their quarry's tail, so violent was the scent of flowers.'[56] The act of Caspersen to thrust a heap of crumpled yellow cellophane into a suspended light projector also recalls Calasso's Persephone, who gazes into the petals of a yellow Narcissus just prior to her abduction (Figure 18.2).[57] Significantly here both Clark's Apollo and Caspersen/Calasso's Persephone

Figure 18.2 Dana Caspersen in William Forsythe's *Eidos: Telos* (1995).

[55] Nugent (1998), 29.
[56] Calasso (1994), 209.
[57] Ibid.

engage in acts of self-contemplation (as or through Narcissus) that lead respectively to transgression in self-eroticism (Apollo) or to the horror of a chthonic existence (Persephone).

While the climax of *Apollo* presents the ultimate ascent—Apollo's apotheosis, that is his 'becoming' Olympian—in staging the myth of Persephone, *Eidos* presents the ultimate descent: Persephone's abduction to the throne of Hades, that is her 'becoming' chthonic. The subsequent contrast between the realms of Olympus/Parnassus and Hades in Balanchine and Forsythe respectively, can be traced particularly in the diametric lighting design for each ballet. Balanchine's bright, white lighting for *Apollo* creates the luminous realm of Parnassus and renders dancers as Apolline dream figures. The lighting scheme also demonstrates Balanchine's purification of the stage, cleansing the performance space until only the Apolline bodily architecture remains. Forsythe, however, makes a sharp departure from the traditions of lighting classical choreography, and uses a heavy darkness on his stage to explore the notion of abyss. A stygian realm is created in Part II of *Eidos* through a stage lit in patches and shadows. This both obscures the action, creating a disorientating and shifting focus (Dionysiac chaos dominates), but also transplants classical bodies from the radiance of a brilliantly lit proscenium, to the murky and nebulous underworld of Greek mythology.

The mythological Dionysus brings his own association with the Greek underworld; not least of all through a biographical link provided by Persephone, the Queen of Hades. According to one birth-myth for the god (in this case Dionysus is identified with the child Zagreus), Persephone is in fact his mother, and Zeus his father.[58] The accompanying myth of Dionysus/Zagreus' dismemberment by the Titans at the command of a jealous Hera, is also significant to the choreography of *Eidos*. Reflecting on this narrative, Walter F. Otto recognizes Zagreus as 'the "chthonic" Dionysus';[59] and as Silk and Stern have pointed out: '[f]or Nietzsche's "Apolline", read *Olympian*, and for his "Dionysiac" read *Chthonic*.'[60] In light of Silk and Stern's reading of Nietzsche's Dionysus, and bearing in mind the god's association with dismemberment, rather than invoking Dionysiac energies through a narrative of death *per se*, the Dionysiac enters *Eidos* largely through the recurring motif of destruction.

Eagleton observes how a duality of destruction and creation form within the Dionysiac experience:

---

[58] See Raymond Guess's note (n. 76) to Nietzsche's (1999), 52, invoking of the Zagreus myth, in addition to Calasso (1994), 204.

[59] Otto (1965), 191.

[60] Silk and Stern (1981), 180–1. However, Silk and Stern do question Nietzsche's placement of Dionysus within a strictly chthonic pantheon, on account of the god not being directly involved with the role of death in the ancient world: '[Dionysus] may have been a very destructive god, but neither in his Greek, nor in his Nietzschean guise does he have any clear links with death' (Silk & Stern (1981), 182).

as the high priest of Dionysus, Nietzsche finds in tragic art a frenzy, chaos, excess and horror which takes pleasure in both creating and destroying—the domain, we might say, of *Thanatos* or the death drive, where we can reap sadistic *jouissance* from misery and carnage secure in the consolation that this eternal flux of strife, savagery and rebirth will never pass away.[61]

The 'sadistic *jouissance*' of eternal flux is brought to the fore in the main mythological reference of *Eidos*. Persephone is uniquely Dionysiac in that she destroys the balance of the birth/death circuit by assuming, in lieu of death, an unprecedented coexistence between earth and Hades. Persephone's existence breaks the ultimate mortal boundary separating life from death and she suffers an eternal negotiation between descent and rebirth. As Calasso's narrator remarks of Persephone's transgression of 'law and order' mortality: 'from now on, it was a question not only of accepting life in a single immutable form but of accepting the certainty that the form would one day disappear without a trace.'[62] It is in this line of text, relating the consequence of Persephone's contravention of the birth/death system, that we may source the significance of Forsythe's title for the work. *Eidos: Telos*: where discrete 'form' here meets its 'end' in the obscurity of Dionysiac flux.

The proclamation of an 'end' (*telos*) in the work of a postmodern artist such as Forsythe, becomes significant if we take into account postmodernity's fascination with both the end of a trustworthy and ordered reason (the stability of significa-tion is destroyed through the poststructuralist project) and also with 'the end of time'. Klaus Scherpe asserts the importance of the idea of 'the end' to 1980s postmodern discourse, through a consideration of apocalypse as the inevitable finale to Baudrillard's age of hyperrealism. Here Scherpe finds:

an anticipation of the end, [a] wishing for the sudden event of total destruction in place of the deadly 'waiting.' . . . 'playing with the apocalypse' is an integral part of postmodern social philosophy.[63]

Eagleton reformulates this assertion, stating that 'the late modern age finds something incorrigibly naive about hope. It is considerably more embarrassed by it than it is by announcements of apocalypse'.[64] Indeed, the late twentieth century has heralded its fair share of announcements of apocalypse: the antici-pated nuclear holocaust of the Cold War; the distinct responses of individual loss and widespread paranoia surrounding the AIDs crisis of the 1980s; and more recently the official warnings of a threat of global terrorism and the consequences of global warming. The apocalyptic promise of these events finds cultural expression in postmodern discourse that announces the end of an enlightened

---

[61] Eagleton (2003), 54.
[62] Calasso (1994), 212.
[63] Scherpe (1986–7), 101.
[64] Eagleton (2003), 40.

(what Nietzsche described as 'Socratic'), modern thought steeped in rationality, and cultivates its replacement by favouring a Dionysiac destruction of form and reason.

Forsythe's own movement idiom extends this shift towards destruction of form, by providing choreography for the destruction of the absolute body. Particularly Forsythe puts an end to the Apolline form of the individual and aggregate body as constructed in classical ballet technique, through dismantling the harmonious system of classical coordination. During the 'structured improvisations'[65] developed in the course of work on *Self Meant to Govern*, the dancers were asked to explore the prescription of classical shapes through the geometrical framework of the *icosahedron*, a polyhedral structure made up of twenty faces of equilateral triangles.[66] The major significance of this model as a modification of classical coordination is the removal of one central point around which to organize movement. Instead, we have the introduction of multiple centres for movement initiation that are constantly shifting around the body according to a crystalline network of points, which consequently instils a movement logic characterized by isolation and fragmentation of parts. In this way, Forsythe destroys the balanced coordination of classical form and reaps the potential the human body has for 'extraordinary proliferation and perfect disorder'.[67]

What Forsythe arguably also choreographs here is a kinetic embodiment of the mythic Dionysus, in that these bodies appear to be driven by—to borrow from Eagleton—a 'Dionysian fury which tears individuals apart'.[68] Dionysus is associated with dismemberment, and particularly *sparagmos*, where bodies are dismantled and total human 'form' is destroyed under the stress of ecstatic assault.[69] This may be drawn out through the god's two birth myths: his 'birth' by Semele, who is destroyed at the very act of conception, and his mutilation by the Titans after birth by Persephone. Dismemberment occurs again in the god's later influence upon the Maenads, who at the height of their Dionysiac intoxication, as the *Bacchae* relates, rend limbs from both animal and human victims. This *sparagmos* has been identified as central to postmodern theatrical treatments of the ancient text and Forsythe's fractured, body-splintering choreography provides a corporeal analogue.[70] His idiom in *Eidos:Telos* performs the destruction and fragmented reconstitution of the composed individual, replacing

---

[65] Fensham (2002), 73.

[66] Forsythe draws his use of the *icosahedron* from the research of Rudolf von Laban, a Hungarian born dance theorist and pedagogue, and forefather to the German *Ausdruckstanz* movement.

[67] Forsythe cited in Brandstetter (1998), 49.

[68] Eagleton (2003), 54.

[69] *Sparagmos*, the ancient Greek cultic technique of tearing the sacrificial victim's body apart, is discussed in relation to Dionysus in Otto (1965), 192.

[70] Fischer-Lichte (2004), 330–1 and 340, expands on the Dionysus/dismemberment association in terms of both Nietzsche's Dionysiac, and the previously discussed *Berliner Schaubühne's* 1974 production of the *Bacchae* directed by Grüber.

harmonious and solid Apolline form with a discordant and dissevered production of the dancing body.

CONCLUSION: THE DIONYSIAC IN CONTEMPORARY CLASSICISM

Both visually, in the physical vocabulary of a radicalized classical technique and audibly, in the central sonic presence of Stravinsky's *Apollon*, the *Stravinsky Project* and *Eidos: Telos* declare their Apolline heritage as oriented through Balanchine's 1928 pinnacle of neoclassicism. What these works also declare, however, is a transformation of the Apolline form of classical ballet into a site for choreography of the Dionysiac condition. The Dionysiac does appear quite differently in the work of Clark and Forsythe, as is appropriate for a god whose sphere of influence is characterized by its very diversity.[71] We may turn to Otto, who, in recognizing the complexity of the figure of Dionysus, provides a summation of his spirit that frames both Clark's and Forsythe's engagement with the Dionysiac:

> Dionysus was the god of the most blessed ecstasy and the most enraptured love. But he was also the persecuted god, the suffering and dying god.[72]

Clark's *O*, with its divine protagonist and *Mmm...*, with its sacrificial victim, both choreograph the sensuality, eroticism, and rapture that invest the experiences of an ecstatic Dionysiac body. Forsythe's *Eidos: Telos*, by contrast, with its obscure staging and central, tragic narrative, choreographs the darkness and violent uncertainty, which beset the oblivion of Dionysiac suffering. These works ultimately represent both dimensions of the Dionysiac condition, that which Nietzsche describes as '[t]hat repulsive witches' brew of sensuality and cruelty'.[73]

What is most striking in both Clark's and Forsythe's choreography is that neither artist abandons their paradigmatically Apolline 'mother tongue', the idiom of classical ballet. Both choreographers invest their work, as typically postmodern artists, with a Dionysiac 'madness, transgression, desire and disruption';[74] but they also maintain, through their chosen formal means of presentation, the clarity, beauty, and craftsmanship that only a fundamentally technical form such as classical ballet can preserve. While this is not the clinical and ultimately formal language of Balanchine's Modernist Apolline classicism—

---

[71] See Otto (1965), 49: '[t]he most distinguished poets and thinkers sensed in this diversity a reality of inexpressible depth.'
[72] Ibid.
[73] Nietzsche (1999), 21.
[74] Eagleton (2003), 55.

Clark's counter-cultural, and Forsythe's self-interrogating classicism are both designed to speak to an altogether different culture—both artists keep their choreography at all times steeped in classical technique. They succeed in this way to suggest a new legacy for the performance of ancient Greek ideologies; striking a contemporary balance between the Apolline and Dionysiac where the perceived instability and chaos of their contemporary culture is expressed in the 'clarity and firmness'[75] of the classical language. What Clark and Forsythe achieve here is a choreography of classicism for their own times, where 'Dionysos no longer speaks in the form of energies but rather as an epic hero, almost in the language of Homer'.[76]

[75] Nietzsche (1999), 46.
[76] Ibid.

19

Caryl Churchill and Ian Spink: 'Allowing the past... to speak directly to the present'

Richard Cave

[It] was a classic case of pigeon holing: one of the source materials for *A Mouthful of Birds* was Euripides' tragedy, *Bacchae*, and as soon as anyone attempts to stage that play, they have [to] call in a movement expert. They feel that a choreographer is the only person who can deal with the kinds of problems the play sets a cast and director: people being torn apart or going mad.[1]

This is Ian Spink's mischievously light-hearted view of how he entered into a series of collaborations with the playwright, Caryl Churchill. That was in 1986; four further projects have developed their creative relationship over some thirteen years, in which they have also continued their independent careers in drama and dance. The feature that unites all their joint stagings is a preoccupation with the degree to which the mythical hovers on the edges of contemporary experience: informing, perhaps shaping or explaining, always a decided *presence*. Two of the collaborations, *A Mouthful of Birds* (1986) and *Lives of the Great Poisoners* (1991), draw explicitly on examples of Euripidean tragedies; one, *Hotel* (1997), more chamber opera than play, on what one might term the mechanics of a feature of classical tragedy in performance; one, *Fugue* (1988), a work for television, on a form of closure in Greek culture, dating back to Homeric times. (The fifth project, *The Skryker* (1994), shares with the others a preoccupation with the archetypal, but that which is more specifically rooted in later European fairytale and folklore.)[2]

---

[1] Spink and Cave (1995), 297.

[2] This was less a creative collaboration in the fullest sense of the term as it is applied to the other classically derived projects discussed in this chapter, since Churchill had been working independently on the play for a number of years before its staging at the National Theatre. Because of his extensive work with Churchill, Spink was employed as movement director and choreographer, helping to realize this complex and challenging text, but he had no direct impact on its composition. Spink's cheeky remark about the circumstances in which he came to work with Churchill on *A Mouthful of Birds* applies more to his actual input on *The Skryker* than to the earlier collaboration.

The focus of this chapter is not on the role of the choreographer in modern revivals of Greek tragedy, nor on classical Greek material as source for modern dance works, but the place of dance within certain postmodern collaborative experiments in total theatre, which have necessitated a fertile crossing of borders between disciplines to extend powers of expression in theatre in ways that dance, drama, or opera in their traditional divisions could not attempt. To realize such ambitions required the evolution of a new type of performer, willing to develop his or her powers of expressivity within the whole body, vocally and physically, the better to be capable of confidently bridging the conventional boundaries between genres and the techniques separately developed to perform them.[3] On both these counts, the collaborations began approximating to the vocal and physical demands made of performers in classical theatre, as we currently understand them to have been. What is not clear from the writings and observations of the collaborators is the degree to which this line of discovery may have been a conscious aim, or just an inevitable consequence of working on Greek tragic themes from a basis of common notions about the methods and conditions of original Greek performance.[4]

What needs to be stressed is the importance of the collaborative process as chosen working method of composition and the importance of improvisation within that process. That it was a true collaboration involving a balancing of contributions from playwright and choreographer (and on occasions, composer, designer, and lighting designer too, as the essays preceding the text of *Lives of the Great Poisoners* make clear) is not particularly evident from the published texts of the various projects, where indications of the dance components are to be gleaned from the tersest of stage directions and where music, either composed or improvised by the cast (if it appears at all), takes the form of an independent score situated after the text. This *text* in other words is at a far remove from the performance text, a situation that has troubled Churchill for its privileging of one component over a greater whole:

this book [*Lives of the Great Poisoners*] gives more weight to the sung and spoken characters because description and photographs can only give a glimpse of what was going on physically throughout the piece.[5]

---

[3] In the past there have been dancers who have pursued careers in acting subsequent to their careers in dance (Helpmann, Shearer, Gable), but the work of Spink's company, Second Stride, has developed a generation of actor-dancers of remarkable versatility and daring (Stephen Goff, Philippe Giraudeau, Lucy Bethune, Sally Owen). For a fuller discussion of this aspect of Spink's achievement, see Cave (2004), 63–72.

[4] Churchill has observed that an influence for her personally on the way that *Lives of the Great Poisoners* evolved was Brecht's *Seven Deadly Sins* with its requirement that the central role of Anna be played by both a singer and a dancer. She did not follow such an influence slavishly, however, since in the collaborators' approach to the *Medea*-inspired section of *Lives* the roles of Medea, Jason and Creusa are assigned to an opera-singer, actor and dancer respectively. See Churchill (1993), viii.

[5] Ibid., ix.

It is too a situation about which Spink has voiced a certain chagrin:

The idea of the author in the traditional sense obviously does not work very well in these kinds of pieces.[6]

In the one instance where his contribution has been recorded (a video of the danced episodes in *A Mouthful of Birds* designed to function as a means of gaining copyright for his choreographic invention), the result is a series of fragments taken out of context and the body of the full play in performance, so that the appropriateness of the movement style and the organic placing of dance within the total structure have in large measure to be guessed at. Again, the quality of delicately balanced sharing that is the requirement of good collaborative practice is not adequately demonstrated or reproduced.

It requires of the theatre or dance historian a considerable feat of imagination to piece the component features together into some semblance of the unity that was so impressive when experiencing the works in performance.[7] The directions, framed significantly by Churchill not Spink in the published texts, are brief (chiefly, one supposes, because she does not feel herself competent to describe the physical dimension or maybe her chosen style here denotes an apologetic embarrassment at resorting to language to define movement, particularly when it is not of her devising), but they are not uninformative: they indicate the positioning of the danced elements, sometimes provide a scenario of the content (as in the Lena sequence, 'Psychic Attack' in *A Mouthful of Birds*), or through a skilful use of adverbs ('tenderly'; 'dangerously') imply the emotional quality that the choreography should ideally convey (as in Paul's episode, 'Pig', from the same play). But they do not indicate the duration of each danced episode, how it is to be integrated into the spoken or sung dialogue that it either accompanies or displaces within a given scene, or what the preferred style of movement or type of body language might be (and there is a major issue here, given the plethora of modern dance idioms available and Spink's known iconoclasm as a choreographer).

It is the synthesis and its effects and consequences that are lost after performance, much as is the case with the original performing traditions of classical tragedy. One can but assemble extant data (the published texts, photographs, comments, interviews, and essays by the contributing artists and information about parallel works that they were engaged in severally and completing within

---

[6] Spink and Cave (1995), 303.

[7] I have been fortunate in being allowed temporary access by Peter Mumford for private research purposes only to video recordings that he made of *A Mouthful of Birds* and of *Lives of the Great Poisoners*. These are single-camera recordings made in poor lighting conditions during the dress rehearsal for each of these shows; like all such videos, they are helpful only if used as an aid to reinforce memory of the performances. They are not a valuable archival record of the events portrayed, because of the distance of the camera in each case from the performers and the dim, fog-like effect of the recording being made under theatrical, not cinematic or televisual lighting.

the same period as the collaborations, video recordings, musical scores, publicity materials, reviews, academic critiques, one's own and other spectators' memories) and weigh these against each other to approximate a sense of what actually occurred on stage and how it was received.

Crucial to any interpretation is an awareness of the theatrical background behind the experience that Churchill and Spink particularly brought to their shared endeavour: a background that in both their cases privileged improvisation as a means to creativity (she with Monstrous Regiment and Joint Stock; he with Second Stride), which consciously involved a sharing of inspiration and ownership of the resulting performance with the members of their casts. This requires of everyone involved an openness and honesty that do not defer to traditional hierarchies within the theatre.[8] At its best such a process allows a pushing against and challenging of known boundaries (personal and social, theatrical and cultural), which hopefully will result in a reaching out towards new potential within all those categories. Rehearsals under such conditions become journeys of discovery for everyone involved, where the group effort generally overrides any one individual's commitment and input. The remarkable aspect of the collaborators' decision to rehearse in this way is their ensuing choice to devise and embody strategies within the resulting performances to communicate the exact and exacting nature of the journeys undergone by cast, writer and choreographer to audiences and invite them to share both the process and the rewards, the movement towards new levels of insight and a committed openness. The resulting extension of awareness may be exhilarating or disturbing (particularly when that openness leads inexorably in two of the later collaborations to a questioning of the ideologies that appear to underpin certain conventions or performing techniques inscribed in classical Greek tragedy).

In turning from generalization to given instances, it might be best to begin with the second of the collaborations, the television dance-drama, *Fugue*,[9] since this

---

[8] My reasons for choosing the word, 'openness' are clear from an answer Spink gave when in interview I questioned whether Churchill has a 'clear sense in her own imagination of what she wants to see on the stage'. He responded immediately with a negative ('No, she does not have a picture of what the work will look like. That's what I like about her so much') and then he explained: 'She is very generous; she will continue to follow you, as you search out the way of visualising or realising what the material could yield or become.' Pressed with a further question whether she ever exercises a right of veto, the response was again a firm negative. To enforce his view, Spink then compared her approach to collaborating with that of David Lan, co-author with Churchill on *A Mouthful of Birds*: 'He had seen very precisely how his scenes would be set up and staged. I found that a problem sometimes. I was written into those scenes and had to create movement material for them . . . I seem to recall hearing the line once or twice: "This is not what I want".' Spink has not subsequently collaborated with Lan. See Spink and Cave (1995), 299.

[9] *Fugue* was commissioned for Dance-Lines 2 for Dance on 4 in 1988. I have been much influenced in the ensuing analysis of this work by repeated viewings of the programme, often in the company of students, by conversations with Ian Spink in preparation for our public discussion at the *Border Tensions* conference at the University of Surrey (see Spink and Cave (1995) for an edited transcript of that event) and by accounts of *Fugue* in Jordan and Allen (1993), 193–4 and in Jordan (1992), 204–5.

presents many of the structural and thematic issues just outlined with a startling clarity. This is a consequence of the piece being a first experience for Spink of creating (as distinct from adapting) for television so that he had to fulfil the roles of choreographer, director and director for television. Being a novice in the last role meant that in his view not enough time had been devoted in the recording process to linking material of a kind that in editing might be deployed to make for smooth transitions between sequences. This results in the finished broadcast version in a staccato crosscutting, which, while initially it might prove alienating, in time establishes its own compelling rhythm and texture. Rather than seducing the spectator/viewer into a state of openness, *Fugue* insists on it: one has to make one's own connections between the acted or danced images that rapidly fire across the screen. To a remarkable degree the viewer assists in the shaping of meaning, a meaning structured on two premises: one thematic (the situation is a death in the family and the subsequent funeral); one technical (both collaborators' engagement with Bach and the form of the fugue). Spink had already essayed the form in *Some Fugues* (1981), and had returned to Bach again that same year as an accompaniment for *Coolhaven*; Churchill, curious about a choreographer's licence to play with repetition as a means to structuring movement patterns into a sustained dance, wanted to explore the degree to which she could shape formal groupings of words into subtle variations on distinct phrases.

We watch an elderly man collapse in death, his wife telling each of their offspring, now adult, of the event, their sharing the news with each other, the family assembling, the funeral and the sombre tea party that follows. Inevitably memories surface like snapshots of the past, as the children recall instances of their father's authoritarian invasions of their privacy; some revelations, especially of his creativity and his attempt once to abandon the family (both formerly kept secret) prompt reappraisals. In technical terms, curt snatches of dialogue, chiefly phone conversations ('Mum says he'd just got out of the bath'; 'He didn't leave a note. It wasn't his fault') where voices, faces, vocal registers, and the social ambiences change but the words stay largely constant, alternate with mimed tableaux (the old man falling down stairs; him looming dangerously over his children, which is made more sinister and poignant by one's noting that the children are played by their adult selves).

A narrative is implied in *Fugue* but not chronologically developed: memories intercut the imparting of information or intrude into the tea ceremony; the repetitions are stressed by appropriately reiterated phrases of Bach. The cumulative effect is to portray the family, living and dead, as trapped in a common past that, structured by petty cruelties, envies, frustrated desires, now leaves them as prey to grudges, resentments, malice, uncharitableness. Neither funeral nor tea ceremony is an adequate recognition of the potential for change, for release (even though at least one of the memories has a positive quality in showing the antics of the family at the beach) because, patently, neither has been truly a form of closure.

As the music, heavily fragmented, moves into the development section of the fugal subjects, fantasy intrudes: we see the surviving family members burning the father's body on a heroic pyre (the epic event is sited with surreal logic on the parkland opposite the parents' terraced house); sand invades the house; and in the longest sustained passage of dance, which picks up and develops all the movement material from the opening sections of the piece, the adults, definitely recognizable as their grown-up selves, play as children at the seaside; importantly, they play for the most part independently, lost in their own imaginative worlds. Seemingly closure has been achieved through the invocation of the Homeric rite of passage with its pyre and subsequent funeral games. Seemingly too the children of the family have found release, have undergone a process of catharsis, through accessing their capacity for play (or in therapeutic terms through embracing the child within).

What ultimately is seen as wanting in the family's life at its moment of crisis is any sense of the sustenance to be drawn from honouring their situation as archetypal: there is throughout the first half of *Fugue* a mounting sense of the need for such an engagement and frustration at the group's uncertainty at how to make the necessary connection. The intrusion of the surreal brings with it a potential answer; but the very nature of the surreal (the incongruity of the pyre in a recognizably bourgeois, urban setting; the children at their games being represented by adult performers) problematizes the ending with layer upon layer of irony. Is this a genuine insight or one travestied in its realization? What is an appropriate response: laughter at the absurdity of it all or awe at the transformations depicted? Have the adults embraced emotional innocence and psychological freedom in claiming the right to be childlike or are they indulging in escapist triviality by becoming childish? Is the overwhelming irony of the ending a reflection of our culture as incapable of confronting emotion through a profound fear of finding it a mask for sentimentality? Or is the ending a critique of contemporary culture that, for all the lip-service paid to Freud, Jung, and their followers, still resists connection with the archetypal and so has lost the power to discriminate between cliché and authentic experience?

We find here only questions evolving into yet more questions by way of an ending, and no firm resolution: but, while the questioning remains, the potential for psychological health lies still within reach. The shaping of the ending is a matter of choice for the viewer/spectator: all avenues, positive and negative, to a secure ending are laid open and that very openness is ultimately the challenge. I have outlined *Fugue* in such detail, partly because it is not easy to access, but more because it deftly introduces many of the themes and creative issues that will occupy the rest of this study.

Susan Leigh Foster in introducing the volume, *Choreographing History*, argues that 'writing the historical text, rather than an act of verbal explanation, must become a process of interpretation, translation, and rewriting of bodily texts'.[10]

---

[10] Foster (1995), 9.

Noticeably she distances the intended work from the logocentric, stressing that interpretation, translation and rewriting should ideally embrace the physical: the resulting text must have a bodily dimension. This is the approach of the collaborators[11] with *A Mouthful of Birds*: it is no straight account or explanation of Euripides' tragedy, since that would risk reductive simplifications; rather their engagement with the *Bacchae* is from a multiplicity of perspectives and through a variety of theatrical styles and genres, in every case privileging the expressive power of the body.

Rather than being a recreation of the myth underlying the Greek text, *A Mouthful of Birds* directly confronts it and does so through a consciously fragmented structure, which explores a range of possible manifestations of the myth within an advanced bourgeois society. (The world of the play touches on the European Union, first-generation black British, feminism, the decline of state religion, consumerism, noise in a technological era.) The original myth that inspires Euripides defines the consequences of the advent of a god within a community that chooses to deny his existence or power. In the modern world the conflict is between the individual and the archetype, which from a position of cultural 'progress' it is tempting to dismiss as primitive. History (as culture and as myth) is viewed in the dance-play not as *passé* but as a still vital, determining presence, such as it is in the world of psychotherapy, where, most clearly in the field of Jungian analysis, its presence and its relation to the archetypal has to be *admitted* (in both senses of the word: 'confessed' and 'allowed to enter'). This entrance of the archetype is what we observe in *A Mouthful of Birds*.

There are but seven performers, each assigned a major role. The play opens with a rapid series of brief scenes in which one by one the characters speak a phrase, which is a kind of verbal talisman for them severally; they then enact a short episode defining the routine of their daily life, which encompasses the chosen phrase within the dialogue and to some degree explains its meaningfulness to them currently. The seven are then each given an extended 'act' or episode, which shows their routine being challenged by a form of possession (alcohol-addiction, passion, obsession with the past, fear, violence, spiritual or psychic invasion, ecstasy); each faces a rift in the self and the need to shape a new identity through an experience of trauma. The play ends with the seven appearing in turn to outline in a frank confession (direct address) to the audience how their lives have changed as a consequence of experiencing possession.

These fragmentary lives are given thematic cohesion by the device of staging interludes between the major scenes, which outline through short episodes of dance, mime, and ritual the narrative-line of Euripides' tragedy. The focal figure

---

[11] The text of the play has come to be thought of as by Churchill alone, but as she admits frankly in her Introduction to a collection of her plays for dancers: 'the writing is as much David Lan's as mine, and, as with other Joint Stock shows, it owes a great deal to the company.' See Churchill (1998), vii.

in these interludes is always Dionysus, a being of consummate physical grace ('He is played by a man. He wears a white petticoat').[12] The characteristically succinct stage direction offers what is likely to be the sum of a spectator's initial experience of the figure: awareness through two stark facts of the character's androgyny. At the end of each interlude, which manifests his growing power within the story of his relations with Pentheus and Agave, Dionysus selects the next of the modern characters to undergo transformation. By way of introduction, they each speak again the talismanic phrase with which they first announced themselves. The ensuing sequence then shows each facing what Churchill in her introduction to the play terms 'an undefended day',[13] a day in which all habitual defences, values, inherited cultural conditioning, and social restraints that determine one's self control are abandoned, consciously, unwittingly, wilfully, or on impulse; and the *id* reigns shamelessly, since 'there is nothing to protect you from the forces inside and outside yourself'.[14]

To answer the question why the creative and directorial group in their initial planning turned for inspiration to Euripides' *Bacchae*, Churchill describes how the collaborators' original decision, much influenced by her input, was to contest what she deemed at that point in time the essentializing feminist trope that men are inherently violent, women inherently passive. Once women and violence became the subject of their debate, then Euripides' plays generally and *Bacchae* in particular were continually referenced. Quickly the spectrum of questioning widened to consider the contexts of women's violence to others and to themselves; violence as a means to female empowerment; and, following on from arguing over the degree to which violence is gender-specific, where lie the 'softer' images of male sexuality (the ways men manifest intensity of passion, are capable of embracing ecstasy, engage in dance as liberating, or realize the feminine in themselves, the anima, creatively).

The particular structure of linked episodes described above was evolved to present the debate as just that for audiences: not to offer answers but to stimulate further questioning and discussion.[15] I have stressed the nature of that structure because it brilliantly illuminates Roland Barthes's contention that there is a 'constant game of hide and seek between meaning and form that defines myth'.[16] Here a spectator faces seven wide-ranging variations on a given theme

---

[12] Ibid. 3.
[13] Churchill and Lan (1986), 5. This, the first printed text of the play, was on sale as the programme throughout the run of Joint Stock's production. (This way of offering audiences the text of a new work is the usual practice at the Royal Court Theatre.)
[14] Ibid. 5.
[15] My account of the rehearsal processes that went into the making of *A Mouthful of Birds* draws on Churchill and Lan's accounts of their work on, and intentions in creating the play to be found in their various introductions to the programme and published texts and my discussions with Ian Spink (all cited above); also on the principles and rehearsal practices of Joint Stock Theatre Company, as recounted in Ritchie (1987).
[16] Barthes (1972), 128.

that is the myth enshrined in *Bacchae*, though that greater theme is only gradually, if systematically revealed through the sequence of interludes; the 'meanings' proffered are multiple and multivalent, because the myth hovers always behind and within the modern-day dramas but in a manner that avoids the risk of its influence being seen as restrictive or essentializing (when the inevitable consequence would be that the drama in performance would become overly predictable).

All seven actors from the main episodes dance in the interludes but no precise parallels are drawn between the ancient and modern roles they impersonate. (Good musical variations are ones where the theme is wittily intimated, hinted at; where the variation exists in an imaginative association with the theme that inspired it.) Only the dancing Dionysus, the man in the petticoat (and not Pentheus or Agave) crosses occasionally the temporal and stylistic divide and becomes to some degree a constant in a spectator's shaping of meaning.

What of the place, function, and style of dance in all this? Ian Spink is a highly eclectic choreographer but a dominant influence on his creativity has been Merce Cunningham and his new 'pure' dance vocabulary with a tendency to emphasize the importance of movement for its own sake.[17] Spink's work particularly reflects Cunningham's interest in questioning the traditions of gender-inflected movement in both classical ballet and in the work of his one-time mentor, Martha Graham, and his concern with ritualizing everyday or pedestrian movement. But Spink was also of the generation that profited richly by the upsurge of interest in contact improvisation and, from that, the potential of improvisation as a mode of invention.

His works have demonstrated a delight in mixing styles to the point where his distinctive 'voice' might best be described as one involving a conscious fusion, a flexibility to move away from one style at any point in his invention in order to explore tangents, reversals, oppositions in style. Here creatively in dance terms is the exact complement of the openness to experience that *A Mouthful of Birds* is representing in its psychological, emotional, and social themes. A pertinent example of this is to be found in the episode focused on Dan, a vicar, whose recurrent personal phrase is 'I don't believe God is necessarily male'.[18] Given that, it is not surprising that Dan along with his dog-collar is clad in a petticoat over trousers and sandals (he was so dressed in the original production, though that detail is not carried through into the printed stage directions).[19] Nor is it surprising that this is the first occasion on which Dionysus enters the modern world: in the initial production they circled each other with absolute eye-contact

---

[17] While a young dancer in Australia, Spink had taken daily class with Cunningham's company while they were on tour there and this remained a lasting influence. For a detailed examination of this background, see Cave (2004).

[18] Churchill (1998), 23. The whole episode centring on Dan is to be found 23–7.

[19] The text printed with the programme (Churchill and Lan (1986), 38, 40) carries two photographs from this sequence that show distinctly how Dan was dressed for this production.

so that the audience could register the tokens of a similar androgyny and an effect, seemingly, of inherited power.

I wish to dwell on this episode in some detail, since it is potentially the most difficult of the sequences to gauge simply from the published text but also because (a daring enterprise) it engages specifically with Dionysiac ecstasy. What was clearly for Greek audiences a credible and profoundly complex experience is decidedly difficult to communicate to a modern audience. Numerous recent productions of *Bacchae* have failed in their attempts to realize a believable state of ecstasy in their handling of the chorus, being either pedestrian because overly literal in matching the imagery of the text or embarrassing in their attempts to realize what it is supposed will evoke impressions of a total abandonment of the self. It is here that Spink's free-flowing, pliant, ever-changing style came into its own as depicting a dancer's ability to live so deeply in the moment of the dance that the movement is an extemporized playing out in the body of that inner identification.

Good contact improvisation communicates from dancers to spectators a mounting physical exhilaration. The style requires each partner to sustain a consummate awareness of the other's body-weight and the disposition of the body-mass throughout the given skeleton. When that is achieved, then it is possible for the partners confidently, shamelessly to take risks with balance, supporting and catching: there is joy in risk, a communal ecstasy in and through the dance and the levels of trust that it requires. The result is a form of transcendence of the body's limits in the partners' giving and receiving themselves to and from each other. The imagery suggested by the continually close bodily contact may to a spectator seem wonderfully erotic, but the acute degree of awareness required of the participants intimates a balancing discipline. There is a sense of a profound intimacy coupled with a rare objectivity, as the focus must always be on the dance and not the individual dancers. This was the style pursued in Dan's episode to a degree that was liberating and disturbing in equal measure: liberating in its immediate effects; disturbing in its consequences.

Dan dances with both female and male partners, whom he brings to his home; they are people of sheltered, closeted, frightened or puritanical mindsets; he seats each of them in a chair and using chair or partner as his support, he dances for them but always with their seated forms as centre of a kind of physical adoration or worship; they are the focus of his absolute, undeviating awareness and attention; their situation, at once spectator and participant, frees them into an ecstasy so intense, so emotionally overwhelming, that they die. Put into words, this sounds preposterous, comic, absurd, grotesque. Danced, the situation is seductive, mesmeric, tender, since each of his dances is a giving of Dan's self to the seated one, his body-lines drawing spectators' attention continually to his partners', as in turn their consciousness opens up to their own potential for transcendence.

There are several instances within *Bacchae* that may have afforded the inspiration for Dan's episode: there is Semele's desire to see Zeus in his full godhead at the moment of consummation, which resulted in her death by fire; and there is the more extended exploration in the tragedy of Dionysus' power to enchant Pentheus to reveal his innermost, hidden, feared, and repressed self to the god, which leads inexorably to his murder. So much for the liberating aspects of the sequence; the ethical issues implicit in what one is watching are, however, deeply disturbing (even though there is no physical violence), not least in what is implied about *compliant* victims. Churchill and Lan might have framed the episode as a scenario for dancing and left the question of an appropriate response either to Spink to define through his choreography or to the spectator. Instead they chose to foreground the question of judgement and in a quite remarkable fashion.

All the danced material is framed within a divided playing space by extended conversations between two prison warders, a man and a woman, from which we come to realize that the danced episodes are situated in time past and that Dan has been convicted of murder, that the deaths continue within the prison cells, that the authorities are uncertain whether to class Dan as male or female and consequently have been moving him/her between institutions. To the prison officers Dan is a 'case', an object that rouses their disbelief and weary distaste; they talk of him in a brutally stark language and, when they get an opportunity to read Dan's private diaries, they do so in a jeering tone ('Call this handwriting? You wouldn't think he'd been educated at all').[20] Their choice of language invites judgement, not because it *places* Dan or defines his psychology but because it exposes the degree to which the warders are constricted within their concepts of what is *normal*. The mode of voicing their judgement at once discredits it, particularly since it is juxtaposed with the dance that the audience is simultaneously watching in another part of the stage space.

Juxtaposing danced and spoken drama in this way (where do spectators choose to place their attention?) evokes something of the mystery of the Dionysiac experience and the degree to which it lies outside or beyond modern codes of value, which too quickly condemn it as shocking, shameful, or sensational. Dance, ritual, and stylized movement patterns are used repeatedly throughout *A Mouthful of Birds* in this way as strategies to liberate spectators from privately conditioned or from traditional patterns of response and to invite openness to other possibilities of interpretation.[21] Dance in these contexts is metaphoric, poetic, allusive, suggestive, compelling of a spectator's attention yet resistant to

---

[20] Churchill (1998), 26.

[21] In the next sequence entitled 'Pig', the audience observes a Eurocrat who becomes passionately enamoured of a pig; the passion and the man's fascination for the creature are evoked through dance, which is often required to be staged against the flow of chat of the man's family, friends and colleagues, who see him as an occasion for innuendo and derogatory jokes. For a full discussion of this episode, see Cave (1997), 81–105.

overly precise and so potentially reductive definitions; it eludes the judgemental pressures that reside in words.

Arguably the most surprising of Spink's choices of dance idiom for the initial production was that for telling within the eight interludes the narrative outline of *Bacchae*. It was the closest he came to Cunningham's idiosyncratic style: cool, supremely controlled, performed as if to some deep internal rhythm, which endows movement with intimations of the hieratic. The performance began with Philippe Giraudeau as Dionysus dancing in this mode, alone in a world seemingly apart; his 'possession' of Agave was his imparting that style of moving to her; on seeing this, Pentheus judged it to be aloof, withdrawn, subversive; it excited his anger because it was clearly a mode of self-expression he could neither share nor understand.

The distanced quality of this aspect of the performance meant that the myth was rehearsed as a re-enactment; even at its horrifying climax with a murder and dismemberment, the story did not dominate the audience's awareness at the expense of the seven modern life stories, even though elements of the myth resonate through all of them. The chosen dance idiom placed the rendering of the myth seemingly outside the constraints of time and history, yet that idiom in no way questioned the rightfulness of the myth's permanence as a cultural icon. To re-order Barthes's terms: the myth in this work is the form that gives complexity of meaning to each of the modern lives. Dance and forms of physicality in *A Mouthful of Birds* offer a connection between modernity and myth. I am reminded at this stage of my discussion of Thomas Moore's commentary on the work of the Jungian analyst, James Hillman; referring to Hillman's contention that '[u]ntil the soul gets what it wants, it must fall ill again', Moore observes: 'The therapist attends to the soul . . . One looks for the myth of the symptom. . . . A symptom is an opportunity as well as a suffering. The therapist has to find its poetry and its dramatic form.'[22] The god who presides over this form of therapy, he sees as Dionysus. The expressivity of the body in its range of potential styles for moving, I would argue, performs such a cathartic healing in *A Mouthful of Birds* by freeing those seven represented, angst-driven lives from pejorative containment as 'cases'. It allows each of them uniquely to *be*.

If the structuring devices free the audience from the pressure to judge in *A Mouthful of Birds*, those in *Lives of the Great Poisoners* seem designed to activate moral discrimination. Drama and dance are now supplemented with music and song, as an *a capella* choir and a trained opera singer augment the cast of performers and the collaboration was extended to include Orlando Gough, the composer.[23] Again as in *A Mouthful of Birds* we see represented a range of life

---

[22] Moore (1990), 72.

[23] An equally important collaborator was Antony McDonald, the stage designer, who was included in the initial planning sessions and devised in response to these a sharply raked playing space, occupying much of stage-centre and stage-left, backed by two vast, white screens (their tops cut on a sharp diagonal) on to which appropriate imagery was projected. The strange angles of it all evoked increasingly in the spectator the idea of the world sliding downward into moral chaos.

stories, all, as the title intimates, perpetrators of murder by poisoning; but in the new work we experience an intricate weaving of historical periods: the Edwardian London of Dr Crippen; mid-eighteenth-century Paris that was the scene of Madame de Brinvilliers' activities; and ancient Corinth, site of Medea's vengeance, while through the action roams the figure of the twentieth-century scientist, Midgley, the industrial chemist, who by inventing CFC gases and leaded petrol threatened the life of the planet. An interesting question posed by the title is how precisely one should interpret the epithet, *great*? Does it indicate the degree of notoriety? Is it to be assessed in terms of the largest number of victims or the intensity of the motivation to murder? The question remains teasingly unanswered.

It seems the function of dance and song within the piece, and especially their particular rhythms, is to create a distinct moral atmosphere in each sequence. We witness three crimes of passion, yet the Crippen episode is reduced to music-hall vaudeville (the victim, the doctor's wife, Cora, was a music-hall singer and friend of Marie Lloyd); Medea's story is presented as grand opera with balletic interlude; and Brinvilliers lifestyle is rendered as an absurdist black farce with its multiple acts of treachery, infidelities, and double-crossings, its endless administering of poison and taking of antidotes. Gough's music adapts readily to the changing demands for pastiche of period styles.

The thematic focus is the motivation for the will to murder. In the case of the three main poisoners, murder becomes an expression of the ego: Crippen makes a bid to revive his ailing libido by using murder as the means to legitimize his adulterous liaison with Ethel, his lover; for Medea murder is an impassioned reassertion of a damaged, because ill-treated self; for Mme de Brinvilliers murder is pursued for its own sake, a manic round of poisonings that has become mechanical rather than motivated, feeding only her lust for power and control over others. But threading his way through their scenes there is always Midgley, the seeming innocent, naively unobservant of what he is witnessing or even participating in (it is Midgley, appropriately, who takes Medea's present of the lethal dress to Creusa): if naivety here is to be taken as a correlative of scientific objectivity, then it defines, and to some degree determines in him a total want of moral sense or historical insight.

The dance sequence that I wish to investigate in detail within these contexts is the central episode in Medea's section, involving the death of Creusa. History tends to privilege the murderer in terms of achieving a lasting name. Who remembers the name of Crippen's wife, beyond perhaps a few historians of popular theatre? Brinvilliers' countless victims included her family (nameless,

---

Unfortunately little of his contribution is extant beyond some photographs of the production, which tend to privilege the performers rather than the stage space, though there is one of part of the designer's model box and some of the projected images. See Churchill et al. (1993). None of the photographs is reproduced in the later publication of the text in Churchill (1998).

and achieving definition only by their particular relationships with her) and the unknown criminals and hospital patients, who suffered at her hands. In artistic representations attention is centred on the murderer to a degree that displaces or marginalizes the victim, which is especially the case in Greek tragedy where violence is relegated to offstage space as a required dramatic convention.[24]

Murder is the erasure of a body, of an individual; yet conventional forms of dramatic representation serve to compound the crime (only scenes of protracted torture allow the victim the space before death in which to establish an identity). In Creusa's onstage death in *Lives of the Great Poisoners*, spectators are required to watch and imaginatively engage with the victim's experience of murder as the process in its horror is defined through dance and mime. Creusa's dance renders onstage what is conventionally held to be unstageable: a body is deployed to enact the consumption of a body by fire. What is particularly unnerving for an audience is that most of the cast of characters are onstage viewing the event, themselves constituting a similar body of spectators. The theatre audience observes the range of the characters' responses: Medea is triumphant; Creon is in a frenzy of grief; the chorus of poisons show sadistic delight; Midgley is blank with incomprehension.

The whole performance of *Lives of the Great Poisoners* invites a critique of modes of representation and the moral attitudes they promote and it also invites an audience to interrogate how morally they respond to traditional codes and conventions. All the theatre styles used in the piece whether drawn from high or from low culture are immediately recognizable to a cultured audience and all are complicit in the dis-inscribing of the individual sacrificed to another's passion. Who exactly determines what is and is not stageable or stageworthy and why? Who chooses the privileged focus of a drama and why? What ethically are the consequences of such choices, especially when they have hardened into accepted (and expected) conventions?

Creusa's dance of death is free of such constrictions: the abject is for once placed centre-stage to challenge historical concepts of decorum. Being unexpected, it has a greater immediacy than any other episode in the performance. The character cannot describe her plight (as dancer and as victim she is the silenced one) but she has access to other means of expression: a body can best express a body's invasion by a process that cannot be arrested as it inexorably eliminates all vestige of that body's expressivity and denies to it any lasting token of what constitutes its humanity. Because the medium and its codes of signification are unfamiliar to many spectators (and not specifically *translatable* even to other trained dancers), meanings cannot be extrapolated by habitual modes of

---

[24] Cassandra in Aeschylus' *Agamemnon* is a notable exception, where her prophetic status allows her to give voice to a vision of her horrifying experience of entrapment and death before the event, so that spectators marvel the more at her stoic acceptance of her fate and her calm exit into her enemies' palace in full knowledge of what will befall her.

interpretation: spectators must either resist the demands of the medium altogether, or allow the medium to take complete possession of their imaginations. If
the latter route is pursued and the victim allowed centrality, then the instigator of
the violence is progressively destabilized morally. Medea is triumphant: 'I love
this rage'[25] (the phrase, given but once in the printed text, is repeated eight times
in the sung score and is set to an intricately varying, descending chromatic line
that insinuates about itself at the top of the soprano's register). But the effect for
all its operatic display is hollow, rhetorical, banal, after the event just witnessed:
Creusa's sudden appalled realization of what is actually happening; the flailing
hands that evoke at once the terrified struggle to tear the dress away and also
the flames that are engulfing the body; the violent contractions and expansions,
the impossible balances as pain wrenches and racks her physique in inconceivable
agonies, the final stillness, prone on the sheet already prepared as a shroud by
the Chorus of Poisons. The abject has 'spoken'.

Dance in this instance allowed the collaborators to move behind the mythical
material to interrogate one of the conventions of classical Greek performance of
tragedy. Though it may seem odd to end this essay with a discussion of *Hotel*
(1997), the last collaboration between Spink and Churchill, I would argue that
the work can be interpreted as a further interrogation of a classical theatrical
convention: the chorus.

Hotel comprises two short parts, which feature a group of thirteen singers
along with two dancers; the first, 'Eight Rooms', shows various couples and
loners going to bed in a hotel and rising for breakfast; the second 'Two Nights'
positions the singers as observers of the dancers, who, it is to be supposed, are
alternate occupants of the same room. Both sequences involve dance and sung
lyrics that deploy an enigmatic, poetic text. In a brilliant creative conceit, the
sixteen rooms of the opening piece are condensed into the one stage space, which
presents the featurelessness of a contemporary hotel; the singers move within the
same performance area but have to *suggest* that they are simultaneously inhabiting
a number of different rooms. The couples have truncated snatches of conversation and play out familiar, pedestrian routines of behaviour, which indicate long
acquaintance with each other. The pairs are aware of each other's presence within
the space but of no-one else. Fifteen performers moved within a confined area
but had eye-contact with only one other person onstage.

Dance in the conventional sense of the term had no place in this piece and yet
it would be wrong to assign to Spink simply the role of director. While the
movement style was wholly realistic in its evocation of unpacking, watching
television, picking up toothbrush and towel prior to exiting to the bathroom and
so on, the staging required the spatial awareness and ingenuity of Spink's
choreographic artistry if there were to be no untimely collisions, no crossings

---

[25] Churchill (1998), 216.

through other people's sight-lines, which would immediately break the illusion that each given couple were inhabiting the space alone. The enacted illusion required the performers to communicate a sense of separateness and isolation between the pairs, but the technical realization of that illusion required within the whole group a consummate and undeviating awareness of themselves as an ensemble.[26]

The couples and the singletons were variously characterized in the programme as 'Silent', 'US', 'Affair', 'Old French', 'Gay', 'Drunk', but their presence in the space was functional (the hotel offered each a bed for the night) and the anonymity of the place steadily imposed itself on them, draining them of individuality as they went through the common rituals of preparing for bed. The music offered a counterpart to this, as what at first seemed random phrases shared by the various couples steadily interwove to form dynamic blocks of harmony or dissonance, before finding a place within the vocal texturing where melodic individuality was lost. For spectators this was to experience a process of depersonalization as a chorus came into being: particular vocal timbres were still recognizable, certain words, snatches of melodic lines or sustained notes were vaguely identifiable but a group identity had asserted itself within which a humdrum individuality was subsumed.

In these terms, 'Eight Rooms' could be interpreted as a meditation on the demands made on performers when coming together to form a dramatic ensemble, musical chorus or *corps de ballet*, the required loss (so far as that is humanly possible) of private personalities in the shaping of a commonality of aesthetic purpose. (How suggestive that French term, '*corps*', is with its embracing of an entire company within but the one body!) That gleams of personhood are briefly apprehended only stresses what is lost to the overriding discipline of the form. 'Eight Rooms' takes us behind the scenes, as it were, to show us the chorus (of singer- dancer-actors, like their Greek forebears) in formation. As such the piece revitalizes a dramatic convention that is too easily taken for granted, because it is too easy to marginalize the performers of the chorus, given the anonymity that their function demands of them. Spink and Churchill right the balance by

---

[26] In conversation with me, Ian Spink described an incident in rehearsals for the Brinvilliers section of *Lives of the Great Poisoners*, which in retrospect might have provided the inspiration for the basic concept of 'Eight Rooms': 'Some of the scenes were highly complex. For example, towards the end in the section dealing with Mme de Brinvilliers there is a gambling party involving considerable intrigue between the various characters. This involved characters having to move across stage to make connections with an accomplice or confidant. These characters were all singing while moving into their different formations, and all the time a rather bizarre ballet for the dancers was taking place between them. Some kind of logic had to be followed, and I had to keep taking the dancers away to alter their material so that it would fit within the larger stage patterns of movement. The actors had to concentrate on whom they were watching as distinct from whom they were talking to and on where they were positioned within the stage space. Within all this complex action the card game continues to be played. Devising the scene felt like trying to put some amazing jigsaw puzzle together.' See Spink and Cave (1995), 298; and a photograph of this moment in the production reproduced in Churchill et al. (1993), 49.

reminding modern-day spectators of the complex integration of performative skills of which a player in the chorus (traditionally) must have been a masterly exponent.

If 'Eight Rooms' explores the required conditions of performance for the chorus, 'Two Nights' may be said to investigate their function. In Greek tragedy the chorus are observers of the main action: they comment on events; ruminate on past history in an effort to explain the current crisis; pray to whatever god seems most appropriate to help their limited understanding of the situation that engulfs them; they advise, but rarely influence the course of events; their role is to react not to initiate; largely passive, their lot is to accept the consequences of what is unfolding before them. They *contextualize* the tragedy that they witness. Within the layout of the Greek playing space, they were set apart from the main actors: lower, more grounded.

In 'Two Nights', the singers are united as a chorus; they watch the two dancers, who occupy the main performing space, and provide them with a musical accompaniment (which Gough asserts should neither 'mimic the text' nor 'ignore the text', but 'connect on an emotional rather than literal level').[27] They lurk as a body within the shadows on the periphery of the lighted areas, a heard presence, dimly seen (the dancers seem in turn to be involved in tense, private scenarios that demand they by contrast make no sound).

Churchill's text comprises edited fragments from a diary she found in a hotel room: it was anonymous, but its author became momentarily a presence in her awareness and then vanished, once her reading ceased. The two dancers seem to embody individuals who similarly 'disappeared': they arrive defined by specific appearances (she, for example, has blood on her clothes at first and sports a gun), they struggle with their desperation and then eradicate their former selves (he by the violent means of committing suicide; she by donning a transformingly skimpy red dress and a whole new body language and posture).[28]

The lyrics sung by the chorus reach after possible explanations of what they see, but there can be no literal interpretation of those private worlds inhabited by the dancers, no direct sharing of a means of communication. The experience that motivates the dancers' movements remains inscrutable; the singers can only hesitantly approximate a meaning within the terms and limitations of their own art. Dance here is used to illuminate the distance, the apartness, the bewildered *otherness* that characterizes the formal chorus of tragedy. But far from being defeatist in its effect, this highlights the whole issue of interpretation for the audience: the gaps in the chorus's understanding stimulate a more

---

[27] Text and programme for *Hotel*, presented by Second Stride, Churchill (1997), unpaginated preliminary matter (recto of page iv).

[28] None of these details are recorded in the text; the account here draws on my notes and memories of watching the production compared with reviewers' observations. A collection of reviews of those performances is to be found in *Theatre Record* (9–22 April, 1997), 507–8 and in the following issue (23 April–6 May, 1997), 574–5.

concentrated attention to what the dancers are seeking to convey through their chosen medium of expression. There would appear to be an exact correspondence here to the spectator's relationship with the choruses of Greek tragedy in performance. *Hotel* in its two distinct sections wonderfully reanimates a modern theatregoer's appreciation of the chorus, which directors currently tend to label a 'problem' and handle self-consciously instead of unapologetically as a *given* to which aspects of contemporary experimental theatre practice can give performers and spectators ready access.

All the collaborations between Caryl Churchill as playwright and Ian Spink as choreographer and director with their varying associates leave audiences in a state of open-ended enquiry. They all in various ways bring the past in the form of Greek tragedy (and at times its related culture of performance) to speak directly to the present, but not in a manner that invites reverence for an inherited cultural icon. Rather past and present are brought into a condition of dialogue, where what is of value in the past is renewed rather than merely accepted and where what is troubling, combative or questionable within the ideologies underpinning the conventions of the genre is offered for debate and interrogation. Throughout the collaborations dance is the preferred medium for effecting this coming into a relationship of past with present. Because Spink's choreography deploys a fusion of many styles of dance, there is in his work always the potential for a rich ambiguity, which Churchill's scenarios, plot-lines and dialogue contextualize, support, and augment rather than reduce to cerebral definitions. Her words never seek to extrapolate meanings from his patterned movement. Rather the dramatic structures and the choreography of their collaborations invite spectators of those works to enter that state of mind that Yeats deemed the proper aim to cultivate through performance (and indeed all art-forms): the state of 'excited reverie', where spectators will be at once alert, informed, engaged and, crucially, where they will be stimulated always to question.[29]

---

[29] W. B. Yeats, 'A Prayer for my Daughter' Yeats (1977), 403. Yeats, walking on a wild, tempestuous night, imagines how his infant daughter's life will evolve and his mind is full of a questioning of possibilities. Significantly, the full context of the phrase defines what approximates to a Bacchic experience: 'Imagining in excited reverie / That the future years had come, / Dancing to a frenzied drum / Out of the murderous innocence of the sea.'

V

THE ANCIENT CHORUS
IN CONTEMPORARY
PERFORMANCE

20

Staniewski's Secret Alphabet of Gestures: Dance, Body, and Metaphysics

Yana Zarifi

'The liveliest lecture on semiotics ever produced' is how a reviewer of Poland's leading theatre company, Gardzienice, described their 2002 adaptation of Euripides' *Electra*.[1] Directed by the company's founder and Artistic Director, Włodzimierz Staniewski, the subtitle of the piece is '*Cheironomia*—a Theatrical Essay', literally 'an alphabet of gestures'. Gardzienice's *Elektra* opens with an upstage screen projection of a second-century BCE papyrus with Euripides' music for the *Orestes*. An actor points to the screen and reads out the words; as the reconstructed music is played, the company sing and relate arm movements to the sound-heights depicted graphically on the inscribed music. Subsequently the chorus leader cries out: 'Beautiful!', and the chorus members cup their breasts; 'Muscles!', and they flex their muscles—each move mirroring gestures from a Greek vase-painting projected onto the screen. Shortly, the still movements pick up speed and develop into a vigorous dance (see Figure 20.1).

This gestural vocabulary serves not only to enable the audience to recognize the story-telling interludes during the course of the play, but it also functions as a kind of leitmotif underlying musical composition, plot construction, and the expression of character. The exposition of this vocabulary in the opening scene of the performance is one of many examples of Staniewski's method, which mingles archaeology, literary sources, and metaphor in order to make antiquity palpable.

The *Elektra*'s semiotic lecture and Gardzienice's training exercises based on Greek iconography suggest a deceptively simple correspondence between image, sound, and gesture. The 'alphabet' of gestures is in fact an ingenious theatrical pun belonging to a complex dance language, which has evolved during Gardzienice's manifold intercultural exchanges and performances over a number of years and which has eventually been layered with references to the cultural remnants of Greek antiquity.

---

[1] Soloski (2005). The performance took place at the La Mama Theatre, New York.

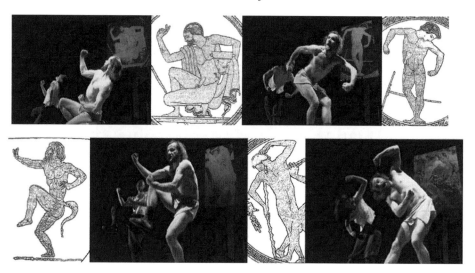

Figure 20.1 Grzegorz Podbieglowski in *Elektra* (2005).

THE SECRET ALPHABET: EASTERN
EUROPEAN PERSPECTIVES

This 'alphabet' of gestures is not simply a set of word–image–movement–sound correspondences, but an ecstatic language rooted in the spirit as much as in the flesh. Moreover, it should not be viewed in isolation, but from the perspective of Staniewski's own idiosyncratic approach to antiquity and to theatre composition, which is rooted in the dramatic tradition of Poland.

Polish drama, especially in the nineteenth century, was visionary, mystical, and unhampered by realistic notions of time, space, and the limiting practicalities which prevailed in western Europe. Poland, having been deprived of a territorial identity for much of its history, had a culture that was primarily defined and sustained by artists who were often also political activists and soldiers, usually in exile or working under censorship. Constant occupation and partition meant that plays which were an outlet for political and metaphysical expression could be staged neither at home nor abroad being either too subversive or too inaccessible. Keeping the idea of a nation alive involved an emphasis on action and a strong metaphysical drive to communicate with a spiritual world deemed to be unattainable through the powers of the Church or State. Polish playwrights—especially those of the nineteenth century—often mingled the metaphysical with the exterior world, mixing the earthly with the unearthly in a way that, though unsuitable for the illusionist staging of their own times, anticipated what we now call total theatre—a theatre that places much emphasis on the body as a means of expression and in which there are no clear divisions between dance, music, words, painting, or architecture.

Nowhere is this articulated better than in the work of Adam Mickiewicz (1798–1855), arguably Poland's greatest literary figure and the main exponent of Romanticism.[2] In his prophetic treatise on the theatre in 1843, known as the *16th Lecture at the Collège de France*, Mickiewicz envisions a theatre that would encompass all the arts—painting, music, architecture—and draw on ancient myth, ancient Greek tragedy, indigenous rites as well as on the latest technology.[3] Mickewicz also drew parallels between Polish winter–spring rites and the Greek Anthesteria.[4] His arch drama, *Forefathers' Eve* (1823, 1832), written in four parts, expresses philosophical and patriotic themes metaphorically, through a biannual folk ritual, *Dziady*, which combines pagan mysticism with the Catholic All Souls' Day. There is no sequential narrative development in the work which is a *mêlée* of dreams, visions, reality, and a representation of rites evoking the spirits of the dead. The drama enacts a battle between angels and demons over the hero's soul, and the hero's struggle to transcend his personal romantic disillusionment to attain patriotic strength is at its centre.

Ancient Greece had been a point of reference for Polish dramatists before Mickiewicz. For example, Jan Kochanowski's *The Dismissal of the Grecian Envoys* (1578) explores national identity through the diplomatic problems posed by Helen's abduction in the Trojan War. He also wrote a moving compilation of laments following models of Aeschylean and Greek lyric poetry.[5] It is important to note that ancient Greek themes in eastern Europe are not necessarily filtered through the western European Renaissance during subsequent centuries. Greek antiquity became associated with a movement in Poland known as the Slavonic Renaissance; and even though the nationalist agenda faded over the years, Greek deities have Slavic faces and Greek 'satyrs inhabit Polish forests'.[6] Classical antiquity in Polish drama is thus often clothed in both pagan and Christian rites as well as the ceremonies from the multiplicity of ethnicities found in eastern Europe (Lithuanian, Ukranian, Byelorussian, Hasidic, to name but a few). These combinations, together with the ecstatic, revelatory, and 'Dionysiac' aspect of ancient Greek culture and religion (filtered partly through Russia), also underpin the often dreamlike, fantastical quality of Polish theatre. This 'ecstatic' aspect, however, was informed by an insistence that portrayals of the ancient world should take account of new and precise knowledge brought by archaeological and other discoveries. The key figure in this so-called 'Slavonic Renaissance', the

---

[2] He is also an important source of inspiration for many leading artists such as Wyspianski, Schiller, Osterwa, Kantor, Grotowski in Poland (to name but a few) and of course Staniewski.

[3] Gerould and Ploszewski (1986), 91–7.

[4] Koliankiewicz (2001), 252–5.

[5] Kochanowski (2001).

[6] Milosz (1983), 60.

erudite and Hellenophile classicist, Tadeusz Zielinski maintained that an academic understanding of antiquity was of primary importance.[7]

The encounter of human and godly beings, spirits, and deities from classical Greek, Polish, and biblical history, including a figure representing both Christ and Apollo, can be found in Stanislaw Wyspianski's *Acropolis* (1903) often restaged—most notably by Witkiewicz (1904) and Grotowski (1969). Wyspianski (1869–1907) was a graphic artist, poet, and set designer who, according to Miłosz, thought in theatrical terms expressing himself not through words but 'with tension of his will and with emotions expressed in colour, movement and sound'. Like Wyspianski, Stanisław Witkiewicz (1885–1939), better known as Witkacy, was also a painter-dramatist. In his Introduction to the *Theory of Pure Form and Theatre* (1920), he proposes a form of theatre analogous to painting which functions 'like an abstract drug, enabling us to experience metaphysical feelings'.[8]

The work of Staniewski, as Alison Hodge has stated, has been 'forged in the persuasive fires' of the same traditions as Wyspianski, Witkacy, and others too numerous to mention.[9] In the performances he has directed and in his associated cultural activities, we find several of the features mentioned above and most characteristically the unusual combination of the ecstatic, the fantastical, and the satirical with an accent on the sort of classicist erudition insisted on by Zielinski. The features linking Staniewski to the wider tradition of physical and metaphysical theatre may be enumerated as follows: first, the inextricability of theatre from pressing spiritual, cultural, and topical concerns; secondly, the lack of division between body and spirit; thirdly, the emphasis on action; fourthly, the focus on the human body as a means of conveying metaphysical urgency; and lastly, the development of an aesthetic, which conflates painting, music, dance, and intense physical expressiveness at the expense of linear verbal discourse.

Staniewski, for example, often describes his method of theatrical composition as that of a painter, sculptor, musical composer, or even of a writer.[10] Discussing the iconography used in the preparation of Gardzienice's performance of *Avvakum* (1983), he says:

> Within traditional Orthodox terminology people didn't talk about 'painting' the icons; they talked about 'writing' the icons, or 'scripting' them.... The artist *writes* an exclamation, a prayer, a lamentation, a challenge to transcendence, to eternity. 'To write' ... is to appear.[11]

This interchangeability is not purely metaphorical; it is in fact a recognition of the hybridity of physical expression in much of eastern European theatre in

---

[7] Zielinksi, (1922).

[8] Quoted in Londré, (1991), 449.

[9] Staniewski and Hodge (2004), 9.

[10] 'The dance of the text', 'the writing of the icon', 'the music of the word', 'the gesture of the word', 'touching the evidence (the fragment of a vase)', 'singing the priming of the canvas', are all phrases used by Staniewski in the course of describing his dramaturgy.

[11] Staniewski and Hodge (2004), 109.

general, where the focus is on releasing an inner power. Staniewski is bent on releasing the 'inner force' of his artistic *prima materia* whether it be an icon, an ancient Greek musical inscription on a papyrus, a Ukranian folk song, or the fragment of a vase.[12]

VASE-PAINTING

The vase for Staniewski is a living fragment of antiquity within what he calls 'touching distance'; and he sometimes refers to the paintings as 'beings' with 'lives of their own', which must be allowed to 'move, escape from the vase, continue the dance within their own momentum.'[13] The dance of Staniewski's Greek productions—*Metamorphoses* (1997), *Elektra* (2002), and *Iphigenia at Aulis* (2007)—is conceived partly out of this metaphysical desire to 'escape from the vase' and partly out of the desire to make antiquity whole again—to piece it together from the fragments which broken vases represent.[14] Though exceptionally erudite and corroborated by historical, philosophical, and literary sources, Staniewski's references to these cultural remnants are, as he himself confesses, uncompromisingly artistic rather than scholarly. He approaches vase iconography more as a painter might than a photographer:

I pick those moves, turns, curves and dynamics which have the most impact. Then, later on, *like a painter*, working with the tempo, rhythm, changes in the dynamics, I use the same gesture but try to transform it into an allegorical language which breaks the realism.[15]

As my close collaborator for my research on Gardzienice, the artist Gayna Wiles explains:

There is a difference between a photographic still, a moment frozen in time, and a drawing which selects the energy of a pose or the key moment for the artist in a sequence of movements. Photographs show the figure caught in a movement. The pose described by the painter is not so much a still as *a choice of the most expressive moment* which

---

[12] Ibid. The icons presented an 'outer radiation', but Staniewski needed to release their 'inner power' and so found 'that this inner force can be retrieved and exposed through animating them, through creating "sung pictures"'.

[13] Staniewski and Hodge (2004), 137, 92. Gardzienice, invited by the Getty Museum in Los Angeles in 2004, performed scenes 'departing' from the celebrated Getty collection of Greek vases which were placed literally within 'touching distance' of the actors (and surrounded by armed guards to make sure that they were not in fact touched—a rule, in fact, broken by Staniewski).

[14] This is how Staniewski describes the process of turning surviving fragments of Greek musical notation into song: '[in the case of each fragment] we had to do with broken pieces—to speak in metaphors—of a broken vase: one piece had a head, on the second piece there was a leg raised ready to dance and on another there was some phallic shape. In order to make that debris, those miserable pieces 'come to life', I asked the actors to sing alternatively the relics of ancient musical notation and the selected ethnic songs from the area of the Ukranian Carpathian Mountains and the Bulgarian Rhodopes Mountains' (Staniewski (2006), 55).

[15] Staniewski and Hodge (2004), 33 (*my emphases*).

Figure 20.2 Courtship Dance of Achilles and Iphigenia. Drawing by Gayna Wiles.

encompasses the story and it must be visually flexible, changing as the viewer changes position.[16]

This echoes Staniewski, who in discussing the retrieval of movement from vases explicitly states that his 'intention is to retain the *essential quality* of the gesture' and that

The postures on the vases came from a forgotten line of life within ourselves—the desire to dance. They are not frozen, static postures: these figures are running, spinning, dancing, flying. The vases show the momentum captured by the painters and sculptors.[17]

Gayna Wiles's drawing of the courtship dance between Achilles and Iphigenia from a live performance of the Gardzienice *Iphigenia* articulates the dynamic three-cornered relationship between vase-painting, drawing from life, and dance (see Figure 20.2). Unlike the all-inclusiveness of the photograph of a live

---

[16] All quotations from Gayna Wiles are taken from private correspondence held by the author (*my emphases*).

[17] Staniewski and Hodge (2004), 33, 129 (*my emphases*).

performance, the painting is focused on what the painter chooses and the 'story' has to take place in a single space with a middle, a front, and a back. Gayna Wiles focuses on the movement and the relationship between the figures. Note how Iphigenia's left foot thrusts the viewer into the picture diagonally upwards, while her right heel seems to stop. She is on the back foot, but her heel and knee indicate that the centre of gravity is about to shift with the wider implication that the balance of her fate is on the verge of being tipped. The angles of her knee seem to be reflected by the corners of the boxes leading to her mother, Clytemnestra at the centre. Achilles is firm. The two main figures are linked by a diagonal line between Achilles' hand near the top left and Iphigenia's foot at the bottom right. The almost vase-like circularity of the shading melts the second figure from the left and the figure on the far right thus emphasizing Clytemnestra's importance in the centre. Unlike a more static black and white photograph or a line drawing, the use of chalk incorporates the idea of shadow. The diagonal lines of the chalk give energy and suggest fleetingness.

Both Gayna Wiles and Staniewski, in this sense, emphasize not only the movement in vase-painting but also aspects of the vase as a three-dimensional object with curved surfaces and shifting distances. As Gayna Wiles explains:

Drawing from life, the centre of gravity is an important tool to understand the dynamics of the figure, how the figure works. An artist is able to balance the mass of the figure against the point of gravity or disorientate the viewer by denying it. The vase painter denies expectation. There is often a ground line in a Greek vase but because the vessel is round and curved the viewpoint constantly changes. The figure can appear to shift. The vase is a functional object and the vase painter makes use of the curve of the vessel to create a sort of perspective, emphasise movement and narrative tension.

In one of Staniewski's pedagogical exercises, where actors assume vase-figure poses within a frame, the viewer's perspective is altered by either shifting the frame or by asking the actors to assume poses which partly exceed the contours of the frame.[18]

The 'performative' value of a vase inheres also in the space between figures. Staniewski draws attention to the space between figures outlined on the vase's surface. He deems this distance symbolic of a dramatic struggle for territory between characters portrayed on the vase, which occurs also between characters in Greek tragedy.[19] Here is what Gayna Wiles writes about vase-painting:

---

[18] This exercise led the 'Vase François' performance by students of the Academy for Theatre Practices (January 2008). It was also part of the preparatory work with vase-paintings for *Metamorphoses.*

[19] From a lecture at the XIIIth Meeting on Ancient Drama at the European Cultural Centre of Delphi, June 2007.

The contour of the figure describes the form of the body, and the relationship between two figures is given meaning by *the dynamic of the space between them*. Close observation from life allows the vase-painter to feel his way into the pose and manipulate the figure so that the viewer can understand human predicament, state of mind, drama of the narrative, physical effort.[20]

Greek vase iconography is a vital source of inspiration for Staniewski: hundreds of vase-paintings from the Geometric to the late Hellenistic periods are scrutinized for expressive hand-movements, for bends of the body, for whirling folds of the costume.[21] An experienced viewer of Greek vases will read these movements in the breathlessly rapid Gardzienice dances as costumes slip off to reveal parts of naked bodies, and as heads and arms tilt at strange angles.

AN ALCHEMY OF CULTURES

But the process of setting 'antiquity dancing'[22] involves not only the cultural remnants of ancient Greece, but also a multifaceted engagement with living performers and performance traditions from several cultures. Developed and distilled through actors' improvisations, Staniewski's alphabet is derived also from music, and from other gestural languages as divergent as the Hindu Sāma Veda of the Jaiminīya school *mudras*[23] and hand movements of Renaissance rhetorical arts.

'Music', says Staniewski, is 'at the core of everything I generate . . . a vital energy and life-force . . . [it is] my co-director.'[24] Before entering the world of antiquity with *Metamorphoses*, *Elektra*, and *Iphigenia*, Gardzienice had generated their performances in close association with indigenous music, rituals, and dances of communities from all over the world.[25] In every instance the music had

---

[20] *My emphases.*

[21] Mainly from the 6th to the 4th cent. BCE. For a series of hand movements from Boardman's Archaic Red-Figure vases which inspired Staniewski see Staniewski (2006), 43.

[22] See Staniewski and Hodge (2004), 137.

[23] Of the four Vedas (sacred texts), three are recited and the fourth, the Sāma Veda, is chanted. There are several traditions of chanting within the Sāma Veda, one of which is the Jaiminīya school who use a syllabic form of musical notation (as opposed to a numerical one) where the syllables are written above lines of the sacred text. There are variations in methods of performance and transmission not merely between schools but also within each school, and the particular branch of the Jaiminīya school whom Staniewski collaborated with, the Keralan Nambudiri Brāhmans, use a purely oral method of transmission and are 'dangerously approaching extinction' (Wayne 1977).

[24] See the accompanying pamphlet to Staniewski (2000), 35.

[25] Explorations and close mutual exchange of performances known as 'expeditions' and 'gatherings', have involved communities from Gardzienice's neighbouring Euro-Asian cultures—Jewish, ethnic Roma, Ukrainian, Lemo, Bielorussian ethnicities—and from places as remote as Lappland, Brazil, South Korea, and Sierra Madre. The company also receive visiting performers from a variety of cultures and performance traditions on home territory. See Filipowicz (1987), Staniewski and Hodge (2004) and Allain (1997). The results of these exchanges can be detected in

been live—it could be heard and felt—and the organic link between gesture and sound could be directly experienced.

The music of antiquity offers no such immediate access. With the disappearance of the ancient performers, the only surviving remnants are the rhythms contained by the song-words of lyric poetry and drama, images of musicians and dancers, and fragments of an elusive musical notation on papyri and stone. So, with approximately half of the fifty surviving musical fragments as starting point, Staniewski and the composer Maciej Rychły set about 'making the stones sing'.[26] The musical fragments included the First and Second Delphic Paeans inscribed on the outer marble wall of the Athenian Treasury at Delphi[27] and musical notation thought to belong to Euripides' *Iphigenia at Aulis*.[28]

Rychły assigned melody lines to the musical signs and built on rhythms of ancient Greek poetry by chanting what seemed like meaningless syllables until, together with the emotional impulses generated by the Gardzienice performers, they built a musical draft.[29] Balkan and Peloponnesian rhythms and songs from the Carpathian and Bulgarian mountains were gradually blended with the Greek paeans, hymns, and dramatic fragments to create the treasure trove of *Metamorphoses'* songs. The ethnic songs used to release the energy in the ancient Greek reconstruction had been chosen on the basis of their function—for instance, lamentation, invocation, wedding celebration. In Staniewski's words: this was in order 'to pour the still fermenting wine into the dry jugs of ancient relics'.[30]

The music was embodied and given life by the actors without betraying its roots in antiquity. Instead of using the composer's musical score, the actors had to devise their own, thereby establishing an inner connection with the notation. Gestures were generated from a combination of impulses from the actors' bodies reacting to the music as well as from the bodies adapting to vase and sculptural images chosen by Staniewski. Actors responded to sound-heights and lengths of the music with their arms, hands, and entire bodies, and audible and visible rhythmic breathing was woven into the overall texture. An extraordinary coherence developed as surrounding sounds of birds and barking dogs were incorporated into the music. The whole company always rehearsed in unison, constantly integrating the composer's material and thus creating a collective

---

the mingling of Kung Fu with the ancient Greek *pyrrhichē* in the *Iphigenia* and in the influence of the Sāma Veda chanters in the *Elektra*.

[26] There are about 50 in all. These fragments also included *The Song of Seikilos*, 1st cent. CE, preserved in the Copenhagen National Museum, inventory no. 14897. See West (1992) doc. 15, 301.

[27] *Second Delphic Paean* composed by Limenius and performed in 127 BCE at Delphi, now preserved in the Delphi Museum, inventory nos. 489, 1461, 1591, 209, 212, 225, 224, 215, 214.

[28] 3rd cent. copy of fragmentary notation to lines 784–92 and 1499–1509 of Euripides' *Iphigenia at Aulis*, see West (1992), doc. 4, 286. For information on the musical sources, see Staniewski (2000), pamphlet, 56–62.

[29] Maciej Rychły, see Staniewski (2000), pamphlet, 9–19.

[30] Staniewski (2006), 55.

experience that was more than its individual parts—as an important collaborator on the project remarked: 'there was no room for *private* breathing.'[31]

In the *Elektra*, the corporeal language which grew out of the 'stone-derived' musical structures of *Metamorphoses* was distilled and developed further to become the alphabet of gestures or the art of *cheironomia*. The conceptual frame for combining graphic representations of musical notation with gesture was not arbitrary: Staniewski had found a precedent for this in Sāma Veda chanting where hand gestures are inseparably connected to the sound lines and to the sequence of syllables associated with the sacred texts. Elaborate hand gestures follow the note, tempo, rhythm, and sung context of the chanting, while at the same time moving vertically and horizontally to match the height and length of the sounds.

Gardzienice also drew on hand gestures from European sixteenth-century works on oratory and rhetoric used in Elizabethan acting.[32] In Gardzienice's creations, philosophical and literary ideas are often actualized in physical movement. When life and history present the director with a new theme and a new aesthetic, the basic physical language changes accordingly and each new project generates its characteristic 'gestus'. Just as *cheironomia* is the prime constituent of the body language in the 'Greek' plays,[33] so too we find whirling in *Sorcery* (1981) and low bowing in *Avvakum* (1983).

The whirling and 'spinning' in *Sorcery* were part of an aesthetic which blended Belorussian, Ukrainian, and Hasidic tunes, wheeling dances and incantations with the ancestral spirit theme, folk wisdom, and occasional lines from Mickiewicz's *Forefather's Eve*.[34] In *Avvakum*, excerpts from the priest's biography and some elements from *Forefather's Eve* combine with Orthodox religious imagery, antiphonal singing from Mount Athos and alternating wild and calm pagan rituals. The low bowing 'gestus', expressing both submission and defiance, was retrieved from the religious icons and based on viewing the body as an allegorical cross.[35]

Elements of previous Gardzienice works often mutate into ones that follow in a process of continual evolution. While there is an intimate connection between physicality and a particular culture, these mutations sometimes reveal performative 'constants' with an immediacy which transcends historical and geographical

---

[31] Tomasz Rodowicz, director of the *Metamorphoses* musical project in Staniewski (2000), pamphlet, 24.

[32] See e.g. the illustrative cuts used to describe the proper use of hands in the art of rhetoric in John Bulwer (1644). This was the first English treatise on gesturing and the main source for subsequent research (e.g. Chambers (1923) fig. 55; Joseph (1951)). See also Władysław Kopaliński's *Dictionary of Symbols*, Warsaw, which is discussed in Staniewski (2006), 55.

[33] *Metamorphoses, Elektra*, and *Iphigenia*. Though there are significant differences between the three pieces in the use of *cheironomia*, Greek vase iconography is the defining source for the creation of the movement language in all three.

[34] Fagin (1977), 103–13.

[35] For an excellent detailed discussion, see Allain (1997), 67–9.

Figure 20.3 Whirling round Dionysos in *Metamorphoses*. Drawing by Gayna Wiles.

specificity. Whirling, for example, features not only in *Sorcery* but also in *Metamorphoses*, where four 'maenads' whirl around a Dionysus figure for an exhilaratingly long time in a crescendo that ends the performance. The whirling permeating the language of *Sorcery* drew on both Hasidic spinning, which expresses the release of an excess of joy, and on the turning of the whirling dervishes,[36] which transcends earthly reality. The same movement in *Metamorphoses* expresses Dionysiac ecstasy. While in *Sorcery* the spinning is derived from living ritual performances, in the *Metamorphoses* it is a delightfully blatant re-animation of the extensive vase iconography which portrays Dionysus surrounded by whirling maenads (see Figure 20.3).[37] Here the whirling on the vases is suggested by swirling costumes, flying hair, and positions of heads and bodies. This iconography has contributed almost as much as the surviving poetry to establish Dionysus as a god of ecstatic dancing who sets the whole of nature in motion.[38]

[36] During the training, several forms of spinning, whirling and circular dancing were explored—prominently amongst these were the whirling dances of the Konya dervishes.

[37] See esp. the 5th-cent. BCE cup painted by Makron depicting maenads dancing around a robed and masked Dionysus column in Beazley (1963), 371, no. 15.

[38] For Dionysus and dance, see Zarifi (2007)), 227–8, 236.

The body can whirl its way to celestial ascent or invite spiritual possession—in either case, whirling expresses the interpenetration of the earthly with the divine that is characteristic of Gardzienice's corporeal language. Furthermore, this language is richly allusive and often has precise connotations. For example, the oppositional tension between submission and defiance in Avvakum's 'bowing' movement distils and anticipates the startling contrasts between sacred and profane, between high and low cultures, between desire and restraint, and between comedy and tragedy which are also characteristic of the later 'ancient Greek' productions.

While gestures are embodied and performed with remarkable fluidity, they also seem to stretch the actors' ranges of physical expression beyond what seems 'natural'. Gardzienice bodies are constantly exceeding the limits of their accustomed ranges of voice or movement. The actors' natural bodies appear to become inhabited by abstract artificial figures from vases and thereby belong to an artistic convention that flouts naturalism. This coexistence of artifice and nature is characteristic of Gardzienice's style of performance which so often combines seemingly irreconcilable differences. Filipowicz's description of *Avvakum* could apply to the *Elektra*:

> The obsessive stream of images is in a process of continuous, kaleidoscopic transformations . . . In this world of instability and endless flux, the images bifurcate, each of them producing . . . irreconcilable connotations . . . Religious rapture suddenly turns into brutal eroticism. A holy procession shifts to a lusty and violent village mob seeking a sacrificial scapegoat. Bodies writhe in paroxysms of pleasure and pain.[39]

IPHIGENIA IN DELPHI

In the summer of 2008, Gardzienice took *Iphigenia at Aulis* and *Metamorphoses* to Delphi in Greece. This was a fitting homecoming because *Iphigenia*, especially, is truly evocative of much ancient Greek theatre practice. There are in Staniewski's *Iphigenia*, as Taplin famously articulated in relation to the *Oresteia* and to Greek tragedy generally, extremely powerful climactic scenes which reverberate thematically and architectonically across the plays—both retrospectively and proleptically.[40] *Iphigenia*'s journey to Delphi, in this sense, forged the Company's intimate correspondence with Greek tragedy, and which this milestone production makes particularly manifest. For Gardzienice's *Iphigeneia* penetrates even deeper into ancient territory than the Company's two previous Greek-inspired productions. For the first time, Staniewski uses the entire

---

[39] Filipowicz (1987).
[40] Taplin (1985).

Figure 20.4 The Chorus in *Iphigenia*. Agniezka Mendel centre.

Euripidean text[41] and a unifying score by the composer Zygmunt Konieczny.[42] The music is pervaded by a Slavic lyricism with a rich emotional texture.[43] The chorus, as Gayna Wiles acutely observed, 'often appeared to fly with the ecstasy of the dance' (see Figure 20.4).[44]

The *cheironomiai* employed in the *Iphigenia* have by now become thoroughly incorporated into Gardzienice's body language through refined training and several years of repeat-performances. Identifiable gestures emerge time and again, either in flowing movement or with an avowedly semiotic purpose to underline, parenthesize or contrast with the prevailing dramatic mood. For example, the harrowing sorrow of Clytemnestra (Joanna Holcgreber) is expressed

---

[41] Translated into Polish with sequences in English and in the original Greek. Staniewski, however, varies the order of certain choral songs creating different atmospheres, such as a sense of foreboding for the sacrifice or a sense of sinister irony as preparations are made for the marriage that turns out to be a deception.

[42] However, two passages—'Pergamon' (774–93, see nn. 44 and 45 below) and *'All'o Phoibe'*— are sung to ancient sounds 'reconstructed' by Rychły for the *Metamorphoses* project (see n. 22 above). *'All'o Phoibe'*, based on a fragment from the second Delphic Hymn of the 2nd century BCE, is sung after the *pyrrhichē* and before Achilles' scene with Clytemnestra.

[43] Allain (1997), 117. For the distinction between emotional 'Slavonic' and linear 'Western' music, see Czekanowska (1990), 111.

[44] During our discussion of the performance at Delphi 2008.

almost entirely in gestures of lamentation culled from Greek vases, but with a depth of feeling and fluidity which cannot be attributed to simple imitation. Conversely, as Agamemnon is sharpening his knives to sacrifice his daughter, three male members of the chorus standing firm at one side of the stage perform a fast narrative sequence in almost pantomimic sign language, while the rest of the chorus sing to a different and more melodious tempo. This sinister sideshow has a distancing effect which, paradoxically, only serves to bring the violence closer. As so often in Staniewski, the grotesque, rather than undermining or lightening the drama, only makes it darker. Irrepressible self-parody, grimaces and occasional comedy do not detract from an extraordinary fluidity and build-up of dramatic tension leading to Iphigenia's sacrifice.

Images of vase-paintings emanate from the movement of the performers in almost dream-like sequences. For example, when Iphigenia is told she is to marry Achilles, her delight is expressed in the courtship dance (see Figure 20.2). The flexed wrists and flicks of the ankles recall dancers represented on Etruscan vases. Yet no such image was presented to the actors. The movement grew out of their bodies in response to the dramatic situation and, as Staniewski described, 'the love scene escaped from the plot'.[45]

Also in the *Iphigenia*, elements from other performance traditions are more thoroughly absorbed into the 'Greek' imagery. A dance depicting Achilles' Myrmidon warriors blends Kung-Fu martial arts with vase imagery from the Greek war dance, the *pyrrhichē*. In the *Elektra*, on the other hand, sequences such as the fan and sword solos (see Figures 20.5 and 20.6 below) are performed in starkly contrasting styles to point up extremes of violence. The pictures illustrate the enriched visual context for *cheironomia* in the *Iphigenia*. Lighting suggesting Titian and Caravaggio paintings, the lush colours of the costumes and the disposition of the chorus all recall biblical and mythical scenes of sacrifice. At the centre of Figure 20.7, Clytemnestra (Joanna Holcgreber) is performing the gesture meaning 'blood' and the slightly mocking expressions of the surrounding figures, rather than undermining her distress, seem only to enhance it. In this scene, the chorus use the art of *cheironomia* to perform a war between the sexes to the accompaniment of a choral song sung in the original Greek.[46] The song's theme is the destruction of Troy following Helen's forsaking of her husband and comes after a marital argument between Agamemnon (Mariusz Golaj) and Clytemnestra. While at first sight it might seem as if the *cheironomiai* were simply emphasizing the words of the song, they are in fact an embodiment of the deeper motifs at the heart of the *Iphigenia*, which are centred around the perversion of ritual: Iphigenia's failed wedding, the sinister juxtaposition between human and animal sacrifice, the 'fateful' marriages of Clytemnestra and

---

[45] In conversation with the author.
[46] Lines 774–93 of Eur. *IA*. The music for these lines was composed by Maciej Rychły (see nn. 22 and 39) and subsequently incorporated into the score for the *Iphigenia*.

Figure 20.5 Fan-dance from *Elektra* performed by Julia Bui-Ngoc from Vietnam.

Helen, to say nothing of the foreshadowed *hubris* to be occasioned by the excessively savage destruction of Troy.

In another scene, Staniewski brings to the fore the close association between the failed wedding and Iphigenia's doom by moving the passage announcing Iphigenia's sacrifice[47] from the late to the earlier part of the production. Iphigenia (Karolina Cicha) sings these lines in desperate distress and fear in the midst of a scene of bustling and joyous anticipation of the supposed wedding:

> But you, Iphigenia, upon your head
> And on your lovely hair
> Will the Argives wreathe a crown
> For sacrifice.
> You will be brought down from the hill caves
> Like a heifer, red, white, unblemished,
> And like a bloody victim
> They will slash your throat. (1080–93)

[47] Eur. *IA* lines 1080–93.

Figure 20.6 Sword-dance from *Elektra* performed by Julia Bui-Ngoc from Vietnam.

Figure 20.7 Joanna Holcgreber gesturing 'blood' in *Iphigenia at Aulis.*

Cheironomia is thus only one of several components in a dance language where dance functions interchangeably as word, as musical notation, as sound or as painted image but where it is, in every instance, an embodiment of spirit.

MUTUALITY AND THE CHORUS

The ideas of communication between body and spirit and of a spiritual energy which conflates image, speech, and gesture find expression in Adam Mickiewicz's concept of '*parole vivante*'—'living speech'. Mickiewicz's *parole* illuminates both Gardzienice's ecstatic dance language and Staniewski's insistence on what he calls 'mutuality'.

In Mickiewicz's 'Slavonic lectures', there is a striving towards a necessary form of communication to which philosophers, scientists, and the Church have ceased to have access. Katherine Underhill, in a revelatory article shows how Mickiewicz, in his lessons 7–10 of the 1844 Lecture, 'employs images of living speech ('*parole vivante*') to convey central truths' and quotes Mickiewicz referring to the 'call' or 'cry' in which man 'concentrates his entire life'.[48] A contrast is drawn between context-free words with no inherent meaning and 'living speech' which contains meaning infused with divinity. Living speech can be actualized in words but not necessarily. As Underhill remarks:

it can be present in *gesture*, or in a meaningful and burning gaze: it can be a form of communication that emanates from the very body of a man who is filled with that energy. According to Mickiewicz, it is the possession of that energy which enabled the apostles to convert people whose languages they did not speak.[49]

This form of communication, whether a gesture or living speech, is *pulled* from the body by the spirit and, while leaving the body, it does not separate from it. This is how Mickiewicz describes creative inspiration in his lecture 279:

We feel an interior fire ignite in the depths of our being; for an instant this fire penetrates and absorbs our entire organism, putting it so to speak in a state of fusion: and then the spirit pulls from our melted organism an extract, an essence, from which it forms this weightless and luminous globe that we call '*parole*' [living speech] which leaves us, *without separating from us.*[50]

Mickiewicz also emphasizes that living speech is dialogic—that it can only occur in communion with the other in 'a moment of *mutual becoming*'.

Therefore, the engagement of living speech in communication involves not only a body that is inseparable from the spirit, but also, as Staniewski insists, a

---

[48] Underhill (2001).
[49] Ibid.
[50] Ibid. 721. My emphases.

body in a state of mutuality with other bodies. The language of the body is a dialogic language and cannot meaningfully exist in isolation. A 'column of fire' exists between spirit and humans and to keep it burning requires a 'vigilant attention to dialogue'.[51] This image, emblematic of Gardzienice's philosophy and training, is also the key principle orchestrating their choral work.[52] The actors are in constant communion with each other separating only at moments of extreme isolation as, for example, Iphigenia at her sacrifice or Agamemnon as he faces his predicament. Protagonists emerge and dissolve back into the group as their individual identifiable gestus ripples through various members of the chorus.

For example, Achilles begins to run, and the run is doubled, first by a figure on the right and, subsequently, by other members of the chorus. This multiple doubling of bodily movements and *cheironomiai* happens time and again to depict actions and characters mentioned in the songs:[53]

> Swift-footed Achilles I saw—
> His feet like the stormwind—running,
> Achilles whom Thetis bore.[54]

Achilles emerges on the left while the member of the chorus who plays the servant in the prologue performs Achilles running movements: 'a wise man should keep his wife at home'.[55] The chorus splits to perform the war of the sexes as half side with Clytaemnestra and the other half with Agamemnon over the issue of Iphigenia's sacrifice. The prevailing *cheironomia* designates 'towers' (Figure 20.8)

> Then from the citadel's top peak to earth
> He will sack all the dwellings in Troy city.[56]

The chorus acts like a living organism animated by the *cheironomiai*: reappearing gestures punctuate or flow with or against the dramatic currents creating an extraordinary coherence. These gestures form the indissoluble bond, Staniewski's 'mutuality', forging intimate links between text,[57] music, audience and the surrounding environment. The chorus is at the centre of most of Gardzienice's performances and moves seamlessly from scene to scene or from performance to performance between various representations of groups such as 'Plato's family' in *Metamorphoses* or 'the mob' in *Avvakum*. In the *Iphigenia*, however, where the

---

[51] Underhill 718.
[52] For comprehensive discussions of Gardzienice actor-training methods, see Allain (1997), ch. 5 and Staniewski and Hodge (2004), ch. 8.
[53] Photos from a recording of Gardzienice's *Iphigenia at Aulis—based on Euripides* performed at the La Mama Annex, New York, Oct. 2000. Photos by courtesy of the Gardzienice Archive.
[54] Lines 278–85, trans. Charles Walker.
[55] Ibid. 750.
[56] Ibid. 779–80.
[57] Contrary to what Staniewski sometimes encourages us to think in Staniewski and Hodge (2004), 136–7. Although sung and spoken language is present as much for its sound as for its inner meaning, the latter is profoundly linked to the physicality of the performance.

Figure 20.8 Chorus from *Iphigenia at Aulis based on Euripides* (2007).

coherence of the dance language combines with Zygmunt Konieczny's musical composition and with Euripides' poetry, something remarkable emerges—a pre-classical ancient Greek chorus finds a fresh reality on a theatrical level.

A number of structural parallels with pre-tragic Greek performance can be detected. In the indoor performances, Euripides' *parodos* (choral entrance song) is performed almost in its entirety. The chorus, with drums between their legs pounding frenzied rhythms, conjure up characters and scenes mentioned in the song (see Figure 20.9). The effect is a series of dazzling epiphanies in quick succession strongly suggestive of what we know about the Greek dithyramb[58]—the dance-song

[58] The dithyramb, as we know from Aristotle, *Poetics*. ch.4 is antecedent to tragedy and thus retains more playful improvisational elements and community participation than its more 'evolved' literary form in tragedy. These elements, I believe, stem from the origins of the dithyramb itself, rooted in the sacrifice of the bull who became the centre of a musical sacrificial drama in which everyday agricultural activities such as driving and herding cattle (*boelasie*) turn into dance and song and into a costumed ceremony. The animal's death, ecstatic dancing to the accompaniment of *aulos* and *tympana*, together with the consumption of wine, combine to evoke the lightning-like presence

celebrating Dionysus' epiphanic birth amidst thunder and lightning (see Figure 20.9):[59]

> In Boeotia's naval squadron
> I counted fifty ships
> Fitted with blazonry;
> Cadmus on each of them
> With his golden dragon
> High on their poops lifted[60] (253–8)

The emergence of characters and tableaux from the chorus also harks back to the so-called 'origins' of Greek theatre when the protagonist is said to have separated from the chorus.

The combination of theatre artifice[61] with what Halina Filipowicz calls 'insistent corporeality' yields powerful multilayered choric tableaux of sacrificial and wedding rituals. Images such as a prematurely broken Iphigenia being wheeled out from beneath the blood-red skirt of her father—suggesting both birth and death—seem to come straight out of the darkness of antiquity into the midst of a sumptuously lit chorus.

A diametrically contrasting 'ancient reality' was created by Gardzienice's performances of the *Iphigenia* and *Metamorphoses* in the natural surroundings of Delphi.[62] In Greece, *'stasima'* (stationary choral songs) from the *Iphigenia* were performed *en route* at locations marked out for their mythical associations: for example, at the edge of Punishment Rock from which Aesop is said to have been hurled, and outside the entrance of the Corycian cave dedicated to Pan and the Nymphs. The procession ended with a performance of *Metamorphoses* at the entrance of a village church in the valley below the Corycian cave.[63] The processing chorus became part of the panoramic views of sea, valleys, and olive

---

of Dionysus. This evocation, extends to poetic inspiration for the composition of the dithyrambic song itself. In a well-known fragment, the 7th cent. poet Archilochus says: 'I know how to lead the first song of lord Dionysus, the dithyramb, when my wits are lightning-struck (*synkeraunotheis*) by wine' (Archil. fr. 120 W).

[59] In myth, thunder (drums) and lightning (wine-induced inspiration) accompany the birth of Dionysus from Zeus' thigh. Note how 'the gouache and line create a strong black and white graphic image to evoke the dramatic effect of group energy', and how the perspective describes the plotting of the stage (Gayna Wiles in our private correspondence about Figure 20.9).

[60] Eur. *IA* 253–8.

[61] Gayna Wiles explains how Staniewski's stage design contributes to the creation of theatrical 'artifice' by denying spatial expectation: 'Staniewski is working with real bodies and a flat stage. The boxes arranged in a raked flexible space, change the ground line. Working with a variety of box heights allows flexibility and the possibility to deny spatial expectation.'

[62] As part of the 'Culture and Environment' artistic events held by the ECCD at Delphi, 4–12 July 2008.

[63] At the church of Aghia Triadha in the region of Delphi. *Metamorphoses* opened with the braying of a live donkey on 'stage' and involved the transformation of a Christ-figure with a heavy cross into Dionysus with a phallic pole. The reaction of the audience which included the local priest was surprisingly warm given the potentially 'blasphemous' connotations. I was told that the dancing, humour, and energy of the performers had prevailed: 'they did not behave like stars like our [Greek] actresses do,' said a nearby farmer.

Figure 20.9 *Iphigeneia at Aulis*' dithyrambic chorus. Drawings by Gayna Wiles.

groves and the song of cicadas and birds blended indistinguishably with the music—especially with Rychły's 'reconstructed' sequences.[64] The strong presence of animals—goats, boars, and donkeys—in almost overwhelming natural surroundings, the heat and arduousness of the day's journey, participation by the local population, together with songs, dances, and communal meals, blurred many boundaries between ancient and modern, between performers and observers and even between animals and humans. The Greek landscape seemed to be reinhabited by some of the sounds and images which it had relinquished many centuries ago.

CONCLUSION

Staniewski's alphabet is linked to an ancient civilization which as well as occupying a historical period and a specific geographical area is also the space where our 'souls'—though forever elusive—are within 'touching distance'.[65] The path towards that space involves a relentless pursuit of academic understanding which seems to fire rather than extinguish an unusually powerful artistic imagination. Perhaps in the end, the best guide to unravelling the secret alphabet of gestures is a story created by Staniewski himself. As so often, the story is a brew of scholarly allusion and evocative metaphor. The allegory depicts a cart transporting the last rescued treasures of a disappearing civilization. The treasures are the songs of ancient times and the destination of the journey 'shrouded in secrecy' could be the Balkans, or the Carpathian mountains, or Illyria, or the steppes of the eastern borderlands of Poland or all of these. The civilization in which these holy relics were found was the Mediterranean during the fourth and fifth centuries, at the time of Julian the Apostate. The search for hidden treasure took place in many areas of the world which, as Staniewski stresses, are to be understood as belonging as much to a spiritual sphere as to a geographic one. There—in both spiritual and geographic places—and amongst other valuables—was found 'the forgotten art of *cheironomia*'.[66]

Now, Staniewski, with the *Iphigenia* in Delphi returns to restore some of these valuables to the Mediterranean and to the modern world. 'The point', he says, is not to revive some ideological construct but 'to get closer, to be able to touch the people of the epoch.'[67]

---

[64] See above, nn. 22, 24, and 39.

[65] Staniewski in conversation with the author.

[66] From a debate between Włodzimierz Staniewski and Leszek Kolankiewicz led by Grzegorz Ziolkowski in Nov. 2004, see Golaczynska and Guszpit (2006), 108–9.

[67] Ibid. 109.

21

Gesamtkunstwerk: Modern Moves
and the Ancient Chorus

Struan Leslie

British actors have generally been known for their 'scapula-upwards' performances—very cerebral but not very mobile, or at least definitely not in the
lower body. However, in British theatre-training, broadly speaking, rhythm
generally referred to modulations of the voice, not the body. While Jean New-
love, a student of Rudolf von Laban, worked with Joan Littlewood and the
Theatre Workshop in the 1950s, and Rupert Doone, a dancer with Diaghilev,
collaborated with Group Theatre (London) in the 1930s on such productions as
Louis MacNeice's *Agamemnon* and Auden and Isherwood's *Ascent of F6*, this
work was generally sustained by small pockets of enthusiasm as opposed to
professional rigour.

But since the late 1960s and early '70s there has been a steady flow of young
British actors towards continental Europe. They have turned to Paris, and
especially Jacques Lecoq (notably Simon McBurney, artistic director of La
Complicité) and more recently to Poland and to Włodzimierz Staniewski and
the influence of Grotowski (notably Katie Mitchell) to find alternatives. The
result has been an interesting cross-fertilization, with the British cerebral-style
now being re-energized by ensemble corporeal performance modes which have
been developed elsewhere in Europe.

The major change that relates to my professional experience has been the
emergence of the Movement Director on the British theatre scene. Now almost
every West End production (and not just a musical) will employ a Movement
Director who works alongside the Director and with the entire cast. My long-
standing professional relationship with Katie Mitchell, which dates from Strindberg's study of familial interaction, *Easter* at The RSC (1994) and includes
the *Oresteia* (RNT 1999) and work on opera (notably Handel's *Jephtha*, Welsh
National Opera 2003), Chekhov (e.g. *The Seagull*, RNT 2006) and other Greek
tragedies (*Iphigenia at Aulis*, RNT 2004, and *Women of Troy*, RNT 2007), is
a product of this new interest in ensemble movement in British theatre.
From 2009, The Royal Shakespeare Company has shown its own commitment

to these developments by setting up the Movement Department of which I am Head. My background in dance (I trained at the London School of Contemporary Dance and Naropa Institute, Colorado) and my interest in, and collaborations with, artists from other disciplines (both performative and visual) enable me to bring to the theatre, and especially text-trained directors, an understanding of, and a desire to work with, the Wagnerian idea of the *Gesamtkunstwerk*—the 'total theatre' work.

Text, music, and movement—the ancient chorus had multiple skills that they learned in life, and fine-tuned over the best part of a year in the rehearsal process in fifth-century Athens. I have sought to capture that range of expertise and develop it with my performers in productions of the ancient tragedies that I have worked upon in recent years. The chorus as ensemble theatrical grouping has received much attention in the last twenty or so years—from directors and choreographers as well as academics. But it is a real challenge to make an ancient Greek chorus connect with today's cultural expectations and norms. How might these connections be achieved? This chapter looks at the various attempts I have made, in collaboration with directors such as Katie Mitchell, Neil Bartlett, and Nicholas Broadhurst, to make these connections and to give choruses once again the kind of prominence that they enjoyed in the ancient world. More importantly, perhaps, it is my experience with ancient tragedy that has led me to take the skills required of ancient dancers into modern plays, especially opera, as well.

BEGINNINGS

After some twenty years of working with the idea of the chorus in many contexts, I am now drawn to examine what it is that makes me engage with choruses so passionately and where it all came from. Notions of the collective, affinity, and communal experience abound in my past. The spectacle of the massed pipes and drums entering the arena at Pitlochry Highland Games, and the patterns of unison movement in the sets of Scottish country dancers as they weave and turn in a church hall, were probably my first experiences of this collective sociophysical experience. Singing Brahms, Handel, Fauré in a school choir as a boy and young man, and performing on stage with one hundred other Boy Scouts in *The Gang Show*, singing and executing simply choreographed unison movement, gesture, and spatial organization—I can now see these as formative 'choric' experiences. These collective events, whilst not fully answering to the definition of chorus, do share some choric aspects and they clearly have a link to the type of theatre and performance that engages me.

My early dance experiences with choreographer, Royston Maldoom, as Dance Artist in Residence in the community of Fife and Tayside, Scotland (1982–5) were of an ensemble nature not of the soloists/*corps de ballet* structure of the classical ballet world. Maldoom's work such as *Area Without Measure* is without doubt 'choric'; and his recent *Rhythm Is It!* project to Stravinsky's *Le Sacre du Printemps/ Rite of Spring* (with Simon Rattle and the Berlin Philharmonic and 250 young people in Berlin) is another example of his creative use of some aspects of choral performance. Even now I identify more with, and have more interest in, the *corps de ballet* than the athleticism of the soloists because there is more a visceral connection for me there.

From working with Maldoom, I progressed to a fully vocational dance training at London Contemporary Dance School, then a Graham-based modern dance training. Here the individual was encouraged and not the collective. Former Graham dancers, Jane Dudley and Nina Fonaroff, and dance educationist, Janet Wilkes identified my broader interest in the application of movement and encouraged my exploration beyond the world of choreography and dance. It was at LCDS that my most formal experience of the physical chorus occurred through my good fortune to study with guest artist, Ernestine Stodelle, a dancer with Doris Humphrey. Stodelle undertook to recreate, in my graduating year, two works by Humphrey, *Waterstudy* and *Shakers*. These two works are undoubtedly, in different ways, choral pieces: *Waterstudy*—an abstract work that, like Da Vinci's drawings, explores and examines the different qualities of water to the accompaniment of a solo drum; and *Shakers* was based on the physical rituals of the religious group based in western Massachusetts. *Waterstudy* had at its core the use of breath—the basis of Humphrey's technique was fall and recovery supported by the cycle of the breath. Working in unison, we, the 'chorus' rose and fell, ran and jumped, connected through this common impulse of the breath. Similarly, the use of breath as stimulus was employed in *Shakers*, where it was harnessed to ideas of community and character. Here too, there was a 'choral' experience for both performer and audience. The use of breath has become an important tool in my preparation of actors for choral work.

My early teaching experiences at Scottish Ballet 'Steps Out' under Rosina Bonsu, working with large groups of young people, the elderly, and people with disabilities, encouraged me to look at the group for purely practical reasons. Here working with large groups for ten hours over four days meant that the collective or choral was often the most effective means to realize our aims and the easiest way to communicate ideas and themes to an audience, a society of relatives of the performers. In addition to this community-based choric awareness, my work has benefited much from my teaching alongside Professor Bob Jarvis in the Faculty of the Built Environment at the University of the South Bank, London, where I have been able to encourage students to explore the important role that space has in determining movement and physicality.

However, the major catalyst for the development of these ideas has been my collaboration with Katie Mitchell (Figure 21.1). As part of her NESTA

Figure 21.1 Chorus from *Oresteia Part II*, directed by Katie Mitchell.

research project,[1] we have explored the physicality of emotion; and for me, in particular, the work of the Portuguese-American neuro-scientist, Antonio Damasio has been of specific use in my developing practice. Damasio, amongst others, has identified emotion as primarily physical: the rules of chemical engagement mean that we respond bodily before the brain understands what we are feeling: you see a bear, run, and *then* experience fear. The identification by Damasio and his colleagues of the primary emotions has led to the development of specific somatic exercises in the training of the actor. In life, our initial, physical responses are unconscious—our recoil from the heat of the flame, the foul smell; these reflex reactions are not stored in our memory banks. To all intents and purposes, they do not happen because we are not aware of them. Since they are unconscious, the actor does not know they are happening in life, and so they are not usually part of their performance. As part of my work as a movement director and director, I have sought to 'reinstate' these reflexes in the

---

[1] Mitchell was a recipient of a joint Fellowship with James MacDonald from The National Endowment for Science, Technology, and the Arts (NESTA) to undertake research into the nature of rehearsal and production methods. This included exploration of late Stanislavskian practice regarding situation, movement, and emotion, and the results have appeared in Mitchell (2008).

moves of the chorus. This engages the audience with their own subconscious as they watch and recognize subconsciously these movements on stage.

PRACTICE

My work in the theatre has sought to wed movement to both speech and song and my model for this has increasingly become the ancient theatre, where the speaking, singing, and dancing body was the norm. All my work has at its core a belief that in order for the actors to be communicating and operating at full capacity, they need to have an understanding and connection with their whole self and the environment in which they are working. The body is a communicating tool that instinctively supports what we are saying—and sometimes not, if we are lying, just as those politicians' 'tells' exhibit the physical ticks of betrayal.

Chorus work in Britain has rarely been successful in the past, sometimes seeming like a group of women loitering at the back of the stage, waiting for something to happen. This has been often down to sheer financial constraints and rehearsal time. Choral work is not part of the sustained training of actors, singers or dancers, each of whose training has a specific set of skills that pertain to their specific form, but at no point does it reach the level of total skill demanded by the ancient tragedians of their performers. Since these skills have been divided up in our modern creative culture, in training the chorus for particular productions, I am striving to combine specific elements of the training from each of the separate disciplines to create my ideal of the *Gesamtkunstwerk*.

The practice I have developed is based around an increased physical awareness and connectivity to the self and the space and the geography in which the performer is working; and specifically in relation to choral work, it means building a connected, collective, and individual physicality. Over time our bodies have found the most efficient way to do what is required in daily and working life—this is what I call the 'habituated' body. This is further exacerbated by the fact that in performance, the body works primarily in isolation. My job is to facilitate the connectivity of the performer to both their own body and to their co-performer. Part of this is achieved through engaging them in a kind of 'wrap around, IMAX' total spatial/sensory awareness training with a 360 degree body awareness at the core—imagine standing at the core of a spherical library and being aware of each book on every shelf and being able to access its information with ease.

The work here has been developed in relation to Mitchell's ideas around, and concerning the need for, the fourth wall. The wall is always in place in the imagination of the actors until it is removed in order that the chorus can speak to the people beyond that wall. But even then the theatrical world continues as the audience become characters in the eyes of the chorus. In order to facilitate this, the body here is conceived of in the broadest context possible—in both architectural/environmental space (as in the warehouse space designed by Bunny Christie for the RNT *Women of Troy*) and with anatomical and somatic physical information gleaned from other artistic (sculpture) and physical (sport, athletics) media. In addition, there is the awareness that comes through self-examination and understanding which the training of a dancer, involving self-criticism, entails.

How do I prepare the performers to work in this role? To make a chorus, you need initially to create a community of people. Yielding and reacting are the two greatest constituents of the job; and if any young artist asks me if they should take a job in a chorus, the answer is always a resounding 'yes', because this is probably the most difficult and rewarding job a performer can have. Connecting to each other and yet being one is not being part of a mob: it is being a slice of society. The aim is to promote sensitivity and awareness of others and of the self in order to bring about greater connectedness within the group.

First this comes through the breath: self-awareness leads to awareness of the breath of others. The performers practise walking and balancing their own 'bubble space' with that of others and they shrink their own 'bubble' in accordance with others. The yielding to the impulse of another is perhaps the most challenging task, but it is important to remember that the modern chorus is a collection of individuals working as a community—it is not about establishing uniformity but communality. This was clear in my work on Neil Bartlett's adaptation of *Oliver Twist* (Lyric Theatre, Hammersmith and American Repertory Theatre, at Harvard, Cambridge, MA, Theatre for a New Audience, New York and Berkeley Repertory Theatre, CA 2007), where the ensemble modulated between chorus, ensemble, and individual character work. The training was focused on flexibility, agility, and musical dexterity in tandem with physical connectivity and clarity between the ensemble of thirteen actors. So here, with training, we came close to the choral idea. Here Thespis stepped out and then back again.

The nearest equivalent I have come across in the contemporary world to the technically 'fully rounded' ancient performer is the member of the operatic chorus, and especially members of the Welsh National Opera Chorus. Like the ancient chorus, this chorus works together and 'lives together' and as such forges a 'community' like no other I have come across. Whilst their levels of skill are not equal—their singing of necessity surpasses any other skills they have in movement and speaking—they have demonstrated through their work that they have the greatest potential to reproduce the unity of skills that we associate with the ancient chorus. They are versatile in that they are asked to dance and have new choreography created on them; and the directors they work with make acting demands upon them that are in certain cases rigorous. The dancer, by contrast, may well be trained collectively in classes of twenty to thirty, but they work individually within the group and they definitely have no voice training. After

Bausch, Forsyth, and Anderson's The Cholmondeleys and The Featherstone-haughs, however, there are possibilities for collective physical dance performance and training outside the classical norms of the *corps de ballet.*

CHORUSES IN PRODUCTION

As the movement/chorus director, I am present throughout the whole rehearsal period, regardless of the form. In opera, I am present for the initial exploration of a scene in which the chorus is present, but not as protagonist, so that I can then direct them in relation to the focus of the events the audience witnesses. In Handel's oratorio, *Jephtha,* the protagonist struggles with the realization that he must sacrifice his daughter. In the 2003 production, the chorus physically move as a collective of individuals with the text, 'What is, is right', in order to convince Jephtha of the necessity of this for the greater good. Each individual member of the chorus has a role to play, each character they create is part of a community. And so they are bound together with Jephtha as their collective focus—the fourth wall behind him—and beyond that we, helplessly watching this world, struggle with their ideal. The scene was constructed without the chorus and then we were directed to respond to the situation.

In another context, in the opera *Oedipe* by Georg Enescu, directed in collaboration with Nicholas Broadhurst in 2006 at Theater Bielefeld, the chorus of eighty-plus men, women, young people, and children were directed to create family units to tell the story of Oedipus. These groups then cross-related—kids playing with those from other families, then coming together to be a flock of sheep during Oedipus' encounter with the shepherd who saved his life as a child. Similarly the scenes here were explored without the chorus. They were then brought in after rehearsals where they had constructed their new families. For a classical play, by contrast, the work is more simultaneous and the chorus develop alongside the protagonists. With *Oedipe,* the limitations of time and the size of the opera chorus (thirty to eighty people) make this often impossible. Regardless of the differences in the preliminary stages, the work is ultimately focused around the releasing of the chorus so that it reacts and yet remains in the situation.

In the development of the chorus of women in *Iphigenia at Aulis* and *Women of Troy,* the benefits of a long-term ensemble were made clear. *Iphigenia* had a double life, first in Dublin at the Abbey Theatre in 2001 and later at the RNT London in 2004. In Dublin we began to explore the movement aspect of the chorus but ultimately in the production we relied upon the choral connectivity to communicate the situation these women found themselves in—as if hostages in Agamemnon's office. When it came to the second production in London, the question more specifically arose as to how to embrace the idea and role of choral dance from the original Greek productions of these plays. With the production set in the 1950s, the image of the women evolved into them being some sort of 'Women's Institute' or guild—a group who know each other socially.

Five members of the company from *Iphigenia at Aulis* continued with us in our work on *Women of Troy*. Others in the company had worked with us in other ways on other productions—*The Seagull*, *Oresteia*—and so they too had a connection and understanding of the process leading to the creation of the work. In fact only two members of the *Troy* ensemble had not worked with either myself or the director, Katie Mitchell before. We, however, continued the general training and incorporated new discoveries and experiments. In *Troy*, the chorus at times embraced the whole ensemble, including queens, princesses and Argive soldiers. As a result, the training was for the whole company and so we ended up with a larger choral group with a greater impact, both psycho-physically and visually. These Trojan women have handbags containing all the ephemera they would have in life—tissues, purse or wallet, photos of family and children and make-up. The application of make-up became a coping-mechanism, maintaining a sense of self and normality, as had been the case in *Iphigenia* as well (see Figure 21.2).

Out of the Trojan women's social cohesion arose a way of addressing the dance element of the original Greek chorus—social dance would have been a part of these 1950s women's normal lives as they would have gone out dancing with

Figure 21.2 Chorus from *Iphigenia at Aulis*, directed by Katie Mitchell.

their husbands and each other. So that when in time of need and stress they recalled their families, they danced a form the audience know and identify—a partner dance; but they danced it alone. Here the chorus makes a collective response in order to normalize and comfort themselves in the situation. The use of social dance became the signifier of something other, unspoken yet visible, and physically felt by the audience.

CONCLUSION

The contemporary cultural engagement with the idea of the chorus does I believe reflect the fact that society is now reacting to events both local and global with a greater sense of community. My ongoing journey of collaboration and discovery has been in part mirrored by the cultural shift from the 'me-culture' of Thatcherism to the new-Blairite 'me-ism' which followed the big events of the 1990s and the first decade of the new millennium (with the Eco-movement, the death of Diana, 9/11, and 7/7). Even the global reaction and the sense of unity around the election of US President Barack Obama could figure as part of this.

The chorus is primarily reactive: they are told about an event and they react to that telling at one and the same time. We have all been part of this world chorus, in some sense. The awareness required to achieve choral integrity by the performer reflects this. We are all witnesses to events on the world stage as they unfold before our eyes on rolling-news broadcasts. In my work now, while I collaborate with a new ensemble of forty-four actors at The RSC for three years, there is time to explore the creation of new performance work with the chorus as protagonist, when Thespis will return once more to the group from which he emerged sometime at the end of the sixth century BCE.[2]

---

[2] Since writing this piece, I have worked with Neil Bartlett on *Everybody Loves a Winner* for the Manchester International Festival 2009.

22

Red Ladies: Who are they and What do they Want?

Suzy Willson and Helen Eastman

Red Ladies is a performance piece by the Clod Ensemble—a theatre company which places music and movement at the heart of all its work.[1] *Red Ladies* features a chorus of eighteen women dressed identically in red headscarves, black trench coats, red stilettos, red vanity cases, and sunglasses. It has two elements: first, they infiltrate the city with a series of interventions, then they perform 'a theatrical demonstration in four movements' inside a theatre.

Red Ladies first appeared in Trafalgar Square in 2005 as part of British Architecture Week. Since then, they have appeared at the Institute of Contemporary Arts, Warwick Arts Centre, The Serralves Museum in Portugal, OFS, Oxford, the British Library and on the streets of London, Oxford, Coventry, and Porto. The most recent version of the 'theatrical demonstration' for 2008 features poetry by Peter Oswald.

HE: *It's unique to watch a chorus on stage as a sole visual focus. Was this a specific attempt to explore chorus as the protagonist of the piece?*

SW: Yes it was. I have always been fascinated by the theatrical potential of the chorus in Greek tragedy. The chorus is always present on stage—a powerful force within a dramatic space. When there are fifteen people doing an identical action it becomes huge—a slight bowing of the head is magnified to become a profound expression of loss. There are so many possibilities for movement within a chorus, different units and groups can move in harmony despite differences of identity, appearance or opinion. I like the way the chorus can exist on the edge of the city

---

[1] Clod Ensemble was created by director Suzy Willson and composer Paul Clark. Over the last ten years, the company has created a huge range of performance projects, workshops and events across the UK and internationally. Productions include—*Under Glass, Silver Swan*, and *Greed*. They make performance for traditional theatre spaces, festivals, and galleries as well as creating projects and curating work in places where art does not usually or regularly happen, including medical schools and centres for the elderly (http://www.clodensemble.com).

and express itself in a form removed from the everyday language and rhetoric of that city. I am drawn to the way the chorus can operate in a poetic register, a heightened form involving both music and abstract movement.

We live in a culture and at a moment in history that has almost fetishized 'the individual'. Through watching a chorus we can, perhaps, step back from the psychology of the individual and observe the behaviour of a group, seeing them like a herd of animals, a swarm of locusts, an army of ants, or a flock of geese. Red Ladies are an emergent phenomenon. We looked at some of the recent scientific and philosophical work being done concerning emergence; exploring the idea that complex behaviour in the natural world (including human society) can occur without any leader prescribing it. The classic example is of a flock of starlings that will swoop in magnificent unison, but without any one bird making the decision to lead. Our piece doesn't deny leaders exist, or suggest that we don't need leadership, but it does celebrate the beauty and industriousness of phenomena where there is no single leader.

I am also interested in the idea of the chorus as witness. When we see the chorus in a tragedy, to some extent the chorus externalizes the inner turmoil of the hero and echoes the emotional trajectory of a tragedy. In the tragedies that interest me the chorus has no agency—it does not take action. And because the chorus members are not representatives of power but of the people, often marginalized voices that are rarely heard or seen, there is always a tension between their emotional involvement in and exclusion from the centre of the action. I was interested in this in relation to politics today—how many people feel politically impotent in the face of big business, government and the media. We were interested in whether or not the group did in fact have power, whether the very acts of witnessing, watching, remembering, re-enacting, lamenting were powerful, creative, political acts in their own right.

In recent years, an overwhelming catalogue of tragic public events and recent natural disasters (the war in Iraq, the New Orleans tornado, 9/11, the tsunami etc.) has been mediated through our television screens. We have seen human beings acting collectively in the face of catastrophe and displaying vast public outpourings of grief. We are bombarded by information everyday and sometimes it is hard to find time to reflect on events or relate them to our everyday reality. *Red Ladies* attempts to create this reflective space. They place world events (war, floods, volcanoes) in the context of the everyday. They knit, they cook, and they wait. The Red Ladies step back from the world and help to lead the audience into a place of contemplation. Meditating on the past and the future and taking a long view of suffering and violence may, to some extent, help to stabilize the present.

HE: *To what extent did you draw on female choruses of the past? Both the theatrical ones such as Greek choruses, T. S. Eliot's choruses, and actual choruses—say, groups of women in history?*

SW: I have always been very interested in politics and how groups of people unite to fight a cause. When women come together in public it is perhaps more powerful because they do not usually have a political voice, which is as loud or visible as men. We don't usually see women in groups in public, especially in uniform—they tend to gather indoors.

We researched different groups of women—the Amazons, the Women's Institute, miners' wives, choruses of debutantes, models, beauty queens, the Korean army, showgirls, and prostitutes. The Suffragettes who believed in 'agitation through symbol' particularly inspire me. (There is an artist called Leslie Hill who has described the Suffragettes as the first performance artists, which I think is a fabulous idea.) The Red Ladies owe a debt to this idea of symbolic agitation—they want to stir things up, they are creative provocateurs.

For me, putting ideas, attitudes, and beliefs in some kind of historical context reassures me that change and transformation is always possible and indeed inevitable. And in a way *Red Ladies* pays tribute to the women who have gone before by referencing them.

A chorus can also illuminate private individual experience by magnifying it. There is a scene in *Red Ladies* when everyone takes on a repetitive movement reminiscent of hysterical movement. There is something about bringing the private madness that many women experience on their own to a group that gives it power, makes it visible and somehow therefore makes it easier to deal with.

In terms of theatrical choruses, we didn't closely reference any particular Greek tragedy or the particular performative functions of the chorus in authentic Greek drama. For me, the most effective choruses are found in dance, for example, Pina Bausch's version of *Le Sacre du Printemps* (*The Rite of Spring*), the work of William Forsythe, the chorus lines of the Moulin Rouge, and the Busby Berkeley musicals. I am often rather frustrated by the use of chorus work in UK theatre productions—the chorus often seems to be a bit of an appendage. This, perhaps, says something about our text-based theatre tradition, which does not always use movement and choreography to its full potential. That being said, it is great to see emerging companies and artists who are interested in blurring these boundaries and are committed to a more 'total' theatre practice.

HE: *How do you go about getting such a diverse group of women to work together?*

SW: The first challenge is actually casting a chorus piece for eighteen women. We were determined to get women of different ages, ethnicities, shapes and sizes and we auditioned over one hundred women. It requires a certain sensibility to work in a chorus—you have to be ready to listen and to trust that you will be seen and heard. A chorus is powerful if it is made up of strong individuals. Each individual has to become more powerful and more present, rather than becoming diluted, weaker or hiding in numbers.

Each Red Lady brings a very different skill and quality: there are dancers, there are people who are good at text, there are people who are very funny, others who are good at leading. Everyone has their place in the chorus and brings their own history, story, and unique body. During the process the performers have to adopt the same rules of engagement as the Red Ladies do: be kind to each other, give each other the benefit of the doubt, listen, pay attention, show up. We worked with quite a few independent artists who are used to leading their own process (for example, Kazuko Hohki, Silvia Mercuriali, Heidi Rustgaard), and it was interesting how well they took to being one small part of a large chorus. It is clear that having a robust sense of your own ideas isn't necessarily an impediment to working well in a group.

To find a common movement vocabulary we worked with neutral masks—a training tool developed by Jacques Lecoq and mask-maker Amleto Sartori. Working in neutral mask helps performers to strip away outward mannerisms, habits, vanities and attitudes, opening up the performer to the space around her. It encourages a state of discovery and openness, an energetic, dynamic, articulate body, and an awareness which enables a performer to be present in a chorus without drawing attention to herself.

Lecoq's pedagogy is based in imitating the movements of nature and then transposing these to dramatic situations. For example: if I am playing a scene where I am angry, I do not start psychologically; instead, I can simply take on the movement of fire. If my lover has left me I can embody a sunset. If I am playing a strong leader, I find a mountain inside my body. If my world is in chaos, I embody an earthquake. This precise observation of 'how things move' (not just people but animals, materials, light, the passions, volcanoes etc.) is the basis of his teaching— that we better understand something by embodying it. Much of the choreographic language of *Red Ladies* is drawn from natural phenomenon. We spent hours looking at documentaries about bison migrating, shoaling fish, turtles showing up on a moonlit beach on exactly the same night to lay their eggs, bats spiralling out of caves in South America, ladybirds busying under rocks, bees in hives, and starlings flocking. We also looked at stars, movement dynamics of weather, storms, sunsets, natural disasters, earthquakes. When these movement dynamics are transposed to the stage, they bring rich and contrasting dramatic atmospheres.

Lecoq also developed a series of exercises based on the 'tragedy' of materials. For example, we can observe the nostalgia that a piece of elastic has for its former shape and the fatigue that ensues after many attempts to revisit it; the scars and bruises that a piece of newspaper retains after it has been crumpled; the shocking shattering of a piece of glass; the melancholy of ice melting. If we embody these movement dynamics, we arrive at a tragic movement vocabulary. By allowing the actor to concentrate on the movement dynamics, they do not impose their own psychology on the action and as a result, perhaps, the drama becomes more open for the audience to interpret how they please.

Figure 22.1 Red Ladies getting into a limousine.

All the women learn a basic set of actions: running, knitting, kneeling, lamenting, preening, falling, flocking, waiting, wrestling, jumping. They draw on these throughout the piece. There are moments when the chorus breaks down into separate voices but they are still using the movement vocabulary that they all share, even if they are not in unison. They are still a group, even when the group breaks down.

HE: *What is the aim of the outside interventions and how would you like the audience to respond?*

SW: Red Ladies' public interventions mean different things to different people. One of the quotes that we were inspired by in rehearsal refers to the work of artist, Joseph Beuys:

A provocation should embody a thrust of energy such that the subconscious itself could open up to a new experience, such that indifference could be transformed into interest.[2]

Red Ladies' 'rules of engagement' are to interrupt the everyday, to provoke thought, to amuse, and to transform the meaning of the spaces they inhabit.

[2] De Domizio Durini (1997), 26.

A Red Lady must keep an eye on things, observe how human beings interact with each other, to witness, to decode. They draw attention to the way in which public space is monitored, they watch the watchers and count surveillance cameras. They gather information about the movements of groups. They record speech patterns. They document abusive or bigoted behaviour. They draw attention to the architecture of a city. They encourage people to ask questions: Who are they? What do they want? What do they mean? Why are they dressed like that? *Red Ladies* poses questions about group identity, difference and otherness.

The context for *Red Ladies* is *NOW*—the current political and social climate. The Red Ladies operate at a time when there is an intense public debate about the infringement of civil liberties. They also respond to the current hysteria around national security, ID cards etc., reminding us, perhaps, that it is all too easy to project an idea of 'other', terrorist, criminal on people just because of the clothes they wear or the bags they carry. In a way the interventions attempt to turn the US anti-terrorism slogan 'If you see something, say something' on its head.

For some the image is empowering, for others threatening, for others ridiculous. The Red Ladies are ciphers and they hold up some kind of mirror to the world. They move through the city with great love, incredible style and devastating integrity! They may, unprovoked, create a sense of urgency—evacuating a scene by stretch limousine, helicopter or bicycle.

Everywhere we go we have different responses. The Red Ladies' missions in central London provoked many reactions from amusement, to harassment, to suspicion—one Red Lady was asked by a policeman outside Downing Street: 'How much?'; a gang of kids asked them if they were working for *al qaeda*; a lot of people bought into the whole Bond action fantasy. In London, it can get very edgy. We often have to get police clearance to operate in sensitive areas— especially around Westminster. Some of the interventions become highly charged, especially when there are men in uniform around. On The Mall, the Red Ladies were rendezvous-ing at the same time as the military Beating of the Retreat. This made for some amusing, de-familiarizing exchanges between police and Red Ladies:

POLICEMAN: Why are you wearing that outfit?

RED LADY: Why are you wearing that outfit?

POLICEMAN: I'm a policeman.

RED LADY: And I'm a Red Lady.

Oxford was a different kind of playground. There the power is located in very different places and is associated with knowledge. In Porto, the reception was very gentle—a group of older Portuguese market women became quite euphoric at the sight of such glamorous women knitting in public.

HE: *Feminine takeover of the city. Is there a statement being made there?*

SW: Certainly I think displays of female solidarity can be very powerful and hopeful. It's interesting isn't it, using the F words—femininity and feminism. I would say that *Red Ladies* is not *about* feminism or femininity. In a way these things are given. It is perhaps because it is so unusual to see a group of only women on stage or indeed in public that people think it must be a feminist statement. We are used to seeing groups of men out in public—politicians, soldiers, police, football fans, and builders. When we see these groups we do not say that they are *about* masculinity. Perhaps by seeing a group of powerful women on the street we are led to think about that. It is their difference that makes us notice the norm. There is no idea of Everywoman in our theatre tradition. If a man is alone on stage somehow the piece of theatre is about the world. If there are eighteen women on stage it is interesting that many people assume it must be about them and their gender, rather than about the world.

Many people come up to Red Ladies and are clearly inspired and feel empowered by a strong female presence on the streets. And because their costume is so 'femme' and they carry their sexuality with such confidence, they seem to command respect. They have had occasional catcalls and men shouting 'whores' etc., but when this happens Red Ladies somehow manage to reflect back these remarks (often by their silence) and perhaps surprisingly, often the perpetrators end up apologizing. The performers to some degree feel that they are in solidarity with sex workers, just as they feel they are in solidarity with veiled groups of Muslim women, who are harassed for the clothes they choose to wear. The statement is one of resistance. When we see a Red Lady fly off in a helicopter, is it joyful because somewhere it gives hope? So the statement being made is one of hope. It is a love song. Femininity made visible—a celebration.

HE: *The way they relate to architecture is particularly interesting? They tend to flock to high places. Why?*

SW: High points are positions of power. You can see what's going on for miles around. By placing Red Ladies on top of buildings, it creates the effect that they are everywhere. When you see them on the balconies of a town hall, on top of the Bodleian Library, on buildings of political or cultural significance, you wonder how on earth they gained access to these buildings, how did they get past security?

One of the functions of the Red Ladies is to de-familiarize. We don't often look up at all in our own city. By positioning themselves on strategic points of a building, they encourage people to look—drawing attention to the architecture. So, on the National Theatre in London they drew attention to the quite extraordinary shapes and angles on what many people see as quite a grey and uninviting building. Once again we are trying to create the effect that they are everywhere, that they have things covered and that they are looking out for us. When we are lucky enough to have a helicopter, this is taken to an extreme. The Red Lady gets a bird's-eye view.

I am also interested in how different dramatic territories operate in different planes of space. For example, the genre of clown works on the horizontal plane, whereas melodrama works on a diagonal. Tragedy operates on the vertical plane—it points us in the direction of the gods and to the underworld. It would be great to get the Red Ladies a submarine one day.

HE: *The Red Ladies undertake missions during the technical time required in preparation for the inside performance. How is this different from the usual experience of touring?*

SW: Often when you tour you just arrive in a town and spend all day in a dark theatre and only encounter the audience when they are in their seats. With *Red Ladies* we are able to build a much more layered relationship with the place we are visiting. First, we visit the city on a reconnaissance mission and decide which buildings we need access to, then there are the negotiations with people over the places we want to get access to. Then the interventions themselves allow the performers to experience the city, to meet the people, and to meet people who would never set foot in a theatre. Perhaps surprisingly, the Red Ladies' interventions are not really about public spectacle, although of course there is an element of that. It is the intimate conversations they have with the general public as they move through a city which seem to be where it works most powerfully.

HE: *You call the inside performance piece 'a theatrical demonstration in four movements'. Why?*

SW: We were trying to work out the relationship between the outside interventions and the inside show. There are layers of performance conventions and fantasies to unravel in *Red Ladies*. The conceit of the performance is that the Red Ladies are an international phenomenon—there are millions of them. Sometimes they rendezvous in a city and make their presence felt for reasons I have just described. Several years ago a group of Red Ladies decided that they wanted to put on a 'theatrical demonstration in four acts', which they invited me and other 'auxiliary staff' to facilitate. This device allows the emergent idea of *Red Ladies* to remain intact—there is no leader.

The idea of the theatrical demonstration partly comes from the idea of a Women's Institute cookery demonstration or a political demonstration. It is a kind of Brechtian device allowing the Ladies to explain to the audience what they are about to see before they see it. They ask the audience to experience the show as a demonstration of group dynamics, a showing, a coming together and a falling apart. The idea of a 'theatrical demonstration in four movements' reassures the audience that there is no need to get anxious when there is no obvious dramatic narrative. We wanted to avoid the audience thinking they were about to witness some kind of spy thriller with a movie plot. We wanted to encourage people to see the poetry in the piece.

And the piece literally is in four movements. Paul wrote a more or less symphonic structure, and the action and choreography was paced accordingly. Again, we wanted to encourage the audience to interpret it that way—a piece of music is linear, has a beginning and an end, but doesn't have a plot.

HE: *Music is a very important part of the piece, how did you and Paul collaborate on creating the aural and oral world and how has it developed throughout the project's life?*

SW: The sound and music changed quite radically over the course of the piece's development. Paul was keen to experiment with using 'found' recorded text—fragments of political speeches, TV dramas, sound effects, nature documentaries etc., which would create the world that the Red Ladies were witness to. In the first version of *Red Ladies* we decided to use a live band (a five-piece who were on stage throughout). It was technically quite difficult to get the recorded material to gel with the live music. The hundreds of recorded voices had an almost 'big-brother' effect on some members of the audience, which wasn't what we had intended at all. Plus the musicians' stage presence was so different from the other performers that we felt that the chorus wasn't holding together visually.

So, for the second version the score was rewritten and totally restructured from scratch. We decided to record the score, so Paul could manipulate the recorded material and the 'music' as a single sound world. He spliced the text rhythmical-ly; tuned voices to the pitch of the instruments and pretty much considered the found material another member of the band. Although the music itself was stylistically diffuse (there was a string quartet, a thrash song, a doo-wop number) the idea was to use the recorded material to bind the piece together and to create a dramatic structure. Paul created the entire score before rehearsals started and wrote three sequences that were played live (a violin serenade, a drum solo, and a short piece for fifteen harmonicas).

Paul and I discussed some of the dramatic effects, which the music would be driving. Often these were the classical references—the elegy for the dead, the ecstatic ritual. We used the text and sound effects tactically to try to open up some of the themes at key moments; for example, by having the sound of birds flocking in the very first scene. We agreed on a simple four-part structure but we did not closely collaborate on the microstructure of the music. Paul went away for a month and wrote the score to have its own satisfying musical shape.

HE: *One of the threads running through the piece is the telling of stories. Why? Was this concept a key part of the process?*

SW: We wanted to suggest that there are many stories to be told, not just one. There is a scene in *Red Ladies* where each woman tells the first lines of a story—a story about a memory. It becomes a chorus of stories. Stories are a way of sharing memories and shaping a collective memory. I am interested in how they are told and shared—over a cup of tea or by passing down a recipe rather than printed in a newspaper or history book. In her book *Regarding the Pain of Others*, Susan Sontag describes remembering as an ethical act and as a way to contact the dead. Of course in Greek tragedy the chorus is there to remind us of our history and ancestry, to learn from our mistakes. But remembering is a fine balance because sometimes too much remembering of ancient grief can lead to revenge. These ideas of justice and revenge are interesting to me.

HE: *Peter Oswald's text is packed with classical metaphor; was there a particular choice in relating the work to classical archetypes?*

SW: Using text was an opportunity to highlight some of the themes difficult to draw out in movement alone. It isn't easy to reference the past in movement because movement only really happens in the present. Also, by using classical references, we wanted to encourage the audience to think of the Red Ladies as a kind of tragic chorus.

We asked Peter Oswald to write the text for us because he is an exceptional poet and has such a strong classical knowledge and understanding. The classical material is just one ingredient that he used and he cleverly laced it with references to the immediate past—again trying to create a continuum. The whale being stuck in the River Thames, the First World War, the Trojan War, the underworld, the pyramids, yesterday's shopping list, the Big Bang—can all be mentioned in the same breath. And of course, once a few classical references have been introduced, the audience are more likely to find their own classical parallels, should they be that way inclined. One audience member thought that the Lady reciting the long speech in the middle was Hecuba, another that the Lady who plays a stirring drum solo in the final moments of the show must be Helen of Troy.

The Sibyl of Cumae speech at the end was actually a piece Peter wrote for us ten years ago when we made a piece based on Ovid's *Metamorphoses*. I love the figure of the Sibyl—she offers such a long-term perspective on things. The line: 'I am dust, dust that cannot blow away' in the context of *Red Ladies* seems to be a commitment to being alive, to changing, to surviving.

HE: *How did you decide on the look?*

SW: The idea for the costume came before the show itself. We were interested in the idea of multiple and mistaken identities, and in 2001 we made a sketch called *Babycase*, for three women dressed in this identical outfit. The idea was that the audience shouldn't be able to work out how many of them there were. Then we thought what would it be like to have a whole chorus of them! In fact we still have a fantasy to do a piece with a hundred of them or a thousand one day. For me it is a very amusing outfit, at once glamorous and stylish but also rather ridiculous, camp and cartoon like. It holds so many different identities—the French resistance, Italian cinema, Bond girls, honey-trap spies, prostitutes. But if you see them marching together they are more reminiscent of soldiers, or of a Maoist or a Fascist army. Then, when they are all knitting, they seem more like a group of Bulgarian old ladies. And while they can seem glamorous and sexy, it is worth remembering that they are also veiled—completely covered up from head to toe.

Throughout their 'theatrical demonstration' the ladies are constantly and very consciously shifting identity—wearing a variety of different costumes that resonate with different periods in history. They have an extensive wardrobe and take their personal appearance very seriously; after all, it is one of their most effective weapons of resistance. It is hard work to maintain such high standards—grooming, deportment, and beauty can be as time-consuming, exhausting, and painful as any military drill. And of course the uniform is a mask and as such is very protective for the performers when they are on the street. Even when they 'unmask' in the show, the principle and heightened atmosphere of a masked performance is always there.

HE: *How much of an alternative history is the piece intending to create?*

SW: For me, performance is about creating an alternative present. Although *Red Ladies* may be a filter for the past, it is powerful because it is happening in the moment and it is immediate, ephemeral, and transient. The quote that I always seem to come back to in my work is from Ovid's *Metamorphoses:*

> What we were yesterday and are today, we will not be tomorrow.[3]

---

[3] Ovid, *Metamorphoses*, 15.214.

References

ABEL, R. (1999). 'Introduction', in id. (ed.), *Silent Film* (London), 1–18.

ABBOTT, H. P. (1996). *Beckett Writing Beckett: The Author in the Autograph* (Ithaca, NY).

ACOCELLA, J., L. GARAFOLA, and J. GREEN (1992). '*The Rite of Spring* considered as a nineteenth-century Ballet', *Ballet Review*. 20.

ADLER, N. (1984). 'Reconstructing the Dances of Isadora Duncan in the United States', *TDR* 28: 59–66.

ALBRIGHT, A. COOPER (2007). *Traces of light: Absence & Presence in the Work of Loïe Fuller* (Middletown).

ALEXANDRE, A. and J. COCTEAU (1972). *The Decorative Art of Léon Bakst* [London, 1913], trans. H. Melville (New York).

ALLAIN, P. (1997). *Polish Theatre in Transition* (London).

ALLAN, M. (1908). *My Life and Dancing* (London).

——(1910). *Maud Allan and Her Art, Souvenir Programme* (London).

ALM, I. (1995). 'Humanism and theatrical dance in early opera', *Musica Disciplina* 49: 79–93.

——(1996a). 'Pantomime in seventeenth-century Venetian theatrical dance', in G. Morelli (ed.), *Creature di Prometeo: Il Ballo Teatrale. Dal Divertimento al Dramma: Studi offerti a Aurel M. Milloss* (Florence), 87–102.

——(1996b). 'Theatrical dance in Venetian opera 1637–1660', in A. Chiarle (ed.), *L'arte della danza ai tempi di Claudio Monteverdi: Atti del Convegno Internazionale Torino, 6–7 settembre 1993* (Turin), 95–111.

——(2003). 'Winged feet and mute eloquence: dance in seventeenth-century Venetian opera', *Cambridge Opera Journal* 15.3: 216–80.

ALTER, J. B. (1994). *Dancing and Mixed Media: Early Twentieth-Century Modern Dance Theory in Text and Photography* (New York).

ANDERSON, E. (2008). 'Dancing Modernism: ritual, ecstasy and the female body', *Literature and Theology*. 1–14.

ANDERSON, J. (1984). 'Plotless dance-drama that deals in emotions', *The New York Times* 26 August.

ANDRESEN, C. (1974). 'Altchristliche Kritik am Tanz—ein Ausschnitt aus dem Kampf der alten Kirche gegen heidnische Sitte', in H. Frohnes and U. W. Knorr (eds.), *Die alte Kirche (Munich)*, 1. 344–76.

ANNES BROWN, S. (2007). ''Hail, Muse! et cetera': Greek myth in English and American literature', in R. Woodward (ed.), *The Cambridge Companion to Greek Mythology* (Cambridge), 425–52.

ANON., (1702). *A Comparison of the Two Stages* (London).

——(1722). *The Dancing-master, a Satyr* (London).

——(1954a). 'The Golden Apple: Choreography by Hanya Holm', *Dance Observer* 21.4: 58–59.

——(1954b). 'New musical in Manhattan', *Time*, 22 March, accessed online: http://www.time.com/magazine/article/0,9171,819617,00.html?iid+chix-sphere [02.11.08].

ANTCLIFFE, H. (1926). 'Prometheus in Music', *The Musical Quarterly* 12.1: 110–120.

ANTON, J. P. (ed.) (1997). *Eva Palmer-Sikelianos' Letters on Ancient Drama* (Athens).

APPLETON, W. W. and K. A. BURNIM (1966, eds.). *The Prompter: A Theatrical Paper (1734–1736), by A. Hill and W. Popple* (New York).

ARBEAU, THOINOT (1967). *Orchesography*, trans. by M. Stewart Evans (New York).

ARCANGELI, A. (1994). 'Dance under trial: the moral debate 1200–1600', *Dance Research* 12: 127–55.

——(2000). 'Dance and health: the Renaissance physicians' view', *Dance Research* 18: 3–30.

ARMSTRONG, R. (2005). *A Compulsion for Antiquity: Freud and the Ancient World* (Ithaca, NY).

ASMIS, E. (1991). 'Philodemus's poetic theory and "On the Good King According to Homer"', *Classical Antiquity* 10:1–45.

ASTAIRE, F. (1959). *Steps in Time* (New York).

ASTIER, R. (2007). 'Françoise Prévost: the unauthorized biography', in L. M. Brooks (ed.), *Women's Work: Making Dance in Europe before 1800* (Madison, Wisconsin), 123–59.

AUDEN, W.H. (1976). *Collected Poems* (New York).

AUDOLLENT, A. (1904). *Defixionum Tabellae* [Paris] (Luteciæ Parisiorum).

AUGUSTIN, F. (1924). *De dans in zijn sociale en artistieke betekenis* (Amsterdam).

AUSLANDER, P. (ed.) (2003). *Performance: Critical Concepts in Literary and Cultural Studies*, vol. 1 (London).

AVERY, E. L. (1934). 'Dancing and pantomime on the English stage, 1700–1737', *Studies in Philology* 31: 417–52.

——(1938). 'The defense and criticism of pantomimic entertainments in the early eighteenth century', *Journal of English Literary History* 5: 127–45.

BACON, FRANCIS (1996). *Francis Bacon*, ed. B. Vickers (Oxford).

BALANCHINE, G. (1982). 'The Dance Elements in Stravinsky's Music', *Ballet Review* 10.2: 14–18 [= first published in *Dance Index* 3 (1948)].

BANES, S. (1977). *Terpsichore in Sneakers* (Middletown).

——(1998). *Dancing Women: Female Bodies on Stage* (London and New York).

BANNERMAN, H. (1998). *The Work (1935–1948) of Martha Graham (1894–1991) with Particular Reference to an Analysis of her Movement System: Vocabulary and Syntax* (unpub. Ph.D. diss., Roehampton).

——(2001). 'Thoroughly modern Martha', *Dance Theatre Journal* 17.2: 32–6.

——(2006). 'A dance of transition: Martha Graham's *Herodiade*', *Dance Research* 24.1: 1–21.

——(2007). 'Embodying History/making connections: Frederick Ashton and Martha Graham', *Proceedings: Society for Dance History Scholars 30th Annual Conference co-sponsored with CORD (Centre National de la danse)*, Paris, 21–24 June: 135–40.

BARKER-BENFIELD, G. J. (1992). *The Culture of Sensibility: Sex and Society in Eighteenth-Century Britain* (Chicago).

BARNES, S. (1994). *Writing Dancing in the Age of Postmodernism* (Hanover and London).

BARNETT, L. (1941). 'Fred Astaire: he is the no.1 exponent of America's only native and original dance form', *Life* 11.8 (25 Aug.): 72–85.

BARON, A. A. F. (1824). *Lettres et entretiens sur la danse ancienne, moderne, religieuse, civile et théatrale* (Paris).

BARRETTO, N. (1999). 'The role of Martha Graham's notebooks in her creative process', in A. Helpern (ed.), *Choreography and Dance* 5.2: 53–67.

BARROW, R. J. (2001). *Lawrence Alma-Tadema* (London).

BARTHES, R. (1972). *Mythologies*, trans. A. Lavers (London).

——(1977). 'Diderot, Brecht, Eisenstein', *Image Music Text*, trans. S. Heath (London).

BATE, W. J. (1945). 'The sympathetic imagination in eighteenth-century English criticism', *English Literary History* 12: 144–64.

BATES, W. H. (MD) (1920). 'A lesson from the Greeks', *Better Eyesight: A Monthly Magazine* (June).

BAUD-BOVY, S. (1988). 'Maurice Emmanuel et la Grèce', *La Revue Musicale* 410–11: 109–15.

BEACHAM, R. C. (1994). *Adolphe Appia: Artist and Visionary of the Modern Theatre* (Switzerland and Philadelphia).

BEARD, M. (2000). *The Invention of Jane Harrison* (Cambridge, Mass).

BEAZLEY, J. D. (1963). *Attic Red Figure Vase-Painters*, 2nd edn. (Oxford).

BECKER, E. et al. (eds.) (1996). *Sir Lawrence Alma-Tadema 1836–1912* (Zwolle).

BELLINA, A. L. (1989). 'I gesti parlanti ovvero il recitar danzando. *Le Festin de Pierre e Sémiramis*', in F. Marri (ed.), *La figura e l'opera di Ranieri de' Calzabigi, Atti del convegno di studi Livorno 14–15 dicembre 1987* (Florence), 107–17.

——(1994). *Ranieri Calzabigi: Scritti Teatrali e Letterari*, vol. 1 (Rome).

BENTIVOGLIO, L. (1991). *Il teatro di Pina Bausch* (Milano).

——(1999). 'Utopia Bausch', *La Repubblica* 9 Feb. 1999.

BENTLEY, E. (1983). 'Martha Graham's journey', in R. Copeland and M. Cohen (eds.), *What is Dance? Readings in Theory and Criticism* (Oxford), 197–202.

BENTLEY, T. (2002). *Sisters of Salome* (New Haven).

BESTERMAN, T. (ed.) (1962). *Voltaire's Correspondence*, 78, January–March 1771 (Geneva).

BIRRINGER, J. (1986). 'Dancing across borders', *TDR* 30.2: 85–97.

BLAIR, F. (1986). *Isadora. Portrait of the Artist as a Woman* (New York).

BLANNING, T. (2007). 'The making of history: John Weaver and the Enlightenment', in M. Kant (ed.), *The Cambridge Companion to Ballet* (Cambridge), 78–86.

BLOM, I. (2001). 'Quo Vadis? From painting to cinema and everything in between', in L. Quaresima and L. Vinchi (eds.), *La decima Musa. Il cinema e le altri arti / The tenth Muse. Cinema and the other arts* (Udine), 281–92.

BLOM, P. (2008). *The Vertigo Years:—Europe, 1900–1914* (New York).

BLONDEL, N. (2002 ed.). *The Journals of Mary Butts* (New Haven).

BOADEN, J. (1831–2). *The private correspondence of David Garrick with the most celebrated persons of his time; now first published from the originals, and illustrated with notes, and a new biographical memoir of Garrick*, 2 vols. (London).

BOARDMAN, J. (1974). *Athenian Black Figure Vases* (London).

——(1988). *Athenian Red Figure Vases: the Archaic Period* (London).

——(1998). *Early Greek Vase Painting* (London).

——(2001). *The History of Greek Vases* (London).

BOCCADORO, P. (2005). 'Pina Bausch's *Orpheus* charms the Underworld of the Paris Opera Ballet', in *Culturekiosque*, 5 July, accessed online: http://www.culturekiosque.com/dance/reviews/pina_bausch_orpheus.html [03.01.08].

BONNET, J. (1969). *Histoire générale de la danse sacrée et profane* [Paris, 1723] (Genève).

BORGER, R. (1978). *Drei Klassizisten: Alma Tadema, Ebers, Vosmaer* (Leiden).

Borthwick E. K (1970). 'P. Oxy. 2738: Athena and the Pyrrhic Dance', *Hermes* 98: 318–31.

Bournonville, A. (1979). *My Theatre Life* [Copenhagen, 1848–78] (London).

Bowers, F. (1996). *Scriabin: A Biography* (New York).

Bowlby, R. (2007). *Freudian Mythologies* (Oxford).

Brainard, I. (1996). 'The speaking body: Gaspero Angiolini's *Rhétorique Muette* and the Ballet d'Action in the Eighteenth Century', in J. Knowles (ed.), *Critica Musica: Essays in Honor of Paul Brainard* (Amsterdam), 15–56.

Brandau, R. (ed.) (1976). *De Meyer* (London).

Brandenburg, H. (1921). *Der moderne Tanz* (Munich).

Brandstetter, G. (1998). 'Defigurative Choreography: From Marcel Duchamp to William Forsythe', trans. Marta Ulvaeus in *TDR* 42.4: 37–55.

Braun, M. (1992). *Picturing Time. The Work of Etienne-Jules Marey (1830–1904)* (Chicago).

Brinson, Peter (1966). *Background to European Ballet* (Leiden).

Brissenden, R. F. (1974). *Virtue in Distress: Studies in the Novel of Sentiment from Richardson to Sade* (London).

Brockett, O. G. (1965). 'The Fair Theatres of Paris in the Eighteenth Century: The Undermining of the Classical Ideal', in M. J. Anderson (ed.), *Classical Drama and Its Influence: Essays in Honour of H.D.F.Kitto* (London), 249–69.

Brooks, Lynn Matluck (2003). *The Art of Dancing in Seventeenth-Century Spain: Juan de Esquivel Navarro and His World* (Lewisburg and London).

Brown, B. A. (1991). *Gluck and the French Theatre in Vienna* (Oxford).

Brown, F. (1980). *Theater and Revolution: The Culture of the French Stage* (New York).

Bruyère, J. de la (1962). *Les Caractères de Théophraste traduits du grec avec les caractères ou les moeurs de ce siècle* [Paris, 1688], ed. R. Garapon (Paris).

Buckle, R. (1979). *Diaghilev* (New York).

——(1980). *Nijinsky* [London, 1971], rev. edn. (Harmondsworth).

Bulwer, J. (1644). *Chirologia; or the Naturall Language of the Hand*, ed. J. M. Clancy (London, reprinted Carbondale 1974).

Bundrick, S. D. (2005). *Music and Image in Classical Athens* (Cambridge).

Burette, J. P. (1717). 'Premier mémoire pour servir à l'histoire de la danse des anciens' and 'Second mémoire pour servir à l'histoire de la danse des anciens', *Histoire de l'Académie royale des inscriptions* 1: 93–135.

Burn, L. (2003). 'Words and pictures: Greek vases and their classification', in K. Sloan and A. Burnett (eds.), *Enlightenment* (London).

Burns, Alfred (1974–5). 'The chorus of Ariadne', *Classical Journal* 70: 1–12.

Burns, E. (1972). *Theatricality: a Study of Convention in the Theatre and in Social Life*, New York.

Burnside, F. (1994). 'Michael Clark's *O*', in *Dance Theatre Journal* 11.3: 29–30.

Burrow, C. (2004). 'Shakespeare and humanistic culture', in Charles Martindale and A. B. Taylor (eds.), *Shakespeare and the Classics* (Cambridge), 9–27.

Burt, R. (1995). *The Male Dancer: Bodies, Spectacle, Sexualities* (London and New York).

——(1998). *Alien Bodies: Representations of Modernity, 'Race' and Nation in Early Modern Dance* (London and New York).

Bywater, I. (1920, trs.). *Aristotle: On the Art of Poetry* (Oxford).

CADENBACH, R. (1995). 'Beethoven's Die Geschöpfe des Prometheus', in *Beethoven: Die Geschöpfe des Prometheus*, Teldec 4509–90876–2.

CAHUSAC, L. DE (2004). *La danse ancienne et moderne ou traité historique de la danse* [La Haye, 1754], ed. N. Lecomte, L. Naudeix, J.-N. Laurenti (Paris).

CALASSO, R. (1994). *The Marriage of Cadmus and Harmony*, trans. T. Parks (London).

CALLIACHIUS, N. (1718). 'De ludis scenicis mimorum et pantomimorum' [Patavii (Padua), 1713], in A.-H. de Sallengre (ed.), *Novus Thesaurus Antiquitatum Romanarum*, vol. ii (Hague), 715–67.

CAMPARDON, E (1877). *Les Spectacles de la foire*, 2 vols. (Paris).

CAMPBELL, P. R. (1993). *Louis XIV: 1661–1715* (Harlow).

CAMPION, THOMAS (1607). *A Discription [sic] of a Maske, Presented before the Kinges Maiestie at White-Hall, on Twelfth-Night Last, in Honour of Lord Haye, and His Bride, Daughter and Heire to the Honourable the Lord Dennye [The Lord Hay's Masque]* (London).

——(1967). *The Works of Thomas Campion*, ed. W. Davis (London).

CAPLAN, J. (1986). *Framed Narratives: Diderot's Genealogy of the Beholder* (Manchester).

CARLSON, M. (1998). *Voltaire and the Theatre of the Eighteenth Century* (Westport).

CARPENTIER, M. (1998). *Ritual, Myth, and the Modernist Text: Jane Ellen Harrison's Influence on Joyce, Eliot, and Woolf* (Amsterdam).

CARONES, L. (1987). 'Noverre and Angiolini: Polemical Letters', *Dance Research* 5.1: 42–54.

CAROSO, FABRITIO (1600). *Nobiltà di dame* (Venice).

——(1995). *Courtly Dance of the Renaissance: A New Translation and Edition of the 'Nobiltà di dame (1600)'*, ed., trans. J. Sutton and F. M. Walker, 2nd edn. (New York).

CARROLL, S. (1990). 'Reciprocal representations: David and theater', *Art in America* 78: 198–206 and 259–61.

CARTLEDGE, P. (1997). '"Deep plays": theatre as process in Greek civic life', in P. E. Easterling (ed.), *The Cambridge Companion to Greek Tragedy* (Cambridge), 3–35.

CAVE, R. A. (1980). *Terence Gray and the Cambridge Festival Theatre* (Cambridge).

——(1997). 'Dance and stylised movement as visual codes in drama: a crisis in interpretation' in M. Gibinska (ed.), *Verbal and Non-Verbal Codes in European Drama* (Krakow) 81–105.

——(2004). 'Ian Spink: texts and contexts', *Contemporary Theatre Review*, 14.3: 63–72.

CD-ROM: *'Gardzienice' Practising the Humanities: Theatrical Essay by Włodzimierz Staniewski* (2006).

CD-ROM: *Metamorfozy; Music of Ancient Greece*, Gardzienice (2000).

CHAMBERLAIN DUERDEN, R. (2003). *The Choreography of Antony Tudor: Focus on Four Ballets* (London).

CHAMBERS, E. K. (1923). *Gestures Used in Acting and Rhetoric in Elizabethan England* (Oxford).

CHANSKY, D. (1991). '*The Trackers of Oxyrhynchus*. By Tony Harrison. The National Theatre, London. 7 March 1991', *Theatre Journal* 43: 52–34.

CHAPMAN, GEORGE (1613). *The Memorable Maske* (London).

CHARBONNEL, R. (1899). *La danse. Comment on dansait, comment on danse* (Paris).

CHAZIN-BENNAHUM, J. (1983). 'Cahusac, Diderot, and Noverre: three revolutionary French writers on the eighteenth-century dance', *Theatre Journal* 35: 169–78.

——(1988). 'The radical influence of eighteenth-century theatre on ballet', in D. Trott and N. Boursier (eds.), *The Age of Theatre in France (L'Age du Théâtre en France)* (Alberta), 299–309.

CHAZIN-BENNAHUM, J. (2007). 'Jean-Georges Noverre: dance and reform', in M. Kant (ed.), *The Cambridge Companion to Ballet* (Cambridge), 87–97.

CHERNIAVSKY, F. (1991). *The Salome Dancer, the Life and Times of Maud Allan* (Toronto).

——(1998). *Maud Allan and Her Art* (Toronto).

CHURCHILL, CARYL (1993). 'Introduction', *Lives of the Great Poisoners* (London).

——(1997). *Hotel* (London).

——(1998). 'Introduction' in *Caryl Churchill: Plays: 3* (London).

——and DAVID LAN (1986). *A Mouthful of Birds* (London).

——and ORLANDO GOUGH AND IAN SPINK (1993). *Lives of the Great Poisoners: A Production Dossier* (London).

CLARK, M. and J. BURROWS (1998). 'Michael Clark', in J. Burrows (ed.), *Conversations with Choreographers* (London), 11–14.

——and F. HENDERSON (2007). 'How we met: Michael Clark and Fergus Henderson', in *The Independent*, 9 Sept.

CLASSENS, H. (1988). 'Maurice Emmanuel, Professeur', *La Revue Musicale*, 410–11: 18–19.

CLASSICAL NET REVIEW: Retrieved 2 Dec. 2007 from: http://www.classical.net/music/recs/reviews/s/sny62352a.html

CLIMENHAGA, R. (1997). *What Moves Them: Pina Bausch and the Aesthetics of Tanztheater* (Ann Arbor).

——(2009). *Pina Bausch* (London).

CODY, G. (1998). 'Woman, dog, tree: two decades of intimate and monumental bodies in Bausch's Tanztheater', *TDR* 42.2: 115–31.

COHEN, B. N. (1982). *Biographical Dictionary of Dance* (New York).

COHEN, S. J. (1960). 'Theory and practice of theatrical dancing in England in the Restoration and early eighteenth century, part ii: John Weaver', *Bulletin of the New York Public Library* 64: 41–54.

——(1965). 'A meeting with Rallou Manou', *Dance Magazine* (June): 57.

COLEBROOK, F. M. (1925). 'Why not a British Dance?' *The Link*, 1/4, July: 45.

COLETTE (1954). *Uniform Edition of Works by Colette. Vol.6: The Vagabond*, trans. E. McLeod.

——(1957). *My Apprenticeships, and Music-Hall Sidelights* [*Mes apprentissages*, Paris, 1936 and *L'envers Du music-hall*, Paris, 1913], trans. H. Beauclerk and A.-M. Callimachi (London).

——(1958). *Paysages et Portraits* (Paris).

——(1984a). *Oeuvres*, vol. 1 (Paris).

——(1984b). *Album Colette* (Paris).

CONDILLAC, E. B. DE (2001). *Essay on the Origin of Human Knowledge* [1746], edited and translated by H. Aarsleff (Cambridge).

COOK, R. M. (1997). *Greek Painted Pottery*, 3rd edn. (London).

COPELAND, R. (2004). *Merce Cunningham: The Modernizing of Modern Dance* (New York).

——and B. COHEN (1983). *What is Dance? Readings in Theory and Criticism* (Oxford).

CORSO, RINALDO (1555). *Dialogo del Ballo* (Venice).

COWAN, J. (1990). *Dance and the Body Politic in Northern Greece* (Princeton).

COWPER, WILLIAM (1791). *The Iliad and Odyssey of Homer, translated into English blank verse* (London).

CRAINE, D. (2008). 'Pina Bausch at Sadler's Wells', *The Times*, 15 Feb.

CRAWFORD FLITCH, J. E. (1912). *Modern Dancing and Dancers* (Philadelphia).

CREWDSON, R. (2000). *Apollo's Swan and Lyre: five hundred years of the Musicians' Company* (Woodbridge).

CRISP, C. (1985). 'Michael Clark/ Edinburgh Festival', *The Financial Times*, 14 Aug.

CROCE, A. (1972). *The Fred Astaire and Ginger Rogers Book* (New York).

CROW, T. (1985). *Painters and Public Life in Eighteenth-Century Paris* (New Haven and London).

CULLEN, F. (2006). *Vaudeville, Old and New: An Encyclopedia of Variety Performers in America*, vol. 1 (New York and London).

CUMBERLAND, R. (1806). *Mémoirs of Richard Cumberland* (London).

CURRENT, R. N. and M. E. CURRENT (1997). *Loie Fuller, Goddess of Light* (Boston).

CZEKANOWSKA, A. (1990). *Polish Folk Music* (Cambridge).

DALY, A. (1986). 'The thrill of the lynch mob or the rage of a woman?', *TDR* 30.2: 45–56.

——(1987). 'At issue: gender in dance', letter in *TDR* 31: 22–26.

——(1994). 'Isadora Duncan and the distinction of dance', *American Studies* 35: 5–23.

——(1995). *Done into Dance: Isadora Duncan in America* (Bloomington and Indianapolis).

DAMASKOS, D. and D. PLANTZOS (eds.) (2008). *A Singular Antiquity: Archaeology and Hellenic Identity in Twentieth-Century Greece.* Mouseio Benaki Supplement 3 (Athens).

DAVID, A. P. (2006). *The Dance of the Muses: Choral Theory and Ancient Greek Poetics* (New York and Oxford).

DAVIES, T. (1780). *Memoirs of the Life of David Garrick Esq., interspersed with characters and anecdotes of his theatrical contemporaries, the whole forming a history of the stage*, 2 vols. (Dublin).

——(1973). *Dramatic Micellanies [sic] Consisting of Critical Observations on Several Plays of Shakspeare: With a Review of His Principal Characters, and Those of Various Eminent Writers, as Represented by Mr. Garrick, and Other Celebrated Comedians, with Anecdotes of Dramatic Poets, Actors, and C.* [London, 1784] (New York).

DE DOMIZIO DURINI, L. (1997). *The Felt Hat: Joseph Beuys A Life Told*, trans. H. R. Maclean (Milan).

DEKOVEN, M. (1999). 'Modernism and gender', in M. Levenson (ed.), *The Cambridge Companion to Modernism* (Cambridge), 174–93.

DELAVAUD-ROUX, M.-H. (1993). *Les danses armées en Grèce antique* (Aix-en-Provence).

——(1994). *Les danses pacifiques en Grèce antique* (Aix-en-Provence).

——(1995). *Les danses dionysiaques en Grèce antique* (Aix-en-Provence).

DE MÉNIL, F. (1905). *Histoire de la danse à travers les âges* (Paris).

DE MILLE, A. (1991). *Martha: The Life and Work of Martha Graham* (New York).

DEODATUS, CLAUDIUS (1628). *Pantheum hygiasticum Hippocratico-hermeticum* (Porrentruy).

DE PURE, M. (1668). *Idée des spectacles anciens et nouveaux* (Paris).

DESMOND, J. C (1997 ed.). *Meaning in Motion* (Durham).

DE SORIA, H. (1897). *Histoire pittoresque de la danse* (Paris).

DIDEROT, D. (1965). 'Lettre sur les sourds et muets' [1751], P. H. Mayer (ed.), *Diderot Studies* 7: 37–89.

DILLON, M. (1990). *After Egypt: Isadora Duncan and Mary Cassatt* (New York).

DONI, G. B. (1763). *Lyra Barberina*, vol. 2 (Florence).

DORF, S.N. (2007*a*). 'Greek desires in Paris: Isadora Duncan dances antiquity in the lesbian salon', Winner of Selma Jeanne Cohen Award 2007, accessed online: http://www.sdhs.org/pdf/Samuel_N_Dorf.pdf [24/06/09].

——(2007*b*). '"Etrange n'est-ce pas?" The Princesse Edmond de Polignac, Erik Satie's *Socrate*, and a lesbian aesthetic of music?' in J. Day (ed.), *Queer Sexualities in French and Francophone Literature and Film* [=*French Literature Series* XXXIV] (Amsterdam and New York).

DORIS HUMPHREY INSTITUTE: accessed online. http://www.dorishumphreyinstitute.org/restaging.html [02/12/07].

D'ORLIAC, JEAN (1914). 'Madame Loïe Fuller et son école de danse', *Le Théâtre* 377, September.

DOUGLAS, A. (1995). *Terrible Honesty* (New York).

DOWDEN, K. (1989). *Death and the Maiden* (London).

DOY, G. (2002). *Drapery: Classicism and Barbarism in Visual Culture* (London).

DRAPER, R. P. (1980, ed.). 'Introduction', *Tragedy: Developments in criticism* (Hampshire and London).

DREIER, K. S. (1933). *Shawn the Dancer* (New York).

DU BOS, JEAN-BAPTISTE (1719). *Réflexions critiques sur la poésie et sur la peinture*. 2 vols. (Paris).

——(1748). *Critical Reflections on Poetry, Painting and Music, with An Inquiry into the Rise and Progress of the Theatrical Entertainments of the Ancients*. (trans. T. Nugent from the 5th edn, revised, corrected and enlarged by the author), 3 vols. (London).

DUCHESNE, JOSEPH (1606). *Le Portrait de santé* (Paris).

DUNCAN, I. (1903). *Tanz der Zukunft. Eine Vorlesung* (Leipzig).

——(1927). *My Life* (New York).

——(1928). *The Art of the Dance* (New York).

——(1981). *Isadora Speaks* (ed. by F. Rosemont) (San Francisco).

DUNCAN, D., C. PRATL, and C. SPLATT (eds.), (1993). *Life into Art: Isadora Duncan and her World* (New York and London).

DUNCAN, R. (1914). 'La danse et la gymnastique', *Conférence faite le 4 Mai 1914 à l'Université Hellenique, Salle de Géographie* (Paris).

DURÁN, C. (1994). 'Teatro-Dança de Pina Bausch faz 20 anos', *O Estado de São Paulo IX* (2. 768), 7 Sept., Caderno 2.

DUREY DE NOINVILLE, J-B. (1757). *Histoire du Théâtre de l'Académie Royale de Musique* (Paris).

DYSON, S. (1993). 'From new to New Age archaeology: archaeological theory and classical archaeology—a 1990's Perspective', *American Journal of Archaeology* 97: 192–206.

EAGLEFIELD HULL, A. (1916). 'A survey of the pianoforte works of Scriabin', *The Musical Quarterly* 2.4: 601–14.

EAGLETON, T. (2003). *Sweet Violence: The Idea of the Tragic* (Malden and Oxford).

EASTERLING, P. E. (ed.) (1997*a*). *The Cambridge Companion to Greek Tragedy* (Cambridge).

——(1997*b*). 'A Show for Dionysus', in Easterling (1997), 36–53.

EFTHIMIOU-TSEKOURA, D., K. VOUNELAKI and I. BOUDOURI (1997). *Nelly's body and dance* (Athens / Kalamata).

EKSTEINS, M. (1989). *Rites of Spring: The Great War and the Birth of the Modern Age* (London).

ELIADIS, Ph. (1960). *Greek Cinema, 1906–1960* (Athens).

ELIOT. T. S. (1922). 'Tradition and the individual talent' [1919], *The Sacred Wood: Essays on Poetry and Criticism* (London).

——(1923). 'Ulysses, order, and myth', *The Dial* 75: 480–3.

ELLIOTT, J. K. (ed.) (1993). *The Apocryphal New Testament* (Oxford).

ELLIS, M. (1996). *The Politics of Sensibility: Race, Gender and Commerce in the Sentimental Novel* (Cambridge).

EMMANUEL, M. (1895a). *De saltationis disciplina apud Graecos* (Paris).

——(1895b). *Essai sur l'orchestique grecque* (Paris).

——(1896a). *La danse grecque antique d'après les monuments figurés* (Paris).

——(1896b). 'La danse grecque antique', *Gazette des Beaux Arts* 15: 291–308.

——(1916). *The Antique Greek Dance, after sculptured and painted figures* trans. H. J. Beauley (New York and London, reprinted 1927).

ENTERS, A. (1931–2). 'Dance credos and the "Greeks"', *The Hound and Horn, a Harvard Miscellany* 5: 292–4.

ERBSE, H. (ed.) (1969–77). *Scholia Graeca in Homeri Iliadem*, vol. 5. (Berlin).

ERSKY, F.-A. (1910). *Les danses antiques grecques et romaines. Étude historique* (Paris).

ESQUIVEL NAVARRO, JUAN DE (1642). *Discursos sobre el arte del danzado* (Seville).

EUSTIS, M. (1937). 'Fred Astaire: the actor-dancer attacks his part', *Theatre Arts Monthly* 21.5: 371–86.

EVANS, A. (1930). *The Palace of Minos*, vol. 3. (London).

EWANS, M. (2007). *Opera from the Greek* (Aldershot).

EYSTEINSSON, A. (1990). *The Concept of Modernism* (Ithaca and London).

FABBRI, P. and A. POMPILIO (1983). *Il corago, o vero Alcune osservazioni per metter bene in scena le composizioni drammatiche* (Florence).

FAGIN, H. N. (1977). 'Adam Mickiewicz: Poland's National Romantic Poet', *South Atlantic Bulletin* 42.4: 103–13 (South Atlantic Modern Language Association).

FEHLING, W.W. (2007). *Iraïl Gadescov, danseur célèbre 1894–1970. De opmerkelijke carrière van danspionier Richard Vogelesang* (Delft).

FENSHAM, R. (2002). 'Deterritorialising dance: tension and the wire', *in Discourses in Dance* 1.2: 63–83.

FERNANDES, C. (2001). *Pina Bausch and the Wuppertal Dance Theatre: the Aesthetics of Repetition and Transformation* (New York).

FERRARIUS, O. (1718). 'De Pantomimis et Mimis Dissertatio' [1714], in A. H. de Sallengre (ed.), *Novus Thesaurus Antiquitatum Romanarum*, vol. 2, (Hague), 685–97.

FILIPOWICZ, H. (1987). 'Gardzienice: a Polish expedition to Baltimore', *TDR* 31.1: 137–163.

FISCHER-LICHTE, E. (2004). 'Thinking about the origins of theatre in the 1970s', in Hall, Macintosh and Wrigley (eds.), 329–360.

FLAUBERT, G. (1991). *Three Tales* (Oxford).

FONTEYN, M. (1980). *The Magic of Dance* (London).

FORSYTHE, W. and J. COPELAND (2001). *Eidos: Telos and William Forsythe* (13.12.2001), accessed online: http://www.abc.net.au/arts/performance/stories/s439792.htm [15.12. 2006].

FORSYTHE, W. and M. SAUP (2004). *Binary Ballistic Ballet: FAQs* (04.08.2004), accessed online: http://www.particles.de/paradocs/bbb/faq.html [15.12.2006].

——and J. TUSA (2003). *William Forsythe Director, Ballett Frankfurt*, interview for Radio BBC 3 (02.02.2003), accessed online: http://www.ballet.co.uk/magazines/yr_03/feb03/interview_bbc_forsythe.htm [15.09.2007].

FOSTER, R. F. (2003). *W. B. Yeats: A Life, II. The Arch Poet* (Oxford).

FOSTER, S. L. (1995 ed.). *Choreographing History* (Bloomington and Indianapolis).

——(1996*a*). *Choreography and Narrative: Ballet's Staging of Story and Desire* (Bloomington).

——(1996*b*). 'Pygmalion's No-Body and The Body of Dance', in E. Diamond (ed.). *Performance and Cultural Politics* (London), 131–54.

——(1996c). *Corporealities: Knowledge, Culture and Power* (London and New York).

FOULKES, J. L. (2002). *Modern Bodies: Dance and American Modernism from Martha Graham to Alvin Ailey* (Chapel Hill).

FOULKES, R. (1997). *Church and stage in Victorian England* (Cambridge).

FRALEIGH, S. H. (1987). *Dance and the Lived Body* (Pittsburgh).

FRANCIS, E. (1994). 'From event to monument: modernism, feminism and Isadora Duncan', *American Studies* 35.1: 25–45.

FRANKO, M. (1993). *Dance as Text: Ideologies of the Baroque Body* (Cambridge).

——(1995). *Dancing modernism / performing politics* (Bloomington and Indianapolis).

——(2002). *The Work of Dance: Labor, Movement, and Identity in the 1930s* (Middletown).

FREUD, S. (1900). *The Interpretation of Dreams*, Penguin Freud Library 4 (London).

——(1905). 'Fragment of an analysis of a case of hysteria', in Penguin Freud Library 8: 44–164 (London).

——(1913). 'Totem and Taboo', in Penguin Freud Library 13: 53–224 (London).

——(1916–17). 'Transference', in Penguin Freud Library 1: 482–500 (London).

——(1930). 'Civilisation and its Discontents', in Penguin Freud Library 12: 251–340 (London).

FRIED, M. (1988). *Absorption and Theatricality: Painting and Beholder in the Age of Diderot* (Chicago).

FULLER, L. (1913). *Fifteen Years of a Dancer's Life* (London).

GAGE, M. (1929). 'The Greek choral dance', *Theatre Arts Monthly* 13.8: 569–78.

GAGER, J. G. (1992). *Curse Tablets and Binding Spells from the Ancient World* (Oxford).

GALLINI, G. A. (1772). *A Treatise on the Art of Dancing* (London).

GARAFOLA, L. (2004). *Legacies of Twentieth-Century Dance* (Middletown, CT).

GARAUDY, R. (1972). *Danser sa vie* (Paris).

GARBER, M. (1992). *Vested Interests: Cross-dressing and Cultural Anxiety* (New York).

GARELICK, R. (2007). *Electric Salome: Loïe Fuller's Performance of Modernism* (Princeton and Oxford).

GARELLI, M.-H. (2006). 'Gestuelle et danse dans le monde antique. Deux questions de bibliographie', *Pallas* 71: 151–67.

——(2007). *Danser le mythe: la pantomime et sa réception dans la culture critique* (Louvain).

GAUNT, W. (1975). *Victorian Olympus* [1952], (London).

GENNÉ, B. (1996). *The Making of a Choreographer: Ninette de Valois and Bar aux Folies-Bergère* [= *Studies in Dance History*, no. 12] (Minneapolis, MN).

GENNEP, A. VAN (1909). *The Rites of Passage* (repr. 1960) (London).

GENTHE, A. (1920). *The book of the dance* (Boston).

——(1929). *Isadora Duncan: Twenty-Four Studies* (New York and London).

GEORGIADES, T.G. (1956). *Greek Music, Verse and Dance*, trans. E. Benedikt and M. L. Gümllner (Cambridge).

GERMAIN, S. (2005). 'Le Suppliant', in Paris Opéra Ballet Programme for *Orpheus et Eurydice* (Paris).

GEROULD, D. and L. PŁOSZEWSKI (Autumn 1986). 'From Adam Mickiewicz's *Lectures on Slavic Literature*, given at the College of France', *TDR* 30/3: 91–7.

GIESE, F. (1927). *Körperseele. Gedanken über persönliche Gestaltung* (Munich).

GILDON, C. (1970). *The Life of Mr. Thomas Betterton, the Late Eminent Tragedian* [1710] (London).

GILES, S. (1988). *Fred Astaire: His Friends Talk* (London).

GILMAN, R. (1975). *Decadence: The Strange Life of an Epithet* (New York).

GILMAN, S. L. (1995). 'Salome, Syphilis, Sarah Bernhardt, and the modern Jewess', in L. Nochlin and T. Garb (eds.), *The Jew in the Text: Modernity and the Construction of Identity* (London), 97–120.

GINNER, R. (1922). 'The Position of Dancing in the Education of Ancient Greece', An Address read by Miss Ruby Ginner at the last 'Dancers' Circle Dinner' 17 Dec. 1922: Ginner Papers BB/N/10 Scrapbook 1921–31.

——(1926). 'The Athletic Festivals of Greece', *The Link*, 2/2, October: 14–15.

——(1933). *The Revived Greek dance. Its art and technique* (London).

——(1936). 'The Jubilee of the Revived Greek Dance', *The Link* 2 (new series no.2), March 1936 [=Special Issue 'The Greek Drama Festival']: 4–7.

——(1960). *Gateway to the Dance* (London).

GLIKSOHN, J.-M. (1985). *Iphigénie: de la Grèce antique à l'Europe des Lumières* (Paris).

GLYTZOURIS, A. (1998). 'Delphic Festivals (1927, 1930): The revival of Ancient Greek dance in *Prometheus* and *Suppliant Women*', *Istorika* 28–29: 147–70.

GOFF, B. (1999). 'The violence of community: ritual in the *Iphigenia in Tauris*', *Bucknell Review* 43: 109–25.

GOFF, M. (1994). 'Dancing-masters in early eighteenth-century London', *Historical Dance* 3.3: 170–23.

——(1995). '"The art of dancing, demonstrated by characters and figures": French and English sources for court and theatre dance, 1700–1750', *The British Library Journal* 21.2: 202–31.

——(1998). '"Actions, manners, and passions": entr'acte dancing on the London stage, 1700–1737', *Early Music* 26.2: 213–28.

——(2005). 'Steps, gestures, and expressive dancing: Magri, Ferrère, and John Weaver', in R. Harris-Warrick and B. A. Brown (eds.), *The Grotesque Dancer on the Eighteenth-Century Stage: Gennaro Magri and His World* (Wisconsin), 199–230.

GOFFMAN, E. (1974). *Frame Analysis: an Essay on the Organization of Experience* (Cambridge).

GOLACZYNSKA, M. and I. GUSZPIT (eds.) (2006). *Theatre-Space-Body-Dialogue: Research in Contemporary Theatre* (Wrocław).

GOLDHILL, S. (2002). *Who needs Greek? Contests in the Cultural History of Hellenism* (Cambridge).

GOLDHILL, S. (2010). 'Who killed Gluck?', in P. Brown and S. Ograjenšek (eds.), *Ancient Drama in Music for the Modern Stage* (Oxford).

GOODDEN, A. (1986). *Actio and Persuasion: Dramatic Performance in Eighteenth-Century France* (Oxford).

——(2001). *Diderot and the Body* (Oxford).

GORCE, J. DE LA (1990). 'Guillaume-Louis Pécour: a biographical essay', *Dance Research* 8.2.

GORING, P. (2005). *The Rhetoric of Sensibility in Eighteenth-Century Culture* (Cambridge).

GOUDAR, A. (1773). *De Venise: Rémarques sur la musique et la danse ou Lettres de Mr G... à Milord Pembroke* (Venise).

GOULD, J. (2001). *Myth, Ritual, Memory and Exchange: Essays in Greek Literature and Culture* (Oxford).

GRAHAM, M. (1959). *Blood Memory* (New York, reprinted 1991).

——(1973). *The Notebooks of Martha Graham* (New York).

GRENE, DAVID and RICHMOND LATTIMORE (eds.) (1955). *Euripides 1: Alcestis, Medea, The Heracleidae, Hippolytus* (Chicago and London).

GRIFFITH, M. (1983). *Aeschylus: Prometheus Bound* (Cambridge).

GRIMM, F. M. VON, et al. (1879). *Correspondance littéraire, philosophique et critique* (Paris).

GUEST, I. (1996). *The Ballet of the Enlightenment: The Establishment of the Ballet d'Action in France, 1770–1793* (London).

HAAS, R. B. (1976). *Muybridge: Man in Motion* (Berkeley).

HALL, E. (1989). *Inventing the Barbarian* (Oxford).

——(1999). 'Introduction' to *Euripides: Iphigenia among the Taurians, Bacchae, Iphigenia at Aulis, Rhesus* (Oxford).

——(2004). 'Introduction: Why Greek tragedy in the late Twentieth Century?', in Hall, Macintosh, and Wrigley (eds.), 1–46.

HALL, EDITH (2007). 'Putting the Class into Classical Reception', in L. Hardwick and C. Stray (eds.), *A Companion to Classical Receptions* (Oxford), 386–97.

——(2008*a*). *The Return of Ulysses: A Cultural History of Homer's Odyssey.* (London).

——(2008*b*). 'Ancient Pantomime and the rise of ballet', in Hall and Wyles (eds.), 363–377.

——(2008*c*). 'Pantomime: a lost chord of ancient culture', in Hall and Wyles (eds.), 1–40.

——, F. MACINTOSH, O. TAPLIN (eds.) (2000). *Medea in Performance 1500–2000* (Oxford).

——, F. MACINTOSH, and A. WRIGLEY (eds.) (2004), *Dionysus Since 69: Greek Tragedy at the Dawn of the Third Millenium* (New York and Oxford).

——and F. MACINTOSH (2005). *Greek Tragedy and the British Theatre 1660–1914* (Oxford).

——and R. WYLES (eds.) (2008). *New Directions in Ancient Pantomime* (Oxford).

HALL, F. A. (1914). 'A comparison of the Iphigenias of Euripides, Goethe, and Racine', *Classical Journal* 9: 371–84.

HALLIWELL, S. (1998). *Aristotle's Poetics* (Chicago).

HANNA, J. (1988). *Dance, Sex and Gender* (Chicago and London).

HANSELL, K. K. (1998). 'Noverre, Jean-Georges', in Selma Jean Cohen (ed.), *International Encyclopedia of Dance*, vol. 4 (New York), 694–700.

HANSELL, K. K. (2002). 'Theatrical ballet and Italian opera', in L. Bianconi and G. Pestelli (eds.), *Opera on Stage*, trans. K. Singleton (Chicago and London), 177–308.

——(2005). 'Eighteenth-century Italian theatrical ballet: the triumph of the *Grotteschi*', in Harris-Warrick and Brown, 15–32.

HARDING, J. (1979). *Artistes Pompiers. French academic art in the 19th century* (London).

HARDISON LONDRÉ, F. (1991). *The History of World Theatre: from the Restoration to the Present* (New York).

HARRIS, M. H. (1979). *Loïe Fuller: Magician of Light* (Richmond).

HARRISON, J. E. (1912). *Themis. A study of the social origins of Greek religion* (Cambridge).

——(1913). *Ancient Art and Ritual* (London).

HARRIS-WARRICK, R. (1998). 'Recovering the Lullian divertissement', in S. McCleave (ed.), *Dance and Music in French Baroque Theatre: Sources and Interpretations* (London), 55–80.

——(1999). '"*Toute Danse doit Exprimer, Peindre . . .*": Finding the Drama in the Operatic Divertissement', *Basler Jahrbuch für historische Musikpraxis* 23: 187–218.

——(2005). 'Introduction', in R. Harris-Warrick and B. A. Brown (eds.), *The Grotesque Dancer on the Eighteenth-Century Stage: Gennaro Magri and His World* (Wisconsin), 3–14.

——(2007). 'Dance and representation in the operas of Lully', in M. Biget-Mainfroy and R. Schmusch (eds.), '*L'esprit français' und die Musik Europas: Entstehung, Einfluss und Grenzen einer ästhetischen Doktrin: Festschrift für Herbert Schneider / L'esprit français et la musique en Europe: émergence, influence et limites d'une doctrine esthétique* (Hildesheim), 208–18.

——and B. A. BROWN (2005, eds.). *The Grotesque Dancer on the Eighteenth-Century Stage: Gennaro Magri and His World* (Wisconsin).

——and C. G. MARSH (1994). *Musical Theatre at the Court of Louis XIV: Le Mariage de la Gros Cathos* (Cambridge).

HART, R. (1991). 'Classical Greek dance: Ruby Ginner method', in A. Raftis (ed.), χορός και Αρχαία Ελλάδα, vol. 2 (Athens), 213–17.

HARVEY, S. (1975). *Fred Astaire* (New York).

HAU, M. (2003). *The Cult of Health and Beauty in Germany. A Social History, 1890–1930* (Chicago).

HAUSAMANN, T. (1980). *Die Tanzende Salome in der Kunst von der Christliche Frühzeit bis um 1500* (Zurich).

HEARTZ, D. (1967–8). 'From Garrick to Gluck: the reform of theatre and opera in the mid-eighteenth century', *Proceedings of the Royal Musical Association* 94: 111–27.

HECK, T. (ed.) (2007). *A Treatise on Acting, from Memory and by Improvisation* (1699) by Andrea Perrucci, trans. and ed. Francesco Cotticelli, Anne Goodrich Heck, Thomas F. Heck., Bilingual Edition in English and Italian (Lanham).

HEDGCOCK, F. A. (1912). *A Cosmopolitan Actor: David Garrick and his French Friends* (London).

HEILBRUN, C. (1990). *Hamlet's Mother and Other Women* (New York).

HEITNER, R. R. (1964). 'The Iphigenia in Tauris theme in drama of the eighteenth century', *Comparative Literature* 16.4: 289–309.

HELPERN, A. (ed.) (1999*a*). 'Martha Graham's early technique and dances: The 1930s, a panel discussion', *Choreography and Dance* 5.2: 7–32.

HELPERN, A. (ed.) (1999*b*). 'The dance theatre pieces of the 1940s: A conversation with Jean Erdman and Erick Hawkins', *Choreography and dance* 5.2: 33–40.

HEUBECK, ALFRED, STEPHANIE WEST, and J. B. HAINSWORTH (1988–92). *A Commentary on Homer's Odyssey* (Oxford).

HEWITT, A. (2005). *Social Choreography: Ideology as Performance in Dance and Everyday Movement* (Durham, NC).

HIGHFILL, P. H., K. A. BURNIM, and E. A. LANGHANS (1973–93). *A Biographical Dictionary of Actors, Actresses, Dancers, Managers and other Stage Personnel in London, 1660–1800,* 16 vols. (Carbondale).

HINCKS, M. A. (1906). 'The dance in ancient Greece', *Nineteenth Century and After* 59: 447–57.

——(1907). 'The dance and the plastic arts in Ancient Greece', *Nineteenth Century and After* 61: 477–89.

——(1909). 'Representations of dancing on early Greek vases', *Revue Archéologique* 14: 351–69.

——(1911). 'Le kordax dans le culte de Dionysos', *Revue Archéologique* 17: 1–5.

HINDSON, C. (2007). *Female Performance Practice on the fin-de-siècle Popular Stages of London and Paris: Experiment and Advertisement* (Manchester).

HOARE, P. (1997). *Oscar Wilde's Last Stand: Decadence, Conspiracy, and the Most Outrageous Trial* (London).

HODGE, A. (2000). 'Włodzimierz Staniewski: Gardzienice and the naturalised actor' in Alison Hodge (ed.), *Twentieth Century Actor Training* (London and New York), ch. 12.

HODGINS, P. (1992). *Relationships between score and choreography in Twentieth Century Dance: Music, Movement and Metaphor* (Ceredigion).

HODSON, M. (1985). 'Ritual design in the new dance: Nijinsky's *Le Sacre du Printemps*', *Dance Research* 3.2: 35–45.

——(1986). 'Ritual design in the new dance: Nijinsky's choreographic method', *Dance Research* 4.1: 63–77.

HOFFMAN, E. (1994). 'Pina Bausch: Catching intuitions on the wing', *The New York Times* 11 Sept.

HOFMANNSTHAL, HUGO VON (1964). *Selected Plays and Libretti*, ed. M. Hamburger (London).

HOGHE, R. (1986). *Pina Bausch—Tanztheatergeschichten* (Frankfurt).

——and S. TREE (1980). 'The Theatre of Pina Bausch', *TDR* 24: 63–74.

HOLDEN, S. (1989). 'Documentary Look at Pina Bausch', *The New York Times* 7 July.

HOLLAND, P. (1996). 'The Age of Garrick', in J. Bate and R. Jackson (eds.), *Shakespeare: An Illustrated Stage History* (Oxford), 69–91.

HOLMSTRÖM, K. G. (1967). *Monodrama, Attitudes, Tableaux Vivants: Studies on Some Trends of Theatrical Fashion 1770–1815* (Stockholm).

HORST, L. and C. RUSSELL (1961). *Modern Dance Forms in Relation to the Other Modern Arts* repr. 1967 (San Francisco).

HOXBY, B. (2005). 'The doleful airs of Euripides: the origins of opera and the spirit of tragedy reconsidered', *Cambridge Opera Journal* 17: 253–69.

HOWE, D.S. (1996). *Individuality and Expression: The Aesthetics of the New German Dance, 1908–1936* (New York).

HUGO, VICTOR (1979). *Quatrevingt-treize*, ed. Yves Gohin (Paris).

HURST, I. (2006), *Victorian Women Writers and the Classics: The Feminine of Homer* (Oxford).

HUXLEY, A. (1937). *Ends and Means: An Inquiry into the Nature of Ideals and into the Methods Employed for Their Realization* (New York).

HYNES, S. (1968). *The Edwardian Turn of Mind* (London).

IK = (1968-). *Inschriften griechische Städte aus Kleinasien* (Cologne).

INGLEHEARN, M. (2008). 'Dancing Masters: Professionals or Businessmen?', in B. Segal (ed.), *Dancing Master or Hop Merchant? The Role of the Dance Teacher through the Ages*. Early Dance Circle Conference, 23 Feb. 2008 (London), 49–60.

ISHERWOOD, R. M. (1981). 'Entertainment in the Parisian fairs in the eighteenth century', *Journal of Modern History* 53: 24–47.

——(1986). *Farce and Fantasy: Popular Entertainment in Eighteenth Century Paris* (Oxford).

JACQUIN, R. (1988). *L'esprit de Delphes : Anghelos Sikelianos* (Aix en Provence).

JAMES, M. R. (1924). *The Apocryphal New Testament* (Oxford).

JAMES, R. (2008). *The Maud Allan Affair* (London).

JAUSS, H. R. (1970). 'Literary history as a challenge to literary theory', transl. E. Benzinger, *New Literary History* 2.1: 7–37.

JENKINS, I. (2008). 'The past as a foreign country: Thomas Hope's collection of antiquities', in D. Watkins and Ph. Hewat-Jaboor (eds.), *Thomas Hope: Regency Designer* (New Haven and London).

——and K. SLOAN (1996). *Vases and Volcanoes: Sir William Hamilton and his Collection* (London).

JENKYNS, R. (1980). *The Victorians and Ancient Greece* (London).

JENYNS, S. (1729). *The Art of Dancing* (London).

JESCHKE, C. and G. VETTERMANN (1995). 'Isadora Duncan, Berlin and Munich in 1906: just an ordinary year in a dancer's career', *Dance Chronicle* 18.2: 217–29.

JOAD, C. E. M. (1948). *Decadence: A Philosophical Enquiry* (London).

JOHNSON, D. (1989). 'Corporality and communication: the gestural revolution of Diderot, David, and *The Oath of the Horatii*', *Art Bulletin* 71.1: 92–113.

——(1993). *Jacques-Louis David: Art in Metamorphosis* (Princeton).

JOHNSON, J. H. (1995). *Listening in Paris: A Cultural History* (Berkeley, Los Angeles and London).

JOHN-STEINER, V. (2000). *Creative Collaboration* (Oxford).

JONES, INIGO (1973). *Inigo Jones: The Theatre of the Stuart Court*, ed. S. Orgel and R. Strong, 2 vols. (London).

JONSON, BEN (1925–52). *Ben Jonson*, ed. C. H. Herford, P. and E. Simpson, 11 vols. (Oxford).

JORDAN, S. (1984). 'Ted Shawn's Music Visualizations', *Dance Chronicle* 7.1: 33–49.

——(1992). *Striding Out* (London).

——(2007). *Stravinsky Dances: Re-visions Across a Century* (London).

——and D. ALLEN (eds.) (1993). *Parallel Lines: Media Representations of Dance* (London).

——and G. MORRIS, (2004). *Ashton to Stravinsky: A Study of Four Ballets* [Television Roehampton TVR] (London).

JORY, J. (1981). 'The Literary Evidence for the Beginnings of Imperial Pantomime', *Bulletin of the Institute of Classical Studies* 28: 147–61.

JOSEPH, B. L. (1951). *Elizabethan Acting* (Oxford).

——(1959). *The Tragic Actor* (London).

JOSEPHS, H. (1969). *Diderot's Dialogue of Language and Gesture: Le Neveu de Rameau* (Columbus).

JOWITT, D. (1985). 'Images of Isadora: the search for motion', *Dance Research Journal* 17: 21–9.

——(1987). 'The impact of Greek art on the style and persona of Isadora Duncan', *Proceedings of the Society of Dance History Scholars, 10th annual conference.* University of California, Irvine, 13–15 Feb. 1987 (Riverside), 195–201.

——(1988). *Time and the Dancing Image* (New York, Berkeley, and Los Angeles).

JUNGMANN, I. (2002). *Tanz, Tod und Teufel: Tanzkultur in der gesellschaftlichen Auseinandersetzung des 15 und 16 Jahrhunderts* (Kassel).

KABBANI, R. (1988). *Europe's Myths of Orient* (London [1986]).

KANT, M. (ed.) (2007). *The Cambridge Companion to Ballet* (Cambridge).

KARAMANOLAKIS, V. (2008). 'University of Athens and archaeological studies: the contribution of archaeology to the creation of a national past (1911–1932)', in D. Damaskos and D. Plantzos (eds.), *A Singular Antiquity: Archaeology and Hellenic Identity in Twentieth-Century Greece* (Athens), 185–95.

KARAYIANNI, S. S. (2004). *Dancing, Fear and Desire: Race, Sexuality, and Imperial Politics in Middle Eastern Dance* (Waterloo).

KAVANAGH, J. (1996). *Secret Muses: The Life of Frederick Ashton* (London).

KELLY, C. (Summer, 1989). 'Classical tragedy and the "Slavonic Renaissance": the plays of Vjačeslav Ivanov and Innokentij Annenskij compared', *The Slavic and East European Journal* 33.2: 235–54.

KERN, S. (1975). *Anatomy and Destiny* (Indianapolis).

KHUDEKOV, S. N. (1913). *Istoriya tanchev*, vol. 1 (St Petersburg).

KILINKSI, K. (1990). *Boeotian Black Figure Vase Painting of the Archaic Period* (Mainz am Rhein).

KING, K (2005). 'The Dancing Philosopher', *Topoi*: 103–11.

KIRK, G. S. (1985). *The Iliad: A Commentary*, vol. 1. (Cambridge).

KISSELGOFF, ANNA (1984). 'Dance: A Graham Premiere', accessed online: http://www.nytimes.com/1984/03/01/arts/dance-a-graham-premiere.html [21/12/07].

——(1988). 'Phaedra's Tragedy in 2 Retellings', accessed online: http://www.nytimes.com/1988/10/20/arts/review-dance-phaedra-s-tragedy-in-2-retelli. [21/12/07].

——(1989). 'Triple bill by Graham Company', accessed online: http://query.nytimes.com/gst/fullpage.html [21/12/07].

KLEIST, HEINRICH VON (1810). *On the Marionette Theater*, trans. Idris Parry.

KOCHANOWSKI, J. (2001). *Laments*, trans. S. Baranczak and Seamus Heaney (New York).

KOLANKIEWICZ, L. (2001). 'Polish spectacles and the religion of Dionysus', *Konteksty*, 55.1–4: 252–5.

KOVACS, D. (2002). *Euripides VI: Bacchae, Iphigeneia at Aulis and Rhesus*, ed. and trans. (London and Cambridge, MA).

KOZEL, S. (1997). '*The Story is Told as History of the Body': Strategies of Mimesis in the Work of Irigaray and Bausch*, in Desmond (1997), 101–9 (Durham).

KRAMER, L. (1990). 'Culture and musical hermeneutics: the Salome complex', *Cambridge Opera Journal* 2.3: 269–94.

KUHNS, D. F. (1997). *German Expressionist Theatre* (Cambridge).

KUNZLE [ASTIER], R. (1974/5). 'Pierre Beauchamp, the illustrious choreographer', *Dance Scope* 9.1.

KURTH, P. (2002). *Isadora Duncan: A Sensational Life* (London).

KURTZ, D. C. (ed.) (1985). *Beazley and Oxford*, Lectures delivered in Wolfson College, Oxford, 28 June 1985 (Oxford).

——(2000). *The Reception of Classical Art in Britain* (Oxford).

LABAN, R. (1948). *Modern Educational Dance* (London).

——(1950). *The Mastery of Movement* (London).

LADA-RICHARDS, I. (2003*a*). '"Mobile statuary": refractions of pantomime dancing from Callistratus to Emma Hamilton and Andrew Ducrow' *International Journal of the Classical Tradition* 10.1: 3–37.

——(2003*b*). 'A worthless feminine thing? Lucian and the "optic intoxication" of pantomime dancing', *Helios* 30.1: 21–75.

——(2004*a*). 'Authorial voice and theatrical self-definition in Terence and beyond: the Hecyra Prologues in ancient and modern contexts', *Greece and Rome* 51.1: 55–82.

——(2004*b*). 'Μύθων Εἰκών: pantomime dancing and the figurative arts in imperial and late antiquity', *Arion* 12.2: 17–46.

——(2007). *Silent Eloquence: Lucian and Pantomime Dancing* (London).

LAGRAVE, H. (1979). 'La pantomime à la foire, au Théâtre Italien et aux boulevards (1700–1789). Première approche: historique du genre', *Romanistische Zeitschrift für Literaturgeschichte/Cahiers d'Histoire des Littératures Romanes* 3: 408–30.

LAMBRINOS, F. (1997). 'The filming of the Delphic festivals', *Istorika* 26: 135–44.

LAMOTHE, K. L. (2005). 'A God dances through me: Isadora Duncan on Friedrich Nietzsche's Revaluation of Values', *Journal of Religion* 85: 241–66.

——(2006). *Nietzsche's Dancers: Isadora Duncan, Martha Graham, and the Revaluation of Christian Values* (New York).

LANDORMY, P. (1943). *La musique française après Debussy* (Paris).

LAPORTE, J. DE and S. R. N. CHAMFORT (1776). *Dictionnaire dramatique, contenant l'histoire des théâtres, les règles du genre dramatique, les observations les plus célèbres, et des réflexions nouvelles sur les spectacles* (Paris).

LATTE, K. (1913). *De saltationibus graecorum capita quinque* (Giessen).

L'AULNAYE, FRANÇOIS HENRI STANISLASDE (1790). *De la Saltation théatrale, ou recherches sur l'Origine, les Progrès, and les effets de la pantomime chez les anciens* (Paris).

LAVER, J. (1969). *Modesty in Dress* (London).

LAWLER, L. B. (1927). 'The ancient Greek dance: the maenads', *American Journal of Archaeology* 31: 91–2.

——(1931). Review of *La Danse grecque antique*, by Louis Séchan, *Classical Philology* 26: 222–3.

——(1941–2). 'The dance of the Holy Birds', *The Classical Journal* 37: 351–61.

——(1942). 'Four dancers in the *Birds* of Aristophanes, *Transactions of the American Philological Association* 73: 58–63.

——(1944). 'Beating motifs in the Greek dance', *The Classical Outlook* 21: 59–61.

——(1946). 'Portrait of a dancer', *The Classical Journal*, 41.6: 241–7.

LAWLER, L. B. (1947–8). 'A dancer's trophy', *The Classical Weekly* 41: 50–2.

——(1948). 'Snake dances', *Archaeology* 1: 110–3.

——(1952). 'Dancing herds of animals', *The Classical Journal* 47: 317–24.

——(1957). '"She could have danced all night—"', *The Classical Outlook* 34: 54–5.

——(1964). *The Dance in Ancient Greece* (London).

——and A. E. KOBER, (1945). 'The "Thracian Pig Dance"', *Classical Philology* 40: 98–107.

LAYSON, J. (1983). 'Isadora Duncan: a preliminary analysis of her work', *Dance Research* 1: 39–49.

LAZZARINI, J. and R. LAZZARINI (1980). *Pavlova. Repertoire of a Legend* (New York).

LC 5: The National Archives, London: Lord Chamberlain's papers: Warrant Books General, 1671–1675 (5/140–141), and Petitions 1671–1697 (5/190).

LC 7: The National Archives, London: Lord Chamberlain's papers: Miscellaneous, 1673–1797 (7/3).

LEAF, W. and M. A. BAYFIELD (eds.) (1898). *The Iliad of Homer* (London and New York).

LECOMTE, N. (2007). 'The female ballet troupe of the Paris Opera from 1700 to 1725' in L. M. Brooks (ed.), *Women's Work: Making Dance in Europe before 1800* (Wisconsin), 99–122.

LEDERMAN, M. (ed.) (1975). *Stravinsky in the Theatre* (New York).

LEKAIN, H. L. (1801). *Mémoires* (Paris).

LELOIR, M. (1951). *Dictionnaire du costume* (Paris [repr. 1992]).

LEPECKI, A. (2006). *Exhausting Dance: Performance and the Politics of Movement* (New York and London).

LEVINSON, A. (1929). *La Danse d'Aujourd' hui* (Paris).

——(1991). *André Levinson on Dance: Writings from Paris in the 20s*, ed. J. Acocella and L. Garofola (Hanover and London).

LEVIEN, J. (1977–78). 'Sources of Style in the Dances of Isadora Duncan', *Ballet Review* 6: 44–9.

LEWIS, WYNDHAM (1969). *Wyndham Lewis on Art: Collected Writings 1913–1956*, ed. W. Michel and C. J. Fox (New York).

LEY, G. (2003). 'Modern Visions of Greek Tragic Dancing', *Theatre Journal* 55: 467–80.

——(2007). *The Theatricality of Greek Tragedy: Playing Space and Chorus* (Chicago).

LIEVEN, P. (1936). *The Birth of the Ballets-Russes* (London).

LINDLEY, D. (1979). 'Campion's Lord Hay's Masque and Anglo-Scottish Union', *The Huntington Library Quarterly* 43.1: 1–11.

——(1986). *Thomas Campion* (Leiden).

——(2004–2009). 'Campion, Thomas (1567–1620)', in *Oxford Dictionary of National Biography*, accessed online: www.oxforddnb.com, [11/05/07].

LISTA, G. (1994). *Loïe Fuller, danseuse de la Belle Epoque* (Paris).

LITTLE, M. E. and C. G. MARSH (1992). *La Danse noble: An Inventory of Dances and Sources* (Williamstown).

LOCKHART, J. (1817). 'Remarks on Greek tragedy', *Blackwood's Magazine*. May.

LOEWENTHAL, L. (1979–89). 'Isadora Duncan in the Netherlands', *Dance Chronicle* 3: 227–53.

——(1993). *The Search for Isadora: The Legend and Legacy of Isadora Duncan* (Pennington).

LONSDALE, S. H. (1995). 'A dancing floor for Ariadne (*Iliad* 18.590–592): aspects of ritual movement in Homer and Minoan religion', in J. B. Carter and S. P. Morris (eds.), *The Ages of Homer: A Tribute to Emily Townsend Vermeule*, 273–84 (Austin).

LONDRÉ, F. H. (1991). *The History of World Theatre: From the Restoration to the Present* (New York).

LORET, J. (1877). *La Muse historique* (Paris).

LUTTRELL, N. (1857). *A Brief Historical Relation of State Affairs from September 1678 to April 1714*, 6 vols. (Oxford).

LYNHAM, D. (1950). *The Chevalier Noverre, Father of Modern Ballet* (London).

LYONS, D. J. (1997). *Gender and Immortality: Heroines in Ancient Greek Myth and Cult* (Princeton).

LYOTARD, J-.F. (1984). *The Postmodern Condition: A Report on Knowledge* (Minneapolis).

MAAS, J. (1975). *Gambart, prince of the Victorian art world* (London).

MCCARREN, F. (2003). *Dancing Machines: Choreographies of the Age of Mechanical Reproduction* (Stanford).

MACAULAY, A. (1981). 'Alistair Macaulay: Dance', in *Ritz,* April.

MCCLEAVE, S. (1998). 'English and French theatrical sources: the repertoire of Marie Sallé', in S. McCleave (ed.), *Dance and Music in French Baroque Theatre: Sources and Interpretations* (London), 13–32.

MCDONAGH, D. (1974). *Martha Graham: A Biography* (London).

MCDONALD, M. (1992). *Ancient Sun, Modern Light: Greek Drama on the Modern* Stage (New York).

MACDONALD, N. (1983). 'Isadora, Chopin and Fokine', *Dance and Dancers* 408 (Dec.), 30–32.

MACDOUGALL, A. R. (1960). *Isadora: A Revolutionary in Art and Love* (New York).

——(1977). 'Isadora Duncan and the artists', in P. Magriel (ed.), *Nijinsky, Pavlova, Duncan: Three Lives in Dance* (New York), 35–63.

MCGANN, J. (1996). *The Poetics of Sensibility: A Revolution in Literary Style* (Oxford).

MACINTOSH, F. (1994). *Dying Acts: Death in Ancient Greek and Modern Irish Tragic Drama* (Cork and New York).

——(2007). 'From the Court to the National: The Theatrical Legacy of Gilbert Murray's *Bacchae*', in C. A. Stray (ed.), *Gilbert Murray Reassessed: Hellenism, Theatre, and International Politics* (Oxford), 145–66.

——(2009). *Sophocles' Oedipus Tyrannus* (Cambridge).

——(2009*b*). 'The "Rediscovery" of Aeschylus for the Modern Stage', in J. Jouanna and F. Montanari (eds.), *Eschyle* (Geneva), 435–68.

MACLEOD, D. S. (1996). *Art and the Victorian Middle Class. Money and the Making of Cultural Identity* (Cambridge).

MCKEE, T. (2007). 'The Reception of Euripides' Hippolytus in the Twentieth Century' (Unpublished M.Phil. diss. Oxford).

MCKINNON, J. (1987). *Music in Early Christian Literature* (Cambridge).

MCLAINE, WILLIAM (1711). *An Essay upon Dancing* (Edinburgh).

MCNEILL, WILLIAM (1995). *Keeping Time Together: Dance and Drill in Human History* (Harvard).

MACPHERSON, D. (1984). 'Spit and polish on the dance floor', *The Sunday Times,* 8 July.

MAGRIEL, P. D. (ed.) (1947). *Isadora Duncan* (New York).

——(ed.) (1977). *Nijinsky, Pavlova, Duncan: Three Lives in Dance* (New York).

MALLARMÉ, STÉPHANE (1945). *Oeuvres complètes* (Paris).

——(2003). 'Ballets' [1886], in B. Marchal (ed.), *Igitur, Divagations, Un coup de dés* (Paris).

MANNLICH, J. C. VON (*c.*1989–93). *Histoire de ma vie: mémoires de Johann Christian von Mannlich (1714–1822)*, ed. Karl-Heinz Bender *et al.* (Trier).

MANNING, S. A. (1986). 'An American perspective on Tanztheater', *TDR* 30.2. 57–79.

——(1991). 'German rites: a history of *Le Sacre du Printemps* on the German stage', *Dance Chronicle* 14–2.3: 129–58.

——(1993). *Ecstasy and the Demon* (Berkeley).

——(2004). 'Sensibility', in T. Keymer and J. Mee (eds.), *The Cambridge Companion to English Literature 1740–1830* (Cambridge), 80–99.

——and M. Benson (1986). 'Interrupted Continuities: Modern Dance in Germany', *TDR* 30.2: 30–45.

MARE, M. L. and W. H. QUARRELL (1938). *Lichtenberg's Visits to England, as Described in his Letters and Diaries* (translated and annotated) (Oxford).

MARICQ, A. (1952). 'Tablettes de défixion de Fiq', *Byzantion* 22: 360–8.

MARMOY, C. F. (1977). *The French Protestant Hospital: Extracts from the Archives of La Providence, 1718–1957*, 2 vols., Huguenot Society of London, Quarto Series 52, 53.

MARSHALL, D. (1988). *The Surprising Effects of Sympathy* (Chicago).

MARSHALL, G. (1998). *Actresses on the Victorian Stage: Feminine Performance and the Galatea Myth* (Cambridge).

MARTIN, I. (2002). *Le théâtre de la foire: des tréteaux aux boulevards* (Oxford).

MARTIN, J. (1933). *The Modern Dance* (New York).

——(1961). *Days of divine indiscipline. Dance Perspectives* 12 (Autumn).

MARTINDALE, C. (2006). 'Thinking Through Reception', in C. Martindale and R. F. Thomas (eds.), *Classics and the Uses of Reception* (Oxford), 1–13.

——and A. B. TAYLOR (eds.) (2004). *Shakespeare and the Classics* (Cambridge).

——and R. F. THOMAS (eds.) (2006). *Classics and the Uses of Reception* (Oxford).

MASON HAUSER, N. (1983). 'Hanya Holm', in G. Dorris and N. Goldman (eds.), *International encyclopaedia of dance, vol 3* (New York and Oxford), 368–72.

MATTHIESSEN, K. (2002). 'Die Taurische Iphigenie bei Euripides, Goethe und anderswo', in S. Gödde and T. Heinze (eds.), *Skenika. Beiträge zum antiken Theater und seiner Rezeption. Festschrift zum 65. Geburtstag von Horst-Dieter Blume* (Darmstadt), 363–80.

MAVROMATIS, E. (1983). *Bella Raftopoulou: dessins libres d'après les vases Grecs pour les fêtes de Delphes 1925–1927* (Athens).

MAWER, I. (1932). *The Art of Mime* (London).

MAXWELL, J. (2006). *Christianization and Communication in Late Antiquity: John Chrysostom and his Congregation in Antioch*, Cambridge.

MAZO, J. (2000). *Prime Movers: The Makers of Modern Dance in America*, 2nd edn. (Hightstown).

McVAY, G. (1980). *Isadora and Esenin* (Ann Arbor).

MEISNER, N. (1992–3). 'Come dance with me', *Dance and Dancers*: 12–16.

MÉNESTRIER, C. -F. (1658). 'Remarques pour la conduite des ballets', appended to *L'Autel de Lyon . . . ballet dédié à sa Majesté en son entrée à Lyon* (Lyons).

——(1984). *Des ballets anciens et modernes selon les règles du théâtre* [Paris, 1682] (Génève).

MEURSIUS, I. (1618). *Orchestra. Sive, de Saltationibus Veterum, Liber Singularis* (Leiden).

MESK, J. (1908). 'Des Aelius Aristides Rede gegen die Tanzer', *Wiener Studien* 30: 59–74.

MICHELINI, A. N. (1987). *Euripides and the Tragic Tradition* (Madison).

MICKIEWICZ, A. (1914). *Les Slaves: Cours professé au Collège de France (1824–1833)* [LS], Paris: Musée Adam Mickiewicz.

MILHOUS, J. (1991). 'David Garrick and the dancing master's apprentice', *Dance Research* 11.1.

MILHOUS, J. and ROBERT D. HUME (1991). *A Register of English Theatrical Documents 1660–1737*, 2 vols. (Carbondale).

MILIADIS, G. (1998). 'Forty years ago', in Papageorgiou (1998), 95–99.

MILLER, M. C. (1999). 'Reexamining transvestism in archaic and classical Athens: the Zewadski Stamnos', *American Journal of Archaeology* 103: 223–53.

MILLER, N. (1988). *Subject to Change* (New York).

MIŁOSZ, C. (1983). *The History of Polish Literature* (California and London), 159–308.

MITCHELL, K. (2008). *Director's Craft* (London).

MONEY, K. (1982). *Anna Pavlova. Her Life and Art* (New York).

MOORE, T. (ed.) (1990). *A Blue Fire: The Essential James Hillman* (London).

MORDDEN, E. (2005). *Sing for Your Supper: The Broadway Musical in the 1930s* (New York).

MORGAN, B. (1980). *Martha Graham: Sixteen dances in photographs* (New York).

MORINNI, C. DE (1978). 'Loie Fuller: the fairy of light', in P. Magriel (ed.), *Chronicles of the American Dance* (New York).

MORRIS, G. (2006). 'Persephone: Ashton's Rite of Spring', *Dance Research* 24.1: 21–36.

MORRIS, M. (1926). *Margaret Morris Dancing: A Book of Pictures by* Fred Daniels with an Introduction and Outline by Margaret Morris (London).

——(1969). *My Life in Movement* (London).

——(1974). *J.D. Fergusson. A Biased Biography* (Glasgow).

MORRISON, M. (1997). *John Barrymore, Shakespearean Actor* (Cambridge).

MUELLER, JOHN (1985). *Astaire Dancing: The Musical Films* (New York).

MULLALLY, ROBERT (1998). '*Measure* as a choreographic term in the Stuart masque', *Dance Research*, 16.1: 67–73.

MULLAN, J. (1988). *Sentiment and Sociability: The Language of Feeling in the Eighteenth-Century Novel* (Oxford).

MULROONEY, D. (2002). *Orientalism, Orientation, and the Nomadic Work of Pina Bausch* (Frankfurt am Main).

MURPHY, P. (1976). 'Ballet Reform in Mid-Eighteenth-Century France: The *Philosophes* and Noverre', *Symposium* 30: 27–41.

MURRAY, G. (1912). 'An Excursus on the Ritual forms Preserved in Greek Tragedy' in Harrison (1912), 341–63.

MURRAY, P. and P. WILSON (eds.) (2004). *Music and The Muses: The Culture of 'Mousikê' in the Classical Athenian City* (Oxford).

NABOKOV, I. and E. CARMICHAEL (1961). 'An Interview with George Balanchine', *Horizon* 3.3, January, 44–56.

NAEREBOUT, F. G. (1994). 'Whose dance? Questions of authenticity and ethnicity, of preservation and renewal', in A. Raftis (ed.), *Dance beyond frontiers. Proceedings of the 8th international conference on dance research* (Athens), 77–86.

NAEREBOUT, F. G. (1997). *Attractive performances. Ancient Greek dance: three preliminary studies* (Amsterdam).

——(1998). 'Being Greek on Fourth Avenue. Isadora Duncan put into context', *Choreologica. Journal of the European Association of Dance Historians* 1: 34–47.

——(2001). *La danza greca antica. Cinque secoli d'indagine* (Lecce).

——(2002). '"Nice dance! But is it authentic?" What actually is this authenticity that everybody is going on about?', *Dance as intangible heritage. Proceedings of the 16th international congress on dance research.* Corfu 2002 (Athens), 125–138.

NEARS, C. (1987). 'Errand into the Maze; Cave of the Heart; Acts of Light', *An evening with Martha Graham: Dance from America*, London: BBC2 (video tape).

NEEDHAM, M. (1996). 'Who is Isadora?', *Dance Chronicle* 19: 331–40.

——(1997). 'Louis XIV and the Académie Royale de Danse 1661—a Commentary and Translation', *Dance Chronicle* 20.2.

NELLY (= Elly Sujulzoglu) (1989). *Nelly's Αυτοπροσωπογραφία* (Athens).

NEVILE, J. (2004). *The Eloquent Body: Dance and Humanist Culture in Fifteenth-Century Italy* (Bloomington and Indianapolis).

NIETZSCHE, F. (1961). *Thus Spoke Zarathustra, trans.* R.J. Hollindale (Harmondsworth).

——(1999). *The Birth of Tragedy*, in Nietzsche, *The Birth of Tragedy and Other Writings*, trans. by R. Spiers, ed. R. Geuss and R. Spiers (Cambridge), 1–117.

——(2000). *The Birth of Tragedy*, trans. Douglas Smith (Oxford).

NIJINSKA, B. (1981). *Early Memories* (New York).

NØRSKOV, V. (2002). *Greek Vases in New Contexts* (Aarhus).

NORTHBROOKE, JOHN (1577). *Spiritus est vicarius Christi in terra. A treatise wherein dicing, dauncing, vaine playes or enterluds with other idle pastimes [et]c. commonly vsed on the Sabboth day, are reproued by the authoritie of the word of God and auntient writers* (London).

NOVERRE, J.-G. (1803–4). *Lettres sur la danse, sur les ballets et les arts* (St Petersburg).

——(1807). *Lettres sur les Arts Imitateurs en Géneral et sur la Danse en Particulier.* 2 vols. (Paris).

——(1930). *Letters on Dancing and Ballets*, trans. C. W. Beaumont from the rev., enlarged edn. at St Petersburg 1803 (London).

NUGENT, A. (1998). 'Eyeing Forsythe', in *Dance Theatre Journal*, 14/3: 26–30.

NYE, E. (2005a). 'De la similitude du ballet-pantomime et de l'opéra à travers trois dialogues muets', SVEC 7: 207–22.

——(2005b). 'Poetry and the choric analogy in eighteenth-century France', in E. Nye (ed.), *Sur quel pied danser? Dance et littérature. Actes du colloque organisé par Hélène Stafford, Michael Freeman et Edward Nye en avril 2003 à Lincoln College, Oxford* (Amsterdam and New York), 107–35.

——(2007). 'Contemporary reactions to Jean-Georges Noverre's ballets d'action', *SVEC* June 2007, 31–45.

OAKLEY, J. H. (1998). 'Why study a Greek vase-painter? A response to Whitley's "Beazley as Theorist"', *Antiquity* 72: 209–13.

O'BRIEN, J. (1998). 'Harlequin Britain: eighteenth-century pantomime and the cultural location of entertainment(s)', *Theatre Journal* 50.4: 489–510.

——(2004). *Harlequin Britain: Pantomime and Entertainment, 1690–1760* (Baltimore).

ODENTHAL, J. (1994). 'From Isadora to Pina', *Ballet International*, 34–6.

OLIVIER, J. J. (1907). *Henri-Louis Le Kain de la Comédie-Française* (Paris).

O'MAHONY, J. (2002). 'Dancing in the Dark', *The Guardian* 26 Jan.

OSWALD, G. (1983). 'Myth and legend in Martha Graham's Night Journey', *Cord Dance Research Annual* 14.1: 34–47.

OTT, J. (2005). 'Iron horses: Leland Stanford, Eadweard Muybridge, and the industrialised eye', *Oxford Art Journal* 28: 407–28.

OTTO, W. F. (1965). *Dionysus: Myth and Cult*, trans. Robert B. Palmer (Bloomington and Indianapolis).

PARFAICT, C. and F. PARFAICT (1743). *Mémoires pour servir à l'histoire des spectacles de la foire* (Paris).

PALMER SIKELIANOS, E. (1967). 'What is great theater?' *Eos* 103–7.

——(1993). *Upward Panic: The Autobiography of Eva Palmer Sikelianos*, ed. J. Anton (Amsterdam, Chur, and Philadelphia).

——(1998). 'What is great theatre?', in Papageorgiou (1998), 300–5.

PAPADAKI, E. (1998). 'L'interprétation de l'antiquité en Grèce moderne: le cas de Anghélos et Eva Sikélianos, 1900–1952' (Diss. University of Paris I).

PAPAGEORGIOU, K. A. (ed.) (1998). *Aggelos Sikelianos, Eva-Palmer Sikelianou, Delphic Festivals* (Athens).

PATER, WALTER (1986). 'The school of Giorgione' [1877] in A. Phillips (ed.), *The Renaissance: Studies in Art and Poetry* (Oxford).

PAYNE, H. C. (1978). 'Modernizing the ancients: the reconstruction of ritual drama 1870–1920', *Proceedings of the American Philological Society* 12.23: 162–92.

PAYNE, R. (1960). *The Splendor of Greece* (New York).

PEACOCK, J. (1995). *The Stage Designs of Inigo Jones: the European Context* (Cambridge).

PEACOCK, S. (1988). *Jane Ellen Harrison: The Mask and the Self* (New Haven).

PEARSON, J. (2002). 'Stilling bodies/animating texts: Isadora Duncan and the archive', in R. Gough and H. Roms (eds.), *On Archives and Archiving* (*Performance Research* 7.4) (London and New York), 108–15.

PEMBERTON, E. (2000). 'Wine, Women and Song: Gender Roles in Corinthian Cult', *Kernos* 13: 85–106.

PERLMUTTER, D. (1991). *Shadowplay: The Life of Antony Tudor* (New York).

PERRUCCI, A. (1699). *Dell' arte rappresentativa premeditata ed all' improvviso* (Napoli).

PERUGINI, M. (1928). 'On decadence in art', *The Link* 3/3 (July): 27–9.

PETERS, J. (2008). 'Jane Harrison and the savage Dionysus: archaeological voyages, ritual origins, anthropology, and the modern theatre', *Modern Drama* 51.1: 1–41.

PG = (1844–66). *Patrologiae cursus completus, series Latina*, ed. J. P. Migne (Paris).

PHELPS, R. (1978). *Belle Saisons: A Colette Scrapbook* (New York).

PHILADELPHEUS, A. (1926). 'La danse antique', *L'Acropole* 1: 315–20.

PHILIPPO, S. (2005). 'Clytemnestra's ghost: the Aeschylean legacy in Gluck's Iphigenia operas', in F. Macintosh, P. Michelakis, E. Hall, and O. Taplin (eds.), *Agamemnon in Performance 458 BC to AD 2004* (Oxford).

PHILLIPS, H. (1980). *The Theatre and its Critics in Seventeenth-Century France* (Oxford).

PIERCE, K. and J. THORP (2006). 'The dances in Lully's *Persée*', *Journal of Seventeenth-Century Music* 10.1 (http://www.sscm-jscm.org/v10/no1/pierce.html).

PICHETTI, E. (1914). *La danza antica e moderna; storia, teoria e musica* (Rome).

PIPILI, M. (1987). *Laconian Iconography of the Sixth Century BC* (Oxford).

Pirrotta, N. (1982). 'Classical Theatre, *Intermedi* and *Frottola* Music', in N. Pirrotta and E. Povoledo (eds.), *Music and Theatre from Poliziano to Monteverdi*, trans. K. Eales (Cambridge), 37–75.

Plato, *The Laws*, trans. R. G. Bury. Loeb Classical Library, 2 vols. (London).

POB: *Proceedings of the Old Bailey* 1674–1913. Trial Proceedings (class T) and Summary of punishments (class S). Available at http://www.oldbaileyonline.org [Accessed 30 Sept. 2008].

Pope, Alexander (1783). *The Iliad and Odyssey of Homer: translated by Pope. A new edition. In four volumes.* Vol. 2. (London).

Porter, J. (2005). 'Feeling classical: classicism and ancient literary criticism', in J. Porter (ed.), *Classical Pasts: The Classical Traditions of Greece and Rome* (Princeton and Oxford), 301–52.

Potolosky, M. (ed.) (2004). *Forms and/of Decadence* [=*New Literary History* 35.4]

Pound, E. (1980). *Ezra Pound and the Visual Arts*, ed. H. Zinnes (New York).

Powell, J. S. (1988). 'Dance and Drama in the Eighteenth Century: David Garrick and Jean Georges Noverre', *Word and Image* 4/3–4: 678–91.

——(1995). 'Pierre Beauchamps, Choreographer to Molière's Troupe du Roy', *Music and Letters* 76.2: 168–86.

Power, K. (1999). 'Raging mothers: maternal subjectivity and desire in the dance theatre of Martha Graham', *Journal of Dramatic Theory and Criticism* 14/1: 65–78.

Pratsika, K. (1998). 'Recollections from the First Delphic Festival of 1927', in Papageorgiou (1998), 126–30.

Preston, C. J. (2005). 'The motor in the soul: Isadora Duncan and Modernist performance', *Modernism/modernity* 12/2: 273–89.

Prettejohn, E. (2006). 'Reception and Ancient Art: the Case of the Venus de Milo', in C. Martindale and R. F. Thomas (eds.), *Classics and the Uses of Reception* (Oxford), 227–49.

Prins, Y. (1999), 'Greek maenads, Victorian spinsters' in R. Dellamora (ed.), *Victorian Sexual Dissidence* (Chicago): 43–81.

Prodger, P. and T. Gunning (2003). *Time Stands Still. Muybridge and the Instantaneous Photography Movement* (New York).

Prudhommeau, G. (1949). 'La danse grecque antique', *Revue esthétique* 2: 98–100.

——(1965). *La danse grecque antique* (Paris).

——(1982*a*). *Histoire de la danse*, vol. 1 (Paris).

——(1982*b*). 'Une thèse sur la danse en 1895: essai sur l'Orchestique Grecque de Maurice Emmanuel', *La Recherche en Danse* 1: 21–7.

Price, D. W. (1990). 'The politics of the body: Pina Bausch's Tanztheater', *Theatre Journal* 42: 322–31.

Pruiksma, R. (2003). 'Generational conflict and the foundation of the Académie Royale de Danse: a re-examination', *Dance Chronicle* 26.2: 169–87.

Pruzhan, I. (1988). *Léon Bakst* (Harmondsworth).

Prynne, William (1633). *Histrio-mastix. The Players Scourge* (London).

Raftis, A. (2003). *Isadora Duncan and the Artists* (Athens).

——(2004). *Isadora Duncan and the Artists*, companion volume in English (Athens).

Ragona, M. (1994). 'Ecstasy, primitivism, modernity: Isadora Duncan and Mary Wigman', *American Studies* 35.1: 47–62.

RALPH, R. (1983). 'Restoring dance to Parnassus: the scholarly challenges of eighteenth-century dance', *Dance Research* 1.1: 21–9.

——(1985). *The Life and Works of John Weaver* (London).

RANDI, E. (ed.) (1993). *François Delsarte: le leggi del teatro* (Rome).

RAVELHOFER, B. (2006). *The Early Stuart Masque: Dance, Costume, and Music* (Oxford).

——(2007). 'Burlesque ballet, a ballad and a banquet in Ben Jonson's *The Gypsies Metamorphos'd* (1621)', *Dance Research*, 25.2: 144–55.

——(2010). 'Choreography as commonplace' in D. Cowling and M. Bruun (eds.), *The Role of Commonplaces in Western Europe (1450–1800): Reformation, Counter Reformation and Revolt* (Leuven).

RAWSON, C. (1972). *Henry Fielding and the Augustan Ideal under Stress: 'Nature's Dance of Death' and other Studies* (London).

RAYMOND, T. (1917). *The Autobiography of Thomas Raymond*, ed. G. Davies (London).

RAYLOR, T. (2000). *The Essex House Masque of 1621: Viscount Doncaster and the Jacobean Masque* (Pittsburgh, Penn.).

REID, JANE DAVIDSON (ed.) (1993). *The Oxford Guide to Classical Mythology in the Arts*, 3 vols. (Oxford).

REINACH, S. (1908). 'La danse grecque', *Revue Archéologique* 12.2: 309–10.

RENE, N. (1963). 'Isadora Duncan and Constantin Stanislavsky', *Dance Magazine* 37.7: 40–43.

REYNOLDS, M. (2005). 'Agamemnon: speaking the unspeakable', in F. Macintosh, P. Michelakis, E. Hall, and O. Taplin (eds.), *Agamemnon in Performance* (Oxford), 119–38.

REYNOLDS, N. and M. McCORMICK (2003). *No Fixed Points: Dance in the Twentieth Century* (New Haven and London).

RICHARDSON, Lady Constance Stewart (1913). *Dancing, Beauty and Games* (London).

RIDGWAY, R. S. (1968). 'Voltaire as an Actor', *Eighteenth-Century Studies* 1.3: 261–76.

RIDING, A. (1997). 'Using muscles classical ballet has no need for', *The New York Times* 15 June.

——(2005). 'Mutual Affection grows for Pina Bausch and Paris', *The New York Times* 15 June 2005.

RIIKONEN, H. (1978). *Die Antike im historischen Roman des 19. Jahrhunderts. Eine literature- und kulturgeschichtliche Untersuchung* (Helsinki).

RITCHIE, R. (1987). *The Joint Stock Book* (London).

ROACH, J. R. (1976). 'Cavaliere Nicolini: London's first opera star', *Educational Theatre Journal* 28.2: 189–205.

——(1982). 'Garrick, the ghost and the machine', *Theatre Journal* 34.4: 431–40.

——(1993). *The Player's Passion: Studies in the Science of Acting* (Ann Arbor).

ROATCAP, A. S. (1991). *Raymond Duncan: Printer, Expatriate, Eccentric Artist* (San Francisco).

ROBERT, L. (1938). *Études Épigraphiques et Philologiques* (Paris).

ROBERTS, M. F. (1908). 'The dance of the future as created and illustrated by Isadora Duncan', *The Craftsman* (Oct.), 48–56.

ROGERS, P. A. T. (1984). 'David Garrick: the actor as culture hero', *Themes in Drama* 6: 63–83.

ROMANOVSKY-KRASSINSKY, M. F. (1960). *Dancing in St. Petersburg* (London).

ROMEIN, J. (1976). *Op het breukvlak van twee eeuwen* [trans. as *The Watershed of Two Eras: Europe in 1900*, Middletown, 1978] (Amsterdam).

ROSEMAN, J. L. (2001). *Dance Masters: Interviews with Legends of Dance* (New York and London).

ROSEMONT, F. (ed.) (1983). *Isadora Speaks* (San Francisco).

ROSENFELD, Sybil (1960). *The Theatre of the London Fairs in the Eighteenth Century* (Cambridge).

ROSENFELD, SOPHIA (2000). 'Les Philosophes and le savoir: words, gestures and other signs in the era of Sedaine', in D. Charlton and M. Ledbury (eds.), *Michel-Jean Sedaine (1719–1797): Theatre, Opera and Art* (Aldershot), 39–51.

ROSLAVLEVA, N. (1965). 'Stanislavsky and the Ballet', *Dance Perspectives* 23: 15.

——(1966). *Era of the Russian ballet* (London).

ROSS. BERTRAM (1997). In Robert Tracy (ed.), *Goddess. Martha Graham's Dancers Remember* (New York), 237–44.

ROTH, G. (1955–70). *Diderot: Correspondance*, 16 vols. (Paris).

ROTHWELL, K. S. (2007). *Nature, Culture, and the Origins of Greek Comedy: A Study of Animal Choruses* (Cambridge).

ROUET, P. (2001). *Approaches to the Study of Attic Vases* (Oxford).

RUBINSTEIN, A. L. (1983). 'Imitation and style in Angelo Poliziano's Iliad translation', *Renaissance Quarterly* 36: 48–70.

RUSKIN, JOHN (1869). *The Mystery of Life and its Arts: Being the Third Lecture of Sesame and Lilies* (New York).

——(1904). 'Notes on some of the principal pictures exhibited in the rooms of the Royal Academy: 1875' [Orpington: 1875], in E. T. Clark and A. Wedderburn (eds.), *The Works of John Ruskin*, vol. 14 (London), 263–4.

——(1908). 'Lecture III: Classic schools of painting: Sir F. Leighton and Alma Tadema', in E. T. Clark and A Wedderburn (eds.), *The Works of John Ruskin*, vol. 33 [first published as part of *The art of England. Lectures given in Oxford*, 1884] (London), 319–23.

RUYTER, N. L. C. (1988). 'The intellectual world of Genevieve Stebbins', *Dance Chronicle* 11/3: 381–97.

——(1996*a*). 'The Delsarte heritage', *Dance Research* 14.1: 62–74.

——(1996*b*). 'Geneviève Stebbins and American Delsartean Performance' in Foster (1996*c*), 70–89.

——(1999). *The Cultivation of Body and Mind in Nineteenth-century American Delsartism* (Westport).

SABIN, R. (1944). 'Dance at the Coolidge Festival', *Dance Observer* 11/10: 120–1.

SAFRANSKI, R. (2003). *Nietzsche: A Philosophical Biography*, trans. S. Frisch (New York).

SAID, E. (2003). *Orientalism* (London [1978]).

SALLENGRE, A. H. DE (ed.) (1718). *Novus Thesaurus Antiquitatum Romanarum* (Hague).

SAVAGE, R. and SANSONE, M. (1989). 'Il corago and the staging of early opera: four chapters from an anonymous treatise circa 1630', *Early Music* 17.4: 495–514.

SAVIDIS, G. P. (ed.) (1992). *Kostas Karyotakis, Poems 1913–1928* (Athens).

SAWYER, P. (1990). 'The popularity of pantomime on the London stage, 1720–1760', *Restoration and Eighteenth-Century Theatre Research*, Series 5: 1–16.

SCANLON, J. and KERRIDGE, R. (1988). 'Spontaneity and control: the uses of dance in late Romantic literature', *Dance Research* 6.1: 30–44.

SCHERPE, K. R. (1986–1987). 'Dramatization and de-dramatization of "The End": the apocalyptic consciousness of Modernity and Post-Modernity', trans. Brent O. Peterson, in *Cultural Critique: Modernity and Modernism, Postmodernity and Postmodernism* 5: 95–129.

SCHLUNDT, C. L. (1962). *The Professional Appearances of Ruth St. Denis and Ted Shawn: A Chronology and an Index of Dances, 1906–1932* (New York).

——(1967). *The Professional Appearances of Ted Shawn and his Men Dancers: A Chronology and an Index of Dances 1933–1940* (New York).

SCHMIDT, J. (1982). 'Esel streckt dich!', *Ballet International* 5.4.

SCHNABEL, H. (1910). *Kordax. Archäologische Studien zur Geschichte eines antiken Tanzes und zum Ursprung der griechischen Komödie* (Munich).

SCHOLL, T. (1994). *From Petipa to Balanchine: Classical Revival and the Modernization of Ballet* (London and New York).

SCHOPENHAUER, ARTHUR (1969). *The World As Will and Representation*, trans. E. F. J. Payne, 2 vols. (New York).

SCHREIBER, R. (1984). *The First Carlisle: Sir James Hay, First Earl of Carlisle as Courtier, Diplomat and Entrepreneur, 1580–1636* (Philadelphia: The American Philosophical Society, 1984)

——(2004–9). 'Hay, James, First Earl of Carlisle (c.1580–1636)' in *Oxford Dictionary of National Biography*, accessed online: www.oxforddnb.com [11/05/07].

SCHRÖDER, B. (1927). *Der Sport im Altertum* (Berlin).

SCHULZE-REUBER, R. (2005). *Das Tanztheater Pina Bausch: Spiegel der Gesellschaft* (Frankfurt am Main).

SCOTT, GREGORY (2005). 'Twists and turns: modern misconceptions of peripatetic dance theory', *Dance Research* 23: 153–72.

SCOTT, W. C. (1987). 'The development of the chorus in *Prometheus Bound*' *Transactions of the American Philological Association* 117: 85–96.

SCRIABIN, A. N. (1995). *Poem of Ecstasy and Prometheus: Poem of Fire* (New York).

SÉCHAN, L. (1909). 'Saltatio', in *Dictionnaire des Antiquités Grecques et Romaines*, 4 (Paris), 1025–54.

——(1930). *La danse grecque antique* (Paris).

SEGEL, H. B. (1998). *Body Ascendent, Modernism and the Physical Imperative* (Baltimore).

SEROFF, V. (1972). *The Real Isadora* (New York).

SERVOS, N. (1981). 'The emancipation of dance: Pina Bausch and the Wuppertal Dance Theatre', trans. P. Harris and P. Kleber, *Modern Drama* 23/4: 435–47.

——(1984). *Pina Bausch: Wuppertal DanceTheatre or the Art of Training a Goldfisch* (Cologne).

——(1996). *Pina Bausch—Wuppertaler Tanztheater oder Die Kunst einen Goldfisch zu dressieren* (Seelze-Velber).

——(2001). *Pina Bausch ou l'Art de dresser un poisson rouge* (Paris).

——(2003). *Pina Bausch: Tanztheater: fotos von Gert Weigelt* (Munich).

——(2005). 'De la confiance et de l'amour' Paris Opéra Ballet Programme for *Orpheus et Eurydice* (Paris), 55–58.

SETZER, D. (2006). 'UCLA Library Acquires Isadora Duncan Collection', *UCLA News-room (4/21/06)*, http://www.newsroom.ucla.edu.

SHAKESPEARE, WILLIAM (1983). *A Midsummer Night's Dream*, ed. Harold F. Brooks (London).

——(1994). *Macbeth*, ed. N. Brooke (Oxford).

SHAWN, T. (s.a.). *Every Little Movement* (New York).

——(1946). *Dance We Must* (London).

——(1979). *One Thousand and One Night Stands* (New York).

SHELTON, S. (1983). 'Jungian roots of Martha Graham's dance imagery', *Dance History Scholars Conference Papers. Sixth Annual Conference*. Ohio, Ohio State University, 11–13 Feb. 119–132.

——(1990). *Ruth St. Dennis. A biography of the Divine Dancer* (Austin).

SHERMAN, J. (1979). *Drama of the Denishawn dance* (Middletown).

SIDERIS, G. (1976). *The Ancient Theatre on the Modern Greek Stage 1817–1932* (Athens).

SIEGEL, M. (1979). *The Shapes of Change* (Boston).

——(1986). 'Carabosse in a cocktail dress', *The Hudson Review* 39.1: 107–12.

——(1993). *Days on Earth: The Dance of Doris Humphrey* (Durham and London).

SIENKEWICZ, T. (1984). 'The chorus of *Prometheus Bound*: harmony of suffering' *Ramus* 13: 60–73.

SILK, M. S. and J. P. STERN (1981). *Nietzsche on Tragedy* (Cambridge).

SILVERMAN, J. (1977–78). 'Andre Levinson on Isadora Duncan', *Ballet Review* 6: 1–5.

SLATER, W. J. (1994). 'Pantomimes', *Didaskalia* 1.2, accessed online: http://www.didaskalia.net [15/08/08].

SMETHURST, M. (2000). 'The Japanese presence in Ninagawa's *Medea*' in Hall, Macintosh and Taplin (2000), 191–216.

SMITH, A. WILLIAM (ed.) (1995). *Fifteenth-Century Dance and Music. Twelve Transcribed Italian Treatises and Collections in the Tradition of Domenico da Piacenza*, 2 vols (Stuyvesant, NY).

SMITH, D. (ed.) (2000). 'Introduction', to Friedrich Nietzsche, *The Birth of Tragedy* [1872] (Oxford).

SMITH, J. and I. GATISS (1986). 'What did Prince Henry do with his feet on Sunday 19 Aug. 1604?', *Early Music*, 14.2: 198–207.

SMITH, M. (2000). *Ballet and Opera in the Age of Giselle* (Princeton).

SMITH, T. J. (2002). 'Transvestism or travesty? Dance, dress and gender in Greek vase-painting', in L. Llewellyn-Jones (ed.), *Women's Dress in the Ancient Greek World* (Swansea), 33–53.

——(2004). 'Festival? What Festival? Reading dance imagery as evidence', in S. Bell and G. Davies (eds.), *Games and Festivals in Classical Antiquity. Proceedings of the conference held in Edinburgh 10–12 July 2000, BAR International Series 1220* (Oxford), 9–23.

——(2005). 'The Beazley archive: inside and out', *Art Documentation* 24: 21–4.

——(2007*a*). '*Collectanea Antiqua*: Sir John Soane's Greek Vases', in M. Henig and T. J. Smith (eds.), *Collectanea Antiqua: Essays in Memory of Sonia Chadwick Hawkes*, BAR International Series 1673 (Oxford).

——(2007*b*). 'The corpus of komast vases: from identity to exegesis', in M. Miller and E. Csapo (eds.), *The Origins of Theater in Ancient Greece and Beyond: From Ritual to Drama* (Cambridge), 48–76.

SMUTS, M. (2004–2009). 'Howard, Thomas, fourteenth Earl of Arundel, fourth Earl of Surrey, and first Earl of Norfolk (1585–1646)', in *Oxford Dictionary of National Biography*, accessed online: www.oxforddnb.com [11/05/07].

SNYDER, D. M. (1984). 'Theatre as a Verb: The Theatre of Martha Graham 1923–1958' (unpublished PhD diss. Ilinois).

SOLOSKI, A. (2005). *The Village Voice*, 5 April (New York).

SPARKES, B. A. (1996). *The Red and the Black: Studies in Greek Pottery* (London).

SPARTI, B. (1993*a*). *Guglielmo Ebreo of Pesaro: De pratica seu arte tripudii (On the Practice or Art of Dancing)*, ed., trans. and introd. B. Sparti (Oxford).

——(1993*b*). 'Antiquity as inspiration in the Renaissance of dance: the classical connection and fifteenth-century Italian dance', *Dance Chronicle* 16.3: 373–90.

——(1996*a*). 'The function and status of dance in the fifteenth-century Italian courts', *Dance Research* 14.1: 42–61.

——(1996*b*). 'Breaking down barriers in the study of Renaissance and baroque dance', *Dance Chronicle* 19.3: 255–76.

SPENCER, C. (1973). *Leon Bakst* (New York).

SPINK, IAN and R. A. CAVE (1995). 'Collaborations: Ian Spink of Second Stride in discussion with Richard Allen Cave', in C. Jones (ed.), *Border Tensions: Dance and Discourse* (Guildford).

STANFORD, W. B. (ed.) (1947). *The Odyssey of Homer*, vol. 1 (London).

STANIEWSKI, W. (2000). *Metamorfozy: Music of Ancient Greece* (Gardzienice). CD-ROM.

——(2006). *'Gardzienice' Practising the Humanities: Theatrical Essay by Wlodzimierz Staniewski*. CD-ROM.

——and A. HODGE (2004). *Hidden Territories* (London and New York).

STEARNS, M. and J. STEARNS (1994). *Jazz Dance: The Story of American Vernacular Dance* (New York).

STEBBINS, G. (1885). *The Delsarte System of Expression* (New York).

——(1902). *The Delsarte System of Expression*. 6th edn., rev. and enlarged [repr. by Dance Horizons, New York 1977] (New York).

STEEGMULLER, F. (ed.) (1974). *'Your Isadora'. The love story of Isadora Duncan and Gordon Craig* (New York).

STEINBERG, C. (ed.) (1980). *The Dance Anthology* (New York).

STEPHANIS, I. E. (1988). *Dionysiakoi Technitai: sumboles sten prosopographia tou theatrou kai tes mousikes ton archaion Hellenon* (Heraklion).

STEVENS, H. and C. HOWLETT (2000, eds.). *Modernist Sexualities* (Manchester and New York).

STODELLE, E. (1984). *Deep Song: The Dance Story of Martha Graham* (New York).

STORR, A. (1998). *The Essential Jung: Selected Writings Introduced by Anthony Storr* (London).

STRATTON, C. (1916). 'The Greek Influence upon the Stage', *Art and Archaeology* 2.5: 250–63.

STRAVINSKY, I. (1947). *Poetics of Music in the Form of Six Lessons* (Oxford).

——(1975). *An Autobiography* (London).

STRAY, C. (1999). *Classics in the 19th and 20th Century Cambridge Curriculum, Culture and Community* (Cambridge).

STUDLAR, G. (1997). '"Out-Salomeing Salome": dance, the new woman, and fan magazine orientalism', in M. Bernstein and G. Studlar (eds.), *Visions of the East: Orientalism in Film* (London), 99–129.

SVETLOV, V. (= V. Ivchenko) (1899–1900). 'Istoritcheskii otcherk drevnei choregrafii', in *Yezhegodnik Imperatorskich Teatrov* (Yearbook of the Imperial Theatres), 2nd supplement, 29–120.

——(1974). *Anna Pavlova* [Paris, 1922] (New York).

SWANSON, V. G. (1977). *Sir Lawrence Alma-Tadema. The painter of the Victorian vision of the ancient world* (London).

——(1990). *The Biography and Catalogue Raisonné of the Paintings of Sir Lawrence Alma Tadema* (London).

SYMONDS, JOHN ADDINGTON (1880). *Studies of the Greek Poets*, vol. 2 (London).

SZONDI, P. (1980). '*Tableau* and Coup de Théâtre: on the social psychology of Diderot's bourgeois tragedy', *New Literary History* 11: 323–43.

TALMA, F. J. (1883). *Talma on the Actor's Art* (London).

TAPER, B. (1964). *Balanchine: A biography* (London).

TAPLIN, O. (1985). *Greek Tragedy in Action* (Cambridge).

——(1989). *Greek Fire* (London).

TAYLOR, G. (1972). '"The just delineation of the passions": theories of acting in the age of Garrick', in K. Richards and P. Thomson (eds.), *The Eighteenth-Century English Stage* (London), 51–72.

TAYLOR, N. (2001). 'John Weaver and the origins of English pantomime: a neoclassical theory and practice for uniting dance and theatre', *Theatre Survey* 42.2: 191–214.

TAYLOR, PAUL (1997). In Robert Tracy (ed.), *Goddess. Martha Graham's Dancers Remember* (New York), 154–71.

TERRY, W. (1954). 'Dance: golden apple, pink tights', *New York Herald Tribune*, 21 March.

——(1956). *The Dance in America* (New York).

——(1963). *Isadora Duncan: Her Life, Her Art, Her Legacy* (New York).

——(1979). *Ted Shawn, Father of American Dance: a Biography* (New York).

THÉÂTRE MUNICIPAL DU CHATELET (1914). *Loïe Fuller et son école de danse* [Programme for show, May 1914] (Paris).

THEODORAKIS, M. (2007). *The Ballad of the Dead Brother*, accessed online: http://en. mikis-theodorakis.net/article/articleprint/386/-1/63/ [01/12/07].

THIESS, F. (s.a.). *Der Tanz als Kunstwerk. Studien zu einer Aesthetik der Tanzkunst* (Munich).

THORP, J. (1997). 'Your Honor'd and Obedient Servant: Patronage and Dance in London c. 1700–1735', *Dance Research* 15.2: 84–98.

——(1998). 'Dance in late 17th-Century London: Priestly Muddles', *Early Music* 26.2.

——(2005). 'The notion of grace in the early eighteenth century: Mlle Guiot's dances in Lully's *Athys*', in E. Nye (ed.), *Sur quel pied danser? Danse et littérature* (Amsterdam and New York), 91–106.

——(2007). '"So great a master as Mr Isaac': an exemplary dancing-master of late-Stuart London', *Early Music* 35.3.

——(2008). 'Scholars and apprentices: training dancers in London c.1700–1750', in B. Segal (ed.), *Dancing Master or Hop Merchant? The Role of the Dance Teacher through the Ages*. Early Dance Circle Conference, London, 23 Feb. 2008, 61–8.

THURMAN, J. (1999). *Secrets of the Flesh: A Life of Colette* (London).

TODD, J. (1986). *Sensibility: An Introduction* (London).

TOEPFER, K. (1997). *Empire of Ecstasy: Nudity and Movement in German body culture*, 1910–1935 (Berkeley).

TORRANCE, I. (2007). 'Religion and Gender in Goethe's *Iphigenie auf Tauris*', *Helios*: 177–206.

TOUCHETTE, L.-A (2000). 'Sir William Hamilton's "Pantomime Mistress": Emma Hamilton and her Attitudes', in C. Hornsby (ed.), *The Impact of Italy: The Grand Tour and Beyond* (London), 123–46.

TOURS. H. (1963). *The Life and Letters of Emma Hamilton* (London).

TOWNSEND, J. A. (2001). 'The Choreography of Modernism in France: The Female Dancer in Artistic Production and Aesthetic Consumption, 1830–1925' (unpublished Diss. University of California, Los Angeles).

TOZZI, L. (1972–3). 'La poetica Angioliniana del balletto pantomimo dei programmi Viennesi', *Chigiana* 29–30: 487–500.

TREBLE, R. (1978). *Great Victorian Pictures: Their Paths to Fame* (London).

TRENDALL, A. D. and T. B. L. WEBSTER (1971). *Illustrations of Greek Drama* (London).

TREUHERZ, J. (1996). 'Alma-Tadema, een introductie', in E. Becker et al. (eds.), *Sir Lawrence Alma-Tadema* 1836–1912 (Zwolle), 11–18.

TURNER, V. (1967). *The Forest of Symbols*, (Ithaca, NY).

TYDEMAN, W. and S. PRICE (1996), *Wilde, Salome* (Cambridge).

UNDERHILL, K. C. (2001). '*Aux Grands Hommes de la Parole*: on the verbal Messiah in Adam Mickiewicz's Paris lectures', *The Slavic and Eastern European Journal* 45.4: 716–31.

URLIN, E. L. (1914). *Dancing: Ancient and Modern* (London).

VACCARINO, E. G. (ed.) (2005). *Pina Bausch: teatro dell'esperienza, danza della vita* (Milan).

VALÉRY, PAUL (1951). *Dance and the Soul: The Original French Text* with a trans. by D. Bussy [= Paris 1923] (London).

VAN DE PUT, W. (1999). 'CVA: Corpus or Corpse?', in R. F. Docter and E. M. Moorman (eds.), *Proceedings of the XVth International Conference of Classical Archaeology*, Amsterdam 12–17, 1998 (Amsterdam), 428–9.

VAN DER LEEUW, G. (1930). *In den hemel is eenen dans... Over de religieuze betekenis van dans en optocht* (Amsterdam).

VAN SCHAIK, E. (1981). *Op gespannen voet. Geschiedenis van de Nederlandse theaterdans vanaf 1900* (Haarlem).

VAN STEEN, G. (2002). '"The World's a Circular Stage": Aeschylean tragedy through the eyes of Eva Palmer-Sikelianou', *International Journal of the Classical Tradition* 8/3: 375–93.

VARNEDOE, K. (1998). 'On the claims and critics of the "primitivism" show', in D. Shapiro and B. Beckley (eds.), *Uncontrollable Beauty* (New York), 241–59.

VAUGHAN, DAVID (1977). *Frederick Ashton and his Ballets* (London).

VELOUDIOS, TH. (1998). 'Display of pyrrhic dance at 9/8 or "Artozenos" i.e. "Zeimbekikon"', in Papageorgiou (1998), 116–25.

VERSINI, L. (ed.) (1996). *Diderot: Oeuvres*, vol. 4 (Paris).

VICARS, D. (ed.) (1902). *Master Paintings of the World* (Chicago).

VICKERS, M. and D. GILL (1994). *Artful Crafts: Ancient Greek Silverware and Pottery* (Oxford).

VICTOR, B. (1761). *The History of the Theatres of London and Dublin from 1730 to the Present Time*, 2 vols. (London).

VIERECK, G. S. and P. ELDRIDGE (1930). *Salome: The Wandering Jewess* (London).

VINCE, S. W. E. (1957). 'Marie Sallé, 1707–56', *Theatre Notebook* 12.1: 7–14.

VOÏART, E. (1823). *Essai sur la dance antique et moderne* (Paris).

VOLBACH, W. R. (1961). 'Appia's Productions and Contemporary Reaction', *Educational Theatre Journal* 13.1: 1–10.

VOSSIUS, I. (1673). *De Poematum Cantu et Viribus Rythmi* (Oxford).

WALKER, C. R. (1958). *Iphigenia in Aulis in Euripides IV*, ed. David Grene and Richard Lattimore (Chicago and London).

WALKOWITZ, J. R. (2003). 'The "Vision of Salome": Cosmopolitanism and Erotic Dancing in Central London, 1908–1918', *American Historical Review* 108: 337–76.

WALTON, J. M. (1987). *Living Greek Theatre: A Handbook of Classical Performance and Modern Production* (Westport).

WARD, J. (1988). 'Newly devis'd measures for Jacobean masques', *Acta Musicologica*, 60/2: 111–42.

WARK, M. (1999). *Celebrities, Culture and Cyberspace: The Light on the Hill in a Postmodern World* (Sydney).

WARNECKE, B. (1932). 'Tanzkunst', s.v. in *Realencyclopädie der classischen Altertumswissenschaft*, 2. Reihe, 4.2 (Stuttgart), 2233–47.

WASSERMAN, E. R. (1947). 'The Sympathetic Imagination in Eighteenth-Century Theories of Acting', *Journal of English and Germanic Philology* 46: 264–72.

WASSERMAN, W. (2007). Conversation with the American choreographer regarding her work as a young dancer with Manou in Greece, 7 Nov. (New York).

WATSON, K. (1994). 'Time for the tutus to come off', *The Guardian*, 3 May.

WATTS, D. (1914). *The Renaissance of the Greek Ideal* (London).

WAYNE, H. (1977). *Samavedic Chant* (New Haven and London).

WEAVER, JOHN (1712). *An Essay towards the History of Dancing* (London).

WEBB, R. (1997). 'Salome's Sisters: The Rhetoric and Realities of Dance in Late Antiquity and Byzantium', in L. James (ed.), *Women, Men and Eunuchs: Gender in Byzantium* (London).

——(2002). 'Female performers in late Antiquity', in P. Easterling and E. Hall (eds.), *Greek and Roman Actors* (Cambridge), ch.13.

——(2005). 'The Protean Performer: mimesis and identity in late Antique discussions of the theatre', in L. Del Giudice and N. Van Deusen (eds.), *Performing Ecstasies: music, dance, and ritual in the Mediterranean* (Ottawa), 3–11.

——(2008). *Demons and Dancers: performance in Late Antiquity* (Cambridge, MA).

WEBER, C. (2002). 'The Dionysus in Aeneas', *Classical Philology* 97: 322–43.

WEDEMEYER-KOLWE, B. (2004). *Der neue Mensch. Körperkultur in Kaiserreich und Weimarer Republik* (Würzburg).

WEEGE, F. (1926). *Der Tanz in der Antike* (Halle).

WEICKMANN, D. (2007). 'Choreography and narrative: the ballet d'action of the eighteenth century', in M. Kant (ed.), *The Cambridge Companion to Ballet* (Cambridge), 53–64.

WEST, M. L. (1992). *Ancient Greek Music* (Oxford).

WEST, S. (1991). *The Image of the Actor: Verbal and Visual Representation in the Age of Garrick and Kemble* (London).

WHITLEY, J. (1996). 'Alma-Tadema en de néo-Grecs', in E. Becker et al. (eds.), *Sir Lawrence Alma-Tadema* 1836–1912 (Zwolle), 59–66.

——(1997). 'Beazley as Theorist', *Antiquity* 71: 40–7.

WHITLEY-BAUGUESS, P. (1988). *The Search for Mlle Guyot. Proceedings of the 11th Annual Conference of the Society of Dance History Scholars* (North Carolina), 32–67.

WILDE, O. (1989). *The Major Works* (Oxford).

WILES, D. (2000). *Greek Theatre Performance* (Cambridge).

WILSON, J. H. (1961). 'Theatre Notes from the Newdigate Letters', *Theatre Notebook* 15.3: 79–84.

WILSON, M. S. (1990). 'Garrick, Iconic Acting, and the Ideologies of Theatrical Portraiture', *Word and Image* 6.4: 368–94.

WILSON, P. (2000). *The Athenian Institution of the Khoregia: The Chorus, the City and the Stage* (Cambridge).

WIND, E. (1940). 'The sources of David's Horaces', *Journal of the Warburg and Courtauld Institute* 4: 124–38.

WINDREICH, L. (1979). 'Dance of the blessed spirits: Hanya Holm's *Orpheus* at the New Queen Elizabeth Theatre', *Vandance* 7.2: 10–11.

WINGE, J. (1949). 'How Astaire Works', *Film and Theatre Today* 7–9.

WINTER, M. (1974). *The Pre-Romantic Ballet* (London).

WINTHER, F. H. (= F. Winther and H. Winther) (1920). *Körperbildung als Kunst und Pflicht* (Munich).

——(1923). *Der Heilige Tanz* (Rudolfstadt).

WOOLF, VIRGINIA (1992). *To the Lighthouse* [1927] (Oxford).

WOOD, C. (2004). 'Let me entertain you', in *Afterall*, 37–44.

WOOD, D. (1999). *On Angels and Devils and Stages between: Contemporary Lives in Contemporary Dance* (Australia?).

WOODS, L. (1981). 'Crown of straw on little men: Garrick's new heroes', *Shakespeare Quarterly* 32: 69–79.

——(1984). 'Garrick claims the stage: acting as social emblem in eighteenth-century England', *Contributions in Drama and Theatre Studies* 10 (Westport).

YAARI, N. (2003). 'Myth into dance: Martha Graham's interpretation of the classical tradition', *International Journal of the Classical Tradition* 10.2: 221–42.

YAMPOLSKY, K. (1999). 'Kuleshov's experiments and the new anthropology of the actor', in R. Abel (ed.), *Silent Film* (London), 45–67.

YEATS, W. B. (1977), *The Variorum Edition of the Poems of W.B. Yeats*, ed. P. Allt and R. K. Alspach (New York).

ZAJKO, V. (2008). '"What Difference Was Made?" Feminist Models of Reception', in L. Hardwick and C. Stray (eds.), *A Companion to Classical Receptions* (Oxford), 195–206.

ZARIFI, Y. (2007). 'Chorus and dance in the ancient world', in M. McDonald and J. Michael Walton (eds.), *The Cambridge Companion to Greek and Roman Theatre* (Cambridge), 227–46.

ZAVOREL, B. J. (2003). 'Isadora Duncan and the dance', *Prometheus, Internet Bulletin for Art, Politics, and Science* 86: 1–11.

ZEITLIN, F. I. (2004). 'Dionysus in 69', in Hall, Macintosh and Wrigley (2004), 49–75.

ZIELINKSI, F. F. (1922). *The Religion of Ancient Greece* (Oxford).

ZINAR, R. (1971). 'The use of Greek tragedy in the history of opera', *Current Musicology* 12: 80–94.

Index

The index in general follows a word-by-word organisation. Where there are several, or many, productions on similar subjects, e.g. Iphigenia, references to these are preceded by references to the mythical figure, followed by references to the original classical source, and then by the various productions listed alphabetically. The English language version of titles of plays, operas and ballets has been used wherever possible but non-English titles are sometimes indexed in the original language because of the terminology used by different producers and writers.

Footnotes of a purely bibliographical kind have not been indexed (the full bibliography should be consulted) but substantive material occurring in the footnotes has been indexed.